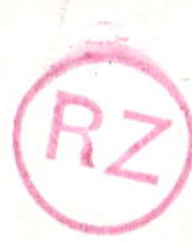

Fig. 2.

Fig. 3.

The Social History of the Decorative Arts

Pottery and Porcelain 1700–1914

The Social History of the Decorative Arts

General Editor: Hugh Honour

Bevis Hillier

Pottery and Porcelain 1700-1914

England, Europe and North America

Weidenfeld and Nicolson

5 Winsley Street London W1

SBN 297 17668 4

Designed by John Wallis for
George Weidenfeld and Nicolson Limited, London
Printed in Great Britain
by Ebenezer Baylis and Son, Limited
The Trinity Press, Worcester, and London

Contents

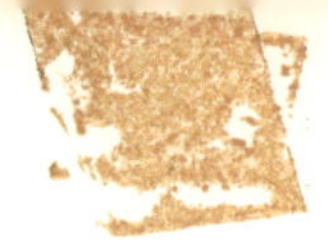

Acknowledgements

The author's principal thanks must go to Mr Hugh Honour, who asked him to write this book and at all stages gave invaluable help and encouragement. He is also greatly indebted to Mr Hugh Tait of the British Museum, who read the proofs and suggested many improvements. Mr Nicholas Orme and Mr Leslie Sherwood also read the proofs and gave much helpful advice.

The author is grateful to the directors and staff of Weidenfeld and Nicolson, in particular to Miss Faith Evans, for their work on this book and for their sympathetic and accommodating approach. His parents read the chapters as they were written and gave him the benefit of their criticisms and suggestions.

Among the many others he wishes to thank for their help are: Mr Michael Archer, Mr David Bindman, Mr Harry Buten, Lord Croft, Mr and Mrs J. K. des Fontaines, Mr Albert Gee, Mrs Moira Gibson, Mr Anton Gill, Mr Geoffrey Godden, Mr Paul Grinke, Mr Reginald Haggar, Mr Graham Hood, Mr John Keay, Miss Alison Kelly, Mr A. J. B. Kiddell, Mr John Mallet, Mr Philip Mansergh, Mr Hugo Morley-Fletcher, Mr John Murray, Mr Anthony d'Offay, Mr and Mrs Richard Ormond, Dr K. G. Robbins, Miss Lilian Russell, Mr Alan Smith, Mr Cyril Staal, Mr E. N. Stretton, Mr Donald Towner, Sir Anthony Wagner, Sir John Wedgwood, Mr H. Weinberg and Mr Derrick Witty.

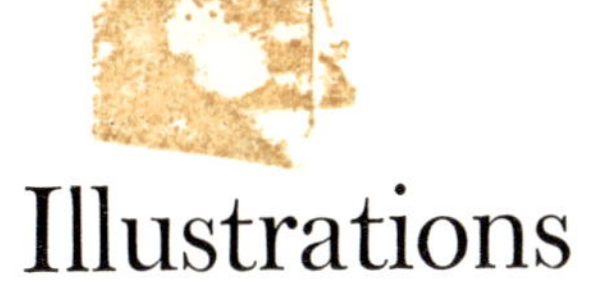

Illustrations

COLOUR PLATES

Social status of the potter
(between pages 26 and 35)

The end of the Baroque
(between pages 52 and 61)

Porcelain

(between pages 68 and 77)

The Rococo

(between pages 92 and 101)

Folk Pottery

North America

(between pages 166 and 175)

Marketing

(between pages 192 and 201)

Collectors
(between pages 270 and 279)

Repairs, reproductions and fakes
(between pages 304 and 313)

Art Nouveau
(between pages 320 and 329)

Amphora coepit
Institui; currente rota, cur urceus exit?

(HORACE, *Ars Poetica*)

I (*opposite*) Josiah Wedgwood and his family at Etruria Hall, by George Stubbs, R.A. From right to left the figures are: Josiah Wedgwood I (1730–95), with one of his vases on a table; his wife Sarah; John, a founder member of the Royal Horticultural Society; Josiah II, MP for Newcastle-under-Lyme; Susannah, the mother of Charles Darwin; Catherine; Thomas, the 'Inventor of Photography'; Sarah and Mary Ann. On the extreme left is the spire of Wolstanton Church.

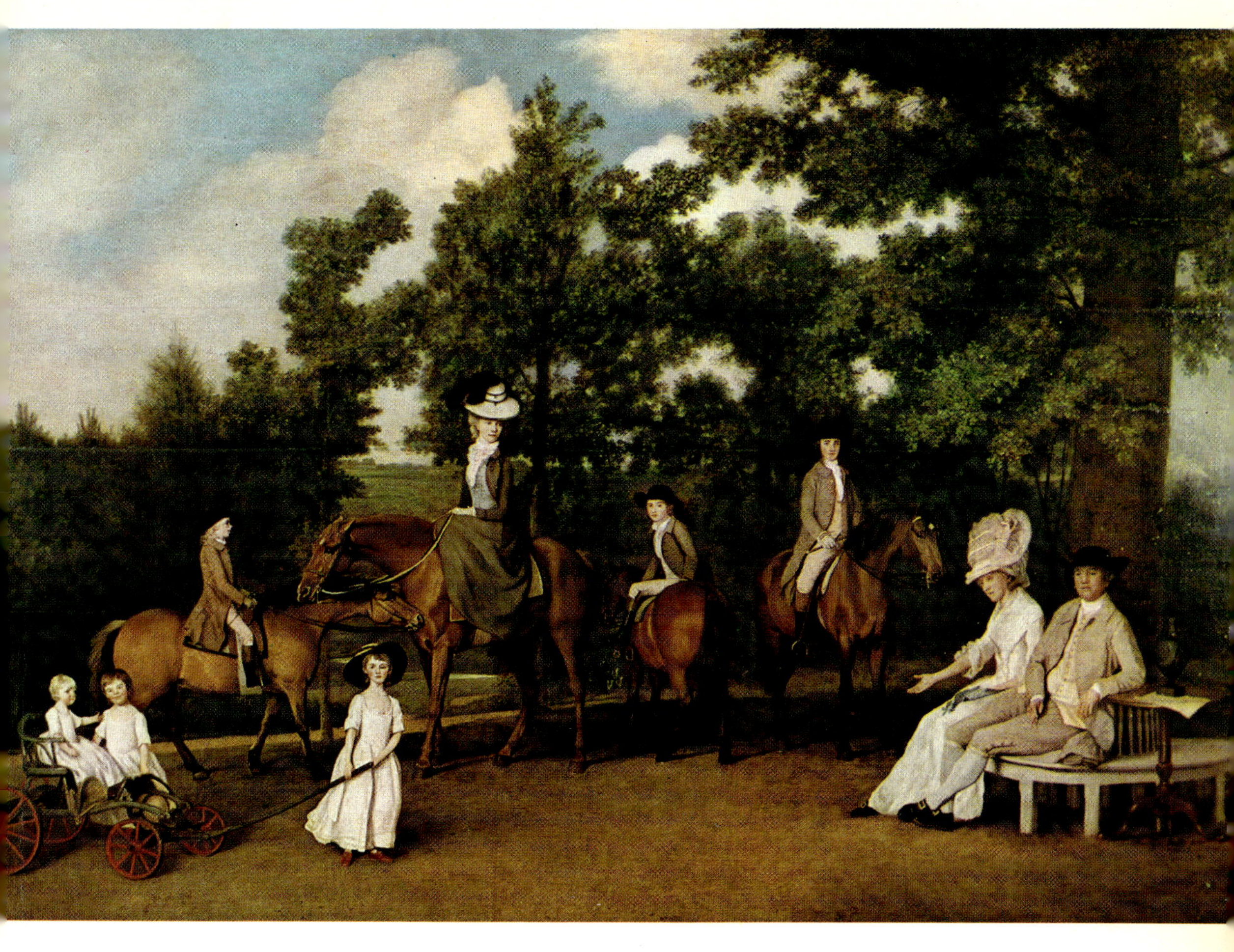

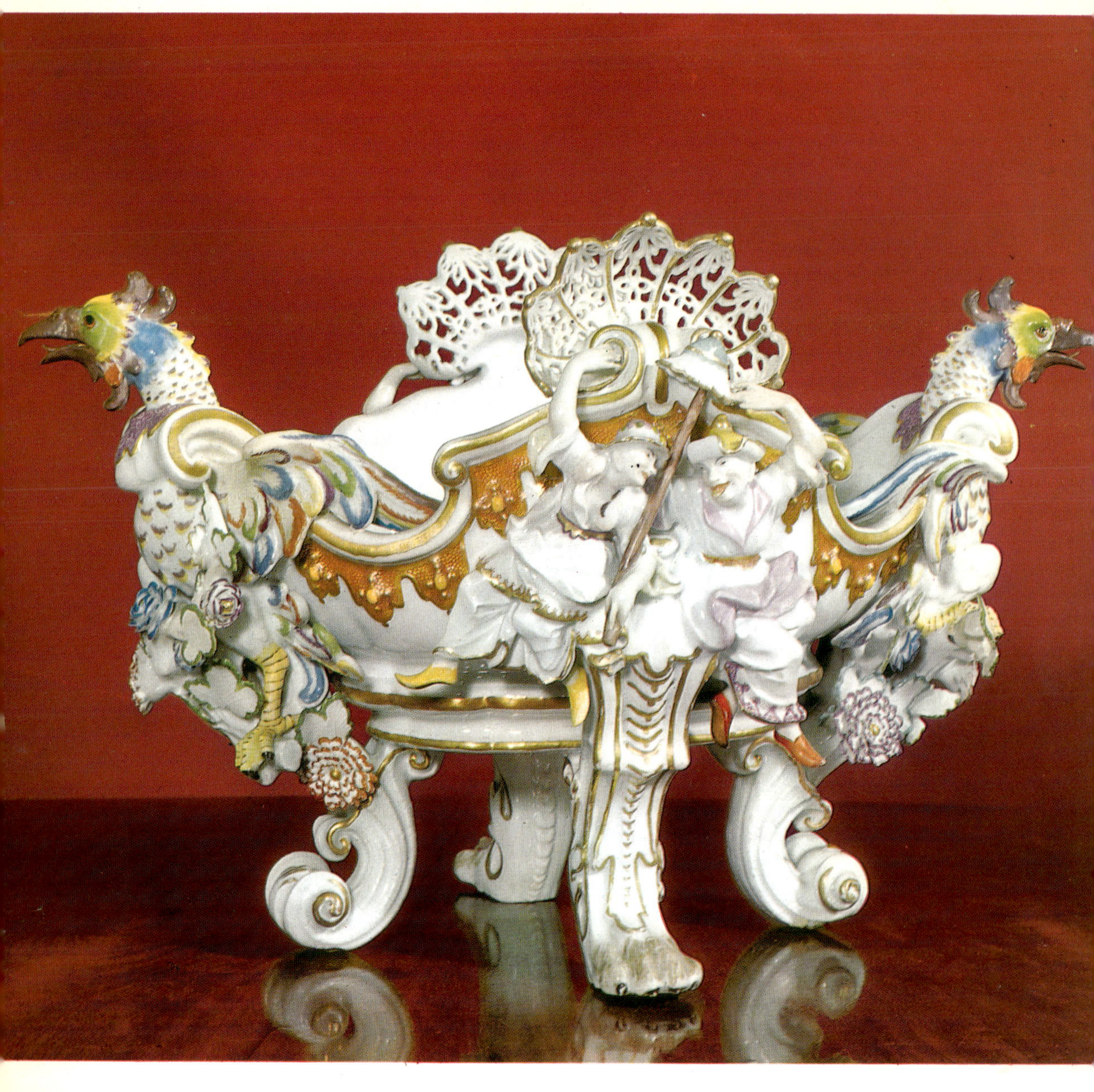

1 Social status of the potter

The Victorians spoke of the 'humble potter' as they spoke of the 'gentle reader' – to suggest social status rather than temperament. 'Common as dirt' was a less cryptically snobbish phrase; a craftsman who worked with clay could not expect much prestige. Browning wrote of 'the salts and silts of the earth' while others pictured it as a Grecian Element in a chiton or as 'the inexhaustible repository of all the vital forces responsible for the manifestations of life and maternity'. But earth seemed less romantic when brought into commerce.

The potter's job was messy and unhealthy. His lungs were injured by clay dust, powdered flints, plaster of Paris, calcined bones and sulphur fumes. He became rheumatic from exposure to high temperatures and rapid transitions of heat, and went blind from the glare of the ovens. The glazer suffered from lead-poisoning; it was only because arsenic is volatilized by heat that its magnificently coloured salts were not widely used.

At the very beginning of our period, in 1700, Bernadino Ramazzini, Professor of Physic in the University of Padua, published his *De Morbis Artificum*, the first comprehensive study of occupational diseases. It included a chapter on the diseases of potters:

> There's scarce any City in which there are not other Workmen, besides those mention'd above, who receive great Prejudice from the Metallick Plagues. Among such we reckon the Potters; for what City, what Town is without such as practise that the Ancientest of all Arts? Now, the Potters make use of burnt and calcin'd Lead for glazing their Ware; and for that end grind their Lead in Marble Vessels, by turning about a long Piece of Wood hung from the Roof, with a square Stone fasten'd to it at the other end. While they do this, as well as when with a pair of Tongs they daub their

II (*opposite*) The Baroque: *a plat de ménage* modelled at Meissen by J. J. Kändler, *c.* 1740. L. 18½ in. H. 11 in.

Vessels over with melted Lead before they put 'em into the Furnace; they receive by the Mouth and Nostrils and all the Pores of the Body all the virulent Parts of the Lead thus melted in Water & dissolv'd, and thereupon are siez'd with heavy Disorders. For first of all their Hands begin to shake and tremble, soon after they become Paralytick, Lethargick, Splenetick, Cachectick and Toothless; and in fine, you'll scarce see a Potter that has not a Leaden Death-like Complexion.[1]

Significantly, Ramazzini added that it was difficult to restore the potters to health, as 'they are commonly pinch'd with another Evil, *viz.* Extream Poverty. So that we are forc'd to flye to the *Medicina Pauperum*, and prescribe such things as at least will mitigate the Illness; advising 'em withal to give over Working at their Trade.'[2] However cheap it was, the *Medicina Pauperum* cannot have been an alluring prospect. In such cases, Ramazzini ordered 'Mercurial Purgatives',[3] 'the Hands and Feet to be anointed with our Rock Oil [petroleum]'.[4] And he preferred 'the simple Filings of Steel infus'd in Wine with Cinamon, to all the Chymical Chalyeats, as being at once more effectual and less chargeable to the poor Wretches'.[5]

Ramazzini says nothing of silicosis and the dust hazard which, in the industrial revolution, was to become the most fatal. Almost the whole of his chapter on potters deals with lead poisoning. But he does also observe that 'this may be said of 'em all in General, that as they all spend their Lives in moist Places, and are still imploy'd in Handling moist Earth, so they are for the most part wan Complexion'd and Cachectick, and a'most always complaining of some Illness or other'.[6] Commenting on this passage in 1778, a French editor of Ramazzini, De Fourcroy, indicated that similar conditions still obtained in Paris:

Les potiers de terre habitent, à Paris, plus dans les faubourgs que dans la ville; il y en a cependant quelques-uns dans celle-ci, mais ils choisissent des rues étroites pour y avoir un logement moins cher. Ils ont tous leurs ateliers dans les salles basses, humides, quelques-uns sur l'eau. La terre humide qu'ils manient pour en séparer les pyrites qu'ils appellent *feramine*; l'eau dont ils arrosent pour la rendre molle, afin de la former en vaisseaux au tour et à la roue, rendent l'air qu'ils respirent humide, peu élastique, et leur occasionnent de la gêne dans la respiration: aussi beaucoup d'entre eux sont-ils sujets aux maladies de poitrine.[7]

In the nineteenth century, two Englishmen wrote books on occupational diseases – the first since Ramazzini – and fortunately for our purposes both lived in potting towns. C. Turner Thackrah wrote his *Effects of the Principal Arts, Trades, and Professions on Health and Longevity* (1831) 'With a Particular Reference to the Trades and Manufactures of Leeds'. Dr J. T. Arlidge, whose *Hygiene, Diseases and Mortality of Occupations* was published in 1892, was consulting physician to the North Staffordshire Infirmary, Stoke-on-Trent. Like Ramazzini, Thackrah is most concerned at the use of lead:

> In the Leeds Pottery we remarked nothing injurious but the department of glazing. Could not the process be effected without the immersion of the hands in the metallic solution? Or could it not be effected by a machine? Or could not some article less noxious be substituted for the lead? On visiting the Derby Pottery, some years ago, I learnt that little lead is used in the composition for glazing, and that the workmen consequently are not injured....
>
> I am told ... by an intelligent manufacturer of earthenware in Leeds, that the comparative cheapness of the leaden glaze is the chief recommendation. Surely humanity forbids that the health of workmen, and that of the poor at large, should be sacrificed to the saving of half-pence in the price of pots.[8]

In Thackrah's work we still find no mention of silicosis. It was left to Dr Arlidge to expose the incidence of what he called 'pulmonary mischief from the dust of potter's clay'.[9] The worst affected were the women who scoured the pots after they were taken from the saggars. They lived in a perpetual cloud of clay dust. Arlidge, whose scientific detachment is tempered by a plangent style reminiscent of the Book of Job, describes them as 'the rougher, more ignorant, and reckless of their sex'.[10] But almost all workers in the potteries were exposed to dust in more or less harmful quantities. The symptoms of the disease known variously as 'potter's asthma', 'potter's consumption' and 'potter's rot' were cavernous breathing, a paroxysmal cough, and, with macabre aptness, a 'cracked-pot sound'[11] when the lungs were tested. At the time Arlidge wrote his book, the mean age at death of male potters aged twenty and over was forty-six and a half years, whilst that of non-potters stood at fifty-four.[12] The deaths of male potters from diseases of the respiratory organs, in relation to their entire mortality from all causes, were sixty per cent in place of twenty-seven per cent as calculated for the male population of the British Isles.[13]

By 1892 it was not only dust inside the potworks which was causing disease. A pall of dense coal dust and smoke hung over the English potteries – the most heavily industrialized potting area in the world. Although the coal-fired bottle ovens have now been replaced by electric kilns, the Potteries folk – always about fifty years behind even their own advances – still sell in their shops the old tragi-comic postcards (Plate 10): 'Firing a Potter's Oven', 'Shadows of the Evening Steal Across the Sky', and, still more *spirituel*, 'The Air Soots Us Well'. The second of these captions is a line from a sombre hymn still popular in the industrial areas of Britain. The fact that D. H. Lawrence adapted a line of the same song for the title of a collection of his poems, *Birds, Beasts and Flowers*, and the fact that it was composed, words and tune, by a Devonshire rector named Sabine Baring-Gould, seem rather to enhance than vitiate its irony as an industrial lament: 'Now the Day is Over'.

Education is the second greatest leveller; but potting scarcely demanded classical erudition. It did not even demand complete sanity. The legend retailed by Simeon Shaw, that Twyford and Astbury gained access to the Elers brothers' works and secrets by feigning idiocy has been discredited,[14] but his statement that 'Their [the Elers'] servants were the most ignorant and stupid persons they could find, and an idiot was employed to turn the thrower's wheel'[15] may derive from a reliable local tradition, and is at any rate plausible.

At the other end of the social and educational scale could be found the first Josiah Wedgwood, a Fellow of the Royal Society, consorting with Joseph Priestley, Erasmus Darwin and Matthew Boulton at the Birmingham Lunar Society, or John Philip Elers himself, an apostate chemist who had been associated with Joachim Becker. But these men were very much the exception. Wedgwood was an auto-didact of genius. Elers had the advantage of high birth: his godparents were Queen Christina of Sweden and the Elector of Mainz, and a picture of the christening is described by Elers's descendant, the novelist Maria Edgeworth, in a letter to her cousin, Captain George Elers.[16] Nothing further from the 'humble potter' of Victorian cant can be imagined; even so, Miss Edgeworth, in breaking the news to her cousin that they were both great-grandchildren of a potter, wrote: 'May be, my dear Coz, your aristocratic blood may shudder at this discovery of which I am nevertheless proud.'[17]

Presumably John Philip Elers was given an education to match his social pretensions. A more orthodox view of the education fit for a potter is suggested by a letter of 1820 from Sydney Smith to his friend Leonard Horner:

> My friend (a potter), to whom we are all so deeply indebted every night and morning, wishes to place a son at Edinburgh, and I have promised to inquire for him. Pray be so good as to tell me the terms of Pillans, and also

mention some good Presbyterian body who takes pupils at no great salary. Never mind whether Whig or Tory, philosopher or no philosopher; a potter has nothing to do with such matters; all I require is that he should be steady and respectable, and that the young fashioner of vases and basins should have an apartment to himself, in which he may meditate intensely on clay.[18]

Social status of the potter

The young potter was a Wedgwood, as we learn from a letter of 1821 to John Murray:

> How little you understand young Wedgewood [*sic*]! If he appears to love waltzing, it is only to catch fresh figures for cream-jugs. Depend upon it, he will have Jeffrey and you upon some of his vessels, and you will enjoy an argillaceous immortality.[19]

Sydney Smith was of course too much a wit to intend these remarks seriously; but their humour largely derives from the pastiche of a current social prejudice.

To most people, the potter's end product was not impressive. Doubtless Dr Johnson was considered to have won the following exchange by his squashing reply: 'Johnson called the East-Indians barbarians. BOSWELL: "You will except the Chinese, Sir?" JOHNSON: "No, Sir." BOSWELL: "Have they not arts?" JOHNSON: "They have pottery." '[20] At his most ambitious the potter could make, so it seemed, nothing more than a poor man's substitute for marble or bronze statuary and wares of precious and other metals. As Ramazzini observed, 'If we had not the way of glazing Earthen Vessels, what a great charge would the World be put to in Pewter and Copper Vessels both for the Kitchin and the Table'.[21] Although they incidentally achieve a pleasing artistic character of their own, copper and silver lustre wares and the various copies of Il Fiammingo (Plates 14–17) were a direct exploitation of the demand for surrogate valuables.[22] But not every potter was prepared to accept without demur the role of imitator. In 1705, when Johann Friedrich Böttger, the failed alchemist, was relegated by the Elector Augustus of Saxony to the position of ceramic experimenter, he wrote above his door in disgust:

> Gott, unser Schöpfer,
> hat gemacht aus einem Goldmacher einen Töpfer.
> [God, our creator, has turned a goldmaker into a potter.]

By the late nineteenth century the potter was manufacturing drainpipes and lavatory bowls as well – no social recommendation, however socially valuable.

Although potting was unhealthy, uncerebral, and low-ranking among crafts, it had a certain mystique. It was popularly presumed, what Ramazzini called it, 'the Ancientest of all Arts'. Victorian writers were obsessed with the romantic notion of 'the first potter'. The most delightful exercise in this branch of dogmatic speculation was an essay by Grant Allen in *Longman's Magazine* (July, 1885):

> To be sure, the primitive savage, unversed as he was in pastes and glazes, in moulds and ornaments, did not pass his life entirely devoid of cups and platters. Coconut shell and calabash rind, horn of ox and skull of enemy, bamboo-joint and capacious rhomb-shell, all alike, no doubt, supplied him with congenial implements for drink or storage. Like Eve in the Miltonic Paradise, there lacked him not fit vessels pure; picking some luscious tropical fruit, the savoury pulp he chewed, and in the rind still as he thirsted scooped the brimming stream. This was satisfactory as far as it went, of course, but it was not pottery. He couldn't boil his joint for dinner in coconut or skull; he had to do it with stone pot-boilers, in a rude kettle of puddled clay.
>
> But at last one day, that inspired barbarian, the first potter, hit by accident upon his grand discovery. He had carried some water in a big calabash – the hard shell of a tropical fruit whose pulpy centre can be easily scooped out – and a happy thought suddenly struck him: why not put the calabash to boil upon the fire with a little clay smeared outside it? The savage is conservative, but he loves to save trouble. He tried the experiment, and it succeeded admirably. The water boiled and the calabash was not burnt or broken. Our nameless philosopher took the primitive vessel off the fire and looked at it critically with the delighted eyes of a first inventor. A wonderful change had suddenly come over it. He had blundered accidentally upon the art of pottery.

Even when a writer was dealing with something far removed from primitive pottery, he would still drag in a reference to the first potter. Writing under the title 'Sèvres' in the *Art Union Monthly Journal* of April, 1847, Dr W. Cooke Taylor put forward his theory about the first pot, with not a mention of calabash or skull of enemy:

> The exercise of plastic art in soft clay must belong to the very infancy of mankind; it would be naturally suggested by the impressions made by the feet or hands in the soil when moistened by a shower of rain. This conjecture is corroborated by our finding that the earliest fictile establishments were placed in the neighbourhood of rivers, more or less subject to periodical inundations; the Babylonians, the Egyptians, and the Etrurians became potters from their vicinity to the Euphrates, the Nile and the rivers of Northern Italy. The discovery that the forms given to the moist clay might

be rendered permanent by heat and pressure, was indicated by Nature herself wherever an inundation occurred; the soil became hardest where footprints had fallen. From the observation of this natural fact to its artificial imitation was a simple step; it was only necessary to press the clay more regularly and to expose it to the direct action of the solar heat. As population spread into the more temperate and colder zones, it was an obvious suggestion, that the diminished action of the sun should be compensated by the artificial heat of fire....[23]

Social status of the potter

The interest in a 'first potter' was essentially religious. The idea of a first potter and a first pot could be equated with the doctrine of a first creator, a Prime Mover, and the making of the first man. And the potter who created could also destroy. The most sustained use of the metaphor was in Edward Fitzgerald's translation of *The Rubaiyat of Omar Khayyam* in which the 'clay population' are made to represent questions of immortality:

> And, strange to tell, among the Earthen Lot
> Some could articulate, while others not:
> And suddenly one more impatient cried –
> Who is the Potter, pray, and who the Pot?
>
> Then said another – Surely not in vain
> My Substance from the common Earth was ta'en,
> That he who subtly wrought me into Shape
> Should stamp me back to common Earth again.

In the Bible, too, there are several variations on the parable. Isaiah 41, 25: 'He shall come upon princes ... as the potter treadeth clay.' Romans 9, 21: 'Hath not the potter power over the clay, of the same lump to make one vessel unto honour and another unto dishonour?' Revelations 2, 27: 'And he shall rule them with a rod of iron; as the vessels of a potter shall they be broken to shivers.' Jeremiah at the potter's house (Plate 4) was a favourite example: 'Then the word of the Lord came to me, saying, O house of Israel, cannot I do with you as this potter?' And later Jeremiah was told to get a potter's earthen bottle, and by the symbolic act of breaking it in front of the elders to foreshadow the destruction of Judah and Jerusalem. The wares in the potter's house are curiously prophetic of those at Messrs Minton's in the late nineteenth century, when, closely allied to a fundamentalist interpretation of the Bible, there was a pedantic-romantic interest in biblical *objets*, a constant descent from the sublime to the meticulous. Terracotta water-jars (Plate 5) became yet another indispensably useless object for the Victorian home, though no crinolined materfamilias was to be seen carrying one on her head from the well.

Apart from the wider religious associations, potting had a mythology of its own. Other industries have had their miracles and martyrs. Steam had James Watt's kettle and the death of Huskisson. Textiles had Hargreaves's Spinning Jenny and the 'little slaves of the mills'. Positive and negative electricity were discovered because Robert Symmer wore two pairs of stockings. The principle of vulcanization was suggested by rubber and sulphur bubbling on Charles Goodyear's stove – a miracle which, despite its pagan name, has a distinct reek of Christian martyrdom ('For that staunch saint still prais'd his Master's name,/While his crack'd flesh lay hissing on the grate').[24]

Potting could boast no martyr as distinguished as Spinoza, who died from inhaling powdered glass when working as a lens-grinder; but a favourite *chanson de geste* was of Bernard Palissy, who stoked his kiln with his own furniture to continue his experiments, and who was imprisoned in the Bastille as a Protestant heretic.[25] A picture in Arthur Mee's *Children's Encyclopaedia* shows Palissy throwing floorboards into the furnace while his wife and children expostulate with him. Another is captioned: 'The Dying Palissy Rebukes with Dignity the Feeble King of France who had Doomed him to Die in a Prison Cell.' Mee dispatches him with a resounding zeugma: 'He triumphed over the obstinate clay and the tyranny of his times.' Josiah Wedgwood's achievement was the more remarkable because his leg was amputated. William De Morgan impaired his health in searching for the lost secrets of Persian lustre. But the supreme ceramic martyrdom must be that of the legendary Chinaman Pousa, a kind of wholesale Mucius Scaevola, who threw himself into the oven when the last sticks of furniture had been burnt, to complete the firing of an exquisite bowl. The chemical reaction of his bones was said to have produced a glaze of unmatchable beauty. A Minton plaque of this self-sacrifice, built into the Ceramic Gallery of the Victoria and Albert Museum, has been concealed beneath a veneer of plain plaster to prevent it competing for attention with the exhibits.

With Pousa, said Moncure Conway (author of that intrepid book *Travels in South Kensington*, 1882), 'began the list of wondrous accidents with which the history and traditions of pottery abound'.[26] Simeon Shaw describes two of them. One was the alleged discovery of salt glaze when 'a strong lixivium of common salt, to be used some way in curing pork' boiled over and glazed the sides of an earthen vessel.[27] The

Social status of the potter

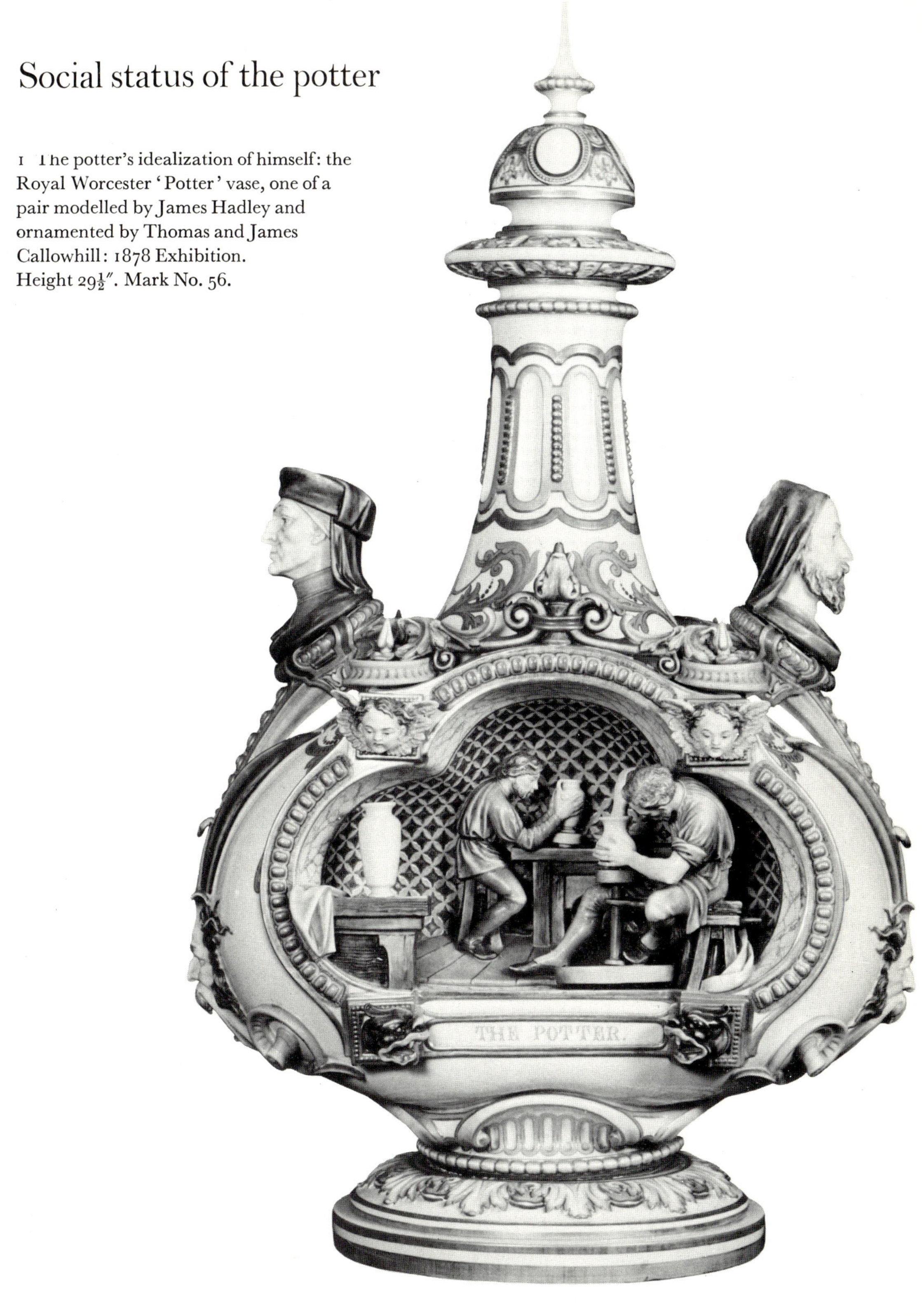

1 The potter's idealization of himself: the Royal Worcester 'Potter' vase, one of a pair modelled by James Hadley and ornamented by Thomas and James Callowhill: 1878 Exhibition. Height 29½″. Mark No. 56.

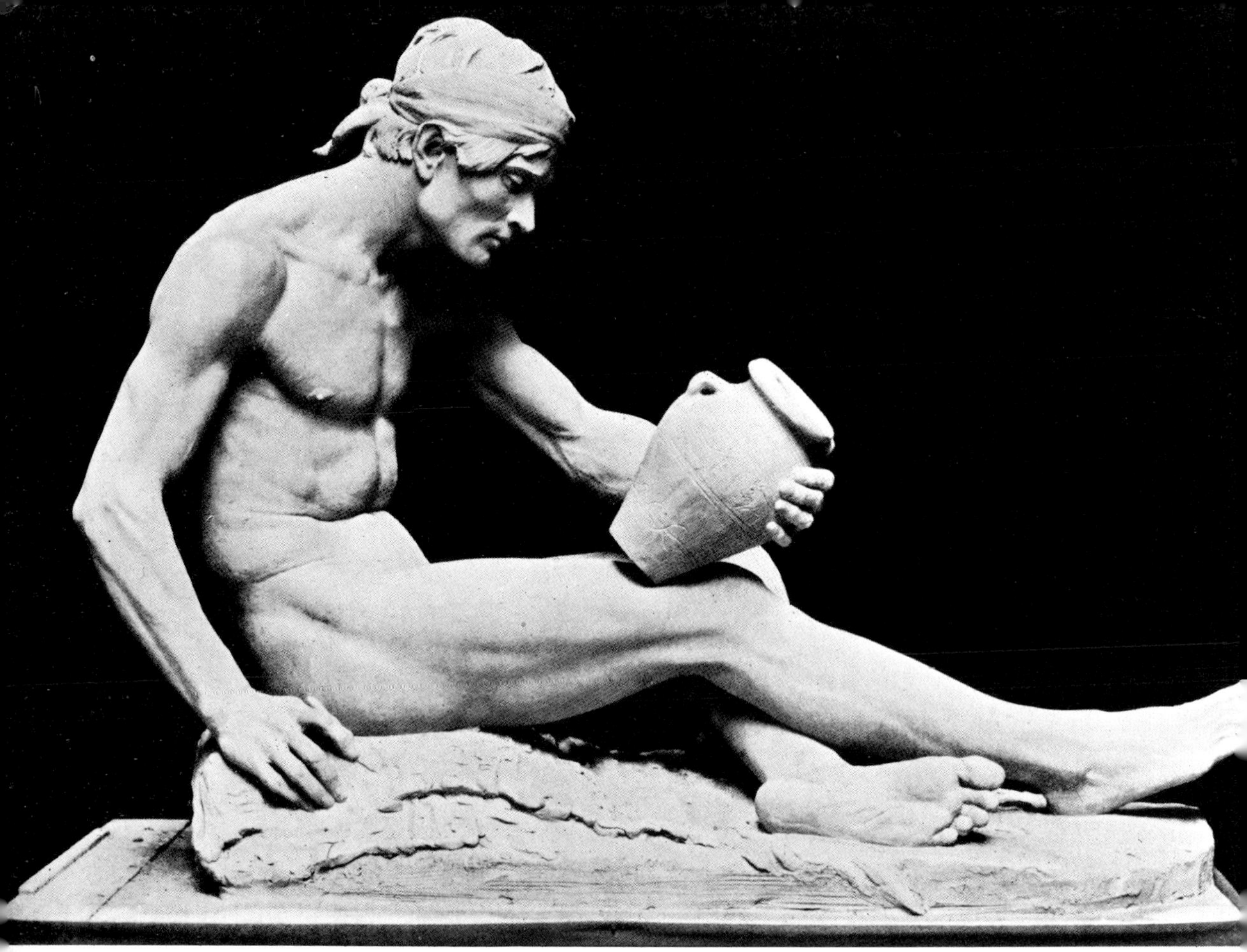

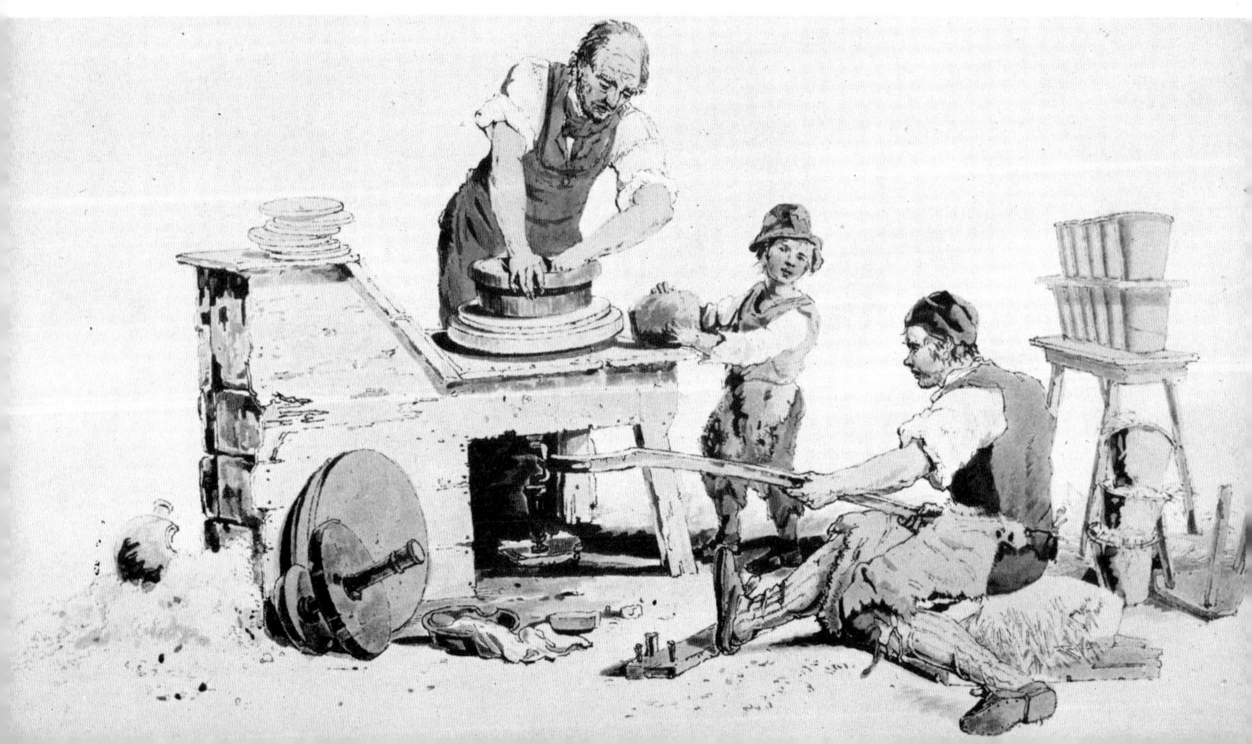

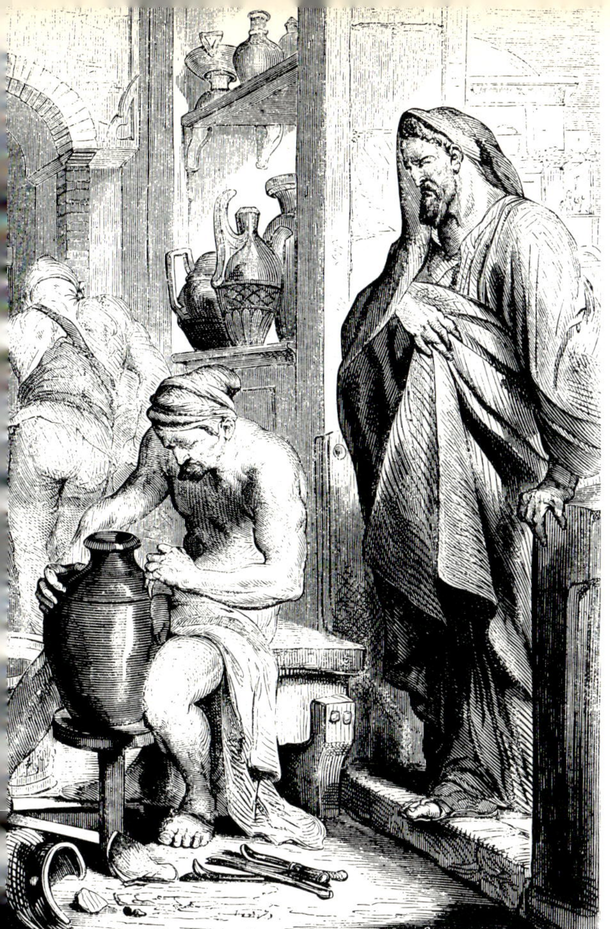

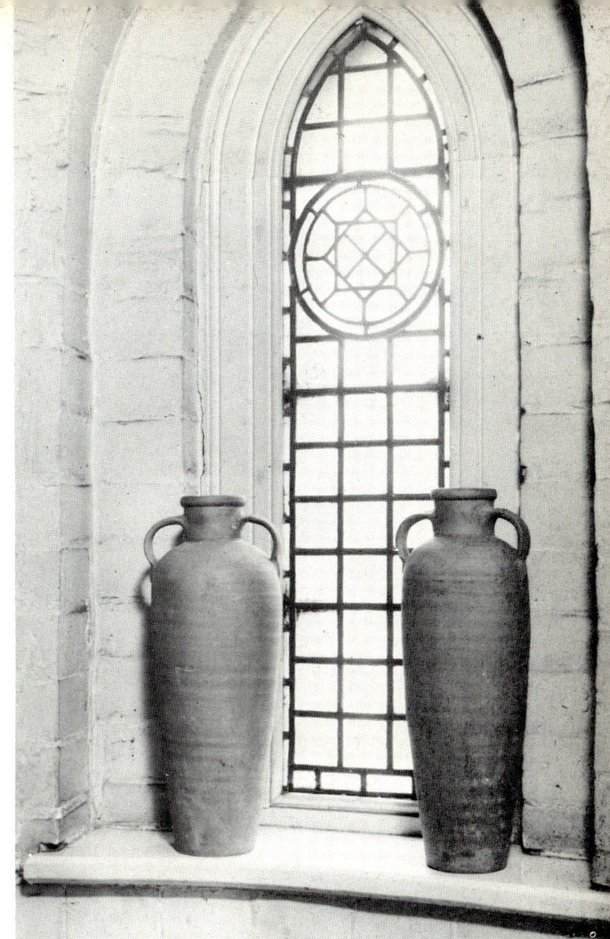

4 (left) Jeremiah at the Potter's house (Jeremiah, xviii, 3). Wood-engraving by M. V. Sears after H. Castelli, from a Victorian family bible published by Cassell. See p. 25.

5 (right) Two terracotta vases of 'biblical' form, height 16″. The window behind them is by Robert Anning Bell (1863–1933). See p. 26.

2 (opposite top) Idealization: 'The Potter' by F. W. Pomeroy, exhibited at the Royal Academy, London, 1899.

3 (bottom) Reality: 'The Potter', plate 1 of W. H. Payne's *The Costume of Great Britain* (1808).

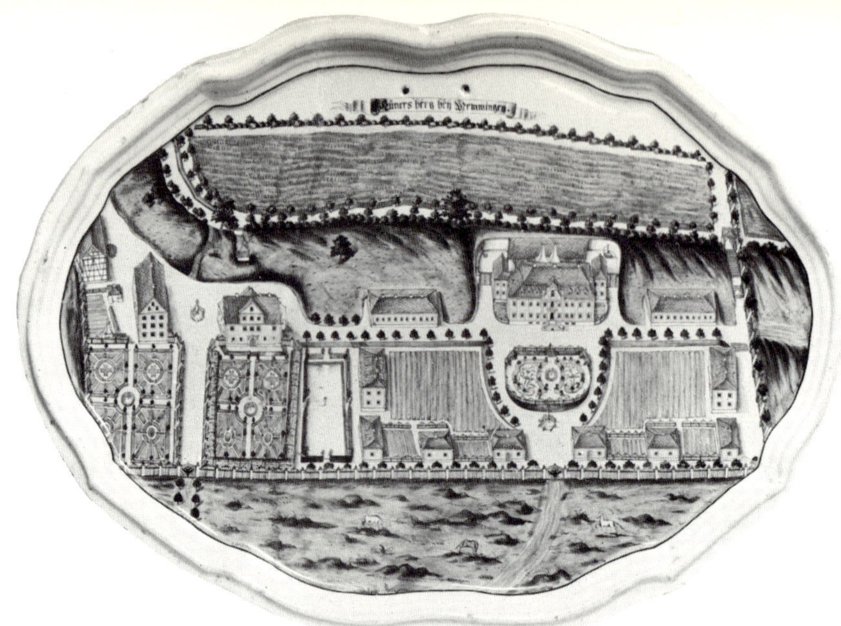

6 Houses of workmen at the Künersberg porcelain factory can be seen in the foreground of this view of Baron Küner's estate, near Memmingen, on a Künersberg *plateau* of *c.* 1760. Length $20\frac{3}{4}''$, width $14\frac{3}{4}''$. See p. 39.

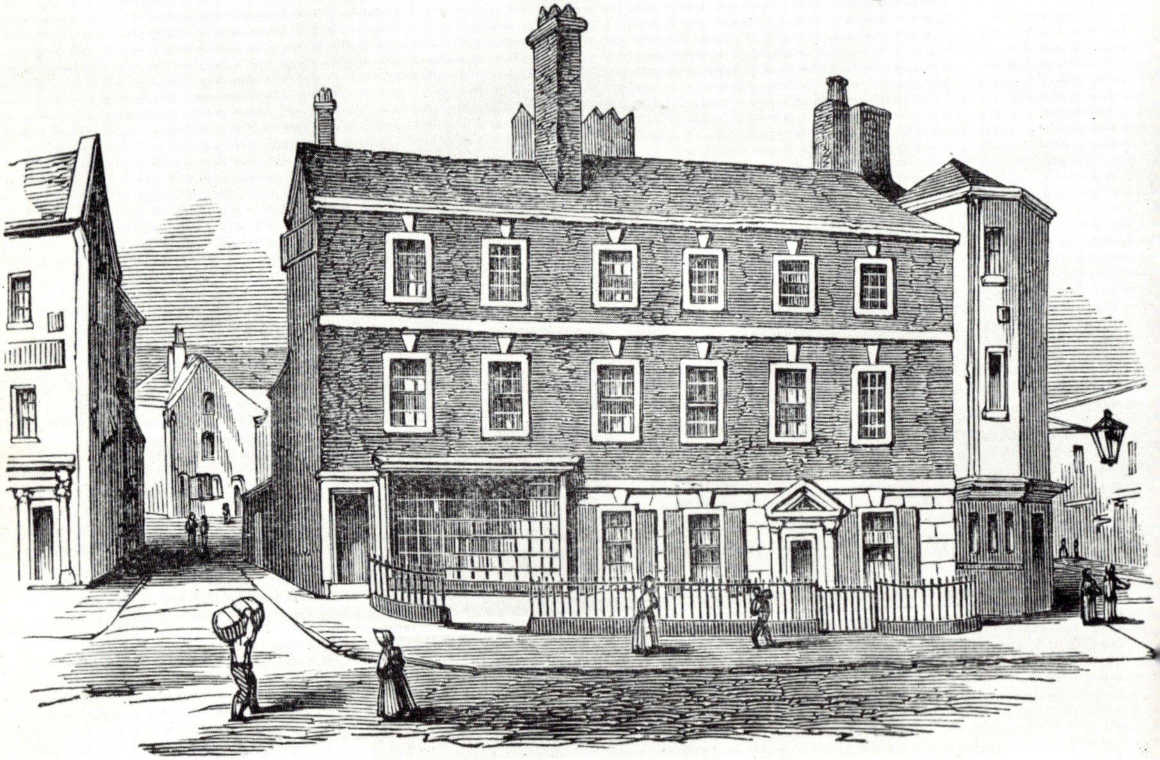

7 The house of an English master potter: Thomas Shaw, alderman of Liverpool. From Joseph Mayer's *History of the Art of Potting in Liverpool* (1871). See p. 39.

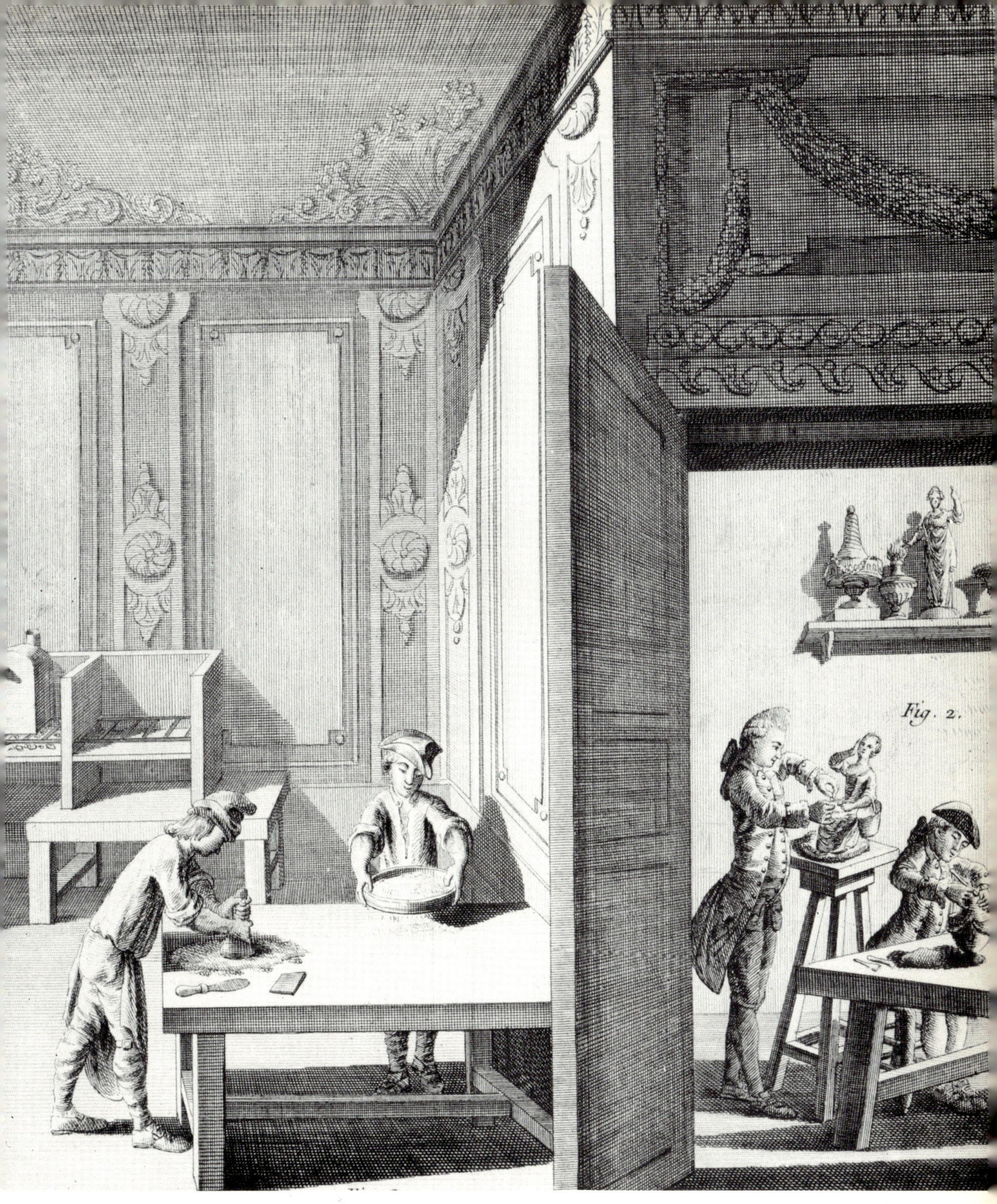

8 A scene from the Sèvres factory in the eighteenth century, showing the social difference, in costume, between modellers and workmen. From the Comte de Milly's *L'Art de la Porcelaine* (1777), published as part of Diderot's *Encyclopédie*.

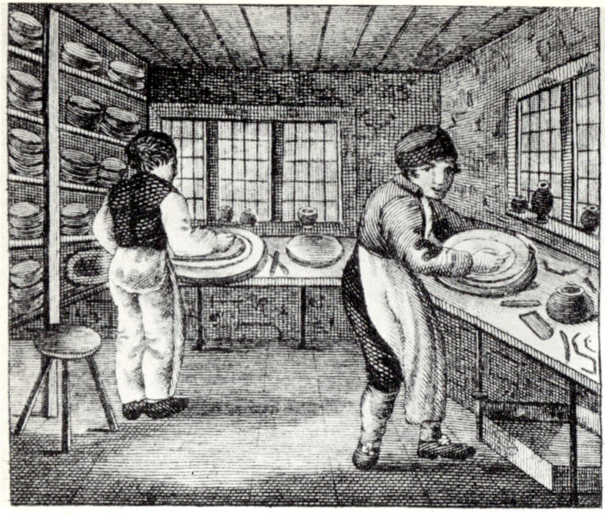

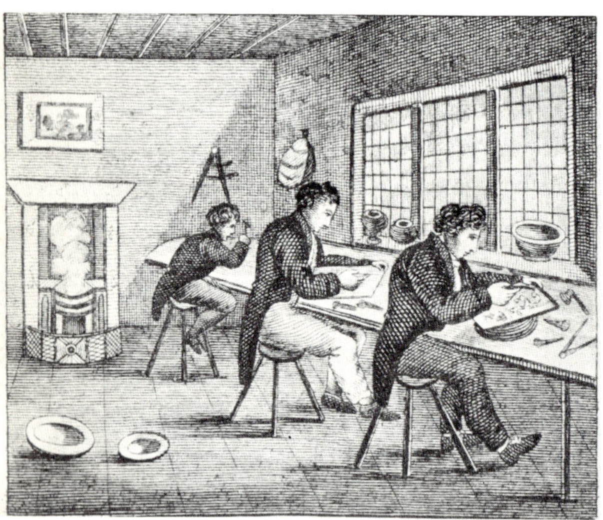

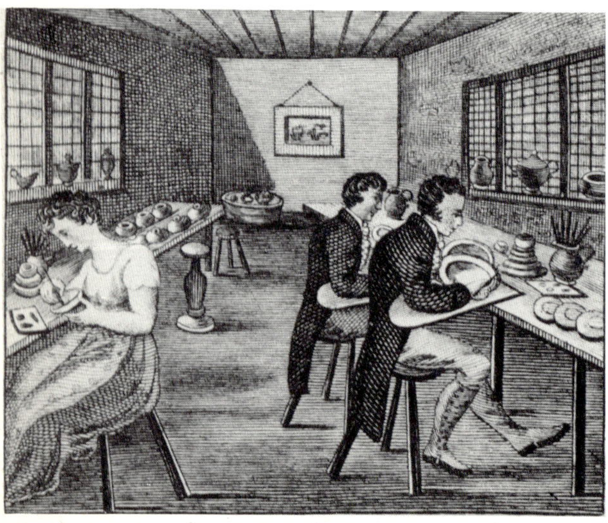

9 Enoch Wood's factory, Staffordshire: from *A Representation of the Manufacturing of Earthenware*, published anonymously in 1827. The social differences in costume between moulders (top), engravers (centre), and painters (bottom) are very marked.

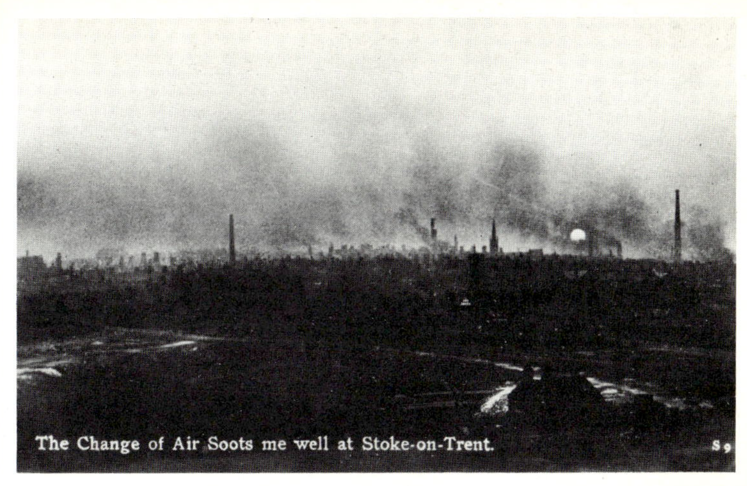

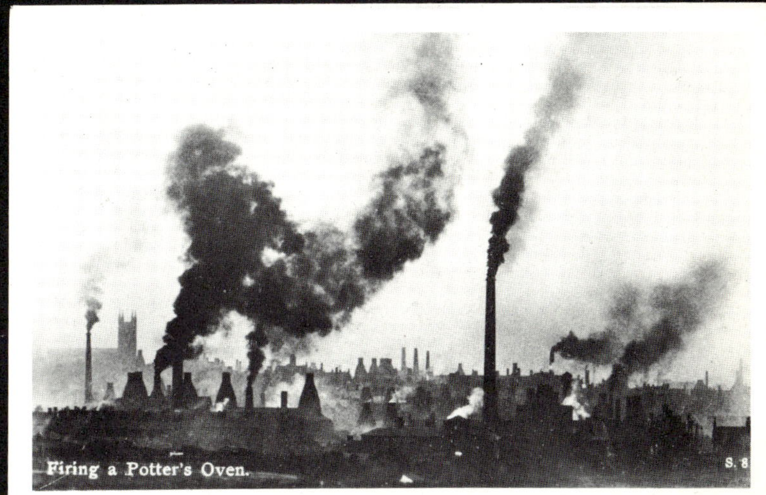

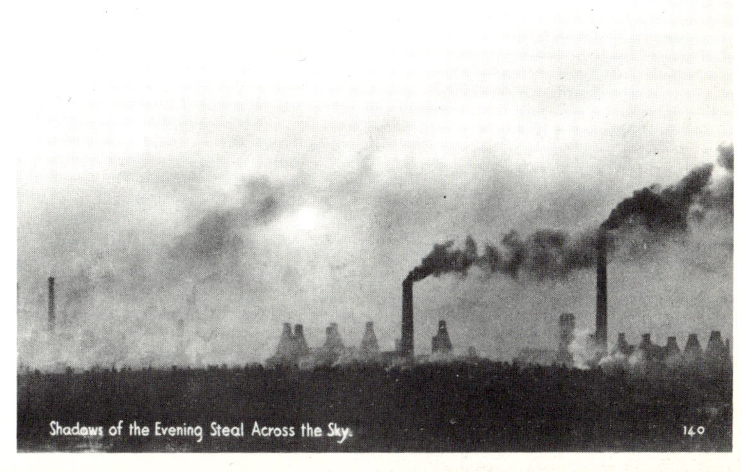

10 'Although the coal-fired bottle ovens have now been replaced by electric kilns, the Potteries folk – always about fifty years behind even their own advances – still sell in their shops the old tragi-comic postcards.' See p. 22.

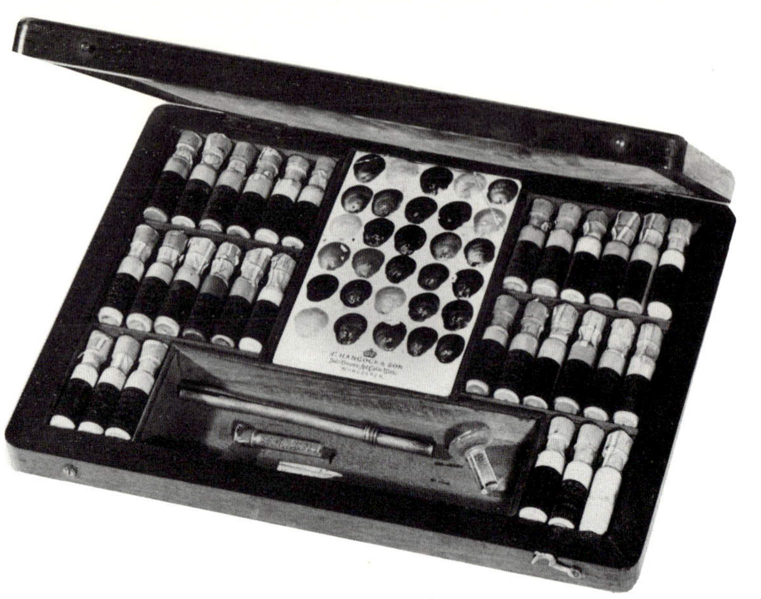

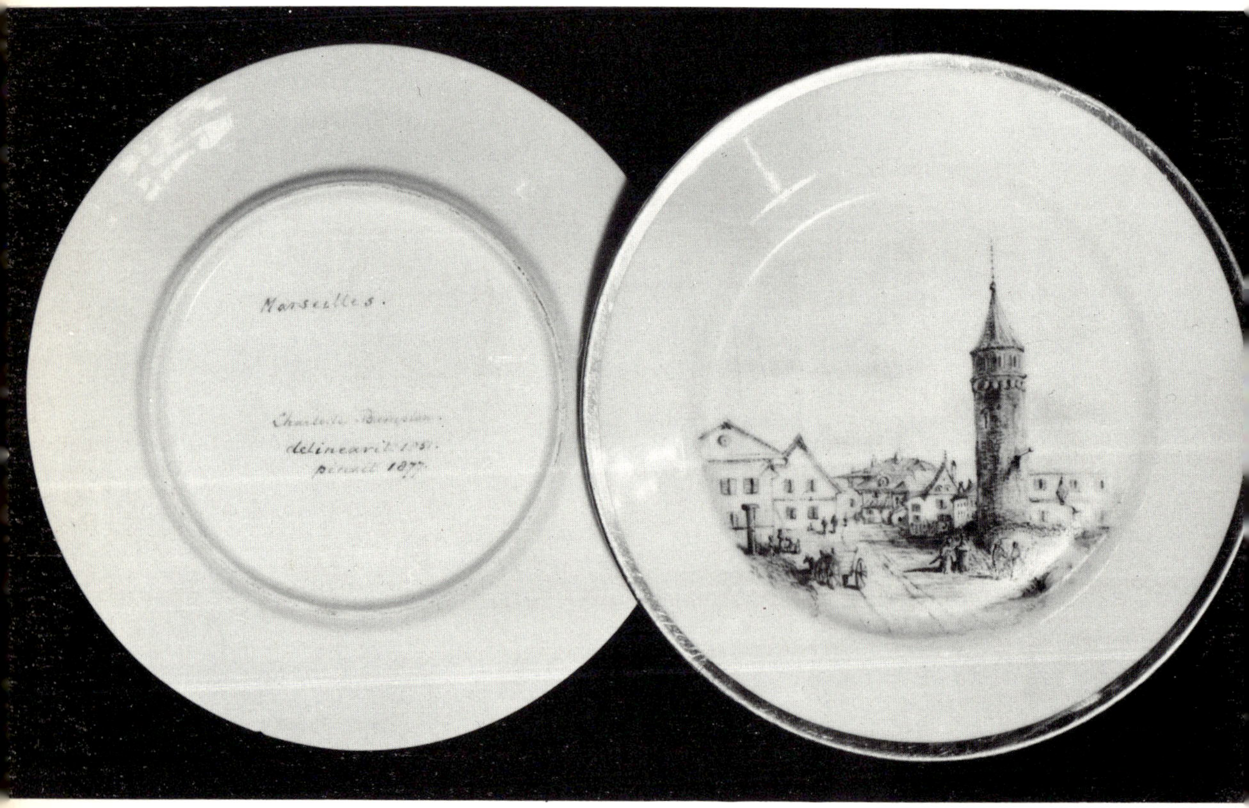

11 and 12 Amateur work: (top) a box of china colours by J. Hancock and Son of Worcester, used by Charlotte Bampton in 1877 to paint plates from sketches made by her in Europe between 1845 and 1870; (bottom) two of the porcelain plates. Diameter 8″. That on the left is inscribed 'Marseilles. Charlotte Bampton. delineavit 1851. pinxit 1877'. See p. 45.

other was the alleged origin of flint ware, when Thomas Astbury noticed that the pulverized calcined flint used by a Doncaster hostler to make a horse's eyes discharge, was white and clayey.[28] Serendipity extended to the collecting as well as the manufacture of ceramics. After describing the martyrdom of Pousa, Moncure Conway writes:

Social status of the potter

The South Kensington Museum has carried out in its own case this tradition of happy accidents, having been remarkable for its good-luck. Some instances of it are in the Ceramic Gallery. Some years ago a terrible explosion of gas occurred in the house of the famous art collector and dealer, Mr Gambart, at St John's Wood, by which the housemaid was killed. M. Alma Tadema was a guest in the house, and he had the presence of mind to open a window when he first perceived that gas was escaping, by which means the disaster was mainly limited to the dining-room. In this room were two large cabinets filled with splendid specimens of Flemish 'graybeards', beakers, and similar wares, and some of the best were smashed. As the fragments were about to be cleared away, a friend of Mr Gambart's, who was also connected with this museum, brought him an offer from the institution of £800 (as I have heard; at any rate, a sum that was generous) for the collection, broken and unbroken, and it was gratefully accepted. The skilled workmen at the museum have put the bits together with such adroitness that it requires a practised eye to distinguish the wares that suffered.[29]

Yet another 'happy accident'; yet another martyrdom. *Vita brevis....*

The apocrypha of ceramics – religious mystique and industrial mythology – qualified the potter as a decent artisan who would earn his place in the kingdom of heaven if he kept obediently to his station in life and did not aspire to a liberal education or the squire's daughter. The one permissible means of social advancement was patronage. There were two kinds of patron. On the one hand there was the prince or nobleman who put up capital for a factory or bought many shares in the business, perhaps provided it with a monopoly or 'privilege' in his state, and made up its losses from his own pocket. But equally important was the customer who bought large services of ware or commissioned elaborate portrait busts, centrepieces for the banquet table, or presents for royalty and ambassadors.

Orry de Fulvy founded Vincennes in the belief that a porcelain factory would enable him to recoup his gambling losses. But although a successful factory could be a valuable source of income for its patron, as Meissen was for the Electors of Saxony, the motives of the patron were often princely amusement and prestige rather than profit. Karl Eugen, Duke of Württemberg, who founded the Ludwigsburg factory in 1758, said that for a prince of his rank a porcelain factory was 'an indispensable accompaniment of splendour and magnificence'. It has been said of Charles III of Bourbon, King of Naples and Spain, the founder of Capodimonte (1743), that 'porcelain, next to hunting, became his favourite pastime'.[30] That Prince Albrecht Ernst of Oettingen-Oettingen should have chosen his menagerie-garden as the site of his porcelain factory at Schrattenhofen (1737) indicates the role of the ceramics factory as a status symbol and luxurious curiosity for princes. It belonged with the private zoo, with Ludwig of Bavaria's collection of freaks, with the armies of giants kept by Frederick William I of Brandenburg and his son, Frederick the Great. (Augustus the Strong actually bartered a regiment of Saxon dragoons for forty-eight of Frederick William's porcelain vases.) The attempt to produce wares and ornaments of outlandish size was part of the same cult, and one could almost regard it as more than fortuitous that the chief modeller appointed in 1790 at Frederick the Great's Berlin factory was called Johann Riese (John Giant). Ceramics were a game : the prince would try to beat the previous record. Ceramics were prestigious : the prince would try to outdo his fellow rulers. At Meissen, Kändler made huge porcelain models of Augustus III, and life-sized animals and birds – a porcelain menagerie – for the *Japanisches Palais*. In 1783 Louis XVI ordered from Sèvres a vase which cost 70,000 livres. Five feet high, and decorated with 'Atalanta's Race', it was intended for the Court of Tuscany, but Louis was so impressed with it that he kept it himself and ordered another. An even larger vase, the 'Cordelier', was made in 1785. In England, where there was no patronage on a grand scale, the proprietor-potters competed with each other; Simeon Shaw tells how an order for 'a very large Punch Bowl', which had been forwarded to 'different celebrated Potters', was finally executed by the Turners' modeller, William Massey. It held twenty-two gallons.[31]

Patronage was proselytizing. The three daughters of Augustus III, King of Poland and Elector of Saxony – Maria Amalia Christina, Maria Josepha and Maria Anna Sophia – married the King of Naples, the Dauphin of France and the Elector of Bavaria respectively, and it was largely at their instance that factories were started at Capodimonte, Vincennes and Nymphenburg. (Maria Amalia brought Charles seventeen Meissen table-services as part of her dowry.) Charles's son, Ferdinand, who became King of Naples, started a porcelain factory there in 1771, and in 1779 proudly sent his father a case of his porcelain.

In England, wilfully isolated, as so often, from movements on the continent, there was only the most nominal royal patronage. This was the main reason why most of the English factories lasted for such a short time. The nearest approach to a patron of the continental type was Sir Everard Fawkener (1684–1778), secretary to George II's son, the Duke of Cumberland, and proprietor of the Chelsea factory from about 1749 until 1758. The lack of patronage in England had two beneficial results. First, there were no crippling monopolies such as the Sèvres one which drove Paul Hannong from Strassburg to Frankenthal in 1754 and which forced the Baron Jean-Louis Beyerlé to sell the Niderviller factory to General Custine in 1770. If Chelsea had been granted the monopoly of soft-paste porcelain, there would have been no Bow, no Derby, Worcester or Longton Hall. Apart from a few clandestine factories, there would have been only a grandiose, puffed-up Chelsea, an English Sèvres with too much money to lavish on vulgar gilding. If Josiah Wedgwood had been granted the exclusive manufacture of jasper, basalt and creamware, we should have few wares by John Turner, William Adams, Humphrey Palmer and James Neale.

Social status of the potter

Secondly, the absence of glamorous patrons allowed the potter-proprietors to be respected in their own right, not just reflectedly glorified as the servants of a prince. Men such as Nicholas Sprimont of Chelsea, a silversmith, Thomas Frye of Bow, a mezzotint-engraver, and Dr John Wall of Worcester, a physician and inventor, were considerable figures even if one forgot that they ran porcelain factories. In any case, the attitude of the English to trade in general was far more indulgent than that of Germany or France. Voltaire (who stayed in England with Sir Everard Fawkener, whom he dubbed 'The Philosopher of Wandsworth') noted in his *Letters Concerning the English Nation* that:

> When the Lord *Townshend* was Minister of State, a Brother of his was content to be a City Merchant; and at the time that the Earl of *Oxford* govern'd *Great Britain*, his younger Brother was no more than a Factor in Aleppo, where he chose to live, and where he died. This Custom, which begins however to be laid aside, appears monstrous to *Germans*, vainly puff'd up with their Extraction. These think it morally impossible that the Son of an *English* Peer should be no more than a rich and powerful Citizen's, for all are Princes in *Germany*.[32]

But perhaps the virtues of patronage outweighed its vices. The prince could annexe to the royal factory men of distinction in auxiliary arts – a court sculptor such as Kändler, a court confectioner such as Haselmeyer at Ludwigsburg, a court miniaturist such as Henrici at Meissen, or even, as with Böttger, a court alchemist. When the Elector Palatine bought the Frankenthal factory in 1762 he imported the court sculptor Konrad Linck as a modeller. Two years later, another court sculptor, Johann Christian Wilhelm Beyer, was appointed *Modellmeister* at Ludwigsburg. Again, royal patronage was a good advertisement. Possibly the princes realized this, for Louis XV himself auctioned Sèvres porcelain to the nobility on New Year's Day, 1759, while in the next reign public exhibitions of Sèvres wares were held at Versailles and Louis XVI unpacked the pieces, breaking several. But certainly the potters realized it: in England, where royal patronage meant little more than the privilege of supplying the gracious patron with handsome services, Wedgwood had the acumen to call his cream-coloured earthenware 'Queen's Ware', while the Turners flaunted the Prince of Wales's feathers as a decorative motif after their appointment in 1784.

Most welcome of all must have been the eleventh-hour *deus-ex-machina* operation which rescued a factory from financial embarrassment, as when Louis XV, in 1763, made up a Sèvres deficit of 96,000 livres (about £12,000). Compared with this largesse, the patronage exercised by the Venetian state in the eighteenth century was hard-headed. After the Vezzi factory came to a disastrous end (1727), the Board of Trade and Senate issued a Proclamation (1728), offering facilities to anyone who would start new factories for *terraglie fine* and porcelain, or who would improve the quality of maiolica; and a similar proclamation followed in 1732, soon after the accession as Doge of Carlo Ruzzini, who, it is believed, may have been one of the directors of the Vezzi company. This was the kind of state encouragement that Houghton had suggested England should exercise. Writing of china manufacture in 1695 he said: 'By my Consent, the Man that would bring it to Perfection, should have for his Encouragment 1000 l. from the Publick, tho' I help'd to pay a Tax towards it.'[33] Henry Delamain, the Dublin potter, was in fact granted precisely that sum by the Irish Parliament in 1753 for having fired delft ware with coals 'as well as was ever done with turf and wood', but he was unsuccessful when he petitioned the English Parliament for similar reward.[34]

The grander the patron, the grander the potter: a good empirical theorem, but obviously not an infallible one, since a very rich patron was quite as capable of maintaining his employees in squalor as a moderately rich one. ('Charitable comme un autre, mais il étoit riche comme mille' was how a French peasant described Louis XVI in August, 1792, when asked by Dr John Moore whether the people would like the king back.[35]) When Johann Peter Melchior, the Höchst *Modellmeister*, was negotiating with Frankenthal, he refused to work 'under officials, but only under the Court'. Another grandee *Modellmeister*, Johann Christoph von Lücke, was engaged by the Vienna factory in 1750 at an annual salary of 1,000 florins and free accommodation. At the other extreme, we find Thomas Whieldon, two years later, hiring 'little Bet Blowr to learn to flower' at a shilling a week. Alderman Thomas Shaw, who ran a pottery business in Liverpool in the mid-eighteenth century, lived in a comfortable Georgian house (Plate 7); but it was not much larger than the model workmen's houses provided by the munificence of Jakob von Küner at the Künersberg factory (Plate 6).

Social status of the potter

Between clay workers (moulders and throwers) and decorators there were differences in pay and working conditions which sometimes caused ill feeling. In 1753 the clay workers at Meissen complained to the inspector Reinhardt that the painters were earning too much and were 'strutting around in fine clothes' while moulders and throwers received only between six and fourteen talers a month.[36] Their own hours, they felt, were too short (6 am. to 6 pm. in summer, and 7.30 am. to 4.30 pm. in winter). Decorators on piecework could work for seventeen hours and earn twice as much. Reinhardt soothingly replied that the painters were endangering their eyesight, and would later suffer for having worked so long in a cramped position. He also argued that when painters were ill they were not paid, whereas clay workers on a monthly salary could continue to draw their pay – a fact which has been ignored in praising Wedgwood for his humanitarian 'innovations'.

The conditions revealed by the Meissen dispute were far from universal. The grander decorators received monthly or yearly salaries, usually, but not always, exceeded by those of the chief modellers. At Meissen, the painter Johann Gottfried Melhorn received thirteen talers a month; the modeller Johann Gottlob Kirchner was engaged in 1727 at 220 talers a year. When the great decorator Johann Gregor Höroldt arrived there in April 1720, he was at first employed at piece rates. He earned six talers in May, eleven talers and twenty groschen in June, forty-nine talers in September and so on until 1729, when he was offered a salary rate of six hundred talers a year. When Samuel Stolzen, the Meissen kiln master, was inveigled away to Vienna by the musician La France, he was promised a salary of a thousand talers a year and a carriage. On 1 January 1751 Lücke, the Vienna *Modellmeister*, was paid his annual salary of 1,500 gulden; Niedermayer, his chief assistant, received six hundred gulden.

Gottlieb Friedrich Riedel, appointed chief painter at Ludwigsburg in 1759, received forty gulden a month. In the same year, Andreas Phillipp Ettner, another decorator, was paid thirty-three florins a month. Johann Goz was employed as a modeller at Ludwigsburg in 1760 at twenty-six florins a month, as were Joseph Nees, a deaf mute modeller taken on in 1759, and Johann Christoph Haselmeyer, the former court confectioner. At Nymphenburg, Franz Anton Bustelli began modelling at four florins a week; this was later raised to five florins and stood at ten florins in 1762. His successor, Dominikus Auliczek, was earning forty florins a week in 1765.

At Gotzkowski's factory, Berlin (1761–3), Karl Jakob Christian Klipfel was engaged to paint flowers and *Mosaik* patterns at 1,100 talers a year; Karl Wilhelm Böhme was employed as a landscape artist at a thousand talers a year. Under Frederick the Great, the chief modeller, Wilhelm Christian Meyer, received 1,500 talers a year, raised in 1764 to two thousand talers; but he could still model a satire on the painter – a monkey in a wig.

But compare these salaries with the wages of the ordinary workman. At Frederick the Great's Berlin factory, a kiln worker received 72 to 336 florins a year, a mill hand 72 to 121 florins, a clay worker 72 to 108 florins, a gold burnisher 96 florins, the woodcutter and nightwatchman 90 florins each. At Meissen the wages of a day labourer preparing clay for the moulds used by the brothers Lücke at Meissen were seventy-two kreutzer for three days. At Frankenthal a thrower could make twenty-five florins, and a day labourer ten florins, a month. At Fulda a clay worker earned eighteen kroner a day, a thrower making small pots and boxes, twenty-four kroner, and moulder and assembler up to sixteen florins a month. At Zürich in 1764 a skilled potter earned five gulden a week, a kiln worker four gulden and a painter six florins.

In 1747 Thomas Whieldon hired George Bagnall as a firer at 5*s*. 3*d*. a week. Samuel Jackson, who threw saggars and fired wares, received 8*s*. a week from 1751. Josiah Spode, the founder of the potting firm, was apprenticed to Whieldon in 1747 at 2*s*. 3*d*. a week – 'or 2*s*. 6*d*. if he Deserves it'. Wages in the porcelain manufacture were higher. When Robert Willcox and his wife (daughter of Thomas Frye of Bow) applied to Wedgwood for jobs in 1769, Wedgwood wrote to his partner: 'His wife and he have got very good wages he says at Worcester, better he believes than he must ever expect again; they would now be content he says both of them at 25*s*. Per week which is low enough if they will be tolerably dilligent.'[37]

In the nineteenth century workmen's associations to obtain better conditions were established in England. Insufficient pay was only one of the potters' grievances. Another was the unfair 'good-from-oven' system, whereby potters were paid only for such wares made by them as came from the kiln in perfect state. The basis of this was the argument that wares flawed in the oven were shoddily made: but often the kiln-packers were careless, and in any case most manufacturers sold off imperfect wares as 'seconds' while giving the workman nothing for them. Annual hiring was another abuse. Potters were hired at Michaelmas for the year. During that year they could not leave their job, but the employer could give them as little as one day's work a week, with payment to match: the system had as much of the mutuality of a bargain as theft. The potters' struggle against these and other abuses, at once heroic and pathetic, is movingly chronicled in Harold Owen's *The Staffordshire Potter* (1901). It is a story of strikes which failed through lack of unanimity, of hysterical Luddism, of misguided attempts to reduce unemployment in the Potteries by establishing a fictile utopia in America – 'Pottersville, USA'. Ultimately the workers won. Annual hiring was abolished in 1865, and a 'good-from-hand' system replaced the odious 'good-from-oven' in 1871. The dangerous processes of the industry were being de-fanged. An amendment to the Factory and Workshop Bill of 1891 extended its provisions, which gave protection to workers in 'dusty processes', to potters as well as textile workers. In 1898 the Home Office ordered an inquiry into lead-poisoning in the pottery manufacture, and as to whether the danger could be diminished or removed by substituting for the carbonate of lead ordinarily used a lead silicate or a leadless glaze. In December 1899, as a result of this investigation, a notification was issued from Whitehall that within six months manufacturers would be expected to have discontinued the use of raw lead entirely.

Social status of the potter

There was one class, largely of decorators, which remained quite unaffected by such morbid considerations: the amateurs. Among the more distinguished dabblers were Ferchault de Réaumur (1683–1757) the scientist, who tried to make porcelain from powdered glass and flour, and the poet Salomon Gessner who painted whimsical ruins on Zürich porcelain. A. O. E. von dem Busch, a Canon of the Holy Cross, Hildesheim, achieved an international reputation[38] with his decoration of Meissen porcelain. He used the highest and lowest forms of carbon for his work, engraving designs on the glaze with a diamond, and rubbing them over with soot (sometimes with Indian ink). His fellow canon J. J. Kratzberg also decorated Meissen wares. The Baroness Beyerlé, wife of the proprietor of Niderviller, painted some of the factory's wares. Sir James Thornhill decorated Dutch delft plates now in the British Museum (Plates 27 and 28).

Two of the daughters of George III fancied themselves as china-painters. Dorothy Margaret Stuart records that Princess Charlotte Augusta Matilda sent her father 'a broth-cup made of Louisbourg [i.e. Ludwigsburg] china after her own design', and adds:

> In the grounds of the chateau [of Louisbourg] was a pleasant house, the Mathildenhof, with a garden of its own, and it was there that she did most of her painting on porcelain, signing each piece on the bottom with her initials, C.A.M. When the Disbrowes were at Stuttgart shortly after her death, 'an oven for baking china' was still to be seen.[39] Some examples of her handiwork are preserved at Frogmore House, large vases, loaded with gold paint, and adorned with landscapes and garlands in monochrome. One particularly 'Wertherish' design shows a mossy tombstone, inscribed *Erinnerung*, on the verge of a gloomy stream.[40]

The Princess Elizabeth, otherwise the Landgravine of Hessen-Homburg (familiarly known as 'Bessie Humbug') painted 'The Triumph of Love' on a Berlin porcelain service.[41] Her original drawings for these designs, including one of Love's flight through the air on an anchor – the anchor of Hope – were naturally hailed as works of genius. The Dean of Westminster, Dr Vincent, congratulated the *Nitidissima Nympha* on the excellence of her handiwork in his election verses at Westminster:

> Lusus docta leves, roseique Cupidinis ortum
> Pinxisse artifici, dulcis Eliza, manu,
> Salve, progenies regum.[42]

These verses were rendered into still more ridiculous English by Sir James Bland Burges (1752–1824), sometime Under Secretary for Foreign Affairs:

> Hail Royal Maid! by whose plastic hand
> Were Cupid's birth and first achievements plann'd;
> Illustrious leader of the graphic train,
> To accept from me this votive chaplet deign.[43]

Wedgwood, always ready to defer to a large enough demand (he even made busts of Voltaire and Rousseau in black to please the clergy, although a Dissenter and liberal himself) made white unglazed 'dry-body' wares for amateurs to try their hand on. The vases shown in

III (*opposite*) English embroidery panel, *c.* 1730–40, showing tea being taken in a garden from porcelain bowls. The man walking up the path is carrying a silver kettle.

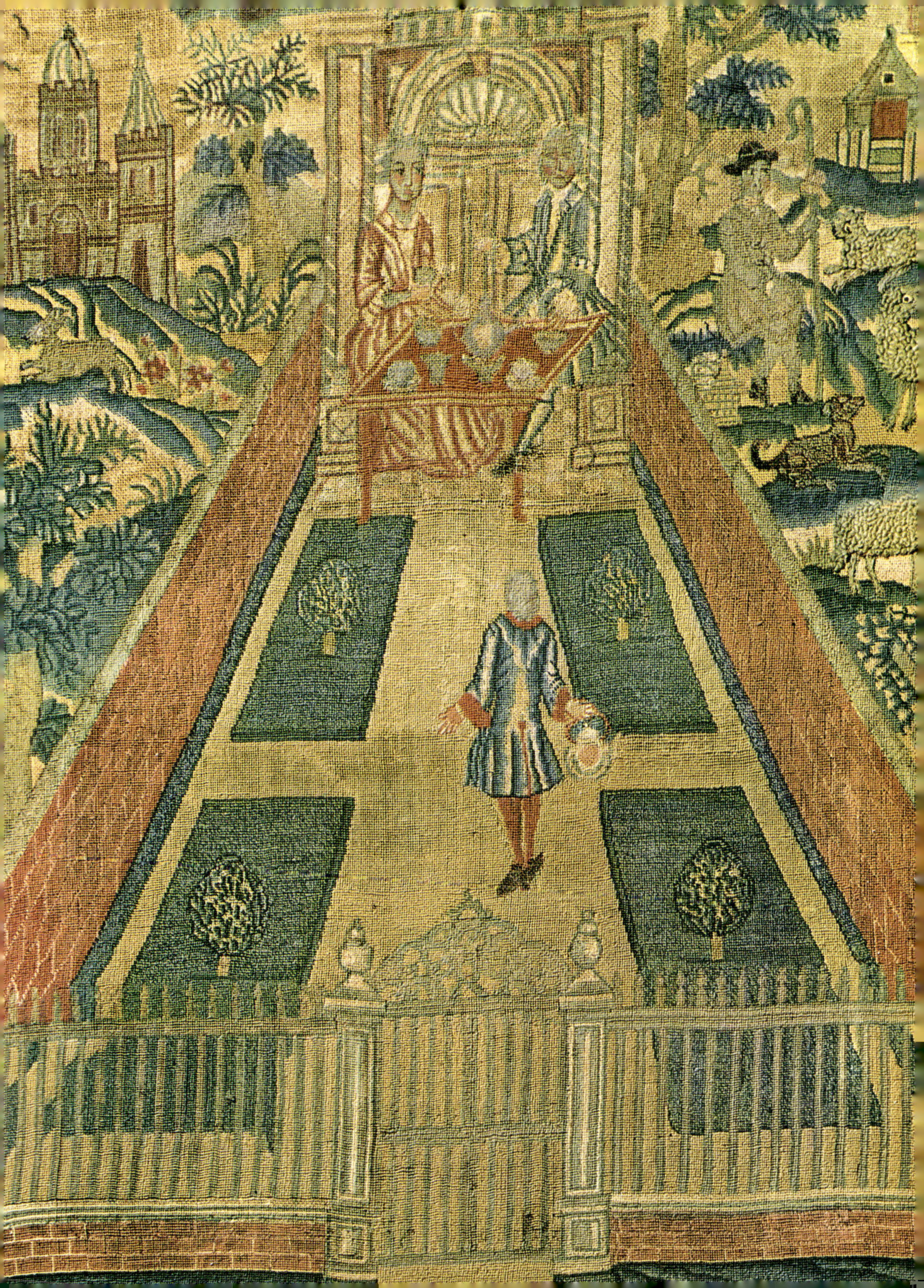

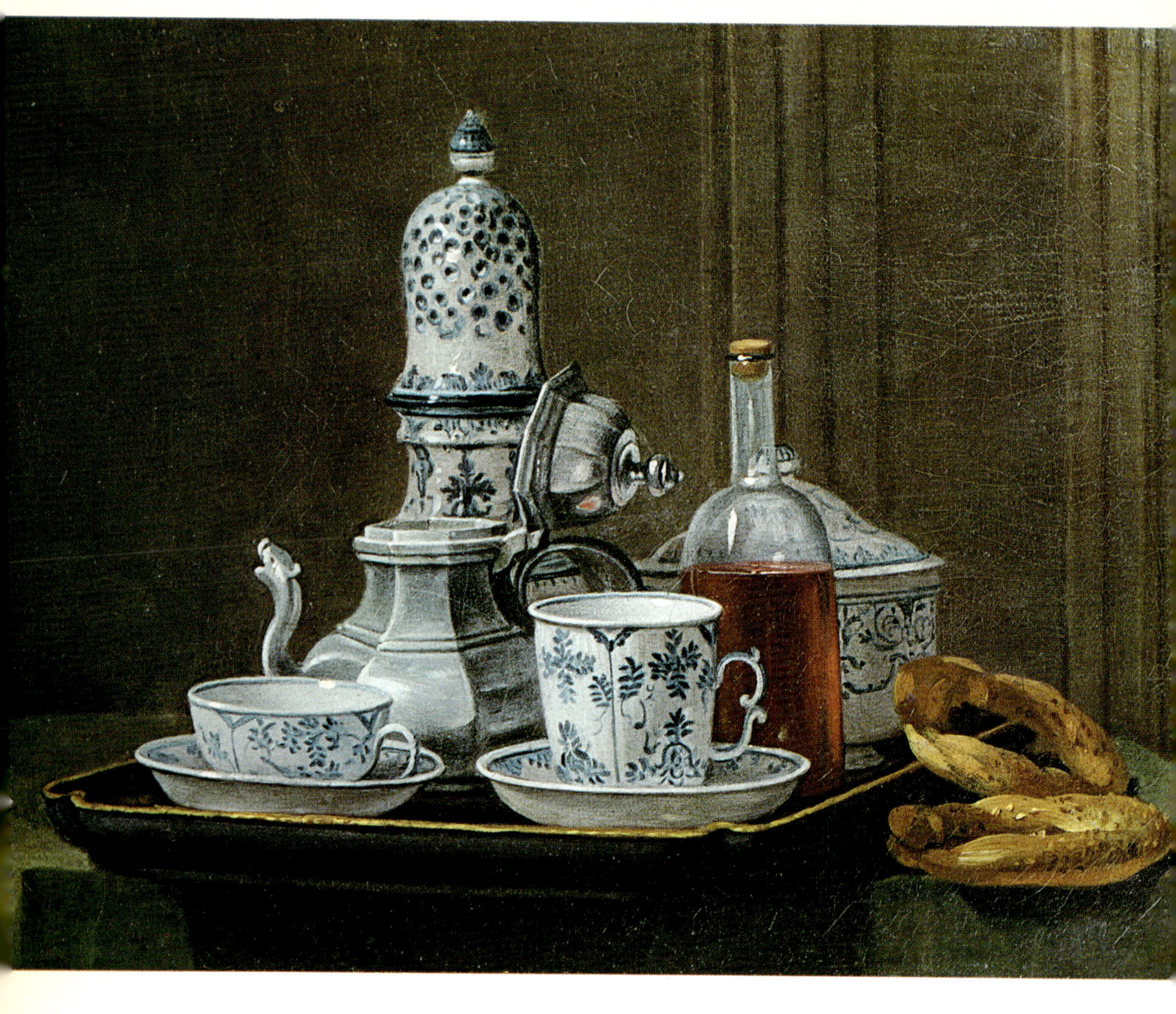

Plate 88 are of the kind to which Wedgwood's London agent referred in a letter of 1796:

Social status of the potter

> The Marchioness of Blandford wishes you to send (along with the things already bespoke) a small vase for Lady's to paint on; what her Ladyship means is made of a white composition...[44]

China-painting became still more popular in the late nineteenth century when Messrs Hancock and Son of Worcester issued a book of *Copies for China Painters* and supplied special paint-boxes (Plate 11) filled with china colours such as 'Sèvres Blue' and 'China Green'. One could buy unglazed menu tablets (1*s*. 3*d*. each), croquet trays (3*s*. and 3*s*. 6*d*.), moustache cups and saucers (2*s*.) and china buttons (2*s*. 3*d*. a dozen). Annual exhibitions of work by Lady Amateurs were held from 1875 at Howell and James's Art Galleries, Regent Street, London, under royal patronage.[45] One of the judges in 1882 was Henry Stacy Marks (Plate 173), himself a skilled amateur decorator of Minton vases (Plate 172).[46] William Owen's *Songs of Labour* were published two years later, but Stacy Marks and the Lady Amateurs seem lustres and continents away from:

> Where the minarets are chimneys;
> Where the towers are potters' ovens;
> Where the plastic clay is fashioned
> Into forms of use and beauty;
> Where the crusted earth is burrowed
> For the wealth of mine beneath it;
> Where the very hills are iron;
> Where grim workers in the metals
> Make the potter's face look whiter
> As they meet him in the highways;
> Where the busy sounds of labour
> Rise, the best of human incense,
> To the throne of the Creator.[47]

IV (*opposite*) 'Still Life of a breakfast table', by Henri-Horace Roland de la Porte (1724–93). The ceramics in use include some Meissen of the Copenhagen pattern.

2 The end of the Baroque

In the baroque period, all the arts aspired towards the condition of grand opera. The richest fulfilment of the style was in palace and castle architecture, heroic tragedy, opera, oratorio and fantastic masques, which, by requiring an imposing congress of art forms, gave scope for the talents of an *uomo universale* such as Bernini.[1] Such a style was not ideally suited to ceramics. Porcelain was too frail, pottery too homely, for its hyperboles and ecstasies; and ceramics cracked in the kiln if used on too grand a scale.

In spite of these limitations, some distinguished sculptors became modellers in porcelain and stoneware; the elevation of pottery into sculpture was part of the general overweening. By the early eighteenth century there were two distinct traditions in baroque sculpture: an extremist tradition, deriving from Italy and Bernini; and a more restrained tradition deriving from Brussels, Antwerp and François Duquesnoy ('Il Fiammingo'). The Bernini school was dramatic, overreaching, conveying an impression of just suspended movement. (When working on his bust of Louis XIV, Bernini had spent some time watching the King play tennis.) The Fiammingo tradition rather expressed the reason of classical antiquity – what Professor Wittkower, referring to Duquesnoy's *Susanna*, calls 'a limpid and temperate simplicity'[2] – a quality which also pervades the work of Duquesnoy's friend, Poussin.

In general, the extremist tradition was directly brought into ceramics by sculptors such as Kändler of Meissen and Massimiliano Soldani-Benzi whose moulds were used at Doccia; while the Fiammingo influence is seen in imitations of his works, ranging from free adaptations to servile copies. It was easier to imitate the sober baroque of Fiammingo than the high-flying baroque of Bernini. In the eighteenth century, the Fiammingo tradition was especially strong in England. Rysbrack and Scheemakers had both been trained in the Antwerp school founded by Duquesnoy's brother after the sculptor's premature death. Both the porcelain factories and the Staffordshire earthenware factories were to make models after Scheemakers's statue of Shakespeare in the Poet's Corner at Westminster Abbey. In the eighteenth and nineteenth centuries models after Fiammingo himself inspired such socially disparate works as the white Chelsea boy's head (Plate 16), the Enoch Wood copy on a bright orange plinth, and a Herculaneum version in which angel wings were sentimentally added, turning the baby into a cherub. Plate 15 shows a nineteenth-century plaster copy, similar to those owned by eighteenth-century sculptors; and examples in plain and bronze-covered terracotta, with in one case a baroque companion bust, are shown in Plates 18–21. A Chelsea sleeping boy dated 1746 in the British Museum, and Wedgwood models of the same subject, are also after Fiammingo. In 1755 the Vincennes factory bought a set of forty 'Figurines par la Rue pour de Service du Roi. D'après Francois Flamant (Fiammingo)'.[3] In about 1770, Gaspare Bruschi, chief modeller at the Doccia factory, freely adapted the *St Andrew* and *St John* set up by Duquesnoy in 1640 under the dome of St Peter's, Rome.[4] These figures, which are over three feet high, are in the Ginori collection, which also includes a great baroque chimney-piece and overmantel with allegorical figures after Michelangelo.

Most of these examples were made long after the baroque had ceased to be the dominant style in Europe. As one would expect, it took less time for baroque influences to reach Germany than to cross the Channel to England: the earliest ceramic versions of the Fiammingo head were in Böttger's red stoneware (Plate 14) and white Meissen porcelain.[5] But there was still a considerable lapse in time. The German states were slow in recovering from the devastations of the Thirty Years War. The Peace of Westphalia (1648), which ended the war, favoured the expansion of France and Sweden. The German recovery began in 1664 with the routing of a Turkish army at St Gotthard by the imperial general Montecucculi. In 1675 the Swedes were defeated at Fehrbellin by Frederick William, the Great Elector of Brandenburg, and in 1683, after the heroic defence of Vienna against the Turks, the city was relieved by a German-Polish army. It was only now that the arts could begin to revive in Germany, and the baroque to develop fully, almost a hundred years later than in Italy or Flanders.

For the first half of the eighteenth century, the supremacy among the

German states lay with Saxony. It began when Augustus the Strong won the Polish Crown in 1697. It declined under his son Augustus III, who might have been known as Augustus the Weak. He virtually left the direction of state affairs to Count Heinrich von Brühl, who also took control of the Meissen factory, and commissioned the great Swan service:

> The new King [says the *Cambridge Modern History*] was, in every respect, the antithesis of his alert, jovial and dissolute father. His character has been admirably symbolized in the famous picture which represents the portly Prince, enveloped in a luxurious dressing-gown, reclining in an easy chair and holding in his lap a tea-cup and saucer.[6]

The cup and saucer were, of course, of the best Meissen porcelain.

The English Ambassador at Dresden, Sir Charles Hanbury Williams, wrote of Augustus III in 1747:

> The King's absolute and avowed hatred of all business, and his known love of idleness, and low pleasures, such as Operas, Plays, Masquerades, Tilts, and Tournaments, Balls, Hunting, and Shooting, prevent both him and his country from making that figure in Europe which this noble electorate ought to do and often has done.[7]

(In the following year, Sir Charles benefited from the king's frivolity when he received a superb dessert service from him.)

To add Saxony to his dominions was one of the most passionate and persistent of Frederick the Great's ambitions. In the Seven Years War he nearly achieved it, when in 1756 Saxony capitulated to him at Pirna. But his own subsequent reverses were so great that he was forced to conclude peace, at Hubertusburg in 1763, on the basis of the *status quo ante bellum.* But after the death of Augustus in the same year, Catherine the Great's candidate, Stanislas Poniatowski, was elected to the Polish throne, and later Poland was divided between Prussia, Russia and Austria. The Saxon supremacy, which had begun with the acquisition of the Polish crown, ended with its loss. But this is to anticipate.

Although, while Germany was distracted by the Thirty Years War and its aftermath, the Italian and Flemish baroque could not find a home there, as soon as the German states began to recover, it was precisely these foreign influences which took root – because Germany had not been able to develop a distinctive and resilient tradition of its own. There was in fact a long tradition of Italian influence on the art of Dresden. Giovanni Maria Nosseni from Lugano (1544–1620) probably collaborated in building the Electoral Stables, the masterpiece of Dresden architecture in the late sixteenth century. He transformed the Gothic choir of Freiberg Cathedral into a princely mausoleum, with sculpted decoration by Carlo de Cesare, a Florentine (1590–3). His three-storeyed banqueting house on the Jungfer – a precursor of Augustus the Strong's Zwinger – was destroyed by a gunpowder explosion in 1747. In the seventeenth century Italo-Netherlandish influences reached Dresden by way of Prague, where Adriaen de Vries worked. The Saxon sculptor Sebastian Walther (1576–1645) was much influenced by his style, especially in the altar of the Sophienkirche at Dresden. The architect Wolf Caspar von Klengel (1630–91) often considered the founder of the Dresden baroque, had not only studied in Italy, but also provided his Dresden sketches and plans with explanatory remarks in Italian. 'Even his looks were foreign, in spite of his pure German extraction,'[8] says Dr Hempel, referring to the portrait by Fehling. Lorenzo Mattielli from Vicenza (1688–1748) made a series of statues for the Roman Catholic Church in Dresden, and carved a colossal sandstone fountain in the gardens of Count von Brühl's palace between 1741 and 1744. A reproduction of this fountain, on a smaller scale, now in the Victoria and Albert Museum, was modelled at the Meissen porcelain factory in 1745 by Kändler, Eberlein and Ehler. It was used as a dessert decoration, and was seen in action by Sir Charles Hanbury Williams at a banquet given by Brühl in 1748.

The most distinguished Dresden sculptor in the Bernini tradition was Balthasar Permoser (1651–1732), and it was through him, indirectly, that Italian baroque feeling was brought into Meissen porcelain. Born near Salzburg, he studied in Florence for fourteen years (probably 1671–85). He came to Dresden in 1689, and was responsible for the mythological sculpture of Augustus the Strong's great palace, Der Zwinger, of which the architect was Mathäes Daniel Pöppelmann, who had arrived in Dresden two years after Permoser. In 1710 Pöppelmann was sent to Vienna and Rome to study palaces and to get expert advice for the proposed palace. He was influenced by Carlo Fontana's buildings for the Vatican, and the Zwinger also included an omega-shaped arena for tournaments, which Pöppelmann called a 'römische Schauburg' (Roman theatre). From 1712 Permoser's chief assistant on the Zwinger sculptures was the court-sculptor Benjamin Thomae, and in 1723 Thomae took on a young apprentice, Johann Joachim Kändler, the future *Modellmeister* of the Meissen porcelain factory. The Zwinger was still uncompleted, and it was only in the previous year that the

East Pavilion had been finished. Even if Kändler did not himself take part in the decoration of Zwinger, he must have been influenced by it. Sponsel, indeed, suggests that 'er mag wohl mehr aus dem Studium der Werke Permosers, als an der Unterweisung Thomaes gelernt haben'. (He may well have learnt more from studying Permoser's work, than from Thomae's instruction.)

The extent to which Kändler was affected by the school of Bernini is very clearly shown in two sandstone tombs carved by him.[9] The earlier was made in 1732 for the Dresden councillor Gottfried Keil (father-in-law of Kändler's *bête noire*, the great Meissen decorator Johann Gregor Höroldt) and his wife Beata Christina Matsius. It depicts Saturn about to overthrow an obelisk – a typical baroque symbol of the transitory. Although Kändler was a clergyman's son, because of his early inclination to the fine arts he had been introduced by his father to the writers and mythology of antiquity. More symbols of transience – winged Saturn, scythe, hourglass – are carved on the other tomb, which is signed 'Jo. Joach. Kändler Konigl. Modellmeister fecit'. It was made for the mother of the poet Johann Elias Schlegel, Maria Schlegel, who died on 30 March 1736. Allegories of muted exaltation, these tombs by Kändler suggest the concept of sculpture attributed to Permoser by Dr Hempel:

> Permoser derived his painterly concept of sculpture, and his virtuosity in the rendering of light and shade and the texture of materials, from Bernini ... like Bernini, he endeavoured to replace the hard and isolating quality of sculpture by the softness and continuity of painting.[10]

For the working-out of such a concept, porcelain, with its softness and fluidity, was in some ways a more apt material than stone. The chiaroscuro would not be too oppressive; muscle, sinew and vein would not start out of the body with such apoplectic emotion, when the asperities of the modelling were lapped in glaze or set off by vivid enamels.

Under the impulse of what the factory archives call the 'römische Bestellung', a number of figures of saints and apostles were made at Meissen between 1735 and 1741 (Plate 23), brilliantly modelled by Kändler and Eberlein. They have not the transcendent quality of Bernini figures, whose heavenward eyes brim with ecstasy and whose draperies seem caught in the swell of an invisible ocean. They are too small to be viewed – as baroque sculpture should be viewed – from different points. But they are completely baroque in tone. In 1735 they received the official sanction of Christendom when a series of them was ordered for Pope Clement XII: coals to Newcastle. Two years later a similar series, also based on statues of apostles in the Lateran Church at Rome, was made for the widowed Empress Wilhelmina Amalia (mother-in-law of Augustus III). To the king's order, an entire altar in porcelain was made for the empress, including a crucifix, a bell, candlesticks and vessels for the Mass. This work, part of which survives in the Künsthistorisches Museum, Vienna, was not completed until 1740 or 1741.

In Italy itself, some magnificent ceramic sculpture was made at the Doccia factory from original moulds by Massimiliano Soldani-Benzi (1656–1740). This sculptor had had an exemplary schooling in the high baroque. His chief patron was Duke Cosimo de' Medici, but he also modelled a portrait of Queen Christina of Sweden (and studied her great art collection). In Paris he met Fischer von Erlach, and Louis XIV, whose portrait he also modelled, 'deigned to speak to him no fewer than seven times'. Like Foggini and other contemporary sculptors, Soldani made copies after the antique in bronze: but as his version of the San Ildefonso *Satyr with a Goat* shows (Plate 91), he invested them with a baroque exuberance. He made the altarpiece for Livorno (*c.* 1692), the bronze ornament for S. Maria di Carignano in Genoa (1699) and for the choir chapel at S. Lorenzo in his home town of Montevarchi (1706–9), and tombs for Malta (1722–9).

A bronze group of Apollo and Daphne by Soldani was a direct adaptation of one by Bernini, and the Doccia factory inventory records a 'Gruppo di Apollo e Dafne con 3 Putti e alberi di Massimiliano Soldani'.[11] A white porcelain plaque,[12] described in one of the early Doccia inventories as 'Time discovering Beauty' (it is actually *Time discovering Truth*) is taken from a model made by Soldani in 1695 for Prince Adam Andreas of Liechtenstein; a bronze version is in Vienna. The Ginori family (who owned the Doccia factory) still possess a Soldani bronze of a *Lamentation over the Dead Christ*, and a white porcelain version, mounted on an ebony pedestal with attached porcelain cherubs, swags and supports, is in the Corsini Gallery at Florence. *The Deposition* (Plate 13) is from a different but similar model. The original dates from about 1700, the porcelain group from about 1750 to 1760. This porcelain composition, which once belonged to that theocratic statesman, Mr Gladstone, was surely one of the most moving sculptures to be made in ceramics since Luca della Robbia, another Tuscan, modelled the *Resurrection and Ascension* in Florence Cathedral.

A set of four Seasons (*c.* 1750–60), some with attachments for candles, are known from the Doccia archives to have been modelled from ivory figures (*c.* 1680) by Permoser.[13] The ivories were at that time in Carlo Ginori's possession, but have since been lost. The porcelain figures survive; already in these works the frivolous affectation of the rococo is overtaking the profound and maudlin affectation of the baroque.

There was a lighthearted side to the baroque itself – though humour usually veered towards malice, the comic towards the grotesque. The *Commedia dell'arte*, or Italian comedy, was an especially popular subject for figures, not only because it gave scope for exaggerated gesture and brilliant colour, but because the patrons of the porcelain factories also, in many cases, patronized the Italian players. When the young Augustus was in Paris in 1687, he saw the troupe of Angelo Constantini, and wrote '... kohme in Paris an divertire mich 6 monat, unterschiedene intrigen besonders in grosser stille mit der Conty, avanture der italienischen comedie'.[14] The *Commedia* formed part of the entertainments during the lavish wedding celebrations of 1719. Sponsel includes in his work on the Zwinger an engraving of a performance of the Italian comedians at Augustus's court. The two characters on the stage are Pantaloon and Harlequin, the two figures most popular with the Meissen modellers. A Meissen harlequin with a tankard on his knee, in Dresden, is dated 1738, and another in the Budge Collection is dated 1740. Italy naturally produced models of the *Commedia*, including the leering Capodimonte Doctor (Plate 24). Bow, which seems to have been more conscious of the London stage than the other English factories (it produced famous models of Henry Woodward, Kitty Clive, and Peg Woffington) made a porcelain Scapino, copied from Luigi Riccoboni's *Histoire du Théâtre Italien* (1728), which also inspired several Meissen figures.

The court dwarfs of Augustus's entourage are recalled by grotesque Meissen figures which were in fact copied from *Il Calotto resuscitato oder Neu eingerichtes Zwerchen Cabinett*, a book published by Wilhelmus Koning at Antwerp[15] in 1716. Dwarfs from the same source were made at other continental factories, notably Vienna and Höchst. The engravings in Koning's book are signed by various artists and have nothing to do with Jacques Callot's work. But a Chelsea red-anchor male dwarf in a tall hat was taken from one of Callot's own engravings, and a female companion dwarf, made a little later, seems to have been an original Chelsea design. The male Chelsea dwarf was reissued by the Derby factory after 1770, with a new male companion, also after a Callot original. This pair, described in the Derby sale catalogue of 1784 as 'grotesque Punches', often have advertisements painted on their large hats, recalling the

The end of the Baroque

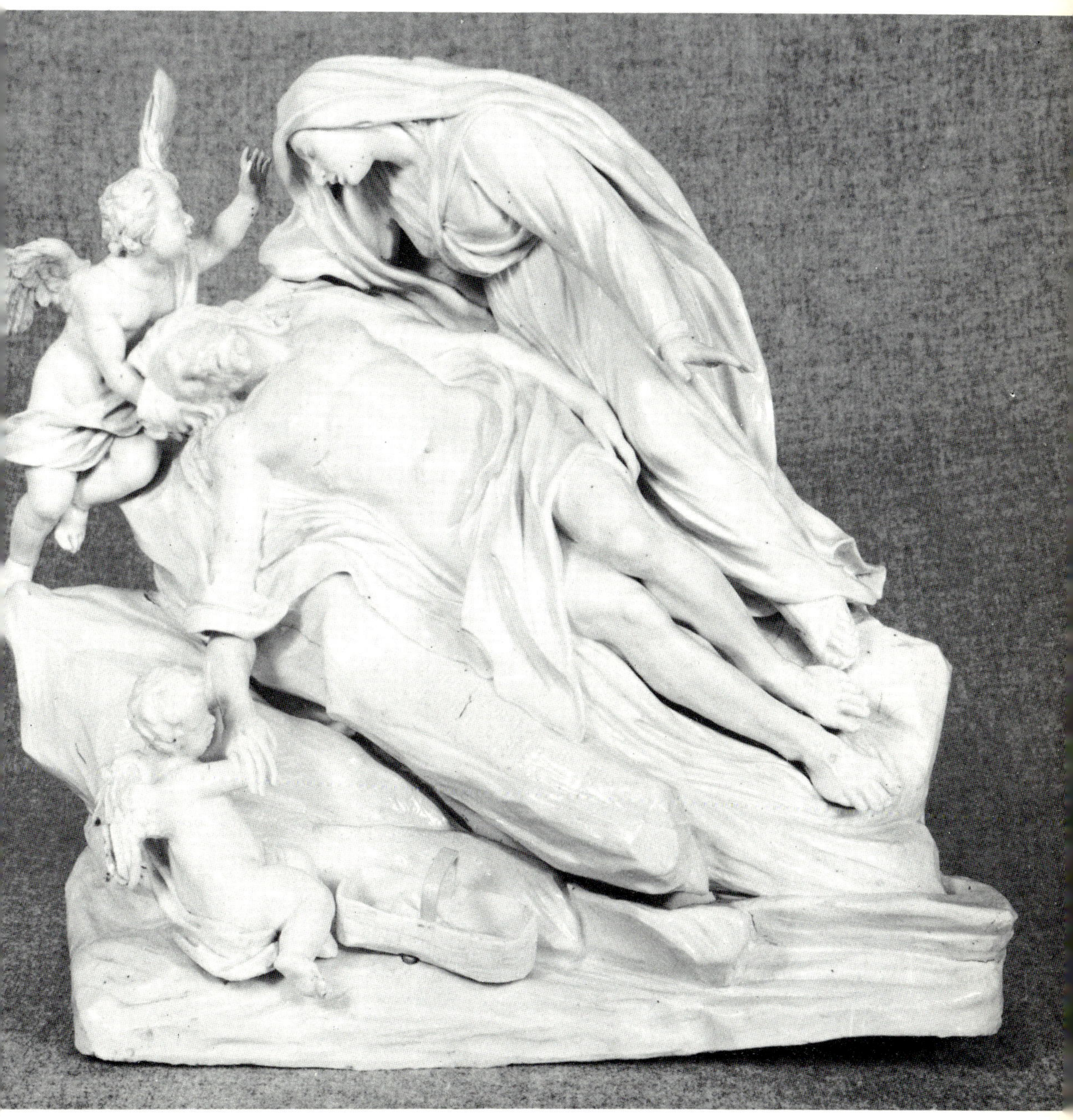

13 The Deposition, Doccia porcelain, from a model by Massimiliano Soldani-Benzi, *c.* 1770. Height 11″. This group formerly belonged to W. E. Gladstone. See p. 51.

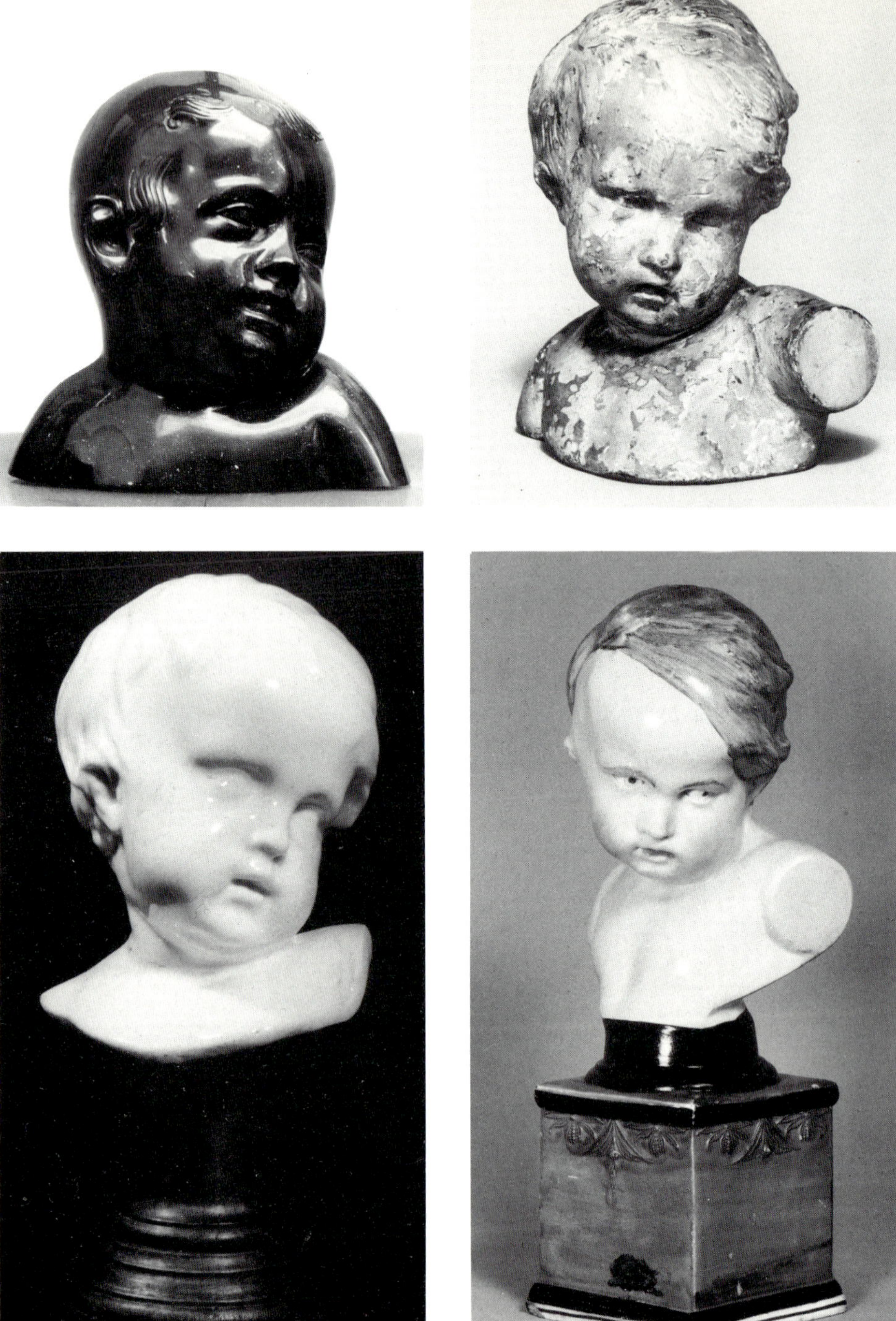

14–17 Four boys' heads after François Duquesnoy ('Il Fiammingo'): (top left) Böttger's red stoneware, Meissen, *c.* 1715; (top right) plaster model by Brucciani & Co., height 7″; (bottom left) Chelsea porcelain, *c.* 1745–50; (bottom right) Enoch Wood earthenware, Staffordshire, *c.* 1830, height 9¾″. See p. 47.

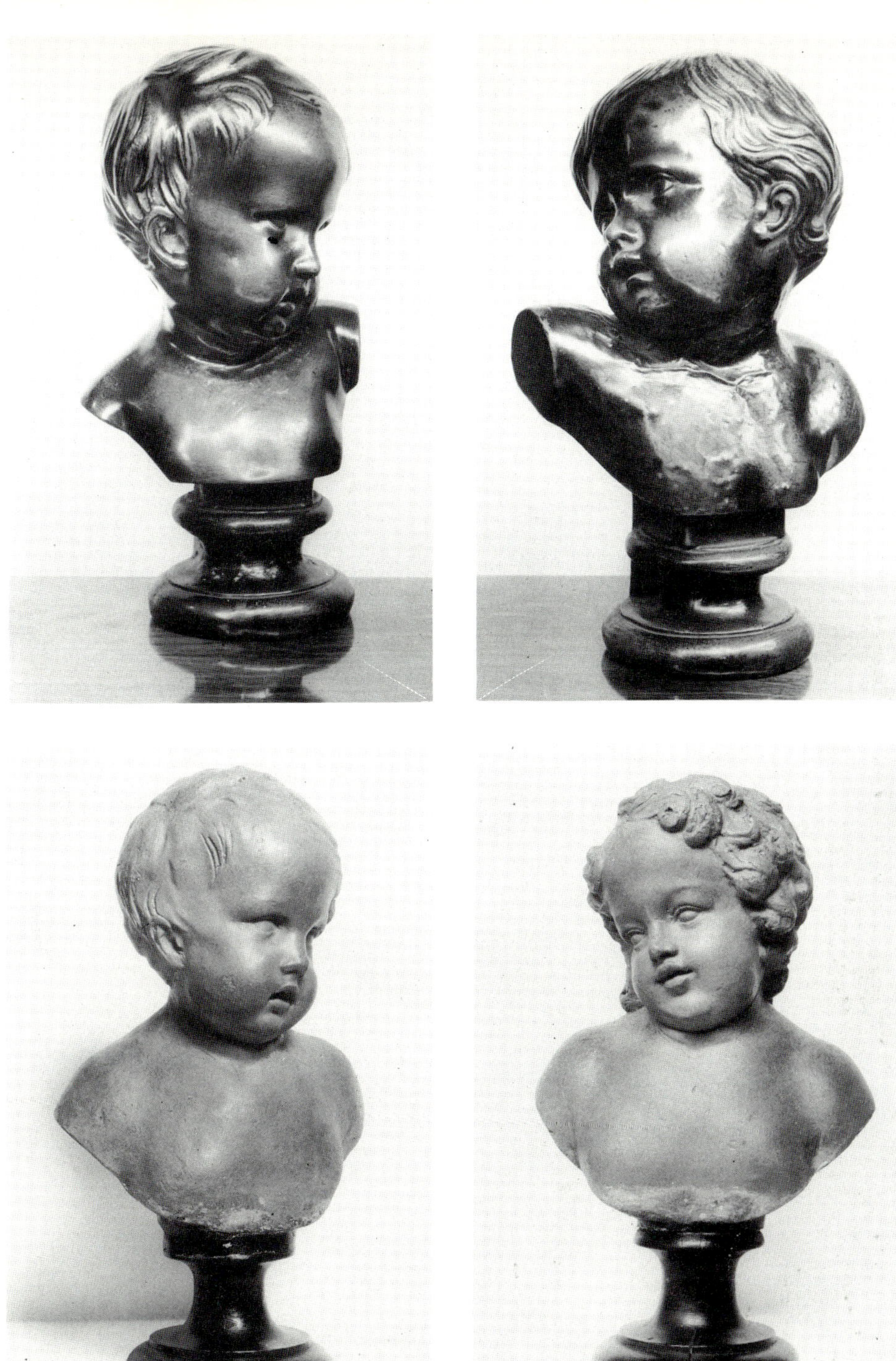

18–21 Four child heads after François Duquesnoy ('Il Fiammingo'): (above) terracottas covered with bronze, height 9″; (below) two companion busts in terracotta, height $10\frac{1}{2}$″ and 10″. See p. 47.

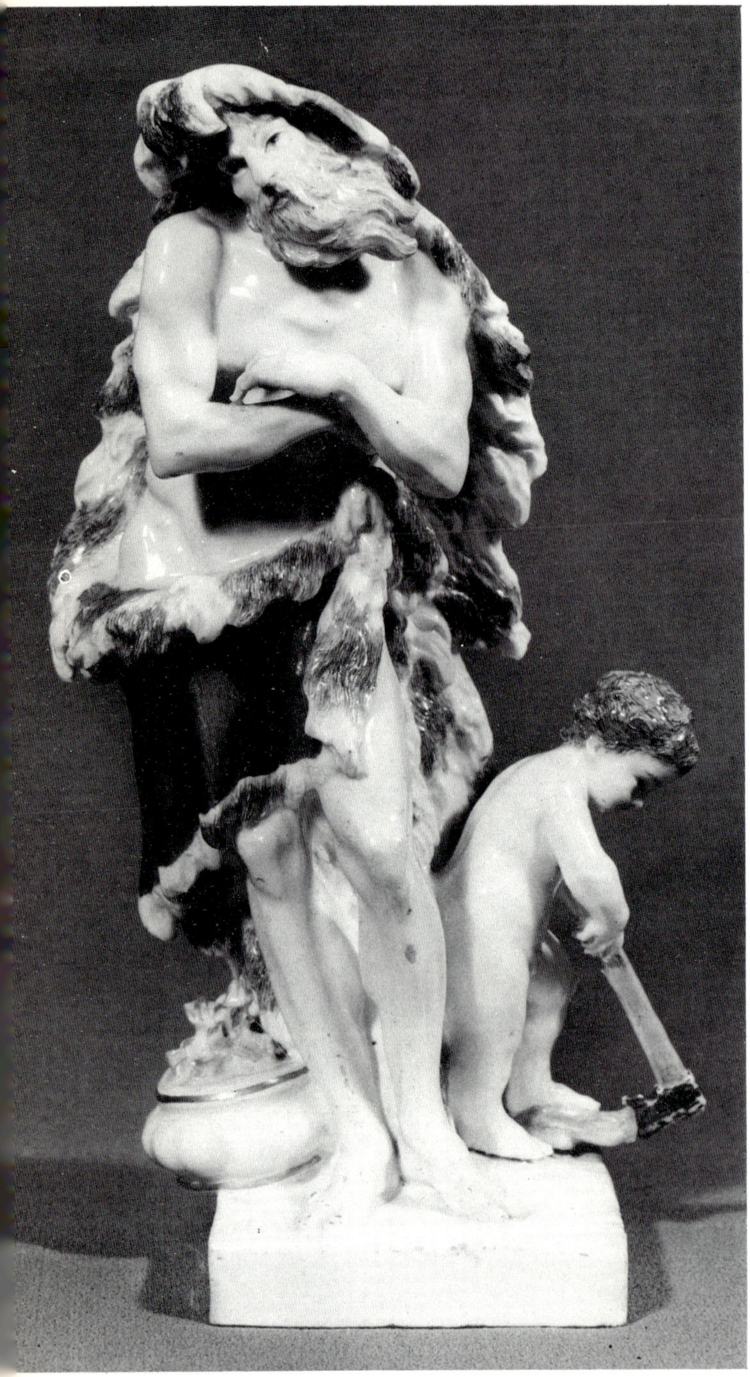

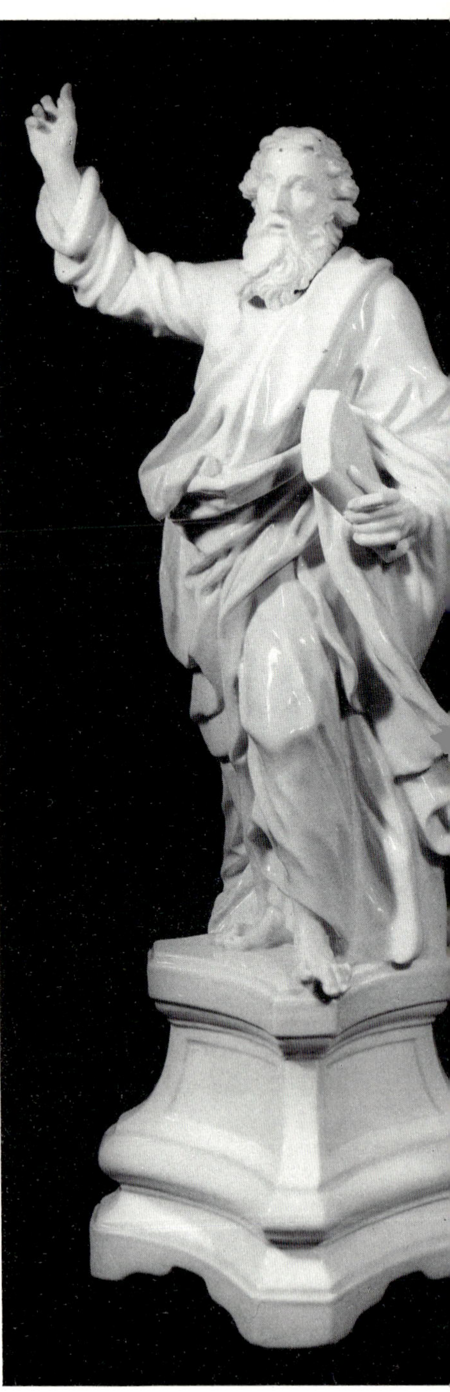

22 (left) Meissen figure of a sea-god, modelled by J. J. Kändler. See p. 103.
23 (right) Meissen figure of an apostle, modelled by J. J. Kändler. See p. 50.

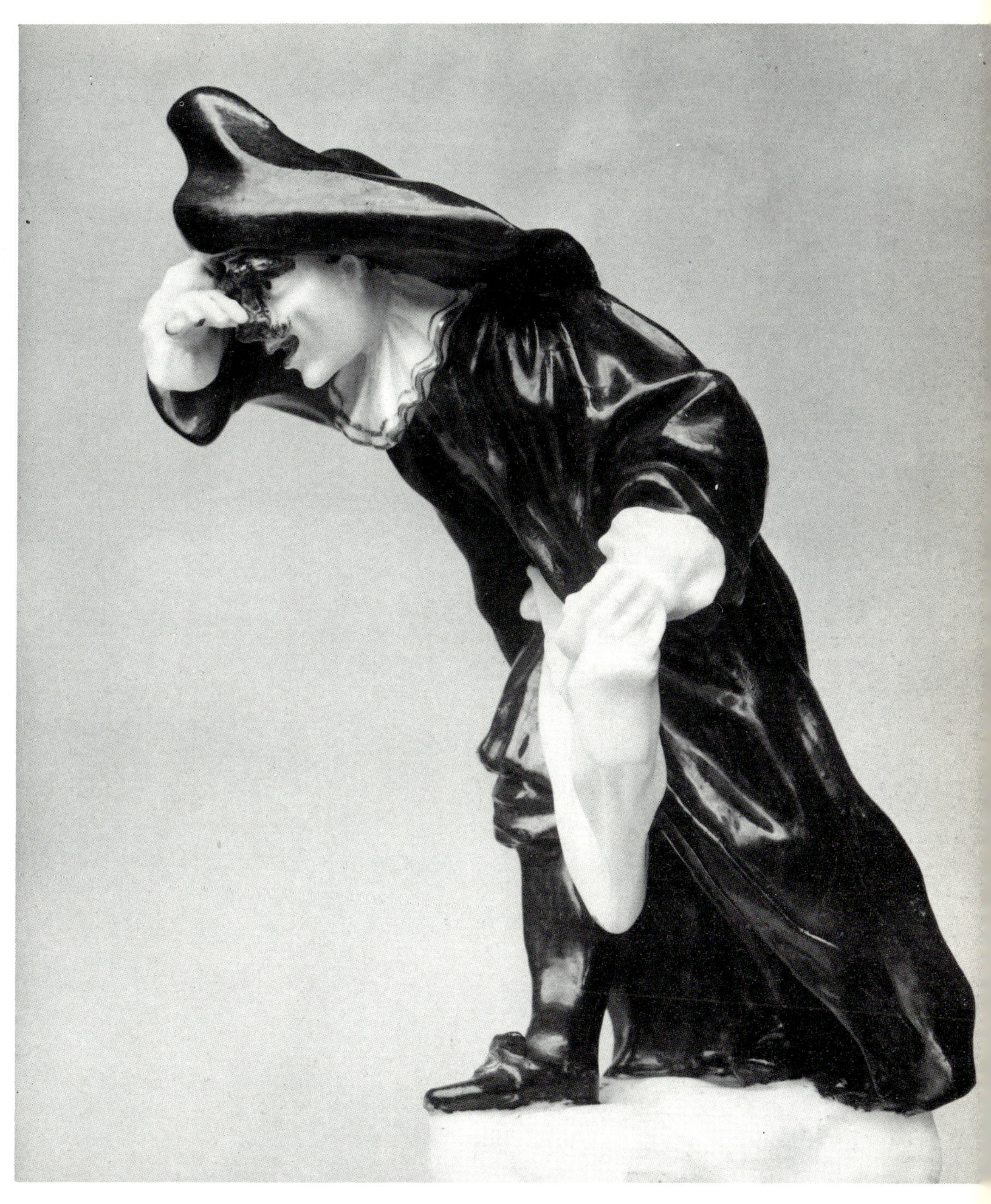

24 Capodimonte figure, The Doctor from the Italian Comedy (after Watteau), *c.* 1750.

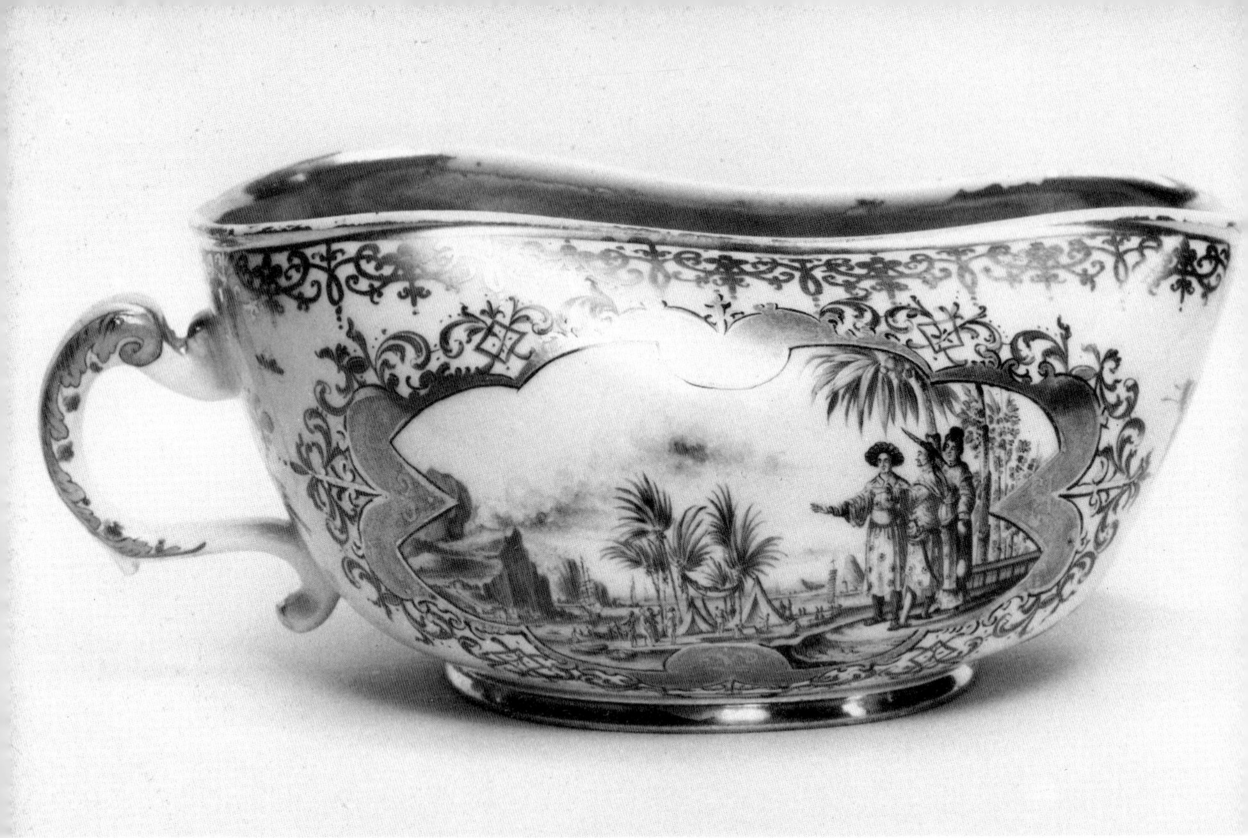

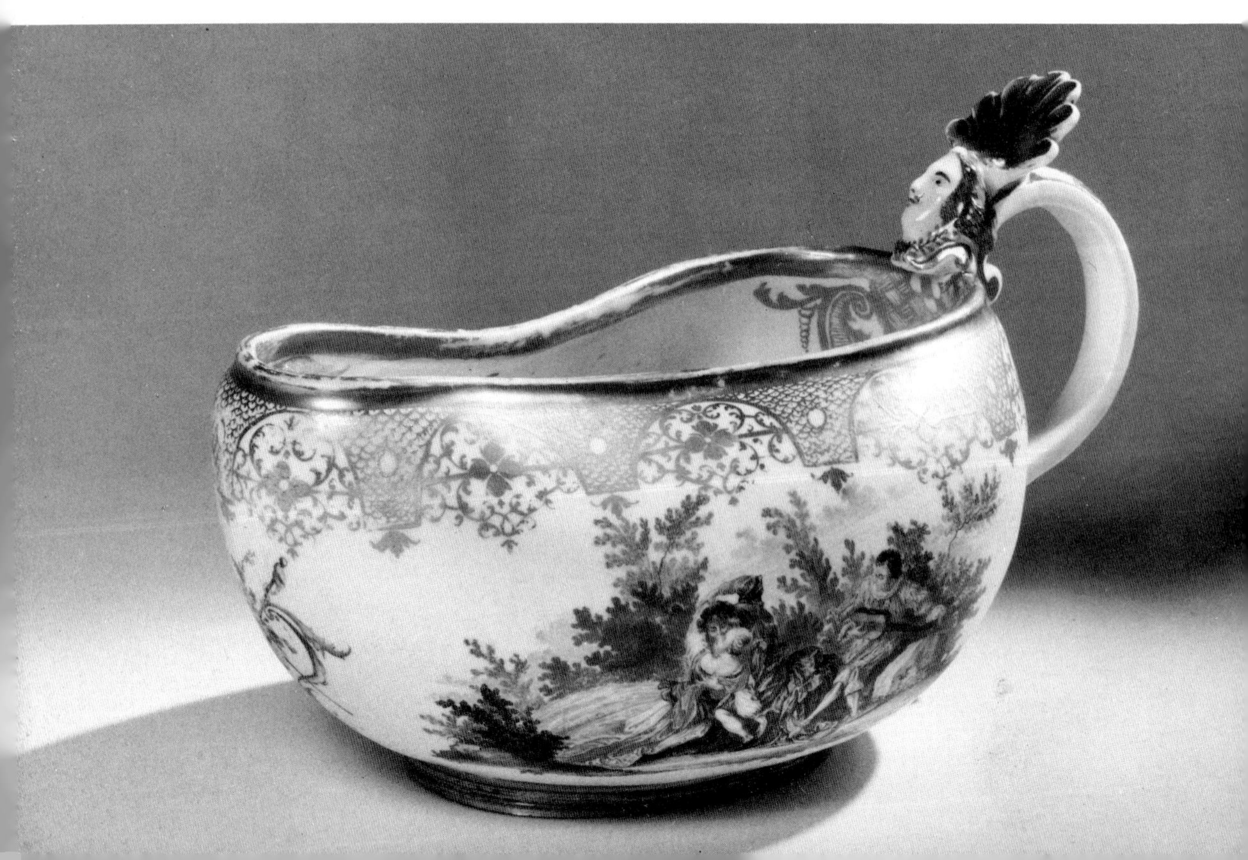

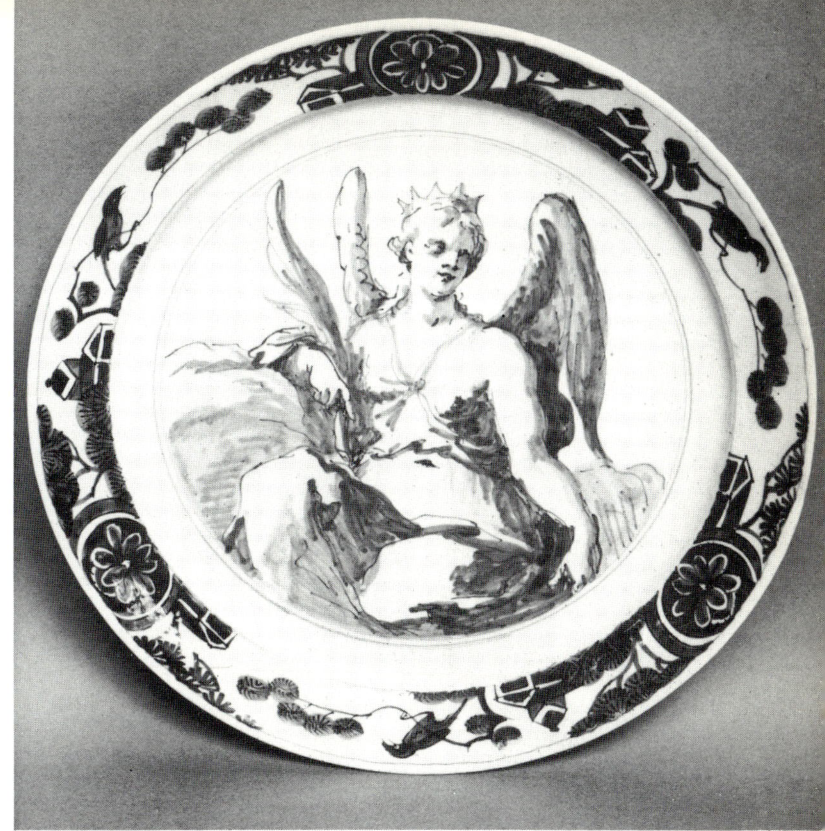

25 and 26 (opposite) Two Meissen bourdalous; (above) decorated by J. G. Höroldt, (below) decorated in Teniers style, *c.* 1738, length $9\frac{1}{2}''$. See p. 62.

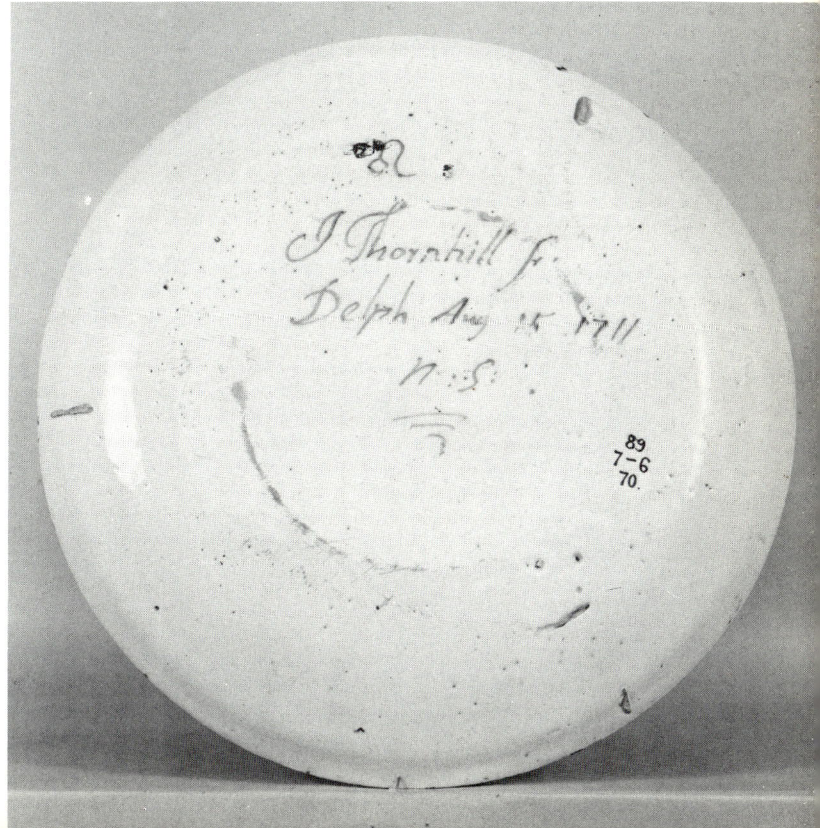

27 and 28 Two Dutch delft plates from a set of twelve painted with zodiacal signs by Sir James Thornhill at Delft in 1711. Formerly in the Mrs Hogarth and Strawberry Hill Collections. See p. 62.

30 'Das Schokoladenmädchen', pastel by J. E. Liotard, *c.* 1743. The girl is carrying a Meissen *trembleuse* held steady by a silver gallery. See p. 63.

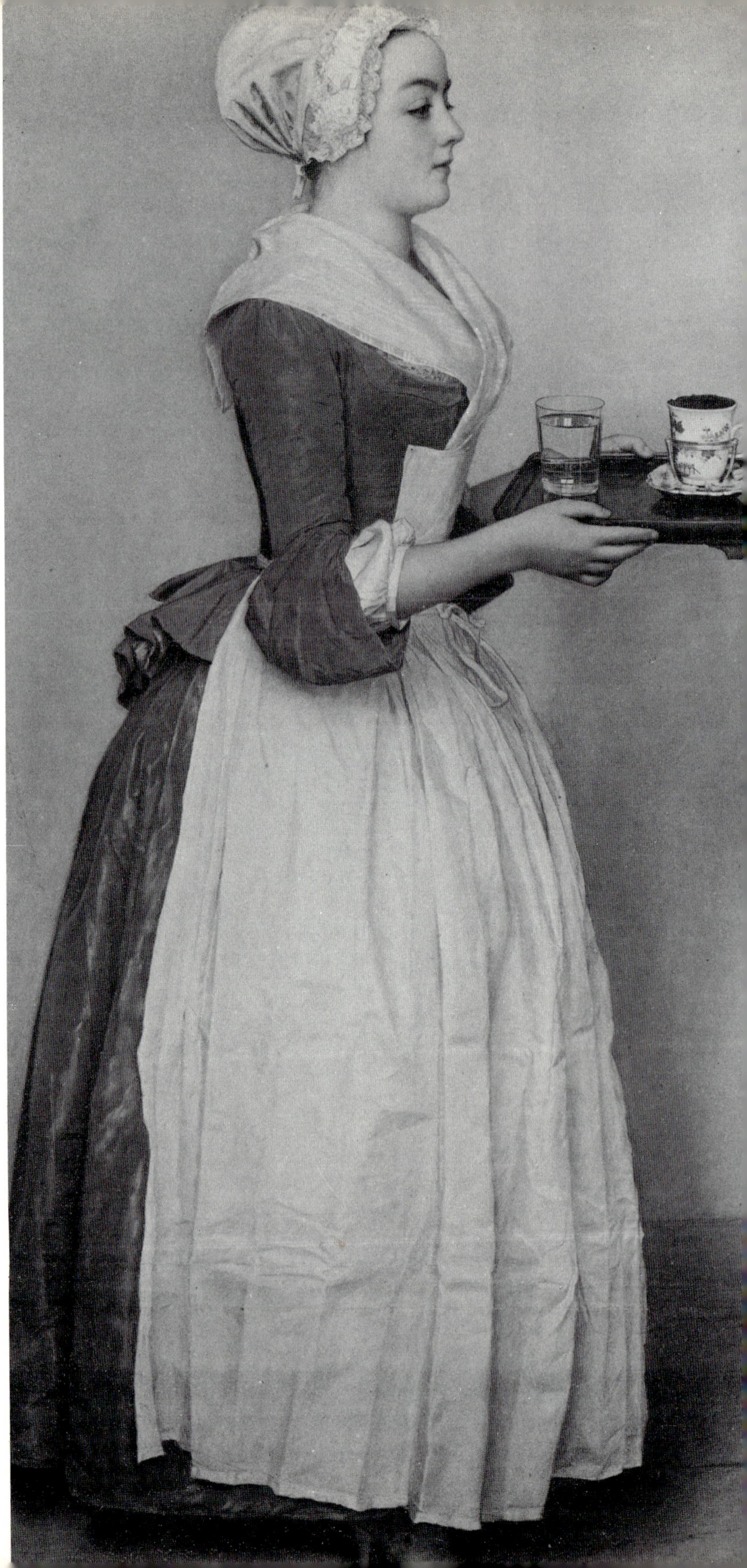

29 Lambeth delft food-warmer, mid eighteenth-century. See p. 62.

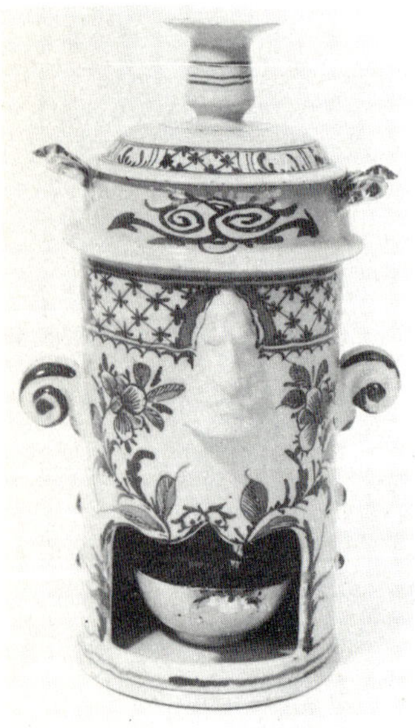

practice of attaching public advertisements to the figures of dwarfs which formerly stood outside the Mansion House in London. For this reason they are usually known as 'the Mansion House dwarfs'; the many forgeries made of them by Samson of Paris show their attraction for collectors.

The fashion for the grotesque and fantastic is equally evident in table wares – in the viciously beaked spout of a teapot in Böttger's red stoneware or the scarlet-polled squawking roosters on Kändler's *plat de ménage* of *c.* 1740 (Plate II). The Chinese figures in the centre of the latter work represent the most common form the exotic took in baroque porcelain. The taste for *chinoiseries* came to Germany from France, together with the aping of the other trappings of Louis XIV's court by the German princes. In gem-like miniatures within cartouches of intricate gilt tracery, the decorator Höroldt portrayed his own captivating vision of Cathay, drained of all barbarism. The scampering beasts of Löwenfinck whose appearance on both silks and porcelain suggests a common engraved source,[16] belong to another oriental arcady. And if, through Kändler's association with the Zwinger, architecture may be said to have influenced porcelain, one scholar has suggested that the debt was repaid, that 'the universal China fashion, intensified in Augustus the Strong with his collection and his manufactory of porcelain, is reflected in the shapes of the roofs and in the painting of the façades' of Pöppelmann's Schloss Pillnitz on the Elbe (1720–3).[17]

Beside the imaginative and exotic baroque there developed a highly formal decoration, of stiff acanthus leaves, pendants and *lambrequins*, laurel sprays, and interlaced strapwork. This resulted largely from the influence of silversmiths and goldsmiths. It was a court silversmith of Augustus the Strong, Johann Jacob Irminger, who was instructed to design the forms and plastic decoration of early Meissen. Consequently most of the cast and hammered ornaments of silverwork were used, such as gadrooning, beading and openwork piercing. And some of the outside decorators, known to factory workers by the more or less opprobrious names 'Pusche', 'Winkelmaler', 'Wildemaler', 'Hausmaler', and (in France) 'Chambrelans', had turned to ceramics from gold and silver.

Hausmalerei such as Ignaz Bottengruber of Breslau and Vienna, Daniel Preissler (1636–1733) and his son Ignaz (b. 1676), Jacob Helchis and the Nuremberg goldsmith Johann Heel, though they might be looked down on by the factory decorators, produced some impressive baroque compositions. Even a cup and saucer could seem majestic when decorated by Bottengruber with military trophies, battle scenes and Turkish prisoners in purple monochrome, like those in the Hamburg Museum, signed in full and dated 1726 – or with bacchic figures in colours within fantastic gilt scrollwork, like those in the Franks Collection at the British Museum. The British Museum also possesses an essay in ceramics decoration by the English baroque painter, Sir James Thornhill. While visiting Delft, he painted six delft plates (Plates 27 and 28) with zodiacal signs – October 1711. He kept a journal of the first part of his tour, but unfortunately the surviving part, in the Victoria and Albert Museum, does not extend to October. On 11 June, however, he noted:

> A little further on is a delicate wood in it a house call'd ye Purveyron & is ye storehouse for Clay of wch the Delph Ware is made.[18]

The plates, which are signed and dated, are painted in a free but simple style; the same zodiacal subjects occur in Thornhill's Painted Hall at Greenwich.

In wares for domestic use, there were three baroque inventions which became rococo institutions: the *veilleuse*, the *bourdalou* and the *trembleuse*. The *veilleuse* is a hollow pedestal on which sits either a covered warming-bowl (*écuelle*) or a teapot.[19] The name derives from the French *veiller*, to keep a night vigil. It originally referred to any night lamp, but later came to apply to a warmer for food or drink, to be available at the bed-side during the night. The Lambeth delft food warmer of *c.* 1750 (Plate 29) is the earliest recorded example. With its grim mask and formal decoration, it is strongly baroque in feeling, though later the *veilleuse* became a vehicle for the more preposterous rococo conceits.

The *bourdalou* took its name from the famous Jesuit preacher Louis Bourdaloue (1632–1704) who between 1670 and 1693 preached at the court of Louis XIV at Versailles.[20] He was so popular that it became necessary for ladies to take their seats hours before a sermon began. So recourse was had to a slipper-shaped chamber-pot which was hidden in the muff and used surreptitiously as occasion demanded.[21] The earliest example known is a Meissen one of about 1730 (Plate 25), decorated by Höroldt. Such a one, according to the Meissen archives, would cost forty talers wholesale, or forty-five talers retail – a gigantic sum when one recalls that Höroldt's monthly salary was only fifty talers. A later Meissen *bourdalou* illustrated by Ducret is painted with scenes from the Italian Comedy. In the bowl is painted a large eye: a similar broad humour is shown in a Sceaux example inscribed inside: 'Ah petit coquin, je te vois.'

The particular application of Bourdaloue's name first appeared in print in the *Dictionnaire de Trévoux* (1771):

> Bourdalou ... On a aussi donné ce nom a une sorte de pot de chambre oblong, dans ce sens il est masculin.

It has been suggested that the English slang 'loo' for 'lavatory', may derive from *bourdalou*: other theories are that it comes from the habit of shouting 'Gardez l'eau!' when about to empty a chamber pot into the street, or from some curious confusion of 'Waterloo' and 'WC'. These arcane matters may be left to the cloacologists, the dryasdusts of the smallest room. But any account of *faïence sanitaire* would be incomplete without a mention of that undisputed French invention, the bidet (according to d'Argenson, French ladies of society might receive visitors while enjoying its use), or the less elegant *chaise percée* or *chaise d'affaires*:

> Two hundred and seventy-five of these horrors [writes Lane] were distributed among the *salons* of Versailles, and it is said that the elderly courtiers of Louis XVIII, returning twenty-five years after the Revolution, were still able to sense the aura of the past. No wonder that in France of the *ancien régime* the pot-pourri vase or *bouquetier* crammed with scented flowers was considered an essential ministrant to indoor comfort.[22]

The name *trembleuse* for a cup kept steady in the saucer either by a raised 'gallery' (sometimes of silver) or by a sunken centre to the saucer, is modern. In the eighteenth century they were called *Schokoladetassen* at Meissen, *Mancerina* in Spain, *Schokoladebecher mit Einsatztasse* in Vienna, *Kronenschale* at Höchst, and, at Sèvres, *tasses à toilette et soucoupes*. A Meissen example of 1730, decorated with flowers in the style of Japanese Arita porcelain, is charmingly depicted in Liotard's pastel of the *Schokoladenmädchen* Elisabeth Baldauf in the Dresden Gallery (Plate 30). Such a cup and saucer would be suitable for a bedridden invalid with trembling hands.

The ceramics manufacture of the early eighteenth century seems to illustrate, in microcosm, the nature of baroque Europe. Politically it was an age of absolutism; and Augustus the Strong took personal control of the Meissen factory, though he was not so autocratic as Frederick the Great later became with the Berlin factory. This royal involvement also shows that noblemen were ceasing to regard the more craftsmanlike arts as unfitted to their rank. This attitude had been pioneered in

Dresden in the sixteenth century, when Count Rochus von Linar (1525–1596), a native of Tuscany, had replied to those who reproached him with being a master mason:

> Certainly, not only do I profess to be one, but I regard it as a great honour and distinction and cannot give sufficient thanks to Our Lord for such grace considering how rare are such gifts and skill, yet how highly necessary in war and peace, and also so honourable and praiseworthy in a knight and soldier that in Italy not only the nobility but also the most distinguished princes and gentlemen study them and willingly offer their services in them to their own glory.[23]

And by 1681, Prince Karl Eusebius of Liechtenstein could write to his son John Adam Andreas:

> You ought to become a perfect architect surpassing Michael Angelo Buonarota, Jacomo Baroccio Daviniola [Vignola], who is our esteemed master, from whom we learnt and accepted the system of the five Orders, Bernini, and others.[24]

Economically, it was the age of mercantilism – the assignment to the State of the central role in shaping economic well-being, by the regulation and protection of commerce. One of the principal mercantilist doctrines was that the State should be, as far as possible, self-sufficient. It was largely because of the wealth of cobalt ores in Saxony that so much early Meissen porcelain is decorated in blue. And it was according to the principles of mercantilism that Augustus's physicist Tschirnhaus, to whom goes some of the credit for discovering porcelain in Europe, searched the country for precious stones and set up mills for grinding and polishing them. The foremost mercantilist statesman, Colbert, has tenuous links with the ceramic manufacture: in 1663 he wrote a memorandum that Edmé Poterat's factory should be brought under royal patronage, though this was apparently never implemented.

Science stands against superstition, astronomy against astrology, chemistry against alchemy. This new rationalism is well represented by the enforced abandonment of Böttger's quest for the Philosopher's Stone and his transference to more rewarding researches. The energy of resurgent Catholicism twists clay into images, recalling the child's definition of a parable – 'earthly-story-with-a-heavenly-meaning'; but ceramics, which had given a dubious immortality to one Jesuit, Cardinal Bellarmine, in pot-bellied 'greybeard' jugs, now give another Jesuit, Bourdaloue, the even more dubious status of a household word.

The end of the Baroque

Porcelain may not be able to give us the supreme flights of the baroque, but it can illustrate its formalism. It shows love systematized, passions played out as classical allegories. It shows humour literally masquerading behind the Cyranesque nose of a *papier-maché* domino, Punch's humpback or the codpiece of Pantaloon. In the age of noble formalism, there is no room for mild deviation: only the freak is acceptable. Where there is not fearful symmetry, there must be fearful deformity. The pearl is flawless, or it is grotesquely misshapen – *barocco.*

3 Porcelain

The quest for a translucent, or, as Dr Johnson splendidly called it, 'semi-pellucid' ceramic was truly baroque. Science had accepted that the earth revolved round the sun; now the potters would cause the sun to shine through the earth. The search for the 'China Stone' which would transmute gross clay into frail china replaced – in Böttger's case, overnight – the hallucinations of alchemy, the search for the Philosopher's Stone that would change lead into gold. Porcelain was sold in the same shops as gold and silver, and was kept in royal treasuries with precious metals and jewels.

At the beginning of the eighteenth century, almost all the porcelain in Europe was oriental. No European potter had succeeded in discovering the secret of Chinese hard-paste porcelain, which was made with *petuntse* (china stone) and *kaolin* (china clay). In the late sixteenth century, a glassy soft-paste porcelain had been made at Florence – the so-called 'Medici porcelain' – but this manufacture seems virtually to have ceased on the death of Francesco I de' Medici in 1587. John Dwight of Fulham, although he was granted in 1671 a patent for the manufacture of 'transparent earthenware commonly known by the name of Porcelain or China and Persian Ware', is unlikely to have achieved more than a fine white stoneware. Two years later, Louis Poterat of Rouen was granted a patent for the manufacture of porcelain, but when he applied to have it renewed in 1694 it was stated that 'the secret was very little used, the petitioners devoting themselves rather to faience making'. Some examples of Poterat's soft-paste porcelain survive, but when he died in 1696, 'crippled in his limbs by the ingredients used in his porcelain', his secret was apparently lost. By 1700, only the St Cloud factory was making porcelain in any quantity. The factory, which was visited in that year by the Duchess of Burgundy, claimed to have made porcelain 'as perfect as the Chinese' since 1693.

Chinese porcelain was brought to Europe by the various East India companies. Much of it was made to order and decorated by the Chinese with European designs, often with armorial bearings. Tureens and platters of about 1765 were painted with the arms of Saldanha de Albuquerque, the aristocratic Bishop of Oporto.[1] Other owners of Chinese armorial wares were the French and Spanish royal families, Duke Leopold II of Anhalt in Germany, and the family of Paravicini di Capelli in Italy.[2] Armorial services were made for Brydges, first Duke of Chandos, in 1713, for Thomas Pitt, Baron Londonderry, in 1719, for Nexton Townshend in 1725 and for Humphrey Parsons, Lord Mayor of London, in 1759.[3] The invoice for a service made for the Peers family in 1731 has been preserved: the service of 700 pieces cost £76.[4]

There were good markets for Chinese porcelain in America,[5] Denmark[6] and Portugal.[7] The most recent evidence on the western market for these wares was provided by the lifting of ten Spanish galleons wrecked off Cape Kennedy in 1715. K'ang Hsi porcelain discovered in these wrecks confirms the existence of a trade route from China through Manila and Acapulco to Spain: the isthmus would have been crossed by mule.[8]

European prints, including Bonnet's 'Le Bain' and Larmessin's 'Peasant Boy' (after Vleugels) were copied by the Chinese with apparent faithfulness, though *galanteries* became subtly more libertine in the Chinese versions. Even Scotsmen appear on Chinese plates, their eyes taking on an oriental slant, the colours of their kilt nearer japonica and filamot than the barbaric originals. A plate in the Musée Guimet, Paris, shows two Scots, one playing the bagpipes.[9] This design may have been copied from a piece of woodcarving at Holyrood Palace, Edinburgh. A bowl in the Espirito Santo Foundation, Lisbon, shows a grimacing Scot on a privy[10] – a satire on the inability of the Jacobites to capture England.

The Chinese copied the armorial bearings and inscriptions sent out to them with minute accuracy. Most of them did not understand what they were copying, and this sometimes led to unfortunate results. A letter preserved in the Goteborg Museum records the fury of the Swedish General Jacob Sederstrom when a service he had commissioned was returned with the words carefully spelled out: 'Agreed. Jacob Sederstrom.' He had torn his signature from a document he had once endorsed and the Chinese artist had laboriously copied out the full text.[11] Again, an English client, in ordering a service, enclosed a sketch of his coat of arms and crest. This was not coloured, but on the sketch the words 'red', 'blue', 'yellow' and so on indicated where these colours should appear. When the service arrived, he found that his handwriting had been carefully copied, but that colours had been added quite arbitrarily.[12] Another story, delightful but perhaps apocryphal, is of a family named Blake whose motto 'Think and Thank' was rendered 'Stink and Stank'.[13]

Japanese porcelain, of which the Dutch East India Company imported the largest quantities, was prized almost as much as Chinese. In *Le Rouge et Le Noir*, Julien Sorel breaks 'an old blue porcelain vase, the ugliest thing imaginable'.

> Madame de la Mole rose to her feet with a cry of distress and came over to examine the fragments of her cherished vase. 'It was old Japan porcelain,' she said, 'it came to me from my great-aunt the Abbess of Chelles. It was a present from the Dutch to the Duke of Orleans when he was Regent, and he gave it to his daughter.' [14]

Because porcelain was precious, it would have been worth the while of European potters in any case to try to discover the oriental formula. But an added impetus to the search was given by the great increase in the drinking of tea, coffee and chocolate in the eighteenth century. As Blegny explained in his *Le Bon Usage du The, du caffe et du chocolat* (1787):

> ... aux Indes & en Europe, il est asses ordinaire de preferer aux tasses ou gobelets d'Argent ou de quelque autre metal que se soit, les chiques de porcelaines ou de fayence, par cette raison que leur bords ne brulent jamais les doigts, & que la facon de tenir ces chiques passe pour une espece de bienfeance.[15]

In England, where the trend was most pronounced, tea-drinking was first made fashionable by Charles II's queen, and was largely confined to the aristocracy. But already by 1699 J. Ovington, Chaplain to His Majesty, could write, in *An Essay upon the Nature and Qualities of Tea*:

> ... the Drinking of it has of late obtain'd here so universally, as to be affected both by the *Scholar* and the *Tradesman*, to become both a private *Regale* at Court, and to be made use of in places of publick *entertainment*....[16]

Duncan Forbes, Lord President of the Court of Session, wrote to Lord Tweedale in January 1743:

> Tea ... is now become so common, that the meanest familys, even of labouring people, particularly in Burroughs, make their morning's Meal of it, and

Porcelain

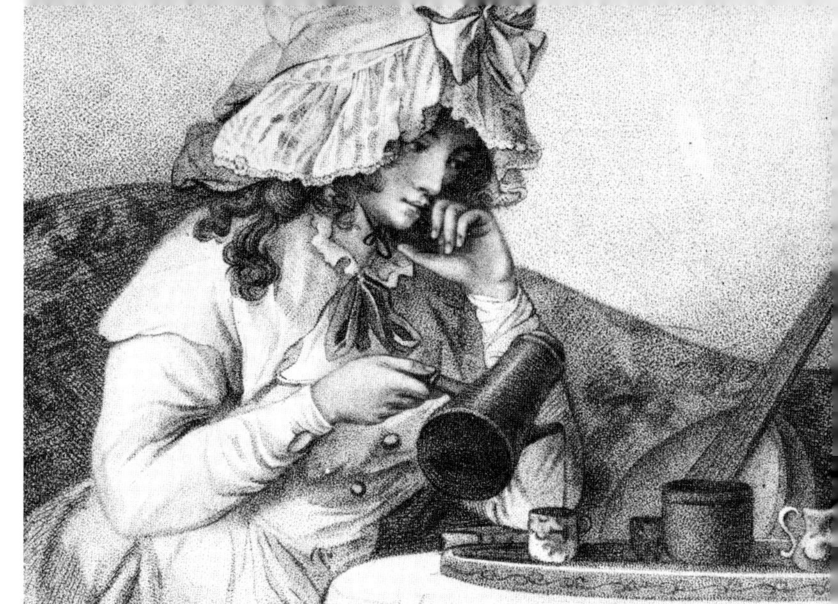

31 Coffee-drinking: 'Morning, or the Reflection', engraving by J. Grozer after W. Ward, 1787.

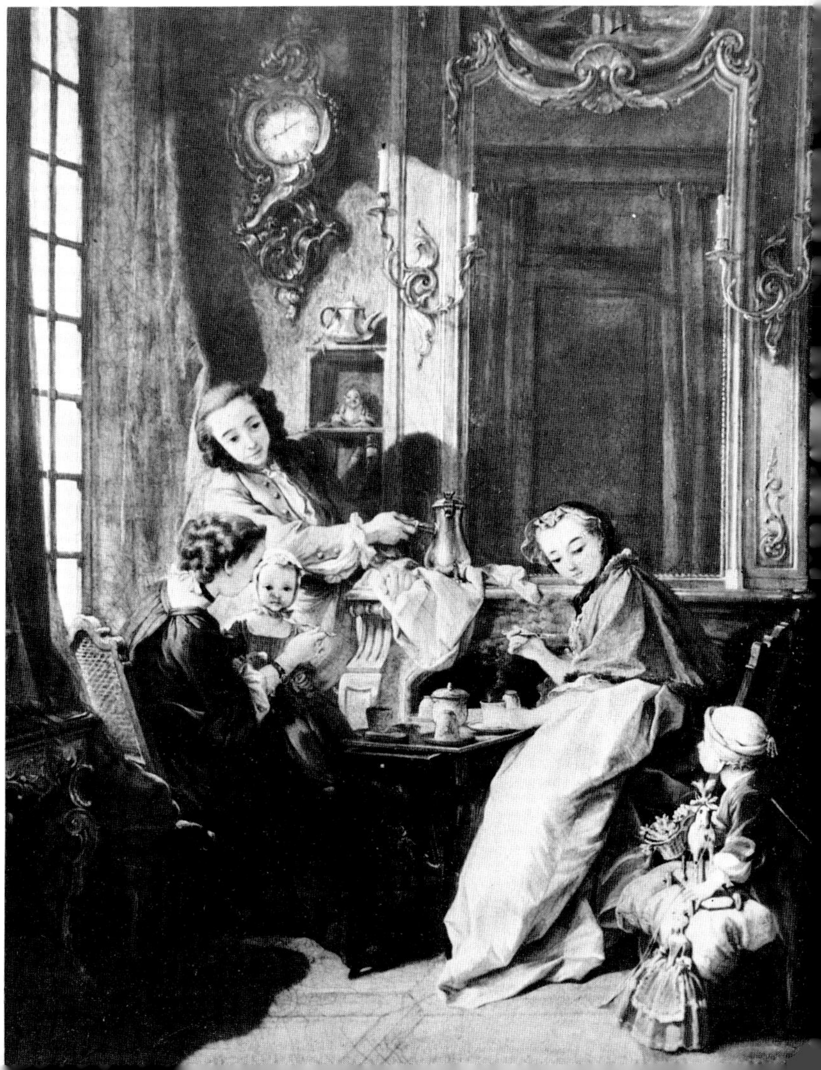

32 François Boucher, 'Le Déjeuner' (signed), 1739.

33 Beggars drinking tea from porcelain cups – a sight which outraged Jonas Hanway, for whose *Essay on Tea* (1757) this was the folding frontispiece. See p. 77.

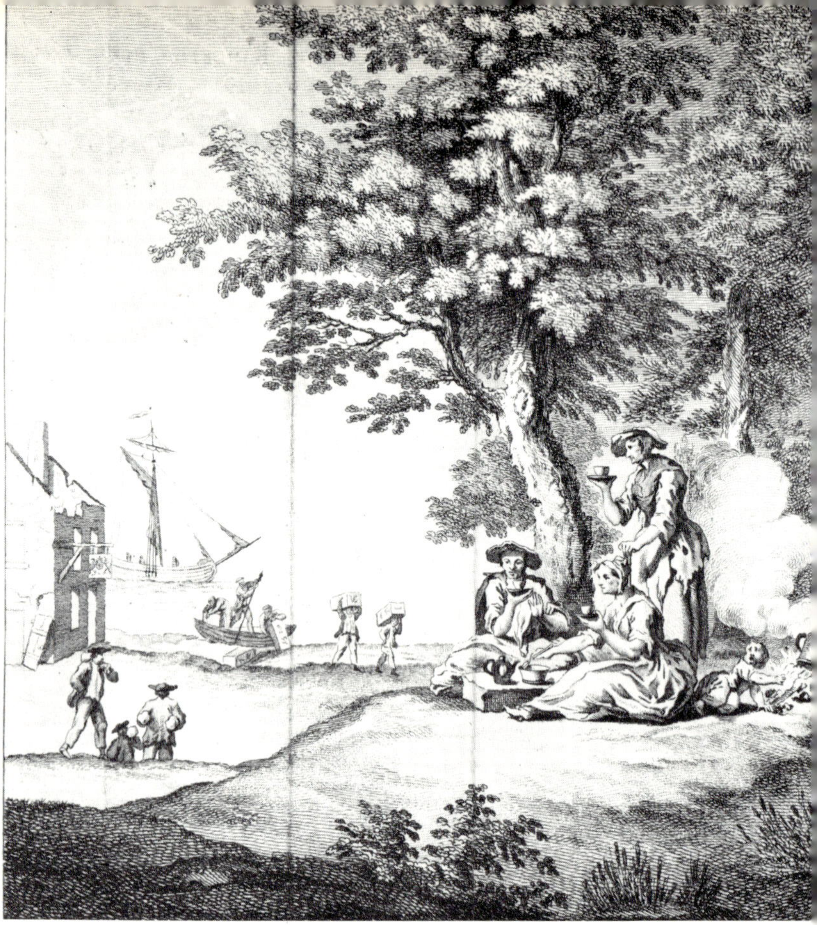

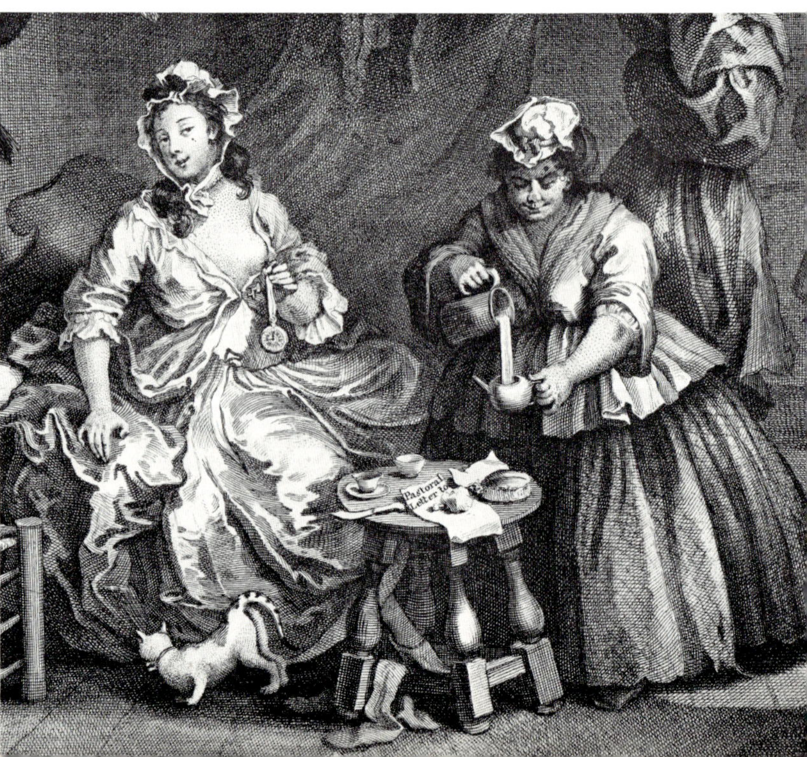

34 'Molls at their tea', a Hogarth print. Note the small size of the teapot and teabowl: tea was still very expensive.

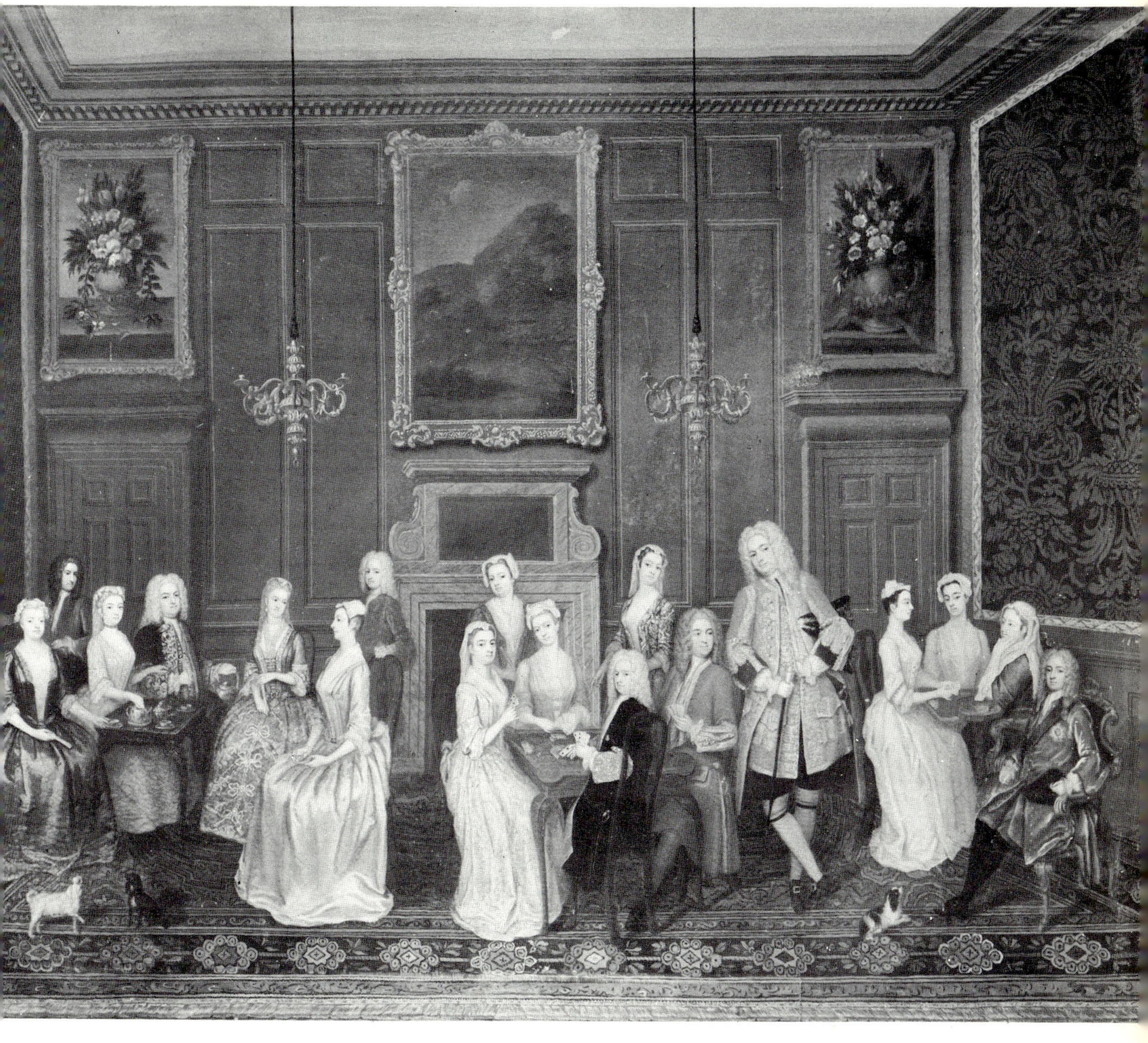

35 Charles Philips, 'A Tea Party at Lord Harrington's House', oil on canvas, 1739. Among the guests are Lady Betty Germaine and the Duchess of Suffolk. See p. 79.

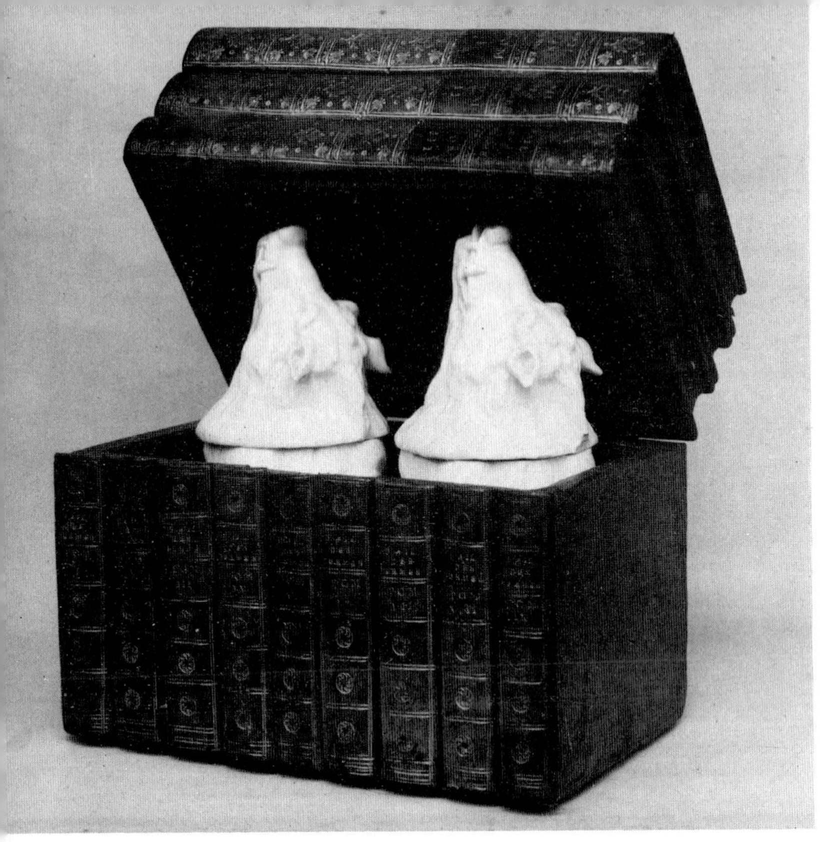

36 Pair of Mennecy porcelain toilette-pots in the form of wild boars, with the original leather case. Mark DCO, *c.* 1750. See p. 85.

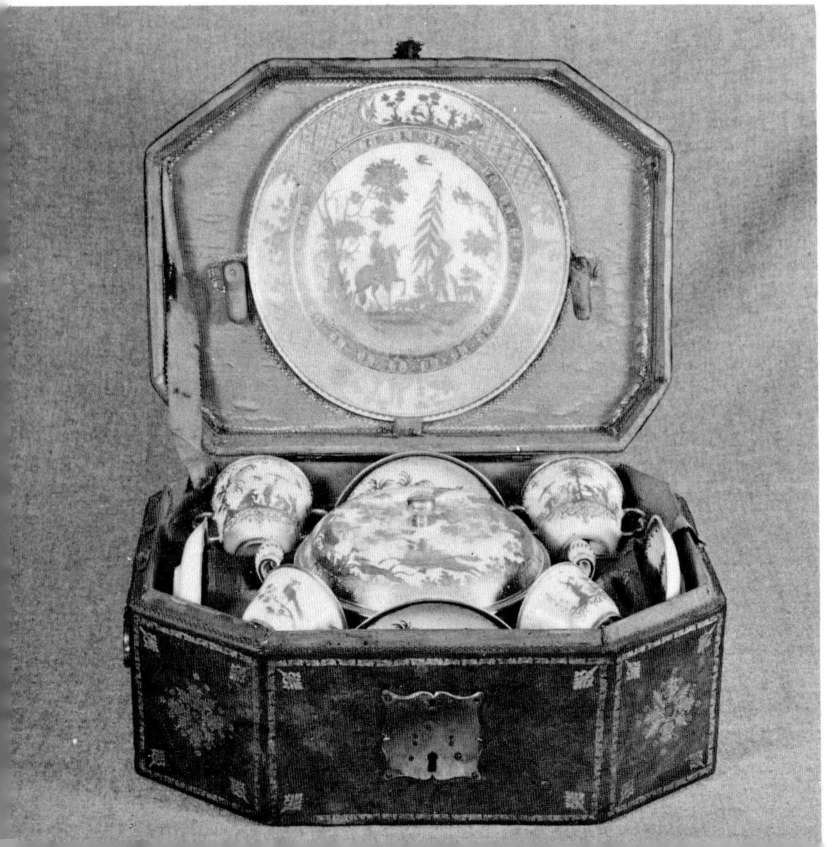

37 Meissen travelling set in leather case, *c.* 1725. The bowl and stand are *c.* 1740. The latter bears the crossed swords mark. See p. 85.

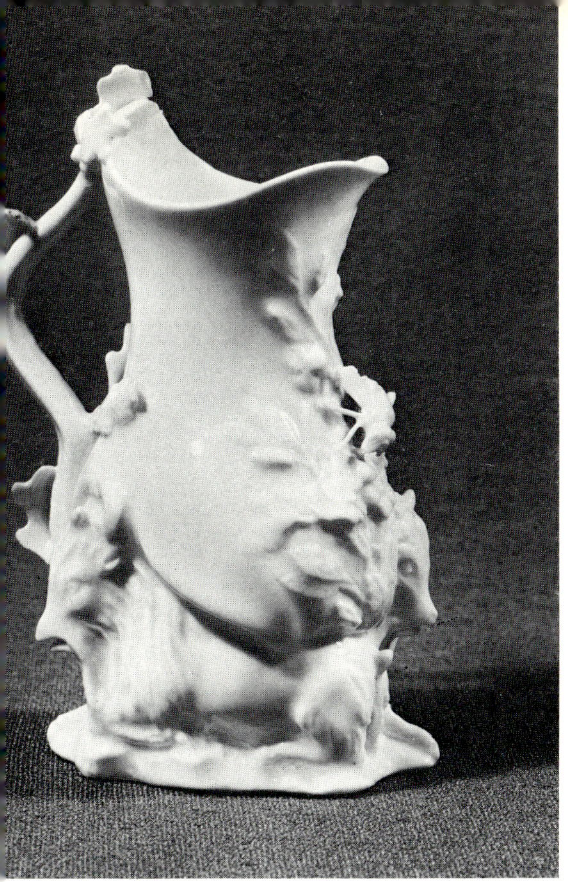

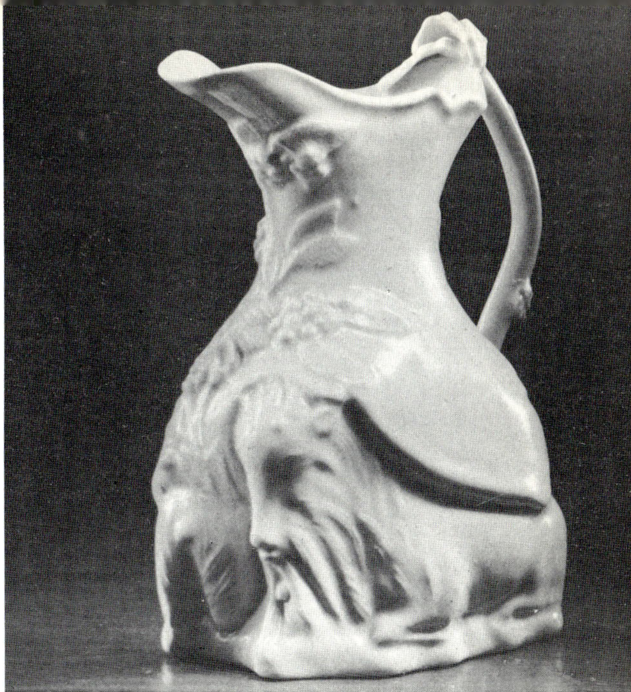

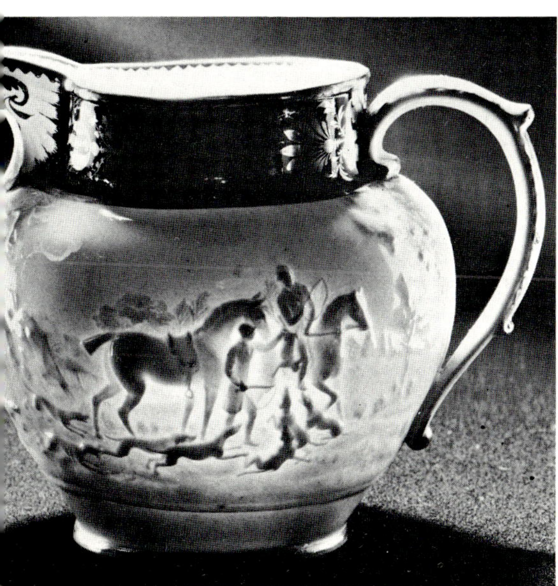

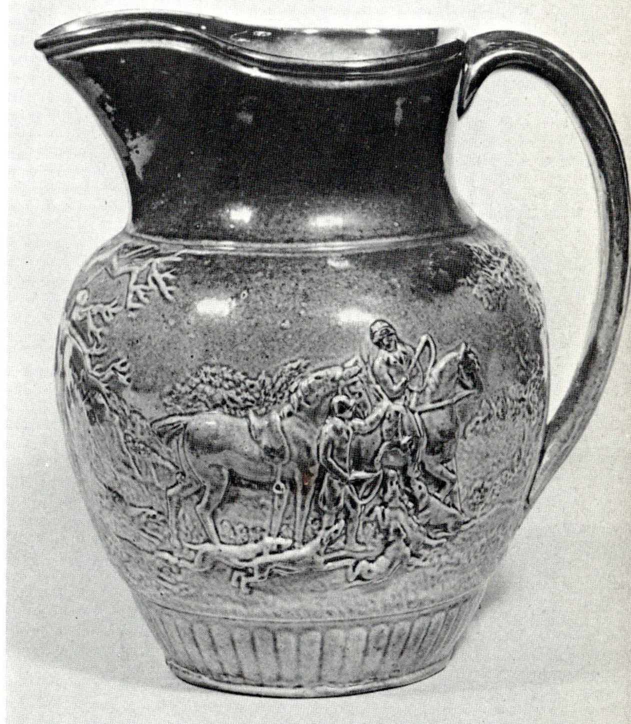

38–41 Social comparisons: (above left) a Chelsea 'goat and bee' jug, *c.* 1745. Mark, incised triangle. Height $4\frac{1}{2}''$; (right) Staffordshire salt-glazed stoneware goat and bee jug, *c.* 1745–50, height $3\frac{7}{8}''$; (below left) porcelain jug, perhaps by Spode, Staffordshire, with blue border and elaborate gilding, *c.* 1850, height $5\frac{1}{2}''$; (right) brown-glazed stoneware jug, perhaps by Doulton, Lambeth, *c.* 1870–80, height $6\frac{3}{4}''$. This design was also used on earlier Wedgwood, Turner and Davenport wares. See p. 120.

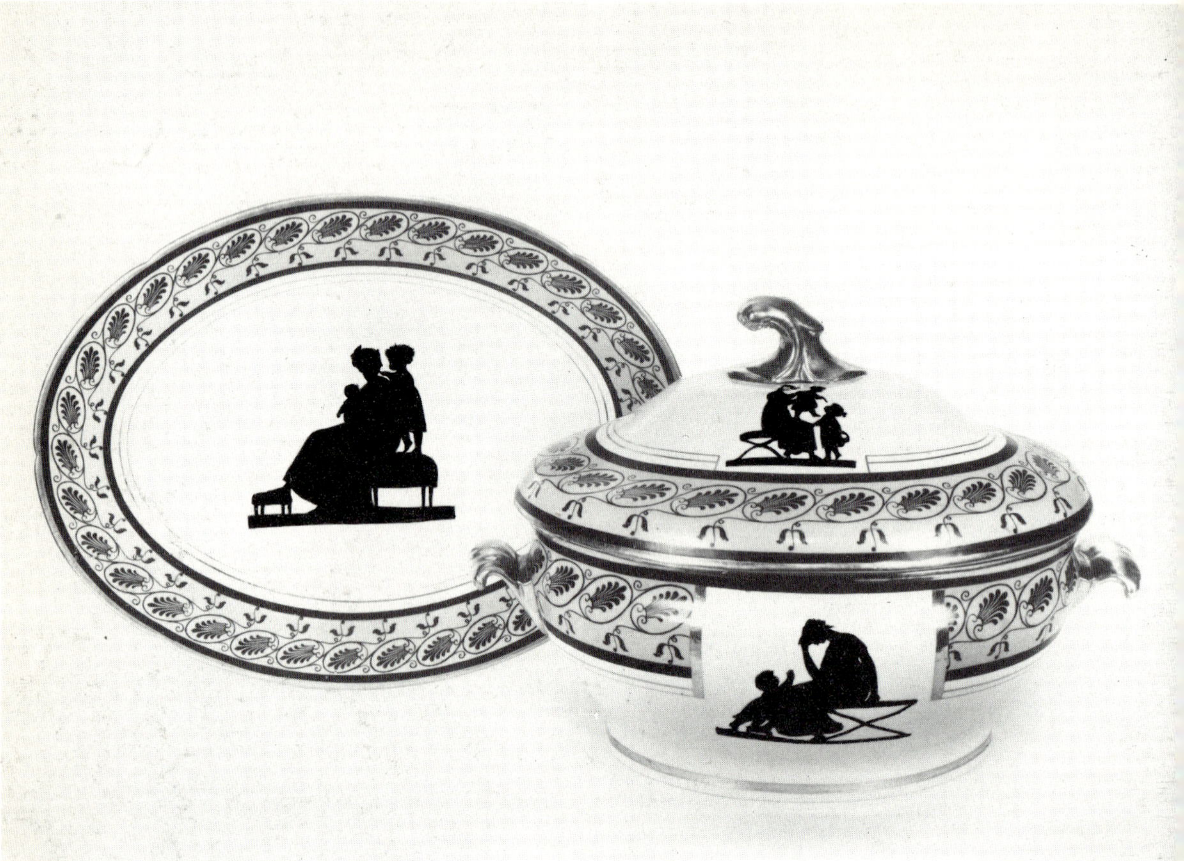

42 Tureen and dish from the silhouette-decorated dinner service made by Coalport, 1805–10, for John Julius Angerstein (1735–1823). Length of dish 15¼″. See p. 86.

43 Worcester cup, early nineteenth century, bearing the crest of the Duke of Sermoneta. A written 'pedigree' has been stuck on the base. See p. 86.

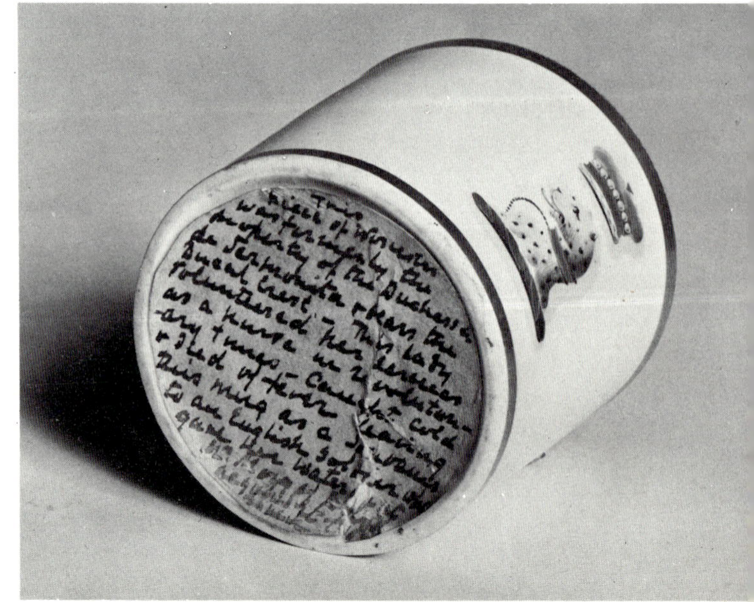

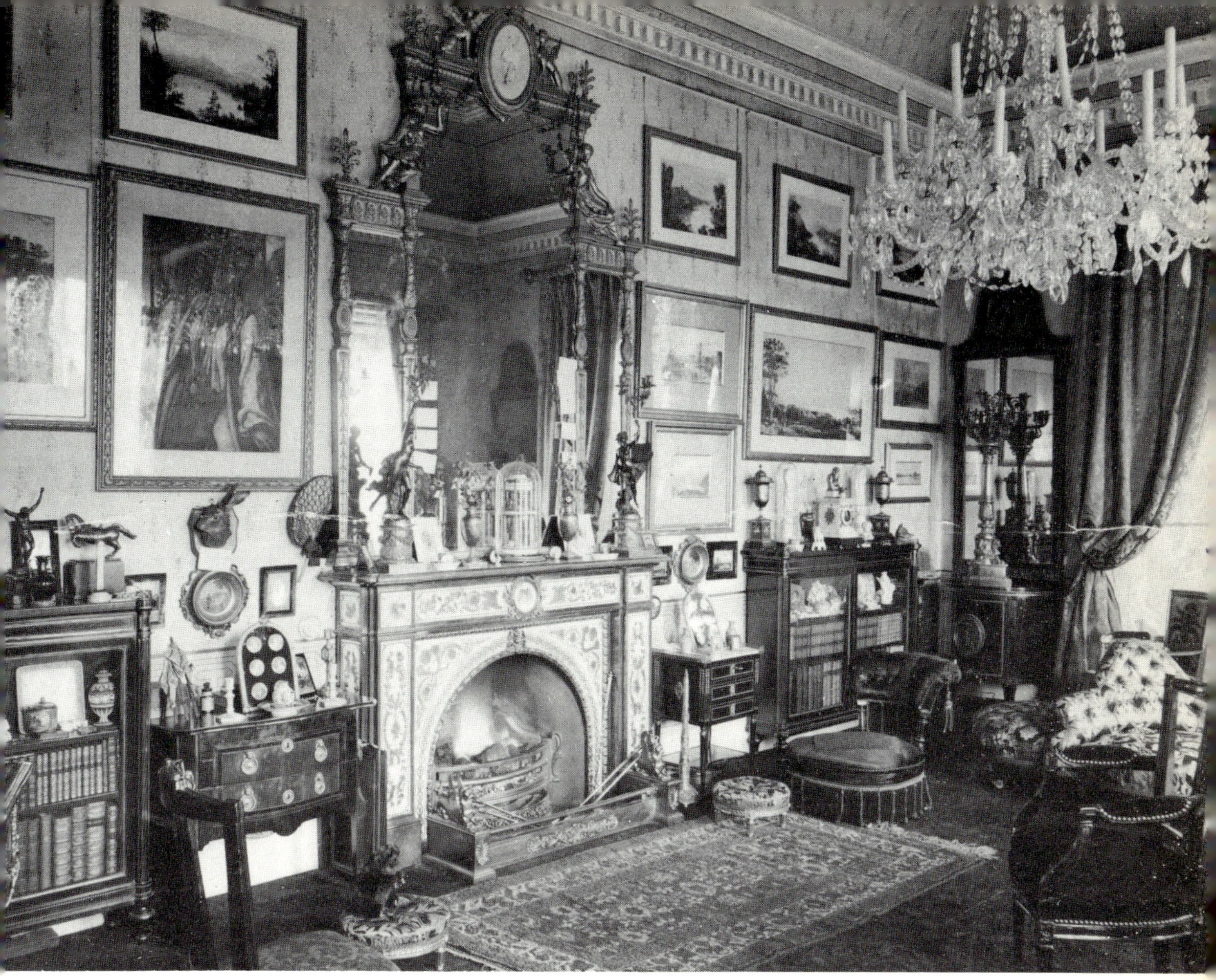

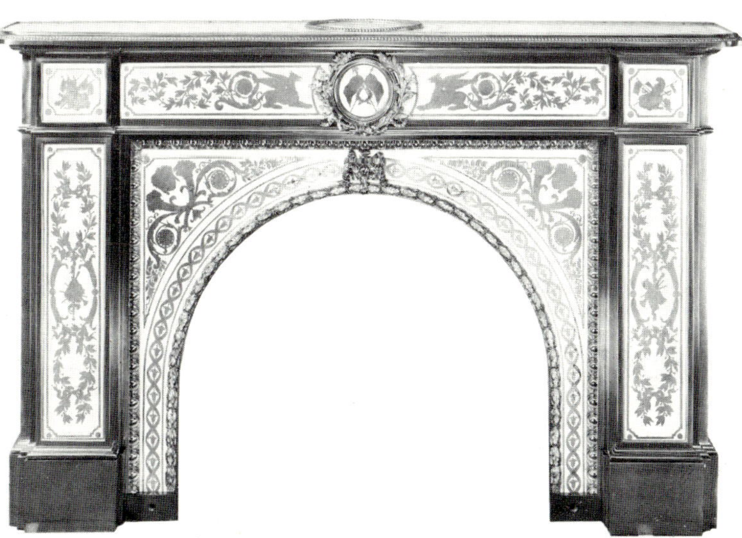

44 and 45 A Copeland chimneypiece made in the early nineteenth century and decorated in Paris. (above) The chimneypiece *in situ* at Hingham Hall, Norfolk, in 1875. See pp. 86–7.

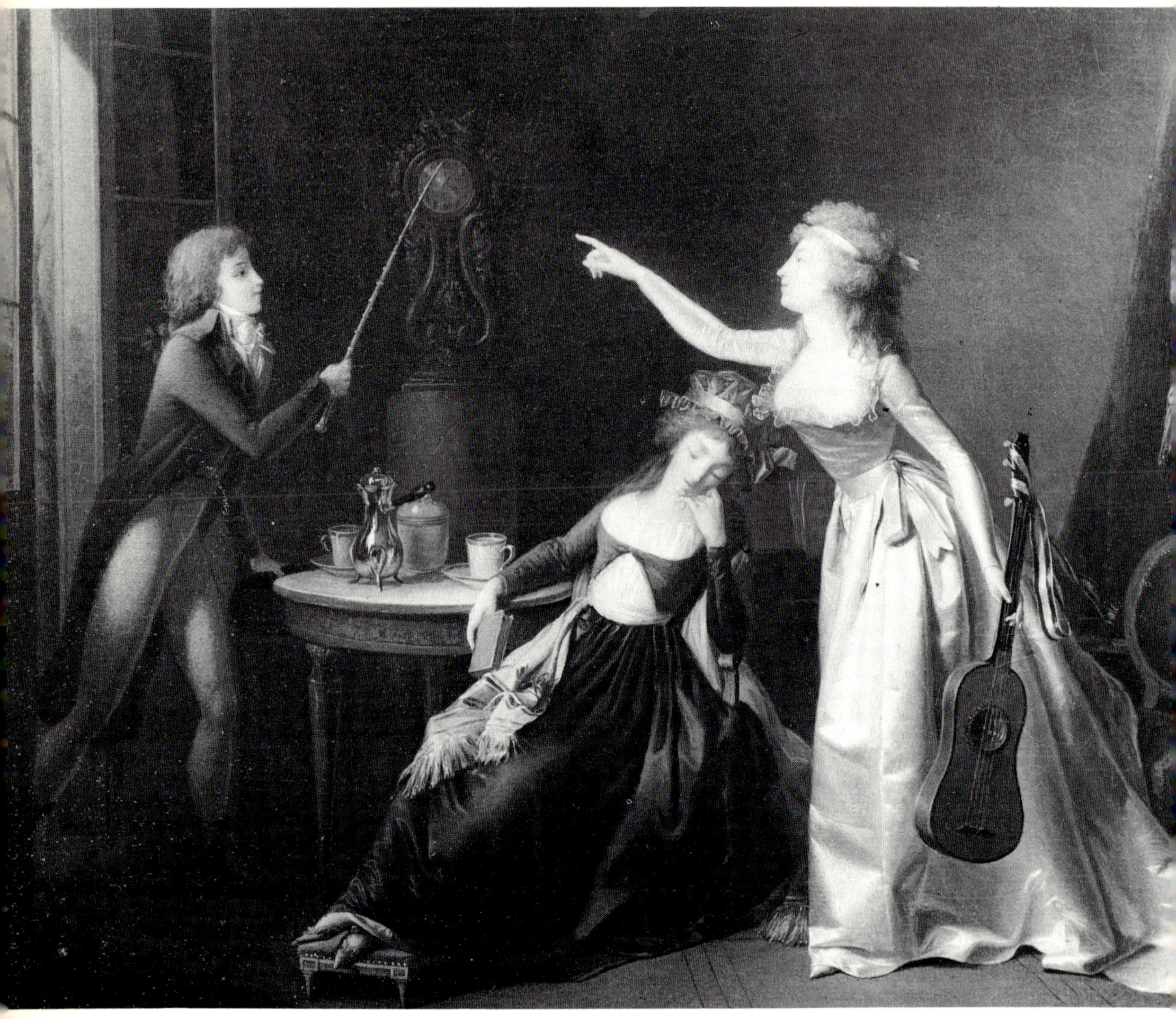

46 Plain French porcelain in a neo-classical setting: 'The Rendezvous' by Jean-Simon Fournier (late eighteenth century). An engraving after this oil painting was made by Alexandre Chaponnier.

thereby wholly disuse the ale, which heretofore was their accustomed drink; and the same Drug supplies all the labouring women with their afternoons' entertainments, to the exclusion of the Twopenny ... at present there are very few Coblers in any of the Burroughs of this Country who do not sit down gravely with their Wives & familys to Tea.[17]

The idea that tea was not suitable for the working classes was echoed by Jonas Hanway in 1757:

To what a *height* of folly must a nation be arrived, when the *common people* are not satisfied with *wholesome food* at *home*, but must go to the remotest regions to please a *vicious palate*! There is a certain lane near *Richmond* where beggars are often seen, in the summer season, drinking their *tea*. You may see *labourers* who are *mending the roads* drinking their tea; it is even drank in *cinder-carts*; and what is no less absurd, sold out of cups to *Hay-makers*.[18]

The frontispiece to Hanway's *Essay on Tea*, from which this passage is taken, shows some picturesque beggars drinking tea (Plate 33). Hanway adds, in another burst of invective:

Tea which should by no means be exposed to the air, being brought from *China* in the packing of *porcelain* to serve the purposes of *saw dust*, or sold in the streets out of wheel-barrows, you must imagine will make a most *delicious* liquor! [19]

Dr Johnson, while defending tea in his most fulminating manner against Hanway's attack, still said:

I have no desire to appear captious, and shall therefore readily admit, that tea is a liquor not proper for the lower classes of the people, as it supplies no strength to labour, or relief to disease, but gratifies the taste without nourishing the body.[20]

Dorothy Bradshaigh, who in 1775 built and endowed a rural almshouse, strictly forbade tea to its inmates. Those who could afford to indulge themselves in an article so unnecessary and expensive, she would 'not allow to be the proper objects of this charity'.[21]

The 'lower classes' could themselves be rather shamefaced about taking to genteel tea, as a passage from John Galt's *Annals of the Parish* (1821) shows:

Before this year [1761], the drinking of tea was little known in the parish, saving among a few of the heritors' houses on a Sabbath evening; but now it became very rife: yet the commoner sort did not like to let it be known that they were taking to the new luxury, especially the elderly women, who, for that reason, had their ploys in out-houses and by-places, just as the witches lang syne had their sinful possets and galravitchings; and they made their tea for common in the pint-stoup, and drank it out of cups and luggies, for there were but few among them that had cups and saucers. Well do I remember one night in harvest, in this very year, as I was taking my twilight dauner aneath the hedge along the back side of Thomas Thorl's yard, meditating on the goodness of Providence, and looking at the sheaves of victual on the field, that I heard his wife, and two three other carlins, with their Bohea in the inside of the hedge, and no doubt but it had a lacing of conek [cognac], for they were all cracking like pen-guns. But I gave them a sign, by a loud host, that Providence sees all, and it skailed the bike; for I heard them, like guilty creatures, whispering, and gathering up their truck-pots and trenchers, and cowering away home.[22]

But by 1784, when the young Comte de la Rochefoucauld visited England, tea-drinking was universal:

Throughout the whole of England the drinking of tea is general. You have it twice a day and, though the expense is considerable, the humblest peasant has his tea twice a day just like the rich man: the total consumption is immense. The high cost of sugar or molasses, of which large quantities are required, does not prevent this custom being a universal one.... It provides the rich with an opportunity to display their magnificence in the matter of tea-pots, cups, and so on, which are always of most elegant design based upon Etruscan and other models of antiquity.[23]

The literary sources, then, point to a great increase in the consumption of tea during the eighteenth century. This suggestion is confirmed both by the tea importation figures[24] – and even these do not take account of a vast smuggling trade – and by the record of the successive taxes on tea by which governments recognized its increasing importance as a source of revenue.

Tea was not popular enough in Britain to be regarded as a source of government revenue until the 1690s, except in a minor degree when, in 1660, an excise duty of 8*d.* a gallon was put on beverages – including tea and sherbet – drunk in coffee houses. In 1695 a tax of 1*s.* in the pound was imposed on lawfully imported tea and 1*s.* 6*d.* in the pound on unlawfully imported tea (that which did not arrive in ships of the East India Company). This was doubled in 1704 and again increased in 1712, when the East India Company were given the monopoly of tea importation so that the Government could collect all taxes from one source. In 1747 the tax was increased, and imports fell. In 1767 the inland revenue duty of 1*s.* in the pound was suspended for five years on black and Singlo teas to increase consumption at home and to encourage export to Ireland and the American colonies. During the next two years there was an increase of more than six million pounds in British and Welsh consumption. Pitt, by his Commutation Act of 1784, repealed the high duties and the inland tax and replaced them by a flat twelve and a half per cent of the value at import. And he put a legal obligation on the East India Company to import enough tea into England to satisfy the demand without raising the price.[25] The Company also had the monopoly of tea importation into America, and it is significant that the first great act of American independence was the Boston tea-party of 1773. In the enviable phrase of Gervas Huxley, Great Britain 'lost an Empire to oblige the East India Company'.[26]

The increasing popularity of tea did not discourage its cult among the fashionable. It might be slopped with abandon by Hogarth's harlots (Plate 34) or stolidly brewed in an earthenware pot by Chardin's serving-maid, but in the salons its fate was kinder:

> 'Tis brew'd and manag'd by the nicest Hands;
> And in a *China* Mash-pot by them stands.
> From thence they draw it in transparent Cups,
> Season'd with Sugar, instead of bitter Hops.
> Great is the wisdom of the sober Sex,
> In chusing Drink that plays no naughty tricks.[27]

In great houses such as Bulstrode or Harrington House, tea-drinking became a hierophantic ritual almost as reverent as the Japanese tea ceremony. Philips's painting of 1739 (Plate 35) shows a Harrington tea party. The first Earl, who is present, had been appropriately compared by Lord Hervey, three years before, to a piece of old china:

> This statesman's fortune (odd as it may sound)
> In that of your old china may be found;
> For first at an enormous price you bought him,
> Then never us'd him, and, laid by, forgot him.[28]

Harrington House was still a temple of the tea cult in the early nineteenth century. Captain Gronow recalled:

> When our army returned to England in 1814, my young friend, Augustus Stanhope, took me one afternoon to Harrington House, in Stableyard, St James's, where I was introduced to Lord and Lady Harrington, and all the Stanhopes. On entering a long gallery, I found the whole family engaged in their sempiternal occupation of tea-drinking. Neither in Nankin, Pekin, nor

Canton was the teapot more assiduously and constantly replenished than at this hospitable mansion.... As an example of the undeviating tea-drinking habits of the house of Harrington, General Lincoln Stanhope once told me, that after an absence of several years in India, he made his reappearance at Harrington House, and found the family, as he had left them on his departure, drinking tea in the long gallery. On his presenting himself, his father's only observation and speech of welcome to him was, 'Hallo Linky, my dear boy! delighted to see you. Have a cup of tea?'

I was then taken to Lord Petersham's apartments, where we found his lordship, one of the chief dandies of the day, employed in making a particular sort of blacking, which he said would eventually supersede every other. The room into which we were ushered was more like a shop than a gentleman's sitting room: all round the walls were shelves, upon which were placed tea-canisters containing Congou, Pekoe, Souchong, Bohea, Gunpowder, Russian, and many other teas, all the best of the kind.[29]

Tea Gardens, such as Bagnigge Wells or Spring Gardens, Bath, made fashionable by Beau Nash, or the more proletarian Bayswater, added to the social attractions of tea-drinking. George Colman wrote:

Bone Tone's the space 'twixt Saturday and Monday
And riding in a one-horse chair on Sunday;
'Tis drinking tea on summer afternoons
At Bagnigge Wells with china and gilt spoons.

George Morland's 'A Tea Garden' (Plate VII) probably shows a scene at Bagnigge Wells. The grotesquely cloche-hatted ladies and their escorts are using an all-porcelain service, perhaps of Worcester manufacture. By now it was usual for the teapot to be of the same ware as the teacups and saucers: manufacturers supplied the complete *équipage*. But in the first half of the eighteenth century, teapots were seldom of a piece with the tea-set, at least in upper-class households. Teapots and coffee-pots tended to be of silver or of Chinese, Dutch or English red stoneware. It is exceptional to find recorded in Lord Bristol's diary as early as 1698: 'For a white Tea-pot & bason for dear wife, £4 – 16 – 9.'[30] But porcelain teapots are shown in use in Tischbein's picture (1756) of his first wife at tea, and in Ollivier's painting (1777) of the court of Prince Conti in Paris, where tea is being taken *à l'anglaise* as the young Mozart plays the clavier. Lord Willoughby de Broke and his family, in Zoffany's painting of *c.* 1780, have a large silver tea urn, but also a porcelain teapot.

By the second half of the century, too, Chinese tea-sets were being superseded by European ones – a trend observed by the Marquis d'Angivillier: 'La porcelaine de Chine n'a plus dans le royaume cette supériorité exclusive qui nous minait et nous mortifiait.' The reason for this was the development of the first European porcelains which could compare with the oriental. At Meissen, a superb white hard paste resulted from the researches of Augustus the Strong's experimenters, the Graf von Tschirnhaus and Johann Friedrich Böttger. It was exhibited in the Leipzig Fair in 1710 and was sold there for the first time in 1713. The earliest reliably dated example is a cup and saucer in the British Museum bearing the arms of Sophia, Electress of Hanover, who died in 1714. Through piracy of the formula, factories were also established at Vienna (1719) and Venice (1720). In France, the St Cloud factory embarked on its most successful period in 1722 with a renewed patent and the patronage of the Duke of Orleans. The Chantilly factory was established by the Prince de Condé in 1725, and another factory, set up in Paris in 1734, moved to Mennecy in 1748 under pressure from the royal factory of Vincennes. The glories of Sèvres were ahead. The Italian factories of Capodimonte and Doccia both began making porcelain on a commercial scale in the 1740s, and the first English soft-paste porcelains of Chelsea and Bow date from the same time. Some idea of the relative domestic status of Chinese porcelain, the best English porcelain, earthenware and delft is given by the journal of Mrs Papendiek, Assistant Keeper of the Wardrobe to Queen Charlotte. Writing of the setting-up of her first home in January 1783, she noted:

> Our tea and coffee set were of Common India china, our dinner service of earthenware, to which, for our rank, there was nothing superior, Chelsea porcelain and fine India china being only for the wealthy. Pewter and Delft ware could also be had, but were inferior.[31]

Coffee was introduced into Italy in 1615 by Venetian traders. Coffee houses were established, and by the early eighteenth century nearly every shop in the Piazza di San Marco, Venice, was a *caffè*. These were patronized by all classes of society, providing the ideal setting for a comedy of manners such as Goldoni's *La Bottega di Caffè* (1750). Coffee was introduced into Marseilles in the late seventeenth century, and in 1672 an Armenian named Pascal opened a coffee stall at the Fair of St Germain. In 1650 the first English coffee house was established at Oxford, and two years later Pasqua Rosée and his partner Bowman opened the first London coffee house in Cornhill. Rosée had previously sold coffee in Holland; regular imports of coffee from Mocha to

Amsterdam began in 1663. The drink was introduced into Germany about 1670, and an English merchant opened the first German coffee house in 1679–80. Bach's *Coffee Cantata* (1732) was written as a gesture of defiance against a royal edict restricting coffee drinking on the grounds of danger to health. The Viennese captured sacks of coffee from the Turks at the great battle of 12 September 1683, and adopted the drink, together with a taste for *turqueries* in porcelain – according to the familiar European pattern, at least as old as the Greco-Persian Wars of the fifth century BC, by which the civilized conquerors guy the bizarre conversions of the 'barbarians'.

The porcelain manufacturers were not slow to encourage the fashion for a separate tea equipage and coffee equipage. There must be coffee sets for the fair Miranda at her morning reflections (Plate 31) and for Boucher's family at their lavish *déjeuner* (Plate 32). Coffee and porcelain are elegantly associated by Johann Peter Uz in a poem of 1753, *Der Sieg des Liebesgottes*:

> Indess prangt Lesbia in ihren kühlen Zimmern,
> die nach dem Garten sehn und reichgekleidet schimmern:
> Und hier versammeln sich, da Spiel und Coffee winkt
> die artigsten der Stadt und wer sich artig dünkt.
> Von allen Lippen rauscht ein fliessend Wortgepränge:
> Die Neuiger schleicht herum in lärmenden Gedränge
> und starrt mit gleicher Lust bald glänzend Porzellan,
> bald einen jungen Herrn und bald ein Möpschen an.
> Die Wirthin geht und kömmt; und all ihr Thun belebet
> der freyen Sitten Reiz, die unsre Zeit erhebet.[32]

Coffee houses were also popular in America. The first licence to sell coffee in the United States was issued to Dorothy Jones of Boston in 1670. The Merchant's Coffee House, established at New York in 1737, became, like its London counterparts, a centre of political intrigue.

Chocolate, or cocoa, was known to Europeans before tea or coffee. The sixteenth-century Spanish conquistadors found that Montezuma 'took no other beverage than the *chocolatl*, a potation of chocolate, flavoured with vanilla and other spices, and so prepared as to be reduced to a froth of the consistency of honey'.[33] But chocolate did not become a fashionable drink in Europe until the seventeenth century. In 1657 a Frenchman opened a shop in London at which solid chocolate for making the beverage could be bought at 10*s*. to 15*s*. a pound. Chocolate houses were established in London, Paris and Amsterdam. About 1700 the English improved chocolate by the introduction of milk. But the cost remained high, because of the high import duties on the raw cocoa bean. Chocolate did not become really popular until 1853, when the duty was lowered to a uniform rate of 1*d*. a pound. Chocolate manufacturers began in the American colonies in 1765 at Dorchester, Massachusetts, using beans brought in by New England sea captains from their voyages to the West Indies.

Because chocolate-drinking was restricted so much to the fashionable classes during the eighteenth and early nineteenth centuries, the porcelain apparatus tended to be of an unusually high quality. At its best, it could include a Meissen *trembleuse* such as the *schokoladenmädchen* Elisabeth Baldauf is carrying in Liotard's pastel (Plate 30), or a superb covered cup from Vincennes decorated with plummeting gold birds on a mazarine blue background (Plate 56). A titillating glimpse of the luxury that attended the most exalted chocolate drinking (and the porcelain in which it was served) is given by Romanet's engraving *Le Bain* (Plate 61):

> De la Lettre ou du Chocolat
> Que préfère Madame ? Ah ma chère Justine,
> J'ai le coeur bien plus délicat
> Plus foible infiniment, hélas ! que la poitrine.

Great momentum was given to the French ceramic industries by the sumptuary laws of Louis XIV, and these indirectly had surprising effects abroad. The idea of sacrificing one's silver in the national interest had been established during the war of 1688 when some massive pieces of silver furniture, including a throne, were sent from Versailles to the Mint. In 1709 the principle was extended into a kind of enforced patriotism. Saint-Simon writes:

> Ce bruit de la vaisselle fit un grand tintamarre à la cour. Chacun n'osoit ne pas offrir la sienne; chacun y avoit grand regret.... Tout ce qu'il y eut de grand ou de considérable se mit en huit jours en faïence, en épuisèrent les boutiques et mirent le feu à cette marchandise, tandis que tout le médiocre continua à se servir de son argenterie.
>
> Le roi agita de se mettre à la faïence; il envoya sa vaisselle d'or à la Monnoie, et M. le duc d'Orléans le peu qu'il avoit. Le roi et la famille royale se servirent de vaisselle de vermeil et d'argent; les princes et les princesses du sang, de faïence....[34]

The nobility ingratiated themselves with the king by sending their silver to the foundry: this was called *faire du bon citoyen* – a phrase curiously anticipatory of the revolution. The duc d'Antin, a sedulous courtier, had a quantity of silver vessels of exquisite workmanship:

> Il courut à Paris choisir force porcelaine admirable, qu'il eut à grand marché, et enlever deux boutiques de faïence qu'il fit pompeusement porter à Versailles.[35]

The furnaces were rekindled in 1759, when Louis XV had about 6,000 marks of his own silver melted down. The court was pressed to follow his example, and the duc d'Orléans sent his silver in a *chariot*. The bourgeoisie resigned itself to the same sacrifice. For six months silver was melted down without cease. Barbier discusses the effects in his journal:

> Il n'est guère possible de se servir de la vaisselle d'argent, surtout en assiettes, quand les princes, les plus gros seigneurs et les gens en dignité seront réduits à manger sur de la vaisselle de faïence.
>
> Cette aventure va ruiner tout le corps des orfèvres ... et en même temps va enrichir toutes les manufactures de faïence et de la porcelaine.
>
> Il y a depuis dix ou douze jours un grand concours de carrosses à un grand magasin de faïences, plus ou moins recherchées, sur le quai de la porte Saint-Bernard, au-dessus des Miramionnes. J'y allai le 30 octobre [1759] acheter des plats et assiettes, et jattes, comme les autres. Le ministre de Paris y étoit avec M. Bertin de Jumillac, frère de M. le lieutenant général de police; et tous les jours, à toute heure, c'est la même chose.[36]

The *London Chronicle* of 26 to 28 February 1760 recorded that:

> On the 5th inst. the Duke of Choiseul, Minister and Secretary of State to the French King, gave an entertainment to all the Ambassadors and foreign ministers residing at Paris, which was served on china and earthenware; his Grace having sacrificed his magnificent service of plate to the wants of the State. M. de Sotomajor, the Spanish Ambassador, paid him 1,100,000 livres for it, and sent it to Madrid in three carriages.

How different from the days when Eléonor d'Etampes de Valençay, Archbishop of Rheims, gave this charming example of Christian humility and charity:

> Trois jours avant sa mort [1651], comme il vit qu'on luy apportoit un bouillon dans une escuelle de fayence, il demanda un plat. On luy apporta un plat de fayence. 'Quoy!' dit-il, 'tousjours fayence!' Il se douta bien que sa soeur avoit pris sa vaisselle d'argent. 'Apportez-moi,' dit-il, 'un bassin.' On luy en apporte un de fayence....[37]

Because the aristocracy turned to ceramics to replace the silver plate consigned to the foundry, ceramics had to improve in quality. And because it was silver that the ceramics were replacing the ceramics tended to take over the styles and motifs which belonged to silver. It is not surprising that the rococo designs of the court silversmith Juste-Aurèle Meissonnier were a dominant influence on eighteenth-century ceramics. Perhaps one might even go so far as to suggest that the two continental silversmiths who founded the Chelsea porcelain factory – Nicholas Sprimont and Charles Gouyn – came to England because they were dissatisfied with the opportunities on the Continent. Certainly early Chelsea was influenced by silver originals: the goat and bee jug (Plate 38) may have been based on a silver prototype by Edward Wood.[38]

Everything was done to suggest that porcelain was, so to speak, worth its weight in silver. *Marchands-bijoutiers* such as Lazare Duvaux sold it with jewels, precious enamels and antiques. Travelling sets were fitted with beautiful leather cases (Plate 37). It was mounted in silver and gold, and imprisoned in wildernesses of ormolu. Voltaire's secretary, Longchamp, relates an incident involving Voltaire and his mistress, Madame du Châtelet, which shows that porcelain was regarded as fit, if not for a queen, at least for a marquise:

> At Châlons-sur-Marne they had a disagreeable experience. Mme du Châtelet always took her own food on journeys, she said to save time, but really to save money. When they arrived at Châlons, however, she felt she would like a cup of soup, so they stopped at the inn. The innkeeper's wife, seeing the beautiful coach, and hearing that it belonged to the Marquise du Châtelet, brought the soup out herself in a china cup with a silver lid. When Emilie had finished, Longchamp was told to carry back the cup and settle the bill. To his horror the woman demanded a louis.[39]

If we compare the porcelain industry of the nineteenth century with that of the eighteenth century, the two most striking differences are, first, a decline in royal patronage, and, secondly, an improvement in technique. The eighteenth-century factories had benefited from a royal patronage which ranged from the grandly squandering to the meanly monopolistic, and which reached its climax when Frederick the Great decreed that each Jew, on his marriage, should buy 300 talers worth of Berlin porcelain. (The philosopher Moses Mendelssohn was obliged to buy a set of porcelain monkeys.[40]) Royal patronage had also meant immense orders of services as diplomatic gifts.

In the nineteenth century, factories had to rely for large orders on public bodies – not remarkable for prodigality or taste – or the private Croesus, such as John Julius Angerstein (1735–1823) for whom the famous silhouette service (Plate 42) was made by Coalport, 1805–10.[41] Angerstein was a millionaire financier and a connoisseur. Aided by his close friend Sir Thomas Lawrence, and by Benjamin West, he made a collection of pictures which were, at his death, to form the nucleus of the National Gallery. By his first wife, Angerstein had two children, John and Juliana, who married the Russian General Sablonkoff. John married Amelia, the eldest daughter of William Lock of Norbury Park, Surrey. The Locks had a circle of cultivated friends, including Fanny Burney and her husband General d'Arblay, Madame de Staël and other French refugees who stayed at Juniper Hall, the nearest large house, during the Terror.[42] The Locks of Norbury were an artistic family, and the eldest son, William, was a painter of some note. His work was admired and encouraged by both Lawrence and Fuseli. Many evenings were spent at Norbury with their guests, including Wedgwood's artist, Lady Templetown, in cutting profiles and sketching. It seems probable that the silhouettes are of Amelia Angerstein and her children, nephews and nieces. The best account of the Lock family and their circle is in *The Locks of Norbury* (1940) by the Duchess of Sermoneta (*née* Lock). An earlier Duchess of Sermoneta – described by Augustus Hare as 'a most ghastly and solemn woman to outsiders'[43] – owned a Worcester mug (Plate 43) on the bottom of which has been pasted a brief pedigree which seems unlikely to be entirely fictional:

> This piece of Worcester was formerly the property of the Duchess of Sermonita [*sic*] & bears the Ducal Crest.– This lady volunteered her services as a nurse in revolutionary times – caught cold & died of fever leaving this mug as a souvenir to an English soldier who gave her water in it. Mr Mogg of Bristol acquired it ... [last two or three words indecipherable].

Like the Angerstein service, the Hingham Hall fireplace[44] (Plates 44 and 45) is a showpiece of nineteenth-century private patronage. It is also a monument to extreme technical accomplishment. Augustus the Strong's baroque schemes for giant and life-sized statues in porcelain had come to grief because the material flawed in the kiln. The blemishes of eighteenth-century porcelain – the grainy or orange-peel texture, the fissures and firecracks, the warping and 'wreathing' – are part of its appeal. Nineteenth-century porcelain lost something aesthetically in achieving technical perfection. But at least it became possible to make huge and flawless panels of the kind used in the Hingham chimneypiece. It was made by the Copeland factory but decorated in France, and in about 1849 it was bought in Paris by John Graham, the art collector, and installed in a corner house in St Alban's Place, Regent's Park. Later it was transferred to 27 Charles Street, St James's. On Graham's death in 1874 it was inherited by his only daughter, Ada Jane, and was moved to Hingham Hall, Norfolk, the seat of her husband, Rawdon Hunter-Murkett. A photograph of that year (Plate 44) shows it *in situ* there. On the death of Ada Hunter-Murkett, the chimneypiece was removed by her only son, and in 1959 was installed by her only surviving grandson in No. 2 Buckingham Palace Mansions, London SW1, whence it was later transferred to the showrooms of Messrs Denys Wrey. Abstracted from its social context, it looks somewhat like a triumphal arch for a dwarf emperor. It hints with only a trace of disdain at connoisseur Graham's establishment in Charles Street and the luxurious 'at homes' of the Hunter-Murketts.

Technical improvement affected the whole range of ceramics. Wares of a quality available only to the few at the beginning of our period were the property of the many by its end. In the first half of the eighteenth century, porcelain was an exciting new invention; in the late nineteenth century, it was taken so much for granted that artist-potters were reacting against its mechanical precision. The history of collecting reflects these trends. In the eighteenth century, porcelain was collected as an exquisite semi-precious substance; but in the nineteenth century and ever since it has been collected largely because it is old. To William Beckford, a piece of good Sèvres made within the previous few years was almost as desirable as a piece of old Chinese porcelain of similar quality, whereas to Lady Charlotte Schreiber, a piece of modern porcelain could seem a contemptible utilitarian object. But already by the end of our period plastics had made their first appearance (bakelite was invented in 1907) and the ceramics factories were worried that these would eventually be the material of most useful wares. Now, in 1968, porcelain itself is beginning to slip back into the range of 'luxury' products.

4 The Rococo

The rococo style grew out of the baroque and became its antithesis. The baroque is unique, as geniuses and monsters are unique; the rococo, as its name almost suggests, is recurrent, repetitive as cuckoo song. Baroque assaults with a new marvel or horror; rococo reassures with yet another curve or trill, infinitesimally varied on the thousand before. There can be banal baroque formulae, just as there can be a rococo genius – Mozart. But baroque depends on originality, at worst descending into the grotesque, for the dramatic effect which is its essence. The 'tragic flaw' of the baroque is pretentiousness. There is a mock-baroque, the equivalent of the mock-heroic in literature. By contrast, the besetting fault of rococo is flippancy. Every *tour de force* is a *jeu d'esprit*, every *maître* a fribble.

The new frivolity was all-pervasive. The grandly symmetrical gowns of Rigaud's ladies gave place to the frothy petticoats of Boucher's. The musical type of the baroque was an architectural fugue; that of the rococo was a tripping sonata, the theme scarcely more than a base for embellishment. Italian dances, wrote Hogarth in 1743, 'in expressing elegant wantonness (which is the true spirit of dancing) have of late years been most delightfully done, and seem at present to have got the better of pompous, unmeaning grand ballets; serious dancing being even a contradiction in terms'.[1] It would be callous to speak of rococo warfare. Death is as much death in scarlet tunics as in khaki battledress. But Professor Butterfield, allowing a fine imagination to outstrip a fine historical sense, has hinted at a concept of rococo warfare:

> The French Revolution puts an end to the gentlemanly warfare – almost the mimic warfare we might be tempted to say – of the eighteenth-century professional armies. It puts an end to the urbane diplomatic game played

with counters by cosmopolitan aristocrats, cynical sometimes, yet too worldly-wise for the last insanities of unforgiving passion.[2]

Even in science, which should be unsusceptible to fashion, a kind of rococo was succeeding a kind of baroque; though it is rather mischievous to say that 'the wonders revealed by the microscope were ... merely a delight for the eye, and the thrilling phenomena of electricity a drawing-room diversion'.[3] Descartes' ponderous theory of vortices was demolished by Sir Isaac Newton. 'A Circumstance which has always appear'd wonderful to me,' wrote Voltaire, 'is, that such sublime Discoveries should have been made with the sole Assistance of a Quadrant and a little Arithmetic.'[4] It was even more diverting to reflect that the inspiration of the theory had been an apple falling on Sir Isaac's head. Nothing was less grave, it seems, than gravity.

How did the new style come into being, and from what did it take its name? Insofar as artists were free agents, it could be seen as a spontaneous reaction against the oppressive grandeur of the baroque by certain *Dessinateurs* of the King of France – Jean Berain (1640–1711), Pierre Cailleteau, called Lassurance (d. 1724), Pierre Lepautre (*c.* 1648–1716) and Claude Audran (1658–1734). But artists were not quite free agents, particularly artists of the King of France, and by a nice paradox of art history it was Louis XIV – that domineering baroque figure – who by dictatorial patronage gave the first impetus to the new style. On 8 September 1699, his architect, Mansart, sent to Fontainebleau a memorandum proposing figures of Diana Pomona, Thetis, Flora, Palès, Ceres, Minerva and Juno for the apartments of the Duchesse de Bourgogne at the Château de la Ménagerie. In the margin of this proposal the King wrote:

> Il me paroît qu'il y a quelque chose à changer que les sujets sont trop sérieux et qu'il faut qu'il y ait de la jeunesse mêlée dans ce que l'on fera. Vous m'apporterez des dessins quand vous viendrez, ou du moins des pensées. Il faut de l'enfance répandue partout. Louis, Fontainebleau, 10 septembre 1699.[5]

And in 1700 Audran began painting the apartments with arabesques, airy scrollwork, tattered cartouches, ethereal canopies – motifs of calligraphic grace anticipating the still less inhibited fantasies of the next generation.

From about the time of Audran's death (1734) the word *rocaille*, which meant rock-work and shell-work for the encrustation of grottoes and fountains, acquired a wider sense as a designation of style. From *rocaille*, the word rococo was presumably derived, on the analogy of *barocco*. A nineteenth-century writer, M.-E.-J. Delécluze, believed he could pinpoint the moment in history when the word was coined. He wrote of a fellow student in the atelier of David:

> Ces expressions : *Pompacour*, *rococo*, à peu près admises aujourd'hui dans la conversation, pour désigner le goût à la mode pendant le règne de Louis XV, ont été employées pour la première fois par Maurice Quaï en 1796–97. Alors ces locutions (on pourrait dire cet argot) n'étaient usitées et comprises que dans les ateliers de peinture.[6]

The genesis of the rococo was in the reign of Louis XIV; but its second and most characteristic phase began in the next reign, with the *genre pittoresque* of J. B. Pineau and Juste-Aurèle Meissonnier (1695–1750), also royal *Dessinateurs*. Meissonnier was a silversmith by training, and a silver candlestick designed by him in 1728 was reproduced in the candlesticks for a rococo masterpiece, the Swan Service made by Meissen for Count von Brühl (1737). Fiske Kimball, in his pioneer work *The Creation of the Rococo* (1943), has written of the Meissonnier candlestick:

> This very work – of which the illustrations are missing in many copies of the engraved folio, and which has escaped the attention of scholars – is the crucial one in the origin of the *style pittoresque*, which shows it fully formed in the hands of Meissonnier – so far as craft objects are concerned – in the year 1728.[7]

Meissonnier's genius for the fanciful is equalled only by certain Mannerists and masters of *art nouveau*. Apart from his influence by direct imitations of his designs, he set a style which had strident echoes as far remote from the original source as Rörstrand, near Stockholm, and the Holitsch factory in Hungary (Plate V). We need only compare the Marseilles tureen (Plate 50) with a Meissonnier design (Plate 49) or the Sèvres inkstand (Plate 48) with his design for an *écritoire de porcelaine* (Plate 47) to see how strong the influence was nearer home. Meissonnier's designs for *salières* are archetypally rococo, since they actually embody the shell-encrustation techniques of the *rocailleurs*. It is etymologically apt that these shapes should so often have been modelled in porcelain, for when Marco Polo, in the service of Khublai Khan, had visited Fukien Province in the thirteenth century, he had named the ware being made by the Chinese potters '*pourcelaine*' – a word which until then had meant 'sea-shells'.

Engravings were the chief vehicle of the new style.[8] The Meissen-Meissonnier link has been mentioned; but the main design which appears on the Swan Service – the glorious arching swans themselves (Plate 57) – was derived from a travel book of 1700 published at Nuremberg by Leonard Buggels. When the Vienna factory was taken over by the State in 1744, the rococo style was adopted as a deliberate act of policy, not, as elsewhere, through the gradual infiltration of rococo motifs. In 1746 a lottery was held to dispose of the old stock; ninety-eight engravings of rococo patterns were bought in 1745 and one hundred in 1746. The naturalistic flowers of Meissen, *deutsche Blumen*, were inspired by engravings published at Augsburg in 1737 by Johann Wilhelm Winmann, *Phylanthus Iconographia oder eigentliche Vorstellung etl. Tausend sowohl einheimischler als ausländischer Pflanzen Bäume und Kräuter*; one of the engravers of this work was the Augsburg *Hausmaler* Bartholomäus Seuter, himself a flower-painter on faience. Gottlieb Friedrich Riedel, employed as chief designer at Höchst, Frankenthal and Ludwigsburg, published at Augsburg (1770) a book of engravings of birds for use in porcelain factories – *Sammlung von Feder-Vieh besonders Haus-Geflügel, nutzlich Fabriquen.* Karl Böhme engraved landscape designs for the use of the decorators at Berlin. A design by Saint-Aubin occurs on a Chelsea vase. Philip Miller's drawings of the Chelsea Physic Garden were the basis of naturalistic flowers on Chelsea porcelain. At Worcester, Robert Hancock made liberal use of engraved books published by Robert Sayer of Fleet Street, including *The Ladies' Amusement or the Whole Art of Japanning made easy* (*c.* 1760) and *The Artist's Vade-Mecum* (1776). Looking at Sayers's elegant figures, it is amusing to recall that he also published *The North Briton* and the obscene *Essay on Woman* for writing which John Wilkes was imprisoned; yet another example of that favourite paradox of historians whereby the eighteenth century is represented, not unwarrantably, as degradation fathoms deep beneath the thin crust of culture – or, as the Elector Palatine described it to Voltaire in a letter of 1756, 'a mermaid, the upper part of whose body is that of a bewitching nymph, while the lower part ends in a loathsome fish-tail'.[9]

More enterprising than the direct copying of engravings by decorators was their translation into the third dimension by modellers. An engraving of *l'Agréable Leçon*, after Boucher, by R. Gaillard inspired figure groups at Sèvres, Vincennes and Chelsea, where, as 'The Music Lesson' it became one of the most effusive works of the gold anchor period. Nilson's engraving of the same subject was probably the source of a Frankenthal group. Coloured engravings by George Edwards were the source of Chelsea figures of birds, and it is known that the Meissen factory also possessed copies of Edwards's engravings. Kändler's lady with a fan and the companion cavalier have been traced to details in engravings, 'Le Baiser Donné' and 'Le Baiser Rendu' by Filloeul after J. B. Pater, and groups of the complete subjects were made at Höchst and Frankenthal.

Engravings were bought by the middle class who could not afford to commission paintings by famous artists, and helped to prejudice their taste in favour of the rococo, more intimate and less obscurely allegorical than the aristocratic baroque. In England, Hogarth's Copyright Act of 1735 freed the artist from the system of particular patronage by forbidding the unauthorized mass copying of engravings. 'Henceforth,' says Joseph Burke, 'his choice and treatment of themes was not dictated by the taste of wealthy individuals: he was free to take the initiative, and appeal to a general public.'[10] A natural result of this emancipation was unrestrained satire of the aristocracy by the middle classes, notably by Hogarth himself, whose 'Taste in High Life' (Plate 180) is an eminently rococo work.

Hogarth was not only a brilliant practitioner of the rococo. He was its greatest contemporary theorist. The artistic canons asserted in *The Analysis of Beauty* are those which distinguish the style. First, asymmetry: 'It may be imagined that the greatest part of the effects of beauty results from the symmetry of parts in the object, which is beautiful: but I am very well persuaded, this prevailing notion will soon appear to have little or no foundation.'[11] The human profile, said Hogarth, is more pleasing than the full face. To avoid symmetry in design – a baroque characteristic – he recommended the use of 'waving' and 'serpentine' lines. Secondly, intricacy: 'Intricacy in form, therefore, I shall define to be that peculiarity in the lines, which compose it, that *leads the eye a wanton kind of chace*....'[12] Closely allied to this principle was that of 'distinctness of parts', an injunction against homogeneity, integration of detail, the architectonic, which again were characteristic of the baroque. 'When you would compose an object of a great variety of parts, let several of those parts be distinguished by themselves, by their remarkable difference from the next adjoining, so as to make each of them, as it were, one well-shap'd quantity or part....'[13] The colours Hogarth preferred were 'retiring shades' and 'tender tints'. He ridicules the idea of the hated 'connoisseurs' that time improves pictures by darkening the varnish: this merely meant, he said, that they 'must have a double

47 (*opposite top*) 'Ecritoire de Porcelaine', designed by Juste-Aurèle Meissonnier.
48 (*bottom*) Sèvres porcelain inkstand, *c.* 1760, designed by Claude-Thomas Duplessis. It was probably a gift by Louis VX to his daughter Marie Adelaide (1732–1800). See p. 90.

The Rococo

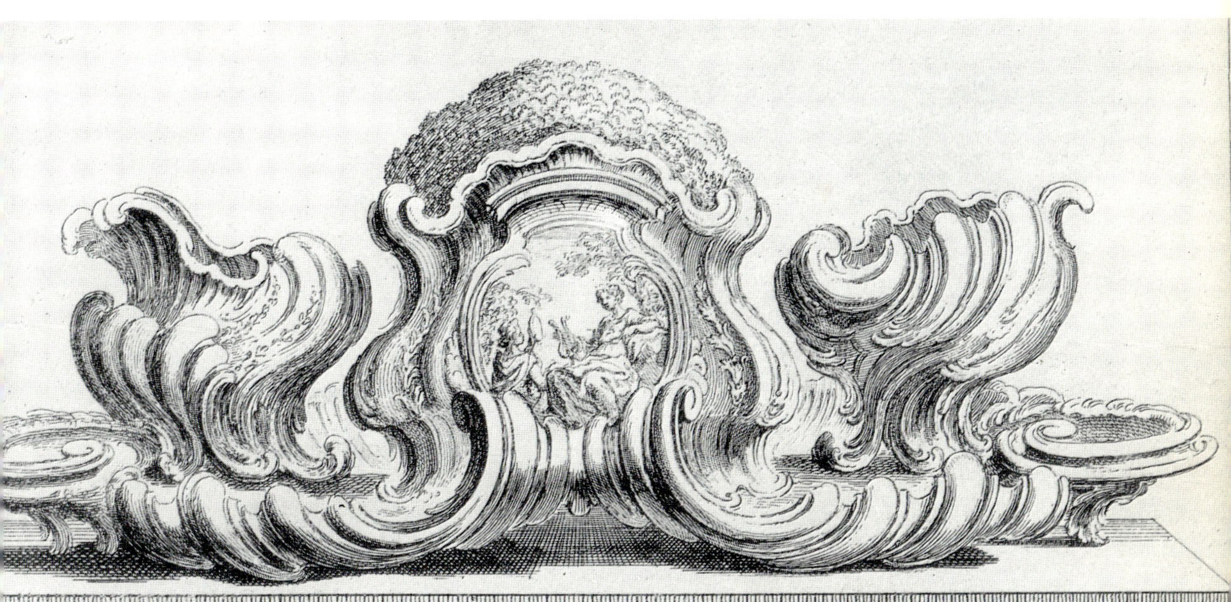

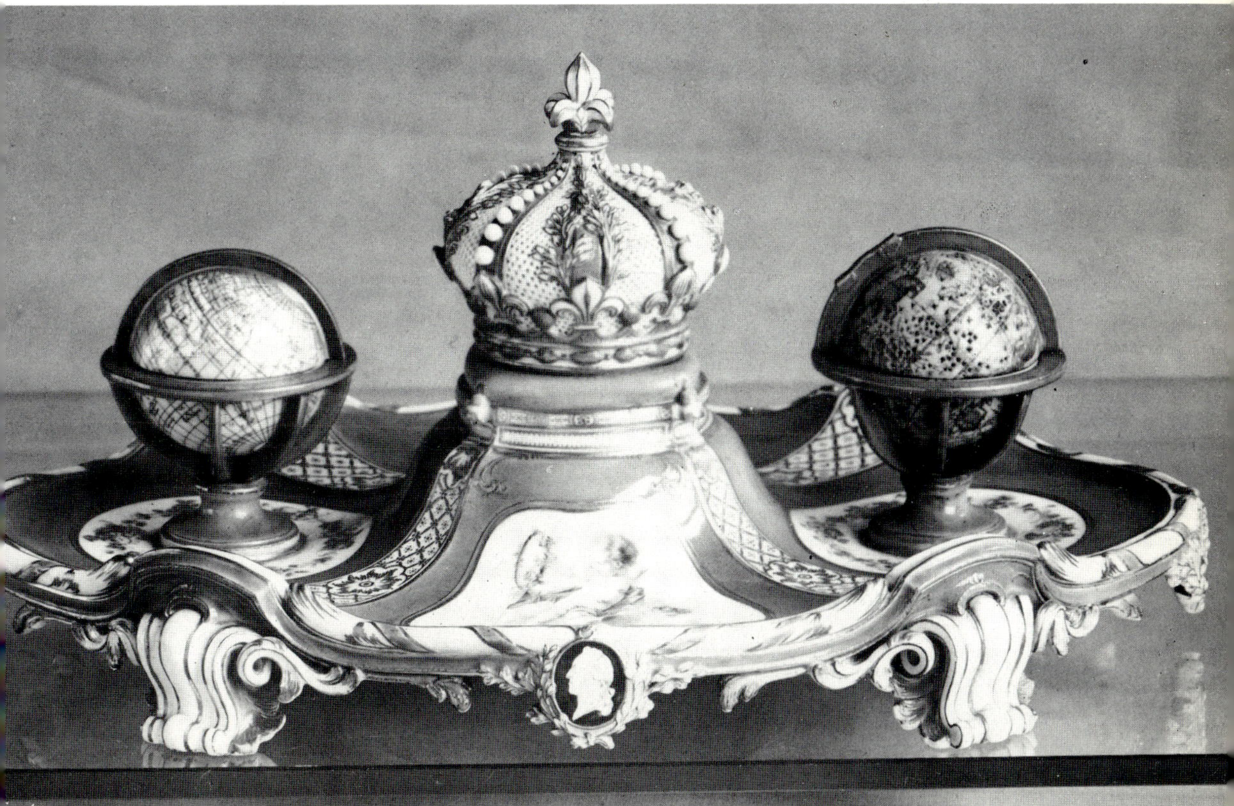

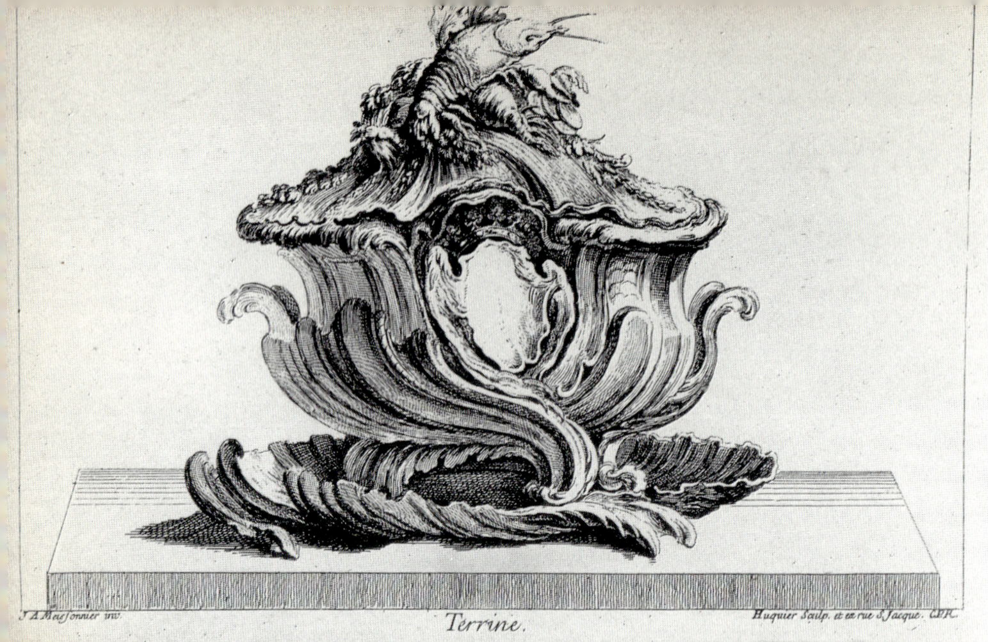

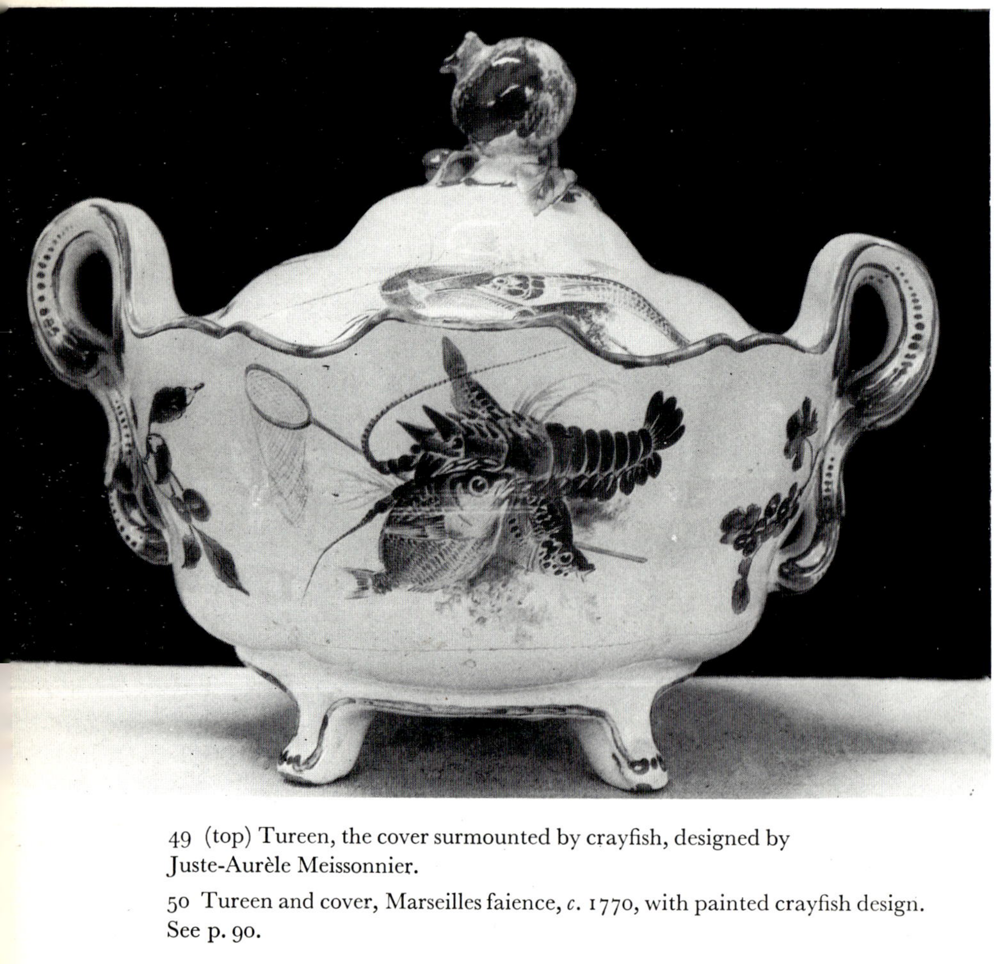

49 (top) Tureen, the cover surmounted by crayfish, designed by Juste-Aurèle Meissonnier.

50 Tureen and cover, Marseilles faience, *c.* 1770, with painted crayfish design. See p. 90.

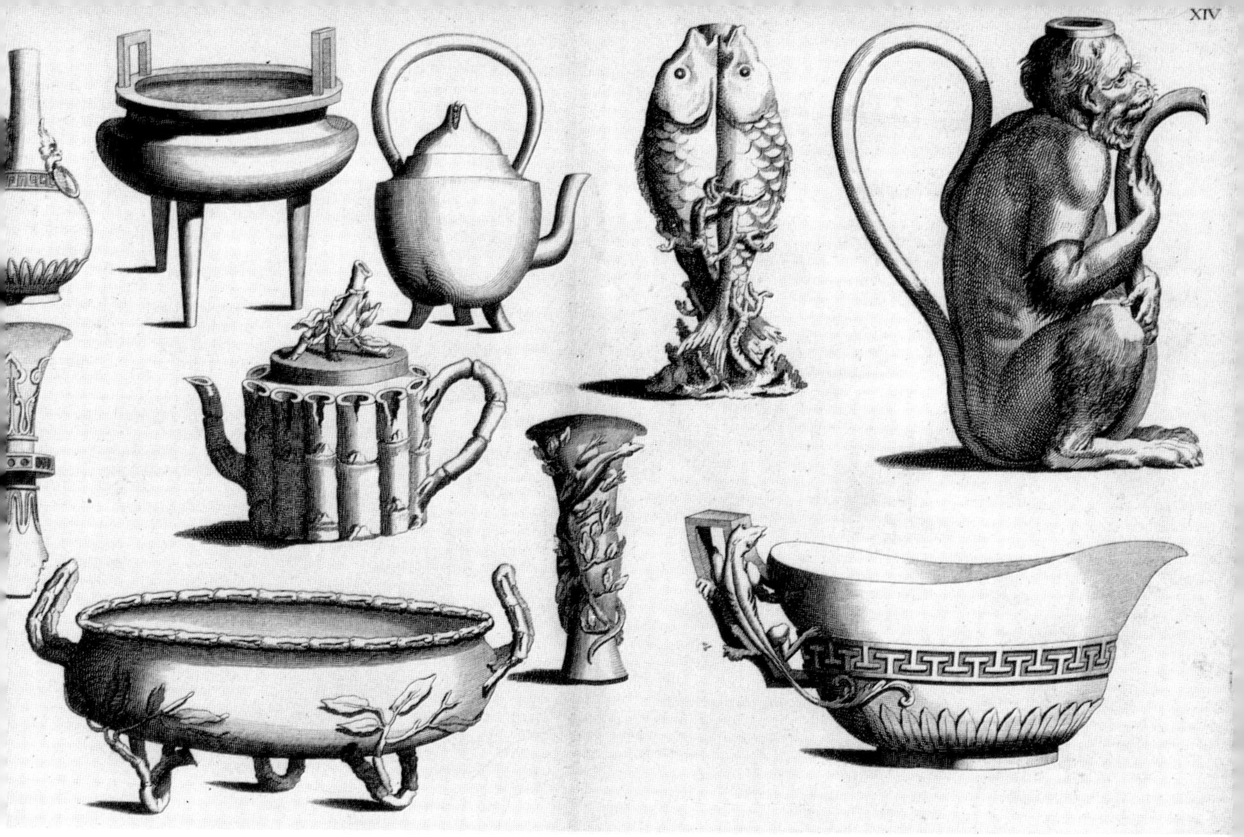

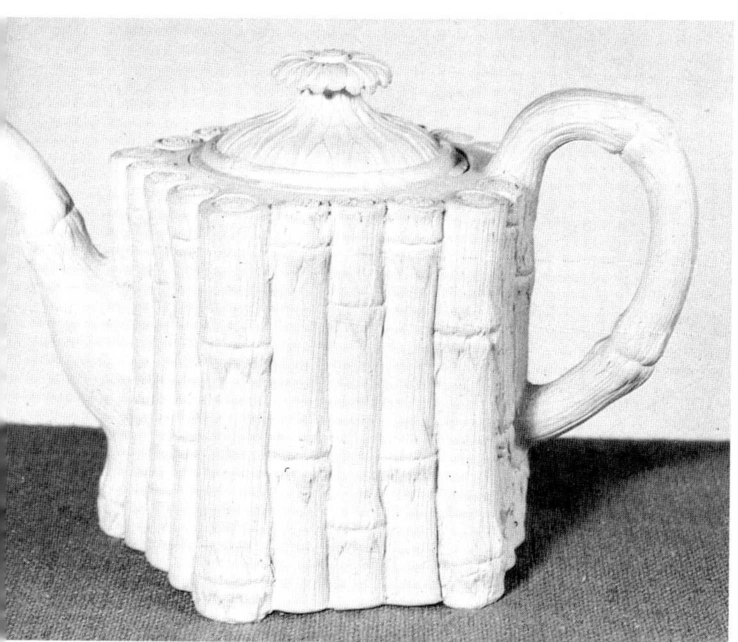

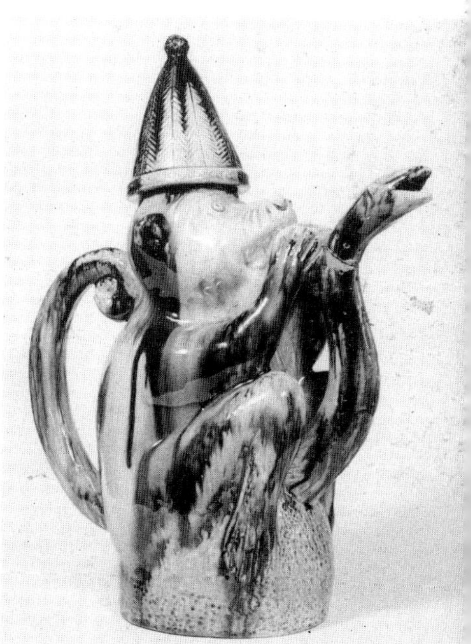

51 (top) A double page from Sir William Chambers's, *Designs of Chinese Buildings, Furniture, Dresses, Machines and Utensils*, 1757.
52 (left) Teapot and cover, cane-coloured stoneware, by John Turner of Lane End, *c.* 1780. Moulded to simulate cane stalks. Mark TURNER impressed and double 'R' impressed.
53 (right) Teapot and cover in the form of a monkey, earthenware decorated with variegated glazes. Second half of nineteenth century, probably French.

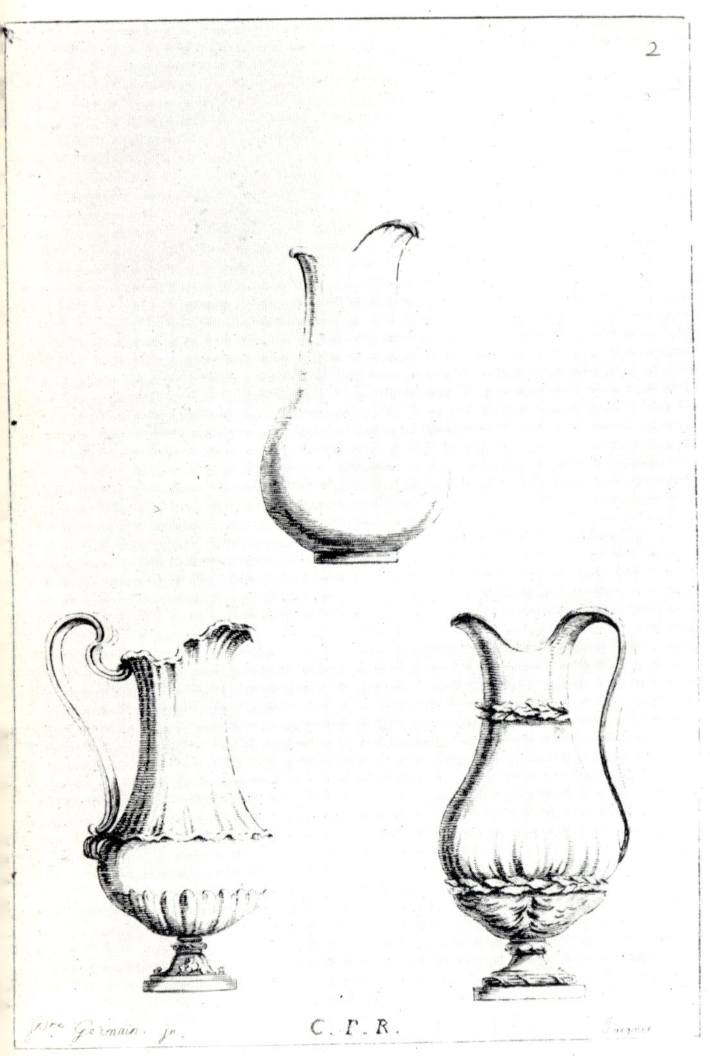

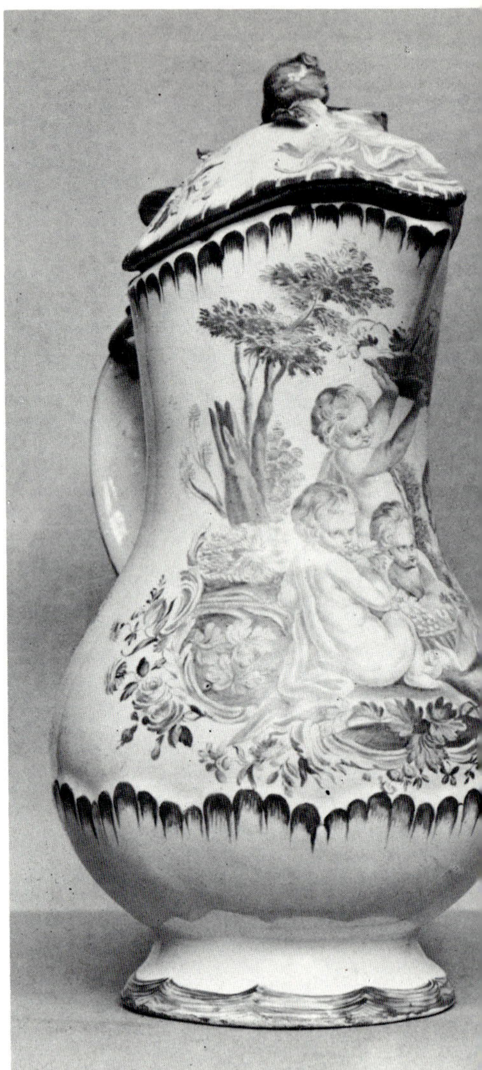

54 (left) Page of rococo ewer designs from Pierre Germain's *Eléments d'Orfèvrerie*.
55 (right) Ewer and cover, Sceaux faience, *c.* 1760.

56 Vincennes chocolate cup, cover and saucer, decorated in gold and royal blue. See p. 83.

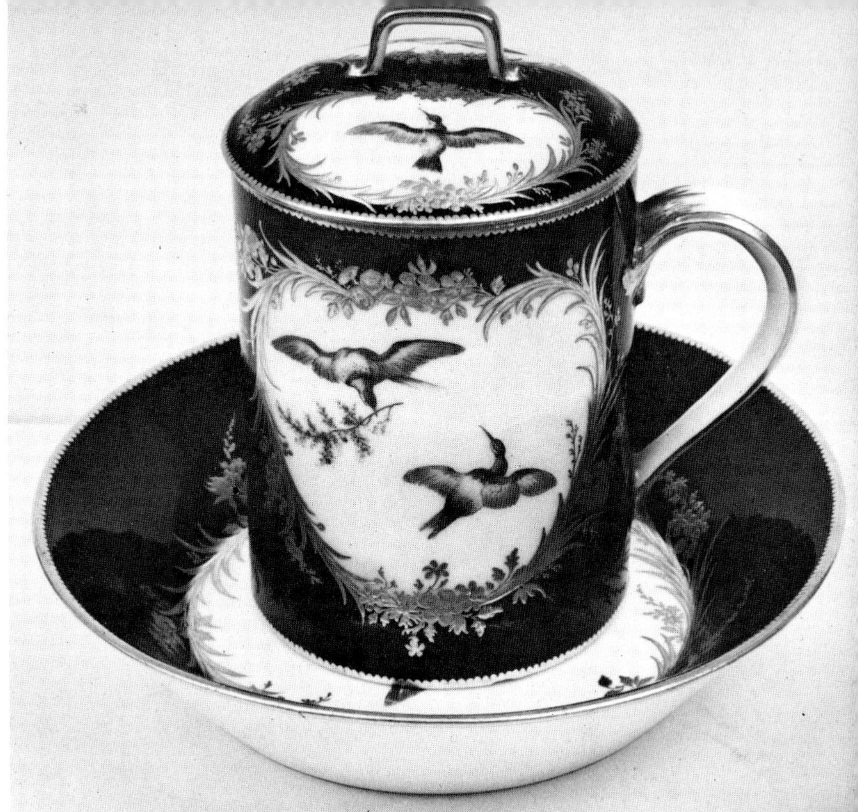

57 Plate from the great Swan Service made by Meissen for Count Brühl. See p. 91.

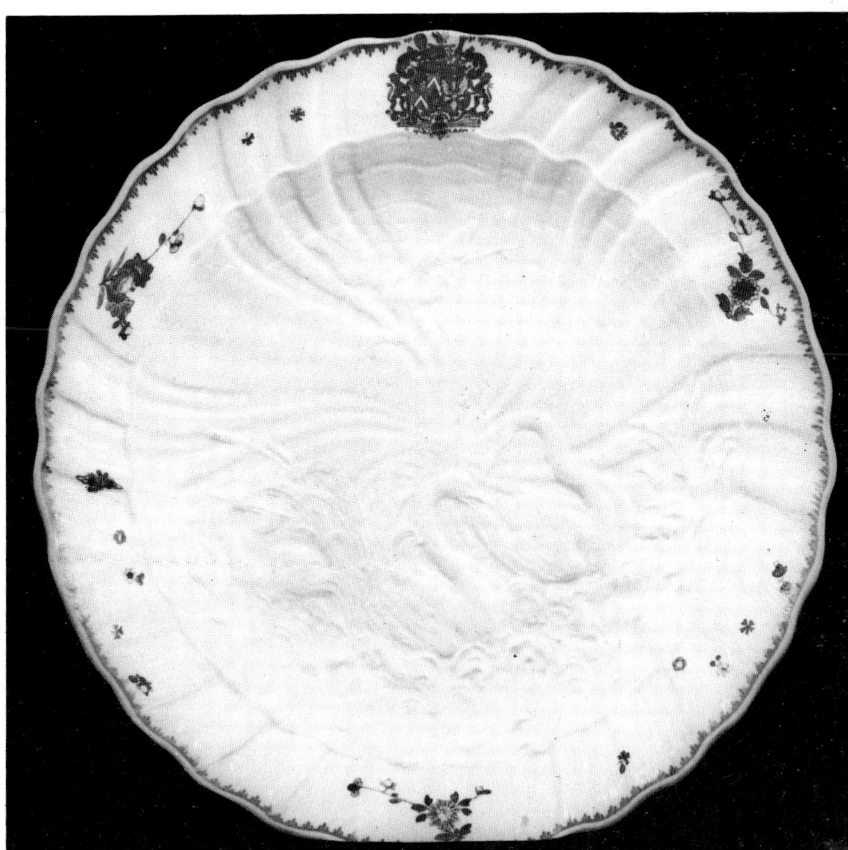

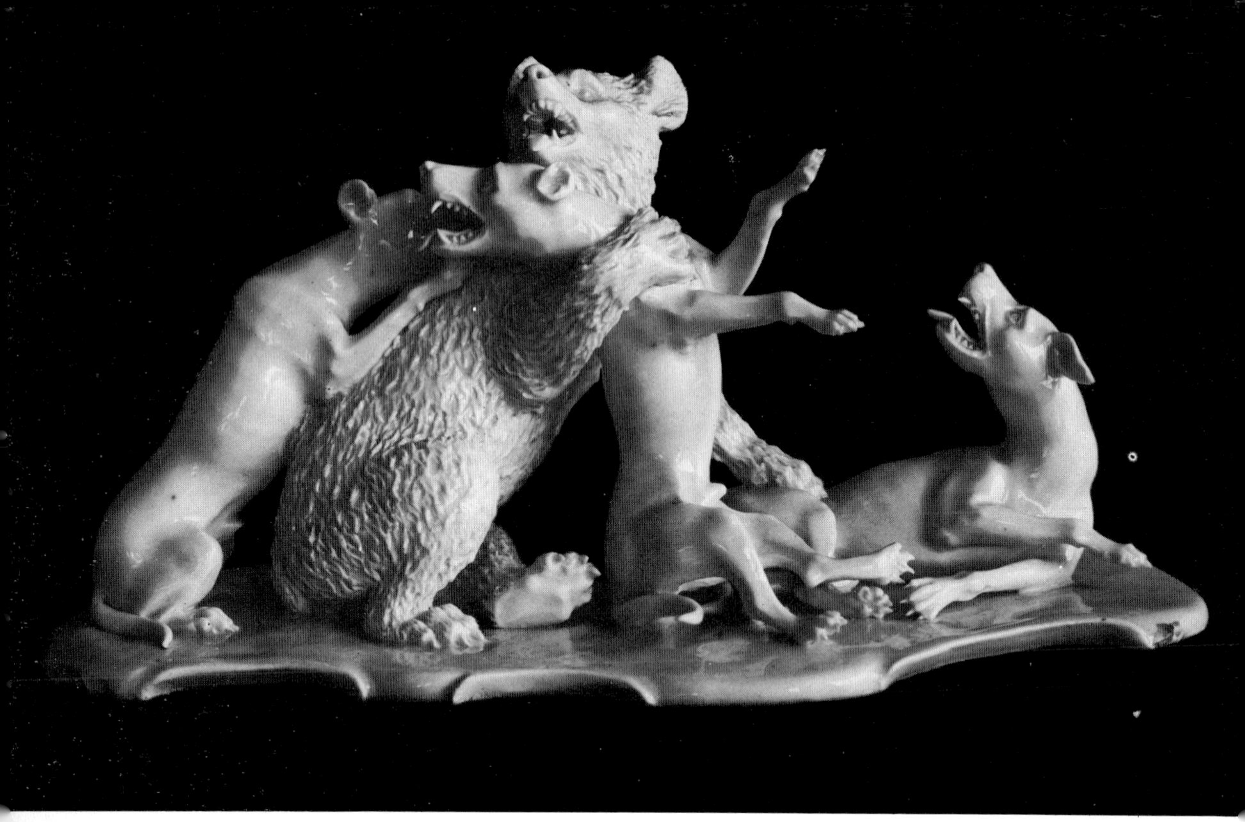

58 Bear-baiting group, Nymphenburg, after a model by Dominikus Auliczek, *c.* 1765.

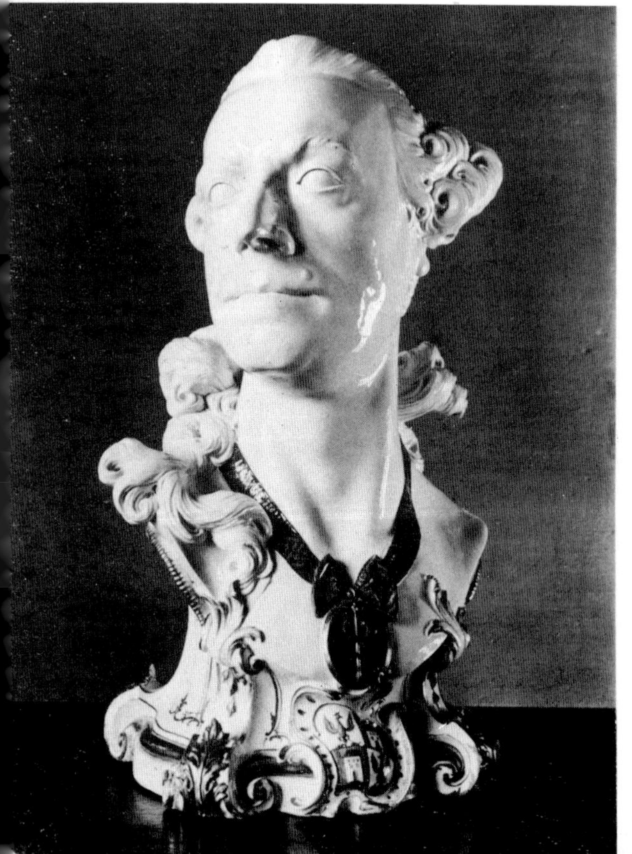

59 Portrait bust of Sigismund, Graf von Haimhausen, modelled by Franz Anton Bustelli; Nymphenburg, 1763. See p. 103.

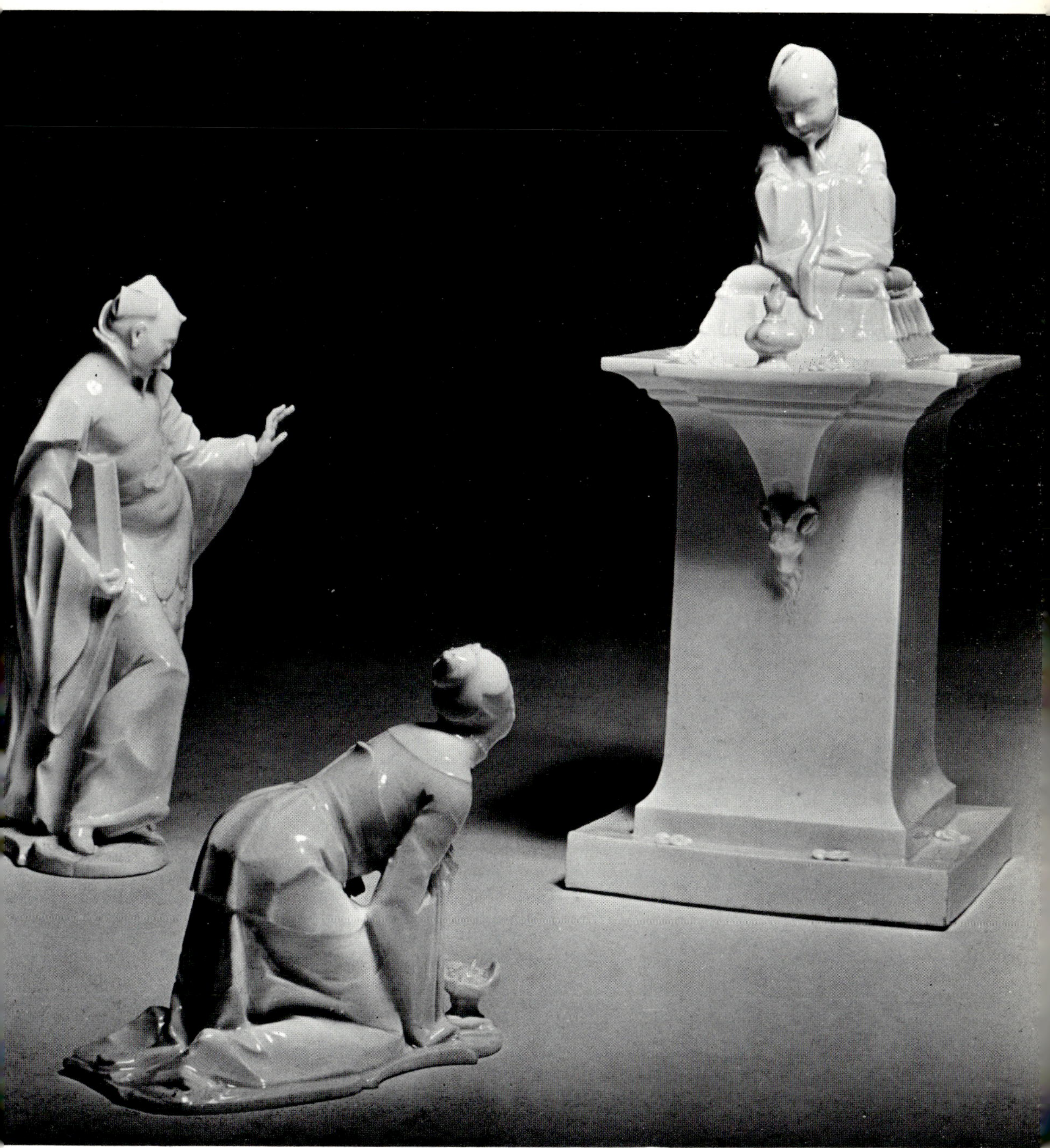

60 Three chinoiserie figures modelled by Bustelli. See p. 106.

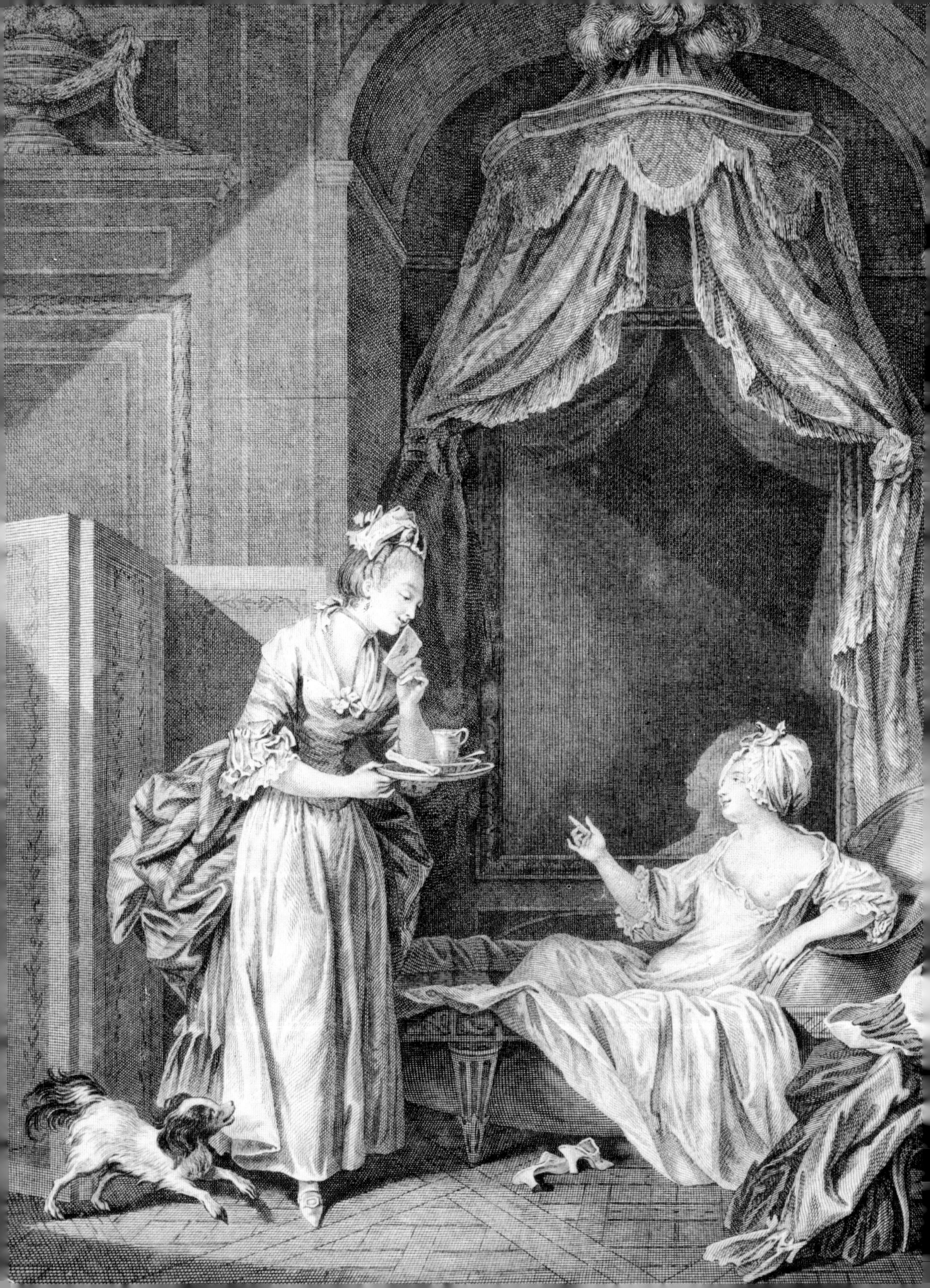

remove from nature'.[14] Faithfulness to nature is his cardinal tenet, and embraces all the others: nature is not symmetrical; its features do not obligingly fuse into an integrated composition; it is not painted in primary colours or seen through a film of brown varnish.

These are the fundamentals of rococo. Hogarth himself was not, surprisingly enough, one of the engravers whose works greatly influenced ceramic designs. The only links that come to mind are his *Midnight Modern Conversation* used as a Fulham design and on Staffordshire saltglaze wares, his cock-pit adapted as a Turner relief, and – still more tenuous – the close copy in Chelsea porcelain of Roubiliac's terracotta of Hogarth's pug, Trump.[15] But the rococo canons laid down in *The Analysis of Beauty* are a convenient starting-point for a discussion of these qualities in ceramics. It was in ceramics that they found most congenial expression. With justice the poor cabinet-maker, working with intractable wood, complained of the interlaced Cs and writhings Ss of rococo: but what material could be more easily fashioned into such designs than infinitely malleable clay?

Asymmetry is found everywhere: in the awry poise of Bustelli's *Commedia dell'arte* figures, the debonair imbalance of Kändler's later models; in the nicely calculated lopsidedness of scrolled porcelain pedestals (Plate 59), the precise artless abandon with which painted flowers are strewn over Chelsea red anchor wares – though sometimes the need to disguise firecracks, rather than any profound aesthetic waywardness, dictated the distribution of sprigs. Intricacy, the second of Hogarth's prescriptions, is equally apparent, in flurries of *bocage*, almost Pre-Raphaelite in their detail, in the exquisite accoutrements of a porcelain hussar, the provender of a Ludwigsburg pedlar, the affectionate detail of the goat and bee jug (Plate 38), the earliest dated production of Chelsea, which, like so many rococo ceramics, may have had a silver protype. As we have seen, Hogarth praised Italian dancing for its 'elegant wantonness' and spoke of lines that should lead the eye '*a wanton kind of chace*'. 'Playful' is the less ambiguous adjective generally applied to the rococo today; but can it have been accident that led W. B. Honey to write: 'Porcelain, with its wanton fragility and delicate plasticity, was especially well fitted to embody an extravagantly decorative style'?[16]

Naturalism, the basic Hogarthian precept, may at first seem an anomaly in this supremely artificial style which twisted mankind into serpentine patterns and portrayed the fruits of the earth as tumbling from ornate cornucopias. (Hogarth wrote of the beauty of 'the goat's

61 (*opposite*) Chocolate drinking: 'Le Bain', engraved by A. Romanet, 1774, after S. Freudebergdel. The chocolate cup is of rococo style. See p. 83.

horn, from which, in all probability, the ancients originally took the extreme elegant forms they have given their cornucopias'.[17]) But naturalism was certainly one of the ingredients of the *genre pittoresque*. When Meissonnier's enemy, the engraver Cochin, attacked him and his allies in the *Mercure de France*, there were strong undertones of irony in his references to their naturalism, although it is for disproportion that they are explicitly castigated:

> Sont priés les orfèvres, lorsque sur le couvercle d'un pot à ouille, ou sur quelque autre pièce d'orfèvrerie, ils exécutent un artichaud ou un pied de céleri de grandeur naturelle, de vouloir bien ne pas mettre à coté un lièvre grand comme le doigt, une allouette grande comme le naturel, & un faisan du quart ou due cinquième de sa grandeur....[18]

Looking at some of the porcelain influenced by the *genre pittoresque*, we can sympathize with Cochin. The huge snails perched on top of certain Vienna teapots are quite incongruous. The bladdery leaves so often painted on Longton Hall plates are scarcely fitting frames for delicate vignettes of castles and ruins. Occasionally we have the feeling that the modeller and the painter are trying to impose on us with a rather silly imitation of the real thing, like Victorian wax peaches, or the rashers of rubber bacon sold in joke shops. A pumpkin which turns into a golden coach is one thing; a melon tureen which splits in two to reveal steaming boiled potatoes is several degrees less enchanting. The Chelsea asparagus *étui* contains pins and needles. But how felicitous the naturalistic could be is seen in the Chelsea botanical plate (Plate VI), with its great crinoline poppies – a work of sumptuous naïveté which could not have been made anywhere but in England. Its colours – pinks, purples, yellows and pale blues – are representative of the pastel shades – Hogarth's 'tender tints' – which in the rococo replaced the masculine red and black of the baroque.

Femininity was in context. Women were acquiring a new importance. Salon and boudoir were centres of political as well as social intrigue. Madame de Pompadour was an *éminence rose*. Women were portrayed as goddesses, graces and muses. Men no longer stared from their portraits, bulging-eyed and autocratic. By artists such as La Tour they were given a feminine charm, with powdery complexions, dimples and winsome smiles. Porcelain figures became arch and skittish. The most brilliant of the rococo modellers was Franz Anton Bustelli, who came to Nymphenburg in 1754. He is to the rococo what Dwight's unknown modellers were to the baroque. His most celebrated work is a set of Italian

Comedy figures. A set of engravings recently discovered by the porcelain restorer Alois Schmid[19] depicts Italian Comedy figures. They were originally published by Martin Engelbrecht in Augsburg, and are conventionally late baroque in style. On the reverse they are covered with drawings, and one page, with a receipt for modelling wood, bears the signature 'Franz Anton Bustelli, 3 Oktober, 1750'. Comparing Bustelli's figures with Engelbrecht's, we can follow the process of imaginative derivation, the very transmutation of baroque into rococo. The penguin-stiff performers become figures of swirling bravura. Bustelli's 1763 portrait of the factory's patron, Sigismund, Graf von Haimhausen (Plate 59) is the quintessence of rococo, from the asymmetrical cartouche of its scrolled pedestal to the military disarray of his curls and the naturalistic wart on his upper lip. (Perhaps we must hail Cromwell as the prophet of rococo?)

Table wares were changing too. With an increasingly refined middle class, table manners became more elaborate and led to a demand for a greater variety of wares – different kinds of tureen, different sizes of plates, sweetmeat trays, pickle dishes, sauce-boats, wine coolers, *salières*, epergnes, porcelain knife handles and so on. Porcelain replaced wax and sugar as a medium for extravagant table decorations. Horace Walpole wrote in 1753:

> Jellies, biscuits, sugar-plumbs, and creams have long given way to harlequins, gondoliers, Turks, Chinese, and shepherdesses of Saxon china. But these, unconnected, and only seeming to wander among groves of curled paper and silk flowers, were soon discovered to be too insipid and unmeaning. By degrees whole meadows of cattle, of the same brittle materials, spread themselves over the whole table; cottages rose in sugar, and temples in barley-sugar; pigmy Neptunes [see Plate 22] in cars of cockle-shells triumphed over oceans of looking glass or seas of silver tissue, and at length the whole system of Ovid's metamorphosis succeeded to all the transformations which Chloe and other great professors had introduced into the science of hieroglyphic eating. Confectioners found their trade moulder away, while toymen and china-shops were the only fashionable purveyors of the last stage of polite entertainments. Women of the first quality came home from Chenevix's laden with dolls and babies, not for their children, but their housekeeper.[20]

An oil-painting by M. van Mytens shows the banqueting-tables at the wedding feast of the Emperor Joseph II and Isabella of Parma, at Vienna in 1760, decorated with many porcelain groups. At Ludwigsburg in 1764, on the birthday of Duke Karl of Württemberg, the table was decorated with a vast porcelain centrepiece, including a lake seventeen feet long and eleven feet wide with Neptune drawn by sea-horses, and grottoes, tritons, naiads and dolphins. Horace Walpole in his (one suspects) hypocritically censorious remarks on table figures, wrote that 'at last even these puerile puppet-shows are sinking into disuse, and more manly ways of concluding our repasts are stablished'.[21] But as late as 1783, Parson Woodforde described a dinner given by the Bishop of Norwich at which:

> A most beautiful Artificial Garden in the Centre of the Table remained at Dinner and afterwards, it was one of the prettiest things I ever saw, about a Yard long, and about 18 Inches wide, in the middle of which was a high round Temple supported on round Pillars, the Pillars were wreathed round with artificial Flowers – on one side was a Shepherdess on the other a Shepherd, several handsome Urns decorated with artificial Flowers also etc. etc.[22]

Porcelain flowers were another product of rococo naturalism. The Vincennes factory made a speciality of them, and they became a craze. By 1748 the flower studios, where forty-five women were already employed, had to be extended; and in 1749 flowers were the greater part of the factory's output. Madame de Pompadour created a winter flower garden of them at Bellevue. The Marquis d'Argenson wrote:

> Le Roi a commandé à la Manufacture de Vincennes des fleurs de porcelaine peintes au naturel avec leurs vases pour plus de huit cent mille livres, pour toutes ses maisons de campagne et spécialement pour le château de Bellevue de la Marquise de Pompadour. On ne parle que de cela dans Paris, et véritablement ce luxe scandalise beaucoup.[23]

The twentieth century has plastic flowers, and houses described by one song-writer as 'little boxes, made of plastic and stuck together with ticky-tacky'. Porcelain flowers complemented porcelain rooms. Ceramic architecture was not without precedent. In the reign of François I, Girolamo della Robbia built the Château de Madrid in the Bois de Boulogne. John Evelyn described it in 1650 as 'most of Earth, painted like Porcelain or China ware'.[24] It was destroyed and ground up for cement during the French Revolution. About 1570 Bernard Palissy built an earthenware grotto in the gardens of the Tuileries, also subsequently destroyed. In the winter of 1670–71 Louis XIV – again anticipating a rococo idea, though not a rococo design – had the *Trianon de Porcelaine* built near Versailles for his mistress, Madame de Montespan. The poet Denis wrote:

Considérons un peu ce château de plaisance,
Voyez-vous comme il est tout couvert de faïence
D'urnes de porcelaine et de vases divers
Qui le font éclater aux yeux de l'univers.[25]

As Denis said, the *Trianon de Porcelaine* was in fact made of faience, not porcelain – of French and Dutch tiles. These materials could not survive the winter frosts, nor Madame de Montespan the King's infatuation with Madame de Maintenon, and in 1687 the building was pulled down.

The eighteenth-century architects in ceramics wisely kept to interior decoration and used porcelain, less vulnerable and more elegant than faïence. The porcelain room built in the royal villa at Portici between 1757 and 1759, and moved in 1865 to the Palace of Capodimonte, may be claimed as the most perfect realization of rococo. It is certainly the masterpiece of the Capodimonte factory. Like the porcelain room at the palace of Aranjuez, made by the Buen Retiro factory when Charles III succeeded to the Spanish throne, it is constructed as a kind of celestial jig-saw puzzle, each of the three thousand interlocking pieces being of a white, flawless porcelain, the joints concealed by festoons, ribbons and musical trophies. Both rooms are unchanged except that the original Portici chandelier, surmounted by a monkey clasping a palm tree, crashed to the ground when a bomb exploded nearby in the Second World War.

The Portici and Aranjuez rooms were in the *chinoiserie* taste. It was inevitable that porcelain, the very substance of which was imitated from, or inspired by, that of oriental wares, should sometimes be directly influenced by oriental designs: this is especially true of Dutch delft and of the Bow *kakiemon* patterns. To some extent the asymmetrical designs of Chinese lacquer and silks, as well as those of porcelain, contributed to the rococo idiom itself. But the rococo was largely autonomous, self-parasitic even, its *chinoiseries* no more than further fantastications of European conceits – the 'vision of Cathay'. It is not to China, but to the apostolic succession of European *chinoiserie* artists – Watteau, Christophe Huet, Boucher and Jean-Baptiste Pillement – that we must look for the source of many oriental caprices in European ceramics. A Bow group of two Chinese kneeling before a goddess was made from an engraving after Watteau. Huet's influence was particularly strong, since his brother, Jean Charles Huet, was the Meissen agent and dealer in Paris. Huet was the master of the *singerie*, and it is not surprising to find a monkey orchestra modelled by Kändler. A print after Boucher inspired a

Vincennes biscuit group of two Chinamen carrying a basket. Paintings in the manner of Pillement decorate a series of tall cups and saucers marked with a gold star, probably made at Doccia; and Robert Hancock also copied Pillement *chinoiseries* at Worcester.

As might be expected, Bustelli created the most delightful of all *chinoiserie* figures, tweaking them into animation and investing them with his dynamic lyricism. There is nothing inscrutable about the Chinese priest (Plate 60); more of Pantaloon than of Confucius in the waggish *noli me tangere* pose. The same uncorrosive satire is directed against the dyspeptic little pagod and the lady making a sacrifice. Bustelli was the nonpareil of rococo modellers; but there were pleasing essays in *chinoiserie* at Frankenthal, Höchst and Ludwigsburg; while Chelsea produced groups of a diabolo game and Chinese musicians, Worcester marked wares of oriental style with pseudo-Chinese characters, and a Staffordshire potter made the boy on a buffalo, a closer approximation to Chinese originals than any of the sophisticated adaptations in continental porcelain.

Chinoiserie did not survive the onset of neo-classicism, neither did the rococo style as a whole. Rather as the tortured convolutions of *art nouveau* were finally superseded by the stark functionalism of the twenties and thirties, already implicit in the designs of Voysey and Mackmurdo, so the rococo gradually yielded to a classicism already discernible in the ruins painted by Salomon Gessner. Like every artistic fashion it was doomed to decadence from the beginning in the mindless cycle of styles which converts art critics into art historians, passionate partisans into Olympian voyeurs. Elaboration could only end in over-elaboration, extravagance in surfeit. The point must be reached where classicism, however antiseptic, would seem a noble refuge from stylistic debauch.

5 Folk pottery

Champfleury, in his *Histoire des Faïences Patriotiques sous la Révolution* (1867), was the first to treat ceramics as, to use his own Gallic hyperbole, 'history frozen by fire'. He showed how valuable a source pottery could be for the history of the peasants, where written documents are so often lacking. Champfleury was also one of the first critics to take a sympathetic attitude towards folk art; but he felt it necessary to defend himself in his preface for having made a study of such crude pottery:

> C'est un art grossier, disent les raffinés. – Soit. – Un bégayement. – D'accord. – Un appel à des principes politiques plutôt qu'à des principes linéaires. – Sans doute.
>
> Pourtant cet art mérite d'être étudié comme les légendes, les traditions, les noëls & les chansons populaires dont il a la saveur.[1]

No such apologia is necessary today. If anything, the tendency to glorify the primitive, which has not lost momentum since Gauguin set sail for Tahiti and the cubists were inspired by African sculptures, needs curbing. The prominence at present given to children's paintings, not as exercises in psychology or as daubs of 'refreshing naivety', but as art, is one of its most betraying manifestations. Before a ten-year-old is given a retrospective exhibition at the Tate, the lesson should be learnt that maturity is reached through an adolescence, more or less painful. If artists cling to the Rousseauist idea that to cultivate the faculties we are born with is to corrupt them, they will continue to make what Sickert, referring to a more sophisticated artist, Monticelli, called 'jewelled mud-pies of fancy'.[2] The prevailing style of twentieth-century painting has been the disingenuous ingenuous.

The true folk artist does achieve maturity, but he achieves it within a certain set of conditions – not all of them limitations. He works in a civilized country, he is not a savage; the word 'folk' implies the existence of a cultured minority, a *beau monde*. But he works away from the centres of culture, of wealth and of fashion, the large cities. This means that he is more or less immune from fashion. When he does absorb a fashion, it is usually years after it has been fashionable. It has become distorted, like a story passed from mouth to mouth: a good example of this process of distortion in folk mythology is the story of the bull in the china shop, which began as a real incident in 1773, was reported in a London newspaper of that year, was being sung and printed as a ballad about 1800–10, and was finally abbreviated into a proverb, which is all that remains of it today.[3]

The folk artist's isolation also means that he is not subject to written criticism. The only criticism to which he is open is that of his customer; the relationship between maker and buyer is usually local and close, though occasionally advantage is taken of a river trade route to reach a wider market, as when Moravian and Slovakian potters use the Danube to supply markets throughout central Europe and far to the south-east. If one purpose of criticism is to influence the artist, non-purchase is probably as persuasive as a caustic newspaper paragraph. Dr Josef Vydra, in his study of Czech folk ceramics, shows how the Anabaptist potters of Moravia were tending in the seventeenth century to defer to their customers' robust taste and abandon the more severe ordinances of their religion. In 1612, the Order had to issue a warning:

> Die Fuergestellten sollten drob halten und nit zugeben, das man so unerbare trinckhgeschüere mache, nach Büchern, Stiffeln und derogeichen geförmört, als ob man nit wüsste, wie man sie zur Fillerey reitzen solle. (The elders should see to it and not permit such dishonourable drinking vessels to be made, in the form of books, shoes and such-like, as if they did not know well enough how to incite to gluttony.)

Other injunctions were against painting 'objects unfitted to us', such as birds and animals, and against putting names on crockery for barbers, 'for it is unnecessary and such crockery is not pleasing for others who come after'.[4]

Where sale as well as production is localized, dependence on tradition is increased. The folk artist has traditions no less intransigent than those of academic art. The fashion in academicism can change, and in recognizable cycles, does; but there is little change in the slow, rhythmic cycle of the seasons. The stability of the peasant environment is reflected

Folk pottery

62 and 63 Original sin and latter-day righteousness: (top) Adam and Eve 'pew-group', salt-glazed stoneware, Staffordshire, early eighteenth century; (bottom) 'tee total' group, earthenware, mid-nineteenth century.

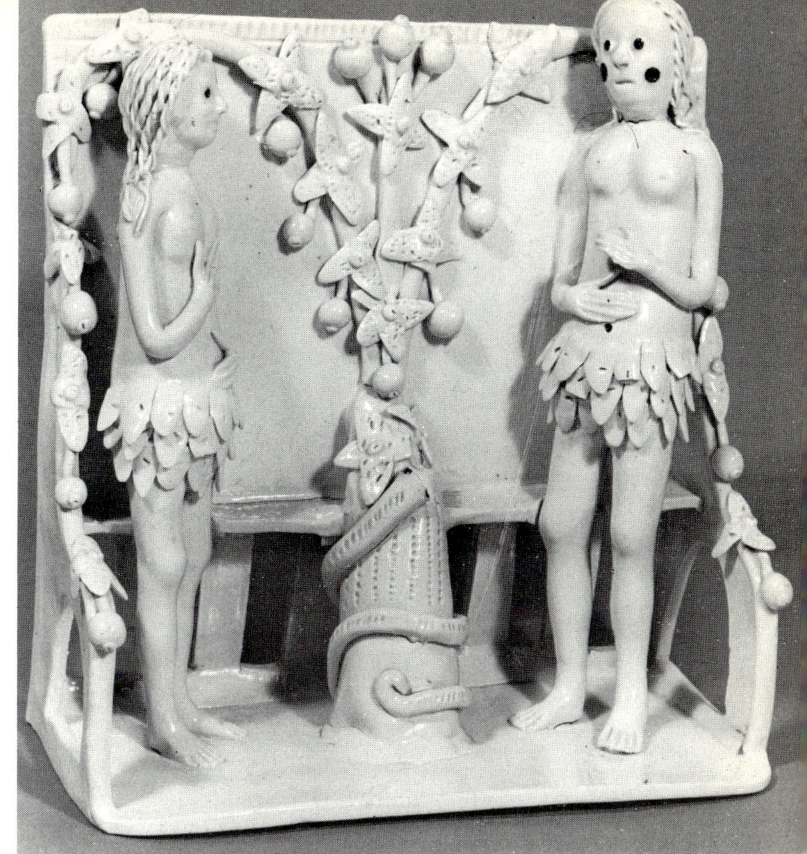

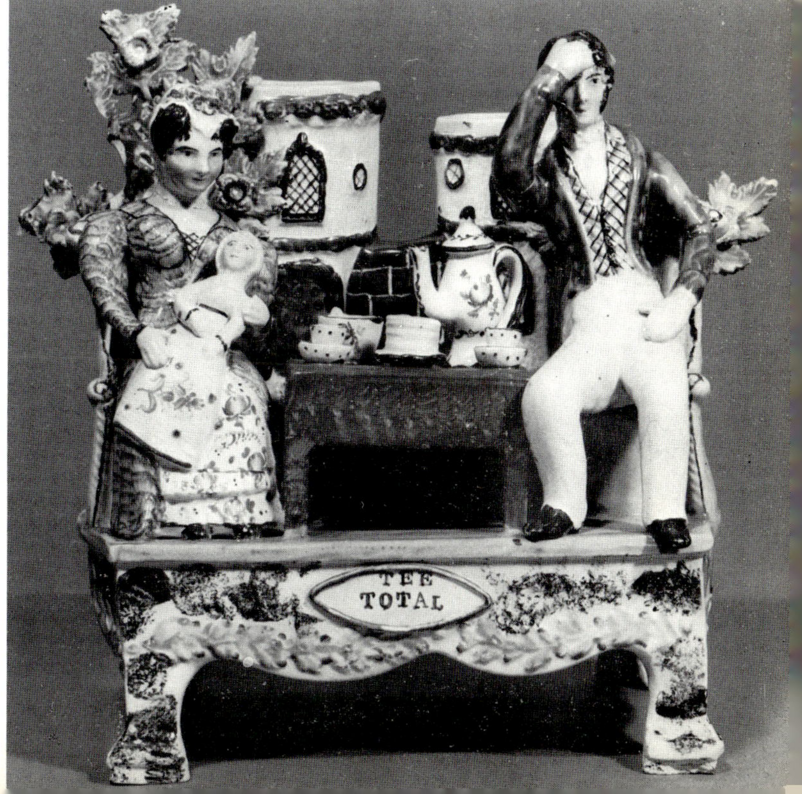

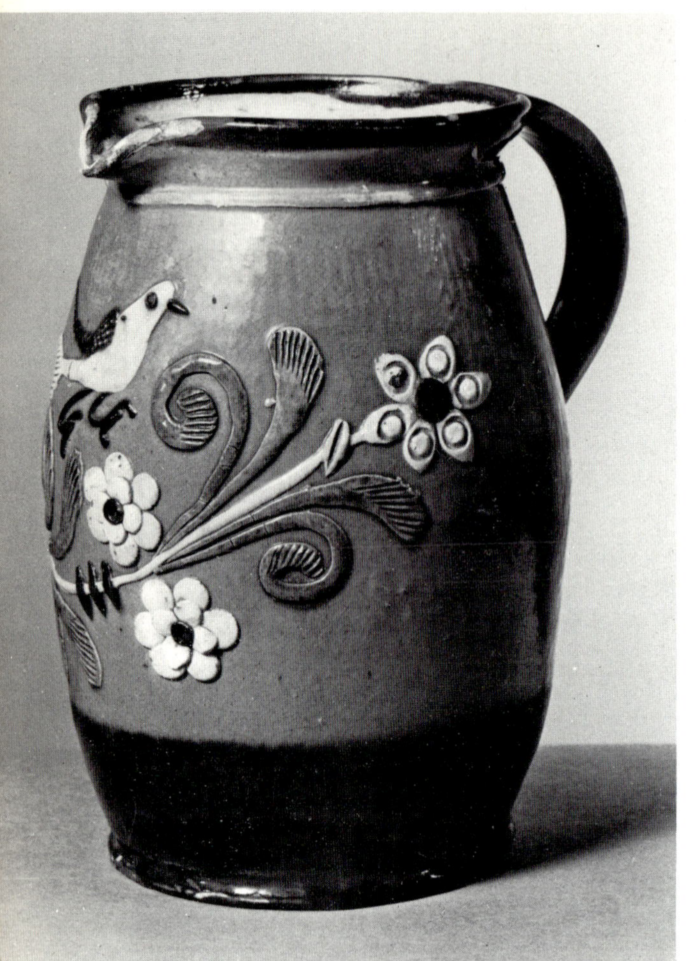

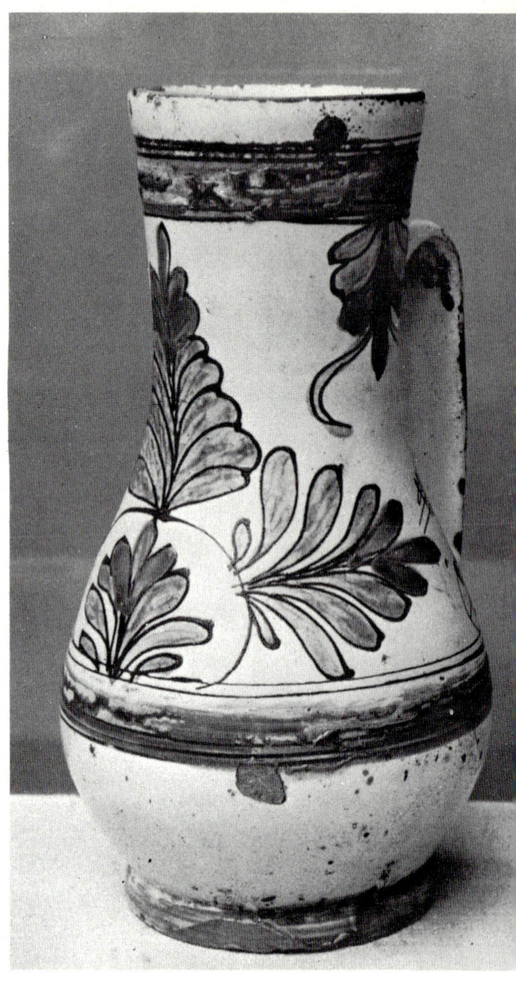

64 (left) German lead-glazed earthenware jug, Marburg, about 1830–60.
65 (right) Moravian earthenware pitcher, eighteenth century.

66 (opposite) Nottingham bear-baiting jug, brown salt-glazed stoneware, *c.* 1700. Compare this rustic model with the sophisticated group by Dominikus Auliczek (Plate 58). See p. 120.

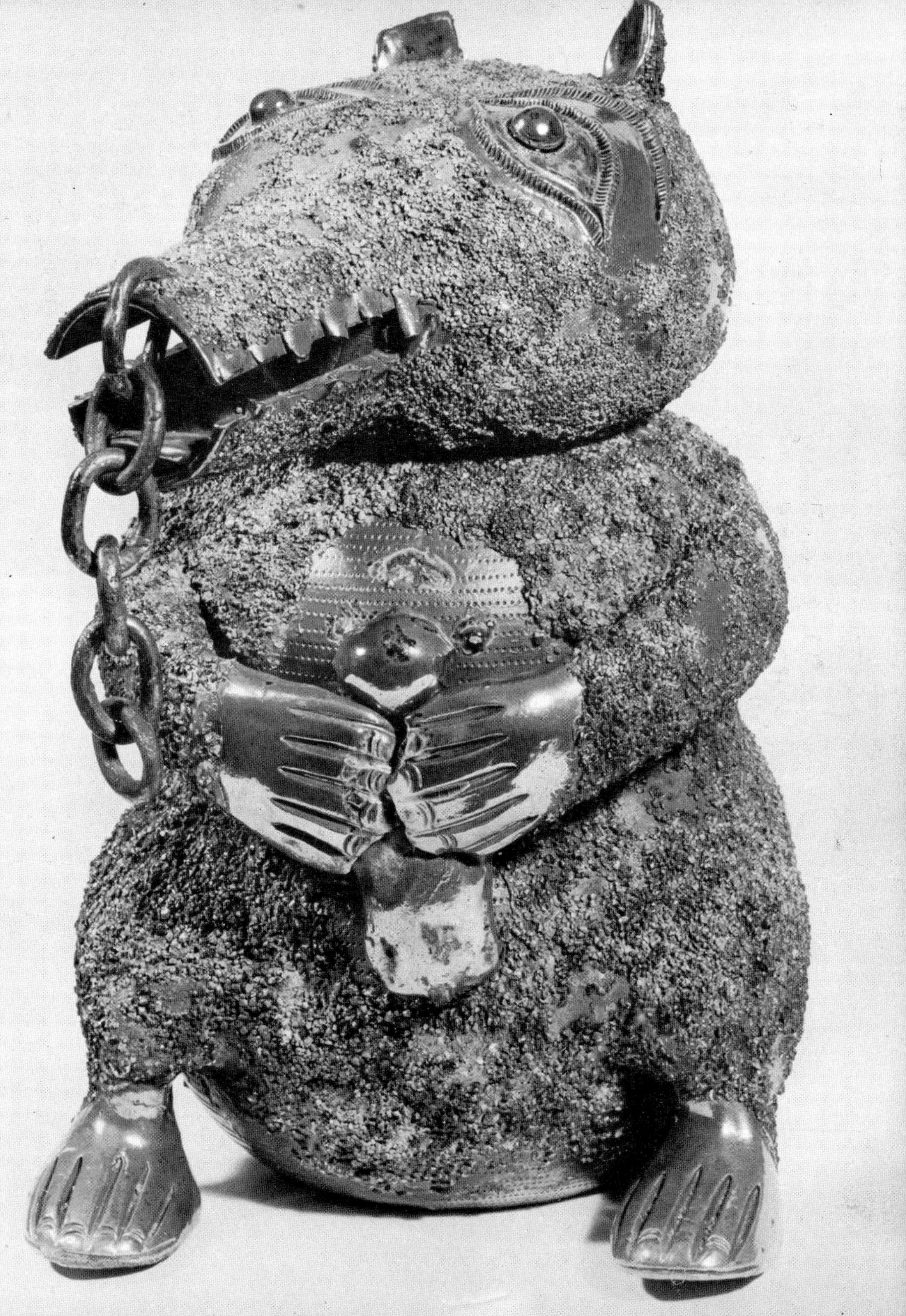

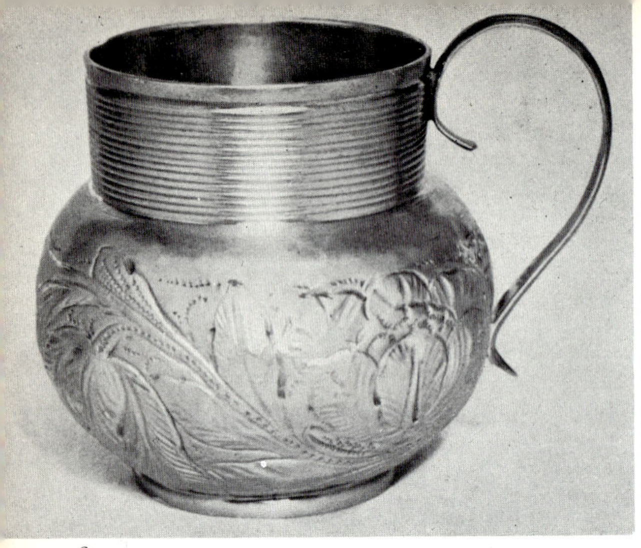

67

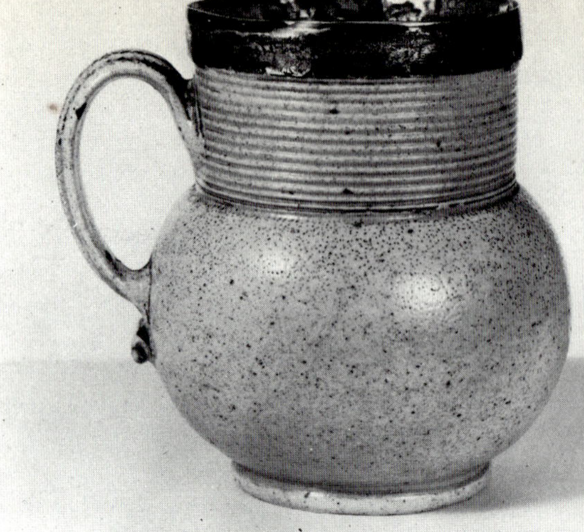

68

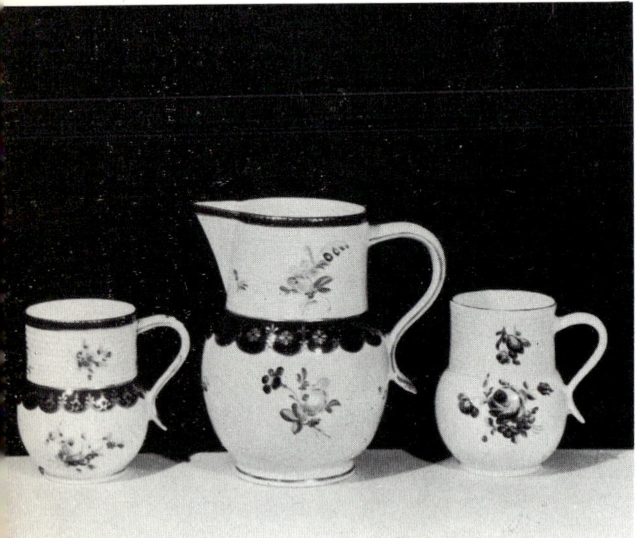

69

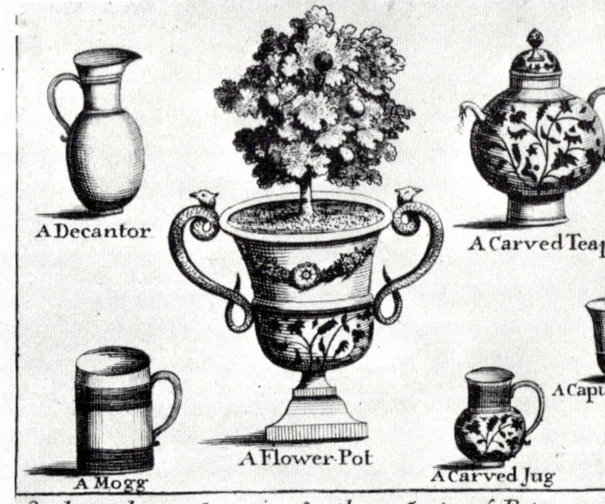

70

67 Silver mug, London 1683. Maker's mark W.S.H. Height $3\frac{3}{4}''$.
68 Fulham mug, Dwight's stoneware, late seventeenth or early eighteenth century.
69 Derby jug, rich blue banding with gilt and floral decoration. Height 6″.
Two small mugs: (left) Chelsea-Derby; (right) Derby, decorated with green flowers.
70 Trade-card of the Nottingham potter James Morley, *c.* 1700. See p. 119.
71 Brown stoneware mug, Nottingham, probably by James Morley, dated 1703.
72 Eighteenth-century mug, Chinese Tehua ware, made in European style.
Height $3\frac{1}{2}''$.
73 Eighteenth-century mug, Chinese Tehua ware, made in European style.
Height $3\frac{1}{2}''$.
74 Chelsea-Derby mug, decorated in blue and gilt.
75 White stoneware mug by the Turner factory at Lane End, Staffordshire,
c. 1780–90. The bands are enamelled in brown.
76 Silver tankard with applied hoops, 1772. Louisa Courtauld and George Cowles.

71

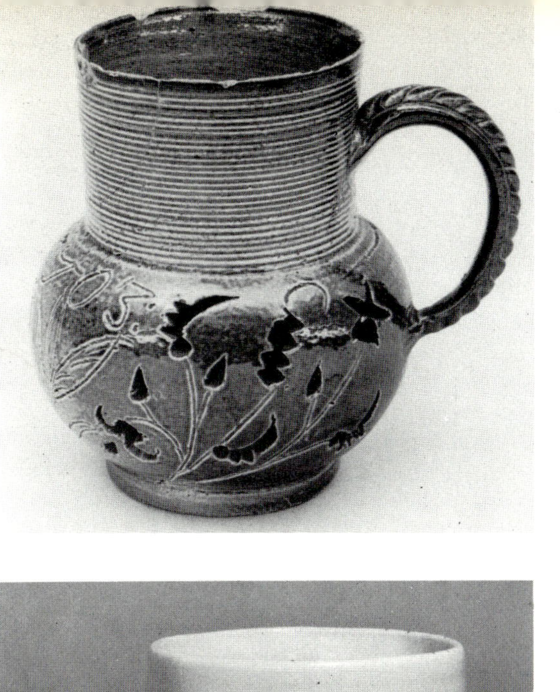

72

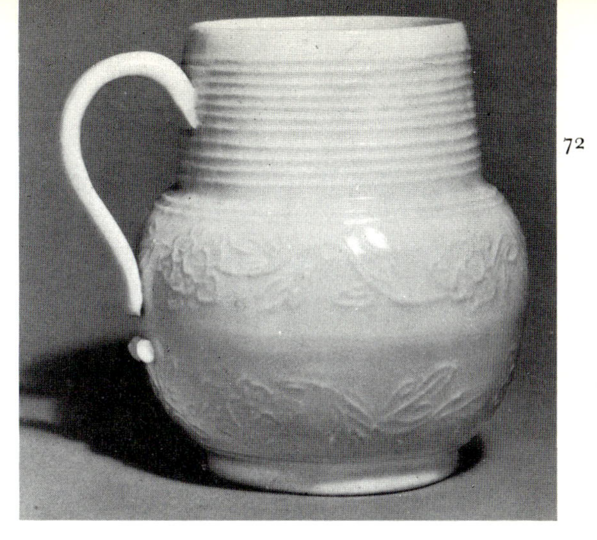

73

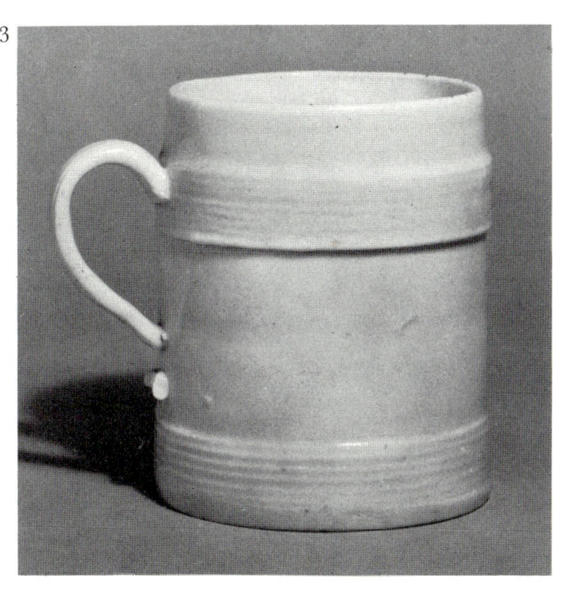

74

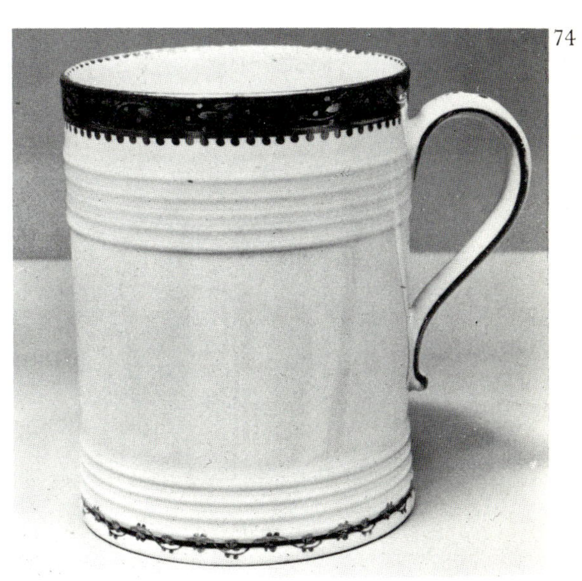

75

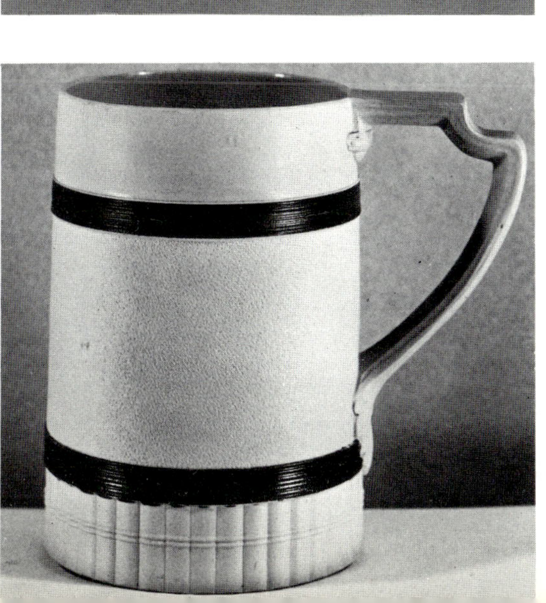

76

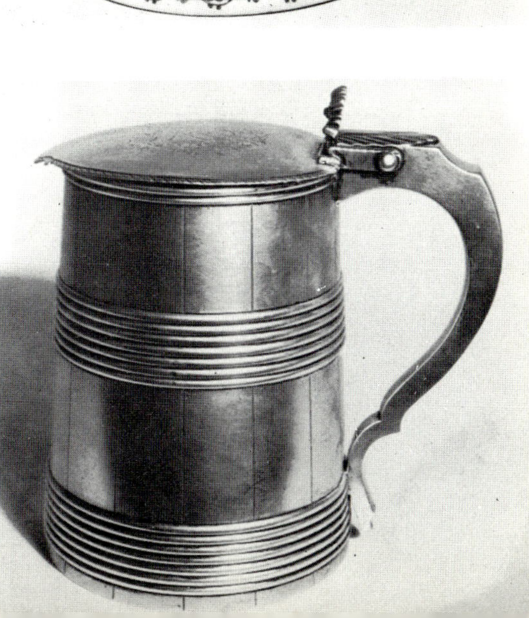

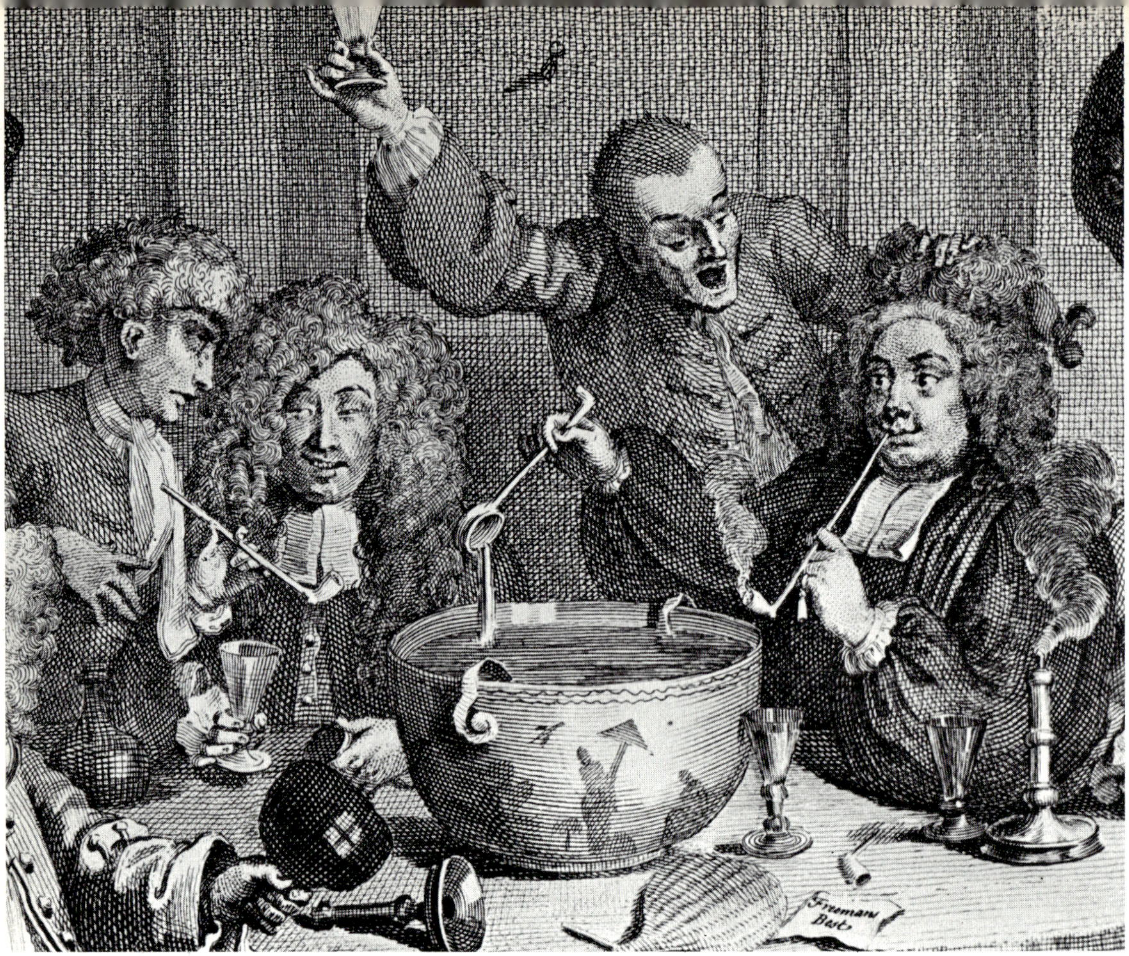

77 and 78 Eighteenth-century punch-drinking: (above) Hogarth's 'A Midnight Modern Conversation'. The punchbowl is decorated with chinoiserie figures; (right) a beldame from Woodward's *Eccentric Excursions* (1797). The bowl is decorated with a prize-fight scene, perhaps that between Humphreys and Mendoza.

79 (opposite top) The Squerryes Court punchbowl, made for John Warde in the eighteenth century. 80 (bottom) Chailey, Sussex, pottery punchbowl, impressed with printer's type filled with yellow slip. Dated 1792. See p. 120.

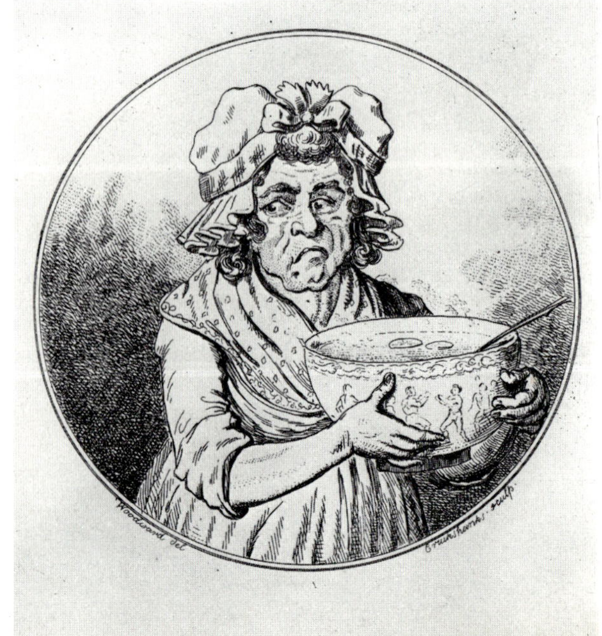

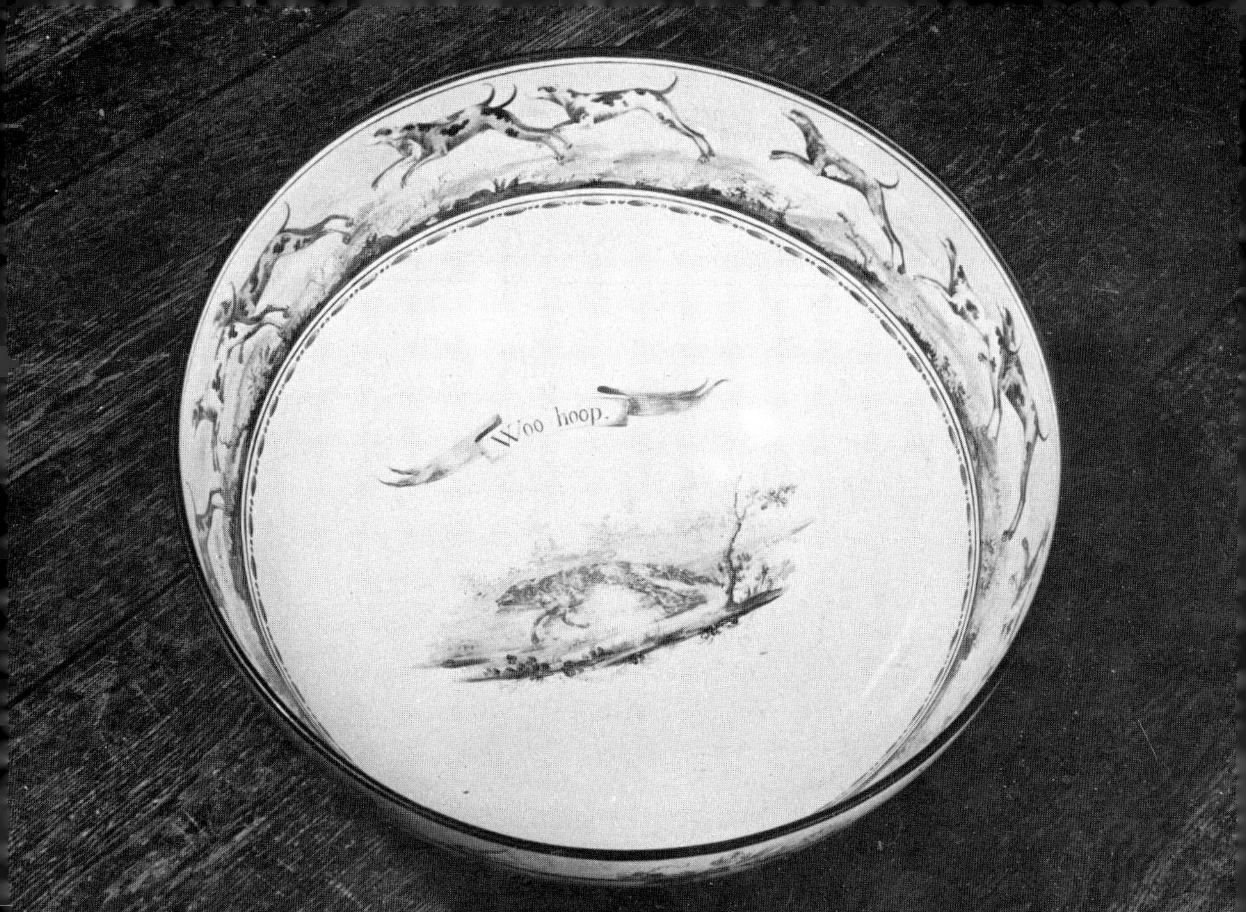

Woo hoop.

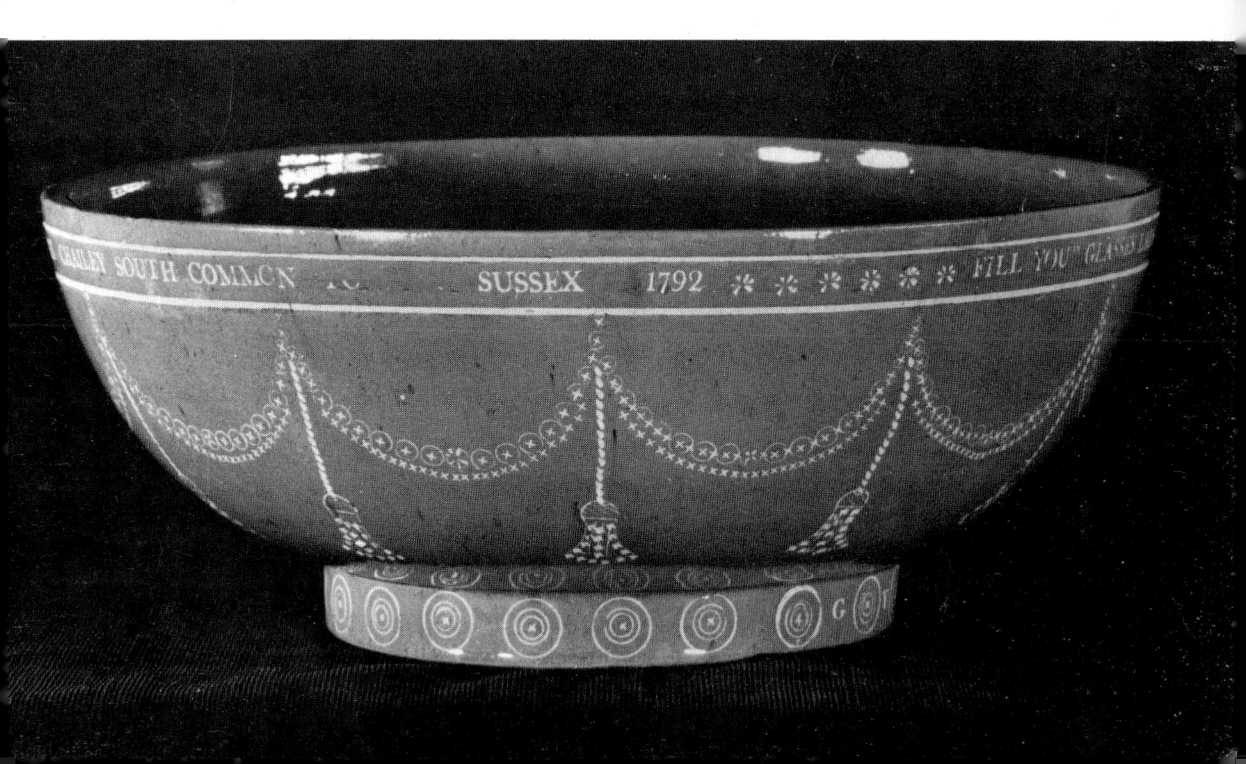

CHAILEY SOUTH COMMON
SUSSEX
1792

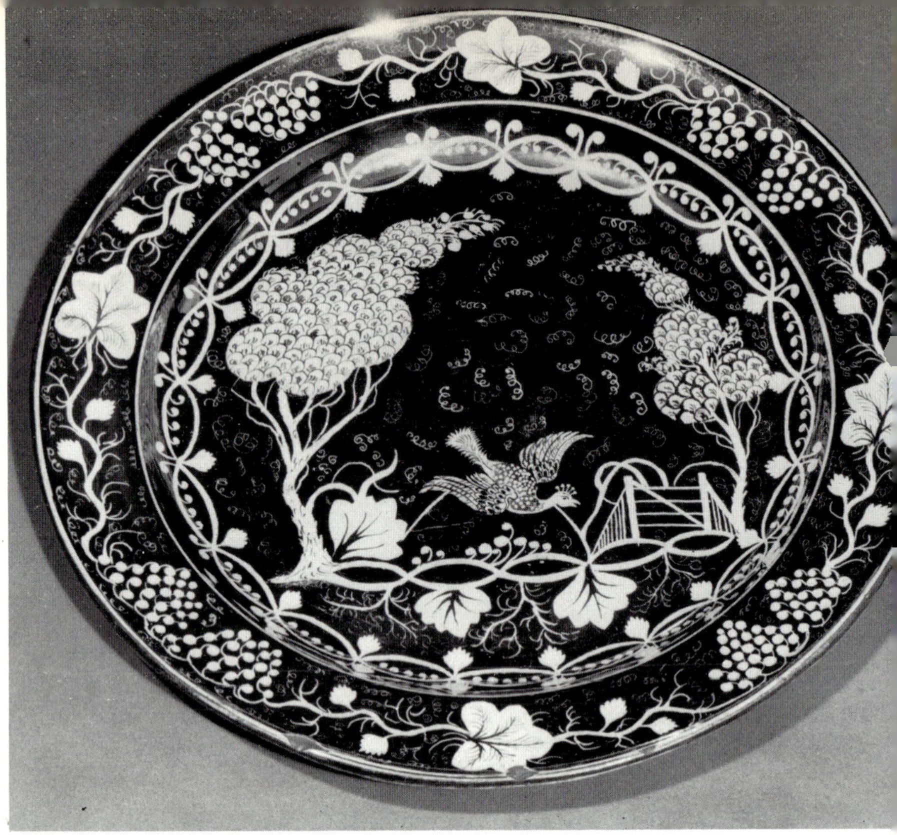

81 Leeds dish, decorated in silver resist lustre.

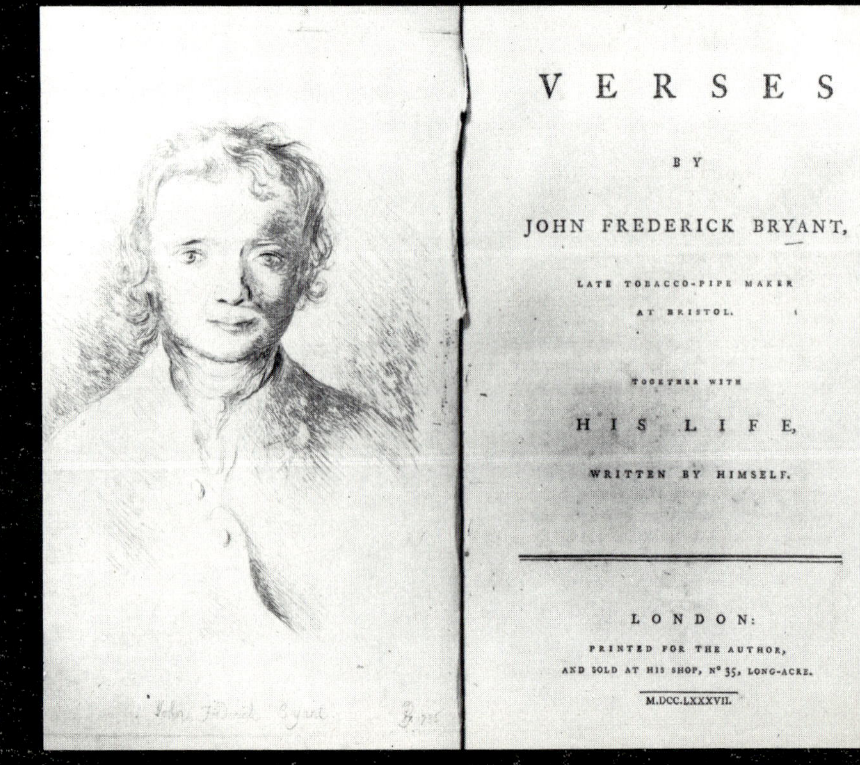

VERSES

BY

JOHN FREDERICK BRYANT,

LATE TOBACCO-PIPE MAKER AT BRISTOL.

TOGETHER WITH

HIS LIFE,

WRITTEN BY HIMSELF.

LONDON:

PRINTED FOR THE AUTHOR,
AND SOLD AT HIS SHOP, Nº 35, LONG-ACRE.

M.DCC.LXXXVII.

82 Title-page and frontispiece to John Frederick Bryant's *Verses* and autobiography (London, 1787). See pp. 121–3.

in a clear predominance of lyrical, peace-loving themes – except in France, where revolution affects the rural as well as the urban workers and gives rise to the *faiences patriotiques* – though even in these the complacent *Vive!* outweighs the denunciatory *A bas!* Religion, another stabilizing influence, enjoins acceptance of the *status quo*, but this does not preclude the ribald antisacerdotalism of the Vicar and Moses, Parson and Clerk, and Tithe Pig groups of Staffordshire or, in France, jugs showing toads in monks' clothing.

Folk art is as ruthlessly decorative as it is ruthlessly functional. Pottery plates sometimes have a mainly decorative value, hung from walls or crossbeams as in the dark cottages of the Bratislava district, Slovakia, or, in France, displayed in a wickerwork *dressoir de campagne* (Plate 111). A comparison between the decoration of folk pottery from different countries – Germany, Czechoslovakia, Russia, England, France, Norway – shows a remarkable similarity in design and techniques. Where we might most expect to find the provincial and idiosyncratic, we find universality. The chief common characteristic in design is abbreviation – the same reducing process as turned the story of the bull in the china shop into a proverb. It is a kind of poetic economy, which derives less from any need for the potter to hurry his work, than from an intuitive deftness acquired by constant repetition of, or variation upon, traditional designs. Everywhere, a roof is a slashing inverted V, rose petals are sickles of carmine. The continuous figure-of-eight border (similar to the device under Queen Elizabeth I's signature) is found both on Toft wares in England and on the Winterthur wares of Switzerland. There is an almost total lack of attempts at illusion. Folk artists, says André Malraux, 'persist in representing what they will never see'.[5]

Equally widespread are the two main decorative techniques used by folk potters – coloured slip, and *sgraffito*, or incised ornament. Whenever these international similarities are discussed, there is a conflict between those who feel they result from the uniformity of the human mind in comparable environments, and those who ascribe them to the spreading of designs and techniques by emigrant craftsmen. Thus, in the case of English slipware, the latter school suggest that slip decoration was introduced by continental workmen in Kent, the nearest point of contact with the Continent, and that it spread first to London and later to the north. They point out that the dates on the wares indicate this order of progress, and that there are records of foreign potters having settled at Sandwich and Maidstone in 1582. The other school claim fragments of slipware found at Kirkstall and Fountains Abbeys, and a fifteenth-century jug found at Wittington Park, Buckinghamshire, as evidence that the manufacture of slipware was an independent development in England.[6] Similarly, in the case of the *sgraffito* wares, the 'uniformity of the human mind' school claim that 'a slip or coating over a red body must naturally (or accidentally, as a mere scratch would show) suggest a pattern in red obtained by incision through the slip'[7]; while the *Völkerwanderung* school suggest that the technique was probably learnt by Italian potters through contact with the Near East, where it had earlier been practised in the lands of Islam and the Byzantine Empire. It is a controversy as perennially absorbing and futile as the disputes as to whether man is naturally good or naturally evil, whether heredity or environment shapes our characters, and whether history is an art or a science.

Ironically, some of the adherents of the 'universality' theory are not, as one might expect, ethnologists of great liberalism, but chauvinists anxious to prove that the pottery of their country has not been tainted by 'foreign strains'. More objective historians tell a different story. Dr Vydra shows how the Anabaptists who came to Moravia from Sicily, Switzerland and Holland to escape religious persecution, brought with them the techniques of Renaissance maiolica, the floral motifs of Dutch delft, and the emblems, cartouches, armorial bearings, legends and figure-of-eight ornament of Winterthur.[8] But the influence was not all in one direction. The Anabaptists, who founded communities on a collective economic basis, and who were popularly known as 'Habaner' – a word etymologically connected with 'Haushaben' – relaxed their puritanism in response to the demands of their customers, and, after 1685, broke away from the collective households as individual master potters, allowing native folk environment to prevail over Haban tradition.[9]

Another well-documented example of foreign influence is the arrival at Strassburg, in 1748–9, of a group of gifted artists from Höchst. Adam Friedrich von Löwenfinck, his wife Séraphie, and his two brothers had been trained as porcelain painters at Meissen. Joseph-Jacob Ringler, who arrived in 1753, had learnt the secret of making hard-paste porcelain at Vienna. Hannong of Strassburg thus became the first *faiencier* in Europe to adopt the full *petit feu* or enamel-painting technique, and while he himself cannot be considered a folk potter, he almost certainly acted as intermediary in introducing the technique to Marseilles, Sceaux and humbler centres of the faience industry.[10]

An enormous amount of peasant wares are associated with drinking – a human activity which even the most obdurate of the *Völkerwanderung* school must presumably admit is universal rather than spread by toping nomads. In Spain, there were the large wine jars or *bucaros*, so much a part of the landscape that we find them celebrated in the *Dorotea* of Lope de Vega, in the *Fortuna con seso* of Quevedo, in the *Bucchereide* (1729) of Lorenzo Bellini, a professor at the University of Pisa, and in the letters of Count Magalotti.[11] English west-country jars of the nineteenth century, probably intended for cider, are shown in Thomas Luny's water-colour (Plate 144). The quality of wine jars varied according to the varying richness of the vine-growing countryside. Dr Vydra writes:

> Decorative maiolica [was] confined to the fertile and vine-growing regions of Moravia and Slovakia ... and spread to the adjoining vinicultural districts of Austria and Hungary. In the much poorer hilly or mountainous districts, the production of this more expensive ware never really secured a footing in competition with cheaper types.[12]

Some folk drinking vessels, such as puzzle-jugs which deluged the unwary or uninitiate with ale, were made solely for peasant use. But most of them had a middle-class or aristocratic equivalent, made of higher-quality pottery, of porcelain, of silver, pewter or other metals. Thus Plates 73–76 show four examples of the double-hooped mug: one of silver, one of Turner pottery, one of Chelsea-Derby porcelain, and one of Chinese porcelain in imitation of an English original. Incidentally, the hoops on these mugs were a purely decorative survival of the hoops which once prevented communal drinkers from taking more than their share: Jack Cade promises his followers that 'seven half-penny loaves shall be sold for a penny; the three-hooped pot shall have ten hoops; and I will make it felony to drink small beer.'[13] Of the six mugs shown in Plates 67–69 and 71–72, one is of silver, one of Fulham stoneware, one of Nottingham stoneware, one of Chelsea-Derby and one of Derby porcelain, and one of Chinese porcelain in imitation of an English model. The Nottingham mug is similar to that shown on James Morley's advertisement sheet of *c.* 1700 (Plate 70), now in the Bodleian Library, Oxford. Since Morley advertises for sale a 'mogg', a 'decanter' and a 'capuchine', it is interesting to find Ralph Thoresby recording in his *Diary* that in 1712 he 'went to see them make the curious Nottingham mugs; he [i.e. the potter] formed one piece of clay into a mug, then immediately into a teapot, then a decanter and in a few moments into six or seven vessels of quite different forms.'[14] In 1693 James Morley had been one of the defendants in the proceedings taken by John Dwight of Fulham to protect his privilege of making stoneware. At Nottingham, too, were made the bear jugs (Plate 66). Artlessly decorated with shredded clay, they are as typical of folk art as gingerbread men studded with raisins, or the million-buttoned bodices of Pearly Queens. These bear jugs remind us of the brutal sports of the countryside: a Staffordshire jug in white salt-glazed stoneware shows a bear hugging a dog to death.[15] Bull-baiting[16] and cock-fights[17] were also popular subjects in Staffordshire pottery, and dog-fights were the favourite sport of the nineteenth-century Staffordshire potters.[18]

A further example of rustic translation is the coarsened salt-glaze version (Plate 39) of the Chelsea goat and bee jug (Plate 38). But folk pottery is not necessarily less refined than pottery made for the upper classes. The hunting punchbowl (Plate 79) made for John Warde, Master of the Pytchley Hunt, whose portrait by Barraud also survives at Squerryes Court, Westerham, Kent, is well made and well painted; but it lacks the extreme finesse of the bowl made by the Chailey Pottery, Sussex, in 1792 (Plate 80), with its inscription beautifully impressed into the clay with printer's type and filled with yellow slip:

FILL YOUR GLASSES LADS AND LASSES
ROUND THE MAYPOLE FRISK AND PLAY
SMILING GLANCING SINGING DANCING
THIS IS CUPID'S HOLLIDAY. THOS
ALCORN CHAILEY SOUTH COMMON
POTTERIES SUSSEX 1792.

The Squerryes bowl is as far from the scalloped silver monteith of the highest class as the Chailey bowl from the 'Drink fair, don't sware' delft pot of the lowest, but still Warde's is a squire's bowl, while the other belongs to the peasantry. Plates 77 and 78 show more representative examples from the two classes. The bowl in use in Hogarth's *A Midnight Modern Conversation* is decorated with elegant *chinoiseries*; that held by Cruikshank's old beldame shows a prize-fight – probably that between Humphreys and Mendoza at Odiham, which appears on a mug dated 1788 in the Willett Collection, Brighton, and on much other pottery besides, in engravings by John Aynsley of Lane End.

Bribery by liquor was common in elections from the Wilkite junketings of the 1770s to the 'Beer and Bible' alliance of the 1870s when the publicans' placards carried the slogan 'Stand by your National Religion and your National Beverage', and Gladstone wrote to his brother, 'We have been borne down in a torrent of gin and beer.'[19] The eighteenth-century electioneering pottery, painted with inscriptions such as 'Sir Francis Burdett for Ever', was bought in quantity by candidates and distributed free to the innkeepers of their constituencies.

Aubrey, writing about 1680, tells us that tobacco smokers at first sported silver pipes, 'but the ordinary sort made use of a walnut shell and a straw.' But by the eighteenth century, the clay pipe had come into general use in all classes, as a comparison between Hogarth's *Midnight Modern Conversation* and Woodward's 'contented innkeeper' shows. Dr Parr, the great Cambridge classical scholar, smoked continually, even in ladies' drawing rooms. He sometimes smoked twenty pipes in an evening and never wrote well without his tobacco. He describes himself as composing his works and 'rolling volcanic fumes of tobacco to the ceiling'. Dr Richardson, in his *Recollections of the Last Half-Century*, tells us that Dr Parr, at the dinner given at Trinity College for the Duke of Gloucester as Chancellor of Cambridge University, upon the removal of the cloth, indulged in his eternal pipe, 'blowing a cloud of smoke into the faces of his neighbours, much to their annoyance, and causing royalty to sneeze by the stimulating stench of muldungus.' Pipes for less erudite smokers might be stamped with dies or coiled and plaited from several feet of clay tubing, again with an intuitive dexterity, not unlike that found in the plaited 'corn-dollies' made for harvest festivals.

In connection with pipe-making, an extraordinary document survives, an account by a folk-artist (albeit a lapsed one) of his life: *Verses by John Frederick Bryant. Late Tobacco-Pipe Maker at Bristol. Together with his Life Written by Himself* (1787). Bryant had the typical background of a folk artist, that is, a father and grandfather in the same trade and district:

> I was born in Market-Street, St James's, Westminster, November 22d, 1753. My father was a native of the city of Bristol, and had been bred a tobacco-pipe-maker, my grandfather and all his family being of that business.

His father, who did not like the trade, had moved from Bristol to London and become a house-painter. There he had met Bryant's mother, who was in service. From the age of 14 months, Bryant was brought up by his maternal grandparents in Sunbury, Middlesex, but in the spring of 1760 he accompanied his father back to Bristol where the old business was taken up. He went to a dame school and learnt to read, then became a packer for his father. His favourite reading was the scriptures, and he observes, with a sincerity which in another might be regarded as sarcasm, 'I could not help lamenting the being born in an age in which portents, prodigies and miracles, with the frequent visibility of God and angels, was not to be seen or expected.' Already, at ten years old, he was writing verses, 'and remember my mother's once laughing heartily, upon finding an invocation to the muses in one of my little attempts; the sublime and interesting subject of which was, the description and character of our turnspit-dog.' Like his father, Bryant was not happy in his job. At one stage he broke away, and joined a press-gang as the alternative they offered him to going on board a man o' war ('my hand with horror embraced the lawless bludgeon'). But eventually he, too, was forced by poverty to go back to pipe-making. 'I went about the country with a hamper of pipes upon my shoulder, in that manner travelling ten, fifteen, and often twenty miles out. This I performed generally twice a-week.' Going to Swansea to consider the prospect of moving there, he met 'a gentleman' at Neath and sang to him some poems of his own composition. The gentleman (whose name Bryant does not give) 'condescended to point out some of my wrong pronunciations, which I have since corrected.' More than that, he became Bryant's patron, and introduced him to some very influential people, who finally enabled him to set up a stationery, book and print-selling business at 35 Long-Acre. His book (Plate 82), published there in 1787, is dedicated to those Benefactors who 'assisted in relieving the Author when in a state of extreme indigence'. They include the Archbishop of York, several bishops, among them the Bishop of Norwich already mentioned as the owner of the table decorations described by Parson Woodforde, a number of peers, and among the rest, that Mr Vanderstegen whose son was tutored by Jane Austen's father, and whose daughters owned the famous Vanderstegen Doll's House, with Chippendale fittings, now in the collection of Mrs Graham Greene.[20]

Like John Clare, Bryant was treated as a rustic freak – the treatment which drove Clare insane. 'The sources of his information', says the unknown writer of a foreword to his book, 'are found to have been a few volumes, chiefly of the English poets, borrowed from different persons; and also some of those books adapted to the capacity of children, from whence his knowledge of Ancient History or Fable is derived.' But Bryant is no Clare. His style is stilted and his allegories are forced. He has not read enough to know when he is using a cliché. All his verse is informed by the terrible frustration of the uneducated: as T. E. Lawrence says of Sherif Ali ibn el Hussein, 'there was a constant depression with him, the unknown longing of simple, restless people for abstract thought beyond their minds' supply.'[21] At best he attains a kind of wry passion when assessing the futility of his aspirations; pathos is locked in a death struggle with bathos:

ON A PIECE OF UNWROUGHT PIPE-CLAY
Rude mass of earth, from which with moiled hands
(Compulsive taught) the brittle tubes I form,
Oft listless, while my vagrant fancy warm
Roves (heedless of necessity's demands)
Amid Parnassian bow'rs, or wishful eyes
The flight of Genius, while sublime she soars
Of moral truth in search, or earth explores,
Or sails with Science through the starry skies:
Yet must I own (unsightly clod) thy claim
To my attention, for thou art my stead,
When grows importunate the voice of need,
Ah then how eager do I urge the flame,
How anxious watch thee mid that glowing fire
That threats my eye-balls with extinction dire!

How ironic that Bryant, with the supposed advantages of a negligible education, should have reacted against his traditional craft environment and aspired all his life to the academic facility then in vogue, while modern artists, with all the resources of the 'museum without walls' at their fingertips, are forever striving to attain naïveté. One begins to doubt the value of divine discontent.

6 Wedgwood, Neo-Classicism and the Industrial Revolution

With John Bryant, we are fast moving away from our definition of folk pottery. Bristol, in the eighteenth century, was the second port of England. But even in the cities, the centres of fashion, there could exist folk enclaves isolated from everything that was fashionable. Like Bryant, the boy poet Thomas Chatterton grew up in eighteenth-century Bristol; but his relatives were still making Bristol delft in a distinctively folk tradition. This anecdote was taken down by Michael Lort in October 1784, among 'anecdotes of Chatterton from his sister':

When he was five years old, he with the rest of his family had a present made him of a Delft cup with some figures or other upon it, by a relation of theirs who made that kind of ware.[1] Chatterton's cup had a lyon rampant; he desir'd however to have an angel with a trumpet 'to *blow his name about*', as he said. I saw the cup which his relation made in compliance with his request, and there is at the bottom of the outside of it T.C.1757 and the angel and trumpet on the side.[2]

Similarly, the antiquary William Bateman grew up in Liverpool, but the mug (Plate 83) which was painted with his surname initial when he was a child, about 1790, at 'the potteries near Liverpool',[3] has more rustic charm than metropolitan elegance. We may even describe as folk pottery the stoneware flip-can made for Alexander Selkirk – the original of Robinson Crusoe – at Fulham in 1703.[4] And it would be hard to deny the folk character of the Dutch delft tiles mentioned in Orton's memoir of Dr Doddridge, the theologian:

I have heard him relate, that his mother taught him the history of the Old and New Testament, before he could read, by the assistance of some Dutch

V (*opposite*) Rococo: a porcelain triton made at the Holitsch factory, Hungary, in the eighteenth century.

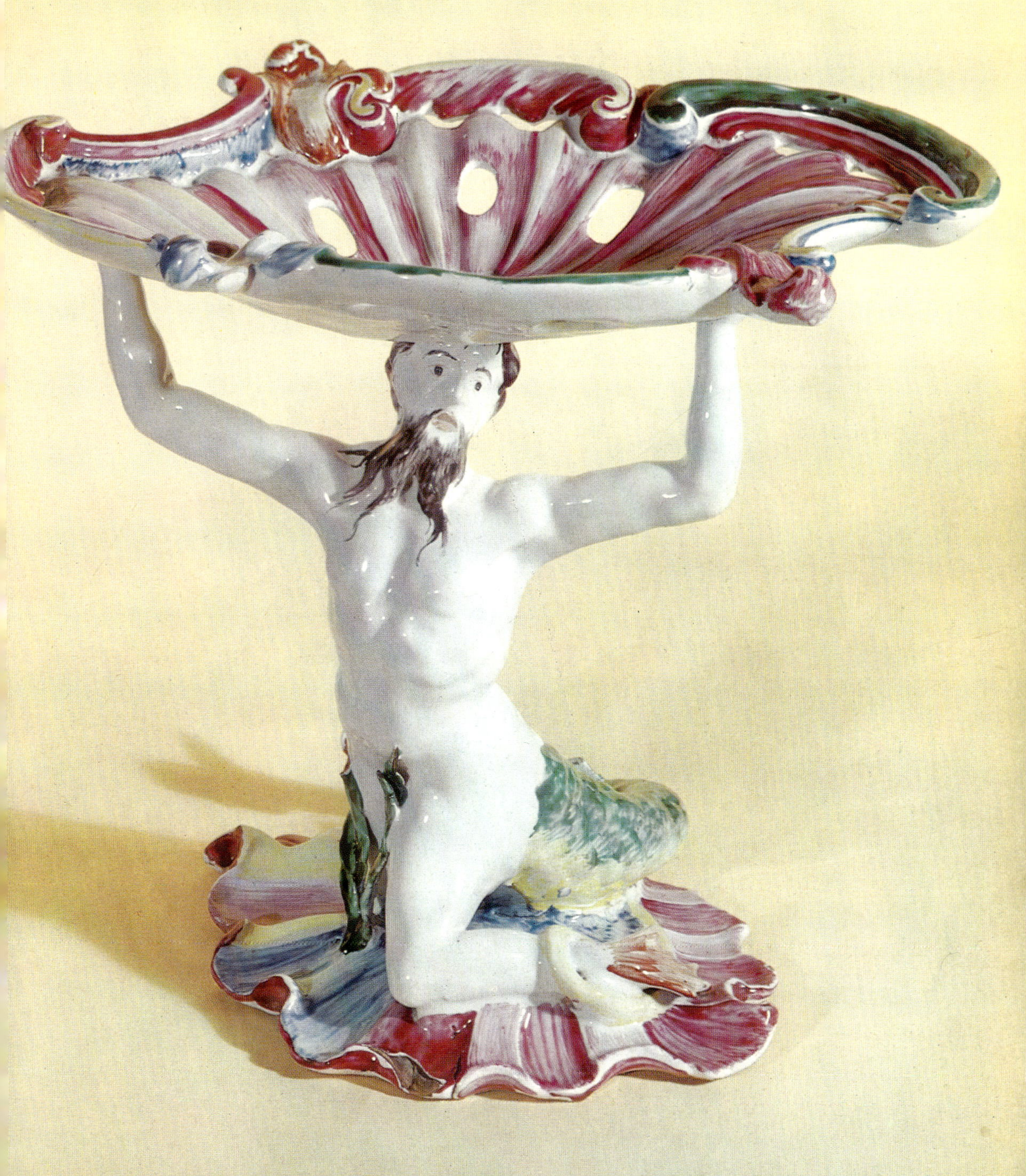

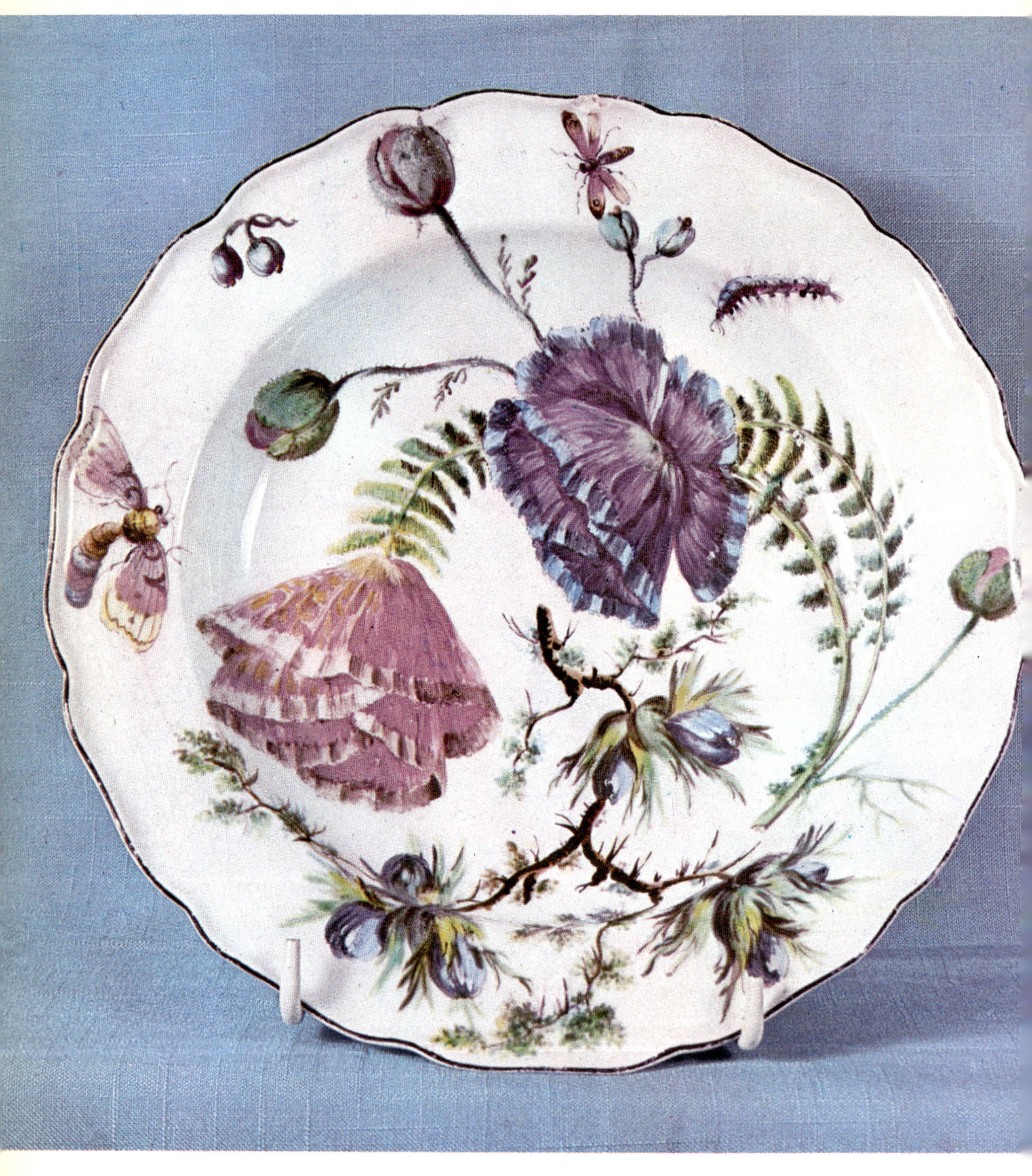

tiles in the chimney of the Room, where they commonly sat: And her wise and pious reflections upon the stories there represented, were the means of making some good impressions upon his heart, which never wore out: And therefore this method of instruction he frequently recommended to parents.[5]

The Dutch tiles at Holyroodhouse Palace were used for the same purpose. In the Holyrood accounts there is a record of 'His Grace Duke Argyle' paying 2*s*. 6*d*. to Robert Baillie in November 1782, 'To one doz. dutch Tyles put in a Chimney', and a further 2*s*. to a mason for setting them with a pan cratch.[6] That a duke should buy Dutch delft tiles does not quite invalidate their folk-ness. Dutch and English delft was in common use in aristocratic households, usually for the more menial purposes. At Bartram-Haugh, the nightmarish mansion of Sheridan Le Fanu's Uncle Silas, it figures in the scene in which Maud Ruthyn re-encounters her loathsome ex-governess:

> Well, one room more – just that whose deep-set door fronted me, with a melancholy frown, at the opposite end of the chamber. So to it I glided, shoved it open, advancing one step, and the great bony figure of Madame de la Rougierre was before me.
>
> I could see nothing else.
>
> The drowsy traveller who opens his sheets to slip into bed, and sees a scorpion coiled between them, may have experienced a shock the same in kind, but immeasurably less in degree.
>
> She sat in a clumsy old arm-chair, with an ancient shawl about her, and her bare feet in a delft tub.[7]

The folk tradition might survive contact with cities, dukes and evil governesses, but it was chronically weakened, though not quite extirpated, by two revolutions: the artistic revolution of neo-classicism, and the Industrial Revolution. Of both of these revolutions Josiah Wedgwood was an outstanding representative in Europe.

By throwing Europe open again to the traveller, the Treaties of Rijswyck which ended the War of the Grand Alliance in 1697 had heralded what might be called the Peace of the Grand Tour. A European tour, including Italy but not usually Greece, which was too far for most, became part of the education of gentlemen, and later of artists. For many of them it was a semi-mystical experience. Even wry, acidulous Gibbon allowed himself a decently Augustan rapture as he sat amidst the ruins of the Capitol 'while the barefooted fryars were singing Vespers in the Temple of Jupiter. . .'[8] (It was actually the Temple of Juno.) John Flaxman, whose visit to Italy in 1788 was largely sponsored

VI (*opposite*) Chelsea botanical plate, *c.* 1755, decorated with large poppies.

by Wedgwood, was disappointed at finding the buildings of Rome less striking than in the prints of Piranesi, but wrote to Romney:

> You will naturally suppose how much I was wrapt in fancy when I saw the Phlegrean plains, where the giants were said to be overthrown by the thunder of Jupiter; the island of the Syrens; the situations of Herculaneum and Pompeia, with the Elysian fields at one view; and walked on the same ground where Homer, Plato, and Pythagoras had been; as well as those venerable professors of the arts of design, whose steps I humbly endeavour to follow.[9]

Fantasy of this *Et In Arcadia Ego* kind was fed rather than discouraged by scientific archaeology and by the published works of men such as 'Athenian' Stuart and Revett, Le Roy and Robert Wood. The most powerful voice among the art historians was Winckelmann, whose researches were made the basis of a dictatorial aesthetic creed. Winckelmann's *Gedanken über die Nachahmung der Griechischen Werke* (1755) was inspired by classical statuary in the possession of the Elector of Saxony. The same sculptures as had influenced the baroque works of Permoser and Kändler were now extolled by the enemy of baroque as a pattern of 'noble simplicity'. 'The Greeks alone,' he wrote, 'seem to have thrown forth beauty as a potter makes his pot.'

Back from Italy, and later Greece, came thousands of casts from the antique, and actual sculptures and vases. Flaxman continues his letter to Romney:

> I must mention excellent news for the arts in England. Colonel Campbell is returning, and brings with him to London three hundred Etruscan vases, many adorned with the finest historical paintings; and a collection of all the plaister casts from the finest antiques he could purchase in Italy. You know by this time Sir Richard Worsley is returned with several valuable bas reliefs he got in Greece, and engravings as well as the original drawings by Pars of the frieze of the temple of Minerva at Athens.[10]

Some of the antiquities which ended up in collectors' cabinets were fakes. Peter Pindar quipped:

> the world reports (I hope untrue)
> That half Sir William's mugs and gods are new;
> *Himself* the baker of th'Etrurian Ware,
> That made our British antiquarians stare.[11]

This refers to Sir William Hamilton, the *mari complaisant* of Nelson's Emma, and British plenipotentiary at the Court of Naples. Since Hamilton was a friend of Wedgwood and Wedgwood's factory was called Etruria, a jibe at the English potter may well be implied. Hamilton was one of the first Englishmen to appreciate and collect Greek vases, and the beautifully printed catalogues of his collections (1766 and 1767, 1791 and 1795) influenced Wedgwood and the styles of Flaxman and Fuseli. The friendship with Hamilton was exploited by Wedgwood as part of his ceaseless publicity campaign. 'Sir William Hambleton, our very good Friend,' he wrote to his partner Bentley in 1776, 'is in Town – Suppose you shew him some of the Vases, & a few other Connoisieurs [*sic*] not only to have their advice, but to have the advantage of their puffing them off against the next Spring, as they will, by being consulted, and flatter'd agreeably, as you know how, consider themselves as a sort of parties in the affair, & act accordingly.'[12]

Wedgwood's role in the neo-classical movement was that of an exploiter, a disseminator, a publicist. He saw the importance of the Herculaneum and Pompeii excavations and the 'discovery' of the Temples at Paestum. Flaxman visited all three within two months of his arrival in Italy. Wedgwood produced direct copies and adaptations of the Herculaneum wall-paintings. He saw, too, how neo-classical pottery could be made a barely dispensable supplement to the neo-classical architecture of his friends Robert Adam and 'Athenian' Stuart. Much given to euphoric grumbling when success was in sight, he complained that 'We were really unfortunate in the introduction of our jasper into the public notice, that we could not prevail upon the architects to be godfathers to our child. Instead of taking it by the hand, & giving it their benediction, they cursed the poor infant by bell, book and candle, & it must have a hard struggle to support itself & rise from under their maledictions.'[13] Apparently some architects unknown had persuaded the Queen that Wedgwood tablets were not fit for chimneypieces. But in general, the jasper plaques sold well enough, and were set in neo-classical mansions from Mrs Montagu's houses in Portman Square (Stuart) and at Sandeford (Wyatt) to Thomas Jefferson's at Monticello, Virginia, and Catherine the Great's palace at Tsarskoe Selo, now Pushkin (Cameron).[14] Another Wedgwood product obviously intended as an architectural accessory was the portrait bust. A Cicero, a Homer or a Shakespeare would sit well in a broken pediment or alcove, and would look better in Wedgwood basalt than in bronzed plaster or the 'artificial stone' of Mrs Eleanor Coade. While staying with Lord Sheffield in Sussex, Edward Gibbon himself decided to order some Wedgwood busts for his library at Lausanne. This was in 1788, seven years after the completion of *The Decline and Fall of the Roman Empire*. In 1792, Lord

Sheffield was asked to settle 'a shameful obsolete bill, my only one, at Wedgewood's [*sic*].'[15]

The aping of the classical had a comic side, which was not lost on one of the smart bluestockings of the Mrs Montagu circle; Mrs Carter wrote to Mrs Vesey in December 1775:

> ... and so Mrs Handcock has no taste for your new invention of a coffee pot. But she is an intolerable commonsense woman. As to her strange objections that the pot has neither spout nor handle, and that the lid will not open, they are certainly quite nugatory; for as it is of a beautiful Etruscan form it answers every essential purpose of a good coffee pot – except the possibility of making coffee in it, which is only a mere circumstance which any one of true genius would easily overlook.

But by 1784 Rochefoucauld could say, certainly with some exaggeration, that the teapots and cups of the rich 'are always of most elegant design based upon Etruscan and other models of antiquity.'[16]

What was ridiculous in 1775 was fashionable less than ten years later; and that it became so was largely Wedgwood's achievement. He interested the connoisseurs in his wares; in 1776, as we have seen, he was trying to flatter Sir William Hamilton into 'puffing' them. He hunted through the English peerage for suitable 'lines, channels & connections' and asked Bentley to search through the Irish peerage with the same object: 'I need not tell you how much will depend upon a *proper* & *noble* introduction.'[17] British diplomats were made ambassadors for Wedgwood and Bentley. In 1778 Wedgwood suggested to his partner: 'Suppose we were to make Sr. Wm. Hamilton a present of an Etruscan tablet ... it would be the best introduction they could have in the country where he resides.'[18] Wedgwood's London showrooms were large and elegant (Plate 98) and became one of the most fashionable meeting places in London. Lord Townshend, writing on 'Squire Hanger', a beau and a macaroni, says:

> At Tattersall's, Wedgwood's, and eke the Rehearsal,
> Then straightway at Betty's he's sure to converse all;
> At Arthur's you meet him, and the mall in a sweat,
> At Kensington Garden's he's posted vidette.[19]

When his copy of the Portland vase – the climax of his neo-classical ambitions – was completed, Wedgwood put it on show and issued engraved tickets of admission. It was the talk of London.

Wedgwood told the public what it ought to want, but he was also prepared to give it what it wanted. To Flaxman he wrote, concerning an 'Achilles' series:

> There is one objection which I am afraid is insurmountable, and that is the nakedness of the figures. To clothe them would not only be a great increase of labour, but would require the hand of an experienced master in the art, and besides, the pieces would not then be a copy of the antique. I know the nudities might be covered with leaves but that is not enough. The same objection applies to the *Judgment of Paris* and the other pieces; and indeed the mode is so general in the work of the ancients that it will be very difficult to avoid the introduction of naked figures. On the other hand it is absolutely necessary to do so, or to keep the pieces for our own use, for none, either male or female, will take or apply them as furniture, if the figures are naked.[20]

This passage is typical both of Wedgwood's sensitivity to public taste, and of his attitude to the artists in his employ. The only time he failed to get an artist to do what he wanted was when he tried to induce Stubbs to design plaques of subjects other than horses: though he did get him to incorporate a Wedgwood and Bentley vase, somewhat incongruously, into the predominantly equestrian and rural portrait of the Wedgwood family (Plate 1).

John Flaxman's father was a plaster-cast seller patronized by Wedgwood. As early as 1771 (when Flaxman was only sixteen) Wedgwood wrote to Bentley: 'Mr Freeman says he knows young Flaxman is a Coxcomb but does not think him a bit the worse for it, or less likely to be a great artist.'[21] In 1775 Flaxman accepted an offer to model tablets for Wedgwood and Bentley, and Wedgwood wrote to his partner, with some consistency: 'I am glad you have met with a modeller and that Flaxman is so valuable an artist. It is but a few years since he was a most supreme Coxcomb, but a little more experience may have cured him of this foible.'[22] And in fact relations between the two improved to the point where Wedgwood could write to Mrs Flaxman, in sending her a drawing of Flaxman by John Jackson (some time after Flaxman's return from Italy in 1794):

> Mr Wedgwood presents his compliments to Mrs Flaxman and has the honour to present her with the portrait of the first artist of the age which from her knowledge of his many other good qualities he flatters himself will be favourably received.[23]

W. G. Constable, in his monograph on Flaxman, shows how Flaxman and Wedgwood worked together, the latter always guiding and correcting as the autocratic patron, the former never attempting to play the temperamental artist. Wedgwood suggested the kind of work he wanted. Flaxman then submitted a drawing for approval, and on receiving this, prepared a wax model. Sometimes he would make a plaster mould from this, but usually this was left to the workmen at Etruria. From this mould, a block mould in biscuit was made, and when this had been worked on by Wedgwood's modellers, it became the basis of the moulds from which the impressions actually fired were taken. Plates 85, 86 and 87 show Flaxman's original sketch, and completed jasper plaques, of *Hector's Body Dragged at the Car of Achilles*. The earliest surviving work certainly by Flaxman in which classical influence appears is the *Dancing Hours*, finished by 1778. The main motif is similar to that of the late Greek or Greco-Roman relief in the Louvre known as *Les Danseuses Borghese*. In 1778 Flaxman also completed the relief which Wedgwood called *The Apotheosis of Homer* (it is now more commonly known as *The Crowning of a Kitharist*). The character of Flaxman's work is a kind of noble naivety – a quality which often accompanies the lack of a sense of humour.

William Blake, a friend of Flaxman and a strong influence on him, engraved a catalogue for Wedgwood. The Herculaneum factory, founded at Liverpool in 1700, also had access to distinguished neo-classical influences.[24] Fuseli exhibited in Liverpool, and frequently visited his friend there, the *litterateur* William Roscoe, sometimes accompanied by the London publisher Joseph Johnson, an uncle of Joseph Johnson the Liverpool engraver, some of whose signed engravings occur on Herculaneum and other pottery. In 1798 Roscoe translated and published a poem by Luigi Tansillo, *The Nurse*. The first edition was going to be illustrated by Fuseli, and in the Picton Library there is a grangerized version with Fuseli's fine drawing. But the edition has an engraving by Moses Houghton, and subsequent editions were not illustrated. A creamware mug in the Liverpool Museum, unsigned and different from these two designs, is entitled *The Mother, from Roscoe's Nurse*.

It was at one time tentatively suggested that a Herculaneum plaque in the Liverpool Museum might have been decorated after one of the lost paintings from Fuseli's Milton Gallery. Fuseli had decided to do single-handed for Milton what several artists had been trying to do for the engraver Boydell with Shakespeare: to produce a gallery illustrative of his works. The venture was not a commercial success, mainly as the result of hostile newspaper criticism, and very few of the paintings seem to have survived. Joseph Johnson of London abandoned a scheme to publish an edition of Milton's works edited by Cowper and illustrated by Fuseli, because Cowper was mentally ill. Because of the Roscoe and Joseph Johnson connections, it seemed possible that the plaque, decorated by William Lovatt with a scene from *Paradise Lost*, might owe its inspiration to a lost Milton Gallery painting. But in fact the style of Lovatt's painting has little in common with that of Fuseli's known works.

The Herculaneum factory was one among the many which imitated Wedgwood. Others were those of John Turner of Lane End and his sons William and John; William Adams; Humphrey Palmer; Samuel Hollins; James Neale; and Lakin and Poole. In the early nineteenth century, the Turner sons became bankrupt and were forced to have sales of their property. The lists of their libraries which appeared in the local Staffordshire press give a good idea of the kinds of book the better neo-classical potters might be expected to own and to use as source books for designs. William Turner's books, sold in 1813, included four volumes of Hamilton's *Antiquities*; seven volumes of 'Herculaneum and Etruscan Antiquities'; the five volumes of Bernard de Montfaucon's *L'Antiquité expliquée et representée en figures* (1719); eighteen volumes of the *Repertory of Arts*; the six volumes of the Comte de Caylus's *Recueil d'Antiquités égyptiennes, étrusques, grecques, romaines, et gauloises* (1762–5); and 'Pergolesi's engravings'.[25]

We know from the accounts of the Turners' London partner, Andrew Abbott, that on 2 November 1782 J. Abbott was paid 10*s*. 6*d*. by the partnership for having bought from Pergolesi '2 Numbers Engravings.'[26] Michelangelo Pergolesi was an engraver and watercolourist who was talent-spotted by Robert Adam in Italy and brought back by him: he worked on the ceilings of Syon House. His principal work, *Designs for Various Ornaments* (1777–1801), influenced furniture design,[27] and was the source of some Turner patterns.

Wedgwood was also much imitated abroad. Arthur Young, at Vicenza in October 1788, wrote: 'My friendly Abbate, continuing his obliging offices, had the goodness to accompany me this morning to a very famous woollen fabric, at present under the direction of an Englishman, and to a magazine of earthenware in imitation of Mr Wedgwood. It is surely a triumph of the arts in England to see in Italy Etruscan forms copied from English models. It is a better imitation than many I have seen in France.'[28] Louis-Victor Gerverot, a much-travelled 'arcanist' or secret-monger, visited Etruria in 1786 or 1787, and took back to Germany neo-classical ideas (realized at the Fürstenberg factory of which he became manager) and also some of the social liberalism of

Wedgwood: he instituted a pension scheme for his workmen and planted flowers round his factory. And Wedgwood's designs were extensively pirated by Sèvres. But the Continental countries also had their own independent neo-classical movements in ceramic art. Naturally the excavations in Italy had a direct influence on Italian porcelain. At the Naples factory, so near the Herculaneum site, a 'Herculaneum service' of 88 pieces was begun in 1781 under the direction of Domenico Venuti. It was sent to the Spanish court in the following year, accompanied by its decorators. As centrepieces, there were busts of Scipio, Seneca, Pallas, Jupiter Ammon and others, and a biscuit group of 'Charles II exhorting his son Ferdinand to pursue the excavations'. An explanatory book of engravings was published by Venuti. In 1785 an 'Etruscan service' of 282 pieces was begun, and in 1787 it was sent to England in the charge of the modeller Tagliolini and John Chisel (or Casely), an English modeller employed by the factory between 1771 and 1804. Another descriptive book was published by Venuti. Much of the service is still at Windsor Castle, though not Tagliolini's centrepiece: 'Tarchon, King of the Etruscans, presiding over gladiatorial contests.' As Mr Arthur Lane has pointed out, the service has an historical, as well as an artistic, importance:

> In 1779 the re-organization of the Neapolitan Navy was entrusted to John Francis Edward Acton, an expatriate Anglo-Irishman who later became Prime Minister of Naples and inherited an English baronetcy. Acton needed the secrets of English naval construction, and hoped that a handsome gift to King George III would open doors to his agents. The Etruscan Service was conveyed to England in the Neapolitan warships Ceres and Minerva, whose commander, the Cavaliere Fortiguerri, obtained permission to visit Woolwich arsenal and Deptford Docks, but was less lucky with Portsmouth.[29]

If Italy had the antiquities themselves, Germany at least had the greatest art critic, Winckelmann, and his disciple Goethe. Goethe, as a nineteen-year-old art student, was awaiting Winckelmann's arrival in Leipzig when the news came that the critic had been garotted at Trieste. 'Goethe, then in all the pregnancy of his wonderful youth,' writes Pater, 'was awaiting Winckelmann with a curiosity of the worthiest kind. As it was, Winckelmann became to him something like what Virgil was to Dante.'[30] Goethe's *Die Leiden des jungen Werthers* (The Sorrows of Young Werther), written in 1774, became the breviary of the neo-classical movement in Germany. The story was suggested by the suicide of a fellow-student at Leipzig, who shot himself while possessed

Wedgwood, Neo-Classicism and the Industrial Revolution

83 (top) Pottery mug made for William Bateman, the antiquary, as a child, *c.* 1790, at 'the potteries near Liverpool'. See p. 124

84 Coffee-pot and cover of red stoneware, engine-turned, together with pedigree. See p. 144.

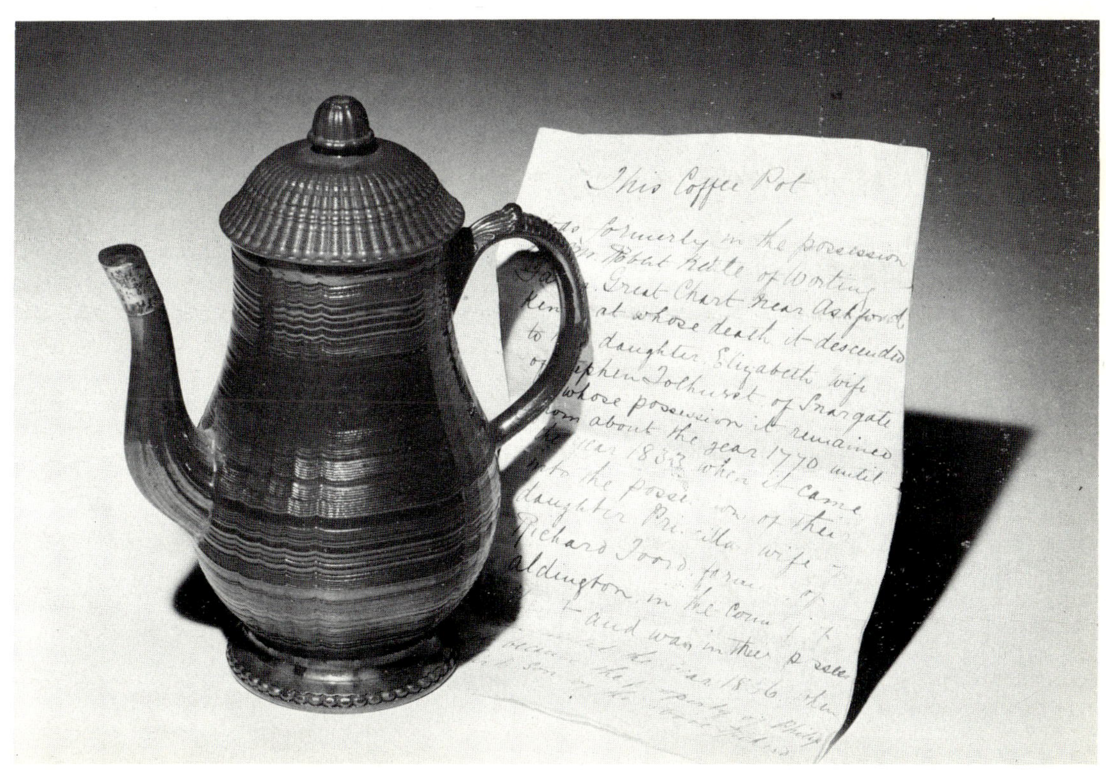

85 (top) Original design by John Flaxman of 'Hector's Body dragged at the Car of Achilles'. Pen and ink.
86 and 87 Two Wedgwood plaques, in blue and green jasper respectively, from the Flaxman design. See p. 132.

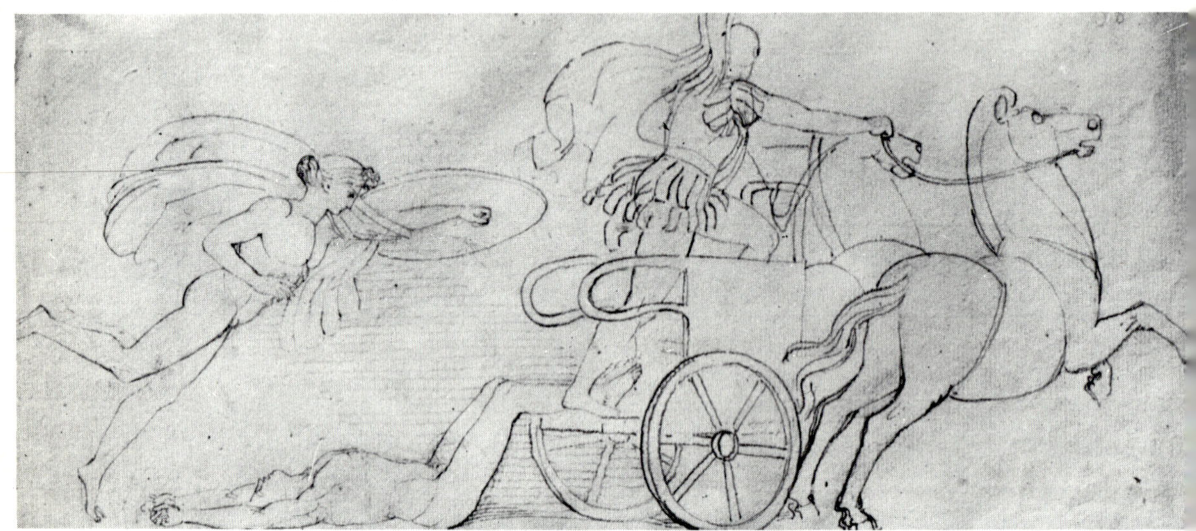

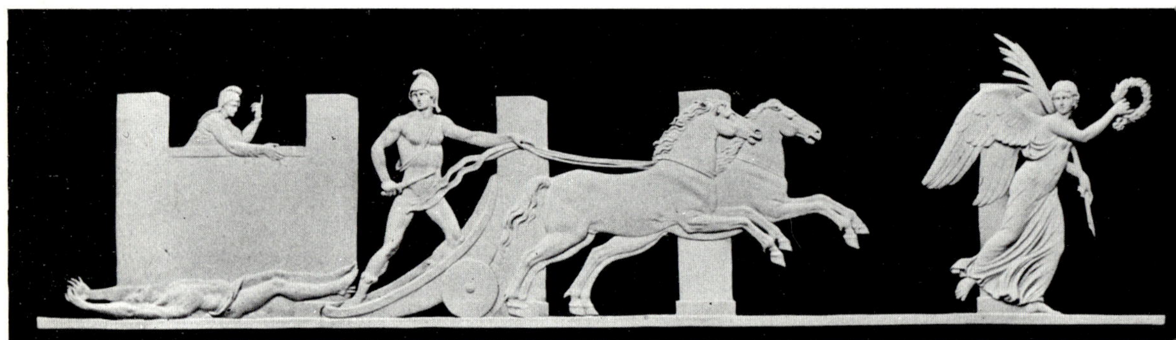

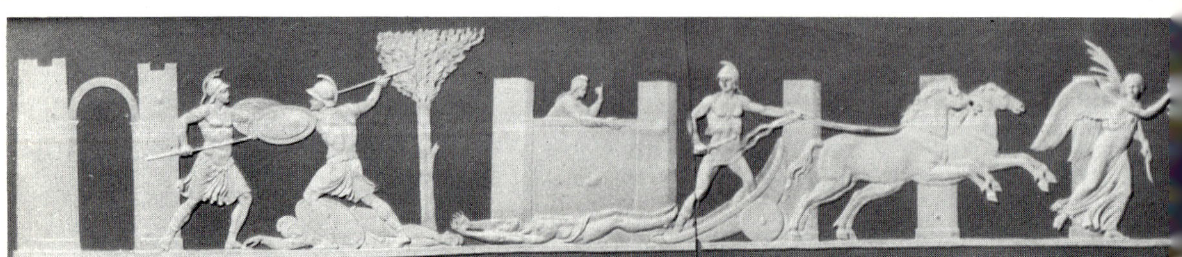

88 (opposite top) Set of vases in white 'dry body' ware, all marked WEDGWOOD impressed. Such wares were originally made for amateurs to decorate with water-colour. See p. 45.
89 (bottom) 'Garniture de cheminée', blue and white jasper, in decadent neo-classical taste. By Lockett of Lane End, Staffordshire, early nineteenth century.

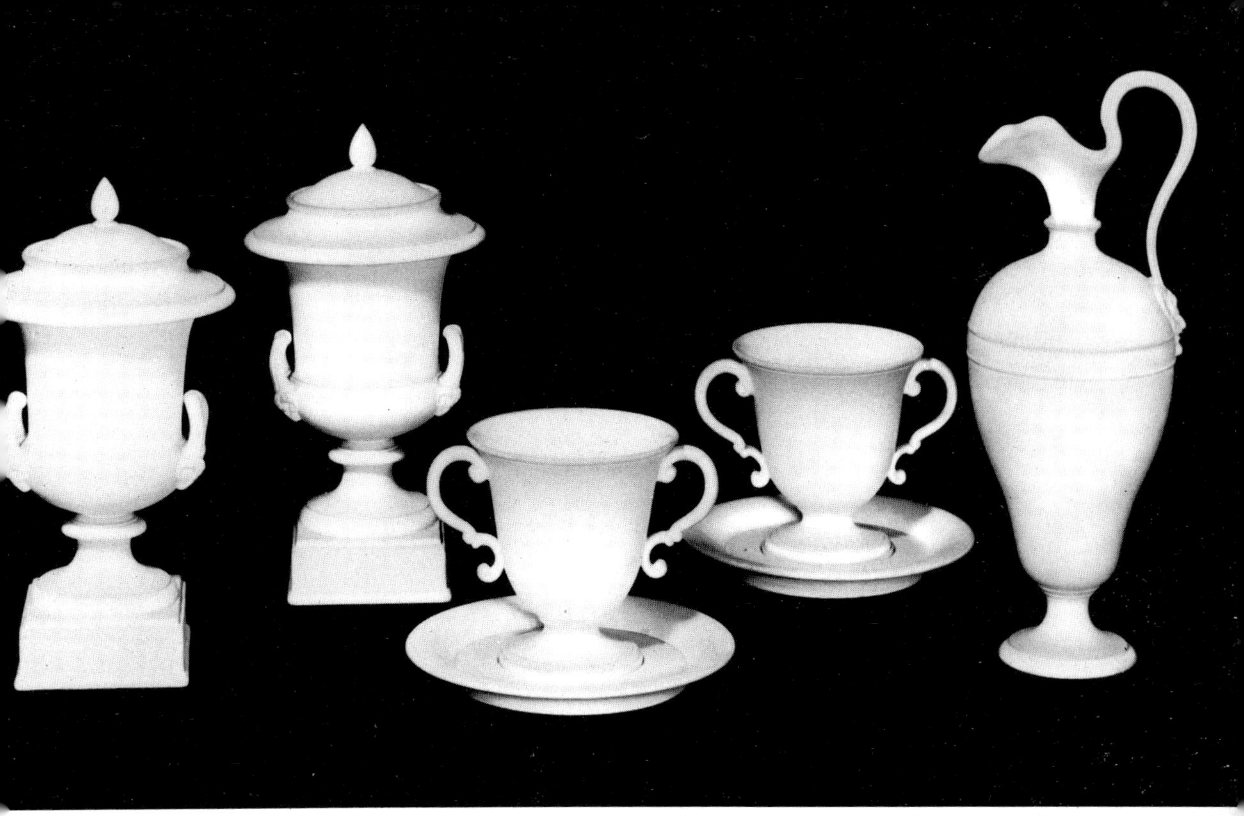

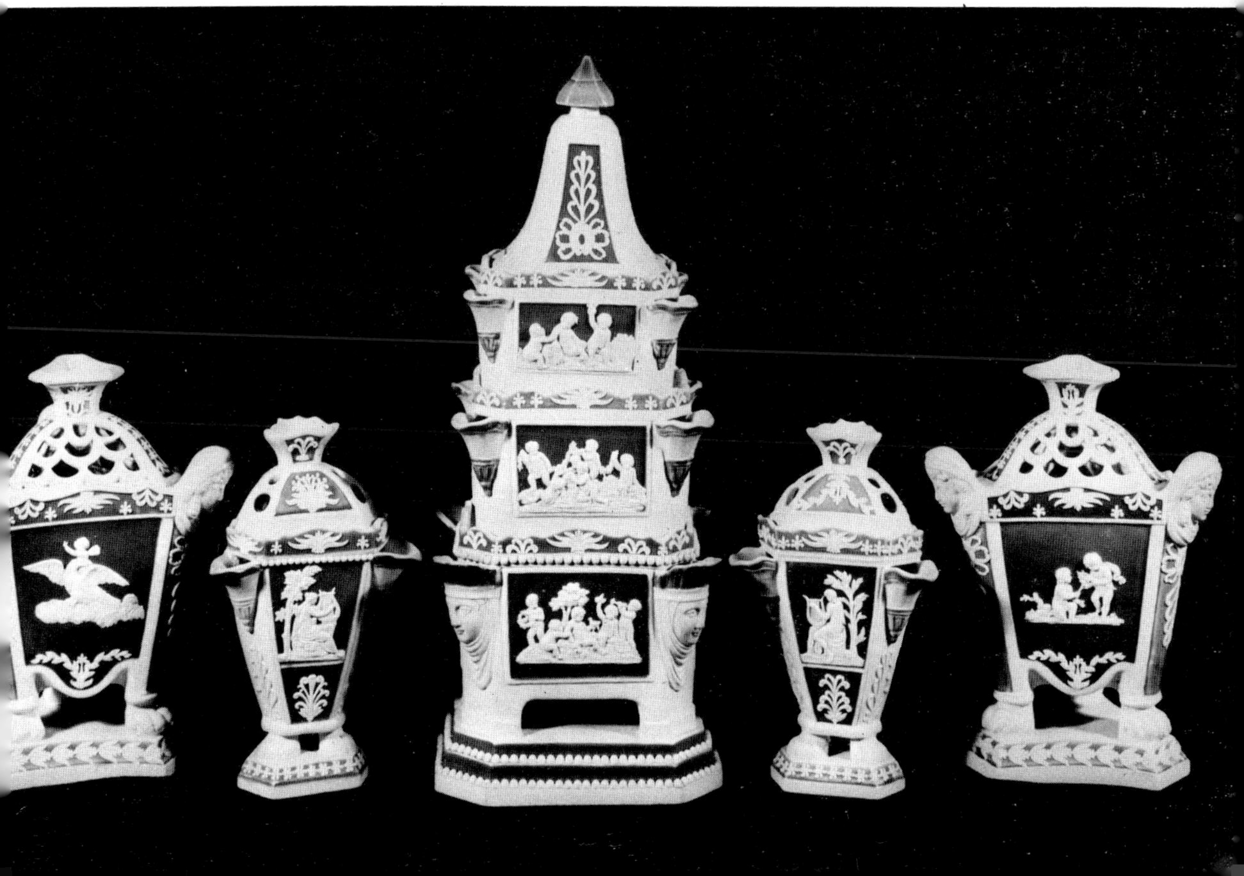

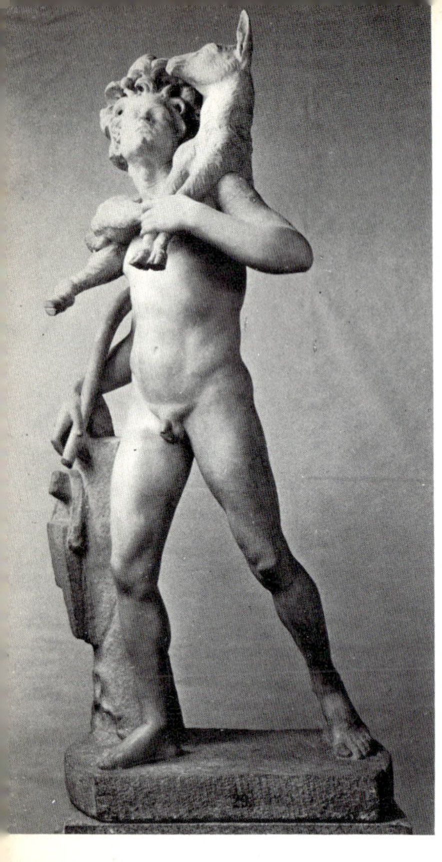
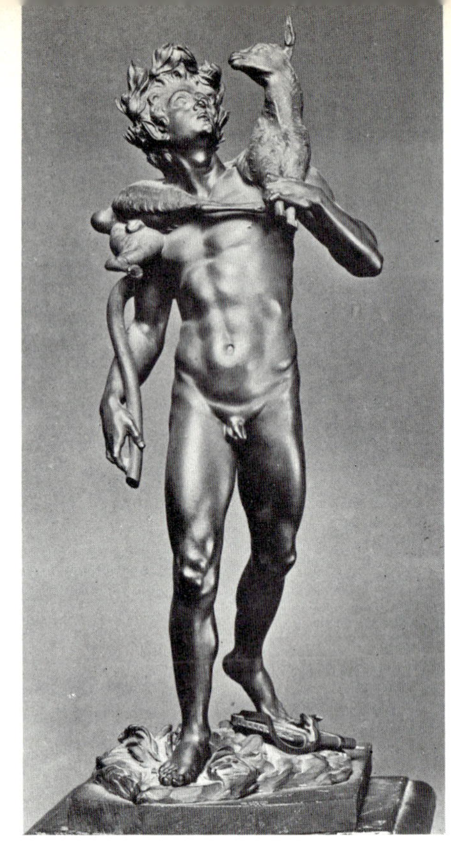

90–93 (top left) The 'San Ildefonso Faun', Greek marble; (top right) bronze version by Massimiliano Soldani-Benzi; (bottom left) clothed porcelain version, Longton Hall, Staffordshire; (bottom right) marble version by J. J. Saly, late eighteenth century. See p. 144.

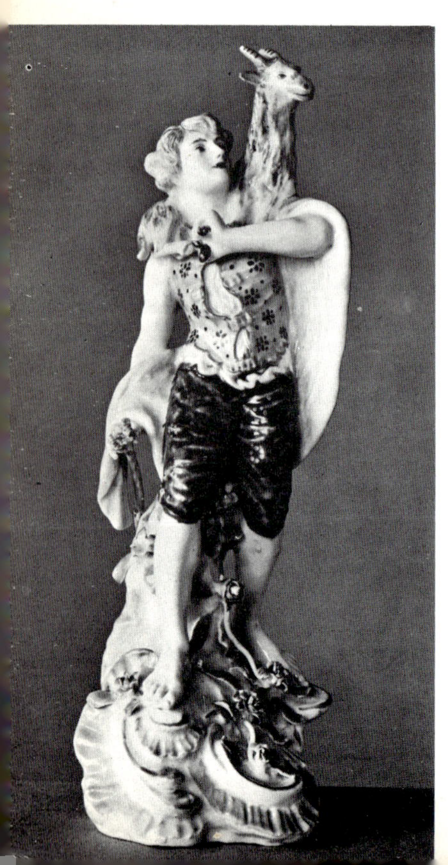
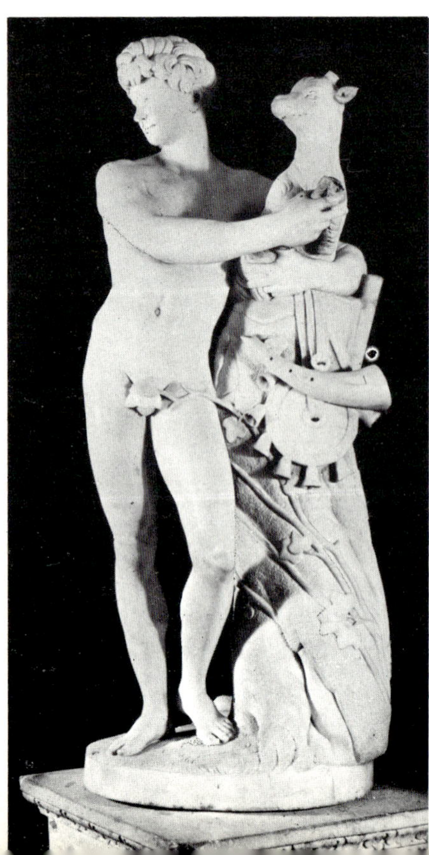

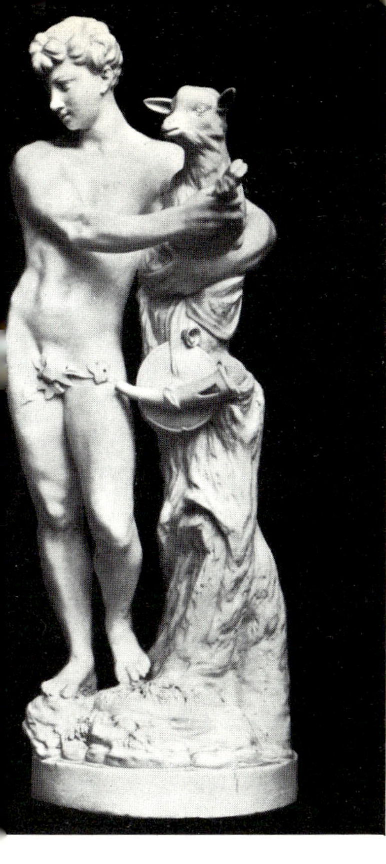

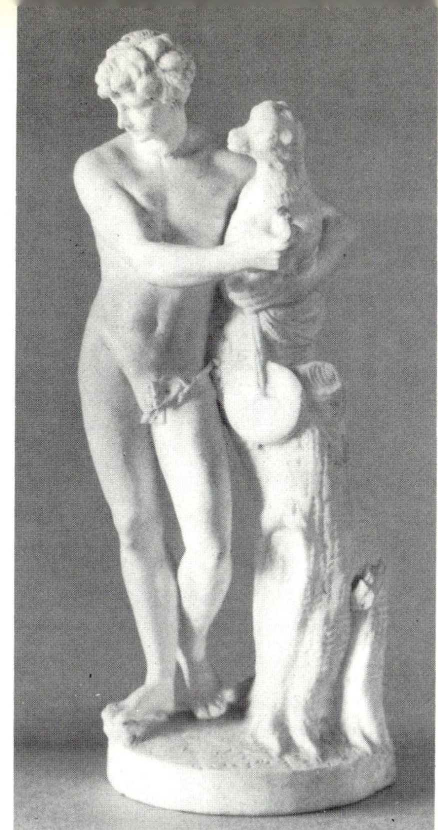

94–97 (far left) Lunéville porcelain version, modelled by J. J. Saly. Mark T.D.L. (for 'Terre de Lorraine'), *c.* 1770, height $8\frac{3}{4}''$; and three versions in Copenhagen porcelain, of varying skill. See p. 144.

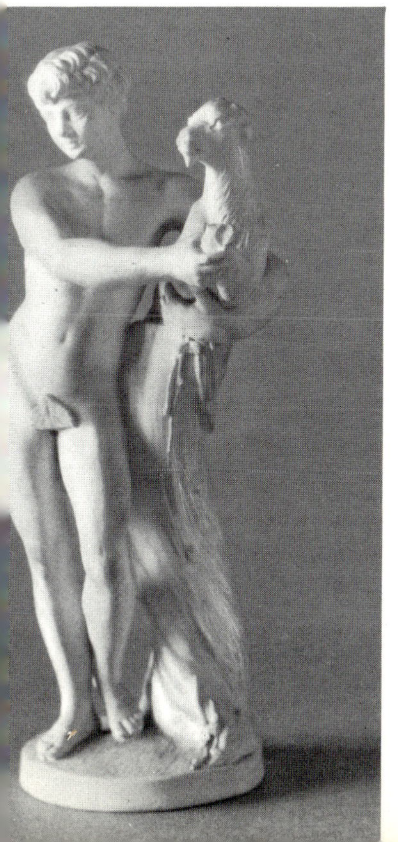

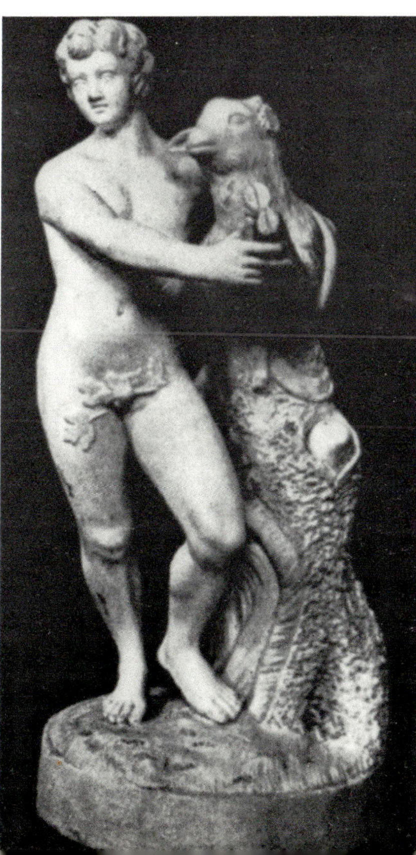

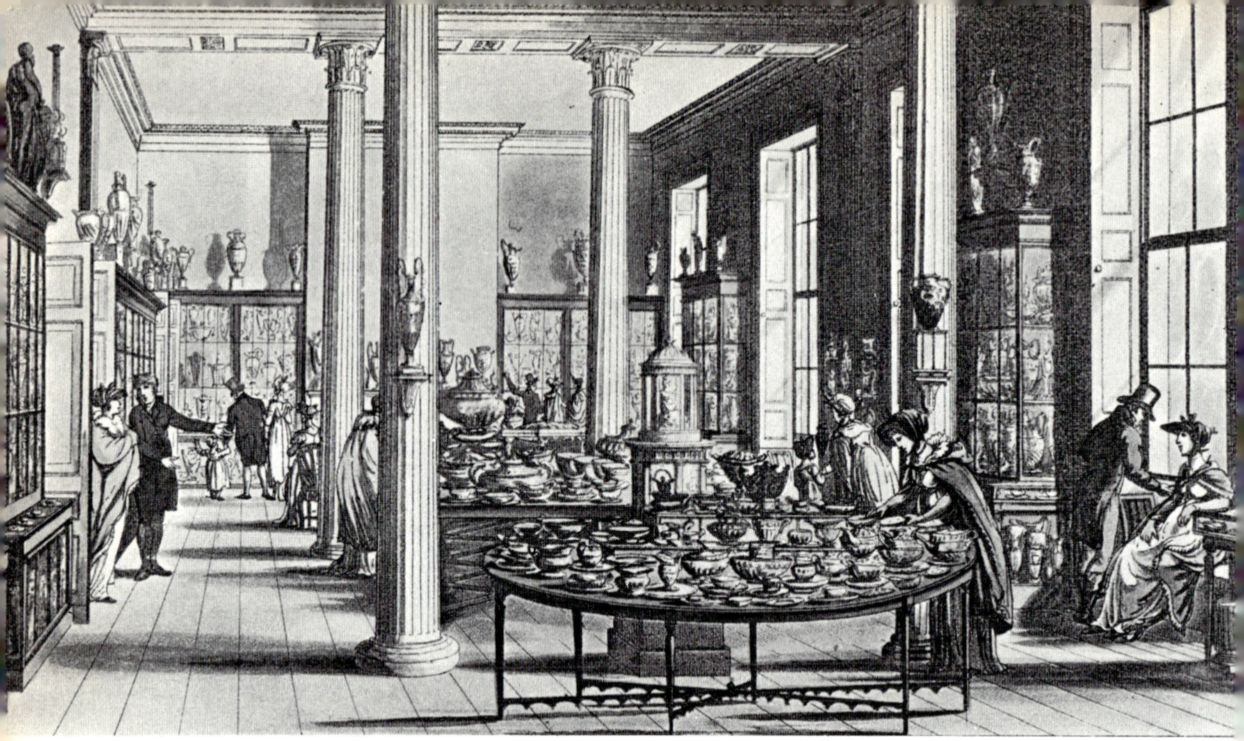

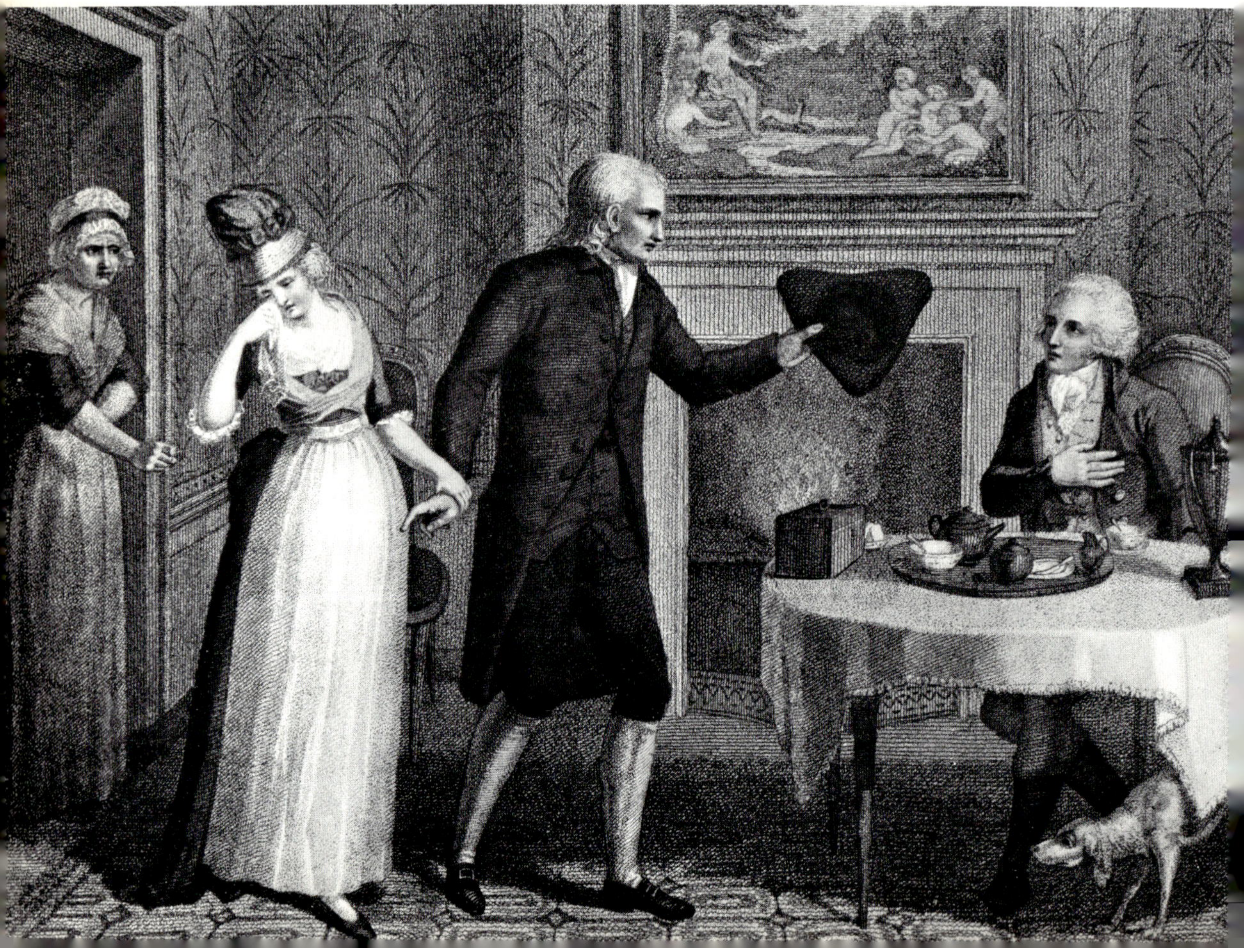

98 (opposite) Wedgwood and Byerley's showroom in York Street, St James's Square, 1809.

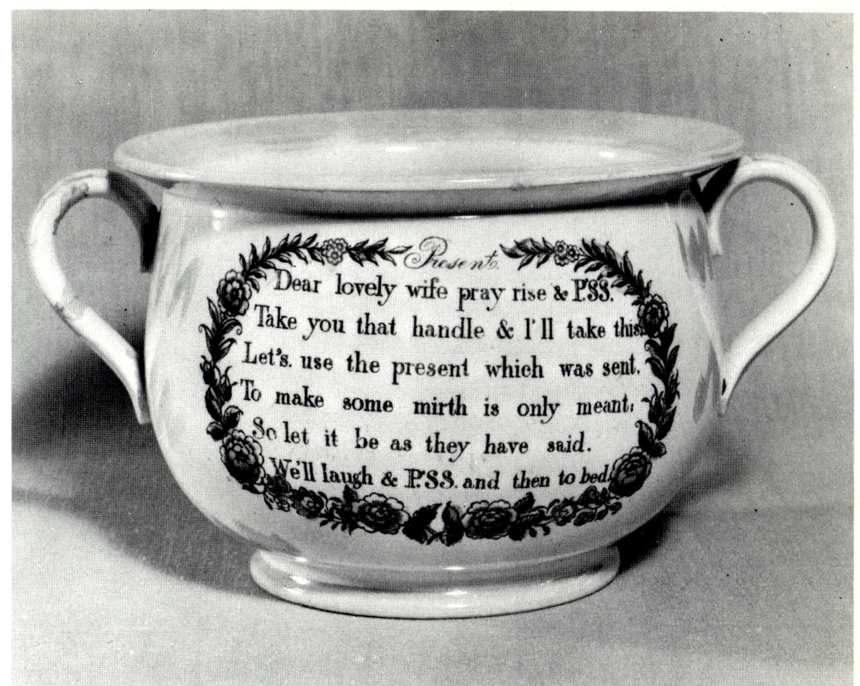

99 (opposite) Black basalt wares in use: stipple engraving by J. Cook after George Morland. A companion print, 'The Accommodation' (not illustrated here), shows what appear to be Wedgwood jelly-moulds on a mantelpiece.

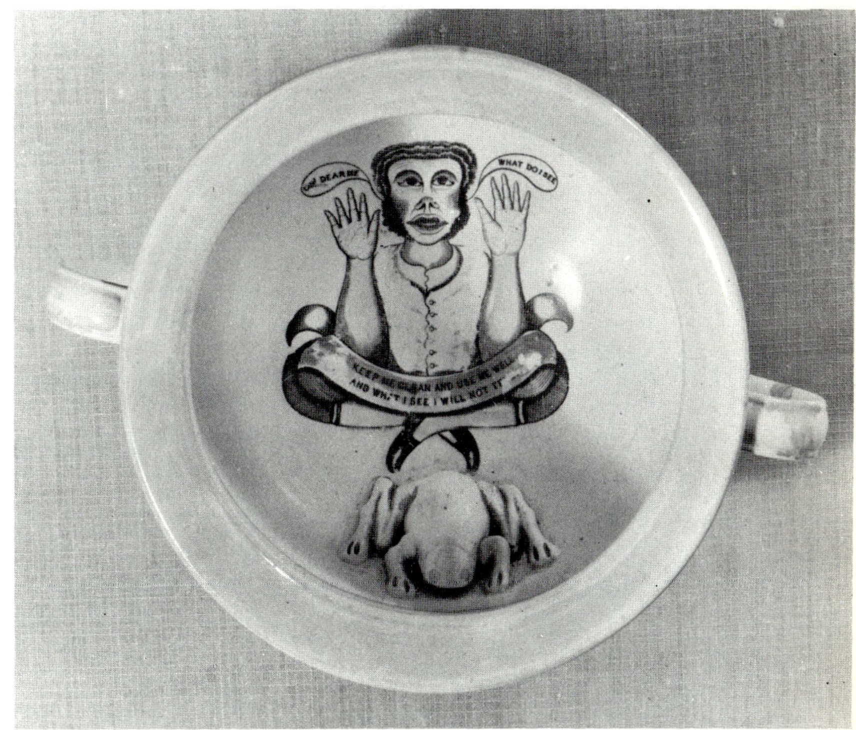

100 and 101 Sunderland double-handed chamber-pot, with modelled frog and printed and lustre decoration.

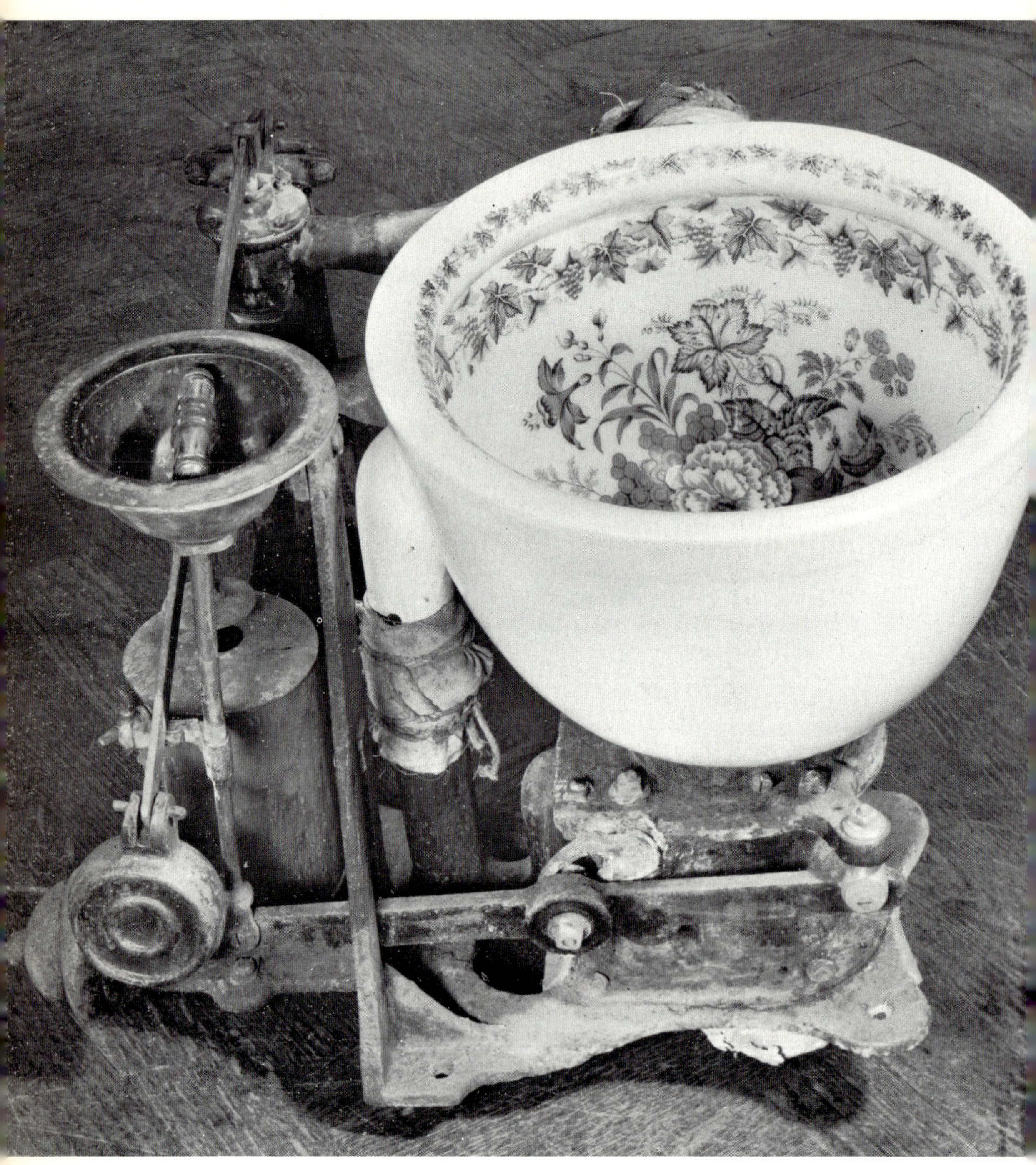

102 Blue transfer-printed lavatory bowl, probably Staffordshire, late nineteenth century. See p. 146.

by a hopeless passion for another man's wife. Subjects from *Werther* were modelled at Meissen by Michel-Victor Acier, were painted on Meissen services, and translated into demure designs for Wedgwood by Lady Templetown.

The porcelain modeller Johann Peter Melchior came to the Höchst factory with a letter of recommendation from Winckelmann himself – despite the latter's belief that porcelain was a frivolous material, fit only for making 'idiotic puppets'. He was also a friend of Goethe and modelled several portraits of him. Melchior moved from Höchst to Frankenthal and there published (1784–9) some articles explaining his concepts of nature and art: *Das sichtbar Erhabene in der bildende Kunst, Der Kunstler am Altar der Grazien*, and *Der grosse Phidias*.[31]

The dewy Salomon Gessner, who painted rococo-classical ruins on Zurich china,[32] wrote the influential *Idylles* of which an approving contemporary wrote: 'The most licentious of his fauns is more virtuous than the shepherds of Theocritus.' Gessner's work has a strong kinship with the Rousseauist sentimentality which insisted on the natural goodness of man and recommended a 'return to nature'. Corollaries to this philosophy were the idea of the Noble Savage and the belief in education through Nature expounded in *Emile* – a belief which in England persisted well into the nineteenth century, with Wordsworth's:

> One impulse from a vernal wood
> May teach you more of man,
> Of moral evil and of good
> Than all the sages can.

– and with William Cobbett's assertion that he had learnt more by sliding down a grass bank than any university could have taught him. The literary expression of the 'back to nature' theme was the pastorale – tenderly erotic philandering in arcadias far from pernicious society: Gessner's *Idylles* were typical. It became fashionable for ladies in high society to affect rustic dress. Marie Antoinette played the shepherdess in the 'peasant village' she had set up in the Trianon park. 'The Queen,' wrote Madame Campan, 'was ravished with the pleasure of inspecting the dairy, watching the cows being milked and fishing in the lake.' In the *laiterie* at Rambouillet, even the pails were of delicate Sèvres porcelain[33]; but Wedgwood supplied wares for the Duc d'Orléans's *ferme ornée* at Raincy,[34] as well as for the aristocratic dairy at Brocklesby Hall, Lincolnshire, now demolished, and for that of Lavinia, Lady Spencer (1786).[35] In 1791 Neale and Bailey, of Staffordshire and St Paul's

Churchyard, London, made dairy wares ornamented with coats of arms for the Castle of Wilhelmshöhe, Kassel, where they remain.

French neo-classicism is largely associated with the political neo-classicism of the Revolution; but already the movement had asserted itself in such works as Saly's Lunéville version (Plate 93) of the San Ildefonso Faun (Plate 90). Saly repeated this model for the Copenhagen factory (Plate 94), who made some maladroit versions of their own (Plates 95–97); it had also been executed in bronze by Massimiliano Soldani-Benzi (Plate 91) some of whose other models, as we have seen, were reproduced in Doccia porcelain; and a clothed rococo example had been made at Longton Hall (Plate 92). Few fauns can have had such a prolonged and varied *après-midi*.

Technique, rather than style, gave Wedgwood supremacy among the European potters. The great technical advance which was the first stage of the Industrial Revolution in ceramics began with the fine red stoneware made in England by John Philip Elers and his brother David in the late seventeenth and early eighteenth centuries. This redware, which could take the impress of delicate reliefs, began to replace the coarse white stoneware of Staffordshire. Wedgwood himself, earlier in his career, made redware. An engine-turned coffee-pot (Plate 84) in this material may be one of his productions. We know something of the social history of this pot from a written pedigree which it contains, though this must be accepted with the usual reservations. The pedigree, shown in the same picture, reads:

This Coffee Pot

was formerly in the possession of Mr Robert Kettle of Worting Farm, Great Chart, near Ashford Kent, at whose death it descended to his daughter, Elizabeth, wife of Stephen Tolhurst of Snargate in whose possession it remained from about the year 1770 until the year 1833 when it came into the possession of their daughter Priscilla, wife of Richard Foord, farmer, of Aldington, in the County of Kent, and was in their possession until the year 1856, when it became the property of Philip third son of the above Richard and Priscilla Foord, and was by him presented to Mr John Kettle Paine, of Oak tilla, Erith, in the County of Kent, on Tuesday April 28th 1874. He died on the 3rd October 1883 when it became the property of his wife, Mary Paine, and she, dying on the 12th December 1903, left it to her daughter Edith Marian Paine of Penthorpe, Coleraine Road, Westcombe Park, Blackheath, S.E.

(*New writing*): On the death of Edith Marian Paine, on October 31st 1933, it passed into the possession of Mr & Mrs C. R. Paine of 17 Christ Church Road, Sidcup, Kent.

Wedgwood's jasper and basalt wares were a natural development of the idea of a lapidary material capable of bearing a bas-relief of perfect definition. Similarly he improved on the old earthenware by adding china clay to it. The result was a creamware which captured the European markets, ruining the delft potters. Wedgwood made direct imitations of the antique almost exclusively as decorative objects. For useful ware his designers merely derived inspiration from the antique as a means to create perfect shapes. This is perfectly in line with silversmiths and furniture makers until the very last years of the eighteenth century.

With his usual acumen, Wedgwood supplied the queen with a service of his creamware and named it 'Queensware'. To present a pottery service to Queen Charlotte was rather like presenting a plastic one to Queen Elizabeth II; but Wedgwood went on to make for Catherine the Great of Russia the famous 'Frog' service, which, he told Bentley, called for 'the most embelished views, the most beautiful Landskips, with Gothique Ruins, Grecian Temples, & the most Elegant Buildings with hands who have never attempted anything beyond Huts and Windmills, upon Dutch Tile at three half-pence a doz.'.[36] He added: 'If you dare attempt and can succeed in this, tell me no more of your Alexanders, no more of your Prometheus's neither, for surely it is more to make *Artists* than mere *men*.'[37] In training artists, in building canals, turnpiking roads, and in factory discipline, Wedgwood was a prime mover.

But perhaps the two most important aspects of the Industrial Revolution in ceramics were, first, the invention of transfer printing, and, secondly, the use of ceramics in sanitation. Transfer printing was first used on English porcelain in the 1750s – including the Worcester mug of 1757 printed with Hancock's portrait of Frederick the Great (then popular in England as our ally in the Seven Years War). This mug is referred to by Carlyle:

> There stands on this mantlepiece ... a small china mug, not of bad shape, declaring itself, in one obscure corner, to be made at Worcester, 'R. H. Worcester 1757' ... which exhibits all round it a diligent potter's apotheosis of Friedrich, hastily got up to meet the general enthusiasm of English mankind.... A mug got up for a temporary English enthusiasm, and for the accidental instruction of posterity. It is of tolerable china, holds a good pint, 'to the Protestant hero with all the honours' and offers, in little, a curious eyehole into the then England, with its then lights and notions, which is now so deep-hidden from us, under volcanic ashes, French revolutions, and the wreck of a hundred very decadent years.[38]

Introduced into Staffordshire, transfer printing was to become the most common method of decorating earthenware.

The use of ceramic pipes for drainage was suggested to Wedgwood in the eighteenth century by the son of John Philip Elers. It was one of the few points at which Wedgwood's vision and taste for heroic enterprise deserted him. He turned the idea down. But in 1842 an engineer, Edwin Chadwick, issued a report on public sanitation and suggested the use of glazed pipes for sewers and house drains. These were at first made by hand, but in 1846 Henry Doulton established a factory at Lambeth for the production of salt-glaze stoneware pipes by machinery. When the Prince of Wales caught typhoid fever in 1870, sanitation became really fashionable. The lavatory in Plate 102, of unknown provenance, is truly princely, with its transfer-printed floral basin and amber handle.

Folk art was not entirely extinguished by the Industrial Revolution. In fact, there emerged a kind of industrial folk pottery, made by factory workers as limited in their surroundings and the sources of civilizing influence open to them as any peasant. Not that they were immune to what was happening in politics. That, after all, affected them, whether by reducing their bread ration or by taking them off to the wars. Jane Austen might not mention the Napoleonic Wars in her novels, but earthenware mugs of the period were covered with brave John Bulls and spindleshanked Boneys. In this time of flour shortage (and bread riots) Wedgwood and the Turners made imitation piecrust from caneware. The crude chimney figures made in Staffordshire from Victoria's coronation onwards give a good idea of the folk heroes and favourite villains: Jenny Lind the 'Swedish Nightingale', General Gordon, Grace Darling, Rush the Murderer. Gladstone, Prime Minister, abstruse theologian, and translator of the *Odes* of Horace and the *Carmen Saeculare*, becomes 'The Grand Old Feller' – a woodman with his axe. And the primeval folk occupation of drinking continues – from wares of mass-produced rusticity (Plate XVI).

7 The French Revolution

Some day a book should be written called *The French Revolution as a Classical Charade*.[1] For whether we believe, with Michelet, Taine and Lefebvre, that the Revolution was largely caused by the misery of the oppressed classes, or, with Tocqueville, Aulard, Jaurès and Mathiez, that it was precipitated by the reactionary aspirations of the bourgeoisie; whether we applaud it with the Marxists or condemn it with the Baroness Orczy, we have to admit the powerful influence of classical precedent. French was the court language of Europe; but education in eighteenth-century France, as in the other European countries, still consisted largely of Latin with some Greek. In 1651 Thomas Hobbes had suggested, from his baroque viewpoint, that one of the most frequent causes of rebellion against monarchy was reading Greek and Roman histories.[2] Shakespeare's *Julius Caesar*, written more than fifty years before, was still more prophetic:

BRUTUS: ... Stoop Romans, stoop,
And let us bathe our hands in Caesar's blood
Up to the elbows, and besmear our swords:
Then walk we forth, even to the Market-place,
And waving our red weapons o'er our heads,
Let's all cry Peace, Freedom, and Liberty.
CASSIUS: Stoop then, and wash. How many ages hence
Shall this our lofty scene be acted over,
In states unborn, and accents yet unknown?[3]

Roman and Greek parallels were invoked by both *enragés* and moderates to justify their actions. 'Brutus' was the smear-word of the reactionaries and the shibboleth of the regicides. Robespierre could think of himself and his colleagues as imitating Lycurgus when they abdicated their power after drafting a constitution. Saint-Just's plans for a national education were based minutely on those of Lycurgus, even down to provisions that children should have a vegetarian diet and sleep on straw mats. Revolutionary victims had the consolation of identifying themselves with Socrates and Phocion. Revolutionary oratory was fatally influenced by Roman precedent.[4] The example of Greece inspired pantheonization and the elaborate revolutionary *fêtes*. Art became political, glorifying the State, and artists became politicians: David, the painter of *Brutus* and the *Horatii*, was President of the Jacobin Club and of the Convention. On 8 Thermidor he made the classic classical gesture of offering to 'drink the hemlock' with Robespierre.

In this artistic climate we might expect French ceramics, usually so receptive to tendencies in the grander arts, to embody propaganda in a classical guise. But this is not quite what happened. In porcelain, there was some classicism, but little propaganda; in faience, much propaganda, but little classicism.

Sèvres represented the luxury and frivolity of the *ancien régime*. When the admirers of Franklin had commissioned from Jean-Baptiste Nini[5] five different medallions of their hero, it was from Sèvres that Louis XVI ordered the chamber pot, set with a similar medallion, which he sent to the Countess Diane de Polignac, one of the Franklin cult.[6] Arthur Young, in describing Madame du Barry's pavilion at Louveciennes on the eve of the Revolution (22 October 1787), shows one way in which Sèvres could be associated in the popular mind with royal excess:

> There is a table formed of Seve porcelain, exquisitely done. I forget how many thousand louis d'or it cost. The French, to whom I spoke of Lusienne, exclaimed against mistresses and extravagance with more violence than reason in my opinion. Who, in common sense, would deny a king the amusement of a mistress provided he did not make a business of his plaything? *Mais Frederic le Grand avoit-il une maitresse, lui fasoit-il batir des pavillons, et les meubloit-il de tables de porcelaine?* [7]

In 1793, it was seriously debated 'si l'on doit conserver la manufacture'. The director Hettlinger, a Swiss geologist who had already been imprisoned for a time because of the accusations of a few *enragé* workmen and wanted nothing more than to return to his native Zürich, admitted (more, one suspects, to show his good revolutionary spirit than from any real conviction) that:

> La manufacture de Sèvres a été la grande ouvrière en luxe de porcelaine, elle en a propagé et entretenu le goût. Elle ne fleurissait pas par le débit

multiplié d'objets usuels et de prix modique, mais de ses ouvrages riches, consacrés à l'opulente vanité qui souvent étaient payés cinq et six fois au delà des frais de fabrication....[8]

But he gave one strong reason why the manufacture should not be suppressed: the skilled workmen would go abroad to sell their talents and secrets. In fact, the Sèvres manufacture was probably saved, ironically enough, by a monarch. Catherine the Great sent 90,000 livres to settle her account. Perhaps there was something to be said for the luxury china after all. Certainly Catherine's unexpected payment 'seemed manna in the wilderness to the Minister of Finance', who therefore opposed the suppression. In January 1794 Wicar, a pupil of David, was named director of the painting ateliers. He resigned and was replaced by another pupil of David. But the very fact that the old painters were retained meant that Sèvres did not become fully classicized. The classicism on Sèvres tea-cups (Plates 115–16) was of the delicate, pretty kind which would have come without a Revolution, the 'rococo classicism' of Salomon Gessner and Hubert Robert. To the old court decorators, it was a fashion, not a style. Besides, as Chavagnac and Grollier observe, 'Le style Romain qui en 1792 devient général, ne s'accommode à cette céramique délicate'.[9] The truly republican workmen – those, no doubt, who had been responsible for getting Hettlinger arrested – were forced to secede from the factory to put their propagandist ideas into clay. In the Paris Exhibition of 1900 was exhibited a group representing 'La République de 1792', executed by renegades from Sèvres who had established themselves in the rue de Charonne.

Right up to 1792, when he was virtually a prisoner, having failed in his attempted flight to Varennes in June 1791, the king was making entries in his minute *petit-bourgeois* script on receipt of Sèvres pieces for the Grand Service de Versailles. This was the last great service produced at Sèvres in soft paste. It was ordered by Louis XVI for the *salle à manger de l'appartement du Roi* at Versailles. The complete service was to have cost 164,390 livres and to have been completed in twenty years, from 1783 to 1803. Up to 1792 only 197 pieces had been finished, at 71,280 livres. The wine-cooler, or *seau à bouteille* (Plate 112) was one of the last pieces ordered by Louis and entered in his accounts.[10]

Soft-paste porcelain, wrote Champfleury, the historian of *faïences patriotiques*, 'etait trop délicate, trop princière, pour une république dont les orateurs invoquaient les moeurs spartiates. Les terres épaisses des fabriques de Paris, de Nevers, et du Nord concordaient davantage avec les tendances démocratiques'.[11] The *faïences patriotiques* provide a record of popular thought and aspirations during the whole Revolution, and although good books, including Champfleury's, have been devoted to these wares, historians of the Revolution do not seem to have appreciated their significance. While chapters have been written on the bloodless academic paintings of David, the true index of popular feeling has been ignored. The faience of the Revolution has nothing in common with *le Beau scholastique.* 'Il se passe d'adjonctions mythologiques, de mascarons et de chimères, de satyres, de végétations fantastiques, de tritons et de tritonesses.'[12] The only classical emblem is the ubiquitous Phrygian cap, the bonnet of Liberty – and that, as reactionaries were not slow to point out,[13] was not a wholly suitable symbol of Liberty. (There were practical difficulties too. It was noted with patriotic disapproval that on some Nevers plates the Phrygian bonnet was shown as black or yellow, in defiance of revolutionary iconology. Du Broc de Ségrange, the historian of Nevers wares, explains: 'La couleur rouge a été peu employée dans la fabrication nivernaise. Comme elle est très-fragilc, elle disparaîtrait nécessairement sous la température des fours de Nevers.'[14])

Usually the main part of the decoration was a written motto. For this reason Champfleury also called this ware *faïence parlant.* Often the motto is accompanied by an emblem. It is significant that the mottoes and emblems are nearly all of an impersonal kind: la Liberté, la Nation, Le Tiers Etat, la Constitution, picks, Bastilles, *arbres de liberté.* Mirabeau is the only statesman to any extent mentioned or portrayed. How different from the English Liberty movement, which was made inseparable from Wilkes's name: 'Wilkes and Liberty', and in default of that, just 'Wilkes' (Plate 117).[15] The only piece illustrated by Champfleury bearing a large portrait of a statesman is a jug transfer-printed at Liverpool with the head of Necker.[16] The French did not naturally indulge in such sentimental androlatry. Edmund Burke expressed the difference between the two nations when he wrote: 'I love liberty as well as any French revolutionary, but I cannot give praise or blame to anything which relates to human actions, and human concerns, on a single view of the object, as it stands stripped of every relation in all the nakedness of metaphysical abstraction.'[17] It is the difference between a nation which achieved a written constitution by revolution, and a nation which achieved an unwritten constitution by evolution. When the English use an abstract phrase they like to be sure that a being of flesh and blood is behind it – as when they call a charwoman 'the daily help'.

The *faïences patriotiques* serve as illustrations to the *cahiers de doléances*

The French Revolution

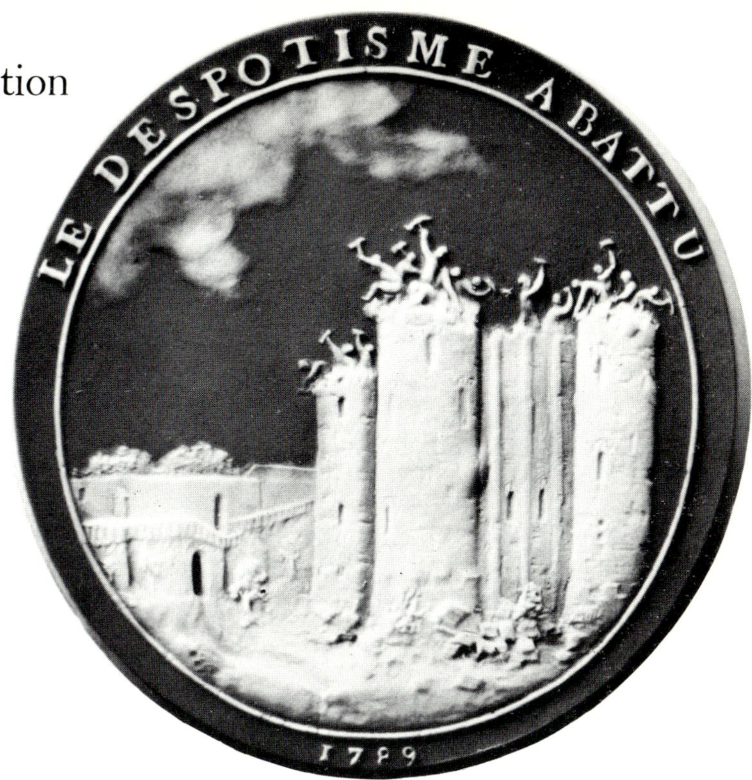

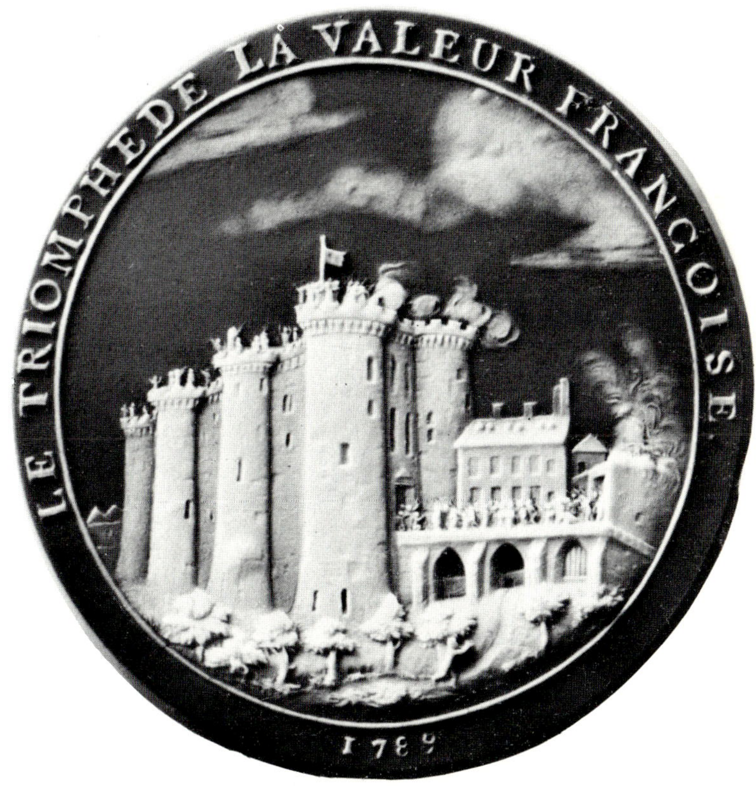

103 and 104 The Bastille medallion made by Josiah Wedgwood in 1789. Blue and white jasper. See p. 160.

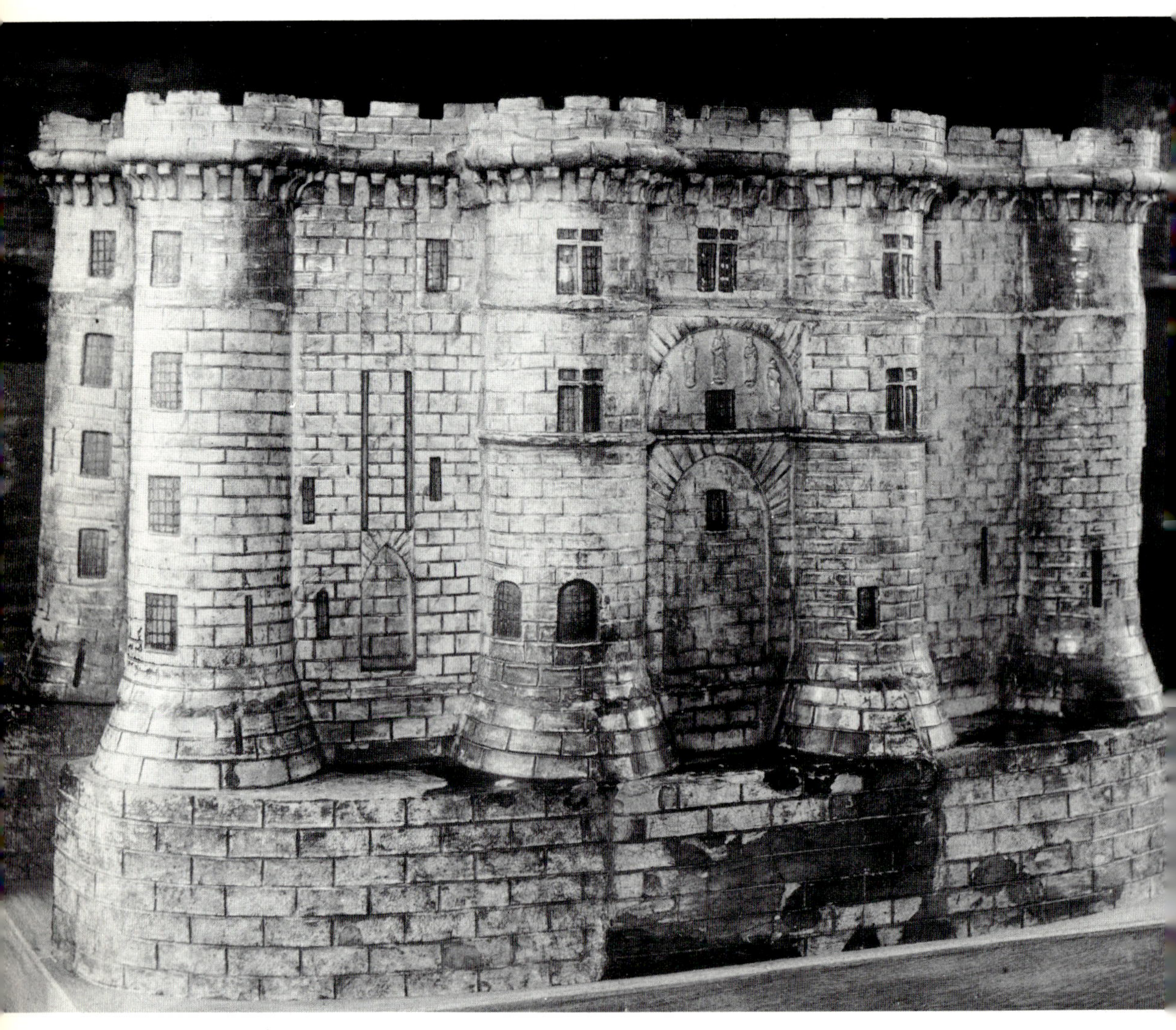

105 Stove in the form of the Bastille, made by Ollivier and presented to him by the Convention. See pp. 159–60.

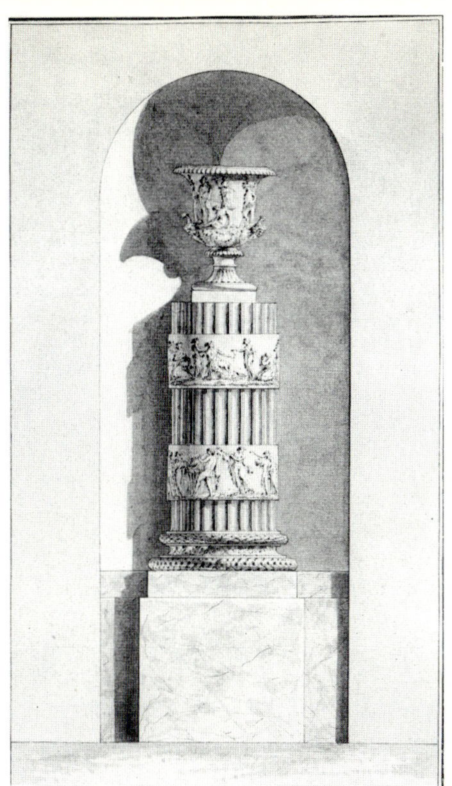

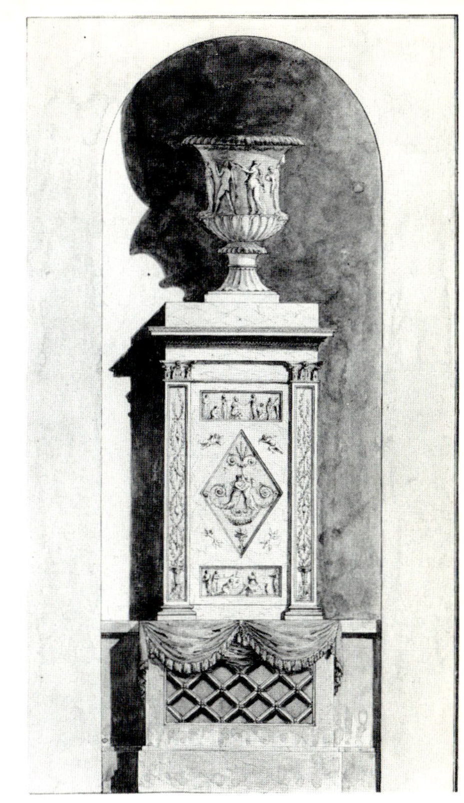

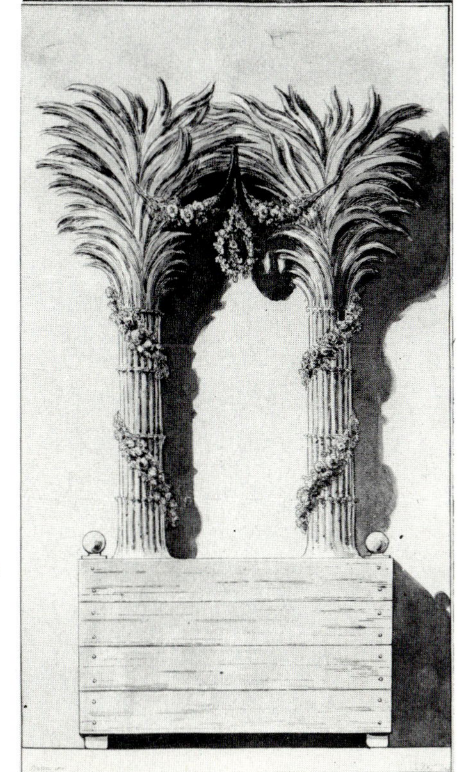

106–8 Three illustrations from the Catalogue of Ollivier's stoves in neo-classical style. See p. 159.

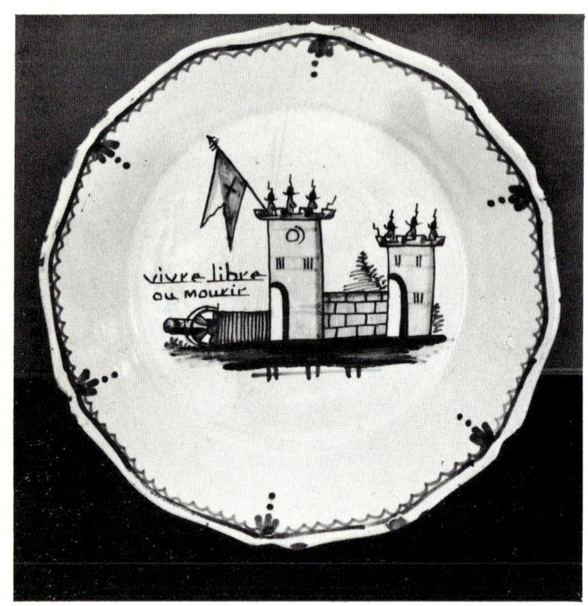

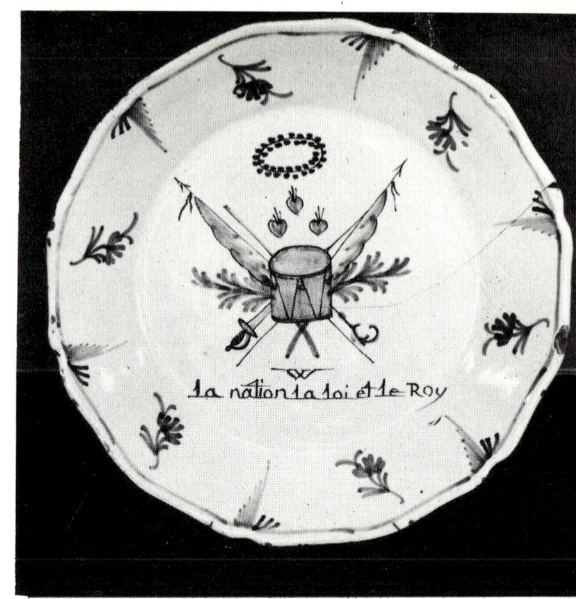

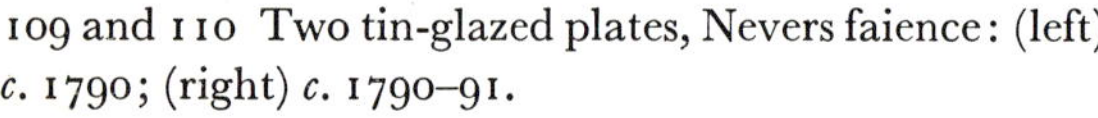

109 and 110 Two tin-glazed plates, Nevers faience: (left) *c.* 1790; (right) *c.* 1790–91.

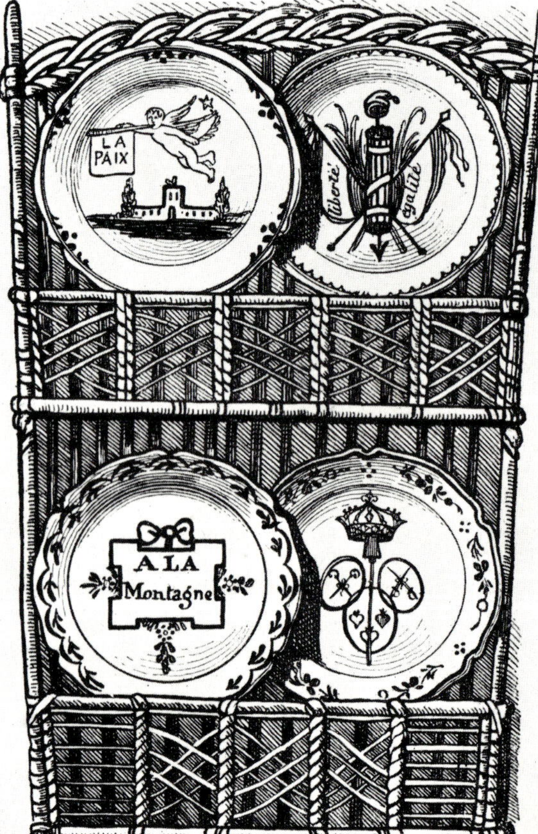

111 *Dressoir de campagne:* wickerwork stand for *faïences patriotiques*. From a drawing by Comte of 1850. See p. 117.

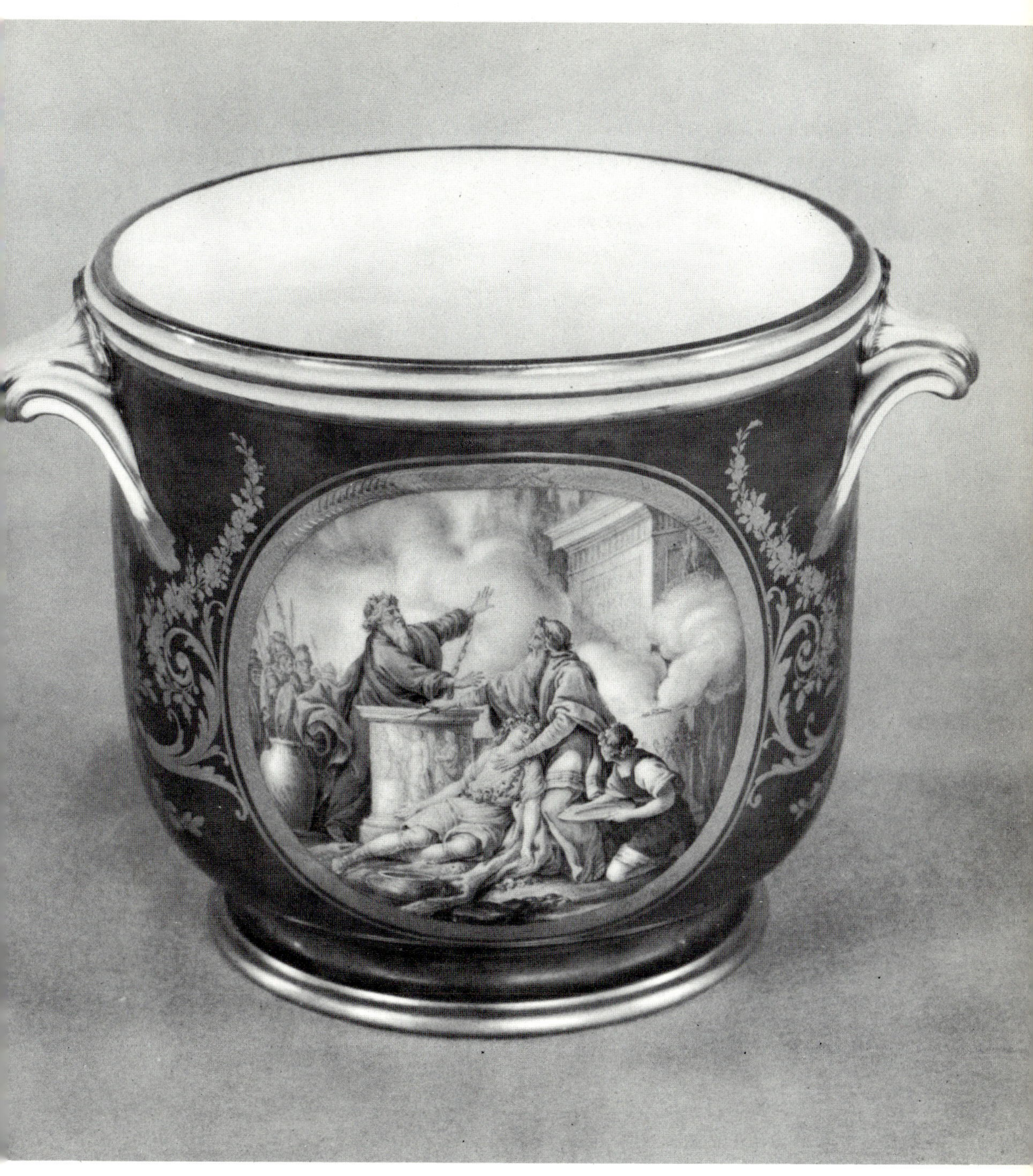

112 *Seau à bouteille* (wine-cooler) from the Sèvres *Grand Service de Versailles* made for Louis XVI. This piece was received by Louis and recorded by him in his accounts in 1791 or 1792, when he was already virtually a prisoner. See p. 149.

VENTE
DE
MEUBLES ET EFFETS
DE LA CI-DEVANT REINE,
PROVENANT DU PETIT TRIANON,
EN VERTU DE LA LOI DU DIX JUIN DERNIER,

Le Dimanche 25 Août 1793, l'an deuxième de la République une & indiviſible, 10 heures du matin, & 4 heures de relevée, & jours ſuivans.

SAVOIR:

Tous les matins. Batterie & uſtenſiles de cuiſine & d'office, ferrailles & meubles communs. *Tous les ſoirs.* Meubles de ſuite, conſiſtans en Lits avec leurs houſſes de différentes étoffes; armoires, ſecrétaires, commodes, tables, conſoles, partie à deſſus de marbre; feux, chaiſes longues, fauteuils, canapés, banquettes, chaiſes à tabourets de damas, lampas, velours de ſoie d'Utrecht, & moquette; faïence, verrerie, porcelaine d'office & de table.

Les autres Meubles de toute eſpèce, & en grande quantité, ſeront annoncés par de nouvelles affiches.

Cette vente ſe fera en préſence des Repréſentans du Peuple, & des Commiſſaires du Diſtrict, au ci-devant Château de Verſailles.

N. B. Les Meubles de la ci-devant Liſte civile peuvent être tranſportés à l'étranger, en exemption de tous droits.

Les Commiſſaires de la Convention Nationale.

CH. DELACROIX, J. M. MUSSET.

DE L'IMPRIMERIE NATIONALE.

PAR CONTINUATION.

VENTE
DE MEUBLES ET EFFETS PRECIEUX
AU CI-DEVANT
CHATEAU DE VERSAILLES,
CONFORMEMENT A LA LOI DU 10 JUIN DERNIER;

En préſence des Repréſentans du Peuple, & des Commiſſaires de Diſtrict & de la Municipalité, dans l'ordre qui ſuit:

SAVOIR;

Le Lundi 30 Septembre 1793, deuxième de la République, & jours ſuivans, les matins, excepté le Jeudi 3 Octobre, depuis dix heures juſqu'à deux.

BEAUCOUP de Meubles ordinaires, comme Houſſes de lits en damas, Fleuret & Siamoiſe, Sommiers de crin, Matelas, Lits de plume, Couvertures, Rideaux de diverſes étoffes, Commodes, Secrétaires, Tables & Bureaux de différens bois, partie à deſſus de marbre; Canapés, Fauteuils, Chaiſes & Bergères de damas, velours d'Utrecht, Moquette & Tapiſſerie, Feux en fer, Chandeliers, Porcelaines, Faïences, Glaces & autres objets.

Le même jour 30 Septembre & jours ſuivans, depuis quatre heures juſqu'à huit.

Superbes Meubles provenant du petit Trianon, & d'un fini précieux:

Conſiſtant en un lit en forme de chaire à prêcher, à bois ſculpté en treillages & chèvrefeuille, peint de couleurs variées, garni de ſes étoffes de baſin brodé, relevées en draperies, ornées de franges, avec Rideaux de croiſée & Siéges aſſortis.

Un Meuble de boudoir en pou de ſoie bleu-cendré, brodé en filet blanc.

Pluſieurs Secrétaires, Commodes, Tables, Encoignures & Toilettes en bois d'acajou & marqueterie, ornés de bronze, précieuſement ciſelés & dorés au mat.

Feux, Bras, Girandoles & Flambeaux de bronze, ciſelés, & dorés au mat, de deſſins du dernier goût, & des plus grands Maîtres.

Superbes Pendules de différentes formes, & du plus beau choix.

Un Meuble de Sallon complet, en velours vert, galonné en or à la Bourgogne, & Franges aſſorties, les bois richement ſculptés & dorés, & d'un genre moderne.

Une Lanterne de ſallon, de forme ronde, de la plus agréable compoſition, en bronze doré au mat, avec mélanges de lapis, pierreries & perles.

Un Meuble complet de chambre à coucher, en pou de ſoie bleu, avec ornemens de cartiſane & franges gris & blancs.

Un Meuble de boudoir à bois doré, les étoffes en pou de ſoie violet, brodé en ſoie nuée, avec camées de ſatin blanc, brodés en ſujets agréables: ce meuble eſt complet, & n'a jamais été mis en place.

Un autre Meuble de boudoir en étoffe cannelée, brodé à rayûres, ſur bois doré, n'ayant pas ſervi.

Douze Chaiſes en Perſe fond lilas, avec pluſieurs pièces ou tapis de Perſe pour rideaux d'une ſalle à manger.

Tapis de pied d'Aubuſſon, de la ſavonnerie & moquette.

Une petite Tente de jardin en acajou, garnie dans l'intérieur en taffetas bleu, avec Tables & Siéges en acajou.

Aſſortimens de Porcelaines de Saxe & de Sèves, du plus beau choix.

Deux Cabinets en glaces pour mettre des porcelaines ou curioſités.

Toilettes montées à tapis de Perſe, & garnitures de laques & porcelaines.

Deux Billards en acajou, galonnés en or, garnis de leurs queues, maſſes & billes, & de porte-lumières en cuivre argenté.

On pourra voir, tous les matins des jours de la vente, les objets ci-deſſus énoncés, qui ſeront expoſés dans les ſalles ſervant de dépôt à la vente.

Il ſera également vendu, à enlever, un ſuperbe Jeu de bagues à la Chinoiſe, avec figures d'hommes & d'animaux, contenant de ſept à huit milliers de fer, belle couverture en plomb doré & ardoiſes.

Le tout ſera vendu au comptant.

CH. DELACROIX.

A PARIS, DE L'IMPRIMERIE NATIONALE.

113 and 114 Two posters advertising the sale of royal possessions, including porcelain, in 1793, following the execution of the King and Queen.

115 and 116 (opposite) Sèvres cups and saucers bearing Revolutionary emblems, including the cap of liberty. These pieces well illustrate that the Sèvres decorators found it difficult to abandon the aristocratic decorative styles of the *ancien régime*. See p. 149.

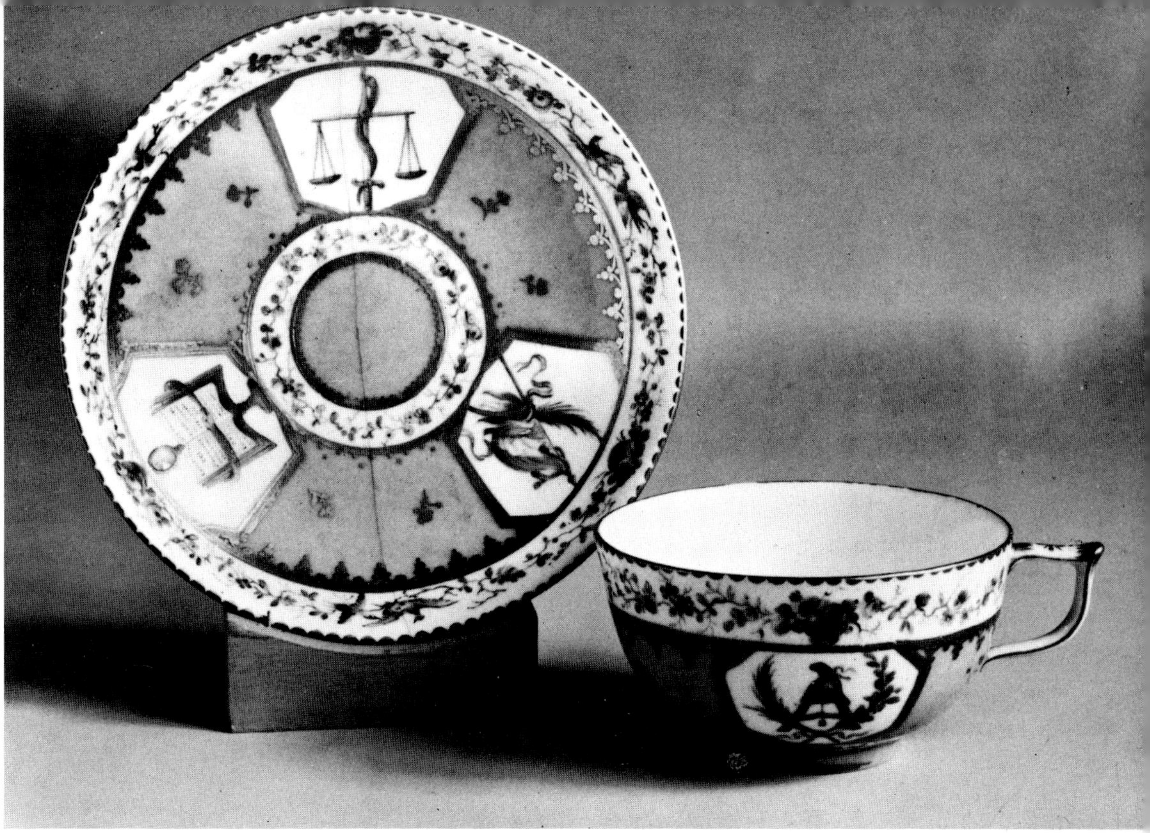

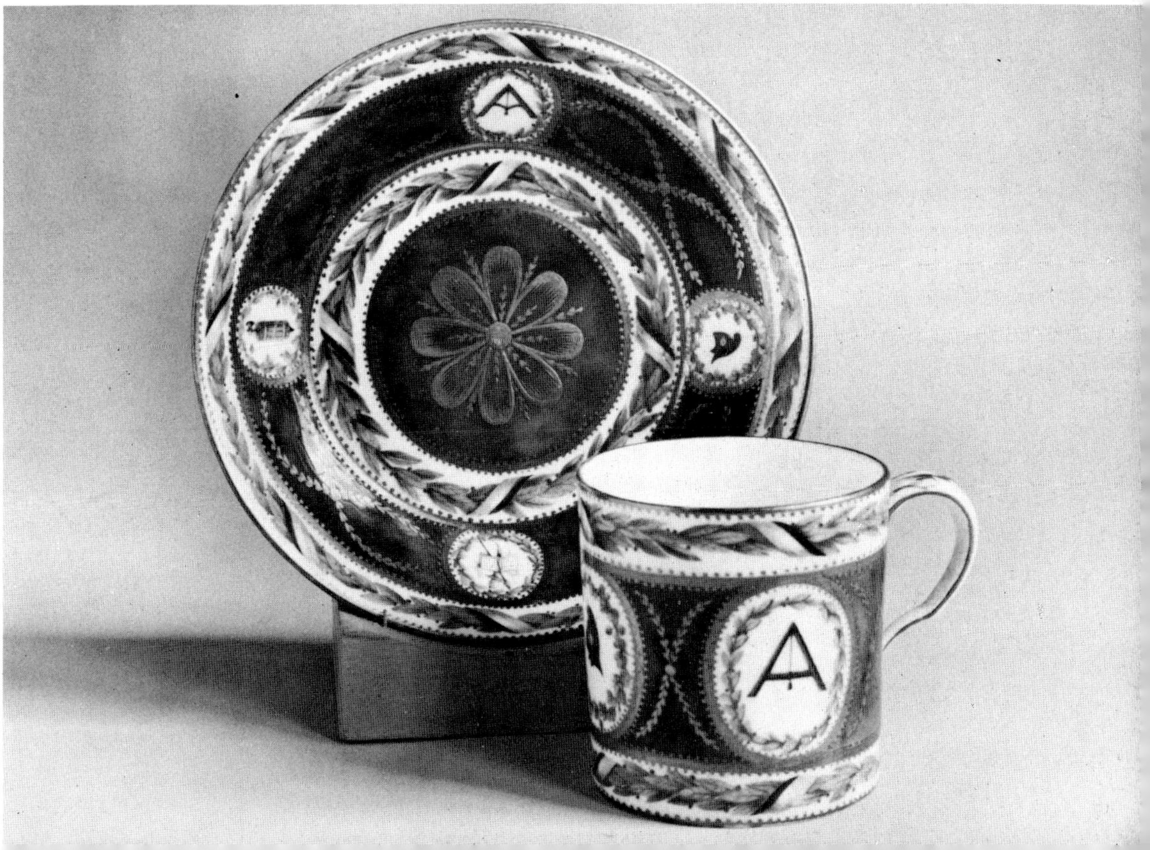

117 Lid of a pomade pot, Leeds creamware. Moulded in relief with a portrait of John Wilkes, with the cap of liberty. See p. 150.

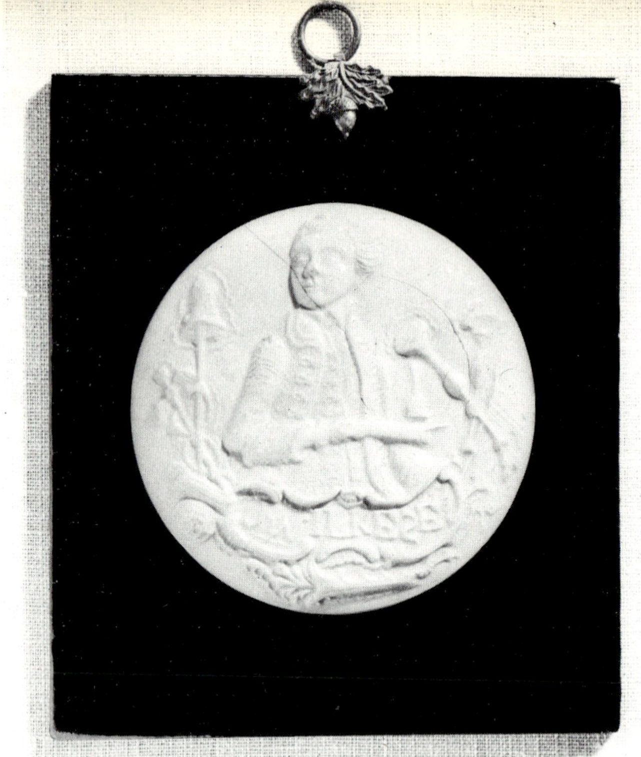

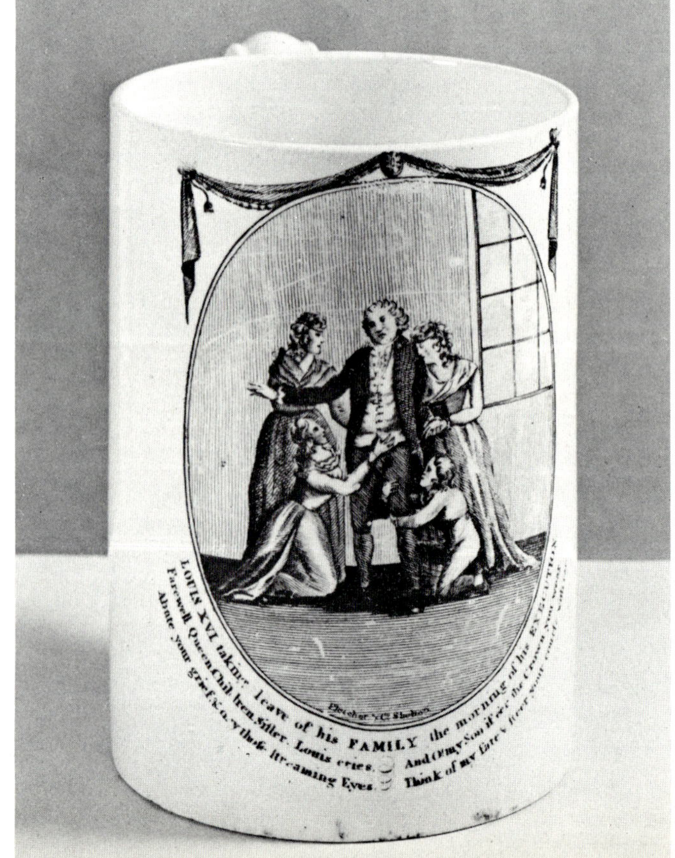

118 'Louis XVI taking leave of his family the morning of his execution'. Transfer design by Fletcher & Co. of Shelton, on a Staffordshire creamware mug of *c.* 1794. See p. 160.

which the electoral assemblies drew up in 1789. One bowl, which shows a peasant bowed down under a cross and a sword (i.e. the clergy and nobility) bears the menacing inscription 'Je suis las de les porter'. The *cahiers* to which potters contributed contained bitter complaints about the treaty of commerce with England. The *cahier* of the master potters of la Nièvre stated that 'Le traité d'Angleterre prive trente-deux mille cinq cents hommes de subsister que leur offraient les manufactures.'[18] French potters had indeed suffered greatly as a result of the treaty. By 1789, sixteen factories in Rouen had disappeared,[19] and 1,500 families were out of work.[20] It is not surprising, therefore, that we hear of potters among the leading revolutionaries. One of them, Ollivier of the Rue de la Roquette, Paris, incited his workmen 'in the most lurid and provocative terms'[21] to take part in the Réveillon Riots of April 1789, the first great popular outbreak of the Revolution.

Ollivier made faience plates decorated with the Phrygian cap surrounded by laurels and bearing the motto 'la liberté sans licence'. He was also a manufacturer of stoves, and the only known catalogue of these is in the Soane Museum, London – *Collection de dessins de poêles de forme antique et moderne, de l'invention & de la manufacture du sieur Ollivier* (Plates 106–8). Ollivier was the subject of a panegyric by Camille Desmoulins, in his *Révolutions de France et de Brabant*:

Espérons nous que bientôt on ne pourra pas plus vanter la supériorité des manufactures d'Angleterre sur celles de France que celle de sa constitution sur la nôtre. J'ai lu déjà qu'on était parvenu dans quelques-unes de nos manufactures à finir les ouvrages d'acier même aussi bien que les Anglais.

J'ignore les progrès de l'art dans leurs manufactures de fayences et de la porcelaine; mais j'ai peine à croire que la perfection en lui supposant les degrès, ait été porté aussi loin que dans la manufacture de M. Ollivier, rue de la Roquette, faubourg Saint-Antoine. En entrant dans les ateliers considérables de cet artiste précieux à la nation et à une multitude d'ouvriers qu'il fait subsister, il est impossible de ne pas rendre hommage aux talents avec lequel il a su convertir des poêles en meubles pleins de goût, et nous venger, par le peu de combustible qu'ils consument et la chaleur qu'ils répandent dans les apartements, de la cherté des marchands de bois....

Ce qui a fait de plaisir à tous les patriotes qui l'ont vu, est un poêle d'une forme absolument neuve, un poêle en forme de la Bastille. C'est exactement la Bastille avec ses huit tours, ces créneaux, ses portes, &c., coloriée au naturel avec des teintes tirées des minéraux & fixées au feu.

Sur la forteresse s'élève un canon, orné à la base des attributs de la liberté: bonnet, boulets, chaînes, coqs et bas-reliefs; les couleurs de la fonte, du cuivre, du marbre, de l'airan, y sont parfaitement imitées et inaltérables.

Les patriotes embrassent M. Ollivier, et les aristocrates eux-mêmes sont forcés de mêler des compliments à d'horribles grimaces. Ce poêle parfaitement a l'Assemblée nationale, dont il est tout à fait digne, si on ne craignait que les noirs et tout le cul-de-sac ne vinssent, dans quelques-uns de leurs accès de rage, chabler sur ce poêle-Bastille, comme le chantre et sa troupe sur le fameux lutrin.[22]

The stove was offered by Ollivier to the Convention, and was duly installed in the Manège. In April 1793 when this meeting-place was abandoned for the Tuileries, the stove, of embarrassing dimensions, was left behind. For a long time it stood in a garden, but was eventually rescued and placed in the Sèvres Museum. It is now preserved in the Musée Carnavalet (Plate 105).

The forces of reaction are also represented in ceramics. The English potters, in particular, had as much reason to be anti-Revolution as the French potters had to be for it. Men like Wedgwood welcomed the revolt of 1789. After the Fall of the Bastille – of which he made a medallion (Plates 103–4) – he wrote to Dr Erasmus Darwin: 'I know you will rejoice with me in the glorious revolution which has taken place in France. The politicians tell me that as a manufacturer I shall be ruined if France has her liberty, but I am willing to take my chance in that respect, nor do I yet see that the happiness of one nation includes in it the misery of its next neighbour.'[23] Wedgwood, with his command of the home market and of other foreign markets, could afford to be complacent; but even he must have been less enthusiastic when in the same month (July 1789) his son wrote to tell him that Messrs Verlingen & Son of Boulogne owed them £380 which they were unable to pay owing to 'the crisis that France & of consequence Commerce, suffers at present, the horrid misery which ravages all the provinces ...'.[24] To a much smaller firm such as that of William and John Turner, the loss of the French market and the non-payment of French debts were crippling. William Turner, who went over to France to collect debts, was imprisoned by the revolutionaries, and only released on the intervention of the English ambassador.[25] John Flight of Worcester, who wanted to go to France in November 1789, wrote to Lord Harcourt to ask whether it was safe. 'His Lordship wrote me a very friendly letter advising me by no means to go to France at present as I should run the risk of being stop'd within the Walls of Paris or perhaps something more disagreable. This determined me not to go.'[26] Popular subjects in England were Louis XVI saying farewell to his family (Plate 118) and Marat being assassinated (Plate IX). In the Lakin and Poole group, Marat is not shown in the *baignoire ensanglantée*, whether from ignorance, prudery or aesthetic preference.[27]

In France, too, reactionary faience was not unknown. When Noël de la Morinière, editor of the radical *Journal de Rouen*, was invited out to dinner with 'un des principaux et des plus pacifiques bourgeois de la ville', he was served food on *assiettes fleurdelisées*. He rose from the table and hurled the plates against the wall.[28] A graver crime against the nation was brought to light by the justice of the peace of the town of Tonnerre. On 27 February 1792, he wrote to the administrators of the department of la Nièvre:

> Messieurs, jeudy dernier, j'ay été prévenu qu'un marchand de fayence qui étaloit sur la foire, avoit entre autres marchandises un saladier dans le milieu duquel étoit écrit: *Vivent les émigrés françois*. Comme on en murmuroit, je m'y suis transporté avec mon huissier; j'ai en effet trouvé ce saladier que j'ai fait saisir et déposer au greffe de la justice.
>
> Ce particulier m'a dit qu'il avoit eu ce saladier à la fayencerie du sieur Petit, de votre ville, où il avoit chargé sa voiture; j'ai dressé procès-verbal de ce fait dont j'ai l'honneur de vous adresser la copie. Je crois devoir le faire pour que vous puissiez faire vérifier les pièces de fayence que l'on fait à cette manufacture, & faire saisir toutes celles qui peuvent être contraires au patriotisme dont tout bon François doit être animé.
>
> J'ai l'honneur d'être, & etc.[29]

The municipal body of Nevers, in its session of the following 5 March, decided that this 'crime exécrable', which could provoke the greatest of all evils, civil war, should be drawn to the attention of the justice of the peace of the section of Couchant, who should make the necessary enquiries and take the necessary steps. But there do not seem to have been any consequences, and it is presumed that Petit, who was proprietor of the manufactory of Bout-du-Monde, at Nevers, escaped. Indeed, the only victim of the guillotine associated with a faience factory seems to have been Count Adam Philibert de Custine, the owner of Niderviller, executed in 1793 for his shortcomings as a revolutionary general.

Another revolutionary general fared better. It is an historical cliché to call Napoleon 'the child of the Revolution'. To lessen the wonder of Napoleon, historians have shown how he inherited a new highly-organized State containing the ingredients of his system – the dictatorship based on the plebiscite. How, also, he took over the methods and motive forces of the revolutionary wars, conscription, moral fervour, the exaltation of an awakened people. How these advantages put him a century in advance of his European enemies, *anciens régimes* which did not dare to call their own peoples into partnership with them to defeat their enemy as this would be a surrender to Jacobinism. And to lessen the crime of Napoleon, they have considered that a dictatorship lay in the dialectic of events themselves; that if there had been no Napoleon, there would still have had to be a *coup d'état* as the logical conclusion of the revolutionary progress from an initial liberalism to a higher distillation of tyranny.

At Sèvres, there was a parallel working-out of the ideas of the Revolution. If the old soft-paste porcelain was 'trop délicate, trop princière, pour une république', if 'le style romain ... ne s'accommode à cette céramique délicate', the hard paste manufactured by Alexandre Brongniart, who was appointed sole director in 1800, was well suited to both. There were mass sackings of the old decorators. To an extraordinary extent, the factory was given over now to the glorification of Napoleon and to supplying his relatives with services of fabulous richness. A porcelain table painted in Etruscan style with 'Homer reciting his Poems to the Assembled Greeks' was sent by Napoleon to his sister Hortense, the Queen of Holland, in 1806. A *Table des Maréchaux* was commissioned by the emperor at a cost of 35,000 francs. For the decoration of this, the miniaturist Isabey – a pupil of David – was summoned to Sèvres to depict Napoleon surrounded, as if by an aureole, by thirteen golden rays, each bearing the name of one of his most glorious victories. Between the rays are thirteen medallions of eleven Marshals of the Empire and two Court dignitaries. The *Table des Maréchaux* was completed in 1810. Two years later, a *Table des Grands Capitaines de l'Antiquité* was finished. Napoleon resisted the temptation to have a cameo of himself placed beside those of Alexander, Caesar, Pompey, Hannibal and the rest.[30] At this time also, many services were given as diplomatic presents, such as the tortoise-shell ground service which Napoleon gave to Lord Malmesbury in 1802 after the Treaty of Amiens, or the 'Olympic' service sent to Russia in 1807. The most spectacular of all the services was the 'Egyptian Service' of 1811–12. The decoration and iconography were taken from sketches made on the spot by Denon during Napoleon's Egyptian campaign, published in his album *Voyage dans la Basse et Haute Egypte* (1802). The great biscuit centrepiece of temples was probably designed by the architect Jean-Baptiste Le Peyre, who, like Denon, was with Napoleon on the banks of the Nile.[31] As soon as it was completed, this service was offered by Napoleon to his divorced wife Josephine, as a consolation present. It was carried, in classical style, to the Château de Malmaison, on six litters, by twelve men. With an equally classical dignity, the empress rejected the present. Six years later it was given to the Duke of Wellington by Louis XVIII.

Châteaubriand, who found himself hating Caesar almost as much as he had hated the 'race of Brutus' (though he was himself a kind of vaudeville Bonaparte) wrote two passages which, while they do not directly relate to ceramics, seem perfectly to suggest the effect of the Revolution. One is the passage in which, musing on Napoleon's execution of the Duc d'Enghien (a direct descendant of the founder of the Chantilly porcelain factory), he describes the desolation of the *ancien régime* at Chantilly:

> That castle, those gardens, those fountains *that were silent neither by day nor by night*, what has become of them? Mutilated statues, lions with a claw or a jaw restored; trophies sculptured in a crumbling wall; coats of arms with faded fleurs-de-lis; foundations of razed turrets; some marble coursers above empty stables no longer enlivened by the neighing of the horse of Rocroi; beside a riding-school, a high unfinished gate: that is what is left of the memories of an heroic race.

The other passage is that in which he describes the room of his lover, Madame Récamier, the subject of David's most famous portrait. These words carry us beyond David and the classical beauty staring from her chaise-longue, beyond Ingres and the huge liquescent eyes of Mademoiselle Rivière, and into the highest Romantic:

> Pointed steeples pierced the sky and on the horizon one could see the hills of Sèvres. The dying sun gilded the picture and entered through the open windows. Madame Récamier was sitting at her piano; the Angelus was tolling; the sound of the bell, which seemed 'to mourn the dying day', *il giorno pianger che si muore*, mingled with the final notes of the Invocation of the Night from Steibelt's *Romeo and Juliet*. A few birds came and settled in the blinds; I was united with the silence and solitude in the distance, across the noise and tumult of a great city.

8 North America

The earliest record of a colonial potter is in a list of the burghers of 'Amsterdam, New Netherland' (later New York) in 1657: 'Dirck Claesen, Pot Baker.'[1] Joshua Tittery, from Newcastle-upon-Tyne, came over to Pennsylvania in 1683 as a glassmaker in the employ of the 'Society of Traders'; in his will he describes himself as a potter.[2] Gabriel Thomas, an English settler, states in his *Historical Account ... of Pensilvania* (1698) that 'great encouragements are given to tradesmen and others.... *Potters* have Sixteen Pence for an Earthen Pot which may be bought in *England* for Four Pence'.[3]

The first colonial potworks on any scale was that of Dr Daniel Coxe, set up at Burlington, New Jersey, in 1688. Coxe was physician to Charles II's queen and later to Queen Anne. He owned a vast tract of land in West New Jersey which carried with it the right to govern, and he was actually the Governor of West New Jersey from 1687 to 1692, although he never went to America. In the office of the Secretary of State at Trenton, New Jersey is an anciently recorded copy of an agreement by which Dr Coxe employed William Gill, 'potter servant' of Lambeth, as a workman at the Burlington Pottery.[4] From this document, signed by Coxe on 23 August 1688, it appears that his manager was John Dewilde, 'Citizen & Potter of London'. At a trial held in London in November 1693 to decide whether certain clay which was being shipped from London to Holland was fuller's earth or potter's clay, Henry deWilde, a London potter, testified that 'about five years since he shipt' some of this clay to 'Pennsylvania where his son had set up a Pot-house'.[5] This shipment would therefore have been made about 1688, the year in which we know John Dewilde set up Dr Coxe's pottery at Burlington. As we also know that John Dewilde called his own son

Henry, it seems very probable that he was the son of Henry deWilde, and that some Burlington ware was made with clay shipped from London to Philadelphia.[6]

Gill, who was to accompany Dewilde to West New Jersey, was to receive five pounds on signing the agreement, the payment of the passage for himself, his wife and children, and a salary of £40 a year. The pottery is mentioned by Coxe in an inventory of property offered for sale in the Jerseys (*c.* 1688), in the Rawlinson manuscripts at the Bodleian Library, Oxford:

> I have erected a pottery att Burlington for white and chiney ware, a greate quantity to ye value of 1200 li have been already made and vended in ye Country, neighbour Colonies and ye Islands of Barbadoes and Jamaica where they are in great request. I have two houses and kills with all necessary implements, diverse workmen, and other servants. Have expended thereon about 2000 li.[7]

In 1691 Coxe sold to the West New Jersey Society of London his entire interests in the Province, including a dwelling-house and 'pottery-house' with all the tools, for £9,000 sterling. It would be unwise to take literally Coxe's claim that 'chiney ware' was made at Burlington. It was a term loosely used at the time. John Dwight of Fulham (who must have moved in similar social circles to Coxe in London, and may well have known him) also claimed to have made porcelain, but his surviving wares are of stoneware, and probably that is what Coxe's factory made, though no documentary examples are known.

But of course the discovery of the porcelain secret was the ultimate aim of the American colonial potters. Porcelain from Europe or China was an extreme luxury. We are told that Madame du Bois, the châtelaine of Maple Grove, a house built in 1757 at Marlborough in Ulster County in the Province of New York, used the first complete dinner service of china in that neighbourhood, and that 'curious housewives from the country round about came journeying thither to gaze with interest on this unwonted piece of luxury'.[8] When the ladies of Plympton, Massachusetts, went to tea with each other in the 1760s, each carried her own tea-cup, saucer and spoon.[9] Before the Revolution, Chinese porcelain, such as the tea-cups from which William Penn is supposed to have drunk his oolong when he visited some of the substantial Friends of Philadelphia in the late seventeenth century,[10] had to be taken to England before being shipped to America, because of the East India Company's monopoly. The first Chinese porcelain to be imported into Boston came on the *Grand Turk*, whose master was Elias Hasket

Derby, a Salem man. Paul Revere, the silversmith (a participant in the Boston Tea Party), who had made a quantity of silver for Derby, was so delighted with the Chinese wares that he used them as models for a silver bowl to be presented to General Shepard 'for his Ability and Zeal in quelling Shay's Rebellion'.[11] Revere also copied Liverpool jugs bearing ship designs, in the 'Revere pitcher'[12] – a rare example of silver taking the lead from ceramics, rather than *vice-versa.*

The first serious, and possibly successful attempt to produce porcelain was made by Andrew Duché at Savannah, Georgia. Duché was born in Philadelphia, Pennsylvania, the son of Anthony Duché, a Huguenot potter. He married in 1731 and settled at New Windsor, South Carolina, in 1735. In July 1737 he was persuaded by Sir Roger Lacey, agent for the Colony of Georgia to the Cherokee Indians, to wait on General Oglethorpe at Savannah. As a result of that interview, he received a grant of £230 and moved to Savannah, where by 1738 he had established a successful earthenware factory.[13]

In March 1739 he made a proposal to the trustees of the colony, recorded in the diary of the Earl of Egmont, one of the trustees:

> Andrew Duche the Potters proposal, setting forth that he had found out the true manner of making porcelain or Chinaware, but needed money (over & above the encouragement formerly given him) to build conveniences and lay in a stock to enable him to make large quantities of it for exportation, which would greatly turn to the Credit and advantage of the Colony, & employ at least 100 poor people in the Town, & many more, if we should procure him a patent for the sole making of it in this Colony & exclusive of all others in any parts of his Majesties Dominions that are or may be annex'd to the Crown of Great Britain for the space of 15 years, wch he hopes will not be refused, as he is the first Man in Europe, Africa or America, that ever found the true material and manner of making porcelain or China ware....
>
> In answer to my Commission to send me over China Cups, he said they would have been ready to send by this opportunity had he been able to build a kiln for that purpose, but till then they cannot be made....[14]

Already we note the exaggeration and evasiveness which characterize all Duché's claims for his porcelain. On 27 June 1739, the trustees in London voted to lay out not more than £12 'in the purchase of a pestle and mortar, lead, smalt, and block tin', which Duché had asked should be sent to him.[15] And certainly Duché managed to impress General Oglethorpe, who on 29 December 1739 wrote to the trustees in London:

> Andrew Duche is the Potter at Savannah who goes on very well there is

North America

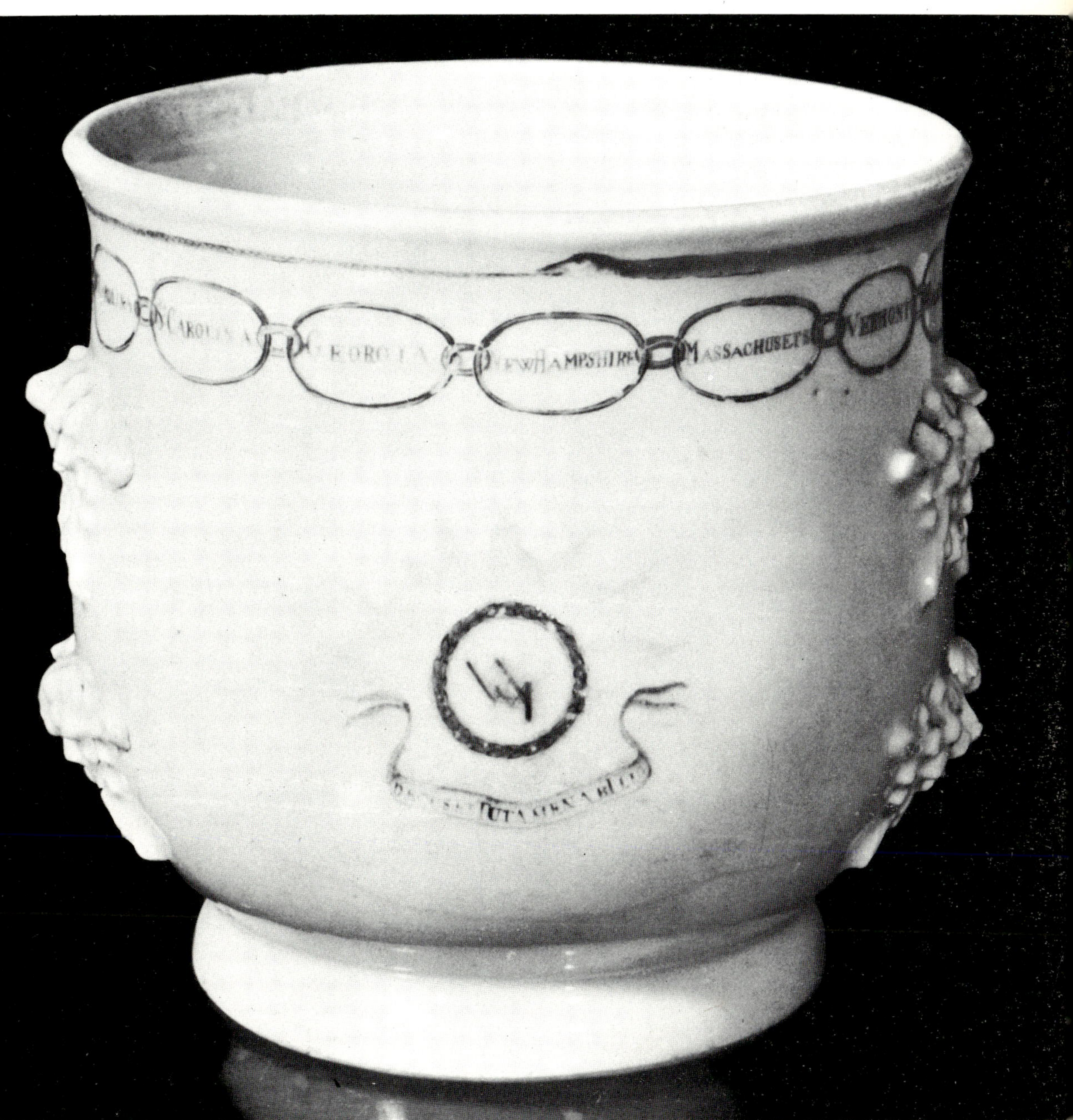

119 Chinese porcelain sugar bowl from a service presented to Mrs Washington, in 1796, by A. E. van Braam Houckgeest. See pp. 181–2.

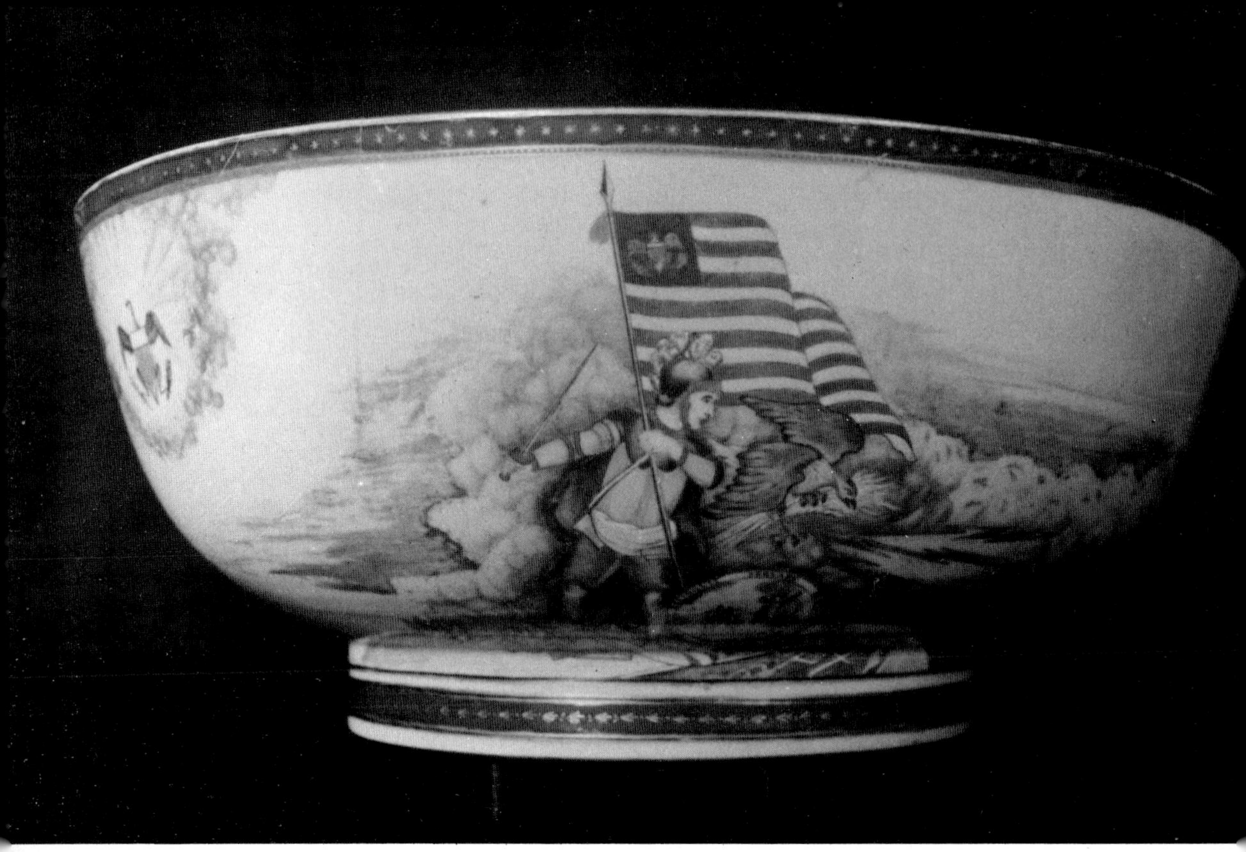

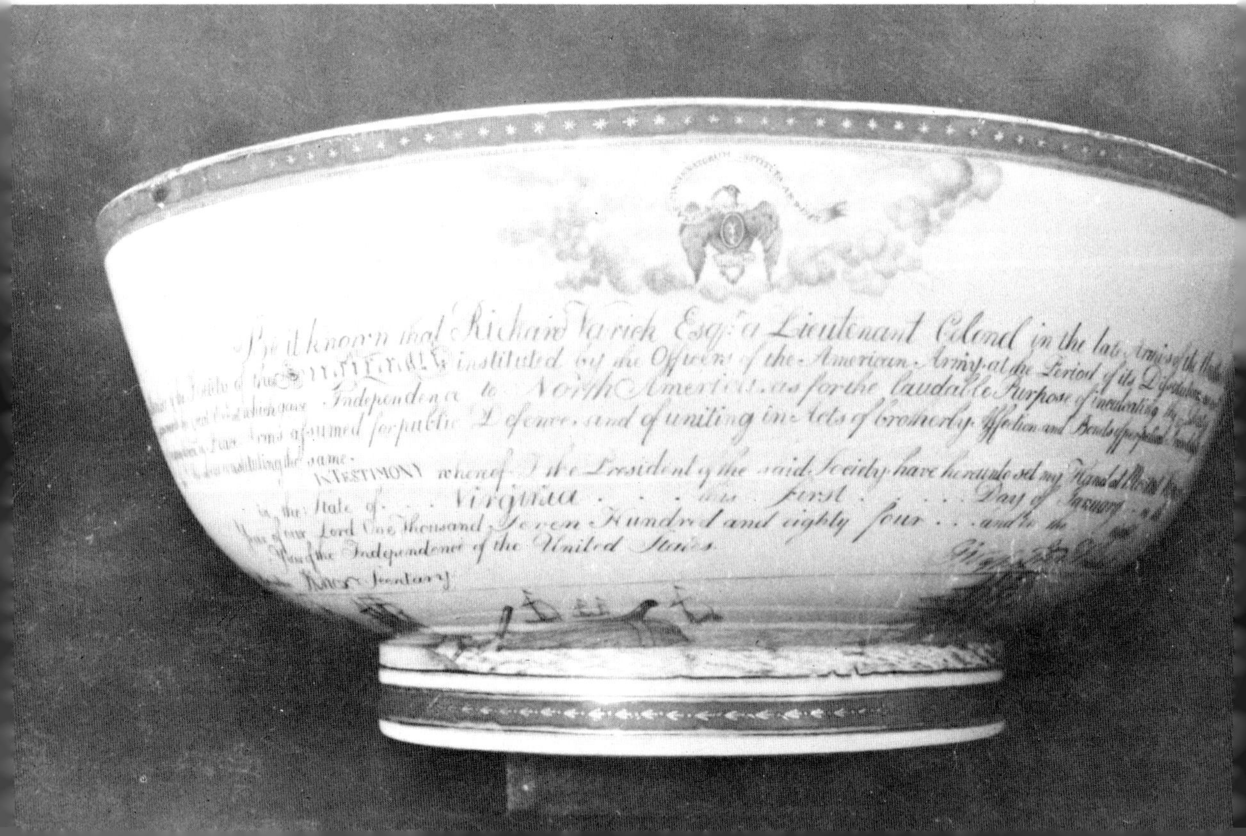

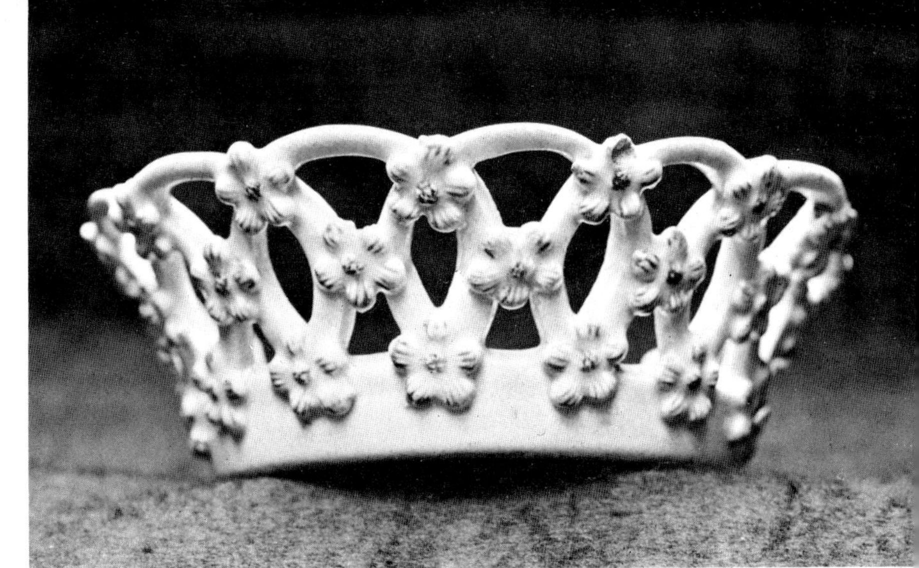

120 and 121 (opposite) Chinese porcelain punchbowl decorated for Lieutenant-Colonel Richard Varick. See p. 182.

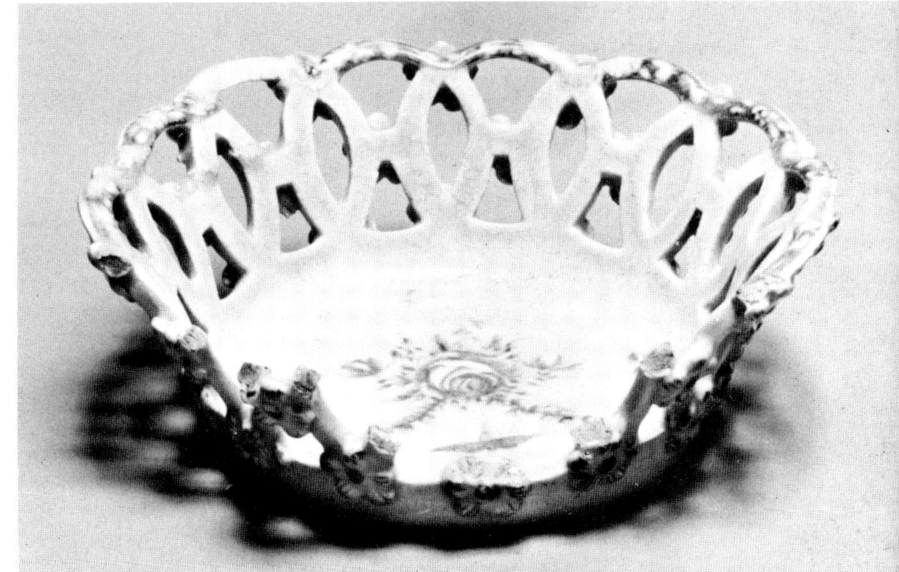

122 and 123 Porcelain fruit basket made by Bonnin and Morris at Philadelphia, 1771–2. See p. 178.

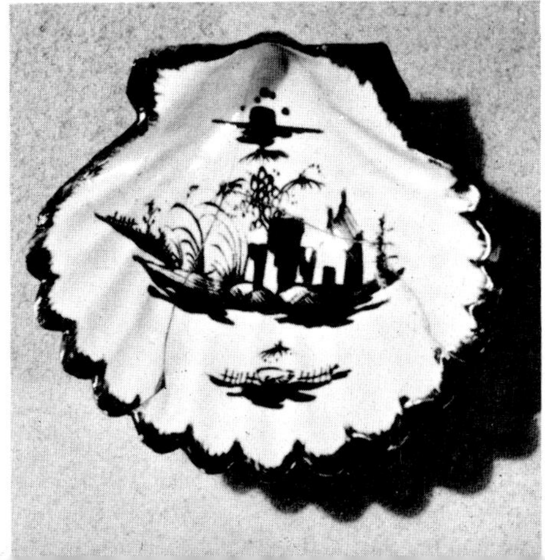

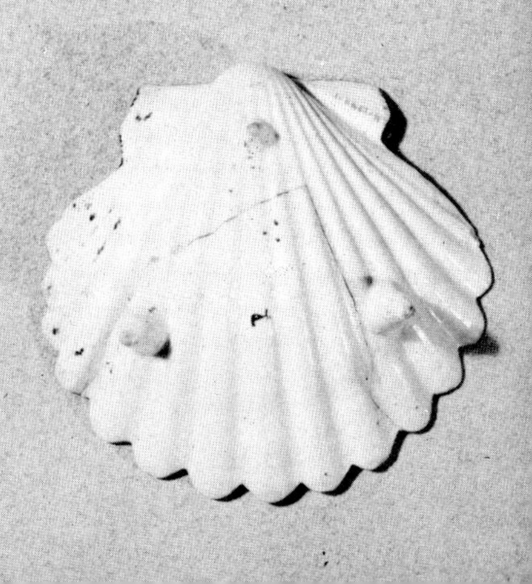

124 and 125 White porcelain salt, made by Bonnin and Morris at Philadelphia, 1771–2. From Walnford, New Jersey (built 1774), formerly the home of Richard Waln Meirs. See p. 179.

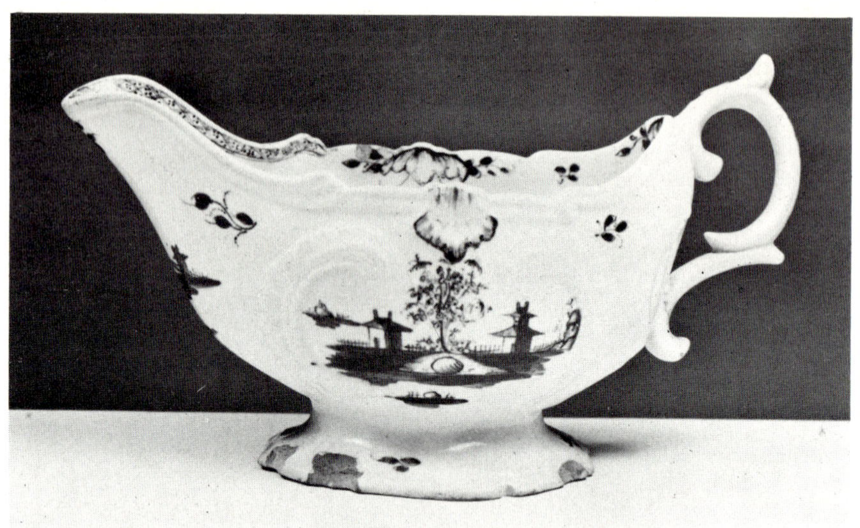

126 Porcelain sauceboat, decorated in underglaze blue, made by Bonnin and Morris at Philadelphia, 1771–2. Mark 'P' in pale blue. See p. 179.

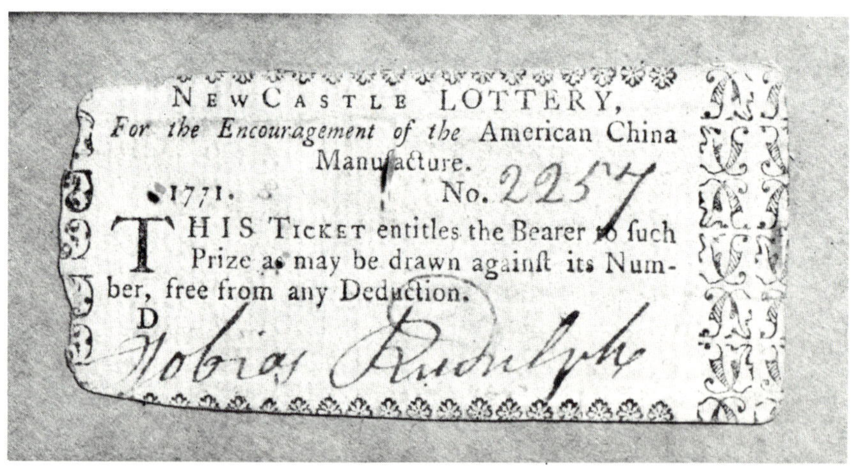

NewCastle LOTTERY,
For the Encouragement of the American China Manufacture.
1771. No. 2257
THIS TICKET entitles the Bearer to ſuch Prize as may be drawn againſt its Number, free from any Deduction.
D
Tobias Rudolph

127 Lottery ticket issued by Bonnin and Morris in 1771. See p. 178.

128 (opposite) Soft-paste porcelain vase made by Dr Henry Mead at New York in 1816. See p. 185.

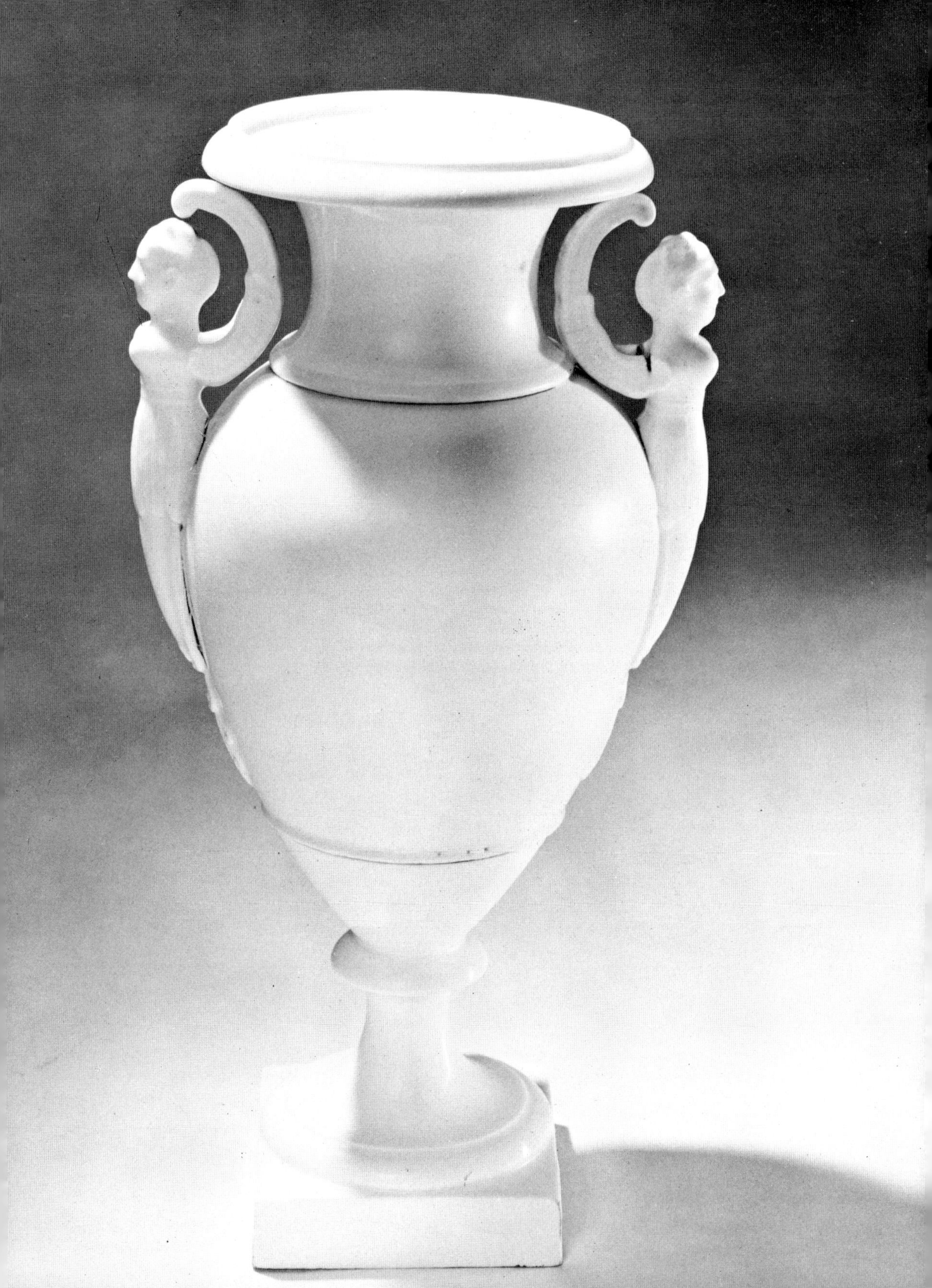

129 and 130 (right) The old waterworks, Philadelphia, at the north-west corner of Schuylkill Front (Twenty-third) and Chestnut Streets, which in 1825 housed Benjamin Tucker's 'American China Manufactory'. Later the factory was moved to the south-west corner of Schuylkill-Sixth (Seventeenth) and Chestnut Streets, and the trade-card (centre) was issued. See p. 185.

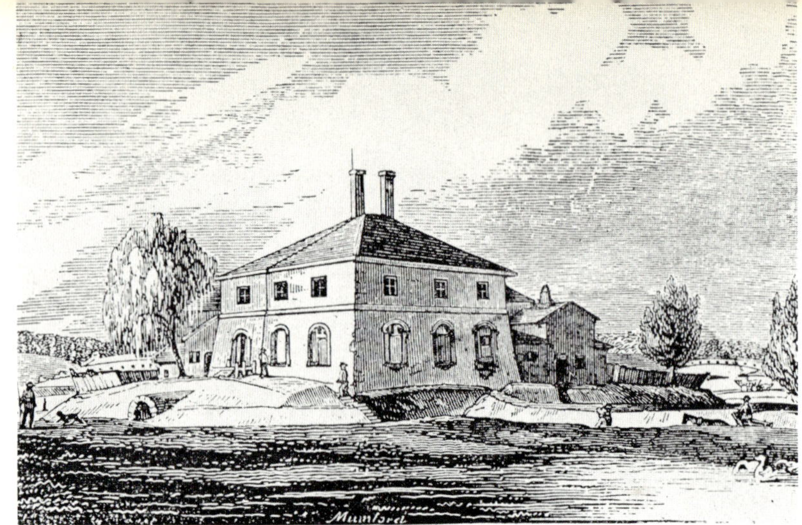

AMERICAN CHINA MANUFACTORY,

S. W. Corner of Schuylkill Sixth & Chesnut Sts.,

OR AT THE DEPOSITORY,

~~*No. 206 Chesnut Street, above Eighth Street,*~~

Where is constantly kept on hand, a superior assortment of CHINA, comprising DINNER SETS, TEA SETS, VASES, MANTEL ORNAMENTS, PITCHERS, FRUIT BASKETS, &c., &c., either plain or ornamented, and of the latest patterns, which may be purchased for Cash, at reduced prices.

ALSO ARE OFFERED FOR SALE,

FIRE-BRICK & TILE,

Of a superior quality, manufactured in part from the materials of which the China is composed.—These have been proved, by competent judges, to be equal to the best Stourbridge Brick.

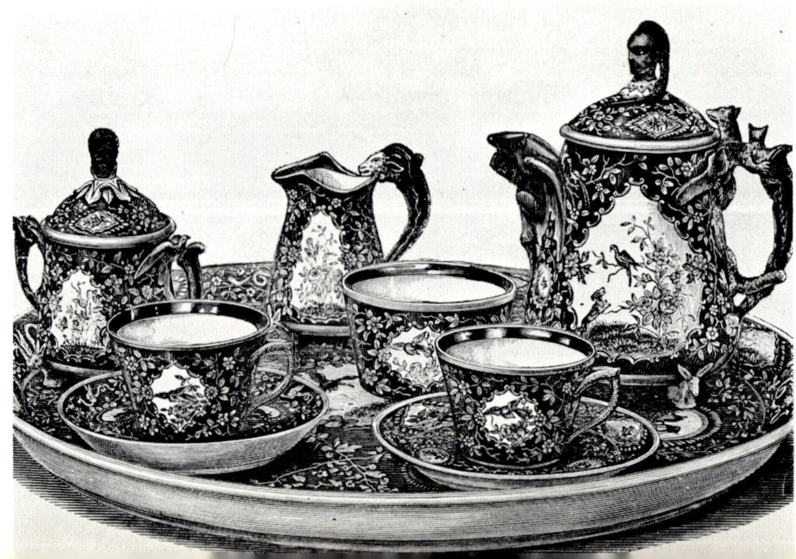

131 'Tête-à-tête' by the Union Porcelain Works, late nineteenth century. See p. 185.

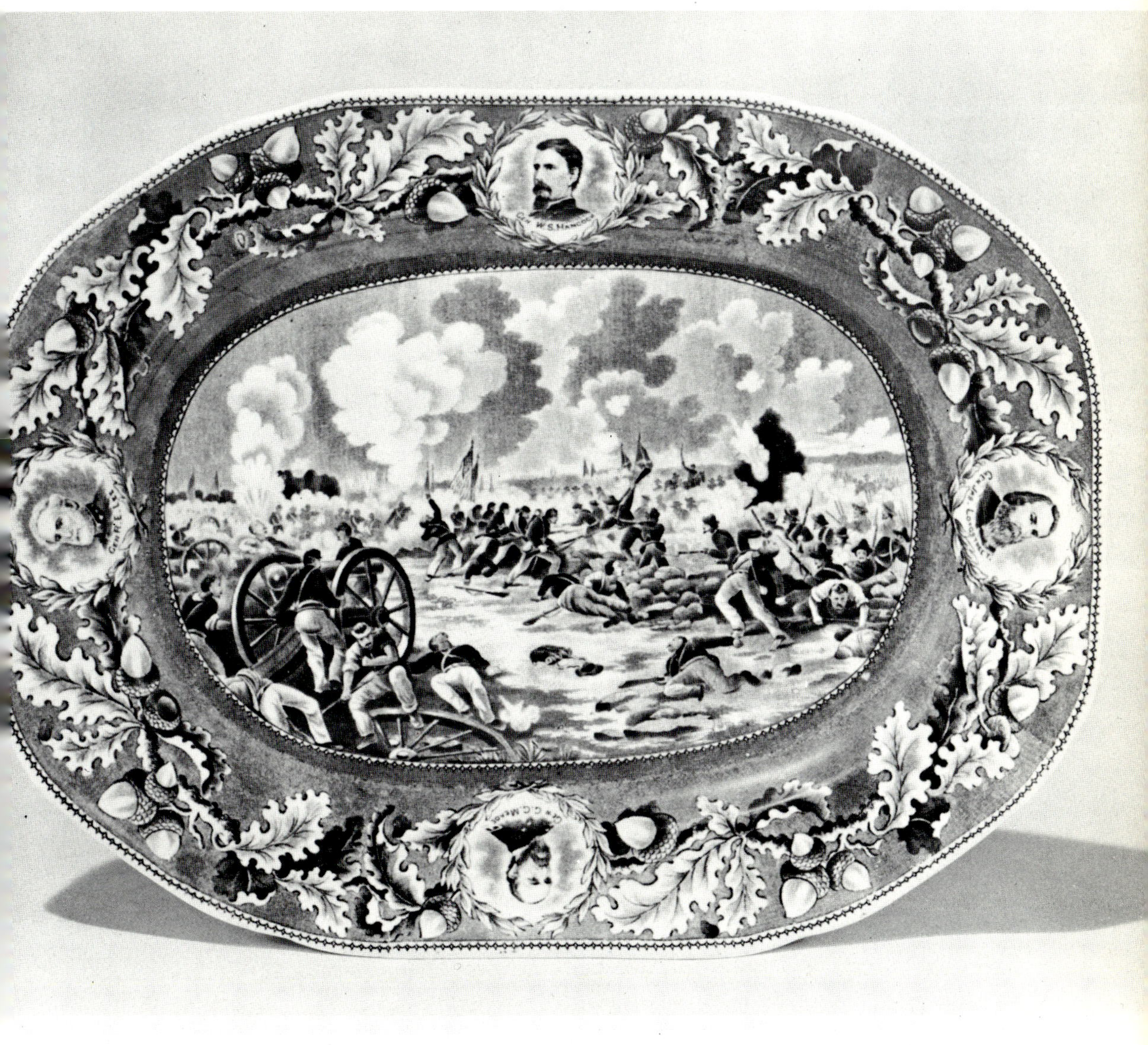

132 Pottery platter with blue transfer print of a scene from the American Civil War. Made by the Edwin Bennett Pottery Co., Baltimore, Maryland, *c.* 1901.

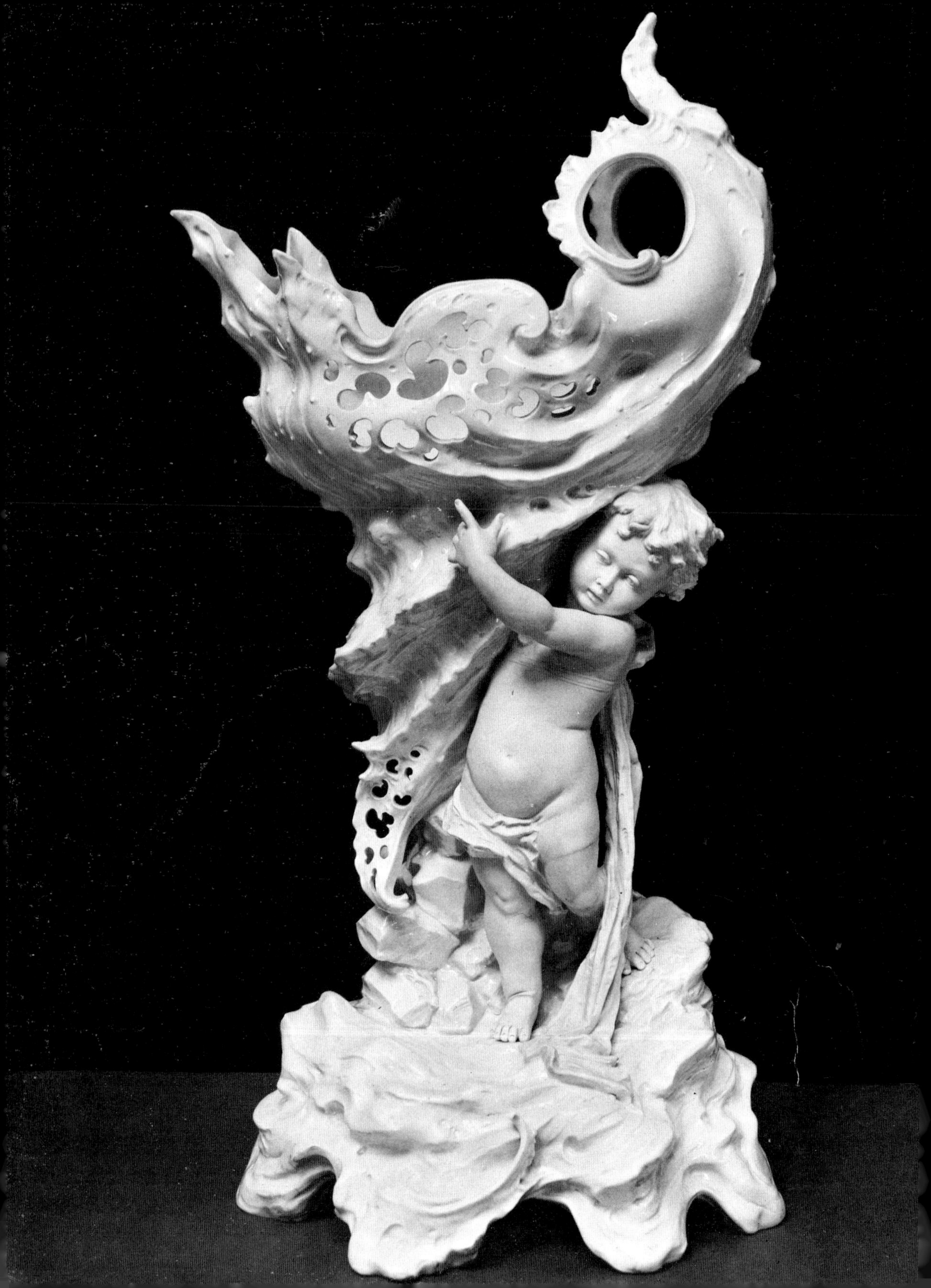

one of the most industrious in the Town & has made Several Experiments which seem to look like the making of China.[16]

William Stephens, secretary of the colony at Savannah, wrote in his diary on 17 June 1741:

> I took occasion to call on Mr Duchee to see some of his Rarities as I had before promised him; but it happened not to be at a right Season for his Kiln was now baking; and from what he told me, I understand all his fine Ware was baking a second time as it ought to be with proper glazing. But he shewed me a little Piece in the form of a Tea Cup with the Bottom broke out, which he said he had passed through one Baking and was yet rough; but upon holding it to the Light, as it was, without any Colouring on it, I thought it was as transparent as any ordinary strong china cups commonly are.[17]

On 29 July 1741, General Oglethorpe wrote to Stephens that Duché had 'come pretty near the Perfection proposed in his Work but is not yet arrived at that Hardness required', and recommended that the colony should make him a further grant of £50.[18] But Stephens was becoming more sceptical of Duché's claims. On 17 August 1741, he wrote in his journal:

> Mr Duchee resolving still to pursue his Intentions of going for England, as soon as he could with Convenience get some Part of his Ware ready to carry with him, to shew to the Trustees, thought fit to send to Mr Jones and me desiring we would come and be present at his forming some of his Clay into useful Cups, etc. We did so and sat by him, whilst he moulded two or three such, about the Size of large Tea-Cups, which were shaped not amiss, neither had either of us any Doubt of his being capable of that before; and they were white, as he also said, they would be transparent, when baked as they ought to be, in like Manner as he had shewn me one a while since that appeared to be so, and was to go through another Baking. But how far it may deserve the Name of Porcelaine, when all is done must be left to Proper Judges, for its present Appearance differs very little (if any Thing) from some of our finest Earthen-Ware made in *England*....[19]

One of Duché's confidants, the minister of the Saltzburger settlement at Ebenezer, near Savannah, recorded in his diary on 21 October 1741, that Duché 'has found out the art of making Chinese ware or porcelain, much cheaper than that brought from China, and yet in quality as good. He is taking many as samples with him to London ...'.[20]

Duché tried to leave Savannah for England in 1742, but was prevented by Colonel Stephens. But with General Oglethorpe's help, he did leave Savannah for Virginia in February 1743 and arrived in London in

133 (*opposite*) Porcelain *jardinière* in rococo revival style, made in West Virginia, 1892.

late May.[21] On 23 September he presented a memorial to the trustees in which he complained of the political treatment he had received in Savannah, but made no mention whatever of his having made porcelain.[22] A letter written at Savannah on 31 October 1744 refers to Duché as still being in England.[23] On 6 December 1744, Edward Heylyn of Bow, merchant, and Thomas Frye, an Irish painter and engraver, took out a patent for making a kind of porcelain with kaolinic clay, described by them in the specification filed on 5 April 1745, as 'an earth, the product of the Chirokee nation in America, called by the natives unaker'.[24] It is difficult to resist the conclusion that they had met Duché.

On 30 May 1745, William Cookworthy of Plymouth wrote to his friend Richard Hungsten, surgeon at Penryn:

> I had lately with me the person who has discovered the china earth. He had with him several samples of the china-ware which, I think, were equal to the Asiatic. Twas found on the back of Virginia, where he was in quest of mines; and having read Du Halde,[25] he discovered both the *Petunse* and *Kaolin*. It is this latter earth, which he says is essential to the success of the manufacture. He is going for a Cargo of it; having bought from the Indians the whole country where it rises. They can import it for £13 per ton; and by that means afford their china as cheap as common stoneware; but they intend only to go about 30 Per Cent under the company.[26] The man is a Quaker, by profession, but seems to be as thorough a Deist as I ever met with. He knows a good deal of mineral affairs but is not *funditus*.[27]

Probably, though not certainly, Cookworthy's unnamed visitor was Duché. There is a close parallel between Cookworthy's assessment of his visitor's religious persuasions – 'as thorough a Deist as I ever met with' – and the Earl of Egmont's description of Duché in his diary as 'a worse believer even than a Deist'.[28] Perhaps it is again Duché who is referred to in Robert Dossie's *Handmaid to the Arts* (1758) where it is stated that kaolin was:

> ... discovered in some mountains on the back of Carolina in great abundance; whither the proprietors of a work near London sent an agent to procure it for them: but he neglecting it for other pursuits, I believe no quantity has hitherto been brought from thence.[29]

There is a curious quirk of syntax which occurs both in Dossie's account and in Cookworthy's, which may or may not be significant. Dossie says the china clay was discovered 'on the back of Carolina'. Cookworthy says it was found 'on the back of Virginia'. It has been plausibly suggested that the London factory mentioned by Dossie was Bow. If

Duché's influence was behind the Heylyn and Frye patent of 1744, what more natural than that they should ask him to procure clay for them on his return to America?

Did Duché himself ever succeed in making porcelain on a commercial scale? It seems unlikely. If he had done, surely we would find more about it in the records and some of his productions would survive. Probably his wares never got beyond the experimental state; though, as he showed samples to Colonel Stephens and told the Saltzburger minister that he intended to take some to London, we cannot rule out the possibility that he showed such pieces to Cookworthy. It certainly seems probable that he would have shown them to Heylyn and Frye in 1744 to convince them of the efficacy of his porcelain recipe.

The earliest American porcelain in existence was made by Bonnin and Morris at Southwark, Philadelphia, between 1769 and 1772. Watson's *Annals of Philadelphia* (1898) states that 'the desire to encourage domestic fabrics gave rise, in 1771, to the erection of a flint-glass manufactory near Lancaster, by which they hoped to save £30,000 to the province. A china factory, too, was also erected on Prime Street, near the present Navy Yard, intended to make china at a saving of £15,000'.[30] In a footnote Watson adds: 'This long row of wooden houses afterwards became famous as a sailors' brothel and riot-house on a large scale. The former frail ware proved an abortive scheme.'[31]

In December 1769 a card or handbill notice was circulated in Philadelphia, then the largest and most important city of the colonies. In it, the proprietors of the new porcelain factory advertised for orders and workmen. The advertisement began:

> NEW CHINA-WARE. – Notwithstanding the various difficulties and disadvantages, which usually attend the introduction of any important manufacture into a new country, the Proprietors of the China Works, now erecting in Southwark, have the pleasure to acquaint the public, they have proved to a certainty, that the clays of America are productive of as good Porcelain, as any heretofore manufactured in Bow, near London, and imported into the colonies and plantations, which they will engage to sell upon very reasonable terms; and as they purpose going largely into this manufacture as soon as the works are completed, they request those persons who choose to favour them with commands, to be as early as possible....[32]

On 26 July 1770, the proprietors advertised for bones, offering twenty shillings a thousand 'for any quantity of horses or beeves shank-bones, whole or broken, fifteen shillings for hogs, and ten shillings for calves and sheep (a proportionable price for knuckle bones), delivered at the china factory in Southwark', and announced that the capital works of the factory were by now completed and in full operation.[33] On 30 October 1770, the *Philadelphia Staatbote* announced the arrival by ship from England of 'nine master workers for the porcelain factory of this city'.[34] The *Pennsylvania Journal* of 1 November 1770 shows that the ship on which they came was the *Pennsylvania Packet* from London.[35] On 10 January 1771, they advertised their first porcelain, and in the same month appealed to the Pennsylvania Assembly for financial assistance.[36] Apparently they obtained none, and in December 1771 a lottery for the benefit of the factory was scheduled to be drawn in New Castle County, Delaware. A ticket for this lottery is in the Brooklyn Museum (Plate 127). On 25 July 1771, Bonnin and Morris had advertised that they had now obtained some zaffre and could supply dealers with blue and white wares.[37]

The mention of Bow in the 1769 handbill; the use of bones in the porcelain formula and of zaffre for underglaze blue; the importing of skilled[38] workmen from London – all suggest a connection with the Bow factory.[39] This has been confirmed by an analysis, at the British Museum, of samples taken from documentary examples of the Southwark porcelain.[40]

The first of the documentary examples, all of which are marked with a 'P' (presumably for Philadelphia) is a fruit-basket of characteristic English design (Plates 122–3), now in the Philadelphia Museum of Art. It was formerly in the Franklin Institute, Philadelphia, having been deposited there in 1841 by Dr James Mease, author of *A Picture of Philadelphia* (1811), accompanied by the following letter:

Mr Gousey Bonnin of Antigua, came to Philadelphia before the American War, and his father having been a correspondent of my father's, they became intimate. What led him to the speculation, I never heard, but in an unfortunate hour, he resolved to undertake the manufacture of China the clay for which he procured from White-Clay-Creek in the State of Delaware, a few miles from the City of Wilmington, and with the aid of five hundred pounds loaned him by my father he erected a long frame building in Prime St southward, which I believe now leads from the navy yard west.

The workmen were doubtless procured from England, and China or Ware of quality of the broken Specimen was made, but to what extent I cannot say: However the news was soon conveyed to England that the manufacture had commenced, when speedily arrived cargoes of the English or Dutch Ware sufficient to supply the demand of the Colony or Colonies. Unable to withstand the competition with the manufacturers in Europe, Mr Bonnin ceased his labours.

The dinner set of his China was all that my father got for his £500.

The quality of it was about equal to the Delft ware of Holland of which much of the American table sets was composed, and which was first imported into England previously to being sent to this Country, the direct trade being prohibited.

February 22, 1841. James Mease.[41]

The basket is not, as Barber, Clement and other scholars have rather curiously suggested, of cream-ware, but of soft-paste porcelain, as are the other examples. Small samples taken from this broken basket have proved, on analysis at the British Museum, to be almost indistinguishable from the Bow paste, with its characteristic bone-ash content. Other examples are a sauce-boat in the Brooklyn Museum (Plate 126), again of typical English shape; a shell-shaped salt cellar (Plates 124–5) loaned to the Philadelphia Museum of Art by the family of Richard Waln, its original owner; a sweetmeat dish, also in the Brooklyn Museum, and a sauce-boat in the possession of Mrs George K. Stout.

Morris withdrew from the undertaking in 1771 and moved to North Carolina, where he died in 1773.[42] In April 1772, Bonnin was advertising for apprentices, and, soon afterwards, for 'fifty wagon loads of white flint stone'.[43] But in the same year the factory closed and the proprietors made a public appeal for charity on behalf of the workmen who had been brought to a foreign country and were left without means of support.[44] In 1774 the effects of the factory were sold, including 'a rolling press for copper plate printing'.[45]

The factory had some eminent clients. On 28 January 1772, Benjamin Franklin wrote from London to his wife in Philadelphia, thanking her for sauce-boats made there:

I thank you for the sauceboats and am pleased to find so good a Progress made in the China Manufactory. I wish it Success most heartily.[46]

A whole breakfast service was bought by Sir William Johnson of Albany, Superintendent of Indian Affairs. Recent excavations at Fort Johnson have uncovered shards of blue-and-white porcelain, and samples of these analysed at the British Museum show the same composition as the other Southwark pieces.

Porcelain was everywhere considered a luxury; but even pottery could be scarce. The Rev. James B. Finlay tells us in his *Autobiography* that in East Tennessee, wooden trays, trenchers and dressed boards were often used in place of dishes.[47] Brother Gottfried Aust began making his first glazed pottery at Bethabara, North Carolina, in 1756, and at a sale in June 1761 'people gathered from 50 and 60 miles away to buy pottery, but many came in vain, as the supply was exhausted by noon. We greatly regretted not being able to supply their needs,' wrote a Moravian diarist.[48] A year later people came from both Virginia and South Carolina to attend the sale.[49]

The demand for pottery was met in three ways: by the development of a folk-type pottery such as that made by the German Mennonites who settled in Pennsylvania; by the establishment of factories for Queen's-ware type pottery; and by importation from abroad, chiefly from England. Wedgwood, the main exporter, was alarmed by the resources that were waiting to be exploited by American potters, and by the emigration of English workmen. In 1765 he wrote to Sir William Meredith, following the emigration to South Carolina of a Staffordshire potter called Bartlem:

> The bulk of our particular manufactures are, you know, exported to foreign markets, for our home consumption is very trifling in comparison, to what is sent abroad; & the principle of these markets are the Continent & Islands of North America. To the Continent we send an amazing quantity of white stoneware & some of the finer kinds, but for the Islands we cannot make anything so rich and costly. This trade to our Colonies we are apprehensive of losing in a few years, as they have set on foot some Pottworks there already, and have at this time an agent amongst us hiring a number of our hands for establishing new Pottworks in South Carolina; having got one of our insolvent Master Potters there to conduct them. They have every material there, equal if not superior to our own, for carrying on that manufacture; and as the necessaries of life, and consequently the price of labour amongst us are daily advancing, it is highly probable that more will follow them, and join their brother artists and manufacturers of every Class, who are from all quarters taking a rapid flight indeed the same way![50]

These fears were groundless. Though the killing of American enterprises may not always have been so callously planned and directed as Dr Mease suggests the end of the Southwark factory was, English wares swamped the market. No American factory of any consideration was established before the Revolution – 'the present wicked and most preposterous war with our brethren and best friends', as Wedgwood called it.[51]

In 1784, two years after Great Britain recognized American Independence, a book was published by Gibbon's friend, Lord Sheffield, entitled *Observations on the Commerce of the American States*. One section was devoted to 'Porcelain and Earthen Ware':

The demand for this article has been great and will increase, except for the most gross kind. The importation has been and must be from Great Britain, on account both of the quality and price.

Attempts to manufacture this article were made at Philadelphia[52] and Boston,[53] but failed. The coarser kinds of earthen ware have been made formerly in Georgia,[54] and latterly in South Carolina[55]; but it is as easy to carry earthen ware from England, as from the Southern to the Northern States, and the high price of labour in America will give England the advantage. Flint, however, a very necessary article for the manufacture of earthen ware of the better kind, is not to be found in any quantity in North America. East India china is sometimes cheaper in Holland than in England. America gets of the coarse kinds from St Croix; but the consumption of china in America is inconsiderable, in comparison to that of British earthen ware; and since the improvements of the latter, it decreases daily.[56]

So Lord Sheffield thought that political independence would make little difference in America's dependence on England for ceramics. It is true that English ceramics continued to be imported in great bulk, including an enormous quantity of blue printed wares made specially for the American market. But Independence did make some difference to American commerce in ceramics. Before the Revolution the American colonies had, naturally, been included in the British colonial system. They had sent goods to the West Indies, and received in payment credit on England, and with this credit had secured the necessary manufactures and supplies from the Old World. Independence, by placing them outside the colonial system, made it necessary for them to look elsewhere for the investment of their commercial capital. But while Independence and withdrawal from the colonial system shut the door to the West Indies, it opened that to the East Indies. For nearly a century the East India Company had held a monopoly of British trade in the entire hemisphere from the Cape of Good Hope eastward to the Straits of Magellan. After the Treaty of Peace this, of course, ceased to be binding on the new nation. Chinese porcelain no longer had to be carried first to England and then reshipped, with all the incident duties and other charges.

The *Empress of China* which sailed from New York for Canton in February 1784 was the first American ship to engage legally in the direct China trade, although Captain Walter Sims – a retired sea-captain who bought 'China Hall', on the Delaware above Philadelphia, on the departure of Andreas Everardus van Braam Houckgeest for Holland, is said to have brought the first Chinese tableware direct from

China to America in 1772. By 1789 fifteen ships flying the American flag were trading with Canton. In 1788 Washington's 'Cincinnati' service arrived, a large dinner service presented by the Society of the Cincinnati to their former commander and first president. In 1796 van Braam Houckgeest landed in Philadelphia with a Chinese tea-set he had especially had made and decorated as a present for Mrs Washington. Some pieces of this set are still at the White House (Plate 119). The design has been twice copied in France, on French china: once for the Centennial in 1876, and once for the Chicago World's Fair in 1893.

> In the centre of each piece appears a medallion of gold bearing the monogram M.W. in square architectural lettering, encircled by a wreath of green leaves, beneath it on a flowing ribbon the motto: *Decus Et Tutamen Ab Illo.* From this central motif radiate the shafts of a sunburst which, terminating in fifteen points, lead the eye to the corresponding fifteen links of a circular chain, thus explaining the motto. In each of these links is the name of one of the fifteen states forming the Union in 1792. Around and about it all, toward the outer edge of the china, is a serpent painted in blue and gold, holding its tail in its mouth, a symbol of unity.[57]

In view of the Civil War, we may regard the serpent as a very appropriate symbol of unity.

As in England, punchbowls were ordered from China, and there are several handsome documentary examples. At some time before 1797, a Tally Ho punchbowl was presented to Captain Samuel Morris by the members of the old Gloucester Fox Hunting Club. The three-gallon Pennsylvania Hospital Punchbowl, decorated with a view of the building, was presented to the hospital by Joseph Saunders Lewis in April 1802, and is still preserved in Philadelphia. A bowl made for Colonel Richard Varick, of New Jersey, now preserved by the Washington Association of New Jersey, at Morristown, is decorated with a meticulous copy of the Colonel's certificate of membership of the Society of the Cincinnati (Plates 120–1). The whole interior of an eight-gallon punchbowl given to the Corporation of New York by General Jacob Morton in 1812 is decorated with a view of the city from Brooklyn, in full colour. An even larger bowl is in the possession of the 'State in Schuylkill', more commonly known in Philadelphia as the 'Fish House' – a social club established in 1732. In 1822 one of the members, Captain Charles Ross, a Philadelphia shipping merchant in the China Trade, gave the club this nine-gallon bowl, which he had had painted in China with swimming perch. La Fayette drank from it when he was the club's guest on 21 July 1825.

VII (*opposite*) 'A Tea Garden' (perhaps Bagnigge Wells). Engraving after George Morland by Mlle Rollet, late eighteenth century.

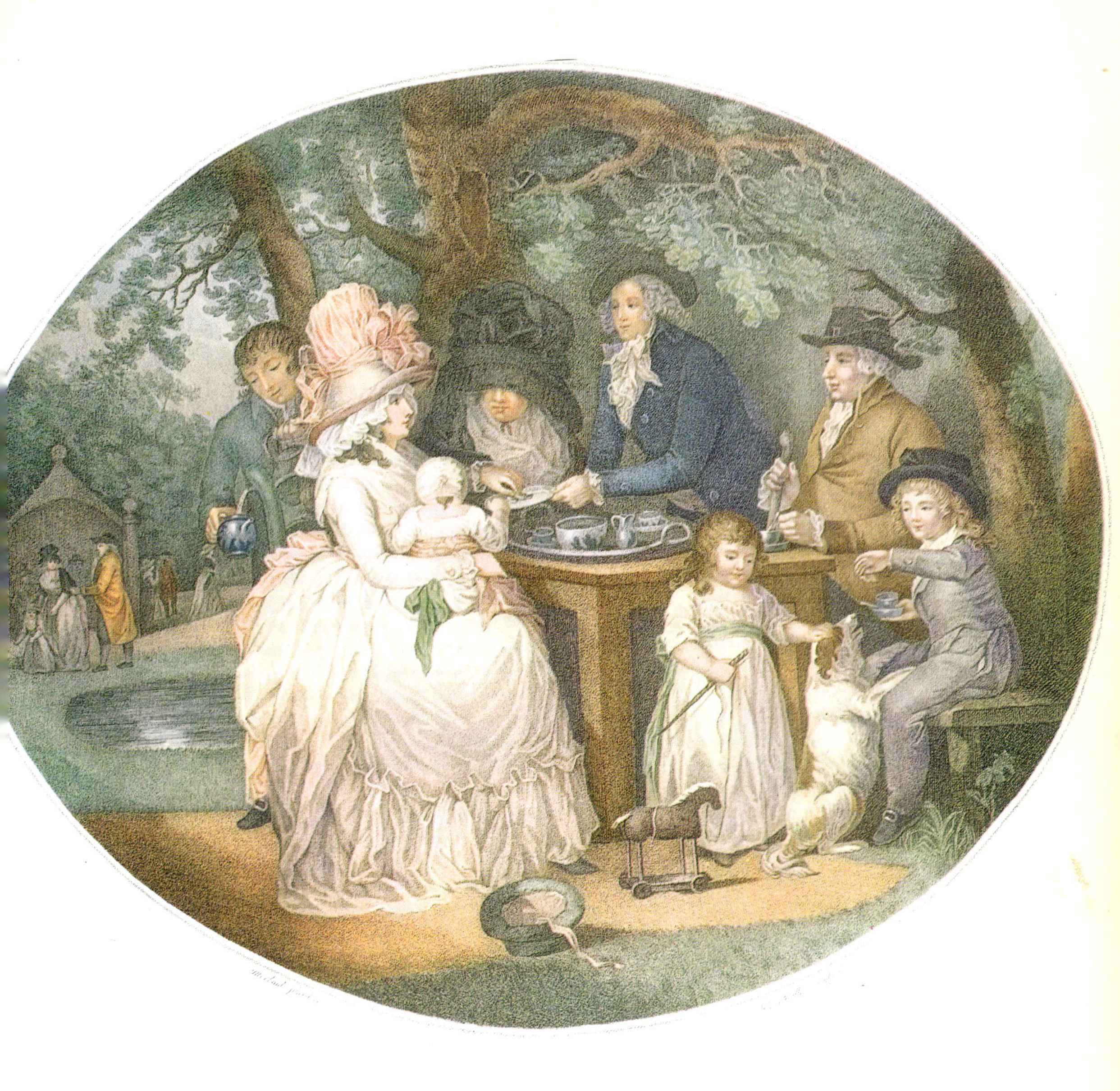

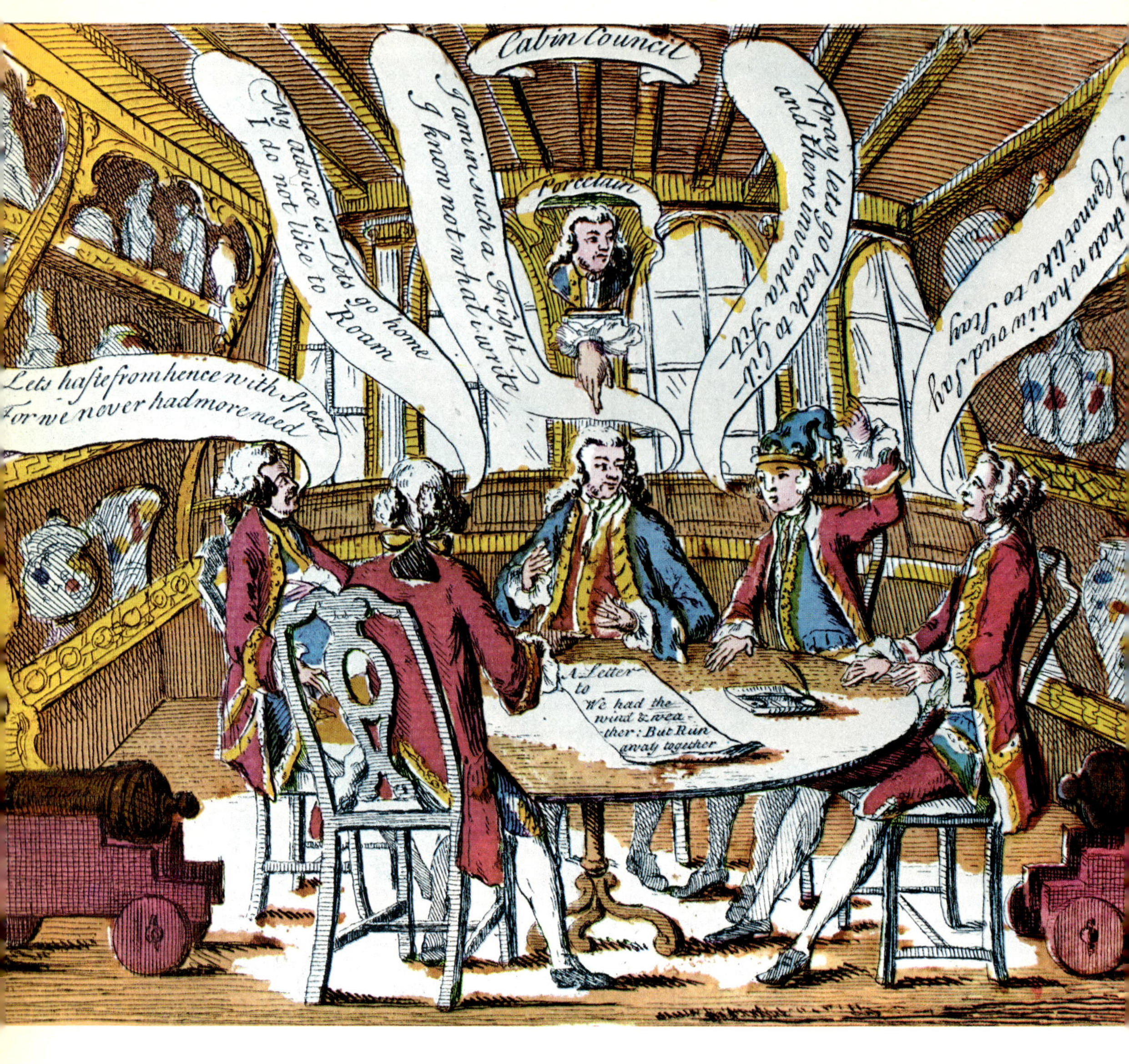
Cabin Council
Porcelain
Lets haste from hence with Speed
For we never had more need
My Advice is Lets go home
I do not like to Roam
I am in such a Fright
I know not what i write
Pray lets go back to Gib
and there invent a Fib
Cannot like to Stay
thats what i would say
A Letter to
We had the wind & wea-
ther: But Run
away together

The effects of the Revolution on the home industry tended to cancel each other out. The Revolution stimulated the American industry temporarily by removing English competition; but many skilled workmen returned to England on the outbreak of trouble, and some potteries went under in the general disruption of the time. With the recognition of American Independence, England made desperate efforts to recover the American market; but the American pottery industry was strengthened by Englishmen who had served under the British flag during the war and who remained there – many of them skilled artisans. Immigration after the peace brought over more expert potters.

It was not until the nineteenth century that any real expansion of the home industry was made. Dr Mead made porcelain in New York City, including a documentary vase (Plate 128) inscribed: 'Finished in New York in 1816.' William Ellis Tucker manufactured a hard-paste porcelain at the old water-works, Philadelphia (Plate 129): his wares were mostly inferior copies of English models. Later the factory was grandly renamed the American China Manufactory (Plate 130). Abraham Miller of the same city was the first to make silver lustre in America. The Ohio valley became the centre of the American ceramics industry following the establishment of potworks by Englishmen such as John Hancock (South Amboy, NJ, 1828), who had served an apprenticeship with Wedgwood's, and by James Bennett from Derbyshire (East Liverpool, 1839). By 1880, East Liverpool alone had twenty-three potteries firing a total of sixty-seven kilns.[58]

The quality of American ceramics was in general low, though an exception must be made for the spirited models of baseball players made by the sculptor Isaac Broome for Ott and Brewer of East Liverpool, or the exquisitely ugly but technically phenomenal 'tête-à-tête set' (Plate 131) made by the Union Porcelain Works at the end of the nineteenth century. There is various evidence that the American potteries could not compete with England in technique. In the Civil War, the Kaolin factory of South Carolina was the only one in the south producing white or porcelain wares,[59] and the Confederate Government had to order china from England, such as the table service used on board the warship *Alabama*, which was ordered from E. F. Bodley & Co., of Burslem.[60] George Ward Nichols, in a book published in 1878, *Pottery: How it is Made*, wrote:

> During the fiscal year ending in June, 1874, we imported of earthen, stone, China and glass-ware, $6,592,360. In the same year we did not export an

VIII (*opposite*) Admiral Byng in his cabin, surrounded by his porcelain collection. From a satirical broadsheet of 1756.

ounce of China ware, and of earthen and stoneware only $59,494, and of glass and glass-ware $631,827.[61]

In 1902, when the White House was restored and renovated under President Theodore Roosevelt,

> ... he determined that the china which was to be purchased then for the new state dining room must be a home product and for several months he swept the country from Maine to Texas and from Florida to California to find a pottery which was equipped to take the Executive order for a state dining set.... At that time it was simply out of the question. There were no American kilns producing china of the quality required.[62]

It was not until 1918 that the White House could get a satisfactory State dining service 'designed by an American artist, made from American clay at an American pottery, burned at American kilns and decorated by American workmen'.[63] But technical facilities were still not wholly satisfactory. George Cartlidge, the Staffordshire potter who had formerly modelled portaits of Great War leaders, wrote:

> In 1919 I was invited to go to America to model a ceramic portrait of the Candidate General Leonard Wood whom I interviewed in Chicago, then I modelled General Harding. I worked for a firm of Tile Manufacturers in Newport, Kentucky doing designs.... *I might add that the Ceramic Portraits I modelled in America had to be brought to England to be manufactured.*[64]

9 Marketing

Like the potter's wheel in the making of pots, the pedlar's basket, in selling them, was an instrument of primeval effectiveness which became rarer, though by no means obsolete, with the mass production of the Industrial Revolution. In an earlier period, the potter had sold his own wares – the travelling potter who appears in the legends of Hereward the Wake, Eustace the Monk, Robin Hood and William Wallace.[1] But by 1686, when Dr Plot wrote his *Natural History of Staffordshire*, the salesman was established in his own right:

> In 24 hours an *Oven* of *Pots* will be burnt, then they let the *fire* goe out by degrees which in 10 hours more will be perfectly done, and then they draw them for *Sale*, which is chiefly to the poor *Crate-men*, who carry them at their *backs* all over the *Countrey*, to whom they reckon them by the *piece*, i.e. *Quart*, in *hollow ware*, so that 6 pottle, or 3 gallon *bottles* make a *dozen*, and so more or less to a *dozen*, as they are of greater or lesser *content*; The *flat wares* are also reckon'd by *pieces* and *dozens*, but not (as the *hollow*) according to their *content*, but their different *bredths*.[2]

The Capodimonte figure of a porcelain-seller (Plate 136) modelled by Giuseppe Gricci, and the German pot-seller (Plate 135) both have loaded 'crates' on their backs.

The richer salesmen had horses and donkeys with panniers. When John Byng visited Lane End in the Staffordshire Potteries in 1792, he observed: 'Hundreds of horses and asses with paniers, are incessantly taking in their lading.'[3] A Cruikshank illustration of 1797 to G. M. Woodward's *Eccentric Excursions* (Plate 142) shows 'Itinerants Dealers in Staffordshire Ware' on the road to Lichfield, the donkeys loaded with panniers. One such dealer was the father of the eighteenth-century novelist and playwright Thomas Holcroft, who wrote in his autobiography:

> My father became, by turns, a collector and vender of rags, a hardwareman, a dealer in buckles, buttons, and pewter spoons; in short a trafficker in whatever could bring gain. But there was one thing which fixed his attention longer than any other, and which therefore, I suppose he found the most lucrative; which was, to fetch pottery from the neighbourhood of Stone, in Staffordshire, and to hawk it through the North of England. Of all other travelling, this was the most severe, and the most intolerable. Derbyshire, Cheshire, Leicestershire, Nottinghamshire, Warwickshire, the towns and cities of Birmingham, Walsall, Wolverhampton, Coventry, Derby, Burton-on-Trent, Litchfield [*sic*], Tamworth, Atherstone, Nuneaton, Lutterworth, Ashby-de-la-Zouch, nay, as far up as Warwick, Stratford-upon-Avon, Daventry, Northampton, Newport-Pagnell, Banbury (I well remember its delicious cakes); and on the east, Stamford in Lincolnshire, Grantham and in short every place within possible reach, or where pottery might be sold, received visits from my father, the asses, and poor me.[4]

Under the direction of a brutal father, Holcroft did much of the work. When he wrote of his hard childhood, he threw off the sententiousness of his literary *persona* and recalled, with realism, the rigours of life as a travelling salesman:

> One day, my ass had passed safely through the clay ruts and deep roads, and under my guidance had begun to ascend a hill we had to cross on Cannock Heath on our way to Rugeley. The wind was very high; though while we were on low ground, I had never suspected its real force. But my apprehensions began to increase with our ascent, and when on the summit of the hill, nearly opposite to two clumps of trees, which are pictured to my imagination as they stood there at that time, it blew gust after gust, too powerful for the loaded animal to resist, and down it came. Through life I have always had a strong sense of the grief and utter despair I then felt. But what a little surprises me is, that I have no recollection whatever of the means by which I found relief, but rather of the naked and desolate place in which I was, and my inability to help myself.[5]

The pot salesman had to be tough. Henry Wedgwood, in his *Romance of Staffordshire* (1879), wrote:

> Unless the pot pedlar was something at fisticuffs, or could take his own part in a scuffle, he was of very little use to this trade. The English have always been proud of boxing, and some of the packmen prided themselves on being able to beat all on the road.[6] Often the coming of these men to Burslem with their mules was looked forward to, as a pitched battle was sure

to take place between the champion potter and the champion pot-seller. Sometimes the packmen would look out for a professional boxer, and bring him with them to the Potteries, in order to make money by getting up a fight. The way that they proceeded was to allow the boxer to introduce himself disguised in some clownish way, and then cunningly get up a dispute with the potters, which would lead to a wager battle. One such battle was long remembered by our Burslem fathers, between one of these boxing pot-sellers and a potter named Unwin. It was fought on the level between Burslem and Hanley, which was oftener then called the 'ridge' than Cobridge. Of this battle Noah Heath[7] composed some verses in honour, although it was fought long before his time, and used to delight his publichouse comrades by their recital.

'How stouker Unwin beat the pedlar,
And made the packmen stare :
Until their looks were dull and flat,
As crazed and cracked ware.' [8]

Henry Wedgwood's stories have to be taken with a pinch of salt-glaze; he was not fastidious in separating truth from legend. One of the chapters which puts most strain on our credulity is that on Ned Saunterer. Ned began as a 'stouker', or handler, but 'Old Toft, who kept the works now held by Mr Pankhurst, and made black ware, used to say that Ned was born for a potseller, and not a potmaker'. Ned took the hint, and became a potseller in 1797:

But Saunterer in leaving a trade which his fathers had followed for generations, and who, father and son, had lived in one cottage to their remembrance a hundred and fifty years, could not do so without a little ceremony. Accordingly he got his tools together, bound them fast with a piece of twine, and after writing upon them his renunciation of the trade of stouker, buried them at the bottom of a coal shaft, adding at once as they went to the depth below his blessing and his curse. Ned went and lay the same afternoon as the burial took place under his favourite elm tree in the Hall Fields, and listened to his companion the throstle.[9]

He bought 'a few articles of the commonest character' from Toft, and with these began business. 'Every day, wet or fine, found him traversing the moors with his little stock of crockery. The greatest distance he went from home was Cheadle market, and with industry he soon got on from a small hawker's basket till he was able to buy a donkey.' He fastened a chain on the donkey's leg whenever he travelled at night, 'and this giving a strange unearthly sound, was likely to work on the superstition of anyone who might have been prowling about'. In addition, he fitted a pair of horns on the ass, to make it look like the Devil. And so effective was the disguise that when Saunterer, on his way home from Cheadle market, surprised two 'body-snatchers' at work, they rushed off in terror, leaving behind their horse and cart. 'From that night Saunterer's position was changed, he was master of a horse and cart as well as a donkey, for neither were ever claimed or enquired about.'[10]

An anecdote from the first edition of *Joe Miller's Jests* (1739), by John Mottley, shows a potseller hoodwinked by superstition himself:

Three or four roguish Scholars walking out one Day from the University of *Oxford*, spied a poor Fellow near *Abingdon*, asleep in a Ditch, with an Ass by him, loaded with Earthen-Ware, holding the Bridle in his Hand, says one of the Scholars to the rest, if you'll assist me, I'll help you to a little Money, for you know we are bare at present; no doubt of it they were not long consenting; why then, said he, we'll go and sell this old Fellow's Ass at *Abingdon*, for you know the Fair is To-morrow, and we shall meet with Chapmen enough; therefore do you take the Panniers off, and put them upon my Back, and the Bridle over my Head, and then lead you the Ass to Market, and let me alone with the Old Man. This being done accordingly, in a little Time after the poor Man awaking, was strangely surprized to see his Ass thus metamorphosed; Oh! for God's-sake, said the Scholar, take this Bridle out of my Mouth, and this Load from my Back. Zoons, how came you there, reply'd the old Man, why, said he, my Father, who is a great Necromancer, upon an idle Thing I did to disoblige him, transformed me into an Ass, but now his Heart has relented, and I am come to my own Shape again, I beg you will let me go Home and thank him; by all Means, said the Crockrey Merchant, I don't desire to have any Thing to do with Conjuration, and so set the Scholar at Liberty, who went directly to his Comrades, that by this Time were making merry with the Money they had sold the Ass for: But the old Fellow was forced to go the next Day, to seek for a new one in the *Fair*, and after having look'd on several, his own ass was shewn him for a very good one, O, Ho! said he, *what have he and his Father quarrelled again already?* No, no, I'll have nothing to say to him.[11]

A certain amount of business was done by barter rather than direct sale. Jonathan Swift, in his *Directions to Servants* (1745), said in his 'Directions to the Waiting Maid':

Two accidents have happened to lessen the Comforts and Profits of your Employment: First, that execrable Custom got among Ladies, of trucking their old Cloaths for *China*.... I think there should be a general Confederacy of all the Servants in every Family, for the publick Good, to drive those *China* Hucksters from the Doors....[12]

Addison had satirized the same custom in *The Lover*:

The common way of purchasing such trifles, if I may believe my female informers, is by exchanging old suits of clothes for this brittle ware. The potters of China have, it seems, their factors at this distance, who retail out their several manufactures for cast clothes and superannuated garments. I have known an old petticoat metamorphosed into a punch-bowl, and a pair of breeches into a tea-pot. For this reason, my friend Tradewell in the city calls his great room, that is nobly furnished out with china, his wife's wardrobe.[13]

By the time Henry Mayhew wrote his *London Labour and the London Poor* (1851–62) barter had almost become the rule in the capital. 'Swop, sir,' he was told repeatedly, 'they all goes in swop.' He took the following statement from one of the 'crocks' (as the crockery and glass sellers were known):

A good tea-service we generally give for a left-off suit of clothes, hat and boots – they must all be in a decent condition to be worth that. We give a sugar-basin for an old coat, and a rummer for a pair of old wellington boots. For a glass milk-jug I should expect a waistcoat and trowsers, and they must be tidy ones too. But there's nothing so saleable as a pair of old boots to us. There is always a market for old boots, when there is not for old clothes. You can any day get a dinner out of old wellingtons; but as for coats and waistcoats – there's a fashion about them, and what pleases one don't another. ... The mistresses of the houses are she-dragons. They wants a whole dinner *chany* service for their husband's rags. As for plates and dishes, they think they can be had for picking up. Many a time they sells their husband's things unbeknown to 'em, and often the gentleman of the house coming up to the door, and seeing us make a deal – for his trowsers maybe – puts a stop to the whole transaction.[14]

A man who went out with a 15*s*. basket of crockery might come back with 1*s*. in his pocket and a huge bundle of old clothes, which he would then convert into cash at the Clothes Exchange in Houndsditch.

The country pedlar, too, did not die out. In 1785 the Staffordshire potters collectively resisted the Government's proposal to abolish pedlars and hawkers. John Burr's painting of 1865 (Plate x) shows a pedlar at the door with general wares. The woman at the cottage entrance is inspecting a porcelain teapot; a flower-vase of characteristic mid-Victorian type stands on the ground by the basket; and we may also note the blue-printed pottery jug with a broken handle standing beside the flowerpot on the stool.

But of course not all ceramics were sold in this way. The *haut ton* would scarcely expect to choose their ornaments, their *blanc de chine* and

Meissen, from a hawker's basket. They patronized the fashionable shops. In eighteenth-century Paris, these were to be found in the rues Saint-Honoré, du Roule, de la Monnaie, de l'Arbre-Sec and the neighbouring streets. It was to this quarter that *les élégantes* came to visit the shop of the *Chagrin de Turquie*, there that the dealers Hébert, Bazin, Bailly, Lebrun, Vigier, Dulac, Poirier, Lhéritier, had their shops. The royal depot of Sèvres porcelain was in the rue de la Monnaie. Thomas-Joachim Hébert, in the rue Saint-Honoré, gave his name to a kind of vase: at Sèvres they spoke of 'la forme Hébert', as they spoke of 'la forme Calabre' and 'la forme du Roi'. The hero of Godard d'Ancour's novel *Thémidore* (1748) says:

> Je n'ose regarder la porte d'*Hébert*; il me vend toujours mille choses malgré moi, il en ruine bien d'autres en bagatelles. Il fait en France ce que les Français font à l'Amérique; il donne des colfichets pour des lingots d'or.[15]

The hero of *Thémidore* was the kind of customer on whom dealers do not look too kindly:

> Nous passâmes chez la belle Bijoutière de la rue Saint-Honoré, d'où, après avoir examiné, critiqué, contrôlé, marchandé mille choses différentes, nous sortîmes, sans en emporter une seule.[16]

It was to such shops that the hero of Baret's *Le Grelot* (1754) was taken for his first lesson in social *savoir faire*. Evidently they were fashionable meeting places; but those who did bring away pieces of china made full use of them as status symbols, as a passage in a novel of 1746, *Angola*, by Jacques Rochette de la Morlière, suggests:

> Parbleu, dit le Marquis, vous avez là une garniture de cheminée superbe; ces cabinets de la Chine sont charmans; est-ce *de la rue du Roule?* Pour moi, je suis fol de cet homme-là; tout ce qu'il vend est d'une cherté & d'un rare ... Mais oui, dit la Comtesse, cela est assez bien choisi.[17]

Another celebrated dealer was E. F. Gersaint. His friend Watteau (who died in his arms) designed him a famous signboard, and his friend Boucher designed him a *chinoiserie* trade-card:

> A LA PAGODE, Gersaint, marchand jouaillier sur le pont Nôtre-Dame, vend toute sorte de clainquaillerie nouvelle & de goût, bijoux, glaces, tableaux de cabinet, pagodes, vernis & porcelaines du Japon....[18]

Gersaint helped to form, and later sold, some of the most famous porcelain collections of his day – those of Antoine de la Roque, the Vicomte

Marketing

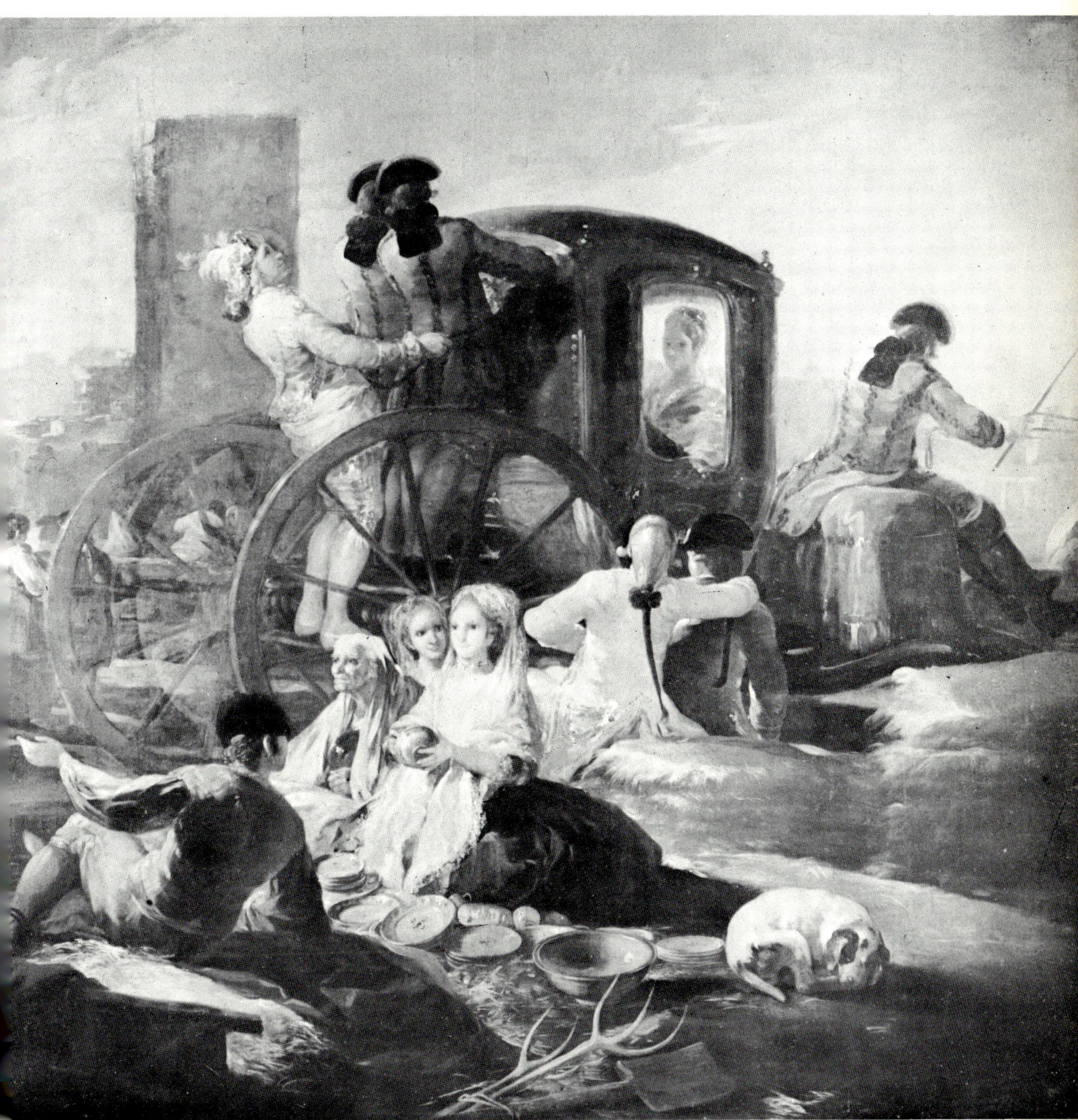

134 Goya, 'El Cacharrero' (the Pot Seller). Cartoon for tapestry, 1778. See p. 207.

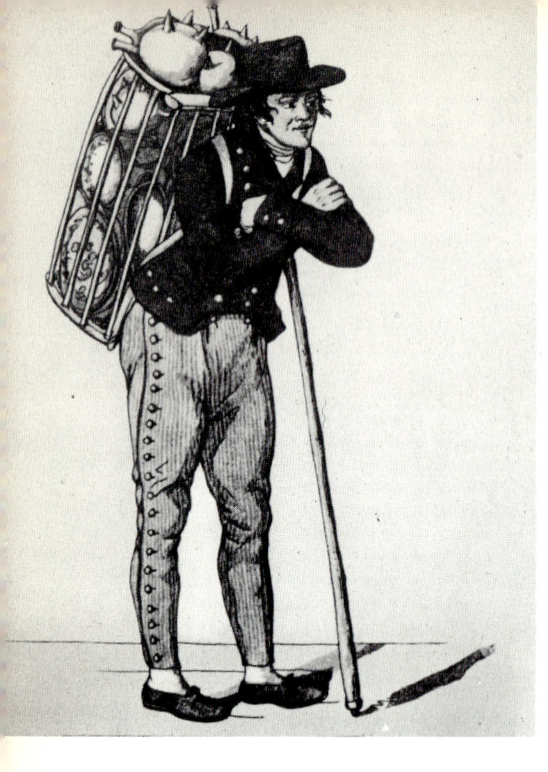

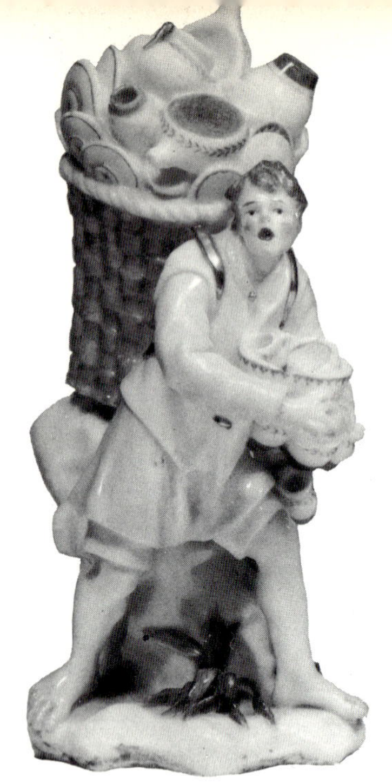

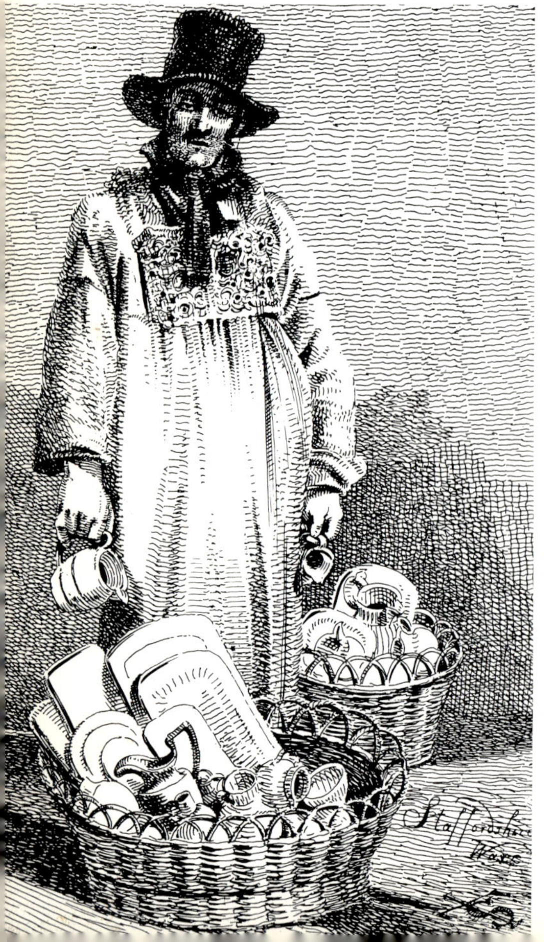
Ware

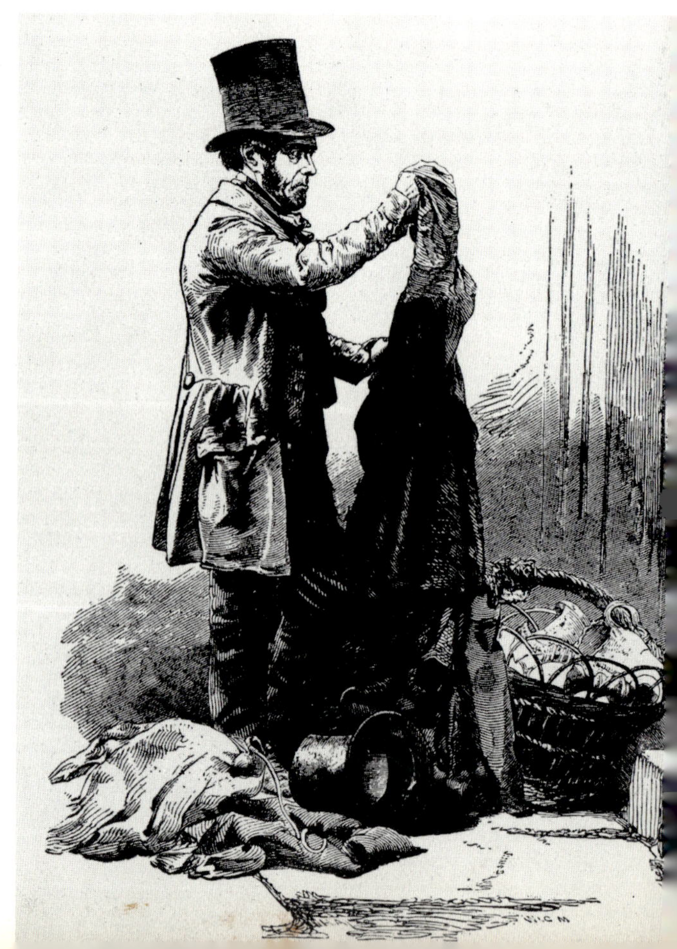

135–38 (opposite, top left) Pedlar of Dresden wares, early nineteenth century; (top right) Capodimonte porcelain figure of a porcelain seller modelled by Giuseppe Gricci, height $8\frac{1}{4}''$; (bottom left) pedlar of Staffordshire wares, late eighteenth century, engraved by Thomas Smith; (bottom right) Mayhew's street-seller of crockery ware, a London figure of the 1860s.

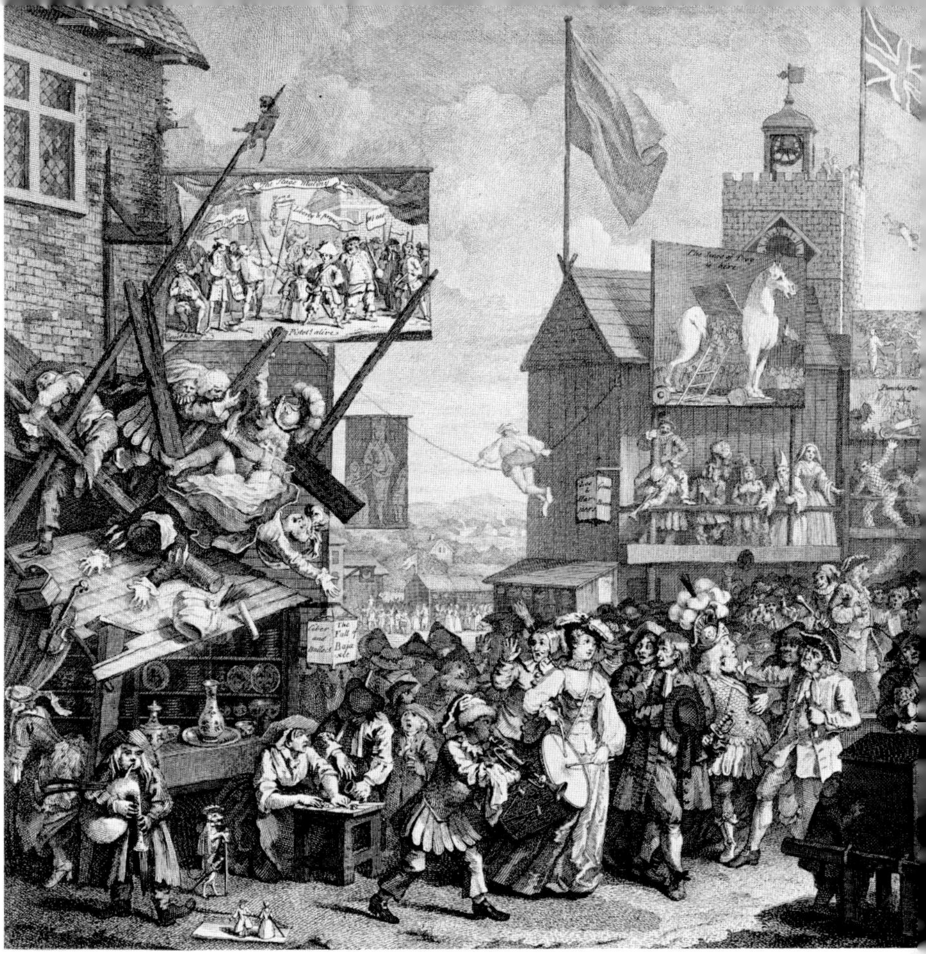

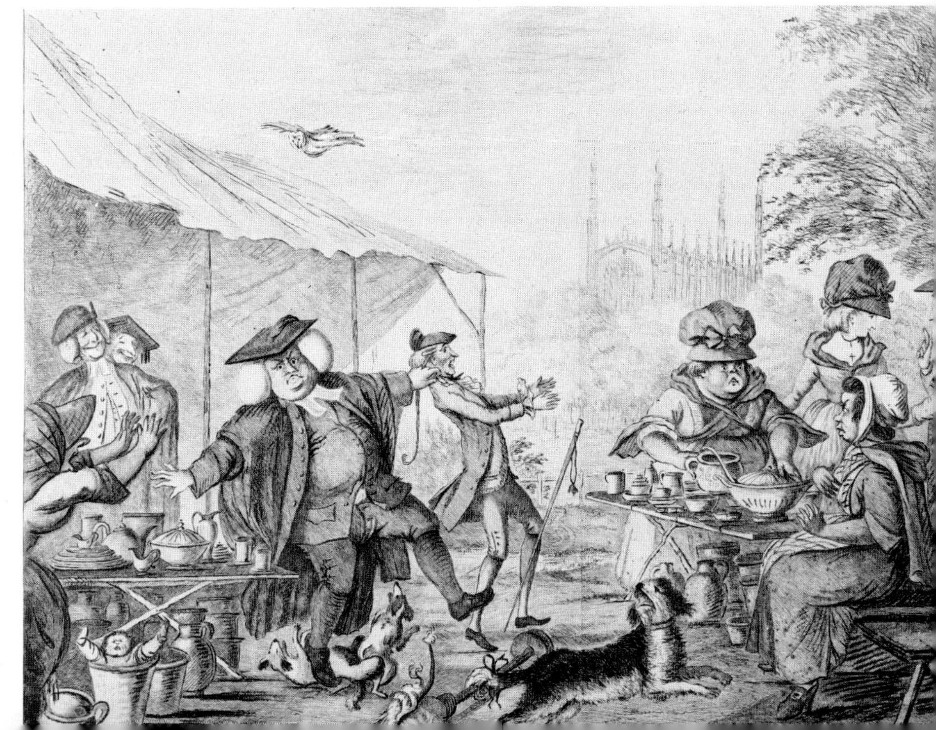

139 (top) 'Bartholomew Fair', a Hogarth engraving. The buskers are collapsing on top of a crockery stall.
140 'Pot Fair, Cambridge', an etching by Bretherton after Bunbury, 1777.

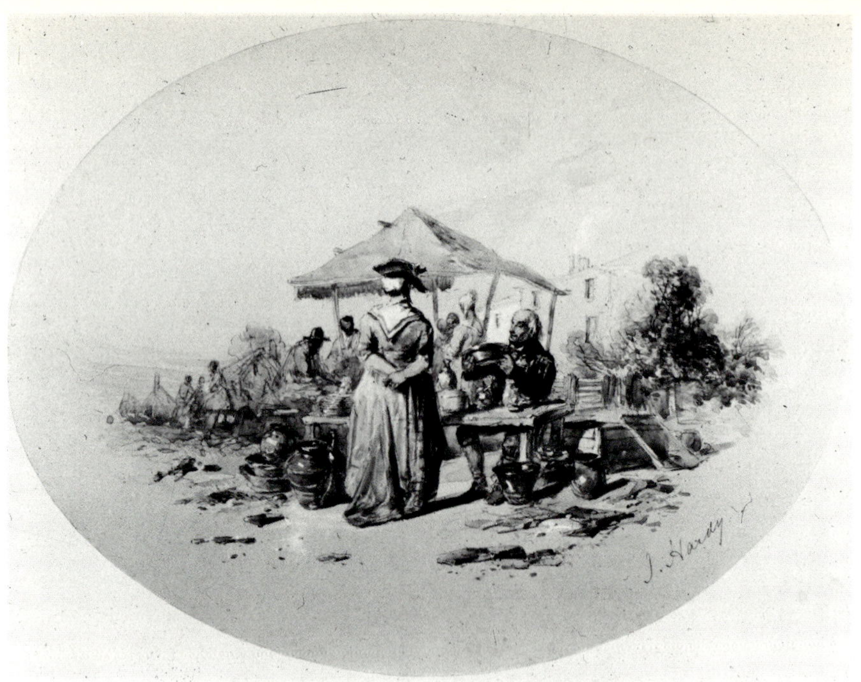

141 Pottery booth at a country fair, by James Hardy junior. Mid-nineteenth century.

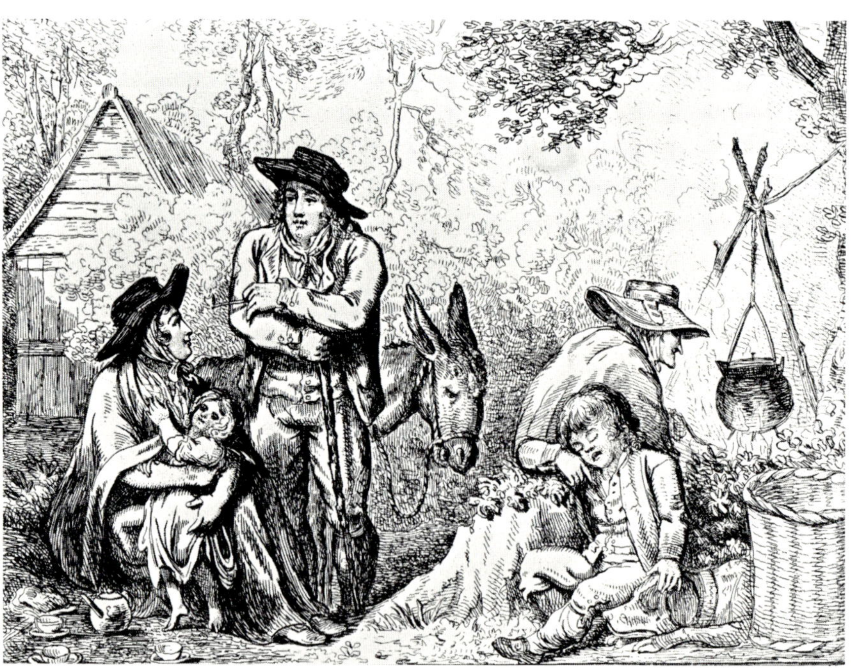

142 'Itinerant Dealers in Staffordshire Ware', from Woodward's *Eccentric Excursions*, 1797.

143 (opposite) 'The Staffordshire Pottery', frontispiece to Enoch Wood's anonymous *A Representation of the Manufacturing of Earthenware* (1827).

Frontispiece.

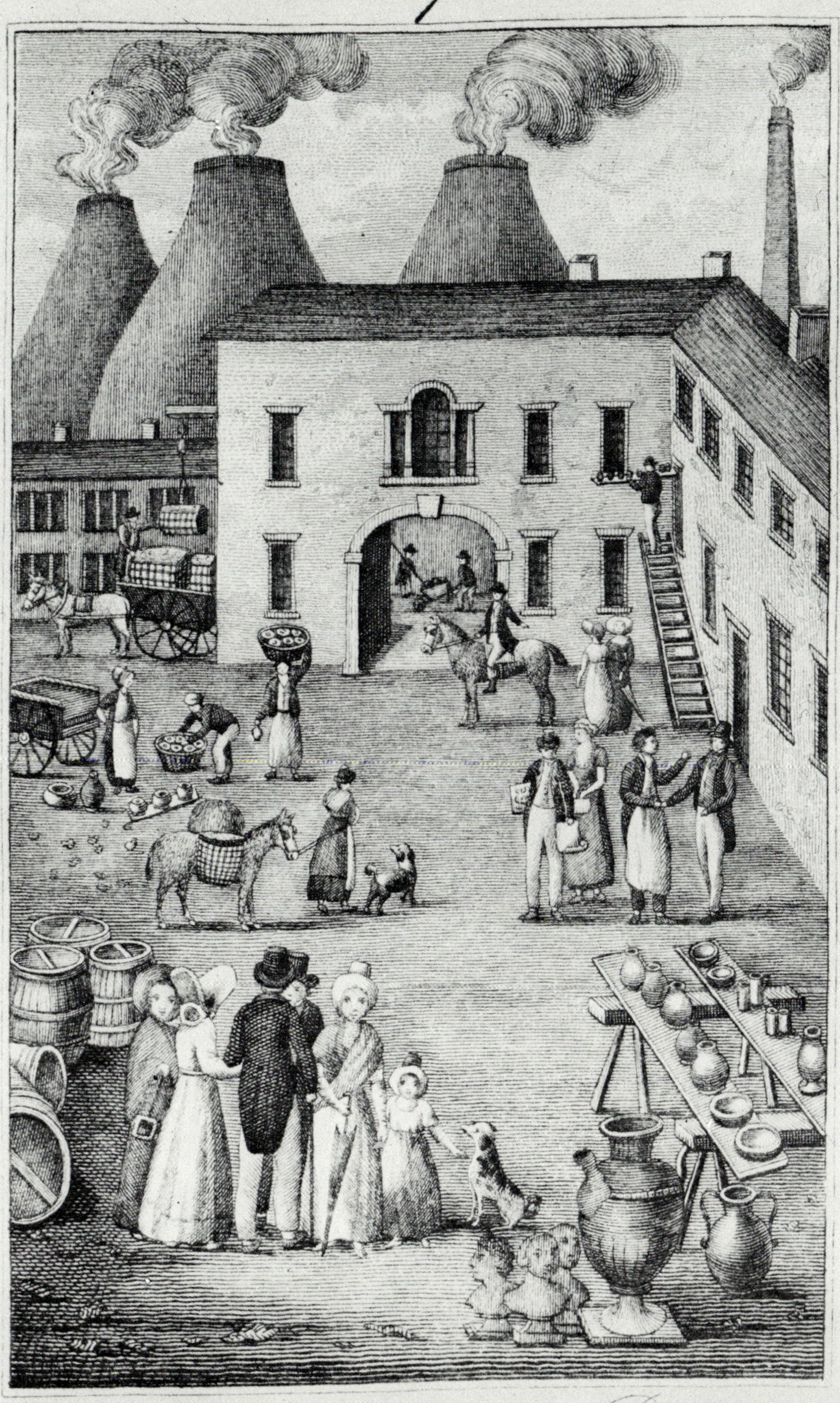

The Staffordshire Pottery

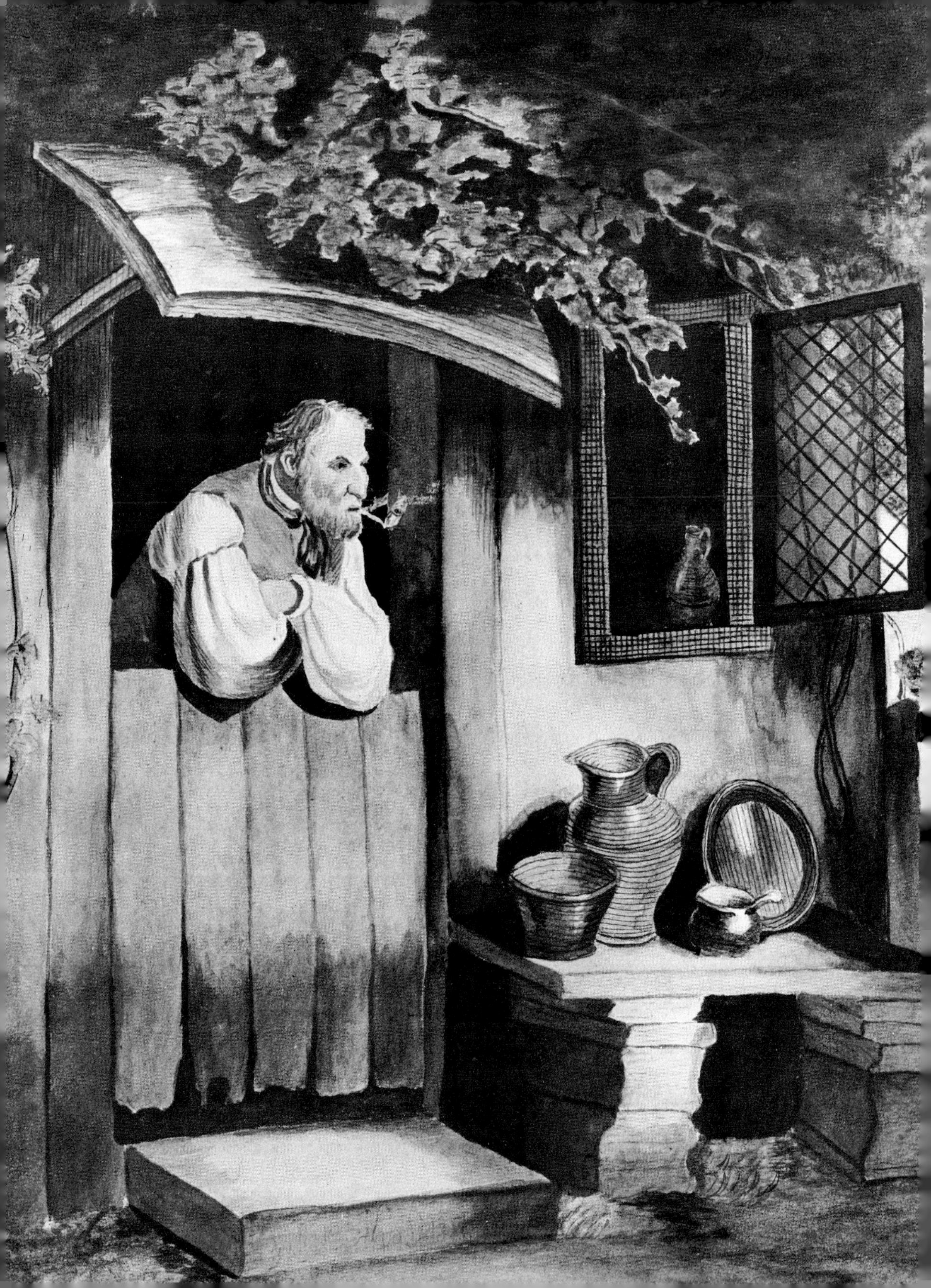

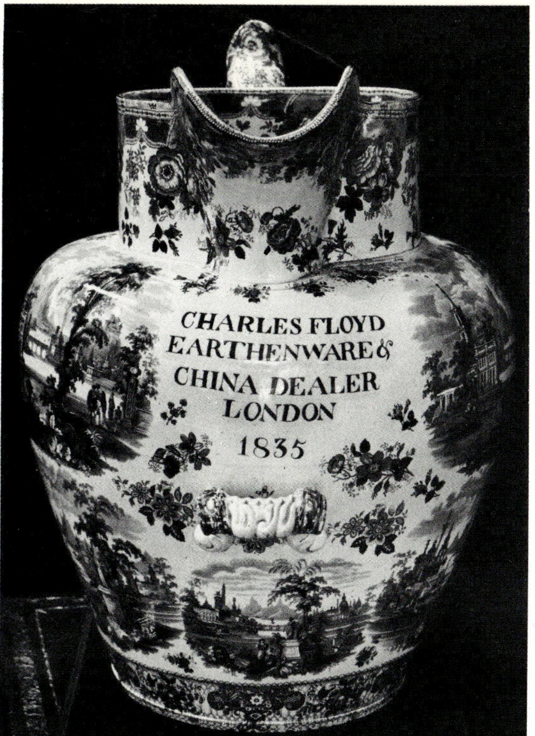

24 *BRITISH WAREHOUSEMAN.* February, 1895.

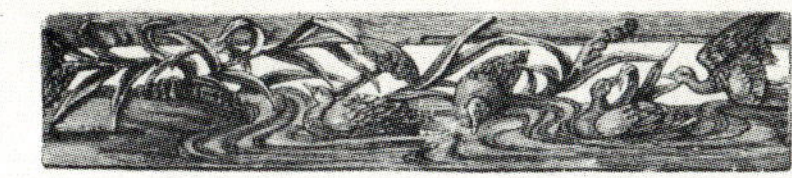

THE "LIBERTY" ART MOVEMENT.

MR. LASENBY LIBERTY is the "man of the moment" in West End trade circles at present, having recently converted the unique business to which, for want of other description, his own name seems to have been universally adopted as the generic definition, into a limited liability company. It is a difficult matter, at best, to beard the British warehouseman in his innermost lair, and often more difficult to get him to believe that his *confrères* throughout the great world of British commerce have the proverbial two-penn'orth of interest in him. Mr. Liberty devotes no inconsiderable portion of a busy and useful life to the service of his fellows, and is himself pleased and interested in every benefit experienced by the trade at large; every honest success of *confrères*, even of such as attempt a measure of rivalry; and every aid afforded by science and mechanics to the improvement of an industry. It is the testimony of every professional interviewer that such men, once convinced, their experience and counsel may throw a ray of light across the pathway of fellow-toilers in the ofttime dreary ways of modern commerce, overmaster a natural aversion to personal publicity, and by their unselfish frankness of expression give great value to the lessons designed to be secured by analysis of their personalities. In this regard the *British Warehouseman* considers the greatest compliment paid to it to lay in the incredulity of several of Mr. Liberty's lieutenants that its representative would be able to reach him, and their compassionate regard for him as prone to "rush in where angels fear to tread"; but Mr. Liberty is an old friend and whilom contributor to this journal, and made a welcome exception in its favour.

The Labyrinth of Crete mildly symbolises the devious pathway which leads from the doors of Chesham House to the *sanctum sanctorum* of its founder. When Prince Regent George of peculiar memory busied himself with the plans of that world-renowned thoroughfare which commemorates his early manhood, he had not the later, nineteenth century man-in-a-hurry in evident view. Or, perhaps the modern architect who has conformed the old buildings at Chesham House to modern requirements is responsible. But,

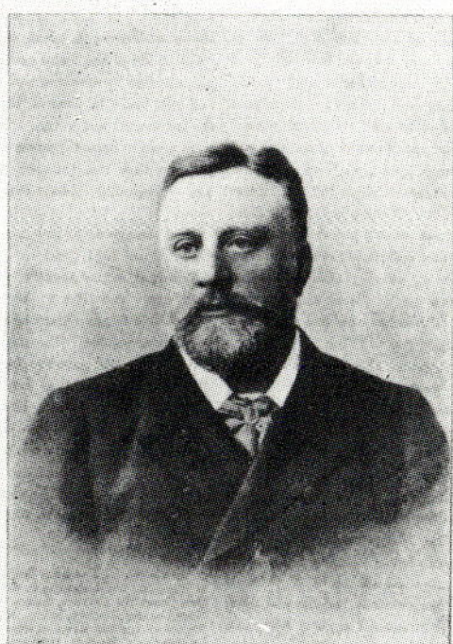

LASENBY LIBERTY, Esq.

144 (opposite) Pottery for sale outside a country cottage. Water-colour by Thomas Luny, probably in Devonshire. See p. 206.
145 (top left) Large earthenware jug, transfer printed in blue, an advertisement for Charles Floyd, a London dealer in ceramics. Dated 1835. Height 24″.
146 (top right) Lasenby Liberty, portrayed in an article in *The British Warehouseman*, February 1895. See p. 212.
147 Magazine issued in 1904 by 'The Little Shop', 1, East 31st Street, New York. See p. 213.

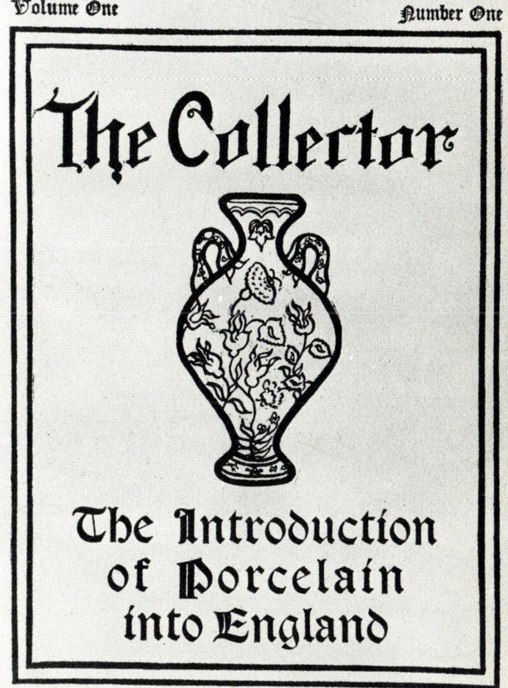

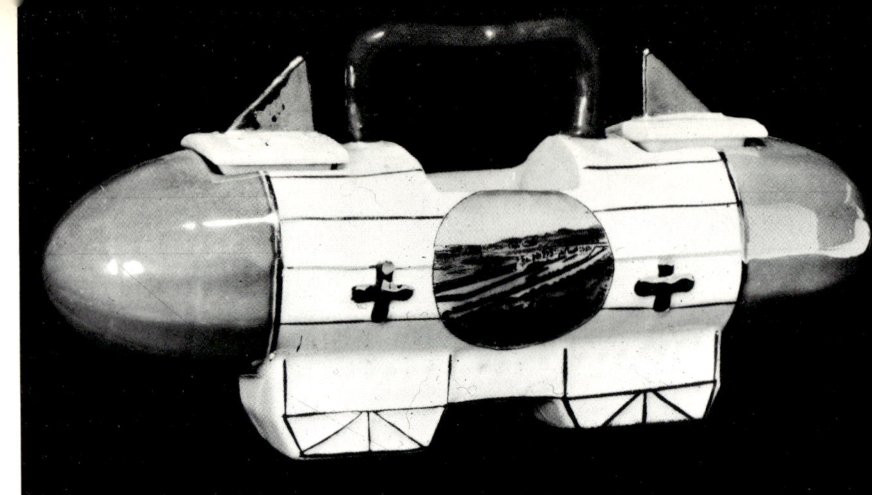

148 and 149 Two Japanese porcelain cruet sets made for the English market: (above) An airship, decorated in blue and orange lustres and with a transfer-printed view of Barry Island on one side, *c.* 1912; (below) A serving maid, decorated in a similar palette. Two china eggs, perforated and corked, serve as salt cellar and pepper pot. Height 5″.

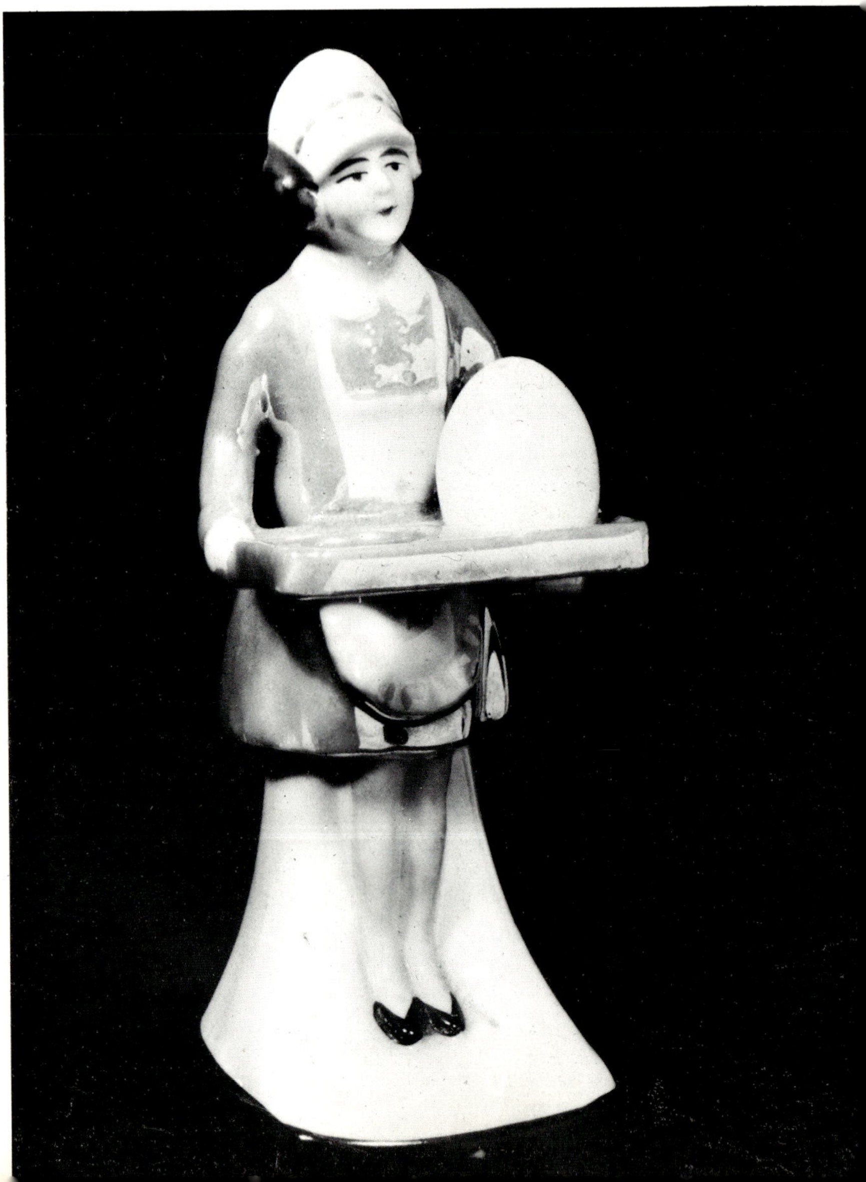

de Fonspertuis and Bonnier de la Mosson. The catalogues to these, with Gersaint's intelligently opinionated prefaces, are valuable relics of early expertise in the study of ceramics.

Gersaint is best known as a picture dealer. It was among his paintings that Watteau showed him. A dealer who specialized in porcelain, and mounting porcelain, was Lazare Duvaux (1703–58), and we are fortunate that two of the work-books in which he recorded his sales have survived. They cover the years 1748–58. But he was described as *marchand-mercier* in the parish registers of Saint-Germain-l'Auxerrois, Paris, when his son was baptized in 1743. Some entries in his books show sums due from 1740, and it is believed that a lost register began at that date. In 1747 he was already supplying goods to the court. His speciality was mounting oriental porcelain in bronze and turning Meissen figures into clocks. He also sold porcelain flowers with bronze stems and leaves, and the bouquets he made up were even perfumed. In 1755 he became *orfèvre-jouaillier du Roi.* Although not a man of letters or a 'scientific' dealer, like Gersaint, he was considered a man of taste. Madame de Pompadour had him arrange the furnishings in most of her houses.

Prices in Paris were high. Here is a sample from Duvaux's *Livre-Journal* for 1753:

March 2 : Mme la Duchesse de Mazarin : Une tasse & soucoupe de Saxe, à fleurs, 12 l.

April 16 : Mme de la Live : Huit figures de Vincennes en biscuit, à 481 l. pièce, 384 l.

April 17 : M. Cony : Un pot à sucre & une théière de Vincennes peints à guirlandes, 48 l.

June 27 : M. de Jullienne : Deux poissons de porcelaine céladon formant des cruches, montés en bronze doré d'or moulu, 960 l.

November 21 : M. d'Azincourt : Une vase de porcelaine jaspée de rouge & bleu, montée en bronze doré d'or moulu, 1,440 l.

One Frenchman who was not prepared to pay such prices without argument was Voltaire. In 1746, according to his secretary, Longchamp, he leapt out of his chair during a quarrel with his mistress, Madame du Châtelet, causing her to drop a cup and saucer, part of 'un superbe déjeûner de porcelaine de Saxe'.

C'était une très grande tasse avec sa soucoupe, dont le dedans était doré en plein, et le dehors orné d'un paysage avec quantité de figures très-bien peints, ce qui formait de charmans tableaux, tant pour l'élégance du dessin que pour la vivacité des couleurs.[19]

Voltaire gathered up the débris and put it on the table; choosing one of the largest pieces, he gave it to Longchamp, and sent him to M. la Frenaye, 'marchand bijoutier au Palais' to match the cup. Longchamp could find no comparable piece, but that which most resembled the broken cup cost ten louis. Voltaire had only given him seven or eight louis, so he asked Frenaye to send along an assistant with three or four of his finest sets, so that Voltaire could choose for himself. The assistant brought six; Voltaire chose the finest, the ten-louis one. Camel swallowers do not strain at gnats: Voltaire, whose daily occupation was questioning the springs of the universe, was not likely to shrink from disputing the price of a coffee-cup. He haggled with determination, but the assistant assured him that M. Frenaye would make no profit by selling at ten louis, and the philosopher was forced to give way. Madame du Châtelet was delighted with the replacement, and the storm in a coffee-cup ended.

An English traveller in France, the querulous Philip Thicknesse (Foote's 'Dr Viper'), was still less attracted by the prices of French china. At St Cloud, in 1766, 'the cheapest thing I could find was a small salladbowl, which, however, cost me a guinea; here I was shewn three small pieces of ornamental china for a chimney piece, that came to a thousand livres'.[20] Eleven years later, we find him equally disgruntled in Paris:

> I saw in a china shop at *Paris*, the figure of the King and Queen finely executed, and very like, in china: the King is playing on the harp, and the Queen dropping her work to listen to the harmony. The two figures, about a foot high, were placed in an elegant apartment, and the *toute ensemble* was the prettiest toy I ever beheld: the price thirty guineas.[21]

In London, as in Paris, the china shop was a fashionable rendezvous. In 1710 Jonathan Swift 'sauntered at China-shops' with the antiquary Sir Andrew Fountaine.[22] *The Spectator* contains a complaint by 'one of the top China women about town' of the trouble given by ladies who turn over all the goods in a shop without buying anything. High prices must have been one of the main deterrents in both countries. Horace Walpole described Mrs Chenevix, from whom he bought Strawberry Hill, as 'a toy woman at Charing Cross, famous for her high prices and fine language'.[23] Thomas Gray, the poet, wrote to Wharton on 16 November 1745, 'Madame Chenevix has frightened me with Écritoires she asks three Guineas for, that are not worth three half pence'.[24] Sending his cousin, Henry Seymour Conway, a Chinese porcelain boar in 1752, Walpole wrote: 'I dare say Mr Cutler or Margas would at least ask twenty guineas for him, and swear that Mrs Dunch gave thirty for the fellow.' And it is to Walpole, also, that we owe the ridiculous anecdote about another dealer, Thomas Turner. After the London earthquake of 1750, Walpole wrote to Horace Mann, on 19 May:

> Turner, a great china-man, at the corner of next street, had a jar cracked by the shock: he originally asked ten guineas for the pair: he now asks twenty, 'because it is the only jar in Europe that has been cracked by an earthquake'.

Turner's stock-in-trade was sold by Christie in 1767, and some of his pieces are in the Schreiber Collection.

Horace Walpole's first mention of Strawberry Hill occurs in a letter to Horace Mann of 5 June 1747. The same pretty passage contains his first mention of Mrs Chenevix:

> I may retire to a little new farm that I have taken just out of Twickenham. ... This little rural *bijou* was Mrs Chenevix's, the toy-woman *à la mode,* who in every dry season is to furnish me with the best rain-water from Paris, and now and then with some Dresden china cows, who are to figure like wooden classics in a library....

Mrs Chenevix's shop, which, according to an advertisement in the *Daily Journal* for 24 May 1733, was 'against Suffolk Street, Charing Cross', is mentioned in the first chapter of Book VIII of Fielding's *Amelia,* the hero of which is lured into a debt-collector's hands by a false report that his wife has been taken ill 'in Mrs Chenevix's'. Mrs Chenevix was the sister of the no less noted toy-woman of Bath, Mrs Bertrand, whose shop is mentioned by Pope in his lines to Lady Fanny Shirley, on receiving from her a standish and two pens ('It came from Bertrand's, not the skies'). In a letter to George Montagu of 18 May 1749, Walpole described a visit from both sisters when Mrs Chenevix brought him the lease of Strawberry Hill to sign:

> I showed them my cabinet of enamels instead of treating them with white wine. The Bertrand said, 'Sir, I hope you don't trust all sorts of *ladies* with this cabinet!' – What an entertaining assumption of dignity!

So much for the social status of even the most eminent china dealers.

A large amount of business was conducted direct by the factories, in the form of commissions from royal and noble patrons and customers. In the eighteenth century the great factories opened warehouses and showrooms to bring their wares before a wider public. The new factory into which Sèvres moved in 1756, designed by Lindel at the order of Madame de Pompadour, included a warehouse for the display of porcelain – as well as a private chapel for the King and other luxuries which altogether cost him over a million livres. The Paris china dealers were unwilling to handle Sèvres porcelain, because of its extreme fragility; they were not allowed for breakages in transit. The china shops made a profitable business of hiring out services for banquets, and they found that there were fewer breakages with Meissen and oriental porcelain than with Sèvres. The dealers also resented the quirkish method by which the factory calculated its charges on the porcelain supplied to them. For convenience in accountancy, all pieces of the same shape – 'la forme Hébert', and so on – were charged at the same price, regardless of the quality of the decoration. This meant that the dealers found it hard to dispose of the less accomplished pieces. It was probably as a result of these difficulties with the dealers that the Sèvres showrooms in the rue de la Monnaie were opened.

In London, Josiah Wedgwood's Newport Street showroom was opened in 1768. On 13 June he wrote to William Cox, his warehouseman and book-keeper: 'I am preparing a Cargo of Goods for your New Warehouse to send by Sea, and have near 1000 Dozen of Plates Biscuit and Gloss[25] for that Purpose.[26] (Sea was the cheapest form of transport.) The Greek Street showrooms were opened in June 1774, when the service made for Catherine the Great was exhibited there. Mrs Delany wrote in her diary, 'There are three rooms below and two above filled with it, laid out on tables, everything that can be wanted to serve a dinner.' In 1782 Turner and Abbott opened their showroom and enamelling establishment in Fleet Street. This showroom was later taken over by Davenport, and in James Findlay's tinted drawing of about 1845[27] the building is shown under the Davenport regime, with wares clearly visible through the windows. Spode's warehouse was in Portugal Street. The reason for the setting up of London showrooms by Staffordshire potters was uncomplicated: Staffordshire, unlike Sèvres and St Cloud, was remote from the capital, unfashionable and inaccessible. Perhaps it was from Wedgwood's or Turner and Abbott's showroom that General Tilney (*Northanger Abbey*, written 1798, published 1818) bought the breakfast set which Catherine Morland admired:

He was enchanted by her approbation of his taste, confessed it to be neat and simple, thought it right to encourage the manufacture of his country; and for his part, to his uncritical palate, the tea was as well flavoured from the clay of Staffordshire as from that of Dresden or Sêve. But this was quite an old set, purchased two years ago. The manufacture was much improved since that time; he had seen some beautiful specimens when last in town, and had he not been perfectly without vanity of that kind, might have been tempted to order a new set. He trusted, however, that an opportunity might ere long occur of selecting one – though not for himself.[28]

Worcester was a more fashionable place than Stoke-on-Trent. There, porcelain shops and showrooms could flourish on home ground. In 1788, when George III was suffering the first mild onset of what used to be regarded as mental derangement, but has lately been diagnosed as a symptom of the rare disease porphyria, he stayed in Worcester with his old tutor, Bishop Hurd (who, like John Turner, hailed from Brewood, in Staffordshire). The only one of the King's curious escapades that concerns us is described by Mr Charles Chenevix Trench in his book *The Royal Malady* (1964):

Next door to Bishop Hurd's palace, where the royal couple stayed, a house was being converted into a porcelain shop. This fascinating spectacle drew the King like a magnet: soon, accompanied by the Queen, he was picking his way through the big rooms, over tools and plaster, wood-shavings and rubbish, asking the masons and carpenters a thousand fussy questions. Not content with their answers, he decided to inspect the work himself and climbed the stairs to the very top floor.[29]

Perhaps this was one of the shops referred to by Robert Southey in his anonymous *Letters from England* (1802):

The main manufactory of this place Worcester is in porcelain, and the shops in which this ware is displayed are as splendid and beautiful as can possibly be imagined. They are equal in length to a common parochial church, and these exquisite works of art arranged in them in the best order upon long counters, around the sides, and in the windows on each side the door which occupy the whole front.[30]

A woman dealer is commemorated in an epitaph published by Horace Walpole's rascally printer Thomas Kirgate at Strawberry Hill about 1791:[31]

An EPITAPH on a Woman who ſold Earthenware.

Bene	VI.
AT. HT. HISST.	Seab AT Eyo
O NELI ESKA	URG.
T. Harin, e. g. Rayc,	RIE FANDD
Hang'd.	Ryy. ov Rey.
F. R.	Esf. or Wha.
O Mabv Syli Fet	TA
O. L.	Vai. . . . Lſa Flo
J. FELESSC.	O Doft Ear Swho.
Lay bye Art	K. Now Sbu
HAND.	T. Ina Ru.
C. LAYSHEG.	NOFY e ARSI
O Th. Erpel	N. S. O.
FAND.	METALL PIT
No W. S. H. E'ſt. Urn	CHERO RBRO
'D. Toe Art	A. D.
H. H. Erſelfy EWE,	Panſhe Inhe
EPI N. G. FRI	R. S. H.
END.	OPMA. yb EAGA.
SLET MEAD	. I. N.

This epitaph (with a few differences in the division of words) had previously been published in the *London Chronicle* of 4 October 1764. According to William Andrews's *Curious Epitaphs*, its subject was 'a poor woman who kept an earthenware shop at Chester'.[32] Decoded, it reads:

Beneath this stone lies Katharine Gray,
Chang'd from a busy life to lifeless clay;
By earth and clay she got her pelf,
And now she's turn'd to earth herself.
Ye weeping friends, let me advise,
Abate your grief and dry your eyes;
For what avails a flood of tears?
Who knows but in a run of years
In some tall pitcher or broad pan
She in her shop may be again.

By contrast with the more lavish showrooms and shops, a small country pottery might give a retired farmer a few articles to put on show outside his cottage. Thomas Luny's water-colour (Plate 144) is of such a scene, and since Luny[33] was a Devonshire artist who painted little but rustic Devon subjects, the wares on show were probably made in one of the local potworks.

Marketing

Much ware was sold at fairs and markets, which pedlars often made their principal bases. Hogarth's *Bartholomew Fair* (Plate 139) shows the collapse of a stall apparently stocked with delft. A Bunbury etching of 1777 (Plate 140) represents the Cambridge pot fair, with Queen's Ware prominently displayed on trestles. Goya's tapestry cartoon of a year later (Plate 134) depicts a pot-seller at the Madrid Fair, showing his wares to two young ladies of fashion, their handsome coach in the background. For fairs were not merely patronized, as humorous prints and picaresque novels might suggest, by roughs and gypsies. The anonymous authors of *La Foire de Beaucaire*, a novel published at Amsterdam in 1708, wrote: 'Ce ne sont pas seulement les Negocians & les personnes du commun qui y trouvent des charmes, la Noblesse y vient chercher mille plaisirs qui suivent un si riche concours.'[34] The fair at Beaucaire was the largest in France. The second largest, which served the north, was that of Guibray, near Falaise. In a supplement to his *Histoire de Falaise*: *Foire de Guibray* (1889), Amédée Meriel shows that in 1704 'Marchands de porcelaine, faïence et cristaux ont apporté pour valeur 10,000 livres; débit, 4,000 livres'. Arthur Young was taken there in 1788, and observed the combined effects of the Eden Treaty and the Staffordshire potters' export trade:

> I found the quantity of English goods considerable, hard and queen's ware; cloths and cottons. A dozen of common plain plates, 3 *livres* and 4 *livres* for a French imitation, but much worse ... a dozen with blue or green edges; English, 5 *livres* 5 *sous*.[35]

In the nineteenth century, a special class of china trinkets was made for sale at fairs – the so-called 'fairings' mainly produced by German firms such as Conta and Boehme of Possneck. These knick-knacks were imported into England; a trade review of 1899 tells us that 'Messrs [Frank] Tuhten & Co. have a large assortment of new figure ware expressly intended for what are known as "sixpenny lines" in the English market. These are especially suitable for fancy stalls, bazaars, watering places and holiday resorts.' In the early twentieth century, the Japanese were the most prolific suppliers of souvenir china, such as the airship and servant-maid cruets (Plates 148–9).

The English market, like the English pedlar, was extraordinarily traditional and unaffected by changes in industry and society. In *Sons and Lovers* (1913), D. H. Lawrence described a scene at Nottingham market:

> She glanced at the dish again. Both she and her enemy, the pot man, had

an uncomfortable feeling, as if there were something between them. Suddenly he shouted:

'Do you want it for fivepence?'

She started. Her heart hardened; but then she stopped and took up her dish.

'I'll have it,' she said.

'Yer'll do me the favour, like?' he said. 'Yer'd better spit in it, like yer do when y'ave something give yer.'

Mrs Morel paid him the fivepence in a cold manner.

'I don't see you give it me,' she said. 'You wouldn't let me have it for fivepence if you didn't want to.'

'In this flamin' scrattlin' place you may count yerself lucky if you can give your things away,' he growled.

'Yes; there are bad times, and good,' said Mrs Morel.[36]

Lawrence's potman reduced his price from sevenpence to fivepence. It says much for the continuity of English market history that the ballad of *Robin Hood and the Potter*, probably written in the reign of Henry VI, shows Robin, disguised as the potter, reducing *his* wares, also in Nottingham market, from fivepence to threepence:

Robyn went to Notynggam
Thes pottes for to sell;
The potter abode with Robens men
Ther he fered not eylle.

Yn the medys of the towne,
Ther he schowed hes war,
Pottys! pottys! he gan crey foll sone,
Haffe hansell for the mar.

The pottys that wer wethe pens feyffe,
He sold tham for pens thre:
Preveley seyde man and weyffe,
Yonder potter schall never the.

Shop dealing, however, had changed in the nineteenth century. On the one hand there were new antique shops with scholarly collector-proprietors, catering for an élite roughly identifiable, in England, with the 'aesthetes'. Murray Marks is representative of this kind of cultured dealer. On the other hand, there emerges, towards the end of the century, a new kind of dealer in contemporary ceramics and popularizer of 'aesthetic' doctrines: Sir Arthur Lasenby Liberty was the first.

Murray Marks was one of those men who take up a profession apparently beneath their attainments and give it a new dimension. He was a

IX (*opposite*) 'The Assassination of Marat', an earthenware group by Lakin and Poole, Staffordshire.

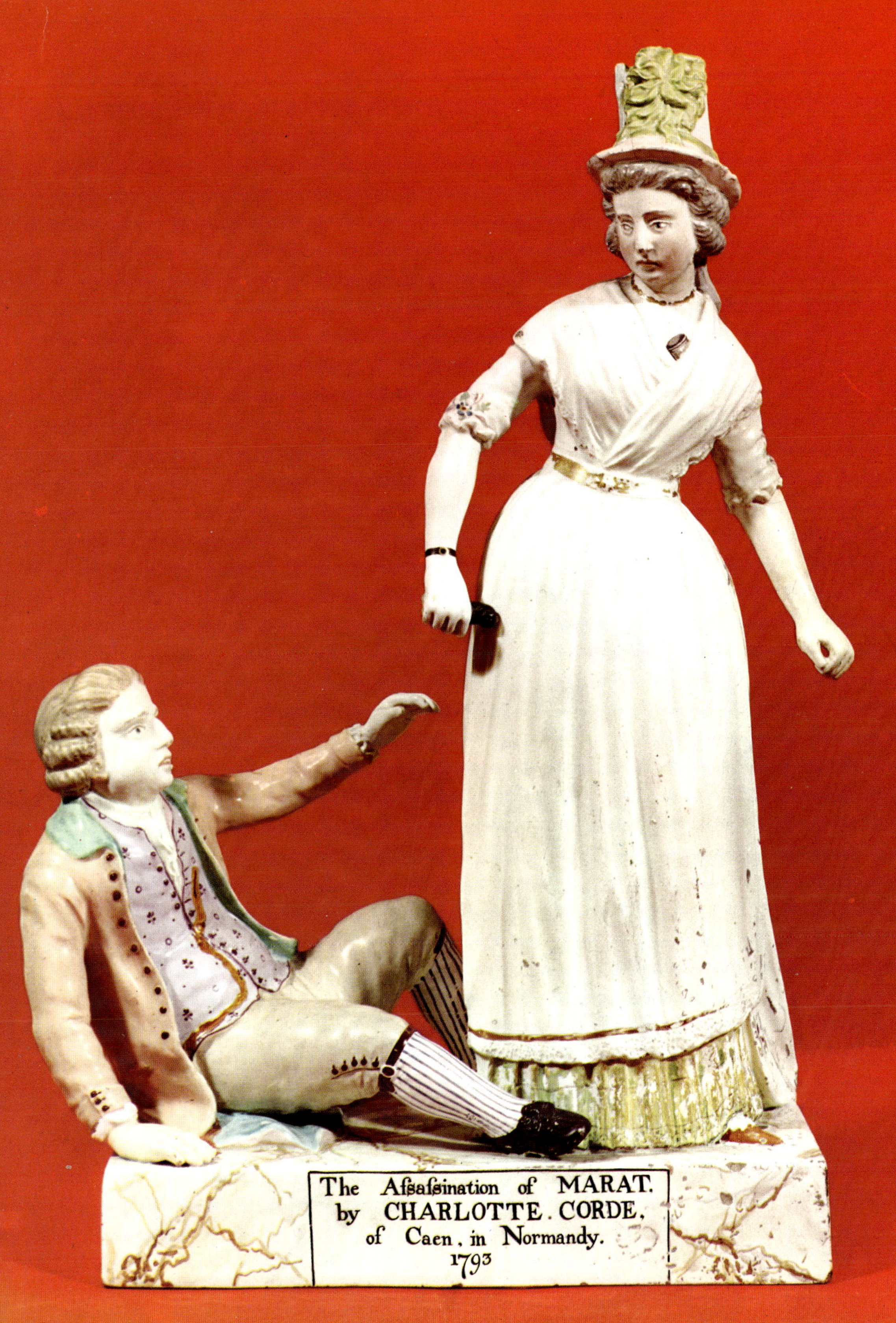
The Afsafsination of MARAT.
by CHARLOTTE. CORDE.
of Caen, in Normandy.
1793

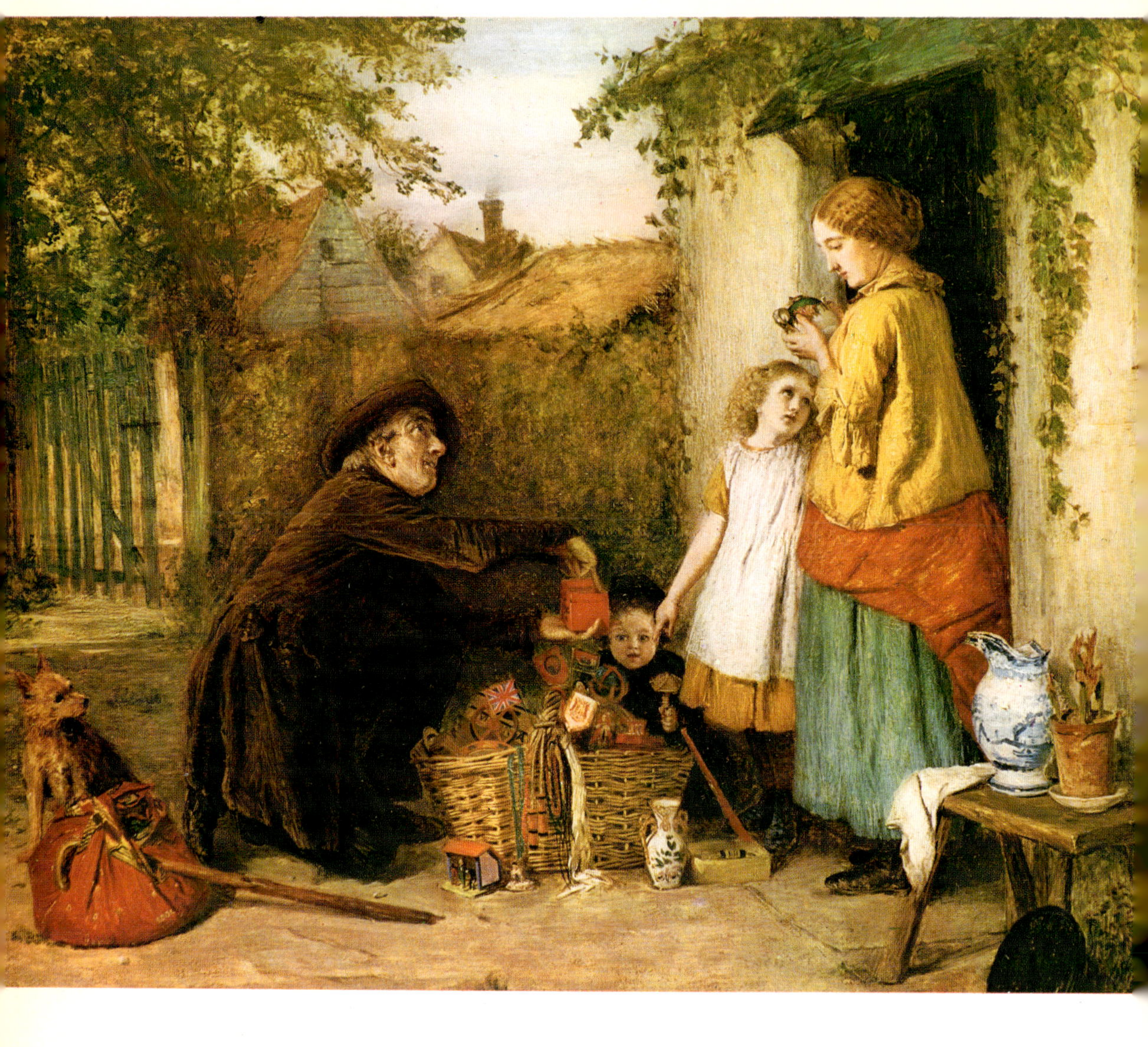

close friend of Schopenhauer, whom he had met in Frankfort, and the two corresponded until Schopenhauer's death in 1860. Marks collaborated with Wilhelm Bode in his work on Italian bronzes of the Renaissance, and helped to compile the catalogue of Pierpont Morgan's bronzes. He was a benefactor of the British, Victoria and Albert, and Fitzwilliam Museums. Ruskin, Swinburne, Rossetti and Millais were his intimates.

We are fortunate in having a good biography of him, published in the year after his death.[37] Marks, born in 1840, was the son of Emmanuel Marks van Galen, a Dutch dealer who had come to England on the advice of Baldock, art adviser to the Prince Regent. The elder Marks had premises at 395 Oxford Street, which he let off to a firm which imported contemporary Chinese goods, Frederick Hogg and Company. Young Marks was attracted by their stock, and set himself to learn about Chinese porcelain. His father refused to let him go to China to look for fine examples, or to start a business of his own. But during one of his father's absences on the Continent, Marks took the law into his own hands. Removing about two thousand pounds worth of goods from the family warehouse, things in which he had a financial interest, he opened a shop in Sloane Street, and by the time his father returned, had made a success of it. When his father retired, Marks took over the Oxford Street premises. He persuaded Pickford's, who occupied the ground floor, to leave, and in 1873 he asked his friend Norman Shaw, the architect, to convert the whole building in the 'Queen Anne' style. Marks's business card is supposed to have been the combined work of Rossetti, William Morris and Whistler. Rossetti designed the Chinese ginger jar and peacock feathers; Morris, the lettering, and Whistler, the background. In scrolls round the gold border the various things Marks dealt in are mentioned: Sèvres, Dresden, Nankin, Oriental, Bronzes, Furniture, Tapestry, Leather, Armour, Carvings, Enamels and Stuffs. The card was printed from six wood blocks – like a Japanese colour print.

Marks was at the centre of the cult for blue and white porcelain, though he did not originate it. That distinction should perhaps go to Félix Bracquemond, also an early enthusiast for Japanese prints. In 1862 Madame Desoye and her husband opened an Oriental shop in the arcades of the Rue de Rivoli, Paris, and the Pennells in their *Life of Whistler* tell us that Manet, Fantin, Tissot, Baudelaire, Solon and the Goncourt brothers were among the early customers. Whistler was also one. He brought back some blue pots and Japanese prints to London and inspired Rossetti with his enthusiasm.

x (*opposite*) 'The Pedlar' by John Burr (1831–93). Dated 1865. The woman at the door is holding a teapot. In front of the basket stands a vase of characteristic mid-Victorian shape.

The only firm importing blue and white porcelain at that time was Farmer and Rogers, who had an 'Oriental Warehouse'. The manager was Lasenby Liberty (Plate 146) who was later to found the great business on the other side of Regent Street. Rossetti strolled in one day, made Liberty's acquaintance, and bought a few pieces of blue china. He eventually sold these to Whistler and introduced Whistler to Liberty.

Passing Marks's window, Rossetti caught sight of some pieces of K'ang Hsi ware. He bought them, and asked Marks whether any more could be obtained. Marks said he could supply him with as much as he wanted. Shortly afterwards Marks went to Holland, bought a quantity of 'blue', and offered it to Rossetti, who was unable to buy the whole collection, but brought along two friends, Louis Huth and Henry Thompson, both of whom became great collectors of blue china. Marks also supplied china for the Garland, Walters, Franks, Grandidier and Salting collections: over 200 of Salting's examples came from his shop.

Sir Henry Thompson (1820–94) was a leading surgeon. He operated successfully on Leopold I, and an operation on Napoleon III is described by Marks's biographer as 'fully successful ... although unfortunately the Emperor's strength did not persist, and he died shortly after it had taken place'. Thompson exhibited at the Royal Academy from 1865 to 1891, and the painting he sent in 1885 showed some of his blue china.

According to Lady Dorothy Nevill, Thompson was the only doctor admitted to London 'society', when the acting and medical professions were barred from it. From 1872 he held 'octaves' at his home in Wimpole Street – small dinner parties which always consisted of eight courses eaten by eight guests at eight o'clock. Marks, who became a close friend of Thompson, selected every piece of his collection, catalogued and arranged it. In May 1878 he arranged an exhibition at 395 Oxford Street of all Sir Henry's blue and white porcelain. The private view was at 11 o'clock on the night of 30 April, and 'a very *recherché* supper was served by Scott's on wonderful blue and white dishes'. The invitation card[38] is supposed to show Rossetti at the mantelpiece and Frederick Leyland at the piano, but the only absolutely recognizable figure is the monocled Whistler.

Of much greater interest is the catalogue of Thompson's collection, issued in May 1878, the first catalogue of a collection of blue and white to be printed. Only 220 copies were issued, of which 100 were for private circulation and 120 for sale. Of the plates, six were by Thompson himself. The remaining twenty-one were by Whistler. The letterpress was by Marks, who wrote the preface and catalogued the 339 pieces.

Presenting the book to a friend, Marks paraphrased the story about Whistler and Velasquez: 'The other day a friend of mine expressed regret that he had not acquired a copy of the catalogue by myself and Whistler; to which I replied, "Why drag in Whistler?" '

The exhibition was a great success – especially the '*recherché* supper'. Byron Webber, in his book *James Orrock, R.I. Painter, Connoisseur, Collector* (1903) describes an 'eminent critic' who 'overflowed with enthusiasm' on this occasion:

> He saw nothing, he could converse about nothing, but this translucent 'Blue'. 'Look at that!' he exclaimed, as a servitor approached, carrying with extreme care, as he had a right to do, a magnificent dish of the true brand. 'Could France, could England produce anything like it? Observe that exquisite pink on that lovely blue!' The exquisite pink was pickled salmon.[39]

Orrock's porcelain collection, which caused him to be known as 'the Admiral of the Blue', was largely formed for him by Marks.

The Thompson collection was sold at Christie's in 1880, and many of the best pieces were bought back by Marks, who also acquired Rossetti's collection for £700 after the artist's death. Most of Whistler's china collection was sold at Sotheby's in February 1880.

Dealers of the Murray Marks type are not found in America until nearer the turn of the century, when there are great collectors to patronize them. By 1904 'The Little Shop', of 1 East 31st Street, New York, was issuing its own magazine, *The Collector.* The first issue dealt with 'The Introduction of Porcelain into England'. The shop's proprietor, A. S. Vernay, promised to deal in future numbers with individual factories, 'and though it would have been more in order to have begun with Plymouth and Bristol, I shall take the liberty of commencing with Worcester, which, from a collector's point of view, is far more interesting than any other'.

We have already encountered Lasenby Liberty, who, at the age of eighteen, had become an employee of Messrs Farmer and Rogers. That was in 1862, the year of London's second Great International Exhibition. Liberty was fascinated by the Japanese exhibits there, the 'oriental revelation'. It was only eight years since Commodore Perry had sailed into Yokohama harbour with a squadron of the United States fleet, ending Japanese isolation, and only six since Félix Bracquemond had looked at his first Hokusai print. Like Marks, Liberty set himself to study oriental art. In 1875 he opened his own shop at 218A Regent Street with a staff of one assistant and one porter. It was a success. Rossetti, Whistler,

Watts, Burne-Jones, Leighton, Millais, Alma-Tadema, Charles Keene, Norman Shaw and Albert Moore were all customers, and even Carlyle and Ruskin were lured into the emporium of fripperies. In less than a year Liberty was able to take over the other half of the premises at 218 Regent Street.

He was not an oppressively modest man. 'Indeed, yes,' he told an interviewer from *The British Warehouseman* in 1895, when asked whether he had influenced Oscar Wilde. 'My "art fabrics" were produced before he became a celebrity. I gave him his opportunity, and he helped me mightily through the publicity he commanded. I am glad to be able to realise that all that world-famous aesthetic movement of fifteen years ago, which had its perihelium in Gilbert and Sullivan's Savoy Opera of *Patience*, was not a cause but a result of my persistence.' There was some truth in the boast. Liberty did for the aesthetic movement what Wilde and the aesthetes could never have done with their meetings and lectures and slim gold-tooled volumes of white vellum. He brought it to the public, a public affluent enough to afford fans, screens and blue china. A Du Maurier cartoon in *Punch* (20 October 1894) showed a hostess of Upper Tooting saying: 'We're very proud of this room, Mrs Hominy. Our own little upholsterer did it up just as you see it, and all our friends think it was Liberty.' And the visitor mutters, *sotto voce*, 'Oh Liberty, Liberty, how many crimes are committed in thy Name!'

Textiles were Liberty's special interest, but he also sold oriental china, 'both ancient and modern'. This ranged from pin trays and fern pots at sixpence each to 'highly finished and important decorative Art Objects, suitable for placing in Halls, Galleries, Conservatories, Stair Recesses, Drawing Rooms, Libraries, Studios, Smoking Rooms &c.' from £10 to £100 each. 'Handsomely decorated Card dishes' on black wood carved stands cost 7*s*. 6*d*., or 25*s*. if of the 'Best Mandarin Quality'. Liberty was largely responsible, also, for the immense popularity of the willow pattern – the poor man's 'blue and white' – though the first Staffordshire version had been made in the late eighteenth century. The doggerel legend of the willow pattern became a nursery rhyme, amply illustrated on the kitchen dresser. The redoubtable Mrs Willoughby Hodgson wrote about willow china in the *Woman's Home Journal*. And as a final indignity a willow plate was inexplicably included in an advertisement for 'Hoven's Hose Holder: A Crusade Against the Garter'.

I cannot end this chapter without an affectionate mention of my first tutor in ceramics, Mr Lickorish, now dead, china dealer in Crawford Street since God knew when. I never knew his Christian name, for only the curious surname was painted above his shop. He dealt only in damaged wares, and was said to be quite disappointed if a perfect piece was brought into his shop. (Legend went further: people wishing to sell china to Lickorish would chip it first to make it eligible.) His prices were amazingly low. I remember, in particular, a handsome Chelsea-Derby bowl, about a foot in diameter, and with the regulation hair crack: ten shillings. By purists, his taste in ceramics was compared unkindly with that of the cockney in food: he liked 'chips with everything'. But those who shared his heresy – that honourable scars do not ruin a work of art – called him 'the Emperor of Broken China'.

10 Revivals – Gothic and otherwise

The favourite occupation of modern art historians and critics is detecting influences. All that disagreeable business of reproaching, rebuking and pronouncing anathemas, of which Ruskin was the master, is replaced by an urbane scholarly game whose object may be to show how far Rembrandt was affected by the Italian Renaissance, or what Mucha owed to Hokusai. For these permissive men, who seem not to mind how painful a work of art is, provided it is derived from another, the nineteenth century is the perfect subject. As Dr Stephan Madsen has written, in his *Sources of Art Nouveau* (1956):

> From about 1820 to 1890 all the styles in Western Europe had been copied, transformed, and recreated; and furthermore towards the end of the century impulses had also been felt from other parts of the world. We may say that the nineteenth century was a repository for the artistic ideas of all countries and all other centuries.[1]

It was a century of revivals. Some of them can be ascribed to a reaction against the industrial revolution; the apparently independent literary, archaeological and religious influences to which revivals have been traced can often be interpreted as part of the same general revulsion. But industry itself, including the industry of ceramics, took control of the revivals. The great international exhibitions which began in the mid-century[2] were anthologies of revived styles, and helped to disseminate them, as did magazines such as the *Art Union Journal*, *Arte Italiana Decorativa e Industriale* and *Sprechsaal für Keramik, Glas und Emil.* Museums bought up the 'best' exhibits, providing at once a model and an ambition for the designer. The exhibitions also created a demand for objects which no one would otherwise have thought of making. The Chevy

Revivals – Gothic and otherwise

Chase sideboard would not have been made if there had not been an Exhibition to show it in – and no one would have paid the huge price demanded for it if it had not been acclaimed by the press as a masterpiece. The ceramic equivalents – two vases, over three feet high (Plate 155), made for the Great Exhibition of 1851 by Charles Meigh & Sons of Hanley, were described in the official catalogue (with unfortunate ambiguity) as: 'Large vases, with portraits of the Queen, and view of the Exhibition Buildings; and of Prince Albert, with interior view.' The juries, in awarding Meigh a prize medal, noted particularly '... some specimens of very remarkable size, especially two great vases, or one piece each ...'.[3] These are now in the Victoria and Albert Museum.

By the second half of the century, the idea of historicism as the natural basis of the arts was so well established that compendious source-books of historical and foreign styles were being published. Owen Jones, in his *Grammar of Ornament* (1856), went so far as to hope that his book would not 'aid in assisting that unfortunate tendency of our time to be content with copying, while the fashion lasts, the forms peculiar to any bygone age, without attempting to ascertain, indeed generally completely ignoring, the peculiar circumstances which rendered an ornament beautiful, because it was appropriate.'[4] But he had the grace to admit that: 'It is more than probable that the first result of sending forth to the world this collection will be seriously to increase this dangerous tendency, and that many will be content to borrow from the past those forms of beauty which have not already been used up *ad nauseam*.'[5] A similar function was served by R. N. Wornum's *Analysis of Ornament* (1856), Dr Christopher Dresser's *Principles of Decorative Design*, and by H. Dolmetsch's *The Historic Styles of Ornament* (1898). As Jones had suggested, these books were to be very influential. They provided the art schools and workmen's libraries now being set up with primers which gave that equivocal subject, art, the respectability of an academic discipline. They ensured that art would not be, to adapt Freeman's famous sneer, 'an easy school for poor men'.[6]

The Classical Revival lumbered on through the century, a wounded chimaera. Its lingering death was caused by successive attacks of the neo-Gothic, neo-Rococo, neo-Renaissance, neo-Baroque and neo-Celtic styles, culminating in the fatal onset of what Walter Crane called 'that strange decorative disease'[7] – *art nouveau*, which itself absorbed elements of all these styles while ostensibly reacting against historicism. The neo-Classical stolidly survived through the 1840s in heavy works by F. & R. Pratt of Fenton, Dillwyn of Swansea, and the inevitable Wedgwood. At the 1851 Exhibition it had a last hour of glory when Thomas Battram displayed an artificial cave filled with terracotta pots, intended to represent an Etruscan tomb. But how far it had already succumbed by the 1830s is well illustrated by a comparison between two teapots, both basalt examples by the firm of Elijah Mayer (Plate 154). That on the left was made about 1780, and has the austere elegance of Hester Bateman silver. That on the right, which looks as if it is about to eat its neighbour, was made to commemorate the Duke of Wellington. It has a lion's head and a snake's tail – chimaera indeed.

The Gothic Revival had two main phases. First came the eighteenth-century Gothick of the dilettantiquarians, Horace Walpole and William Beckford, fancifully picturesque or romantically sinister (both men wrote 'novels of gloomth').Then followed the deadly serious nineteenth-century Gothic of Pugin, Barry and Ruskin, associated with scientific archaeology, 'restoration', and religious movements.[8] Nothing could more suitably illustrate Walpole's favourite epigram, that the world is a comedy to those who think, a tragedy to those who feel, than the difference between these two revivals.

Their influence on ceramics was nowhere near so profound as on architecture or literature. It appeared diluted in vignettes of ruins (Plate 150), or in flashily enamelled jousting scenes. In printed wares, its effect was stronger, since the engraved designs were often derived from works nearer the sources of inspiration. Hawking, one of the accessories of the Gothic landscape, was a popular subject mainly inspired by Sir Walter Scott's novels, which, as serious fiction, were a compromise between fanciful Gothick and moral Gothic. The Eglinton Tournament is depicted on jugs and mugs which may have been sold as souvenirs of it. But there is little trace of the Gothic in dinner or dessert services. ('Thank God !' as Samuel Butler remarked of Mendelssohn's *Songs Without Words.*) Porcelain in general seems to have escaped the hand of the Goths. Pottery was better adapted to the gaunt, angular style, and it is no surprise that this material was also preferred by that direct descendant of the Gothic Revival, the Arts and Crafts Movement.[9]

The outstanding example of eighteenth-century Gothick in ceramics is the set of jasper chessmen designed by John Flaxman for Wedgwood in the early 1780s.[10] Three extracts from a bill he presented are relevant:

Oct. 30th, 1783. A figure of a Fool for Chess	£1 : 5 : –.
Dec. 1st, 1784. Three days employed in drawing bas-reliefs, vases, Chessmen, &c.	£3 : 3 : –.
March 8th, 1785. A drawing of Chess-men	£6 : 6 : –.

Revivals – Gothic and otherwise

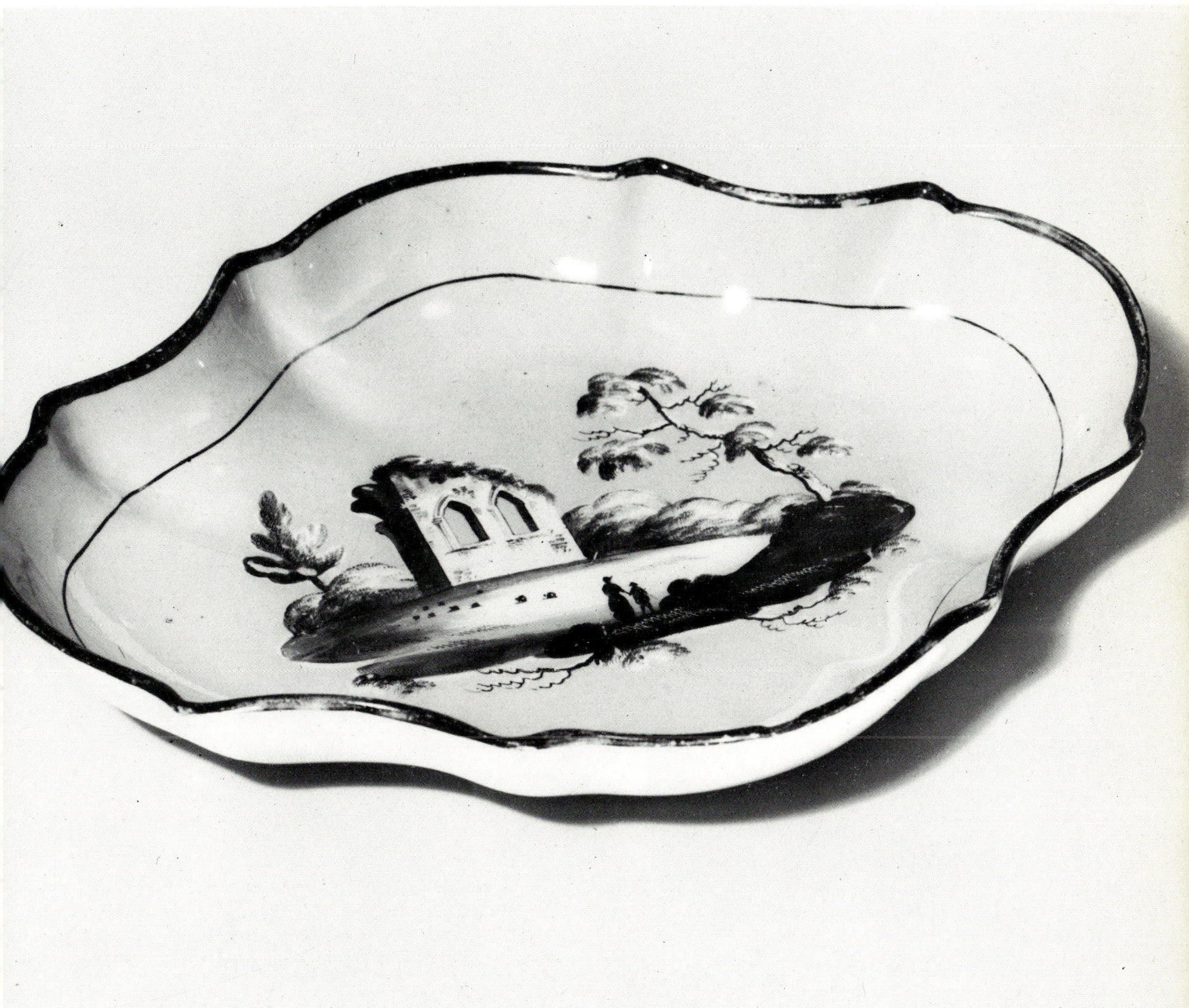

150 Neo-Gothic: a sweetmeat tray, Staffordshire pottery, decorated in thick brown and white enamel on a mushroom ground. Early nineteenth century. Length $9\frac{1}{2}''$, width $7\frac{1}{4}''$. See p. 218.

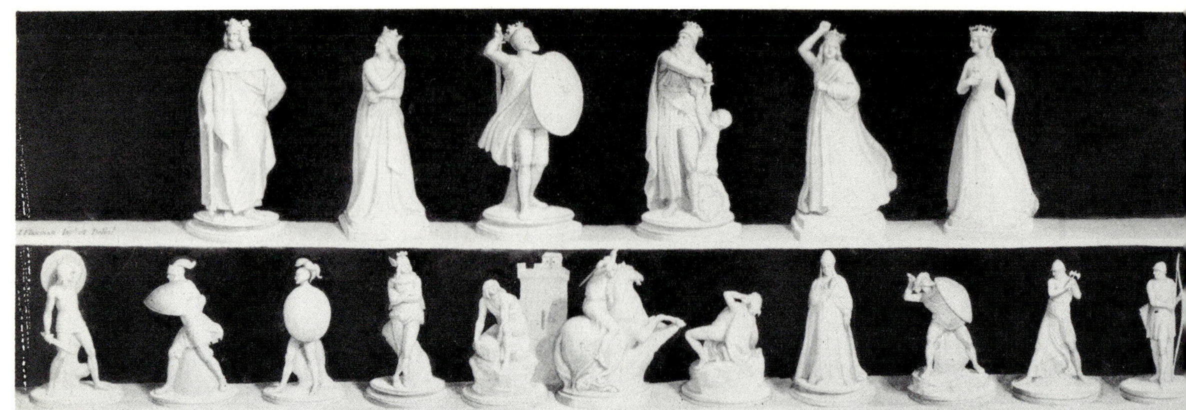

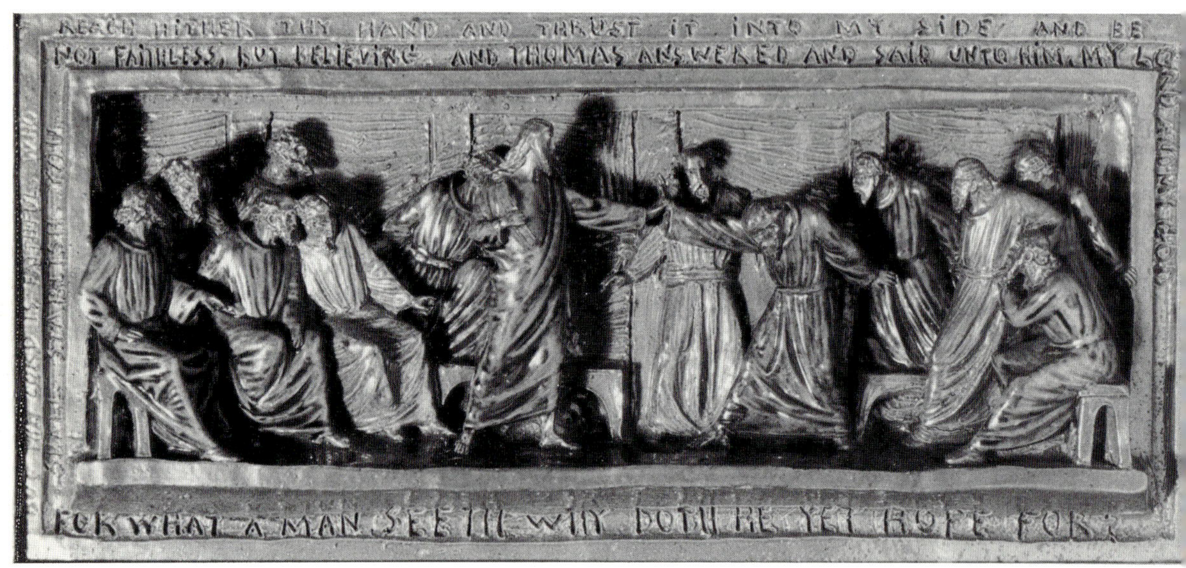

151 (top) Original design by John Flaxman for the Wedgwood chessmen. See p. 218.
152 (centre) 'The Incredulity of St Thomas', by George Tinworth, 1880. See p. 230.
153 (right) American Neo-Gothic: architectural finials made by the Indianapolis Terracotta Company. Late nineteenth century.

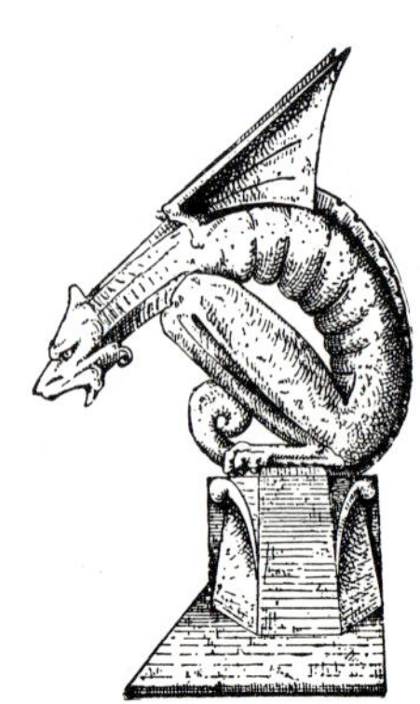
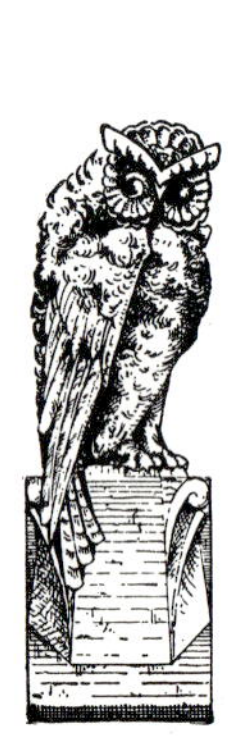
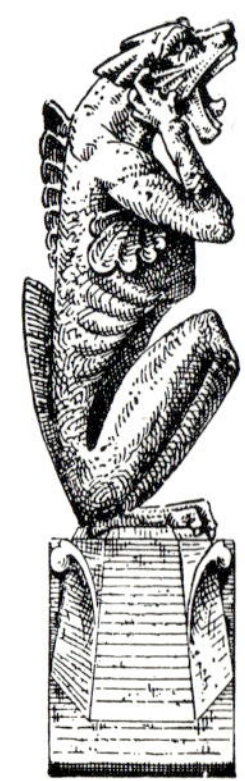

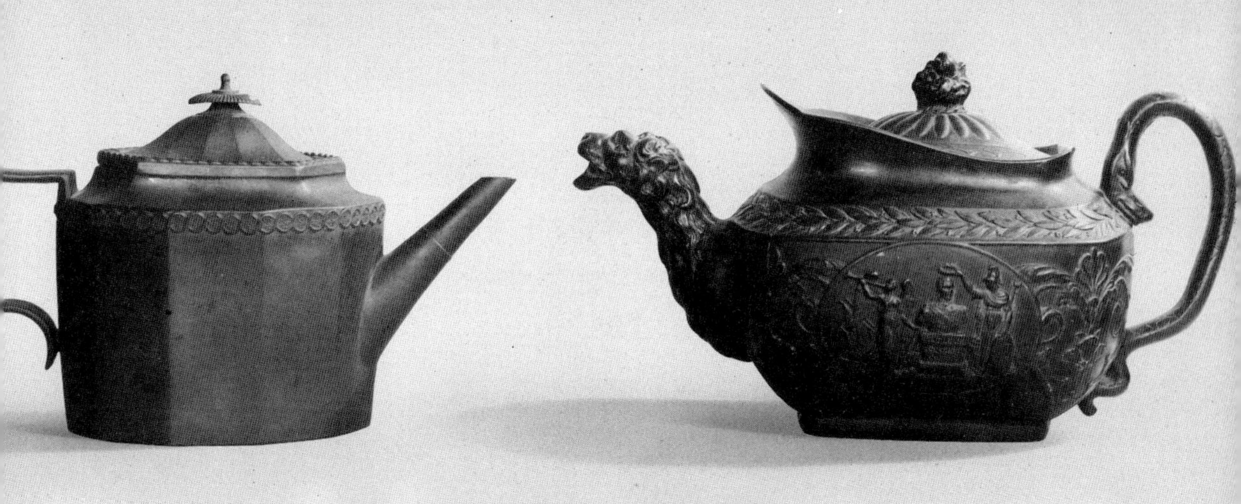

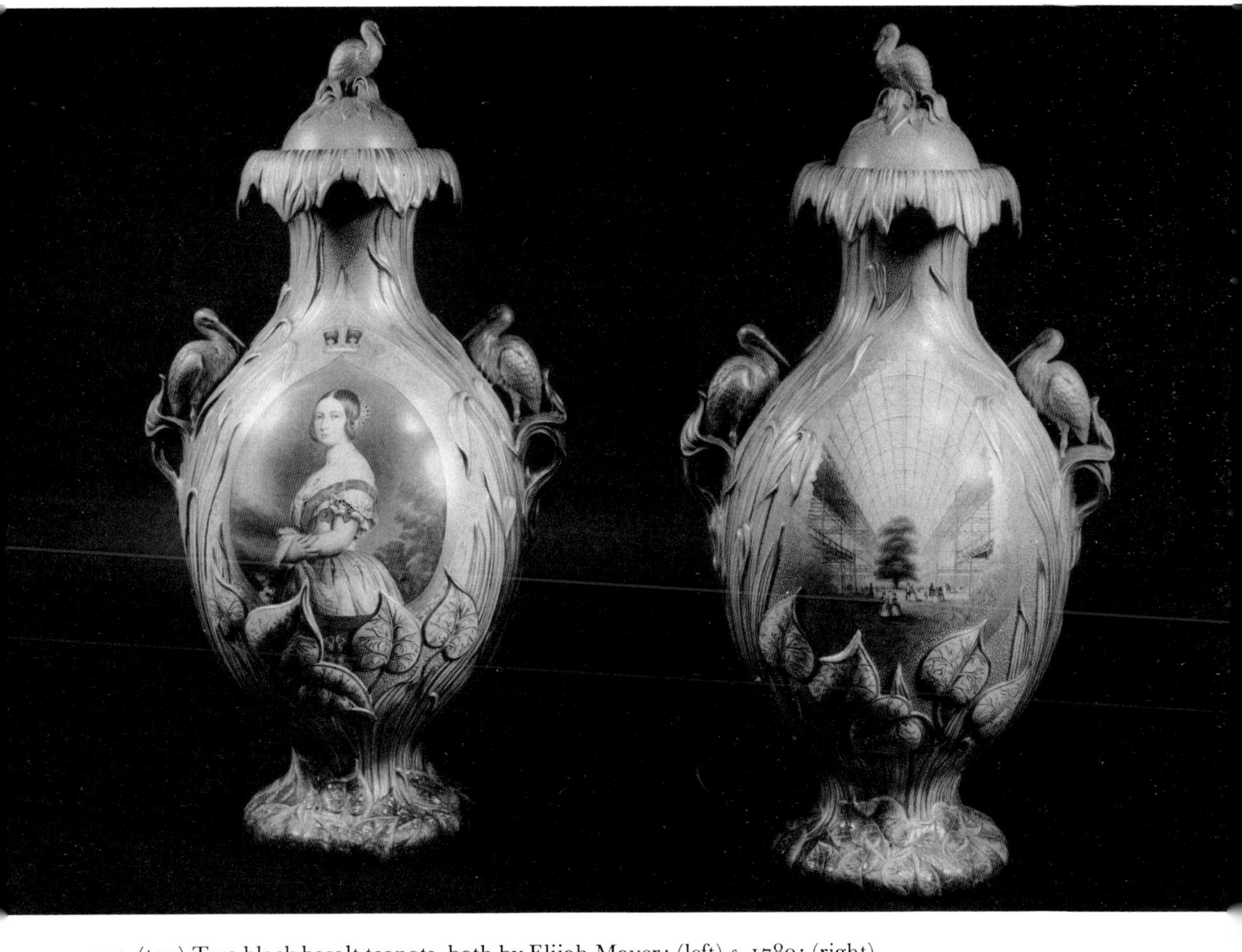

154 (top) Two black basalt teapots, both by Elijah Mayer: (left) *c.* 1780; (right) *c.* 1830. See p. 218.

155 Pair of stoneware vases modelled in relief, painted and gilt. Made by Charles Meigh & Sons, Hanley, Staffordshire, for the Great Exhibition of 1851. See p. 217.

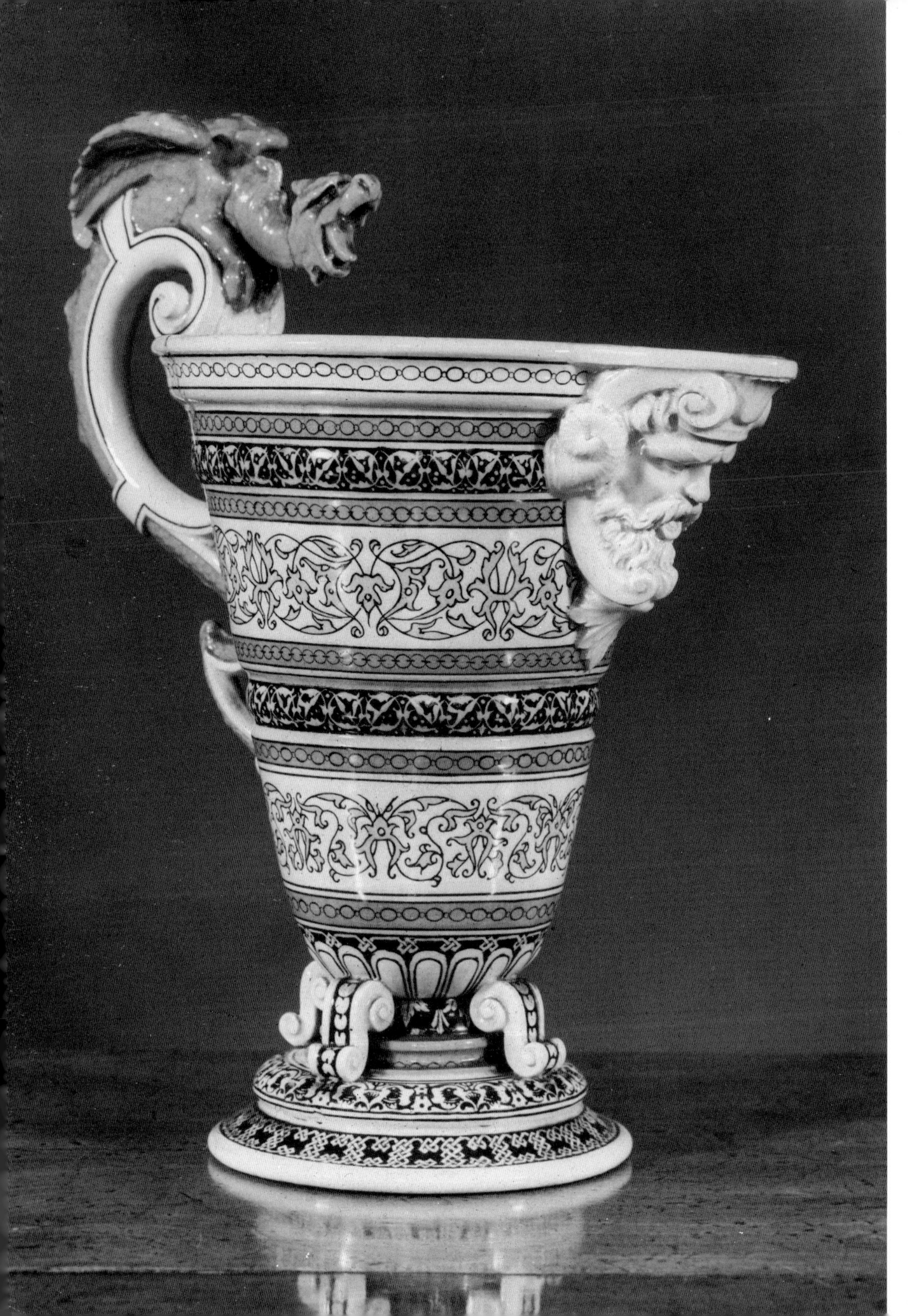

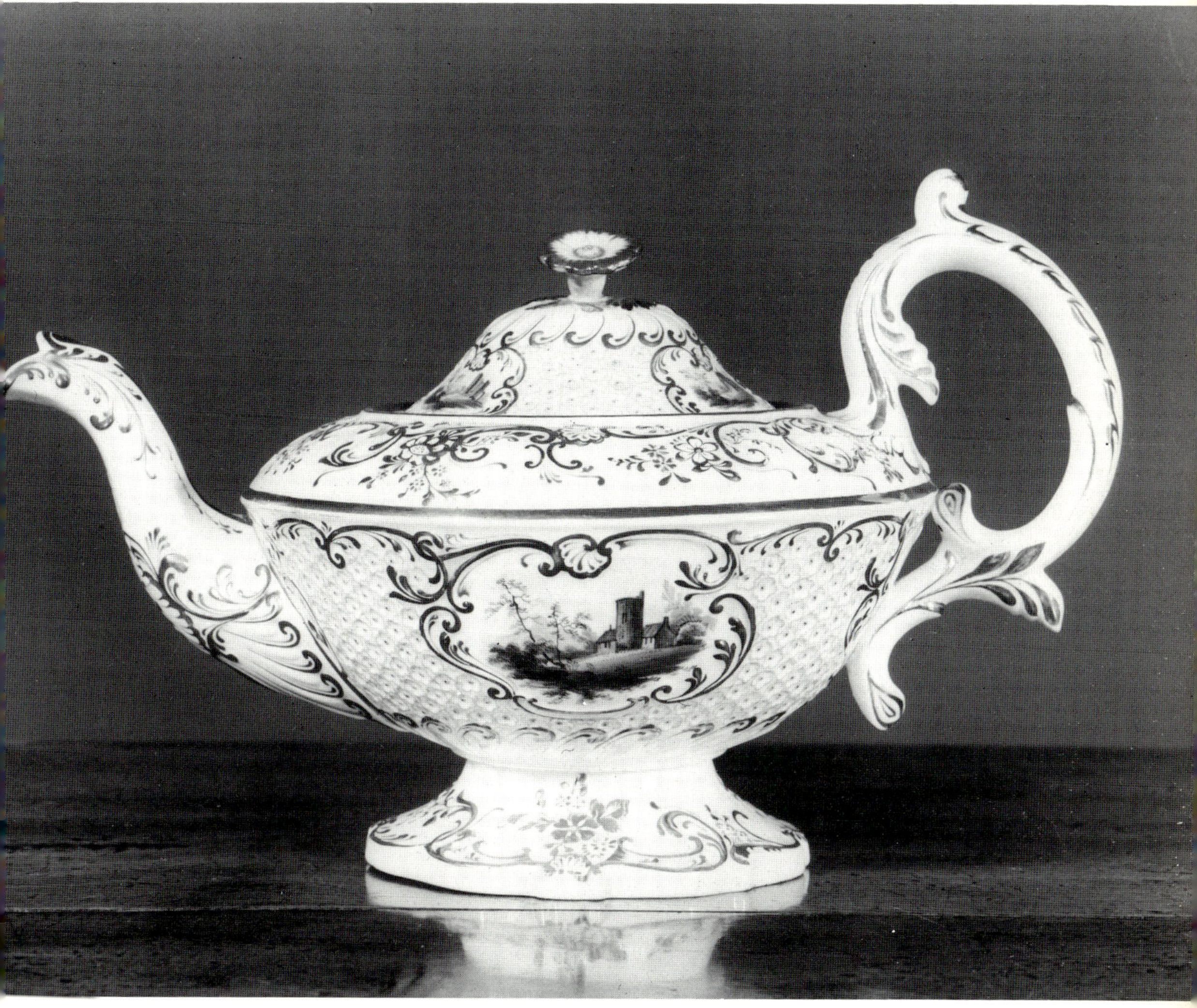

157 Neo-Rococo: A Rockingham-type porcelain teapot, *c.* 1845, probably Staffordshire. Height 6½″. A matching tea-cup (not illustrated here) bears the number 4632. See p. 231.

156 (opposite) Neo-Renaissance: earthenware ewer, decorated in brown and ochre, signed 'C. TOFT. MINTONS 1875'. Height to top of handle: 9½″. See p. 234.

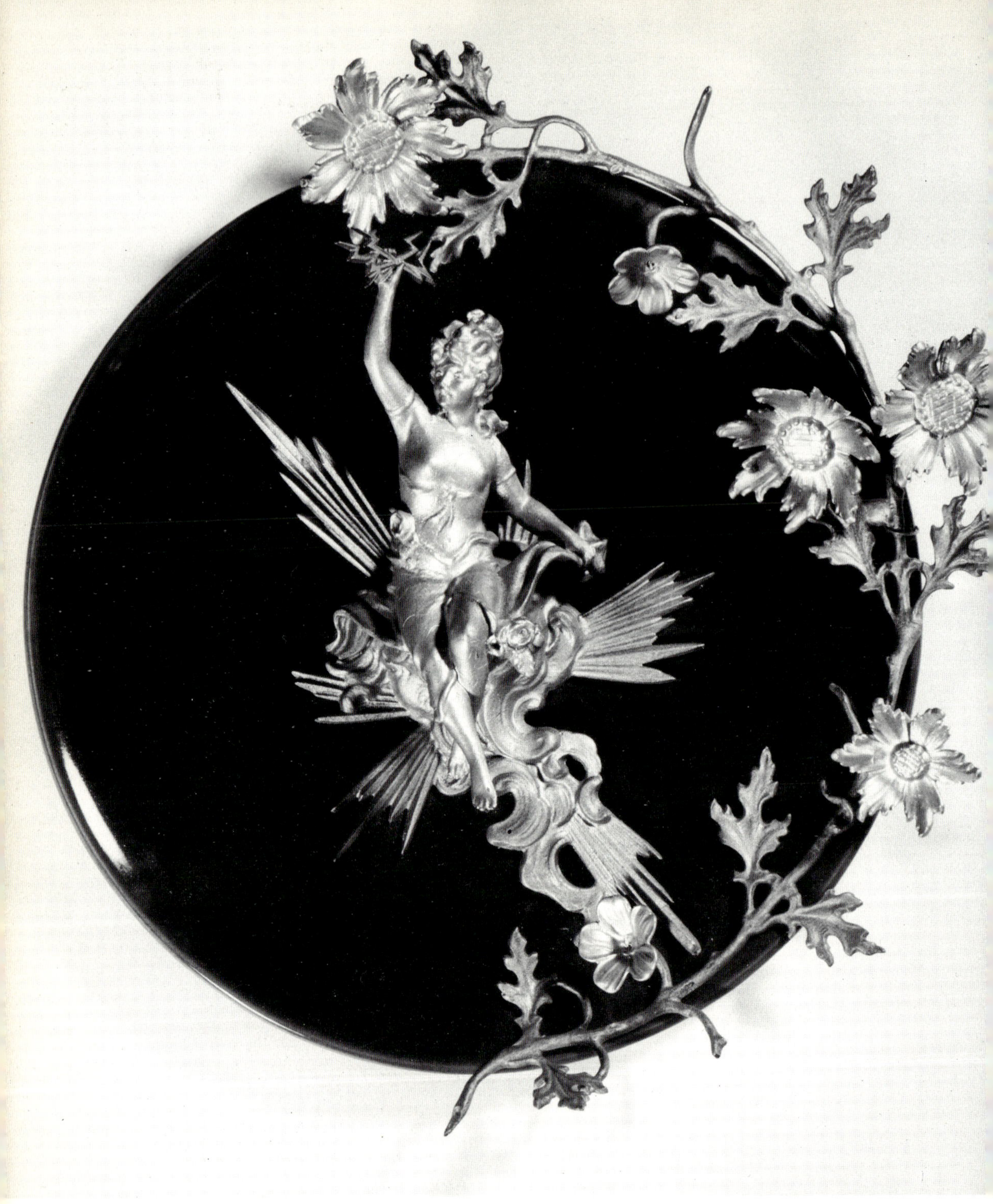

158 Neo-Baroque: red-glazed earthenware plate, diameter 13″, ornamented with ormolu. Probably French, end of nineteenth century. See p. 233.

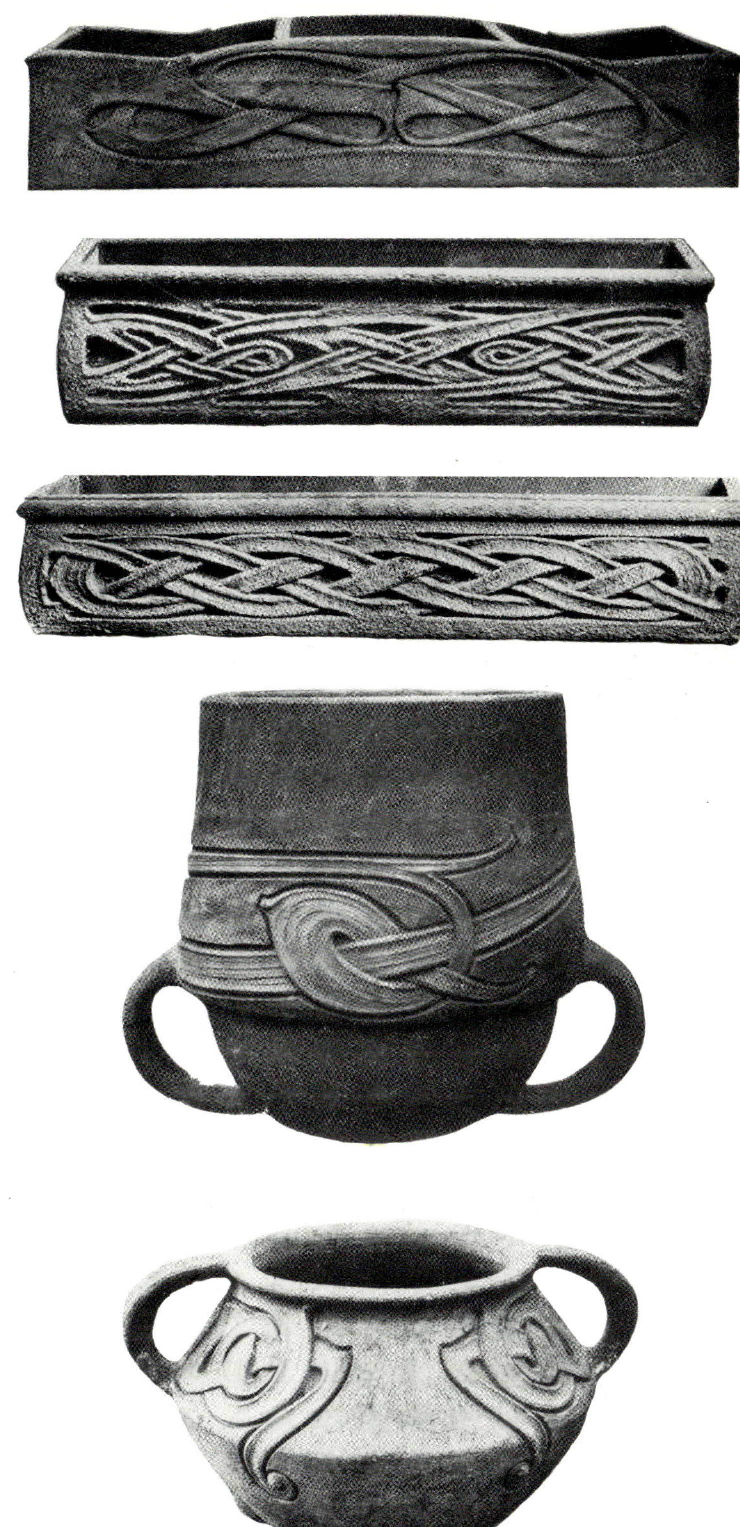

159 and 160 Neo-Celtic: garden pottery, from an undated Liberty catalogue, *c.* 1900. See p. 239.

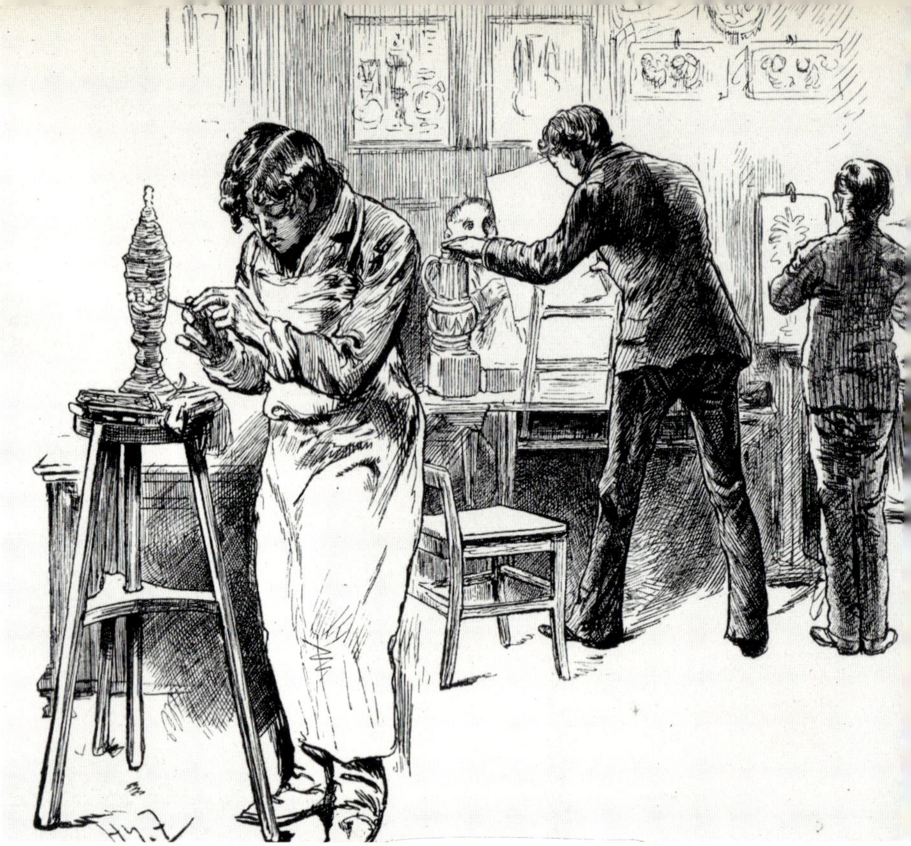

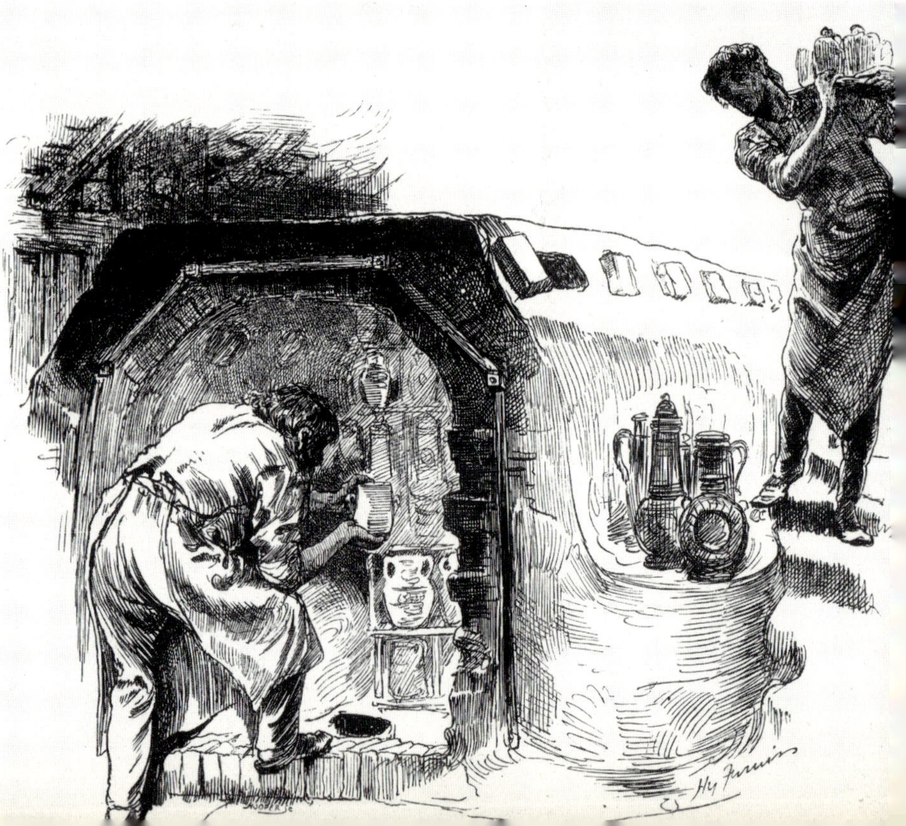

161 and 162
Stoneware revival: two illustrations by Harry Furniss to 'Potters in Rhineland', an article by William Woodall, M.P. for Hanley, Staffordshire, in the *English Illustrated Magazine*, 1890: (top) 'The Technical School'; (bottom) 'Packing the Oven'. See p. 238.

The drawing mentioned in the last entry is in the Wedgwood Museum at Barlaston and shows eighteen pieces (Plate 151). There are three kings, three queens, a knight, a bishop, a castle, a fool and eight different designs for pawns. The drawing is signed 'I. Flaxman, Invt. et Delint'. In the year after it was made, Mr Herbert Croft[11] of Holywell, Oxford, tried to acquire this drawing. On 26 September 1786 he addressed a letter to 'Mr Wedgwood or Mr Byerly, at the Queen'sware Warehouse, Near Soho Square':

Dear Sir,

Tomorrow I shall send you the box and specimen set of chessmen. Enclosed are the keys. My former letters on this subject and the directions I gave your cabinet-maker in Fleet-street,[12] make my troubling you any further on this subject useless, I suppose. But, if you or Mr Byerly wish for anything further, I am at your service. What I originally promised I am also ready to do, when you choose. In return for what I have suggested on the subject, if you will save me the expense of buying a set of the men (since I have half as many children as there are pawns), I shall be obliged to you.

Your medals I still keep, in the hope that you will allow me to be of service in pointing out subjects for a suite of English medals. Pray send me, with the chessmen, the head of my old friend, Dr Johnson[13]; and believe me to be,

Dr Sr very truly yours,

Herbt. Croft.

P.S. If I am in your debt at all, send me the bill also, and I will settle it. Provided you do not hang up Flaxman's drawing of your chessmen, I shall be very glad to give it houseroom among my prints and drawings, and he, I'll answer for it, wd. not be sorry.[14]

Wedgwood wrote to Flaxman from Etruria on 20 February 1784, 'we are getting forward with the Chessmen, and hope soon to send a complete set to Greek Street'.[15] Flaxman wrote to thank Wedgwood for 'the liberal praise you bestowed on my chessman'.[16] Apparently the first pieces were made at the end of 1783 as the Oven Book contains an entry of December 1783 for '8 doz. and 3 Chest Mon blue and white'.[17] A further entry in the same handwriting in February 1784, '5 doz. and 4 Chest Mon, blue and white jasper',[18] is initialled 'D.H.', evidence that Daniel Hollinshead was engaged in producing the chessmen at that time. Another record appears in November 1784: '12 Chest men Gasper Tom Fool'.[19]

The colours of Flaxman's chessmen were blue, white, sage green or cane colour. The pawns were not of a stereotype pattern, but were modelled as warriors, each different. The Kings and Queens may have been based on Kemble and Mrs Siddons. (Flaxman had earlier modelled a portrait medallion of the actress, and one of the Queens, with her arms crossed theatrically, has the same pose.) The 'Tom Fool' was designed to take the place of the bishop in sets exported to France: Wedgwood, who showed vision even in the minute, had discovered that the bishop is 'Le Fou' in a French chess set.[20]

Engravings of some of Flaxman's chessmen were published in William Hone's *Year Book* of 1838. The owner of the set in question, who signed himself 'R.R.', regretted 'that, from the close of Messrs. Wedgewood's [*sic*] establishment in London, no further information relative to these specimens of elegant pottery can be obtained than that "the moulds are still in existence".' Another of Hone's correspondents, 'A.I.', writing in March 1831, contributed a fantasy about the chessmen which transposes them into their natural setting – the atmosphere of a Gothick mystery-novel:

> A few evenings ago, my friend Jamieson called at my chambers to play a game of chess. He has taste in the fine arts, as well as skill in the game, and I produced a set of Flaxman's chess-men, by Wedgewood [*sic*], which I deem it good fortune to possess, and which I think must be the pieces alluded to in the *Year Book*, p. 271.
>
> We had just concluded a game, and were admiring the beauty of the bishop, when a card was brought to my friend. ' 'Tis from a country client,' said he, 'I must attend to him,' 'You can see him in the next room,' I replied, 'and in the mean time I will endeavour to amuse myself with one of Carrera's situations.' Jamieson retired, and I was soon deep in the study of the sixteenth problem. Upon raising my eyes, I was surprised to find my friend's chair occupied by a very quaint looking person, whose style of dress reminded me of Vandyk's picture of the earl of Arundel, only that my visitor's garments did not appear to have been made with quite so much care as that nobleman's are represented to have been.... I was uneasy; for I felt myself in the presence of an unearthly being, and anxiously waited for him to communicate the object of his visit.[21]

Of course the mysterious visitant turns out to be Don Pietro de Carrera (' "My name," said the unknown, "is not strange to you." '), who offers to give 'A.I.' a lesson in the game. ('I bowed, and as stenography is one of the arts I have studied professionally, I instinctively took up the pen I had just used. I was able to write every word that fell from his lips. This circumstance now appears to me to be very extraordinary. The sounds he uttered were in a strange language – it must have been the spirituality of his communication which went straight to my understanding.') Eventually, the Master disappears in a cloud 'from which issued a most delicious fragrance', and Jamieson emerges from behind his cigar smoke, to reproach 'A.I.' for allowing the candle snuffs to reach 'portentous length' and for making hieroglyphics in his sleep.

In the sterner second phase of the Gothic revival, the style begins to have a wider application in ceramics, as in architecture. Gothic jugs in white stoneware became popular. The design of Ridgway's 'Jousting Knights' jug was registered in 1840, that of Meigh's 'Minster' jug, with apostles in niches as on a rood screen or cathedral façade, in 1842. Similar jugs were made by T. J. & J. Mayer, by Cork and Edge, and by T. & R. Boote. A Wedgwood jug of the second decade of the century was perhaps the precursor of this style.

At the same time, there is a new and vast demand for encaustic tiles for ecclesiastical and domestic buildings, modelled on those used in English cathedrals and houses from the beginning of the thirteenth century. A great stimulus was given to this industry by the use of Minton's encaustic tiles in the Palace of Westminster, of which the first stone was laid in 1840. It was as a result of working on sculpture at Westminster that Robert Wallace Martin became the most Gothic of European potters.[22] As a youth he had studied in the studio of John Birnie Philip, a sculptor best known for his work on the Albert Memorial. Philip's earliest sculptural work had been on the new Houses of Parliament, and he had naturally fallen under the influence of Pugin. Working under Philip, then, Martin was likely to be predisposed toward the Gothic. In 1859 Philip offered to take him on as a pupil for a premium of £50, with no salary for the first year. Mrs Martin was prepared to pay the fee, but Wallace would not allow her to sacrifice her small capital, and left Philip's service. But Wallace was related, through an aunt's marriage, to the Barry family. His father worked for the wholesale stationers Barry and Hayward in the City of London (as did Wallace himself for a short time). Mr James Barry showed some of Wallace's drawings and carvings to his brother Sir Charles Barry (1795–1860) who in 1836 had been commissioned to rebuild the Palace of Westminster. A meeting with Sir Charles followed, and Wallace was placed without premium or conditions under Mr Thomas, who was in charge of the stone carving at Westminster.[23]

When Barry had first accepted the great commission, he had arranged for his friend Pugin to be superintendent of the wood-carving. Pugin had directed the formation of a large collection of plaster casts from the most famous examples of Gothic architecture in Europe, to inspire his workmen. Later he superintended the execution of all the woodwork, ornamental metalwork, stained glass and encaustic tiles throughout the building. Although the Houses of Parliament had been formally opened by Queen Victoria in 1852, there was still much decorative work to be done, both on the interior and the exterior. Martin can never have met Pugin, who died in 1852, but he worked under Pugin's chief assistant, Mr Thomas, and among Pugin's plaster casts. This experience left him with a lasting taste for the Gothic. An early ceramic work signed by him is a large vase of 1875, with a caparisoned knight incised into the stoneware with a *sgraffito* technique closely related to that of Hannah Barlow of Doulton's. Beard, discussing the effect of the Pugin casts on Martin's ceramics, suggests that 'his leering birds, his laughing, mocking faces, and his gaping monsters are directly traceable to the monstrous finials, corbels and gargoyles among which he then worked.'[24] Some of the famous 'Wally-birds' are seen in the photograph (Plate 166) of all three brothers at work – which seems to me a greater work of art than anything they made. As a neo-Gothic master of the impertinent grotesque, Wallace Martin has only two rivals, the Indianapolis Terracotta Company in America (Plate 153), and the superb O'Shea who was forced to decapitate the parrots and owls which he had carved on the Oxford University Museum in effigy of members of Convocation.[25]

Like O'Shea, George Tinworth (Wallace Martin's lifelong friend) was a protégé of Ruskin. 'Mr. Ruskin,' said the *Strand Magazine*, 'became as strongly convinced of Tinworth's genius as he is of Turner's.'[26] At the Lambeth School of Art, where he studied with Martin under John Sparkes, he made some colossal terracotta medallions copied from ancient Greek and Sicilian coins. When Ruskin came to give away the prizes, he took one of these medallions as his text for a lesson on the principles of relief. In 1875, Ruskin's praise of three large terracottas of religious subjects exhibited by Tinworth at the Royal Academy, obtained for Tinworth a client, the neo-Gothic architect G. E. Street. Street commissioned him to produce panels for a reredos at York Minster and lunettes for the Guards' Chapel in Birdcage Walk, London. As with Martin, these early experiences in architecture gave Tinworth's later work a strong Gothic bias. His contemporaries thought him a second Ghiberti; and when he died, a London street was named after him.[27]

The rococo revival was the most powerful influence in ceramics for most of the century; the same taste is shown in the vogue for Sèvres porcelain among collectors. It is seen at its most extravagant in the shell-encrusted plates made by Chamberlain at Worcester and in the

'Rockingham' style teapots (Plate 157) made by such firms as Samuel Alcock and Co. and Hilditch and Hopwood. Sometimes the rococo revival outdid the rococo itself. Copies made in the 1870s by Stevenson and Hancock of Derby of the set of child seasons originally made in the eighteenth century by Bristol and John Turner were given scalloped and scrolled pedestals, while the original models had relatively plain bases.

Among the other Hogarthian precepts now being obeyed again is naturalism, as in the large leaves on the Great Exhibition vases by Meigh (Plate 155) and Grainger & Co., both uncannily anticipating *art nouveau*. But it must be added that the most unrococo of potters could also favour naturalism, simply because it *was* natural. Faithfulness to nature went with faithfulness to the natural qualities of one's materials. We find both characteristics in the paintings of the utterly unrococo Pre-Raphaelites, who belong to the neo-Gothic, Arts-and-Crafts tradition. Similarly, the neo-Gothic Martin brothers, who allowed expression to the natural qualities of their coarse stoneware, hunted for new shapes in the vegetable gardens which surrounded their Southall factory:

> The primary source of inspiration [writes Beard] was the *Cucurbitacea ovi fersacada* – the common vegetable marrow – the ribbings of which slightly exaggerated and the mottled skin of which they reproduced with remarkable fidelity in numerous vases ... and it was not long before they added to their repertoire a rough texture based upon cucumber skin.[28]

Cochin, who was so unkind about the French silversmiths' artichokes and celery,[29] would have had a field day criticizing the Martin brothers' pots. Like so much that they did, these aesthetic forays into the vegetable patch have a Marx brothers drollery. But the results are among the most successful of their wares, comparable with Japanese gourd and egg-plant pots.

The neo-rococo suffered fluctuations in power as other styles came into fashion, but it was as strong as ever in the 1890s. In 1896 Gleeson White, the greenery-yallery future editor of *The Studio*, attacked the style in the newly founded magazine *The Quarto*, with the bludgeoning raillery which passed for art criticism at the time:

> The unlooked-for happened, the one period most hated by esthetes, most abhorred by earnest disciples of Ruskin, most degrading to the Eastlake art student, has been revived, with all its lawless ornament and bizarre decoration, and a costume even worse than the period when its last visitation occurred. Here we leave fanciful theory and touch upon painful but absolute fact. A special mission lately undertaken to discover the art standard prevalent in the chief manufactures of Great Britain, yielded one certain truth: in every

branch of industry that touched art productions, the renascence of the Rococo was evident, although deplored. But all the same, there it was, and the old discarded text-books were being ransacked for motives, to be re-arranged for the new fashion. You found carpets and other fabrics woven in patterns of florid character, pottery and glass, furniture and metal-work, were all being shaped in ornate curves, and embellished with the sprawling lawless ornament of the most vulgar decoration that ever grew to be recognized as a style.

The flamboyant and voluptuous curves of this gorgeous and ornate decoration have already conquered the simpler lines of the Queen Anne period, and the spiky stiffness of modern Gothic. The lily and the sunflower are dethroned to allow the extraordinary and unnatural impossibilities of the rococo flora to reign in their stead. The thing like an old-fashioned jam-tart, the foliage like a limp head of celery or an acanthus run to seed, the tortured capital C's writhing in agonies, the wickerwork baskets of ultra-naturalistic flowers, the sprawling rotund cupids, and all the motley motives belonging to this carnival of artistic license, are, for the moment, rampant in our homes. To them, no doubt, will soon come the mythological ceiling, where fat and nude deities defy the laws of perspective, gravitation and decency at once. The sham architectural framework, with the fluttering ribbons, wind-tossed draperies, and general riot of colour and form, is already beginning to dazzle our astonished eyes, and will, ere long, be pronounced 'good form' and entirely high toned. All our carefully-learned sobriety is to be forgotten, and in one rebellious outburst against all canons of taste or principles of design, we are to proclaim the triumph of disorder, and declare the artistic decoration of a third-rate music-hall, the gilded chariots of a travelling circus, and the saloons of a second-rate steamboat, to be alone admirable....[30]

Gleeson White tried to predict what would follow:

What is to be the next style? Herein history and evolution agree. The reaction against unlicensed extravagance will be again followed by a stern despotism, the rabble of the rococo will only yield to a dictatorship with rigid and inflexible convention new to this generation ... classic art, pure and stately, is certain in some shape to sweep away the crew of baser decoration. ... The rococo will have to run its course first, it is true; but its short and hideous 'carmagnole' must end in a new autocracy....[31]

He was, of course, quite right, as the art of the 1920s and 1930s shows. But he misjudged the length of the rococo 'carmagnole', did not foresee *art nouveau*, of which the rococo was to be one of the strongest ingredients, and of which, ironically, he himself, as editor of *The Studio*, was to be one of the chief promulgators.

Contemporary with this rococo revival in England, there was a baroque revival in Germany, and, to a lesser extent, in France. Dr

Hempel pushes the origins of the revival back to the early years of the century, and has a charming explanation for it: 'Once again, as in the seventeenth century, it was the attractive personality of Rubens that paved the way for an understanding of the Baroque. Delacroix was the pioneer.'[32] The idea is appealing; but in fact there is no manifest baroque revival until the second half of the century, and the main impulse would seem to have been the growth of art history. In 1887 Cornelius Gurlitt published his *Geschichte des Barockstils in Italien*; in 1888 Heinrich Wölfflin's *Renaissance und Barock* appeared; and in 1889 another study by Gurlitt, *Geschichte des Barockstiles und des Rokoko in Deutschland* was published. The neo-baroque is best illustrated by the art of Adolf Menzel (1815–1903) and such architecture as Paul Wallot's Reichstag building in Berlin (1884–94) or Charles Girault's *Petit Palais* in Paris (1897–1900). It never took much hold on ceramics (being even more unsuitable for that medium than the true baroque) but appears at its most horrific in a class of French pottery wares with metal additions (Plate 158).

Like the baroque revival, the Renaissance revival of the same period was closely connected with new art histories, especially German ones. In 1860 Jacob Burckhardt's *Die Kultur der Renaissance* was published. In 1868 Lübke's *Geschichte der Renaissance Frankreichs* appeared, and 1873, the year of Lübke's *Geschichte der Deutschen Renaissance*, was also the year in which Walter Pater's book of essays, *The Renaissance*, provoked the furious silence of Ruskin – if anything, more forbidding than his tirades. In a prose like burst plums, Pater gave expression to acute ideas which are still active in art philosophy. And the way in which he evoked Renaissance art was well calculated to work on the Victorian mind, used to sentimental overstatement of all kinds. He might tell his readers, of della Robbia pottery, that 'no work is less imitable: like Tuscan wine, it loses its savour when moved from its birthplace, from the crumbling walls where it was first placed';[33] but he can hardly have been surprised that the Victorian potters produced imitation 'della Robbia ware', when he wrote of it, 'I suppose nothing brings the real air of a Tuscan town so vividly to mind as those pieces of pale blue and white earthenware, by which he is best known, like fragments of the milky way itself, fallen into the cool streets, and breaking into the darkened churches.'[34]

The seven volumes of *The Renaissance in Italy* by John Addington Symonds were published between 1875 and 1886. And German erudition was not exhausted. Another book by Lübke in 1877 – *Der Formenschatz der Renaissance*; in 1880 Hauser's *Stil-Lehre der Architektonischen*

Formen der Renaissance; in 1888 Wölfflin's *Renaissance und Barock*. Art history was becoming less romantically evocative, more analytic. Wölfflin's *Classic Art* (1899) discussed the Italian Renaissance from an almost exclusively formal point of view, quite alien to the larger-than-life, personality-cult approach of Burckhardt and Symonds. The new approach led away from hero-worship, direct imitation and revivals, towards a more cerebral and self-determining art.

But while it lasted, the Renaissance revival had an overwhelming influence on ceramics. In France, the natural derivation was from the French Renaissance, the Renaissance of Azay-le-Rideau and Chenonceau, so beloved by Pater and abhorred by Ruskin. French wares at the Paris Exhibition of 1878 are covered in arabesques. Hero-worship of Bernard Palissy led to the researches and imitative works of Charles Antoine Avisseau (1796–1861) and his pupil Georges Pull (1810–89), the founders of the studio pottery movement in France. In England, Edward Bingham of Castle Hedingham, Essex (Plate 171) was inspired by the life of Palissy, and made unhappy pastiches of his work.[35] Minton's also imitated Palissy; in 1860 the South Kensington Museum acquired an original Palissy ewer, a copy of which it had already bought from Minton's in the previous year. Minton's made Renaissance wares on a more extensive scale than any other firm. They showed 'majolica' at the 1851 Exhibition, and began a Victorian craze closely paralleled in the activities of collectors. In 1856 the *Art Journal* said 'the Minton majolica is one of the most successful revivals of modern pottery.'[36] One Minton majolica dish shown at the 1862 Exhibition is painted with a Roman soldier after Mantegna. Alfred Stevens was the most eminent of the artists who painted their Renaissance wares. They also made the della Robbia pottery, and the 'Henri Deux' (or Saint-Porchaire) wares, the technique of which was a kind of ceramic marquetry, coloured clays being inlaid in a buff-coloured body. Henri Deux ware was also made by Kerr and Binns at Worcester, and by Wedgwoods. Once again, the work of a famous artist on Wedgwood chess sets gave distinguished expression to a revived style. The artist in this case was Walter Crane, who worked at Etruria from 1867 to 1871. The relevant entry in the Museum records reads:

Chessmen and Table.

Chess Table.	Henry II Ware – – – – –	£10 : 10 : –.
Chess Men.	(16) each 10/– – – – – – –	8 : – : –.
„ Pawns.	(16) „ 7/– – – – – – –	5 : 12 : –.
Whole fitted up with Table as the Exhibition Piece –	–	£45 : – : –.

XI (*opposite*) Two nineteenth-century music-sheets showing contemporary ceramics.

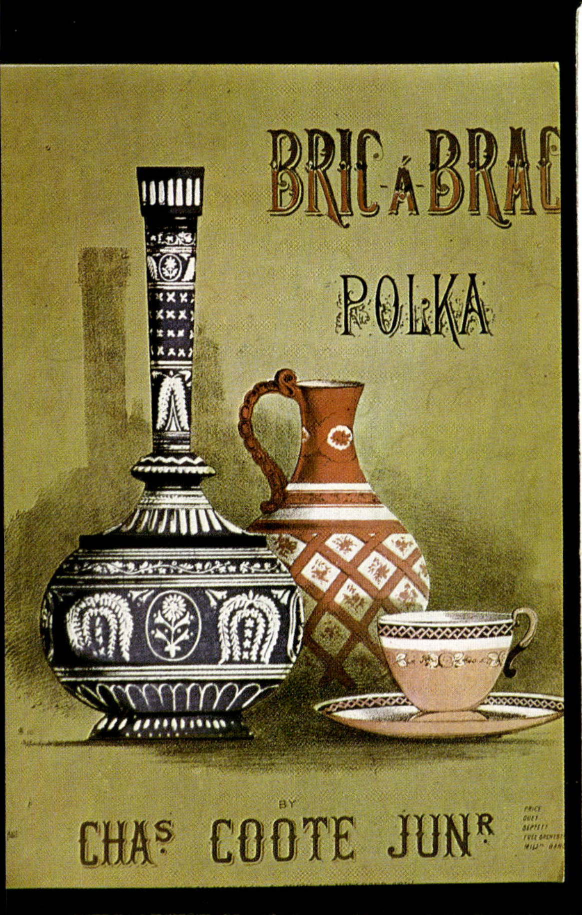
BRIC-Á-BRAC
POLKA
BY
CHAS COOTE JUNR

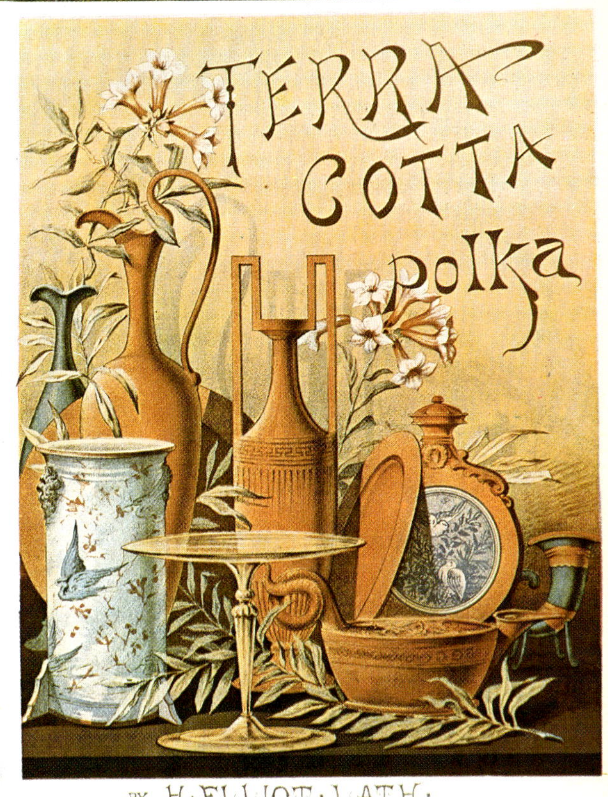
TERRA
COTTA
polka
BY H·ELLIOT·LATH·
ENT. STA. HALL
PRICE 4
London.
SWAN & Co 4, Gt MARLBOROUGH STREET, W.

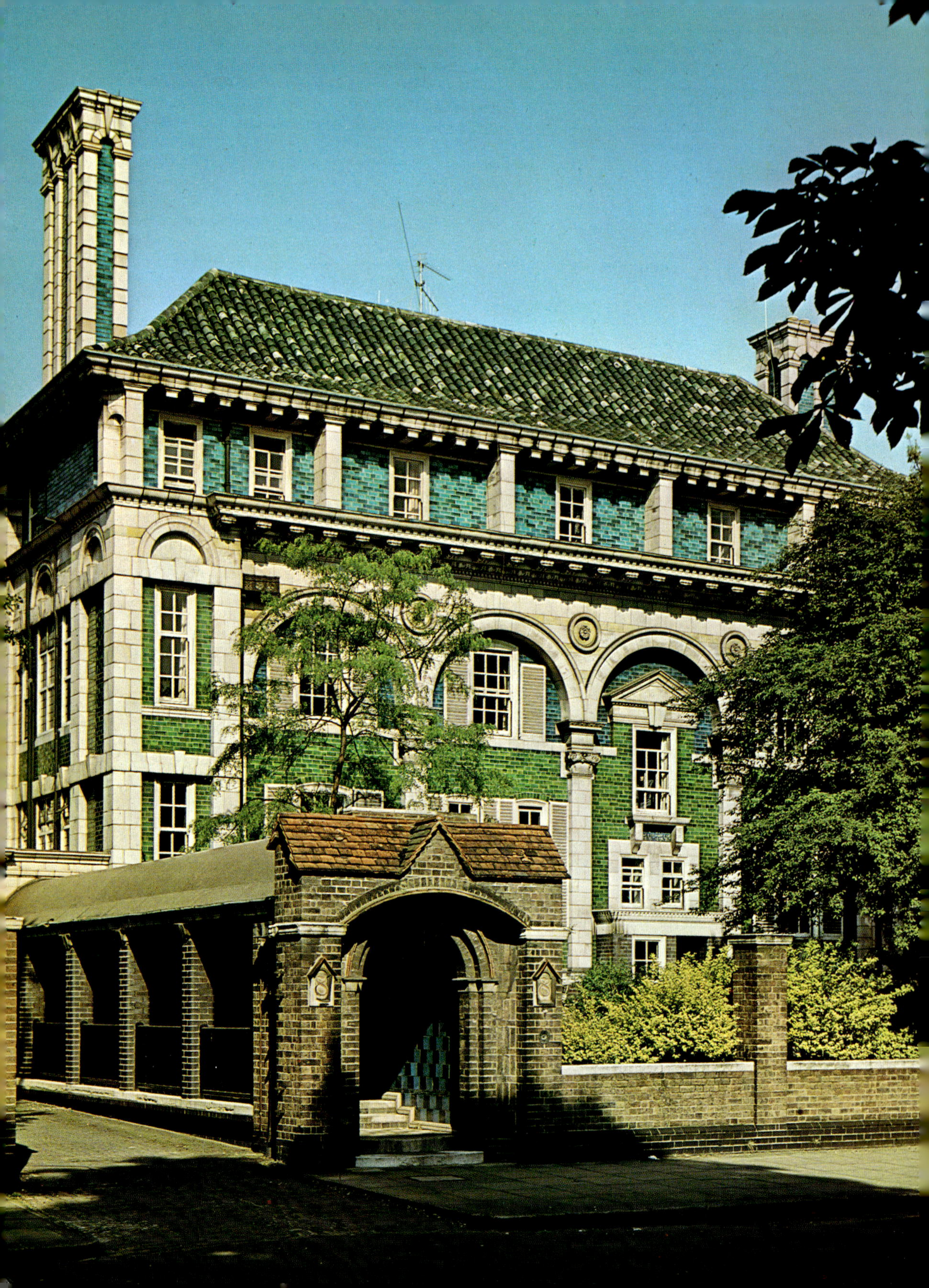

Here, then, is a pioneer of *art nouveau* (some think, *the* pioneer) serving an apprenticeship in historicism.[37]

The Renaissance revival gave the Martin brothers yet another chance to indulge in the grotesque. Between 1880 and 1895 they produced a series of vases, jars and ewers of characteristic Renaissance design. Beard points out[38] that this period roughly coincides with Wallace's friendship with Sir William Richmond Drake (1817–90), Chairman of the Burlington Fine Arts Club, whose book, *Notes on Venetian Ceramics*, had been published in 1868. The Martin brothers' most ambitious work in this style was a terracotta fireplace and overmantel made in 1891 for Buscot Hall, Berkshire. 'Based on Italian Renaissance designs,' writes Beard, 'it consists of a large semi-circular arch surmounted by an oblong panel decorated with Lord Faringdon's arms, and topped by a series of three round-headed coved niches flanked by Renaissance columns.'[39]

Terracotta was one of two ceramic materials greatly revived in the nineteenth century. It was developed by French firms in the 1840s; but at the 1851 Exhibition, several English companies, notably Minton's and F. & R. Pratt, showed large-scale terracottas, and in 1858 Copeland's exhibited two terracotta busts of Minerva and Juno in the Ceramic Court of the Crystal Palace. Doulton's showed large terracottas at the Paris Exhibition of 1867, and, at the South Kensington Exhibition of 1871 their *pièce de résistance* was a fountain designed by John Sparkes and modelled by Tinworth: it was later erected at Kennington Park. In the 1880s and 1890s, terracotta plaques, often ornamented with neo-Renaissance arabesques, were widely used in architecture. The Watcombe Pottery, founded in the 1860s near Torquay, and the Torquay Terracotta Company, founded in 1875, specialized in small terracottas. The novelty of such wares and the fashion for them must have been considerable, as a 'Terracotta Polka' was published (Plate XI). Terracotta was the most suitable material for making the Biblical pots (Plate 5), never more popular than at this time. But the Martin brothers could be relied on to find the quaintest use for any given material. A contributor to *The Colonies and India and American Visitor* of 29 July 1893 wrote:

> A curious and quite original business is now being done in cinerary urns of Martinware. It was Mr Charles Martin's lugubrious duty, a short time ago, to seal up the remains of a gentleman and his wife in two handsome jars prior to their being deposited in the family vault, whence in the dim and distant future they may possibly be unearthed, the spoil of some enthusiastic archaeologist of a race yet unborn.[40]

XII (*opposite*) No. 8, Addison Road, Kensington, London: the house built for Sir Ernest Debenham by Halsey Ricardo. Many of the tiles with which this 'ceramic palace' was faced were supplied by William De Morgan.

The revival of the other material, stoneware, began in Germany in the 1840s. In 1890 William Woodall, Member of Parliament for Hanley, wrote an article in *The English Illustrated Magazine,* entitled 'Potters in Rhineland'. It was illustrated by the *Punch* cartoonist Harry Furniss (Plates 161–2). Woodall wrote:

> Siegburg suffered severely during the wars of the seventeenth century; and the potters, despairing of being able to carry on their industry in peaceful security, finally emigrated to other lands. All attempts to induce them to return to their ruined abodes and desolated town were unsuccessful; but about fifty years ago an enterprising and ingenious potter undertook to revive on the spot the old manufacture. With the aid of ancient moulds, discovered in the neighbourhood, he reproduced the ware of the old types, following closely the old traditions. These revivals found a ready market, by the agency of unscrupulous dealers, as veritable examples, and long held unchallenged their places in public museums and the cabinets of collectors as genuine examples of the much-prized ware of Siegburg.

Woodall described a similar stoneware revival in the so-called *Kannerbacherland,* or German Potteries, in the province of Nassau: 'the blue revival of the *Grès de Flandres* is everywhere *en évidence.*' In the Prussian Royal Trade School, which he visited as a member of the Royal Commission on Technical Instruction, Woodall saw youths learning to make reproductions of sixteenth-century stoneware (Plate 161).

In England, a new interest in stoneware was aroused by the discovery of a cache of Dwight stoneware in a sealed-off chamber in Fulham. This collection was bought from the last representative of the Dwight family in 1862, by Mr Baylis of Prior's Bank, and was sold at Christie's by a later owner, Mr C. W. Reynolds, from 29 May to 1 June 1871. The German wares were also in favour, especially among the Arts and Crafts men, and in the *Art Journal* of 1874 Professor T. C. Archer drew a parallel between the new Doulton wares and the seventeenth-century European stonewares, whose makers, he said, were 'guided by the nature of the material ... and never played tricks with it by trying to make it do more than it was capable of being made to do well.'

The Celtic Revival stemmed partly from the romantic interest in history and archaeology which had contributed so much to the neo-Gothic. This interest often took a national turn, and in Ireland became associated with the Home Rule movement. Scandinavians looked back to the heroic Viking epoch and developed the 'dragon style' based on the motifs of Nordic art. This revival in Scandinavia had hardly any direct effect in England, though William Morris visited Iceland and in 1872 began to translate the sagas, while Sir Lawrence Alma-Tadema, a Friesian, presented his friend Edmund Gosse with Nordic texts. In Great Britain the comparable art of the Celts inspired a new enthusiasm. Queen Victoria was so impressed with the illuminated Book of Kells that she added her own gracious autograph to it. In 1850 the Tara Brooch was found, and Celtic ornament was gradually adopted by silversmiths, goldsmiths and book illustrators. At the 1851 Exhibition, jewellery exhibited by James West & Sons, of Dublin, was described as 'copied from antique Irish ornaments', and at the Dublin Exhibition of 1853, a copy of the Tara Brooch was shown by Messrs Waterhouse of Dublin. In the 1840s, 1850s and 1860s, George Petrie and Henry O'Neill published their works on Irish archaeology. Edward Sullivan's *Facsimiles of National Manuscripts of Ireland* was published in 1876. Lady Charlotte Guest, better known to us as the great china collector, Lady Charlotte Schreiber, translated the Welsh Celtic legends of the *Mabinogion* into English. Gerard Manley Hopkins drew on Welsh poetry for the literary device known as 'cynghanedd'.

But the most passionate phase of the Celtic revival began with the publication of Yeats's *The Wanderings of Oisin, and other Poems* in 1889, followed by *The Countess Kathleen* (1892) and *The Celtic Twilight* (1893). Lady Gregory, George Russell ('A.E.'), Lionel Johnson and George Moore were other Irish writers who contributed to the revival. In 1891, Grant Allen, who had written about the First Potter in *The Fortnightly Review*, wrote in the same journal:

> The Celt in Britain, like Mr Burne Jones's enchanted princess, has lain silent for ages in an enforced long sleep; but the spirit of the century, pushing aside the weeds and the briars of privilege and caste, has set free the sleeper at last.

The revived Celtic style was one of the main sources of Dr Christopher Dresser's Linthorpe designs; but its introduction into popular ceramics was by Sir Arthur Liberty. Liberty's were selling a 'Cymric Silver' in 1900, and their Celtic ceramics, including the garden furniture in 'frostproof earthenware' (Plates 159–60) must date from about the same time. Liberty's 'Barum Ware', 'with Celtic interlacing', is illustrated in their 1908 catalogue of 'Yule-Tide Gifts'.

The origins of two minor revivals, Persian and Arabian, were also mainly literary. Edward Fitzgerald's translation of the *Rubaiyat of Omar Khayyam* was a Victorian best-seller, and had an especial relevance to potters. Mr Hugh Wakefield illustrates a 'Persian' vase by Minton.[41]

William De Morgan was more directly influenced by Persian lustre wares, such as those with which Lord Leighton filled his house at Kensington. Burton's translation of *The Arabian Nights* gave Arabia a pantomime glory, and his *Travels* aroused further interest, in part prurient, as did the Biblical cadences of Doughty's *Arabia Deserta*.

But it must not be assumed that revived styles were merely inspired by immensely popular literary works which would appeal even to the 'humble potter'. Abraham Lomax, in his inside story of *The Royal Lancastrian Pottery, 1900–1938* shows how, at least by that late stage, quite recondite works of art history were being brought to the potter's notice:

> The firm did not overlook the necessity to nourish the mind and spirit of the Art staff. Good books on art and pottery were at their disposal. One of the many fine books provided was the classic work of Sarre and Martin, *Mohammedanischer Kunst* – an expensive work in three volumes containing a great collection of well-chosen examples of Mohammedan art magnificently reproduced in colour.[42]

The future of ceramics, it might have seemed, would lie in an ever more sycophantic dependence on ever more scholarly sources of archaic design. But *art nouveau* took the revived styles in a boa embrace. The 'new autocracy' predicted by Gleeson White supervened. 'Abstracts' (to adopt Hamlet's convenient terminology) succeeded 'brief chronicles of the time'.

11 Artist potters in England

A few artists were able to glorify or romanticize the industrialism of the nineteenth century. In Turner's paintings, steam sports with the elements on equal terms. Factory chimneys belch the same black defiance as the tug of the *Fighting Téméraire*. The smoke in Monet's *Gare Saint-Lazare* billows under the glass like a Constable sky brought indoors. Whistler wrote: 'When the evening mist clothes the riverside with poetry as a veil and the poor buildings lose themselves in the dim sky ... the tall buildings become *campanili* and the warehouses are palaces in the night.'[1]

But the reaction of most artists to industrialism was escape. Gauguin sought the primitive in Pont Aven and Tahiti. In England, the most industrial country, the Pre-Raphaelites put the present resolutely behind them and retired into a medieval fantasy, 'quaint chambers in quaint palaces where angels creep in through sliding panel doors, and stand behind rows of flowers, drumming on golden bells, with wings crimson and green'.[2] William Morris bought Kelmscott Manor in the Oxfordshire countryside, and made it the 'Nowhere' of *News from Nowhere*. The aesthetes took refuge in art itself – *l'Art pour l'Art*. More physically, they escaped into private bohemias where absinthe glittered in thimble glasses and languid hands described epigrams in the air.

The potter must escape too. George Moore inveighed against industrial ceramics:

> The world is dying of machinery; that is the great disease, that is the plague that will sweep away and destroy civilization; man will have to rise against it sooner or later....[3] Capital, unpaid labour, wage-slaves, and all the rest – stuff....[4] Look at these plates; they were painted by machinery; they are abominable. Look at them. In old times plates were painted by the hand,

and the supply was necessarily limited to the demand, and a china in which there was always something more or less pretty, was turned out; but now thousands, millions of plates are made more than we want, and there is a commercial crisis; the thing is inevitable. I say the great and the reasonable revolution will be when mankind rises in revolt, and smashes the machinery and restores the handicrafts.[5]

While Moore damned the present, Wilde idealized the past:

In those days the artist was free. From the river valley he took the fine clay in his fingers, and with a little tool of wood or bone, fashioned it into forms so exquisite that the people gave them to the dead as their playthings, and we find them still in the dusty tombs on the yellow hillside by Tanagra, with the faint gold and fading crimson still lingering about hair and lips and raiment. ... The potter sat in his shed, and, flower-like from the silent wheel, the vase rose up beneath his hands. He decorated the base and stem and ears with pattern of dainty olive-leaf, of foliated acanthus, or curved and crested wave. Then in black or red he painted lads wrestling, or in the race: knights in full armour, with strange heraldic shields and curious visors, leaning from shell-shaped chariot over rearing steeds: the gods seated at the feast or working their miracles: the heroes in their victory or in their pain.[6]

The aesthetes told the potter what he should escape from and to, but practically the back-to-handicrafts movement was led by a Pre-Raphaelite, William Morris. He himself made stained glass, wove and dyed tapestries, and printed books and wallpaper. While the aesthetes saw the artist as a being distinct from the irredeemable bourgeois,[7] Morris saw the artist in every man, and preached a socialism of art by which mass production would be replaced by honest English craftsmanship under each man's vine and fig tree. The beautiful Thames-side churches, he told the potters of Burslem, were the works of 'country bumpkins ... nothing grander than that'.[8]

The potter closest to Morris was his friend William De Morgan, whose ceramic designs have something in common with Morris's wallpaper and textile patterns. He was born in 1839, the son of Augustus De Morgan, Professor of Mathematics at London University, who was said to read algebra books like novels. ('Great Gun, Do Us A Sum', was William's anagram of his name.) William attended the University College School, where Joseph Chamberlain and the younger Tom Hood were his seniors. After three years at the College itself, he was admitted to the Academy Schools in 1859. Among his contemporaries there were the future Sir William Richmond, Henry Holiday, Fred Walker and Simeon Solomon – as Richmond called him, 'that wonderful little Jew who might have risen to any height of distinction if he had chosen to encourage his great gifts'.[9] Now, as later also, De Morgan showed little academic talent, but his stained glass designs were admired. In 1863 he stayed at Bettws-y-Coed with Solomon and Holiday, and with the latter worked on a picture which showed 'the Lady of Shalott floating down the river to Camelot and exciting the wonder of spectators on the bank ... the result was curious and rather beautiful'. This incipient Pre-Raphaelitism was fostered by a friendship with Edward Burne-Jones. With 'Ned' and the others, De Morgan adopted the somewhat ruthless bonhomie of Pre-Raphaelitism, its 'larks', 'pranks', 'good laughs', idiotic puns and the unappealing fake cockney which relied on a copious misplacement of aitches. Pre-Raphaelites were not allowed to wilt. Burne-Jones wrote to him, 'I want you fat and merry, full of rude and coarse jesting, I don't like you to be miserable'. At a party attended by 'little Rudyard Kipling' on Christmas Day, 1873, 'Charles Faulkner and William De Morgan enchanted us all by their pranks', wrote Lady Burne-Jones.

In 1861 the firm of Morris, Marshall, Faulkner and Company was established at 8 Red Lion Square. De Morgan and Solomon made occasional designs for stained glass and tiles. In the basement a small kiln was built for firing these. But De Morgan never joined the Morris enterprise. He set up his own pottery at 40 Fitzroy Square, and the tiles Morris ordered from him were nearly all decorated with De Morgan designs. 'Morris never made but three designs for my execution,' said De Morgan '– the *Trellis and Tulip*, the *Poppy* and another – I forget the name. I never could work except by myself and in my own manner.' Undoubtedly Morris had a great influence on De Morgan, though the uncompromising outline and absence of wishy-washiness that both favoured was probably suggested to both of them, as later to Rouault, by the techniques of stained glass.

At Fitzroy Square, there was a triumph and a disaster, best described by De Morgan himself:

In '72 (or '70) I re-discovered the lost Art of Moorish or Gubbio lustres. It had been re-discovered before in Italy in 1856 – but that I didn't know at the time, or I wouldn't have presumed. It has been re-discovered since, times out of number, and a glorious array of old Italian names, Maestro Giorgio of Gubbio, etc., is always trotted out to mount the re-discoverers on. I never did anything to justify a belief that the *art* of the cinquecento had been re-discovered – it was merely the pigment... Well! – in the course of my re-discoveries, the flame from my kiln discovered a wood-joist in the house chimney of 40 Fitzroy Square, and the roof got burned off.

In 1872, following his father's death, he moved with his mother and sister to 30 Cheyne Row, and built a kiln in the garden, within a shard's throw of the site of the Chelsea porcelain factory, and almost opposite the site of Wedgwood and Bentley's enamelling studio. He still designed some stained glass, including windows with large heads of Shakespeare and Dante for Sir Samuel Marling's home, Stanley Park. But tile and other pottery decoration was now the larger part of his business, and he rented 36 Cheyne Row, known as 'Orange House', as a showroom and workshop. Among his decorators were the interesting primitives Charles and Fred Passenger, and Dr Reginald Thompson, who married De Morgan's sister. Reginald Blunt, who later worked for De Morgan, learnt something of the Chelsea days from the Passengers, and in his book *The Wonderful Village* (1918) described how 'towards evening would often be heard a big voice shouting "Bill!" and footsteps mounting the stairs three at a time like a schoolboy's, which told of the arrival of William Morris with ruffled hair and indigo-stained fingers, keen to discuss some new project or just to hear how things were going with his friend'.[10]

He now began to get important commissions. In 1879 or 1880 he made tiles for the Czar's yacht, *Livadia*, and for the house of Sir William Quiller Orchardson, the artist. By Lord Leighton, the luxurious President of the Royal Academy, he was given a chance to pit his art against that of his ancient exemplars, lustre for lustre. Leighton had made a collection of Saracenic tiles during visits to Rhodes, Cairo and Damascus. These, on his return, were fitted into the Arab Hall of Leighton House, Kensington, begun in 1877 but not finished until 1881; but it was found that there were not enough of the old tiles to complete the work. De Morgan, therefore, was asked to make replicas of the Saracen tiles, and to complete the scheme of decoration with original tiles of appropriate design. Of the result, Mrs Stirling wrote:

> So perfect were his reproductions of the old Syrian ware both in colour and glaze, that it is impossible to distinguish between the ancient and the modern work; while the wonderful blue, intersected by a line of gold, which he employed in the rest of the decoration vies in gorgeousness of hue with the productions of the oriental potters. Nevertheless, this achievement, though an artistic, was not a financial success, for he found himself five hundred pounds out of pocket by it; a fact of which, needless to say, he never allowed Lord Leighton to be aware. But this was only one of the many instances in which

Artist potters in England

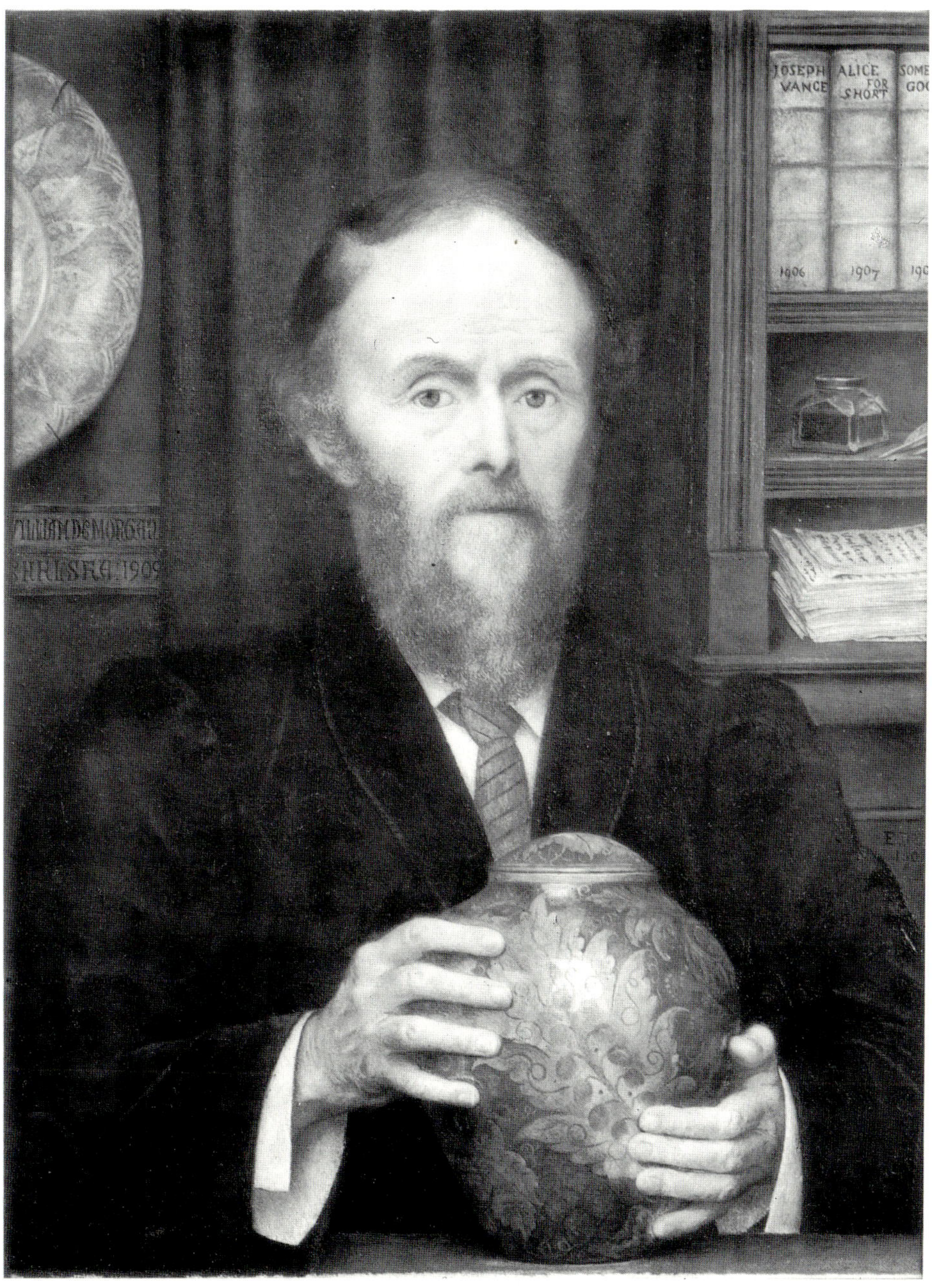

163 Portrait of William De Morgan with one of his lustre vases, painted by Evelyn De Morgan in 1909. The vase is now in the Victoria and Albert Museum.

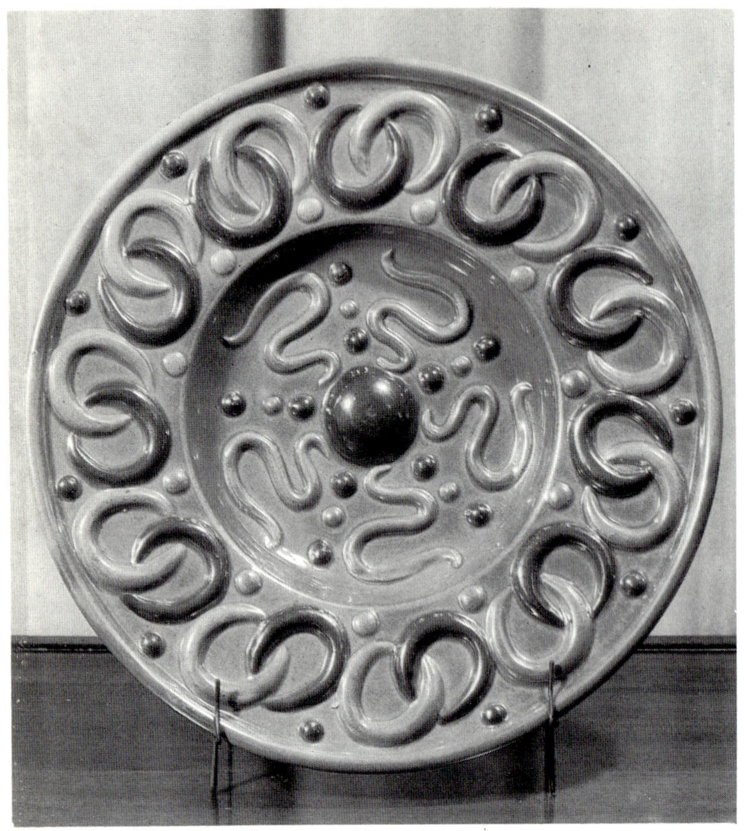

164 (top) De Morgan plate, decorated in blue and copper lustre.
165 (bottom) De Morgan bowl decorated in pink and blue lustre. Mark W.D.M. Fulham. Bought from the factory by the second Lord Swaythling.

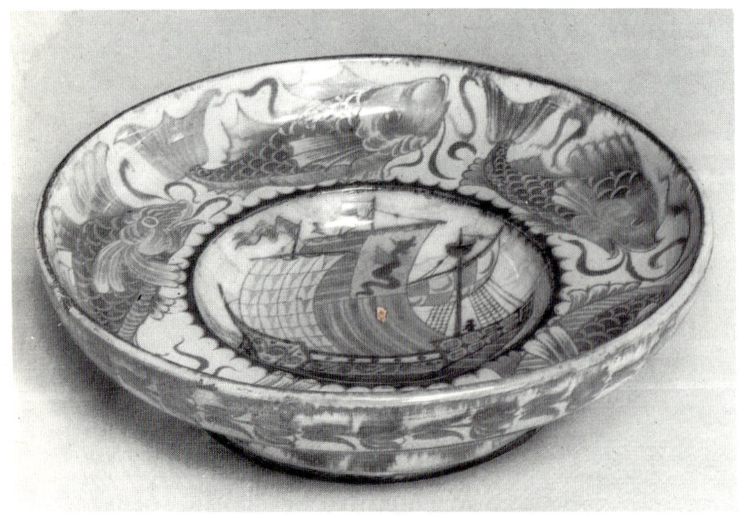

166 (opposite top) Portrait of the Martin brothers, photograph printed on sensitized wood. See p. 230.
167 (bottom) Relief by George Tinworth above the doorway of South Bank House, Lambeth. It shows some of the staff at Doulton's factory, including Hannah B. Barlow, engaged in *sgraffito* decoration of vases.

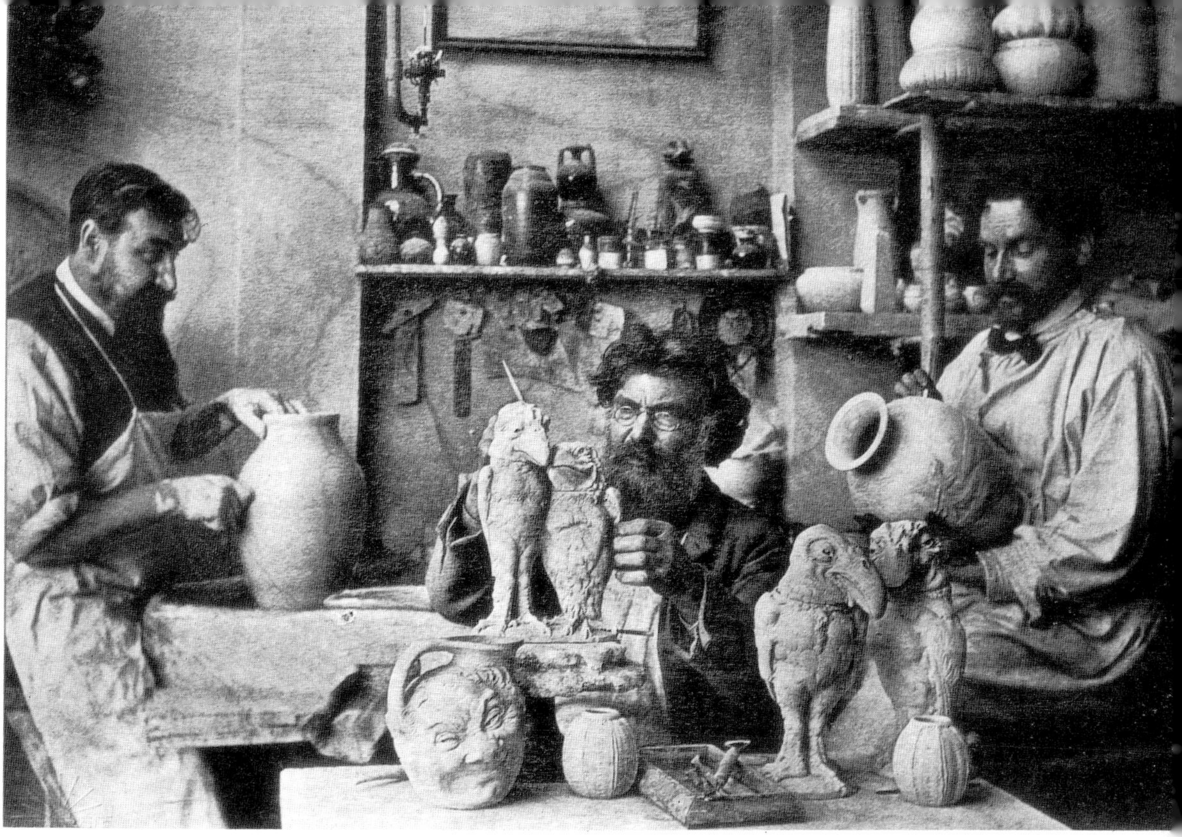

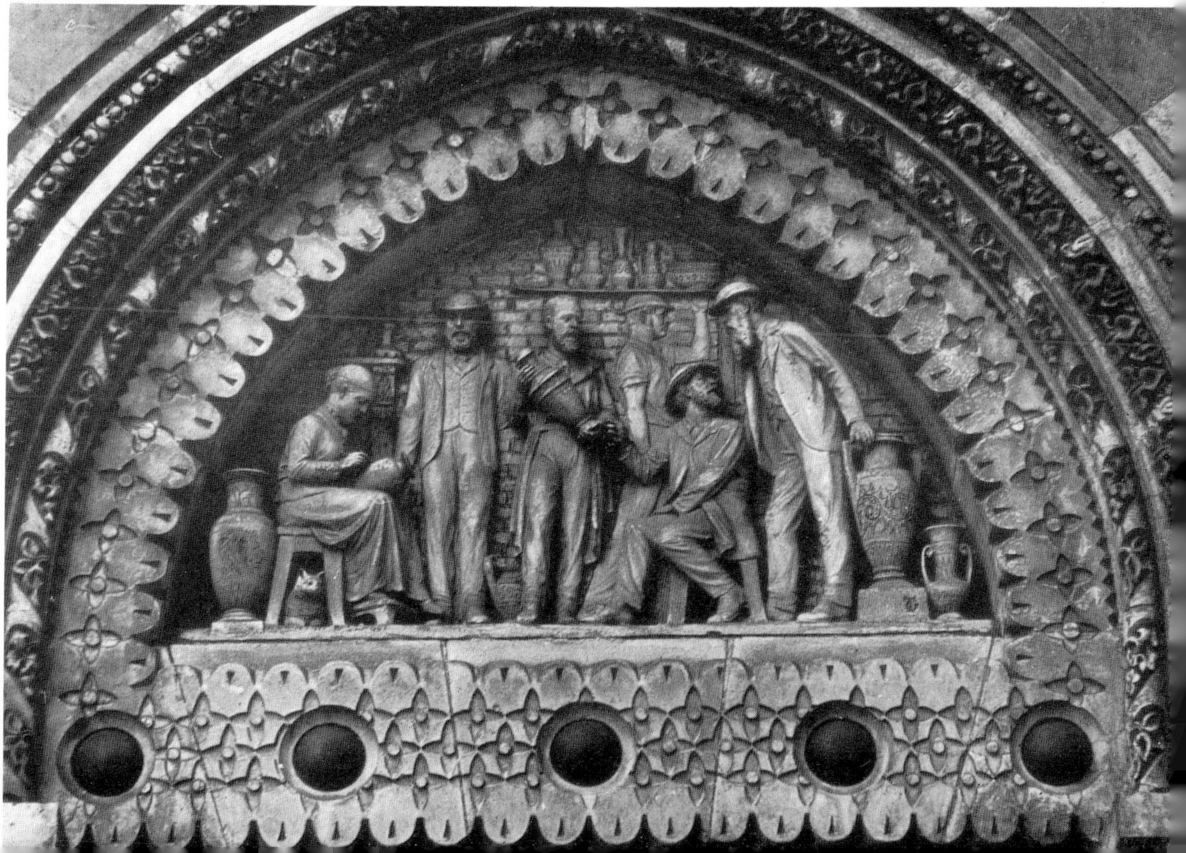

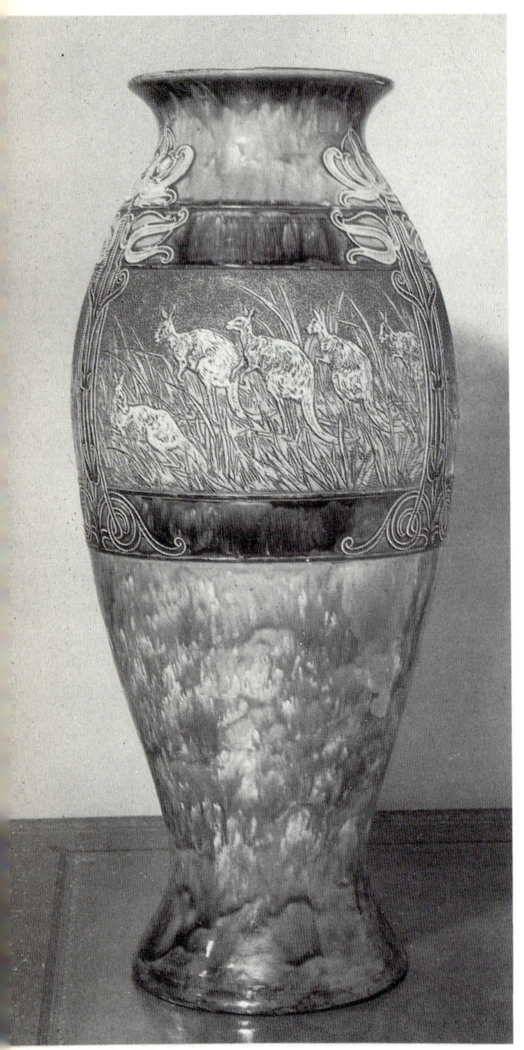

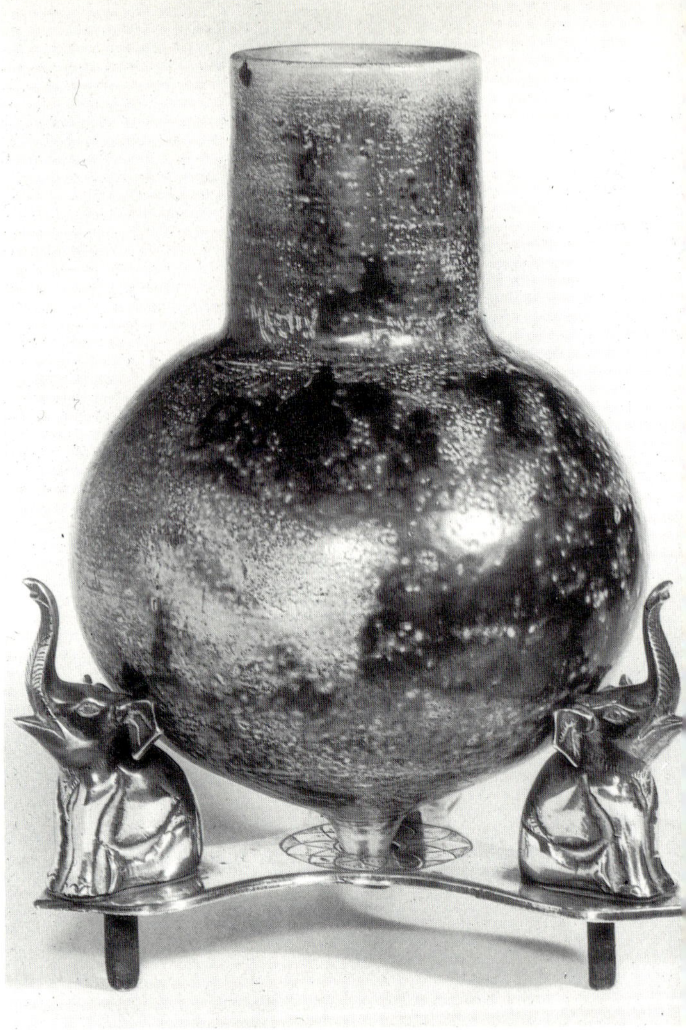

168 (left) Large Doulton vase decorated by Hannah B. Barlow for the Australian market.
169 Martinware amphora, decorated in mottled brown glaze, signed and dated 1911. It was almost certainly sold with the brass elephant tripod.

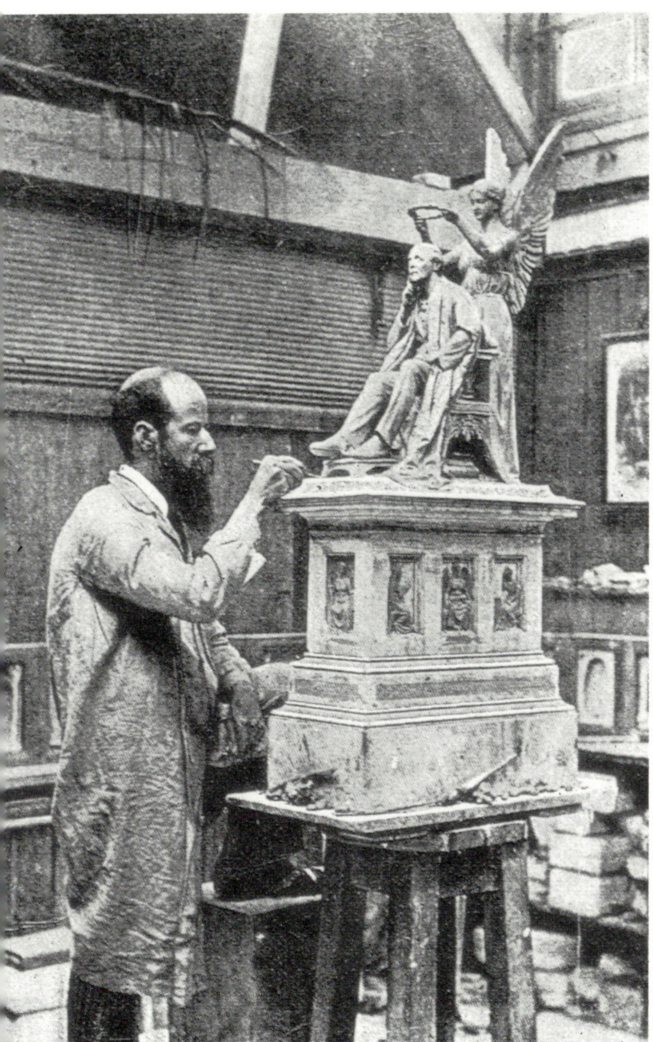

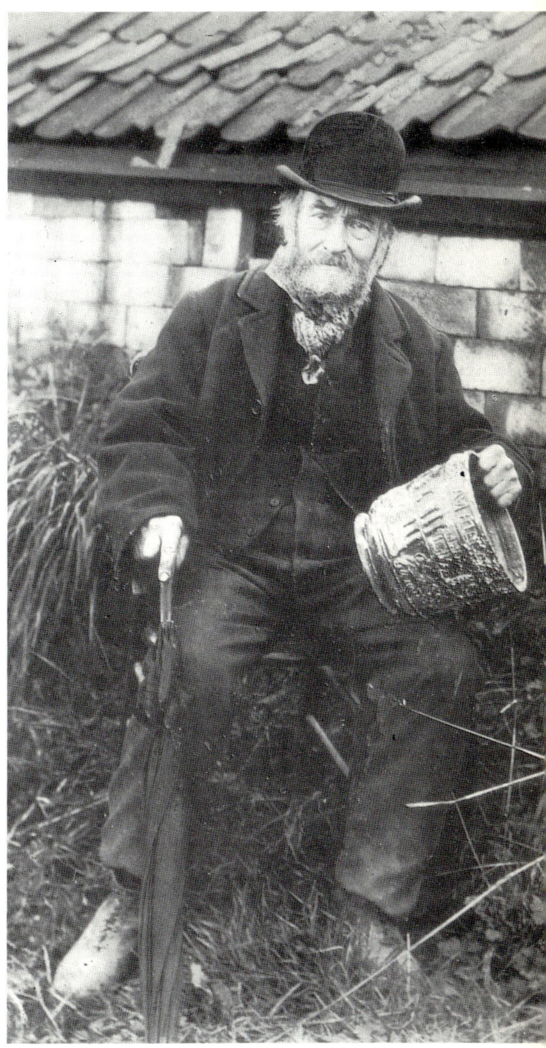

170 (left) George Tinworth working on a sketch model of Professor Fawcett in the studio provided for him by Doulton's at Lambeth. (From a photograph by F. W. Edwards, reproduced in the *Strand Magazine* of October 1891.)
171 Edward Bingham of Castle Hedingham, from a photograph of 1905. He is holding his earthenware reproduction of a Roman green glass racing cup found at Colchester and now in the British Museum. See p. 259.

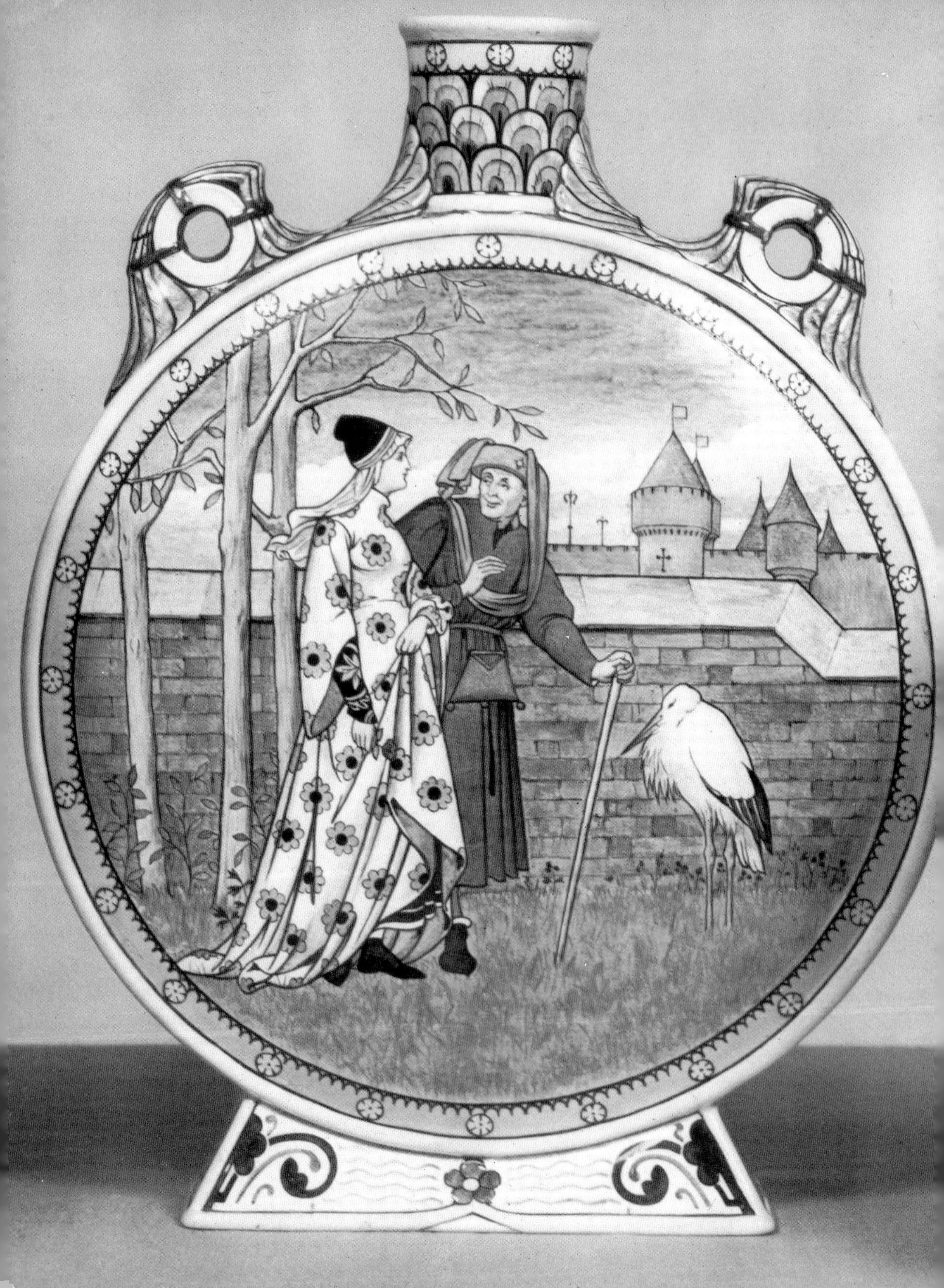

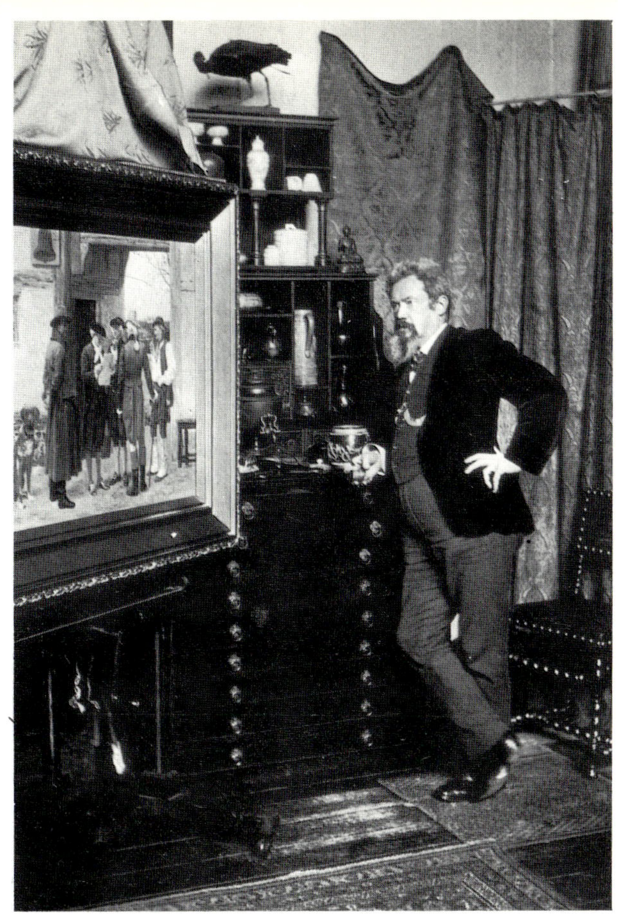

172 (opposite) Vase, earthenware with painted decoration designed by Henry Stacy Marks, R.A., factory date mark for 1877.

173 (left) Henry Stacy Marks in his studio, showing one of the stuffed birds he used as models. See p. 45.

174 'A Medieval Potter', painted by Henry Stacy Marks. Note the stuffed birds, and, in the bottom right-hand corner, a vase of similar shape to that in Plate 172.

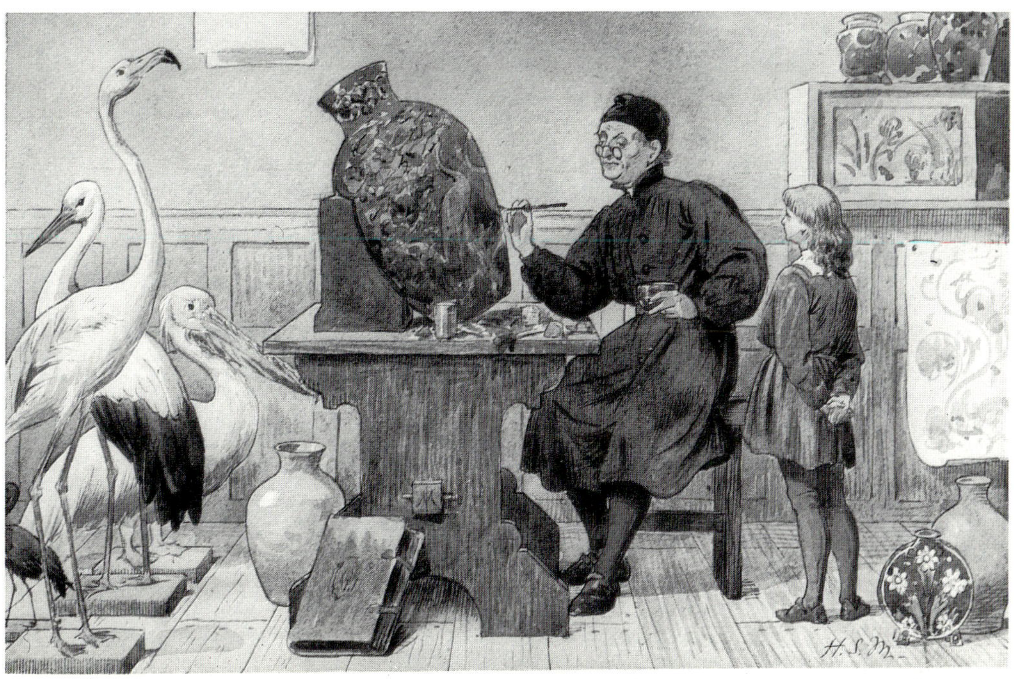

175 and 176 Doulton vase decorated by Frank Butler. The base shows the proliferation of factory marks in the late nineteenth century. See p. 260.

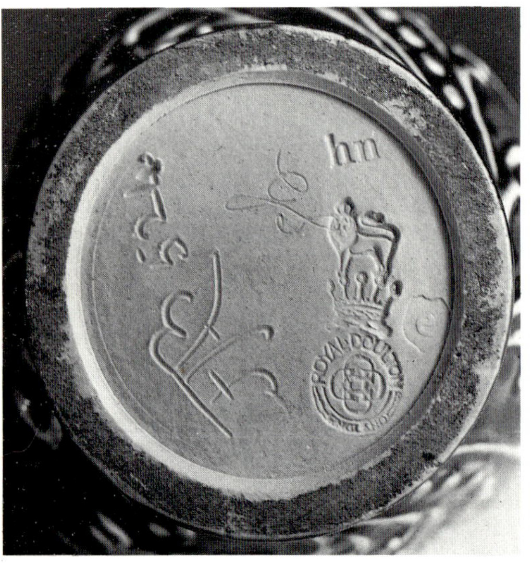

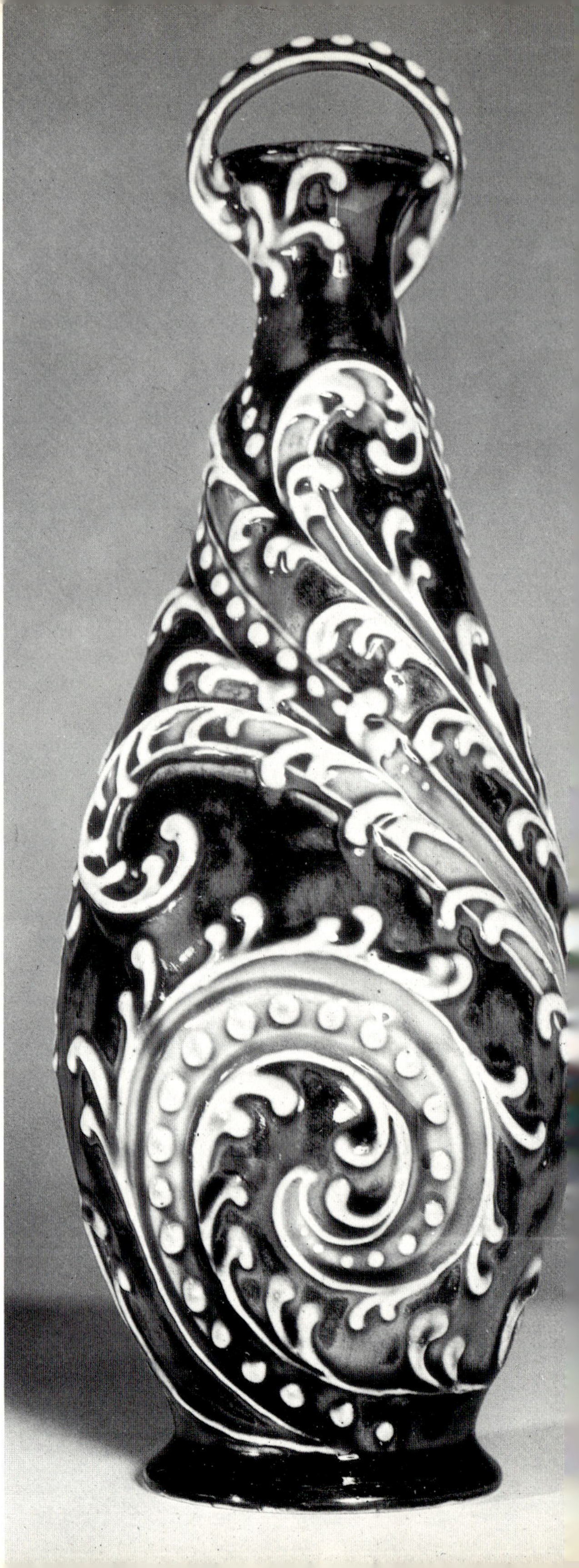

the heavy cost of production either exceeded the retail price that he felt it possible to ask, or else threatened to cripple the perfection at which, with the passion of a true artist, he aimed whatever the outlay.

In the same period he supplied tiles for Bedford Park, Chiswick, the first of the 'garden suburbs',[11] where Morris wallpapers were also extensively used. Mr John Betjeman, with his instinct for *mise en scène*, has placed De Morgan ware squarely in its historical context:

> Yes, it was Bedford Park the vision came from,
> De Morgan lustre glowing round the hearth,
> And that sweet flower which self-love takes its name from
> Nodding among the lilies in the garth.
> And Arnold Dolmetsch touching the spinet,
> And mother, Chiswick's earliest suffragette.[12]

Ostensibly the Chelsea factory was organized on Morris theories, and in rosy retrospect was seen as 'a kind of private guild' with 'a community of interest'. But in effect De Morgan dominated the business and imposed a factory discipline and style as rigorous as Wedgwood's. One of his workmen, a Mr Bale (who had been sent to De Morgan on the recommendation of William Morris), later recalled how he had once decided to finish a pot himself without waiting for De Morgan to give him a design. '*Why did you put that in*?' asked De Morgan.

'I thought it wouldn't matter and would save time.'

'*I thought*,' he repeated, ' – Please understand I don't pay you to think! If you think again, you must think elsewhere!' So much for aesthetic socialism and the artist in Everyman. Bale also tells us that 'Mr Morris was always coming round to get ideas from Mr De Morgan, and would carry off his finest work. Mr De Morgan just let him take it and never bothered. We used to hide fine pots sometimes as we didn't like them going.'

In 1878 Morris had bought a Georgian house at Hammersmith which he named Kelmscott House. It delighted him to think that the same river flowed past both his houses, and in 1880 he, De Morgan and others made the voyage from Hammersmith to Oxfordshire in a small houseboat, 'The Ark' – a trip which provided endless opportunities for Pre-Raphaelite 'pranks' and the manufacture of horrible puns ('Oxford', declared De Morgan, was derived from *Arksford*, so named because 'a narrer mind only wants a narrer 'at – an Ararat'). In 1881 Morris set up his workshops at Merton Abbey, by the River Wandle in Surrey. In 1882 De Morgan followed him there, buying land nearby. But he continued to live at Chelsea and kept his showroom at Orange House until 1886, when it was moved to Great Marlborough Street. In 1887 he married the artist Evelyn Pickering, whose works were so Pre-Raphaelite in style that the initials E.P. on one of her paintings, *Aurora Triumphans*, were altered by a dishonest dealer to E.B.J., so that for twenty years it was believed to be the work of Burne-Jones. Like Gauguin, she was literally an artist-potter. A large head of Pan was modelled by her and decorated by De Morgan.

In 1888 De Morgan went into partnership with the architect Halsey Ricardo, and set up the Sands End Pottery in Fulham. But from 1892 onwards he was forced to spend the winters in Florence, because of the threat of tuberculosis. Naturally this had an unhappy effect on a business which had always owed so much to his personal direction. When the P. & O. Company, following the precedent set by the Czar, ordered a vast consignment of tiles and panels for the liners *Arabic*, *Palawan*, *Sumatra*, *China*, *Malta* and *Persia*, a slightly absurd situation developed in which designs were drawn on paper in Florence and sent to Fulham to be transferred to the tiles. De Morgan was unable to buy paper of the necessary rough quality in Italy, the home of beautiful *cartamano*, so paper had to be shipped out from England. Thin tiles baked in England were sent by post to Florence for his inspection, and a code was established by which he could telegraph instructions to the Fulham staff. In spite of these inconveniences, the Florentine workshop, surrounded by rose gardens and scented pine woods, appealed to the mediaeval romancer and Pre-Raphaelite in De Morgan. Here he could convincingly play the artist-potter, far from the Battersea gasworks, but not too far from the amenities of English villa life with his congenial relatives, the Spencer-Stanhopes, on the Bellosguardo Hill. He hired six or seven Tuscan craftsmen – 'just common *imbianchini*' – and said he 'never had had to do with such hands and eyes'. The liner tiles, which showed scenes from the various countries served by P. & O. lines, were a great success. But Reginald Blunt, writing in 1918, said that all the liners, as well as the imperial yacht *Livadia*, had been sent to the bottom of the sea 'by Hun torpedo'.

Blunt was appointed general manager and 'Chancellor of the Exchequer' at the Fulham works in 1897. Of his three years there he wrote: 'It is, in some ways, a melancholy, though never depressing or despondent, record; for monetary difficulties, chiefly due to the insufficiency of the initial capital, run like a black thread – or rather, perhaps, a hampering barbed wire entanglement – through every page of it.'[13] Before long, men had to be stood off. 'It is melancholy,' wrote De Morgan, 'to think my men should be driving omnibuses.' In 1898 the partnership with Halsey Ricardo came to an end because of Ricardo's increasing architect's practice. In October 1899, De Morgan wrote to Blunt, referring to a commission to tile the dairy at Woburn: 'Our very existence hangs on the completion of the Bedford panels now, and this will scarcely tide us over Xmas. Who would be an Art potter?'

De Morgan's connection with the manufacture ceased in 1905, 'when neuritis gripped my business thumb and stopped my drawing. I threw Art aside after forty odd years'. Iles and Fred Passenger, who had become De Morgan's partners after Ricardo's defection, continued the business until 1907, when the firm came to an end. But from the extinct factory came a spectacular monument to its memory, the most ambitious conception in ceramics since the porcelain rooms of Portici and Aranjuez. In 1905 De Morgan's former partner, Halsey Ricardo, now a fashionable architect,[14] had been commissioned by Mr (later Sir) Ernest Debenham to build a large house in Addison Road, Kensington. In it, according to the *Architectural Review* of March 1907, Ricardo attempted to fulfil two aims 'which stand for a new development in English architecture, and, for aught we know, in the architecture of the world'. First, it was to be a house immune from the destructive effects of a city atmosphere. And secondly, it was 'the initiation of an architecture to be expressed in definite terms of colour'. Out of the derelict De Morgan factory, Ricardo selected a mass of the finest tiles, many of them identical to those which had been used in the P. & O. liners, and incorporated them in the ceramic palace (Plate XII) which still stands at 8 Addison Road (it is now occupied by the Richmond Fellowship for Mental Welfare and Rehabilitation). Mrs A. M. W. Stirling, in her biography of De Morgan (her brother-in-law), gives the impression that all the ceramics used were by him. But in fact the De Morgan tiles were used only for panels of decoration, inside and out. The basement storey, or podium, was faced with blue-grey semi-vitrified Staffordshire bricks, the framework of the structure being carried out in the Doulton glazed terracotta known as Carrara ware, the pinky-cream colour of this material being relieved in the upper stages by darker bands of the same material. Into the panels formed by this framework, glazed brickwork by the Burmantofts Branch of the Leeds Fireclay Company was introduced – the lower panels of a soft deep green, the upper of a bright blue. A dead level uniformity of tint was wisely avoided, by the use of variegated brickwork – but even so, one cannot help feeling that Ricardo's intentions were only too well realized. Totally out of harmony with the other houses in Addison Road, the building looks like a glorified gentlemen's bathroom turned inside out. But the De Morgan tiles are among the best he ever made. Today the building may seem an Edwardian freak, with its archaic telephone system labelled 'Servants' Quarters' (i.e. basement), 'Motor House' (i.e. garage) and 'Winter Gardens' (i.e. conservatory), and the special duct to carry Sir Ernest's cigar smoke out into the shrubbery. Mrs Stirling's description gives a better idea of the impression it must have made originally:

> A long and picturesque entrance-loggia, with columns of granite, tiled in rich blue-green, and terminating in a lunette of flying cranes, leads to a dwelling, the walls of which are lined with tiles in the same peacock colouring, and with panels, friezes and lunettes of rich and elaborate design. Passages and archways show a vista of gorgeous hue like some magic Eastern Palace of Dreams. In the centre rises a hall roofed in by a glittering dome of mosaics; archways and pendentives of gold mosaic throw into bold relief the rich oriental tint of the walls and the frescoes. In the corridors beyond, duplicates of the vanished ships' panels may be seen, great eagles and birds of prey, strange fancies in beast life, rare designs in trailing leaf and glinting foliage. Moreover, against the prevailing brilliance of the background, here and there stand great cabinets full of age-old pottery from Persia and Asia Minor which shine with a mysterious pearly radiance produced by long burial in the earth. And it is interesting to note how those gems of Ancient Art are in harmony with their surroundings and are seen thus in their rightful setting, enhanced by the work of a potter who, separated from the ancient craftsmen by the passing of centuries, is yet linked with them in a community of ideas.

De Morgan was ill and depressed. He was beginning to look like one of the sad old birds he had so often painted on tiles. Two of his best friends had died – Morris in 1896, G. F. Watts in 1904, and it seemed likely that he would not survive them by long. After the Addison Road palace, no more phoenixes rose from the Fulham works, which were converted into a manufacture of Bluebell Polish. But for De Morgan himself there was to be an extraordinary new lease of creative life. Confined to his bed by influenza, he continued a novel of which he had written two desultory chapters in 1901. As he characteristically put it, he turned from pots to plots, tiles to 'tyles' [tales]. The first novel, *Joseph Vance* – the autobiography of an old man in a workhouse – was a best-seller. He was hailed as 'Dickens Redivivus' – though prolixity was really the only quality in which he rivalled Dickens. The working characters in the book spoke in the facetious cockney of which De Morgan and his Pre-Raphaelite friends were past masters. How, one of his admirers asked his wife, had he gained his knowledge of the common classes? Perhaps it was indiscreet to ask? Or perhaps Mr De Morgan, like his father, dabbled in the occult?

His ambition to revive the pottery lapsed. Lady Burne-Jones rejoiced that all the men and furnaces that stood between him and the world had vanished, 'and just your Self is left speaking exactly as you wish'. The irony is, that in his lifetime his pottery sold badly and his novels were best-sellers; while now his pottery is avidly collected but his novels are hardly read.

De Morgan's life was rarefied. He was the son of a professor and spiritualist. At the age of forty-eight he married an artist, and had no children. He had lived idyllically in Florence, but was so upset by some earthquake tremors in 1909 that he came back to England for good. He nowhere touched life so really as in his death. 'Acutely distressed' by the First World War, he was building a model aeroplane in Church Street, Chelsea, on Boxing Day, 1916, when he received a visit from a young officer who had come from France on the previous day. The officer, having read *Joseph Vance* in the trenches, had decided that his first visit in England should be to its author. De Morgan caught trench fever. For seventeen days he raved in delirium, believing that he was a wounded soldier in a hospital in France. He repeatedly asked for his wife, 'while she, poor soul, sat, a frozen image of grief, waiting for the one moment of recognition, the one word of farewell which was never granted'. De Morgan died on 15 January 1917, surely the bizarrest victim of the Great War. He had written a mere hundred thousand words of a novel called *The Old Man's Youth and the Young Man's Old Age*. 'Mr De Morgan,' wrote one obituarist, 'has done what none of his readers will ever be able to do – he has left one of his novels unfinished.' He was buried in Brookwood Cemetery, under a tombstone designed by his wife and inscribed with a sentence which had occurred in one of the letters from 'angels' written on the De Morgans' planchette. In 1918 May Morris unveiled a tablet to his memory in Chelsea Old Church. The inscription told how he had recreated 'in Ceramic work upon his own vigorous designs the colour of the Persian & the lustre of the great Umbrian craftsmen'.

De Morgan's life illustrates, and helps us to define, the character of the artist-potter. He is independent: Bustelli was a greater artist than De Morgan, but he was tied to a factory and the dictates of the factory's patron. He puts art above financial reward – because he can afford to. (This, fundamentally, is why Morris's artistic socialism was delusory. Every man had not the capital to indulge his own ideas.) Not only is the artist-potter unhampered by directives from above; he forbids interpretation from below, as in the case of Mr Bale. He asserts the right of the artist to have his unique conception realized, and no other. He is an artist who has chosen clay as his medium (almost, in De Morgan's case, his canvas), not a potter with artistic aspirations. De Morgan's original designs on paper, preserved in the Victoria and Albert Museum, show him as a powerful and imaginative draughtsman. He did not claim technical originality – 'the sincerest form of imitation', he said, 'is pottery' – but in the butcherous reds and iridescent blues of his lustre wares he expressed something new. If his line is a cat's cradle rather than a whiplash, it can still be claimed as inchoate *art nouveau*, a sedate harbinger of revolution.

The characteristics of De Morgan as an artist-potter are closely paralleled by those of the Martin brothers, who potted, first at Fulham, then at Southall, from 1873 until 1915. They were determined to be independent. Although they had to begin by working for Doulton, they declined his offer to join his permanent staff. Cazin, who met the brothers at Doulton's, was so impressed by Walter Martin's ability as a thrower that he tried to persuade him to accompany him to Paris when he returned in 1874, but without success. Like De Morgan, they produced wares of a romantic archaism, but insisted on a day-to-day originality. They boasted that they had never made two pieces quite identical. 'William Morris', wrote Holbrook Jackson, who met the brothers in 1910, 'would have delighted in these men ... and he would have loved to hear Wallace Martin, clay in hand, discussing enthusiastically problems of life, commingled with a deeply informed technical interpretation of his craft'.[15] The same writer was impressed by the brothers' unconcern over the business side of their trade:

> There is nothing about the little shop of the Martin Brothers at all like modern commerce. Business, you imagine, may possibly take place there, but you feel that the main object is something different. The pots are not arranged like the crockery in an ordinary shop, and there is no effusive display of antagonism towards dust.... They will not approach you as shopmen, and I dare not think what would happen if you attempted immediately to open up commercial relations. I have seen many pieces of stoneware bought of Wallace and Edwin Martin, but I have never seen them *sell* a piece.[16]

Wallace Martin had been a student at the Lambeth School of Art, whose progressive director, John Sparkes, gave his pupils pottery tiles on which to paint in enamels. Another of Sparkes's protégés, and a lifelong friend of Wallace Martin, was George Tinworth, who became by far the most materially successful of the Victorian studio potters. He was paid extravagant attention by critics, first by Ruskin in his *Notes on the Royal Academy* of 1875, then by Edmund Gosse, who wrote a book on him published in 1883. Gosse called him 'a painter in terracotta' and saw in his puritan humour 'a return to the spirit which animated Bunyan and Quarles'. Posterity has not confirmed the contemporary judgment. The reaction began with Richard Bedford's comment in the *Dictionary of National Biography* that 'He took no pains to remedy his lack of education and cannot in any sense be considered a great artist.' But the forbidding religious terracottas have a certain interest as part of the Victorian Gothic revival, and as such are discussed in Chapter 10.

Edward Bingham of Castle Hedingham, Essex (Plate 171) was another deeply religious potter. The walls of the primitive potworks he built for himself just below the castle keep were covered with scriptural texts. He was a mystic who kept a diary of his struggles, failures and visionary experiences. But although Bingham's wares, crudely modelled in local clays, were sold as 'art pottery', he was not in the true sense an 'artist-potter'. He was the kind of anachronism that Richard Jefferies, W. H. Hudson, Edward Thomas and George Bourne liked to find in unspoilt enclaves of rural England, an hereditary artisan of the same kind as the other village craftsmen – miller, blacksmith, cabinet-maker. His father, also named Edward Bingham, had made red pottery at Lambeth from 1775 to 1780, and in 1834 (when his son was five years old) had settled in Gestingthorpe, Essex, where he made, beside plain earthenware, the traditional instruments of rustic amusement, puzzle-jugs and birdwhistles. In 1837 the family had moved to Castle Hedingham, where the potting business was continued. May Morris wrote of William De Morgan:

> His is the story of most of our Arts and Crafts workers of the mid and later nineteenth century – the impulse of invention that seeks for outlet – the invention brought to a dead stop by the loss of tradition in the crafts – the necessity of spending valuable time experimenting in the ABC of an Art, and patiently working it up in the path in which his instinct guides him.

It was not at all like that for Edward Bingham. He learnt the ABC of the craft from his father. At the same time, he felt quite as strongly as the artist-potters the sadness of industrialization – perhaps more strongly, since he was truly part of the tradition that was being destroyed. In 1906 he joined his son in America, and in March 1909 he wrote from New Jersey to a friend in England:

> You speak of the old pottery works, ah, all that is now over. I have not seen a piece of true native clay since I have been here.... I feel and believe my son Edward [feels] too, that we have done with pottery for ever. He is working at a large store in the city as a china packer....[17]

The individual potter was being ousted; but by compensation the factories were employing artists and encouraging them to assert their individuality. Doulton had Hannah Barlow (Plate 168), George Tinworth (Plate 170), Frank Butler (Plates 175–6), and Cazin. At Minton's. M. L. Solon invented his extraordinary *pâte-sur-pâte*. Like Solon, Désiré Leroy, of Derby, had been trained at Sèvres, while Emile Lessore, employed by Wedgwood's, had been a pupil of Ingres. Lessore, in common with De Morgan and other artist potters, believed in an easeful life; as soon as he could afford to, he re-migrated to Fontainebleau, whither crates of Wedgwood wares were sent for him to decorate. In token of the new licence given to the individual, the artist was allowed to sign his own productions[18] (Plate 176), although industrialization is also represented by elaborate factory marks, symbols of competition and prestige, and by registration marks, including date marks, as part of a national codification.

The Arts and Crafts movement of William Morris continued to find adherents in the early part of this century. Among his followers were men like Ananda Kentish Coomaraswamy, Edward Carpenter and Eric Gill. But the idea that the salvation of the arts lay in a revival of the crafts died an unnatural death: the aesthetes won. We encounter the type of the Morris disciple, perhaps for the last time, in the amiable cranks of mid twentieth-century fiction – Mr Anthony Powell's Dr Trelawney, who, like Eric Gill, wears a priestly robe, and Mr Kingsley Amis's Professor Welch, who holds madrigal parties and serves food off chafing-dishes. But from the débris of Morris's theories, preached by hairy-suited Fabians and suffragettes, and hammered into beaten copper overmantels by the Birmingham Guild of Handicraft, one survived: art must be faithful to its materials. The oil painter must not thin out his colours and paint aquarelles in tinted turpentine; neither must the watercolourist use thick impastos of body-colour, as Samuel Palmer had done in 'The Apple Orchard'. The artist must exploit the unique-

XIII (*opposite*) **The potter Albert Dammouse (left) at work in his studio with an assistant. Painted by his brother, Edouard Dammouse, in 1899. Note the poster by Chéret on the wall behind Dammouse.**

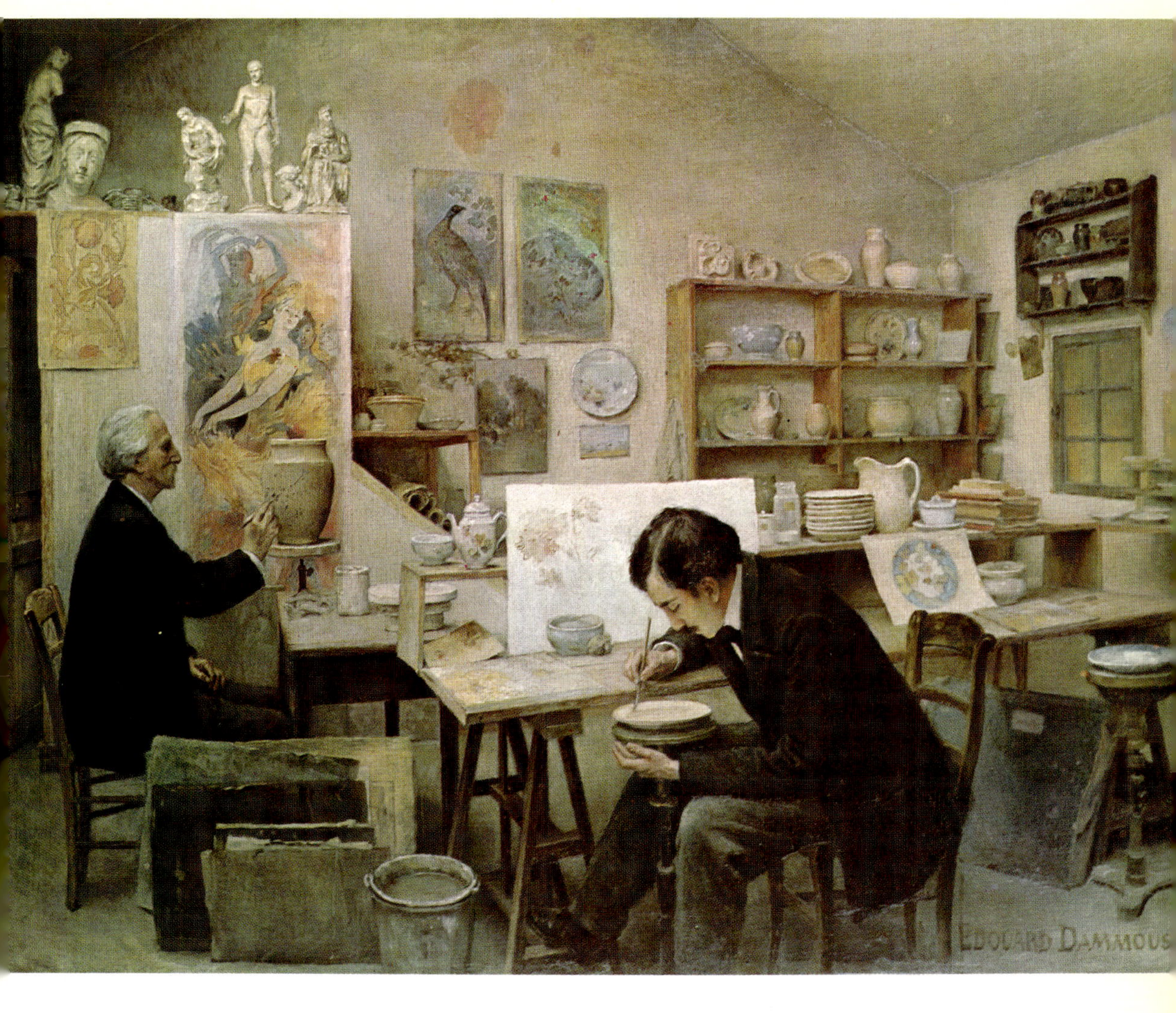
EDOUARD DAMMOUS

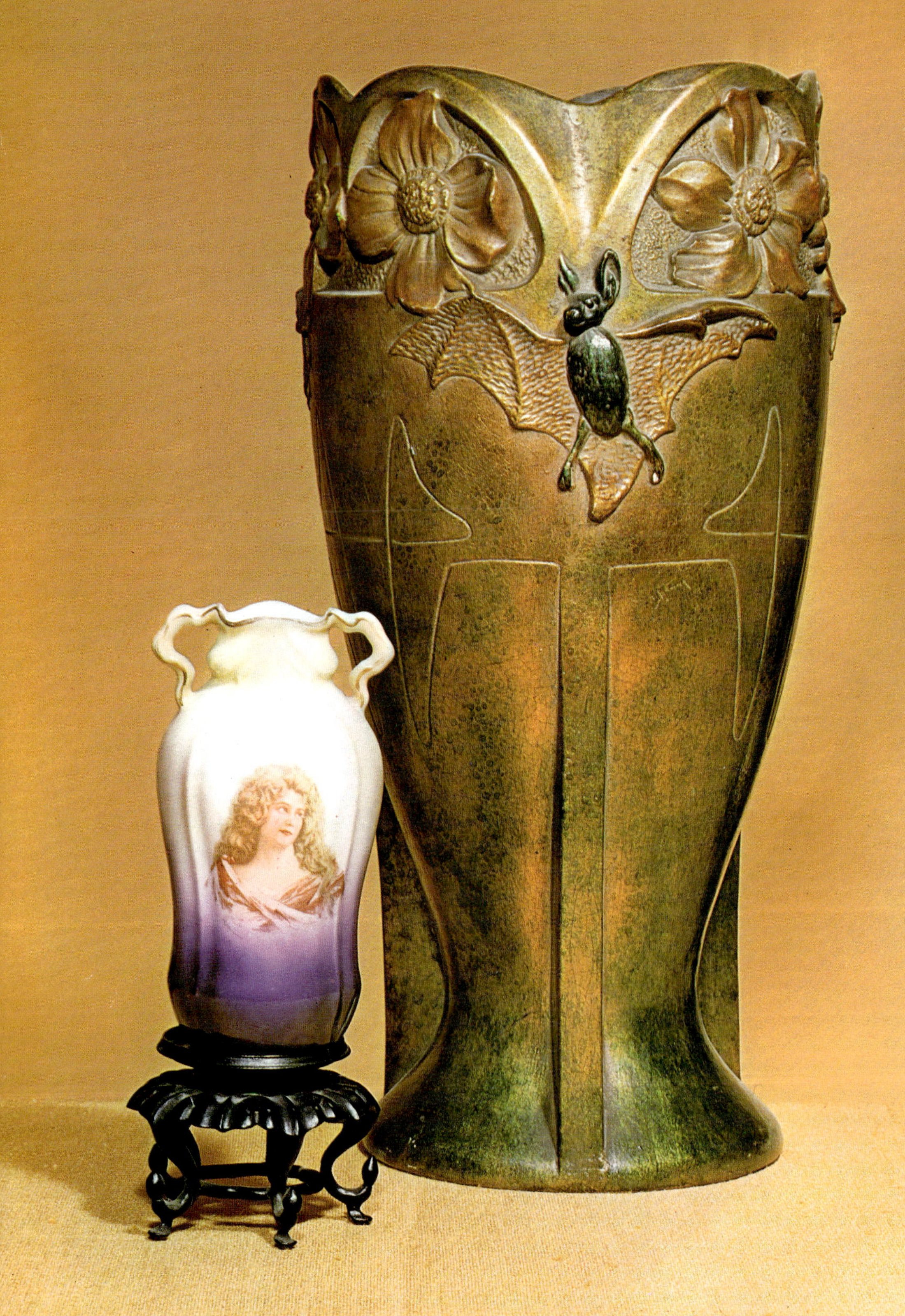

ness of his medium. Heinrich Wölfflin was to coin the word *malerisch*, 'painterly', to describe the arch-especial quality he looked for in a painting. 'Potterly' might ungracefully describe the quality William Morris sought in ceramics. The potter must be faithful to the homely, elemental attributes of the clay:

Try to get the most out of your material, but always in such a way as honours it most. Not only should it be obvious what your material is, but something should be done with it which is specially natural to it, something that could not be done with any other. This is the very *raison d'être* of decorative art: to make stone look like ironwork, or wood like silk, or pottery like stone is the last resource of the decrepitude of art.[19]

Morris added an indulgent but malicious corollary: machine-made wares must be faithful to the machine:

Set yourselves as much as possible against all machine work (this to all men). But if you have to design for machine work, at least let your design show clearly what it is. Make it mechanical with a vengeance, at the same time as simple as possible. Don't try, for instance, to make a printed plate look like a hand-painted one: make it something which no one would try to do if he were painting by hand, if your market drives you into printed plates: I don't see the use of them myself.[20]

Twentieth-century studio potters, led by Bernard Leach, adopted the principle of fidelity to the clay. But they did not take it primarily from William Morris. They took it from the country whose art had already caused a revolution in European painting – Japan. Letting the clay 'speak for itself' was the traditional observance of Japanese potters. The ancient Jomon potters were so concerned to give expression to the material that they worked with almost unwashed clay, leaving in it pieces of organic matter, pebbles and shell fragments.[21] The great Japanese masters, such as Kenzan I, usually avoided symmetry. Before hardening, a round vessel would be coaxed into that slight irregularity which might, in a pun worthy of De Morgan, be described as 'the bias on the bowl'. A jar that came from the kiln unflawed might be discreetly damaged – perhaps on the principle that fragility is one of the distinctive qualities of ceramics – the chip being filled in with gold lacquer. Bernard Leach, the greatest of the English artist-potters, became a pupil of Kenzan VI in 1911, and is entitled to call himself the seventh Kenzan – the equivalent, in the world of ceramics, of an English Pope. But since he did not set up his own pottery at St Ives until 1920, his works do not come within the province of this book.

XIV (*opposite*) Two *art nouveau* vases of unknown provenance. That on the left is glazed in cream and purple; that on the right, with bat design, is predominantly green.

The organization, or rather disorganization, of ceramic making in England has been, since 1914, much the same as that established in the late nineteenth century. On the one hand there have been the artist potters, often working in agreeable places such as St Ives; on the other, the factories, in less agreeable places such as Lambeth and Stoke-on-Trent. The factories have continued to employ artists: Rex Whistler and Eric Ravilious, for example, both designed for Wedgwood's. Increasing use is now being made of designs by art students. Occasionally an artist-potter has become a teacher in an art school, as when Sir William Rothenstein appointed William Staite Murray head of the ceramic department at the Royal College of Art in 1927. In these ways the difference between studio pottery and factory wares has been made less distinct; but no machine has yet been invented to add to a pot the impress of a potter's thumb, the arbitrary play of fire, the extrusion of minerals through the glaze, and the other beguiling imperfections of hand-made pottery.

12 Collectors

Macaulay's strictures on Queen Mary II's china collection have been so often quoted in books on ceramics, that to omit them here would be a startling breach of etiquette:

> In every corner of the mansion appeared a profusion of gewgaws, not yet familiar to English eyes. Mary had acquired at the Hague a taste for the porcelain of China, and amused herself by forming at Hampton a vast collection of hideous images, and of vases on which houses, trees, bridges, and mandarins were depicted in outrageous defiance of all the laws of perspective. The fashion, a frivolous and inelegant fashion it must be owned, which was thus set by the amiable Queen, spread fast and wide. In a few years almost every great house in the kingdom contained a museum of these grotesque baubles. Even statesmen and generals were not ashamed to be renowned as judges of teapots and dragons; and satirists long continued to repeat that a fine lady valued her mottled green pottery as much as she valued her monkey, and much more than she valued her husband.[1]

The remains of Queen Mary's collection are still to be seen at Hampton Court[2] and Windsor Castle. As Macaulay's description suggests, they are predominantly Chinese. They include a number of figures of the goddess Kuan-yin, in the so-called *blanc-de-chine* porcelain from Fukien Province. But Mary also bought Dutch delft,[3] and although oriental porcelain is more prized than any other throughout the eighteenth century, European wares are also collected as the European factories develop. As early as 1745, Gersaint wrote in a preface to his catalogue of Antoine de la Roque's collection:

> A l'égard de la Porcelaine, il semble que depuis celle de Saxe a pris faveur en France, l'ancienne n'a pas été recherchée avec tant d'ardeur qu'auparavant. On ne peut pas disconvenir que la Porcelaine de Saxe ne soit séduisante

à l'oeil par la beauté du dessein, le choix des sujets, l'agrément des formes, la légèreté dans l'exécution de certains morceaux, & le brillant de ses couleurs. Cependant, malgré tous ces avantages, elle n'est regardée par les vrais Connoisseurs que comme du faux en ce genre, & de foibles copies, en comparaison de l'ancienne.[4]

Who were the 'vrais Connoisseurs' to whom Gersaint refers? La Roque himself was one of them. Born at Marseilles in 1672, he became an officer in the Compagnie des Gendarmes de la Garde du Roi. He was severely wounded at Malplaquet in 1709 and was retired with a pension from Louis XIV. He edited *Le Mercure* from 1721 until his death in 1744, and is the villain of one of Browning's less felicitous poems, *The Two Poets of Croisic* (1878):

> the Chevalier La Roque, –
> Eminent in those days for pride of place,
> Seeing he had it in his power to block
> The way or smooth the road to all the race
> Of literators trudging up to knock
> At Fame's exalted temple-door – for why?
> He edited the Paris 'Mercury'.

(In other stanzas, the unfortunate editor is also made to rhyme with 'cock', 'o'clock', 'gold in crock', '*ad hoc*' and 'lady's-smock'.[5])

Gersaint also sold the collection of the Vicomte de Fonspertuis, the basis of whose collection was the élite of the cabinet of General Du Vivier, his uncle. Du Vivier had been a friend of La Fontaine, the author of the *Fables*, and a passage from one of La Fontaine's letters to the Prince de Conti (another china collector) in 1689 shows that Du Vivier already had a china collection at that date:

> Nous en parlions il y a deux jours du Vivier & moi; il me pria de vous assurer de ses très-humbles respects. Nous fîmes des voeux très-particuliers en votre faveur, ils n'étoient oüis que de quelques Idoles Chinoises & du Destin, qui apparemment les exaucera.[6]

Du Vivier was visited nine years later by Dr Martin Lister, who wrote:

> I saw the appartment of Monsieur *Viviers* in the Arsenal; it consists in 7 or 8 Ground Rooms looking into the great Garden; These Rooms are small, but most curiously furnisht, and have in them the greatest variety, and best sorted *China* Ware I ever saw, besides *Pagods* and *China Pictures*.[7]

'M. du Vivier, à l'Arsenal' was one of the 'Fameux Curieux Des Ouvrages Magnifiques' listed in the *Livre Commode* of Nicolas de Blegny (published at Paris in 1692 under the pseudonym of Abraham du Pradel).[8] At the head of the list was 'Monsieur le Duc d'Aumont, rue de Jouy'.[9] His son, Louis-Marie-Augustin, duc d'Aumont (1709–82), First Gentleman of the Bedchamber, was regarded as the greatest porcelain connoisseur of his time. His collection was largely formed from the sales of the Dukes of Tallard and Dancésune, of Julienne de Gagnat and Randon de Boisset, in Paris, and that of Baron Jacob van Wassenaer-Obdam in Holland (The Hague, 1750).[10] But we also encounter him in the *Livre-Journal* of Lazare Duvaux. Characteristic purchases included:

October 22 1751 Un vase de porcelaine violette jaspée, garni à console & terrasse dorées d'or moulu (rendu), 480 l.
November 10 1751 Quatre tasses à anses & soucoupes, pot à sucre & théière de Saxe avec le cabaret verni, 120 l.
May 21 1753 Neuf soucoupes en relief, porcelaines de Vincennes, en blanc à 30s., 13 l.10s.

His collection was sold by Julliot fils and Paillet at Paris on 12 December 1782.

In England, the vogue for old china was equally strong. 'China vessels are playthings for women of all ages,' wrote Addison in 1714. 'An old lady of fourscore shall be as busy in cleaning an Indian Mandarin, as her great-grand-daughter is in dressing her baby [i.e. her doll].'[11] The young couple in Hogarth's *Marriage à la Mode* (1743–5), rejecting, like their creator, the Burlingtonian proprieties, have a mantelshelf groaning with Chinese porcelain. In a painting of 1742 (an engraving of which is illustrated in Plate 180), Hogarth satirized 'the folly of collecting old china'. An old beau and an old lady of the Chesterfield school are gloating over a Chinese bowl and the companion saucer; a large china jar stands behind her; while a black boy, fondled by another lady, holds a pagod. The gentleman is thought to be the foppish Lord Portmore, newly returned from France, while the 'miniature Othello has been said to be intended for the late Ignatius Sancho, whose talents and virtues were an honour to his colour'. The original work was painted to the order of a Miss Edwards, 'who, having been laughed at for some singularities in her manners, requested the artist to recriminate on her opponents...'.

An outstanding English virtuoso of the early eighteenth century was Sir Andrew Fountaine (1676–1753) of Narford Hall, Norfolk. Fountaine was knighted by William III in 1699 and in 1701 accompanied Lord Macclesfield to Hanover to announce to the Elector the Act of

Accession passed by the British Parliament. From there he went on to Italy, buying antiques, including the maiolica which was to be the chief glory of his collection. He succeeded to Narford on his father's death in 1706. In 1714 he made a long visit to Paris, and then again went to Italy, spending nearly three years at Rome and Florence, where he became a friend of Cosmo III, Grand Duke of Tuscany,[12] the last of the Medici princes. In 1718 he sold his collection of medals to the Earl of Pembroke to pay for an enlargement of Narford. In 1727 he succeeded Sir Isaac Newton as Warden of the Mint. He died at Narford in 1753.

He had no children, and at his death his title and collections devolved on a relative of his wife; there is still an Andrew Fountaine at Narford. The collections were not dispersed until 1884, when a sale was held at Christie's. J. C. Robinson, Her Majesty's Surveyor of Pictures, and formerly Art Superintendent of the South Kensington Museums, wrote to the editor of *The Times* on 18 April:

> For a brief space the perennial yet ever changing museum in King Street will present a splendid show. The eager amateurs and dealers of all Europe will be there, and probably America also will join in the hot contention, if, indeed, the shortsighted fiscal regulations of that country do not close the door to the influx of that wealth of which she has most need – America, young and so rich and great, but who deliberately shuts out works of art and sends us dynamite!

In a second letter to *The Times* (2 June) Robinson took occasion to explode an idea which had bedevilled collectors of maiolica right through the eighteenth and early nineteenth centuries:

> The word majolica has not even yet entirely superseded the old-fashioned term 'Raphael ware'. Down almost to our own time the crude idea prevailed that the majolica wares were actually painted by Raphael and his scholars.[13] Doubtless Sir Andrew had some hazy notions of this kind when he formed his collection, for the principal specimens of his procurance at Narford are of the strictly pictorial class of the schools of Urbino and Castel Durante, for which the beautiful engravings of Marc Antonio and his followers mainly furnished the original designs of the painted subjects.

Pope, who doubtless looked with disfavour on Fountaine's friendly relations with the Hanoverian court, attacked him in *The Dunciad*:

> But Annius, crafty Seer, with ebon wand,
> And well-dissembled em'rald on his hand,
> False as his gems and cancer'd as his Coins,
> Came, cramm'd with capon, from where Pollio dines.

But Sir Andrew was a friend and patron of that other anti-Hanoverian, Swift, and the Narford Library formerly contained a number of the Dean's letters and of his drawings for *The Tale of a Tub*, sent to Narford for Sir Andrew's approval, but never returned. Swift himself at one time had a mild fancy for china, and in 1710 visited china shops with Sir Andrew.[14]

Another china-collecting friend and correspondent of Swift's was Lady Betty Germaine. A daughter of the second Earl of Berkeley, Lord Lieutenant of Ireland, she had been brought up in Dublin Castle, where Swift was chaplain. In 1706, at the age of twenty-six, she married Sir John Germaine, who, according to Horace Walpole's tattle, was 'so exceedingly ignorant that he believed his countryman Sir Matthew (they were both Dutch) was author of St Matthew's gospel'.[15] She bore him three children, all of whom died in infancy. When Sir John died in 1718 he left her Drayton, advising her to marry again. But she remained a widow, dividing her time between a house in St James's Square; Knole, where she stayed with her friends the Duke and Duchess of Dorset; and Drayton, where she usually spent about six months in the summer. There is a small, very brown portrait of her at Knole, where her pot-pourri recipe is still in use, but a more attractive souvenir is a portrait in Mr Paul Mellon's collection (Plate 35), *A Tea Party at Lord Harrington's House*,[16] painted by Philips in 1739. Lady Betty is supposed to be the hostess, and at the three tables are a company of her friends, including the Duchess of Montagu, the Duchess of Dorset, Lady Betty's sister-in-law Lady Suffolk, who had married her younger brother George (also present), her elder brother James, Lord Berkeley, and her niece Mary Chamber, pouring tea. Lady Suffolk was another voracious china collector. In August 1732, Lady Betty sent her a present of porcelain with the message: 'You love old china, sure I am venture to say this is really so; I being informed that these are the pictures of our first parents drawn from the life, and at that time of the year that the fig tree ceases to produce leaves.'[17]

Lady Betty's china room is still preserved at Knole, which she seems to have used for the overflow of her collection. Much of her china is still at Drayton. She is known to have had her favourite pieces, with other curiosities, depicted in two paintings, but these have disappeared. To accommodate her vast collection, she had special brackets attached to the stretchers of cabinet stands, and had hanging shelves copied from a design made for the Duchess of Norfolk. They bear her arms and widow's cap. Horace Walpole visited Drayton in 1763:

It is covered with portraits, crammed with old china, furnished richly, and not a rag in it under forty, fifty, or a thousand years old; but nor a bed or chair that has lost a tooth, or got a grey hair, so well are they preserved. I rummaged it from head to foot, examined every spangled bed, and enamelled pair of bellows, for such there are; in short, I do not believe the old mansion was ever better pleased with an inhabitant, since the days of Walter de Drayton, except when it received its divine old mistress.[18]

Horace Walpole stands in relation to Sir Robert Walpole rather as the rococo to the baroque: the child that grows into the antithesis of its parent. Or one thinks of the delicate flower of a great bristling cactus. He is what the eighteenth century calls a dilettante, the nineteenth, an exquisite, and the twentieth, an homosexual. The most amateur psychologist can distinguish the invert traits in his character – the obsessive love for his mother, distaste for his father's saturnalia at Houghton, hero-worship of his cousin Henry Conway,[19] friendships with decrepit ladies who would make no demands on his carnality,[20] irritation with the old Marquise du Deffand when she became too infatuated (love, in her case, was actually blind) and a romantic escapism[21] – even at Eton he was the deviser of a sustained pastorale in which Thomas Gray, the poet, was Orosmades, Richard West and Thomas Ashton were Favonius and Almanzor, while he, aptly enough from our point of view, took the name of Celadon.[22] He flirted with vegetables, 'settled down to enjoy, summer after summer, the growth and blossoming of his lilacs and his syringas, his honeysuckles and his acacias'.[23] In his slighting references to William Beckford, we discern the defensive contempt of the latent for the blatant, the calamite[24] for the Caliph. His nature is more grossly implicit in his uninhibited pre-Freudian fantasies. In his Gothick novel, *The Castle of Otranto*, a 'Knight of the Gigantic Sabre' disconcerts Manfred by arriving with 'an hundred gentlemen bearing an enormous sword, and seeming to faint under the weight of it'. This phallic symbolism is only rivalled by the Oedipal undertones of Walpole's play, *The Mysterious Mother*, which concerns a gentlewoman who takes the place of a maidservant with whom her son has arranged an assignation, and bears him a daughter.[25] One symptom is lacking to make Walpole's a textbook case: the so-called 'changeling syndrome'. Others might doubt his paternity – Lady Mary Wortley Montagu said he 'was generally supposed to be the son of Carr Lord Hervey' – but he was apparently content to be his father's son. One can only suggest that a man of his proclivities, born in any other station of life, might have wistfully imagined himself a Prime Minister's son, shaking hands with the King.

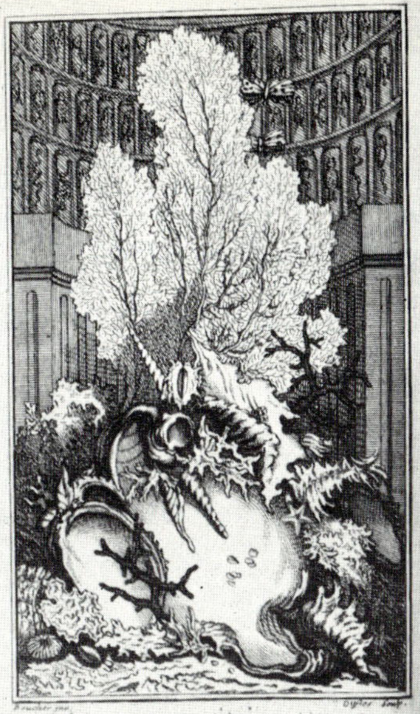

CATALOGUE

RAISONNÉ

D'UNE COLLECTION conſiderable de diverſes Curioſités en tous Genres, contenuës dans les Cabinets de feu Monſieur BONNIER DE LA MOSSON, Bailly & Capitaine des Chaſſes de la Varenne des Thuilleries & ancien Colonel du Regiment Dauphin.

Par E. F. GERSAINT.

A PARIS,

Chez { JAQUES BAROIS, Quay des Auguſtins, à la Ville de Nevers. ET PIERRE-GUILLAUME SIMON, Imprimeur du Parlement, au bas de la rue de la Harpe, à l'Hercule.

M. DCC. XLIV.

Avec Approbation & Privilege.

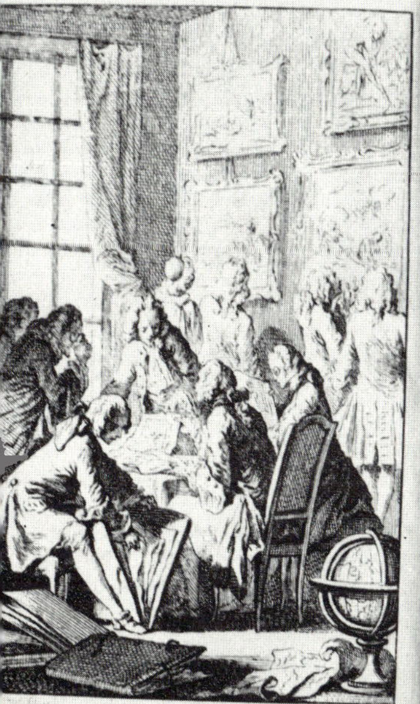

CATALOGUE

RAISONNÉ,

DES BIJOUX, PORCELAINES, BRONZES, LACQS, LUSTRES DE CRISTAL DE ROCHE ET DE PORCELAINE,

Pendules de goût, & autres Meubles curieux ou composés; Tableaux, Deſſeins, Eſtampes, Coquilles, & autres Effets de Curioſité, provenans de la Succeſſion de M. ANGRAN, Vicomte de FONSPERTUIS.

Cette Vente se fera, ſeulement pour la partie des Bijoux; dans les premiers jours du mois de Decembre 1747. les autres Effets curieux ne ſeront vendus que le premier Lundi de Carême 4 Mars 1748. & jours ſuivans.

Par E. F. GERSAINT.

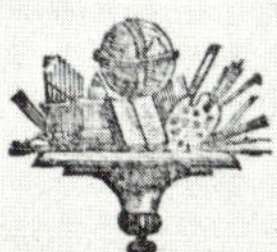

A PARIS,

Chez { PIERRE PRAULT, Quay de Gêvres. JACQUES BARROIS, Quay des Auguſtins.

M. DCC. XLVII.

AVEC APPROBATION ET PRIVILEGE.

Collectors

177 (top) Title-page and frontispiece of Gersaint's catalogue of the collection of Bonnier de la Mosson, 1744. See p. 281.

178 Title-page and frontispiece of Gersaint's catalogue of the collection of the Vicomte de Fonspertuis, 1747. See p. 266.

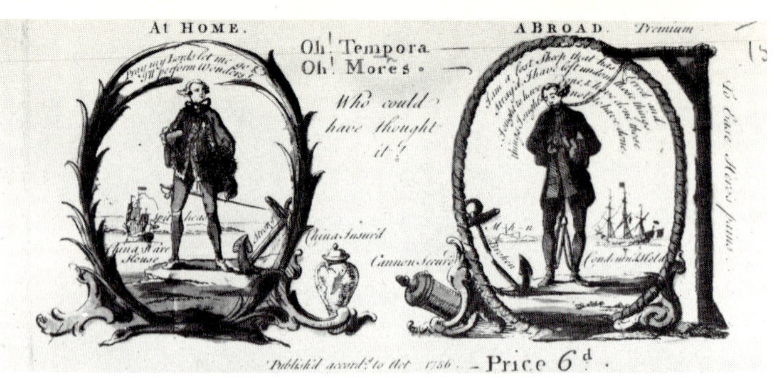

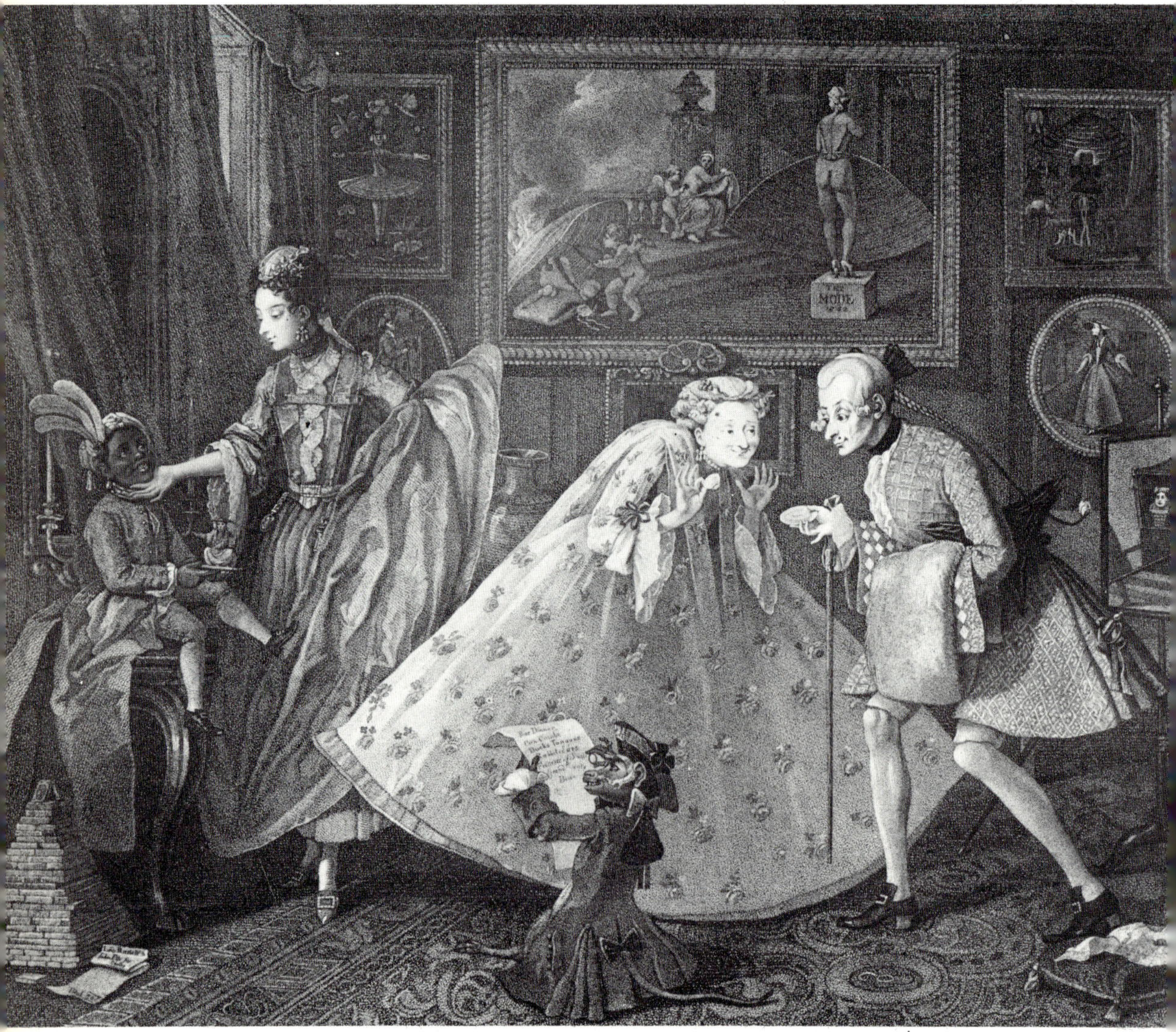

179 (top) Top of a satirical broadsheet attacking Admiral Byng, 1756. The left-hand cartouche includes 'China Ware House' and 'China Insur'd'. See p. 279.
180 'Taste in High Life', an engraving after Hogarth's oil painting of 1742. The man holding the saucer is supposed to be Lord Portmore. See p. 267.

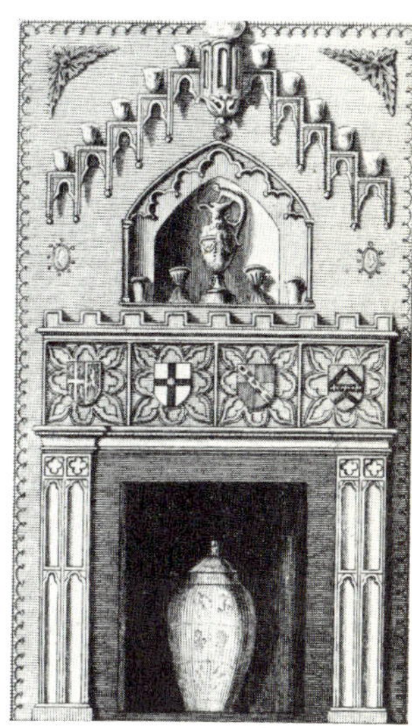

182 Horace Walpole's China Room at Strawberry Hill, from *A Catalogue of the Strawberry Hill Collection*. See p. 280.

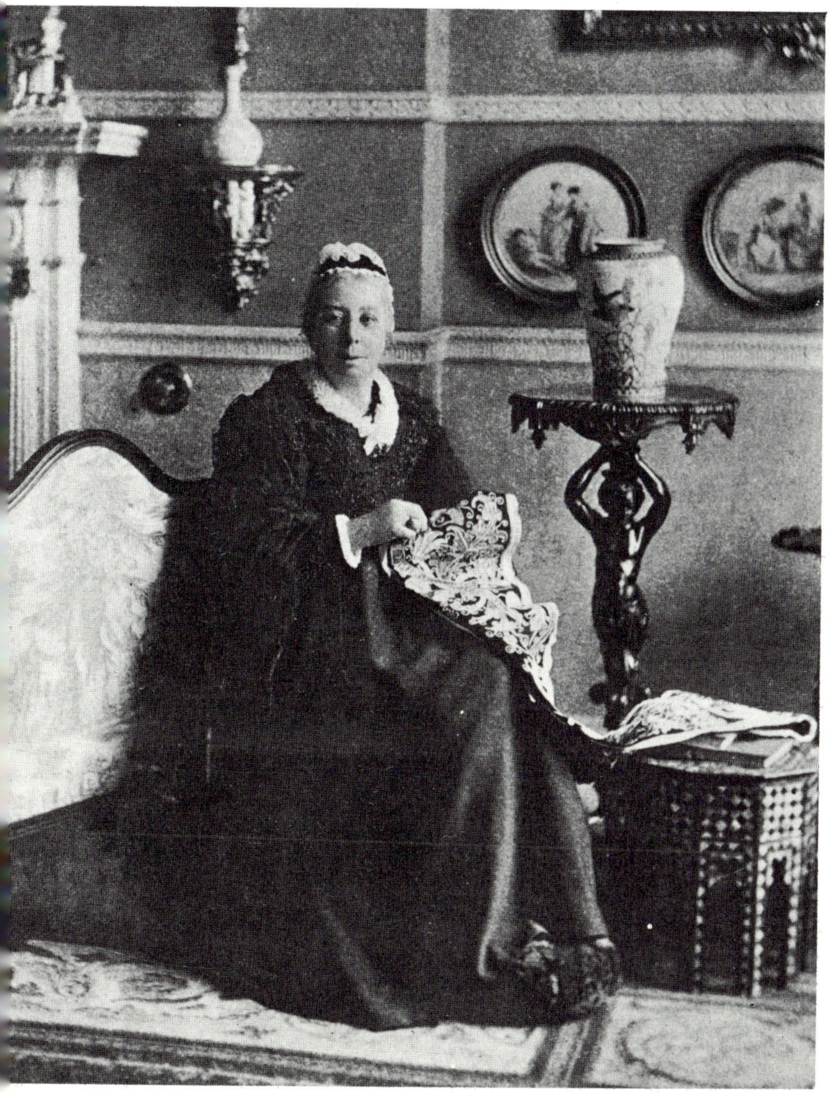

181 Lady Charlotte Schreiber, who formed the great Schreiber Collection now in the Victoria and Albert Museum. See pp. 294–5.

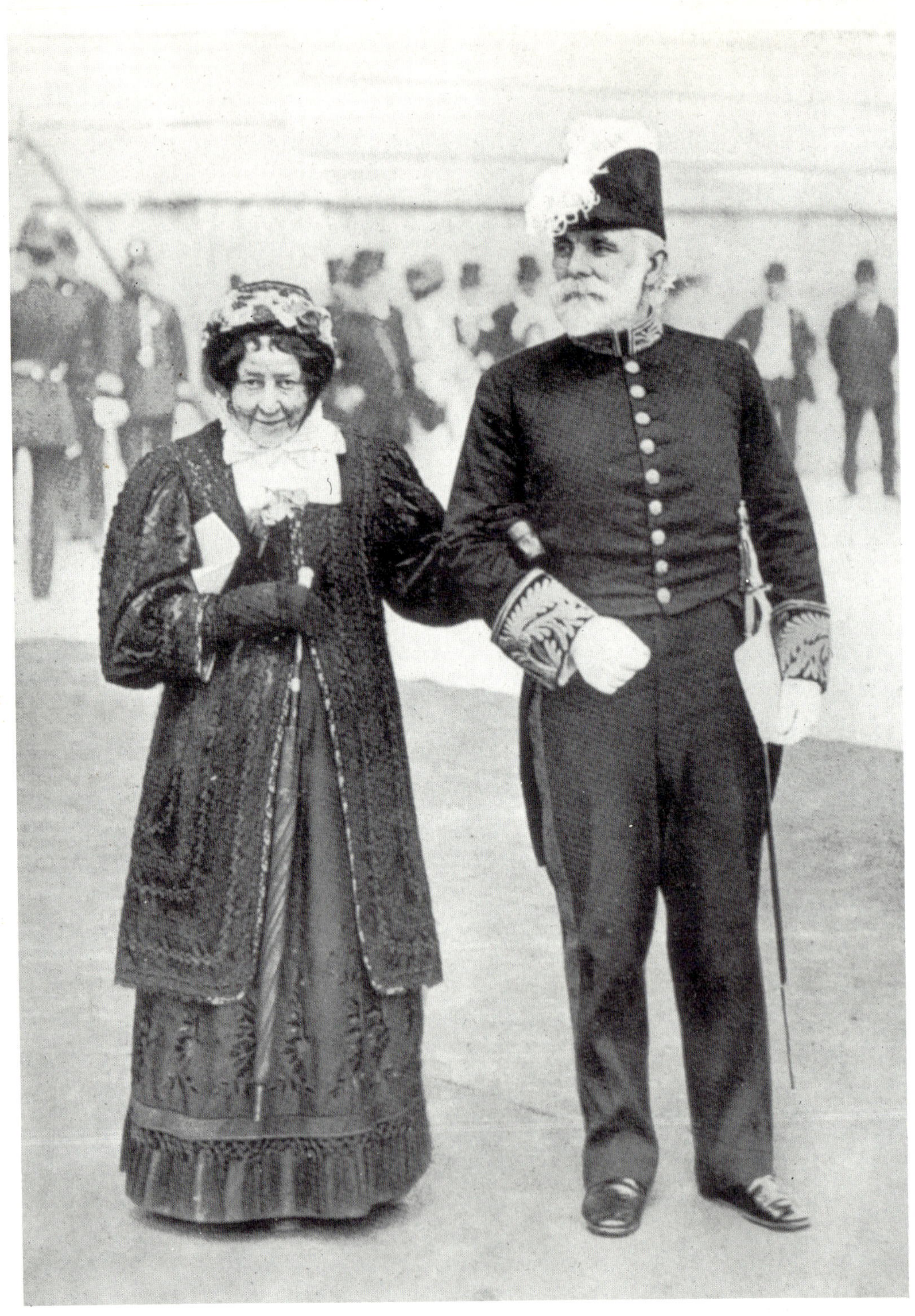

183 Lady Dorothy Nevill and John Burns at the opening of the Victoria and Albert Museum, 26 June 1909. See p. 289.

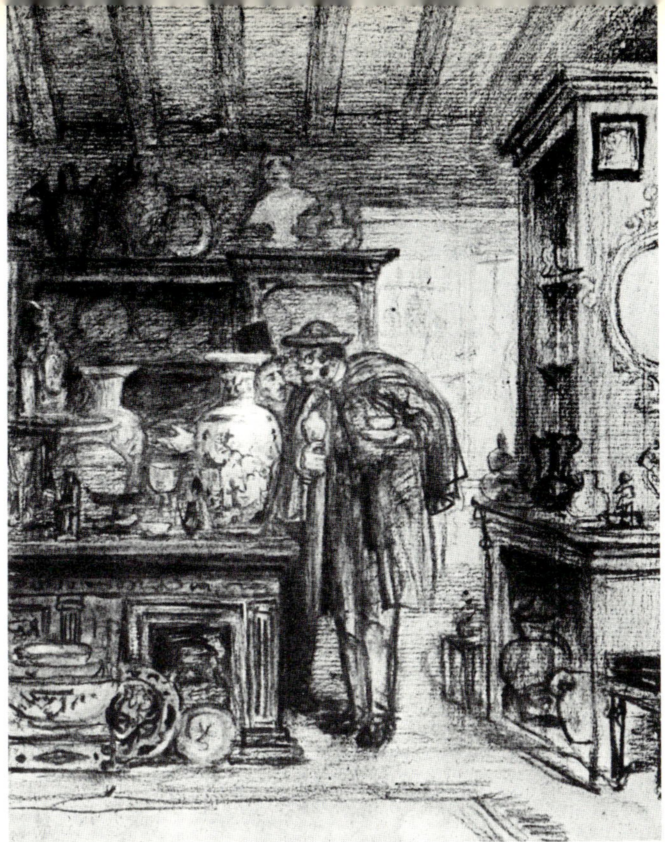

185 Andrew Lang, author of *Ballades in Blue China*. See p. 290.

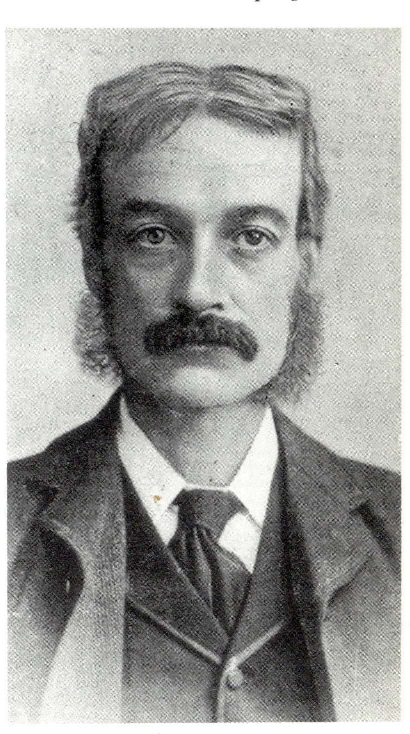

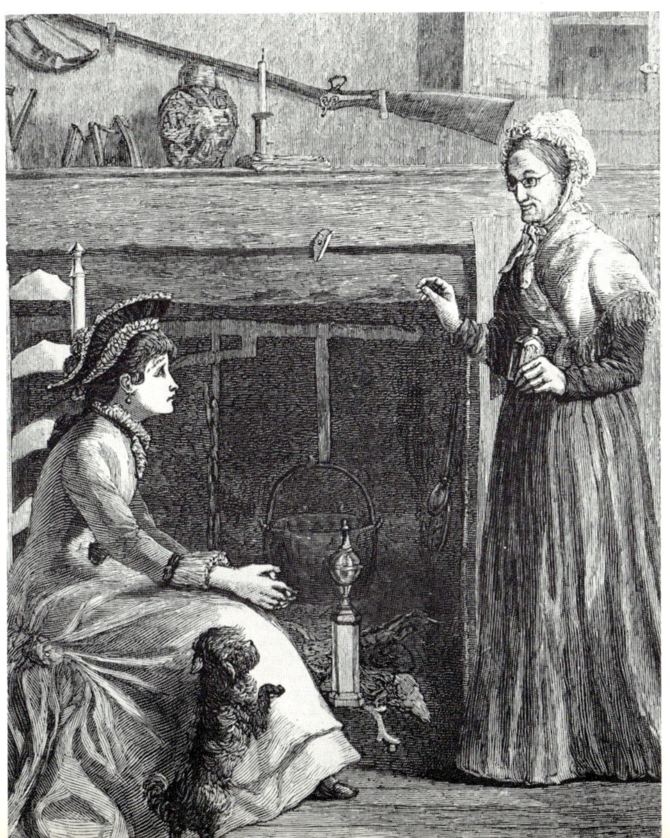

184 (top left) 'Love' by Sir Edward Poynter (later P.R.A.), mid-nineteenth century. Drawn at the Langham Sketch Club, black chalk.
186 'China Hunting at Daisy Farm', from the American book *The China Hunter's Club* by Annie Trumbull Slosson (1878). The old lady is producing a Staffordshire tea-caddy for the girl.

Comte Robert de Montesquiou

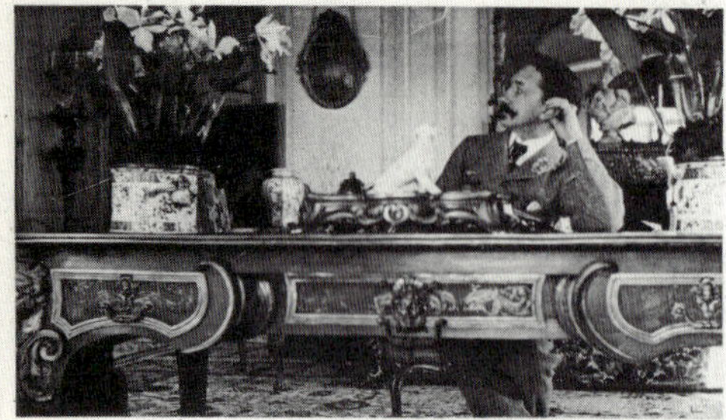

Pays des Aromates

COMMENTAIRE DESCRIPTIF

D'UNE COLLECTION D'OBJETS RELATIFS AUX PARFUMS

SUIVI D'UNE NOMENCLATURE DES PIÈCES QUI LA COMPOSENT

AINSI QUE DU CATALOGUE D'UNE BIBLIOTHÈQUE ATTENANTE

ET ORNÉ D'UN PORTRAIT.

PARIS

H. FLOURY, ÉDITEUR

1900

Les cassolettes légères
Pleines d'aromes défunts
Me semblent les reliquaires
Des odeurs et des parfums.

Des plus sages des fleurettes,
Des feuillages bienheureux,
Elles gardent les squelettes
Sous leur grille et dans leur creux.

À leur souffle qui m'arrose
Ma ferveur s'extasia
Pour l'amour de Sainte Rose
Ou de Saint Acacia.

Robert de Montesquiou

187 and 188 Title-page and manuscript poem, Comte Robert de Montesquiou's *Pays des Aromates* (1900). See p. 296.

189 (opposite) 'The Broken Saucer' by Gertrude Martineau, signed and dated 1894. See p. 296.

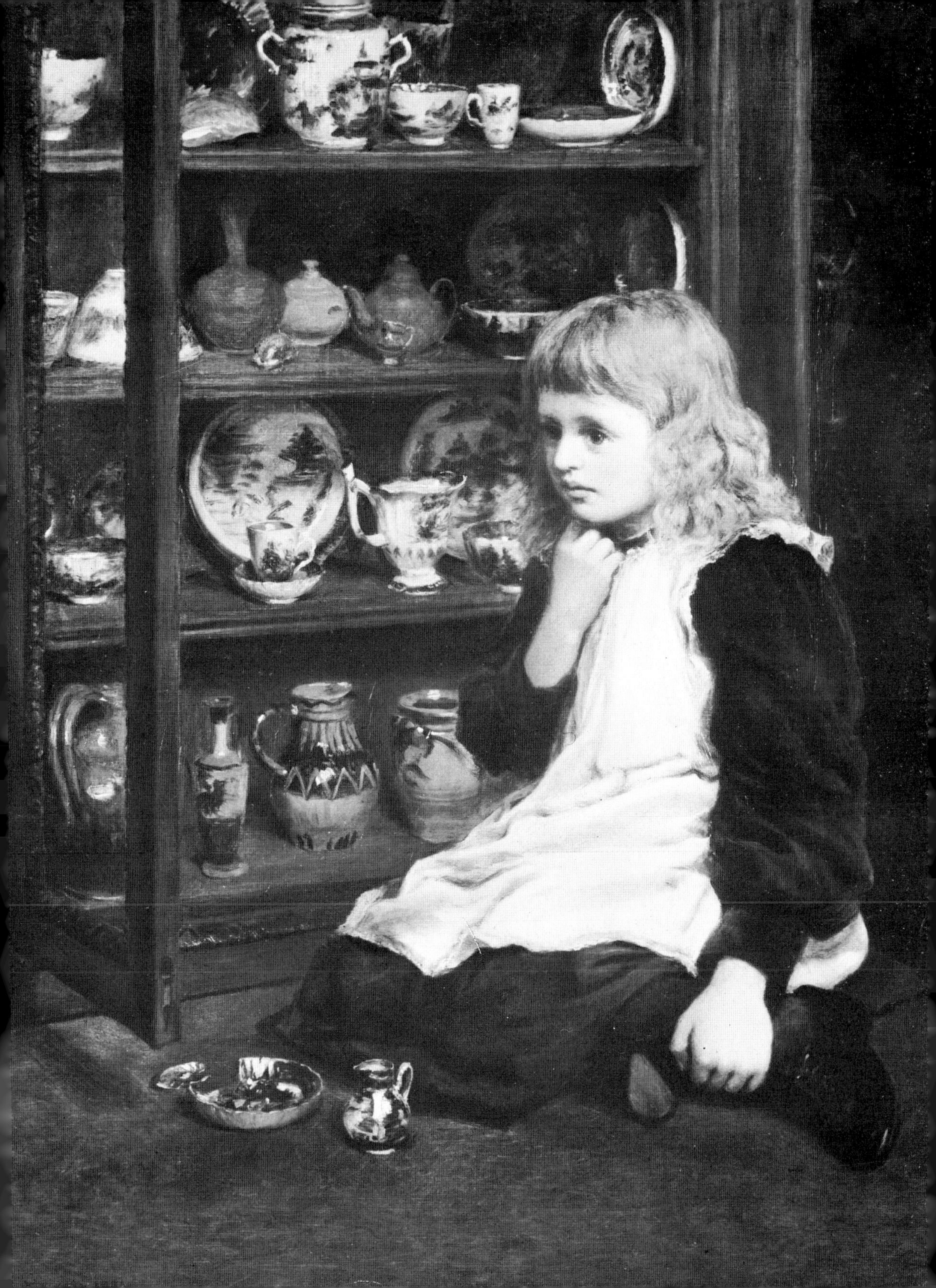

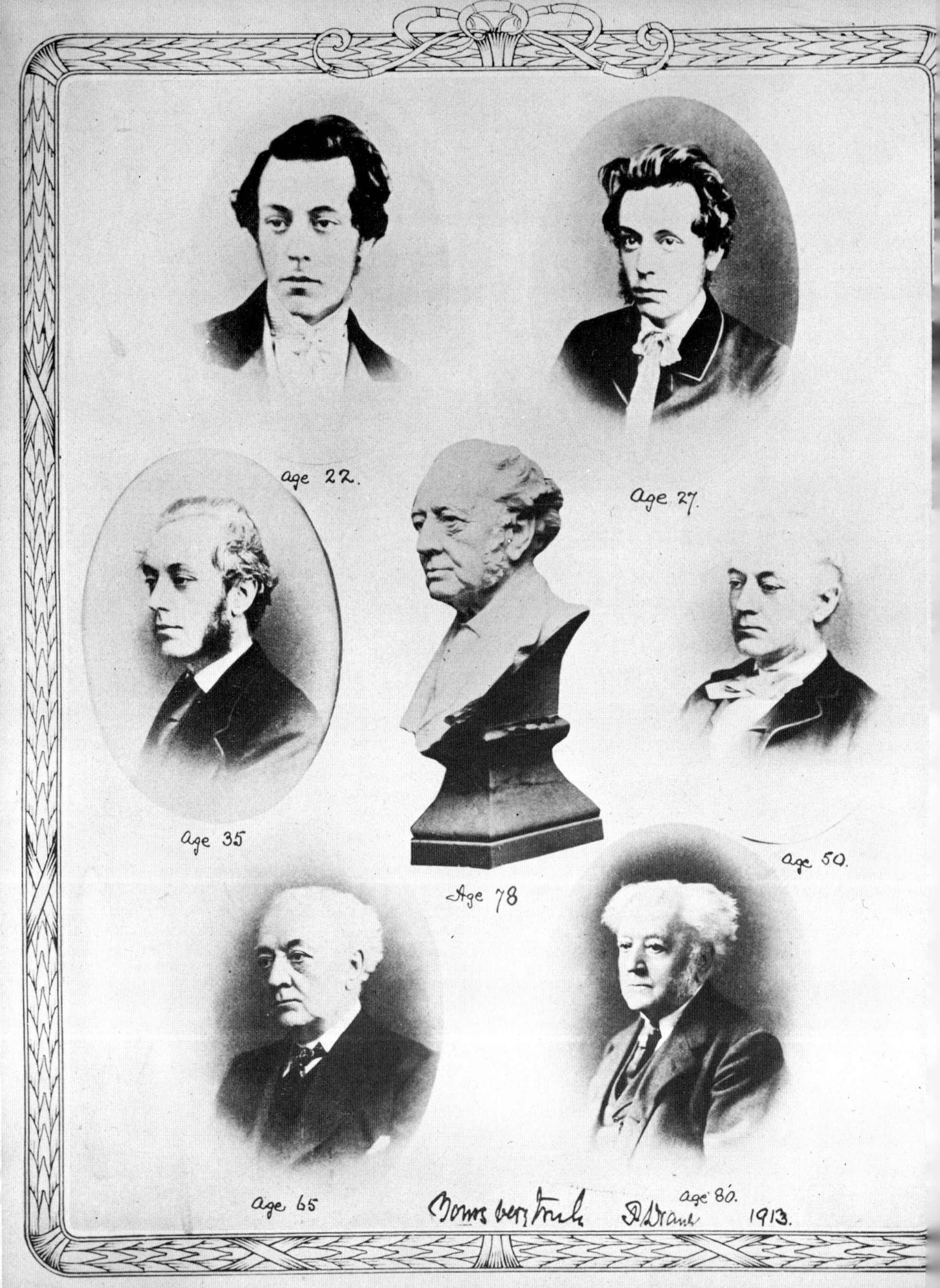
age 22.
Age 27.
age 35
Age 78
age 50.
age 65
age 80.
Yours very truly
1913.

This aspect of Walpole, which his biographers, with false delicacy, have skirted, is relevant to any study of china-collecting, so often regarded (even before Wilde's débâcle) as evidence of 'effeminacy'. Writing in 1807, under the fairly opaque guise of Don Manuel Alvarez Espriella, Robert Southey said, in his *Letters from England*: 'The passion for old china is confined to old women, and indeed is almost extinct.'[26] Untruthful as it was, this comment was perhaps aimed at Charles Lamb, who in his essay on Old China wrote: 'I have an almost feminine partiality for old china. When I go to see any great house, I inquire for the china-closet, and next for the picture gallery.' Mark Twain confessed that:

> The very 'marks' on the bottom of a piece of rare crockery are able to throw me into a gibbering ecstasy; and I could forsake a drowning relative to help dispute about whether the stopple of a departed Buon Retiro scent-bottle was genuine or spurious. Many people say that for a male person, bric-a-brac hunting is about as robust a business as making doll-clothes, or decorating Japanese pots with decalomanie butterflies would be....[27]

In Kipling's poem *The 'Mary Gloster'* (1894) the dying captain says to his son, educated at 'Harrer an' Trinity College':

> The things I knew was proper you wouldn't thank me to give,
> And the things I knew was rotten you said was the way to live.
> For you muddled with books and pictures, an' china an' etchin's an' fans,
> And your rooms at college was beastly – more like a whore's than a man's.

All this, despite an aggressive array of china-collecting marshals, generals and admirals – including the ill-fated Admiral Byng, who is shown in one hostile broadsheet (Plate VIII) sitting in a cabin lined from ceiling to floor with vases and pagods, while in another (Plate 179) he stands by a vase labelled 'China Insur'd', a sinking ship being labelled 'Condemn'd and Sold'.[28]

Byng was condemned to death by a court-martial in 1756, for failing to join battle with the French fleet which was on the point of attacking Minorca. An attempt to save his life was the most spirited and humane act of Horace Walpole's political career, but he succeeded only in gaining a two-week reprieve, and Byng was shot in March 1757. It was, Walpole told Mann, a tragedy 'in which I have been a most unfortunate actor, having to my infinite grief, which I shall feel till the man is at peace, been instrumental in protracting his misery a fortnight, by what I meant as the kindest thing I could do'.[29] Inevitably, Walpole had been out-manoeuvred. His political life was never much more than a froth of

190 (*opposite*) Robert Drane, the founder of 'comparative collecting'. The principle of comparative collecting is well illustrated by this page of photographs from the catalogue (1922) of his collection of Worcester porcelain. See p. 295.

ineffectual faction. Macaulay was not really unfair when, gleefully launching into his second crockery collector, he wrote of Walpole:

> After the labours of the print-shop and the auction-room, he unbent his mind in the House of Commons. And, having indulged in the recreation of making laws and voting millions, he returned to more important pursuits, to researches after Queen Mary's comb, Wolsey's red hat, the pipe which Van Tromp smoked during his last sea-fight, and the spur which King William stuck into the flank of Sorrel.[30]

The storehouse for these treasures, and for his china collection, was Strawberry Hill, Twickenham, the house which Walpole bought from Mrs Chenevix, the toy-woman and china dealer, in 1747. At Strawberry there was a china closet, hung with a 'paper to imitate Dutch tiles' afterwards apparently replaced by actual tiles. In the Preface to his *Description of Strawberry Hill,* Walpole said: 'The following collection was made out of the spoils of many renowned cabinets; as Dr Mead's, Lady Elizabeth Germain's, Lord Oxford's, the Duchess of Portland's, and of almost forty more of celebrity.' It included the Delft plates decorated by Thornhill (Plates 27 and 28) which Walpole bought at Mrs Hogarth's sale. Some 'Raphael or Faenza ware', presents from the Earl of Exeter, 'had belonged to Jarvis the painter, who had a fine collection of the Faenza ware'. (The collection of Jarvis [Jervas] was sold by Heath in 1739.) Historically, though not perhaps aesthetically, the *pièce de résistance* of the china collection was (to quote the 1842 catalogue):

> *The celebrated large blue and white* ORIENTAL CHINA CISTERN, on Gothic carved pedestal, *in which* HORACE WALPOLE'S *cat was drowned,* this gave occasion to Mr Gray, the poet, to write his beautiful Ode, beginning thus:
>
> 'Twas on this lofty vase's side,
> Where China's gayest art has dyed
> The azure flowers that blow;
> Demurest of the tabby kind,
> The pensive Selima reclined
> Gazed on the like below.

Walpole had had a special label printed with Gray's poem at the Strawberry Hill Press. At the 1842 sale the cistern was bought by the Earl of Derby for £42, and it is still at Knowsley, in spite of the suggestion by Mr Edmund Blunden, in a letter to the editor of the *Times Literary Supplement*, that 'cat-lovers everywhere are no doubt waiting to trace and in contemporary fashion to annihilate this relic of medieval barbarism, and no doubt Chinese torture'.[31]

In 1751 Walpole wrote to George Montagu: 'My evening yesterday was employed – how wisely do you think? in what grave occupation? in bawding for the Duchess of Portland, to procure her a scarlet spider from Admiral Boscawen.'[32] Margaret Cavendish Holles Harley (1714–1785), Duchess of Portland, is best known for having supplanted with her own name the famous Barberini-Hamilton vase now in the British Museum. She collected books, pictures, busts, coins, medals, miniatures, jewels and specimens of natural history – including red spiders – as well as china:

The Duchess of Portland (wrote Walpole, in a preface to her sale catalogue) inherited the Passion of her Family for Collecting. At first her Taste was chiefly confined to Shells, Japan & Old China, particularly of the blue & white with a brown Edge, of which last sort she formed a large Closet at Bulstrode; but contenting herself with one specimen of every pattern She could get, it was a collection of odd pieces.

In view of what has already been said of the intimate connection between shells and porcelain, it is interesting to note how many of the eighteenth-century virtuosi were conchologists as well as china collectors. The great French collectors whose cabinets were sold by Gersaint – Fonspertuis, La Roque and Bonnier de la Mosson[33] – were all connoisseurs of shells. The frontispiece to the De la Mosson catalogue of 1744, which includes both shells and porcelain, is a delightful rococo engraving of shells by Duflos, after Boucher (Plate 177). The British Museum copy of the La Roque catalogue formerly belonged to Sir Joseph Banks, President of the Royal Society (who has signed it and noted on the flyleaf: 'Holmskiolds sale at Copenhagen 1794'). Banks was another collector of both porcelain[34] and shells. So also was James West (1704?–72), another President of the Royal Society, and MP for St Albans. West's collection, which was sold in 1773, contained a considerable amount of Meissen and even Chelsea wares. The Duchess of Portland also bought contemporary porcelain, and the frontispiece to Horace Walpole's copy of her sale catalogue was indexed by him not only '(1) The [Portland] vase; (2) The Jupiter Serapis' (which Walpole himself bought); but also '(3) the carp of Chelsea porcelaine'. But the bulk of the Duchess's china collection was oriental. An unusual blue and white Arita dish, now in the possession of the Earl of Ilchester, bears the following eighteenth-century label:

Plate bid for at a sale and obtained by Elisabeth Countess of Ilchester, for £100 against the Duchess of Portland, which was carefully put away when the Duchess visited her for fear of recalling the fact.[35]

Another collecting duchess was Isabella, Duchess of Manchester (1692–1786). A poem of 1740, *Isabella; or, The Morning* by Horace Walpole's friend Sir Charles Hanbury Williams, shows her enthusing over contemporary Staffordshire pottery, brought her by Richard, brother of Viscount Bateman[36]:

To please the noble dame, the courtly 'squire
Produc'd a *tea-pot*, made in Staffordshire:
With eager eyes the longing Duchess stood,
And o'er and o'er the shining bauble view'd:
Such were the joys touch'd young Atrides' breast,
Such all the Grecian host at once exprest,
When from beneath his robe, to all their view,
Laertes' son, the fam'd Palladium drew.
So Venus look'd, and with such longing eyes,
When Paris first produc'd the golden prize.
'Such work as this,' she cries, 'can England do?
It equals Dresden, and outdoes St. Cloud:
All modern China now shall hide its head,
And e'en Chantilly must give o'er the trade:
For lace let Flanders bear away the bell
In finest linen let the Dutch excel;
For prettiest stuffs let Ireland first be nam'd,
And for best-fancy'd silks let France be fam'd;
Do thou, thrice-happy England! still prepare
This clay, and build thy fame on earthenware.'
More she'd have said, but that again she heard
The knocker – and the General appear'd....

'Your servant, Sir – but see what I have got!
Isn't it a prodigious charming *pot*?
And a'n't you vastly glad we make them here?
For Dicky got it out of Staffordshire.
See how the charming vine twines all about!
Lord! what a handle! Jesus! what a spout!
And that old Pagog, and that charming child!
If Lady Townshend[37] saw them, she'd be wild!'

To this the Gen'ral: 'Madam, who would not?
Lord! where could Mr Bateman find this *pot*?
Dear Dicky, cou'dn't you get one for me?
I want some useful china mightily;
Two jars, two beakers, and a *pot-pourri*.[38]

The General, a flesh-and-blood anticipation of Jane Austen's General Tilney in his approval of contemporary Staffordshire wares, was General Churchill, son of an elder brother of the great Duke of Marlborough. There was later a china gallery at Blenheim, but it was not formed by the Churchills. It was fitted out in 1796 with a collection donated by 'Mr Spalding, a valetudinary of moderate fortune':

> Among other varieties are many of the choicest pieces of the old blue and white, and pale japan brown edge, so much esteemed by the curious.... Among many other pieces deserving attention, are a pair of small bottles, once the property of Queen Anne – A large japan tea-pot, a present from Louis XIV to the Duke of Richelieu – Two smaller ones, from the collection of the Duke of Orleans, father to Egalité – Some pieces from the late Princess Amelia's cabinet – many from the Portland Museum, and from the celebrated collection of the Duke d'Aumont, at Paris – a singular piece from the Duke of Argyle's curiosities, in a former reign – several articles from the late Duchess of Kingston's – from Selima, Countess of Huntingdon's – from M. Calonne's – and M. Beaumarchais's collections. Five ornamental pieces, presented by a Nabob to a Governor of Bengal, in the reign of William III, possess uncommon beauty. A large white tea-pot, once in the possession of Oliver Cromwell, will be deemed a curiosity....[39]

The long and fantastic life of William Beckford (1759–1844) leads us from the eighteenth well into the nineteenth century. The antipathy between him and Horace Walpole, the Lord Mayor's son and the Prime Minister's son, has already been suggested. Cyrus Redding, in his anonymous *Memoirs of William Beckford* (1859), wrote:

> Towards the close of Horace Walpole's life, he was annoyed by hearing of the extent of Mr Beckford's collection, and his extravagant purchases, which he said would raise the prices of articles of *virtu* so high, that it would prevent his adding to his own collection, and he became irritated about it, declaring that in all events Mr Beckford should not have anything of his, and he therefore entailed his property on so many that it appeared next to impossible that Mr Beckford should survive them all. Singular to say, Mr Beckford did outlive them all, and purchased many important curiosities, which were conveyed to Lansdown.[40]

In 1822 the public were informed that the weird palace of Fonthill, so long locked up from the eyes of strangers, was to be thrown open in preparation for a sale. Catalogues were issued by Christie's at a guinea each, and 7,200 were sold. One of those who took the opportunity of viewing Fonthill was William Hazlitt. Wherever there is a collector, there is, it seems, someone to chide him. Hazlitt served Beckford as Macaulay served Queen Mary and Horace Walpole:

> It is a desert of magnificence, a glittering waste of laborious idleness, a cathedral turned into a toy shop, an immense museum of all that is most curious and costly, and at the same time most worthless, in the productions of art and nature. Mr Beckford has undoubtedly shown himself an industrious *bijoutier*, a prodigious virtuoso, an accomplished patron of unproductive labour, an enthusiastic collector of expensive trifles – the only proof of taste he has shown in this collection is his getting rid of it.[41]

Hazlitt was wrong. Beckford did not get rid of his collections. In the first place, the Christie's sale did not take place after all; the entire demesne and the abbey, with the contents, were sold to John Farquhar (1751–1826) for £300,000. But when the collections were sold by Phillips in the following year, Beckford reserved or bought in much of them, and made them the foundation of a new museum in Bath. These collections were sold at Bath, after his death, in November 1845. 'Mr Beckford's collection of Oriental china was very extensive,' wrote Marryat, 'and remarkable for very fine specimens of eggshell plates with ruby backs, as well as those of every other description. The mazarine blue and crackle were unique. Of the Japan no such specimens were ever before offered for sale.'[42] But the collection also included much maiolica, Meissen, Sèvres and even some Wedgwood cups and saucers, though these were probably designed, as Gibbon said of the younger Gordian's concubines, 'for use rather than ostentation'.

Beckford was a master of the bizarre; but however nameless the tastes indulged behind the walls of Fonthill – vices which, according to gloating rumour, twice caused the collapse of the abbey's great tower in retribution – they could scarcely rival those of Thomas Griffiths Wainewright (1794–1852), who poisoned four people, including his uncle and mother-in-law, and was transported to Tasmania for defrauding the Bank of England. Born at Chiswick in 1794, he was brought up by his grandfather, Ralph Griffiths, the friend of Josiah Wedgwood[43] and Thomas Bentley. Beckford had studied music under Mozart; Wainewright went to school at the Hammersmith academy of Charles Burney, son of the historian of music. After brief service as a guardsman, he became a journalist, under the pseudonyms 'Janus Weathercock', 'Egomet Bonmot' and 'Van Vinkvooms'. Charles Lamb, who speaks of him as 'kind light-hearted Wainewright', admired his prose, and became his friend. They shared a taste for old ceramics. In the *London Magazine* of December 1821, Wainewright described 'Janus's boudoir', which contained 'several very fine specimens of the Raffaëlle china, particularly a grand dish with the marriage of Cupid and Psyche ... ; some curious brown-biscuit teapots, fillagree-worked; and other crockery, both *cracknell* and *green dragon*; which show their possessor's ample range of taste and antiquarian science'. Wainewright was a talented artist. He was much influenced by Fuseli. William Blake stopped before one of his pictures in the Royal Academy and pronounced it 'very fine'. Swinburne described him as 'powerful with pen, pencil and poison'. Wilde, fascinated as always by the supposed effects of 'sin' on art, wrote an essay on him: 'In one of the beautiful rings of which he was so proud, and which served to show off the fine modelling of his delicate ivory hands, he used to carry crystals of the Indian *nux vomica*, a poison, one of his biographers tells us, "nearly tasteless, difficult of discovery, and capable of almost infinite dilution".'[44] Dickens, who came upon him by chance in gaol, made him the hero of his *Hunted Down*; and he was also the Varney of Bulwer's *Lucretia*. He tried to poison two more people in Tasmania, but his hand seems to have lost its cunning. He died of apoplexy in 1852.

In Wainewright's brief inventory of his ceramics, there is, despite his claim of an 'ample range of taste', no mention of the china most fashionable in the early nineteenth century – Sèvres. The fashion was set by George IV, who bought most of his collection while Prince of Wales, with the help of his French confectioner, Benoît, that of the third Marquess of Hertford (1772–1842), and of Beau Brummell. Hertford, the founder of the Wallace Collection, had a fine Sèvres collection of his own, which included the inkstand (Plate 48) believed to have belonged to Madame Adelaide, sister of Louis XVI. Brummell, too was a Sèvres collector. When he left London and his debts behind in 1816, and sailed for France, his collection was sold by Christie's, who catalogued it with sublime tact: 'A very choice and valuable assemblage of Specimens of the rare old Sèvres Porcelain ... The genuine property of A MAN OF FASHION Gone to the Continent.' Brummell's biographer, Captain Jesse, writes:

> Among the Sèvres china was a pair of oval vases, which sold for nineteen guineas; they were green, with flowers and fruit, and mouldings of burnished gold. A small cup and saucer of the same, eighteen pounds. A ewer and basin, mazarine-blue-and-gold ground, richly ornamented with birds and exotics finely painted in compartments, with the name of each specimen upon them; the handle of this ewer was silver gilt, and the lot fetched twenty-six pounds.[45]

Meanwhile, fatty deposits of buhl and ormolu were accreting in Brummell's new rooms at Caen. A service of Sèvres was locked behind brass-wire doors:

> The designs were most exquisite, and on each plate was represented, in colours chaster than the originals, all the celebrated beauties that held such powerful sway over the courts of Louis the Fourteenth and Fifteenth; and, as they were not few in number, the reader may imagine that his inanimate but elegant harem completely filled his buhl seraglio. These portraits were so charmingly done that the Beau, in the true spirit of a sultan, used to inform his visitors that it was 'almost profanation even to look at these frail fair ones'.[46]

One of the causes of Brummell's quarrel with George IV was a snuffbox. The royal collector was determined to have Brummell's which he particularly admired. He told Brummell to go to Gray's and order any box he liked in lieu of it. Brummell chose one with a miniature of the Prince, but when he called at Gray's he was told that special directions had been sent by the prince that the box was not to be delivered: it never was, nor was the one returned for which it was to have been exchanged. 'It was the fashion in those days,' wrote a friend of Brummell's, 'to indulge in a luxury of snuffboxes. I have seen at Sir George C——d's a tray handed round the table covered with such boxes, to be examined and criticized.'[47] Another snuffbox collector was the dandy Lord Petersham (later Earl of Harrington). He was supposed to have a different snuffbox for every day of the year. Captain Gronow 'heard him once, on the occasion of a delightful old light-blue Sèvres box he was using being admired, say, in his lisping way – "Yes, it is a nice summer box, but would not do for winter wear".'[48] Petersham's reputation as a connoisseur was so persistent that T. H. S. Escott could write in 1907 'he is also the original author of the china mania that endured to our own day'.[49] Sir Guy Laking suggests that: 'One reason for the acquisition of Sèvres, on the part of wealthy English connoisseurs, to the exclusion of other and contemporary productions, was the general and intense antagonism to all Napoleonic forms of art.'[50] This is not altogether plausible. As far as taste was concerned, the fashion owed much to the florid predilections of George IV, but its main basis was not so much taste as opportunity – the opportunity created by the dispersal of great French collections during and after the French Revolution. George IV's collection, Hertford's and Brummell's were all formed as a direct result of the Revolution. So also was that of Edward, Viscount Lascelles (1764–1814), at Harewood House, Yorkshire.[51]

XV (*opposite*) 'The Riddle of Life', gilt vase by Capeque, *c.* 1900.

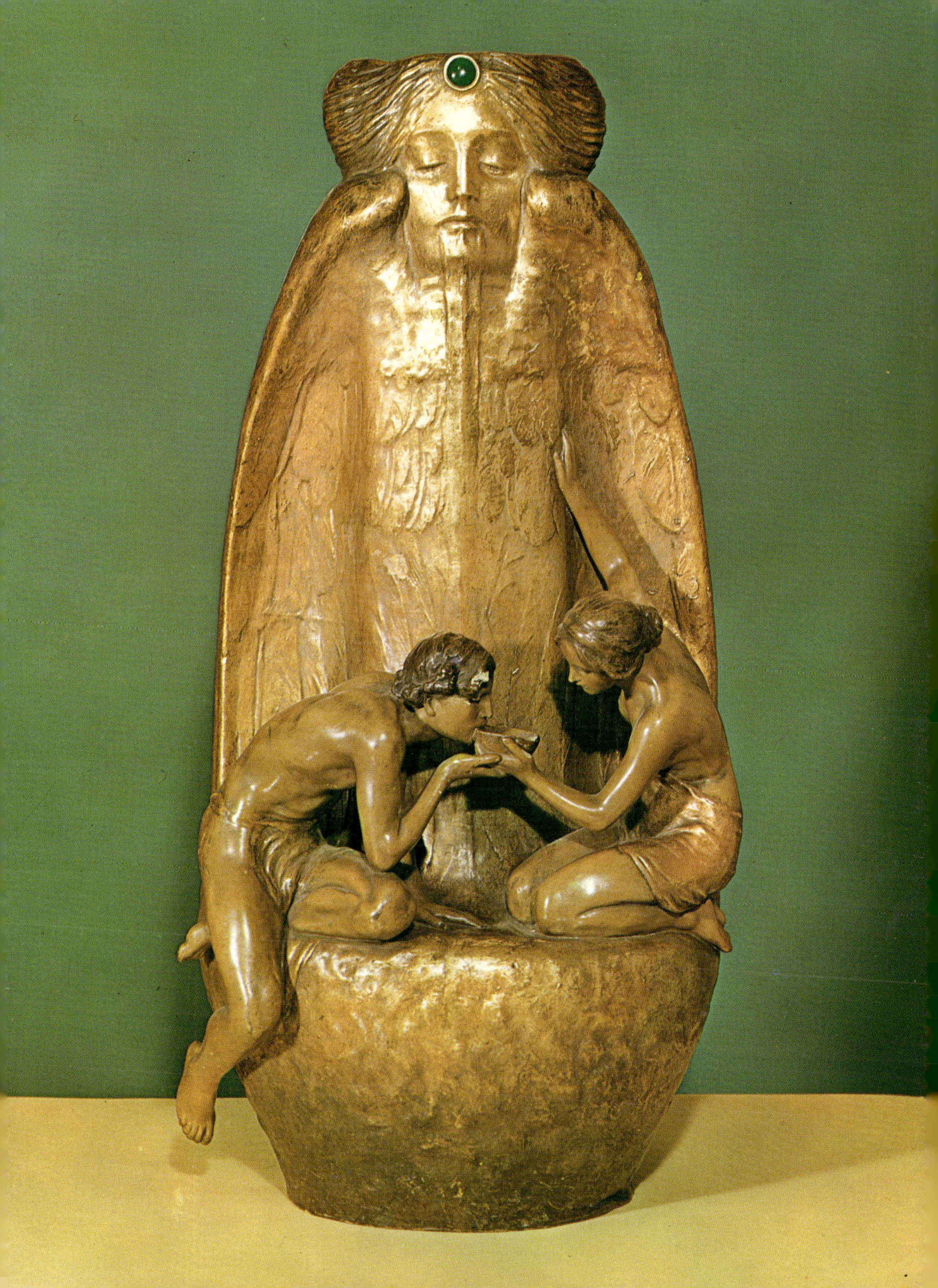

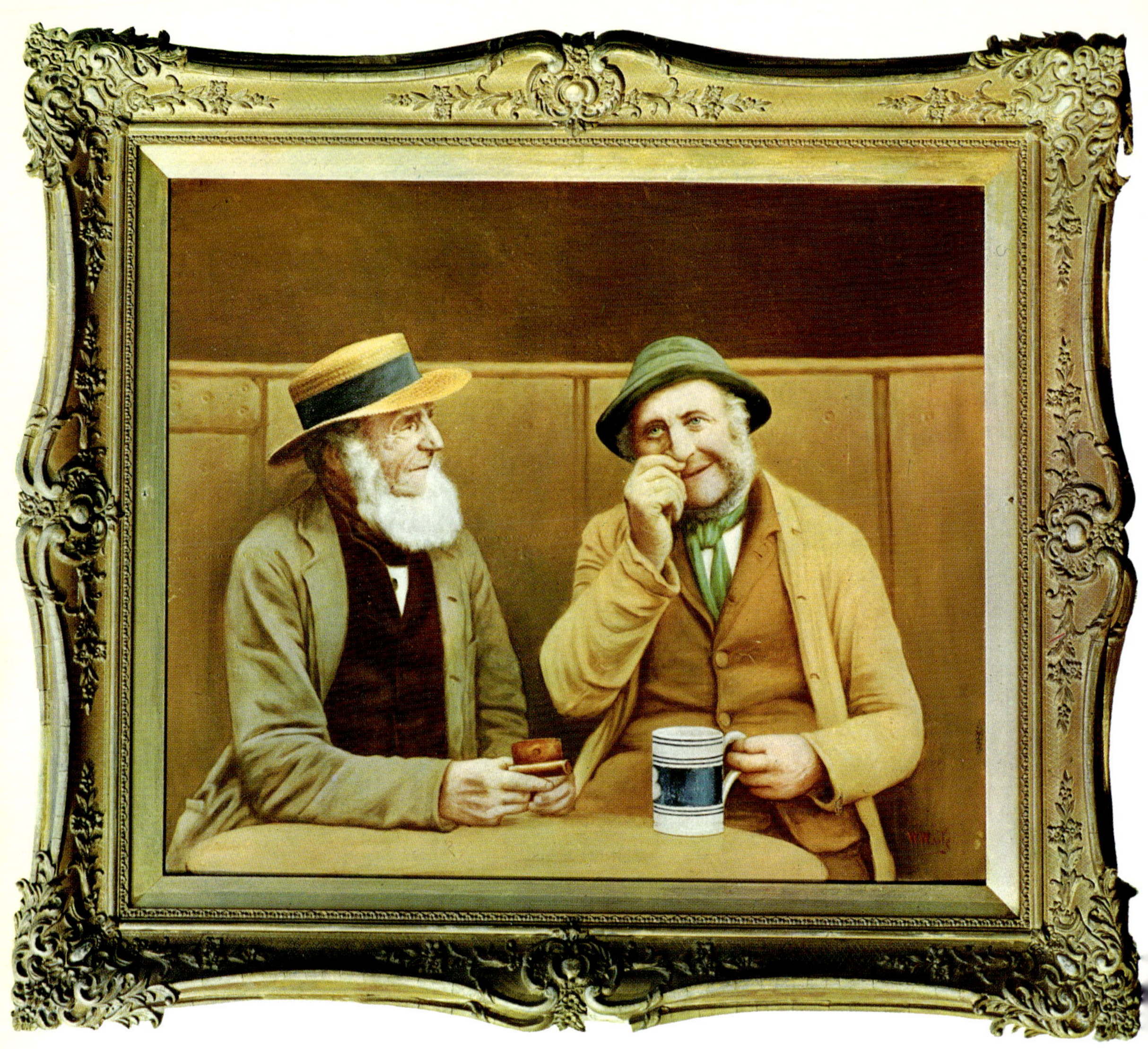

Sèvres remained fashionable. Of the 4,294 objects in Ralph Bernal's sale in 1855, the Sèvres fetched the highest prices. Sèvres was one of the main ingredients in the many embarrassments of riches created by the Rothschild family. Nathaniel Rothschild of Vienna bought his Sèvres from Lord Revelstoke. Baron Ferdinand Rothschild amassed the Sèvres at Waddesden Manor, Buckinghamshire. Alfred Rothschild is described by Lady Dorothy Nevill as 'the finest amateur judge of French eighteenth-century art in England, possesses much beautiful Sèvres in his wonderful collection, which is a monument of what sound judgment and unrivalled taste can effect'.

Lady Dorothy Nevill (1826–1913), of whom I have written at greater length elsewhere,[52] is listed by Marryat as a Sèvres collector, and also appears among the collectors of Italian and English ceramics. Collecting was in her blood. Horace Walpole was her kinsman, and her obsession with him amounted to platonic necrophilia; while her mother was the grand-daughter of Sir Everard Fawkener, patron of the Chelsea porcelain factory. She was one of the great Victorian society hostesses. To her, china collecting was just one of many frittering pursuits. She made skeletons of leaves, bred silkworms and axolotls, experimented with cooking guinea-pigs, made illuminated genealogies and tied Chinese whistles on to pigeons' tails – 'No one but myself, I believe, has ever organized such a winged orchestra'. Between 1906 and 1912 she wrote five autobiographies. She was not peeling the onion, penetrating ever deeper to the core of her being. The simile would rather be a vivacious old lizard shedding one iridescent skin after another. She had Horace Walpole's talent as a gently malicious gossip. There are many accounts of china-collecting sprees. At Winston Churchill's wedding she made her last new friendship – with Edward Cazalet, a sixteen-year-old Eton boy, who collected old porcelain. 'I am so unhappy,' he wrote in March 1913, three years before his own death in the Great War. 'We have just had a wire to say that my dear Lady Dolly died yesterday evening.'

One of Lady Dorothy's friends was the eccentric Marquess of Clanricarde, a millionaire Irish landlord with a reputation for rapacity. The best accounts of him are in Ralph Nevill's *Life and Letters of Lady Dorothy Nevill* (1919) and in Lady Dorothy's own book, *Under Five Reigns* (1910). He was a classic miser. One rumour was that in 1852, when he became attaché to Sir James Hudson at Turin, he made arrangements to sleep in a broom cupboard to save expense. Another said that he was his own tailor; his coat and hat were held together by rough stitching. But, we are told, he was 'not without coquetry': though his tie

XVI (*opposite*) 'The Snuff-taker' by William White of Esher, Surrey, *c.* 1880–1910. The old man on the right holds a mug of the kind made by the 'mocha-ware' factories, though this is a plain glazed example with a white relief.

was secured by a piece of old tape, he wore in it a diamond scarf-pin in the back of which he usually inserted a piece of coloured paper painted by himself with a child's colour-box. He kept an old hard-boiled egg to show his servant the correct size for eggs. At his club he gorged himself with free chutney, and took such flagrant advantage of an old rule that ham should be included in the table service, that 'the too liberal ordinance had to be hastily abrogated'. A cigar, he said, was never at its best until the third time of smoking. When he had smoked an inch he would cut off the end and put the remains away. After the second smoking he would cut off another portion, saving the stump as a *bonne bouche*. It was among these cigar stumps that he kept the Cinquecento jewel, said to be worth some £12,000, which Canning (his grandfather) had brought back from the Mogul's treasury at Delhi. In the same Albany house, Nevill noted, 'valuable pictures were stacked on the floor, while several thousand pounds' worth of Sèvres china was displayed in a rough sort of cabinet which the Marquis himself had knocked up out of old packing-cases. When he moved to Hanover Square he kept his Sèvres in his kitchen.'[53]

Clanricarde had, in an exaggerated form, the collector's cast of mind, not only in his hoarding instinct, but also in his concentration on attractive detail at the expense of large issues. Nevill observed the latter trait:

> His accuracy and remembrance of detail were quite wonderful; on the other hand he had little imagination or breadth of vision. An omnivorous reader, he was prone to attach overmuch interest to detail, and was more interested in sidelights upon the lives of historical personages than in the great events in which they had taken part. The French Revolution, for instance, did not appeal to him at all; 'an unpleasant affair,' he told me, 'which I don't want to read about.' He took very much the same line about the Great War, and when people mentioned it before him would at once change the subject.[54]

Andrew Lang (Plate 185) expressed the same philosophy with lapidary facetiousness:

> The foolish people raging
> O'er Bradlaugh and o'er Bright
> They know not the assuaging
> Of what is 'good' and 'right':
> Of coins that 'scaped the Vandals,
> Of daggers with jade handles,
> Of broidered Syrian sandals,
> Of bowls of Malachite.

Can kings or clergies alter
The crackle on one plate?
Can creeds or systems palter
With what is truly great?

Lang was one of the literary men who collected 'blue' – the blue china before which, in Beerbohm's cartoon, the Sage of Chelsea stood implacably unmoved while Whistler rhapsodized; the blue which was hurled from Oscar Wilde's Magdalen window into the Cherwell by philistine athletes. (Inexplicably, he seems to have missed the opportunity of saying 'If I had served my God as I have served my Ming, he would not thus have left me naked to mine enemies'.)

Blue china was the indispensable chattel of the aesthete. 'I hope I can live up to my blue,' sighed Wilde; and du Maurier, in *Punch*, showed a gormless young couple trying desperately to live up to *their* crockery.[55] In his *Ballades in Blue China* (1880), Lang wrote:

There's a joy without canker or cark,
There's a pleasure eternally new,
'Tis to gloat on the glaze and the mark
Of china that's ancient and blue;
Unchipp'd all the centuries through
It has pass'd, since the chime of it rang,
And they fashion'd it, figure and hue,
In the reign of the Emperor Hwang.

As Mr Roger Lancelyn Green has written, the drawing by Sybil Longman in the large paper edition of 1888 'combines Pre-Raphaelitism and "Blue China" more deliciously than any conscious parody could do'.[56]

Among the leading collectors of 'blue' were Dante Gabriel Rossetti and his mildly evil friend, Charles Augustus Howell. ('Criminally speaking,' said Whistler of the latter, 'the Portugee was an artist.') Henry Treffry Dunn's *Recollections of Dante Gabriel Rossetti and his Circle* (1904) contains a delightful anecdote of the rivalry between them. In a Hammersmith junk shop, Howell found a blue dish – 'it was the blue, the sweet, rich blue, only to be found in the choicest Nankin'. He held a dinner party to show it off, and the 'Chinese worshippers' invited were Rossetti, Whistler, the Ionides brothers, Leonard R. Valpy, George Howard (later Earl of Carlisle), George Price Boyce the water-colourist, Burne-Jones, Morris, old George Cruikshank (1792–1878) and the landscape painter John William Inchbold. Howell was much congratulated on his find. By a typical Pre-Raphelite 'prank', Rossetti concealed the dish under his Inverness cape, took it home and hid it, swathed in models' dresses, in an oak wardrobe. He then invited Howell and the other collectors to dinner, to see 'a piece of "Blue" that I think will rival his'. On the afternoon of the day of the dinner, Howell called at Rossetti's with a factotum. He had guessed pretty shrewdly who had his dish and where it was to be found. After talking to Rossetti for a while, he left him in his studio on some pretext, disentangled his property from the wardrobe, and replaced it with another dish of the same size and shape. At dinner, Howell challenged Rossetti to produce the rival dish:

> As the dish became uncovered, a curious, puzzled expression came over his face, and when it was entirely exposed to view, he stood still in blank astonishment. For a few moments he was silent; then his pent-up feelings burst out in a wild cry.
>
> 'Confound it! See what the spirits have done!'
>
> Everyone rose to look at the dish. A dish it was, certainly, but what a dish! Instead of the beautiful piece of Nankin that was expected, there was only an old Delft thing, cracked, chipped, and discoloured through the numerous bakings it had undergone.[57]

There was nothing very scientific in the collections of Rossetti, Wilde and the other 'blue' men. At its most sophisticated, their attitude was one of informed mysticism. Blue china was just one of the stage props in what Swinburne traitorously called 'the fairyland of fans, the paradise of pipkins, the limbo of blue china, screens, pots, plates, jars, joss-houses, and all the fortuitous frippery of Fusiyama [*sic*]'. It belonged with bombinating temple gongs and the fantasies induced by opium, and it survived well into the Dr Fu Manchu era of the early twentieth century: witness the cover of Hugh Tuite's 1924 novel, *The Secret of the Blue Vase*. Vases were expected to have secrets, not histories: 'blue' and 'choice Nankin' were considered quite adequate designations of what we would call K'ang Hsi, Yung Cheng, or Ch'ien Lung. Just as the French Impressionists bought, and were influenced by, the late, lurid Japanese prints – *crêpes*, as they revealingly called them – with little knowledge of the early masters, so the 'blue' coterie bought export ginger-jars and thought they had the treasures of the ancients in their cabinets. The late Mr Arthur Lane, then Keeper of the Department of Ceramics, Victoria and Albert Museum, gave in a Paper of 1957 an example of this mysticism:

Those were the days of wild, romantic speculation. I note one entry [in the Museum records] : 'Vase with grey crackled glaze. Ancient Chinese.' (I have pursued this piece, and find we have now prosaically labelled it 'Chinese; about 1800–1820'.) [58]

At the same time, there were two far more scientific collectors of Chinese ceramics: Sir Augustus Wollaston Franks (1826–97) and George Salting (1836–1909). Their collections, both of which were bequeathed to the nation, show a preference for eighteenth-century Chinese porcelain of brilliant decorative virtuosity; it was only with the coming of the railway to China that Ming, Sung and T'ang pieces began to be excavated in quantities and appreciated in the West for their three-dimensional qualities, subtleties of shape and glaze.

Salting's collection contained several K'ang Hsi single-colour vases. Edmond de Goncourt observed how this form of porcelain was becoming more popular than the elaborately decorated wares:

> Un singulier phénomène qui se passe au dedans d'un collectionneur de porcelaine !... nous commençons par aimer les porcelaines décorées, puis peu à peu le goût se déplace et va à les porcelaines qui n'ont pour elles que la beauté de la matière. On s'éprend alors des *blancs* pâte tendre, des *bleus turquoise*, des *violet aubergine*, et de là, il n'y a qu'un pas pour se passionner à l'endroit de ces porcelaines ou de ces faïences qui semblent enfermer le marbré d'un papier *peigne* dans une gemme. Les Chinois, ces curieux de pierres dures, sont très sensibles à ces fabrications appelées *yao-pien* (transmutations), à ces métamorphoses d'une porcelaine en un semblant de matière précieuse: métamorphoses obtenues par des combinaisons hasardeuses de feu, de flambage, de courants d'oxygène faisant passer le rouge de cuivre par le violet, par le bleu, par le vert, en des colorations chatoyantes et voltigeantes, et d'autant plus appreciées par les collectionneurs de l'Empire du Milieu qu'elles ressemblent aux langues de feu qui ont léché le vase pendant sa cuisson.[59]

Meanwhile, vernacular ceramics were not being neglected, either by scholars or by collectors. Joseph Marryat's remarkable *History of Pottery and Porcelain* (1850) contained long and important chapters on English wares, and in 1878 Llewellyn Jewitt's two-volume work *Ceramic Art in Great Britain* was published. Eliza Meteyard's *Life of Josiah Wedgwood* appeared in 1865–6. By the time the first French edition of Marryat appeared, Greslou had published his *Recherches sur la Céramique*, Houdoy had written on the faience and porcelain of Lille, Davillier on Moustiers and Marseilles, Dr Warmont de Chauny on Sinceny and Ognes, Lejal on Saint-Amand-les-Eaux, Fillon on Poitou, Vendée, and Tainturier on Alsace, Lorraine. The admirable – and still unsuperseded – *Histoire des Manufactures françaises de porcelaine* by the Comte de Chavagnac and the Marquis de Grollier was first issued in 1906. In 1876 the *Punch* artist Charles Keene wrote to his friend Joseph Crawhall, the bird painter, 'I fancy my taste is much the same as yours in the china way. I'm very fond of the old English .... Blue Japanese seems the fashionable ware for connoisseurs here. I confess I'm rather tired of it'.[60]

The greatest collector of English ceramics – some would say, the greatest of all china collectors – was Lady Charlotte Schreiber (1812–1895). She documented herself almost as well as Horace Walpole and rather better than Lady Dorothy Nevill; she kept a diary from the age of ten until seventy-nine, and her *Journals*: *Confidences of a Collector of Ceramics and Antiques* (1911) are only surpassed as a monument to her by their translucent illustrations in the Victoria and Albert Museum. She was born in 1812, daughter of the sixty-eight-year-old Earl of Lindsey. She was a cousin of the future Sir Henry Layard, the excavator of Nimrud and picture collector: both were grandchildren of the famous Dean of Bristol, C. P. Layard, who was hanged in effigy for selling the bronze eagle lectern of the Cathedral to pay for the repair of the building. Her father died when she was six, and three years later her mother married a clergyman, the Reverend Peter Pegus, an odious man whose part in Lady Charlotte's life seems to have been similar to that of Mr Murdstone in David Copperfield's. At any rate she hated him, and at the age of twenty-one, in 1833, she left home. Meanwhile she had learnt French and Italian, and some Latin, Greek, Hebrew and Persian. Later she mastered Welsh as well, and it was on her translation of the *Mabinogion* that Tennyson based his *Idylls of the King*. He consulted her as to the proper pronunciation of the E in Enid. Should it be short or long? The phrase, 'Geraint wedded Enid' would be all right with the long E, but impossible with the short one. Lady Charlotte pronounced: the E should be short. Tennyson altered the phrase to 'Geraint married Enid'.

Lady Charlotte had charm as well as intellect. She loved the opera, where in 1833 she met the young Disraeli – 'the younger Disraeli', as she called him, being herself a devotee of Isaac D'Israeli's *Literary Characters*. 'We talked about several things,' she wrote. 'He is wild, enthusiastic, and very poetical.... I cannot understand his trying to get into Parliament.' It was at the house of Mrs Wyndham Lewis (the future Mrs Disraeli) that she met the Welsh ironmaster Josiah John Guest, a widower of forty-eight. To the disgust of her relatives, she married this elderly, dissenting tradesman in 1833. It was a happy marriage. She bore him ten children, established him in London society, and took a keen interest in his business. She had a room reserved for her at his London office; 'I have so schooled myself into habits of business,' she wrote, 'that it is more congenial to me to calculate the advantage of ½ per cent commission on a cargo of iron than to go to the finest ball in the world.' Sir John Guest died in 1852. Three years later, Lady Charlotte married her children's tutor, Charles Schreiber. With no great works to manage any longer, and her children growing up, she began her collection.

She had every virtue of a great collector: good taste, intellect and scholarship, enormous wealth, charm for wheedling, a ruthless business sense for haggling and an unhappy fatherless childhood which gave her, perhaps, a desire for the security of old husbands and other old possessions. Her *chasses*, as she called her china-hunts, are described with complete honesty, and though the effect is sometimes unsympathetic, no china collector can really disapprove of the energetic huntress. All's fair in love and antique collecting, and no means were ever so triumphantly justified by their end.

A new way of collecting English china was introduced by Robert Drane (Plate 190), whose collection of Worcester porcelain was sold in 1922. Drane invented 'comparative collecting'. If he found a Worcester bowl decorated with a certain pattern, he would try to acquire a Chinese bowl and a Meissen bowl bearing the same design. In this way his collection became much more than a mere accumulation of pretty things. It showed how different factories copied or adapted each other's designs.

Mr Gladstone was another collector of English ceramics, especially of Wedgwood ware. But his collection, which was sold at Christie's in June 1875, also contained Meissen, Sèvres and Capodimonte porcelain, and a Doccia group of the Deposition, from a model by Massimiliano Soldani-Benzi (Plate 13). His Chelsea tea service (*c.* 1765) is in the British Museum. Gladstone was no dilettante. Lionel Tollemache, in his *Talks with Mr. Gladstone* (1898), quotes an anonymous friend as saying of him: 'He will talk about a piece of old china as if he was standing before the judgment-seat of God'.[61] But in 1898, so shortly after the trial of Oscar Wilde, china-collecting was suspect, and Tollemache felt it necessary to assert the essential manliness of the Prime Minister's collecting:

In the case of Mr Gladstone, this 'feminine partiality', as it were, put on virility through its contact with his eminently masculine nature. How quixotic, or rather, how Quixote-like, how grandly fantastic he was in that infatuation, even as in his infatuation about Helen of Troy! I never ceased to be grateful to the late Lady de Tabley who, one evening when she and I were guests of the Gladstones, espied me *nescio quid meditantem nugarum* in a distant corner, and hurried me across the room just in time to see Mr Gladstone holding up a piece of old china, and to take note of the flashing eye and the Rhadamanthine solemnity with which the great enthusiast was winding up his discourse.[62]

However much the People's William might improve the image of the collector, the people themselves remained pleasantly convinced that the type was monstrous. The collector was an evil fellow who pinned beautiful butterflies to boards, gloated over dead things. Eighteenth-century cartoonists had shown the antiquaries alternately debating the merits of a cracked chamber-pot, brooding over crumbling mummies and skulls, and peering pruriently at pictures of the nude. Conan Doyle, in *The Illustrious Client*, portrayed Baron Gruner, who collected both eggshell Ming and ...

'I tell you, Mr Holmes, this man collects women, and takes a pride in his collection, as some men collect moths or butterflies. He had it all in that book. Snapshot photographs, names, details, everything about them. It was a beastly book – a book no man, even if he had come from the gutter, could have put together.'[63]

Perhaps the nearest flesh-and-blood parallel to Baron Gruner, at least in his sinister public reputation, was Robert, Comte de Montesquiou, the part-original of Proust's Charlus, of Wilde's Dorian Gray and of Huysmans's Des Esseintes. His catalogue of objects associated with smell (Plates 187–8) shows him in characteristic pose, though the canonical portrait is Boldini's of 1897, showing him with the porcelain-topped cane with which he was unjustly alleged to have beaten his way out of a charity bazaar when the Cours la Reine building caught fire in May 1897.[64]

But the public were eventually won over to collecting. By the end of the nineteenth century, almost every suburban villa had its china cabinet. Gertrude Martineau's painting of 1894, *The Broken Saucer* (Plate 189) shows what must have been a familiar domestic tragedy. *Punch* satirized the disruptive effects of 'acute chinamania' in the home:

MAY: Mamma! Mamma! don't go on like this, pray!
MAMMA (*who has smashed a favourite pot*): What have I got left to live for?

MAY: Haven't you got ME, Mamma?
MAMMA: You, child! You're not Unique!! There are six of you (*indicating the rest of the family*) – a complete set!! [65]

What had converted the public was partly the increased aesthetic awareness for which Wilde and the aesthetes had fought, but far more it was the lure of the bargain. The word first appeared in its modern sense in a book title of 1911, when Charles Edward Jerningham dedicated *The Bargain Book* to Lady Dorothy Nevill.[66] But among the incunabula of bargain-hunting, the most striking is surely this advertisement from a 1907 copy of the *Daily Mail*:

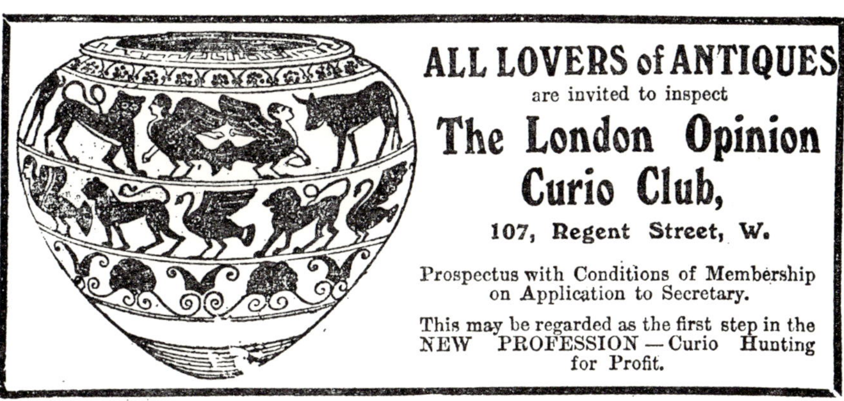

The little professionals had succeeded the *grands amateurs*.

13 Repairs, reproductions and fakes

> I'm very much mistook if Mr Lambert's will be a catch;
> The breaking of the Chiny will be the breaking off of his own match.
> Miss wouldn't have an angel if he was careless about Chiny;
> She never forgives a chip, if it's ever so small and tiny.
> Lawk! I never saw a man in all my life in such a taking;
> I could find in my heart to pity him, for all his mischief-making,
> To see him stand a-hammering and stammering like a zany;
> But what signifies apologies, if they won't mend old Chany!
> If he sent her up whole crates full, from Wedgwood's and Mr Spode's,
> He couldn't make amends for the cracked mandarins and smashed toads.
>
> TOM HOOD, *The China Mender*

The proverbial nightmare of the pot seller is a bull in a china shop. Recalling the exploits of Zeus under that somewhat unsubtle incognito, one might well believe it a myth, born perhaps of some weird misassociation of Paul Potter and his famous painting of a bull at the Hague. But in fact the proverb, which is not found in print before the nineteenth century, appears to derive from a real incident no earlier than the eighteenth century. Mr Aubrey Toppin, Norroy and Ulster King of Arms, has discovered this notice in the *London Packet* of 17 March 1773:

> This morning an over drove bullock rushed into the *China Shop* of Miss Powell, opposite St Andrew's Church, Holborn, where he frightened the lady into an hysterical fit, and broke a quantity of glass and china.

The story passed into folk tradition. A writer calling himself 'Dr Dryasdust', in *Bentley's Miscellany* for 1844, quotes the Secretary of the Society of Antiquaries, who at a recent meeting had told how, between thirty and forty years back, he had heard the elder Grimaldi sing a song in which the adventures of a bull in a china shop were 'broadly and comically related'. Dr Dryasdust himself had found a broadsheet copy of the ballad, printed by the Catnach Press with an appropriate wood engraving:

SONG THE BULL IN THE CHINA-SHOP

On Holborn Hill, the first of May,
The truth I do declare, sir,
A furious Bull did run away,
Which made the folks to stare, sir;
This Bull was stout, this Bull was strong,
He ran and made no stop, sir,
Till, horns and all, he rush'd headlong
Into a china-shop, sir!
  Tol de rol, &c.
The cups and platters there he dish'd
And knock'd the mugs about, sir!
The china-men they swore and fish'd,
But could not get him out, sir;
And such a clatter made he then,
And such a great uproar, sir,
With sheriffs, mayor, and aldermen,
Was never heard before, sir!
  Tol de rol, &c.

History repeats itself. *The Morning Post* of 21 October 1933, states that a bullock ran into a china shop at Fakenham, Norfolk, on the previous day, when the Queen and the Princess Royal were there. Her Majesty is reported to have said that she had often heard of a bull in a china shop, but had never seen one before.

The counterpart of the cataclysmic accident was deliberate breakage on a grand scale. This was practised not only at the fair, where the crockery shy offered an inexpensive catharsis of petty frustrations, but in the salons of the elegant and their imitators. In *Thémidore*, Godard d'Ancour describes how French prostitutes expressed fashionable (or real) anguish when the officers left for the army:

Une heure se passa à badiner, à chanter, à faire partir les bouchons, & à casser quelques porcelaines. C'est le goût des Dames de condition: depuis le départ des Officiers pour l'Armée, elles font les Petites-Maîtresses, & se plaisent dans des soupes où l'on fait carillon: elles trouvent un esprit infini à briser un miroir ou une table, ou à jetter des chaises par les fenêtres. Les filles du monde n'ont-elles pas droit de copier dans ces expéditions les jeunes Marquises, puisque celles-ci les copient dans leurs intrigues? [1]

The china repairer could hardly cope with the ravages of bulls run amok or of distracted marquises and courtesans, but there was still enough casual damage to give almost full-time employment to such as John Parry, whose advertisement sheet of 1793 (Plate 191) is preserved in the Lysons collection in the British Museum. Parry, of No. 9, Hatton Wall, Hatton Garden, London, was a versatile businessman. He described himself as 'China Burner and Riveter'. He would handle and spout teapots, clean or repair glass ornaments and lustres. He made and sold pomatums. And he would provide music for town or country at the shortest notice. The advertisement ends with an elaborate sustained metaphor in verse, in which broken plates are compared with broken pates, and the same remedy is prescribed for ceramic as for human ills: 'burning'.

In the case of humans, burning meant cautery, a drastic, but still very common, treatment.[2] In the case of china, it meant that a frit, or glaze, fusing at a low temperature, was used as a cement, and the piece fired in a muffle kiln. This was the method of Coombes of Queen Street, Bristol, the repairer whose name is most frequently found inscribed on the base of repaired pieces. Pountney, in his *Old Bristol Potteries* (1920), tells us how Coombes and another Bristol man, Daniel, executed repairs as a profitable sideline:

> From the middle of Joseph Ring's period until about 1820, or a little later, there were two men, Coombes and Daniel, who went from one pottery to another firing the kilns for the pottery proprietors. They were styled 'china burners' and their process was to ignite the six or eight fires surrounding the kiln, after the doorway had been built up with fire-bricks or fire-clay, and to tend these fires until the maximum heat had been acquired, which was estimated in a bricked-up trial hole which was opened for testing purposes, and bricked up again after the examination. In the Bristol Museum were two Oriental porcelain plates, and one saucer, until quite recently wrongly described as having been made at Bristol, marked on the back with the names of one or the other of these two men, and their trade and address below the name. Daniel as a rule called himself, a 'china burner', whereas Coombes generally used the words 'china mender'. Their process in mending was to dip the fragments of ware into a glaze and stick them together, probably supporting the articles on a mound of clay, so as to keep the edges together. These would be put into the 'trial hole' and left to be fired with the rest of the ware. The result would be a good and invisible joint.[3]

Coombes was working from Queen Street as early as 1780 – the date inscribed by him on a repaired Bristol *sucrier*[4] – and was still living there in 1805.[5] We get some idea of what he charged from an inscription on the base of a repaired Chinese sauceboat: 'Coombes, China Mender, Queen Street, Bristol 1778 at 1s od.' (Plates 193–4).[6]

A more obvious method of repair was glue, although this tended to soak into the edges of the fracture and leave a stain which emphasized the break. The cements of which Robert Dossie gave recipes in his *Handmaid to the Arts* (1758) sound more like witches' brews. One contained green vitriol, dung of horses, the blood of any animal, some short hair and the scoria or clinkers of a smith's forge. Another, specially prescribed for china repairs, had as its main ingredient glue boiled in distilled vinegar, to which was later to be added a beaten clove of garlic, half an ounce of ox-gall, powdered sandarac and other exotic substances. Dossie himself showed a becoming scepticism in remarking: 'I see no reason why common vinegar should not be equally proper for this purpose with the distilled; nor indeed am I very certain that vinegar improves at all the cementing property of the composition.'[7] The adhesive most recommended by Dossie for china and pottery was made of grated Suffolk cheese, quicklime and skimmed milk. He also states that: 'drying oil with white lead is also frequently used for cementing china, and earthen ware; but where it is not necessary the vessels should endure heat or moisture, isinglass glue with a little tripoli or chalk, is better'.[8]

Garlic and white lead, two of Dossie's ingredients, recur in *The New Family Receipt Book* of 1810. One prescription is: 'Garlic stampt in a stone mortar; the juice whereof, when applied to the pieces to be joined together, is the finest and strongest cement for that purpose, and will leave little or no mark if done with care'.[9] The same book states: 'Excellent cement for broken china may be made from a mixture of equal parts of glue, white of egg, and white lead.'[10]

Modern cements – often transparent, stainless, and so effective that if the mended piece is dropped again it usually breaks in a different place – have not only superseded the horrible concoctions of Dossie. They have also replaced the old metal repairs of the eighteenth and nineteenth centuries. Father Martinius Martini, a Jesuit missionary to China, described the manufacture of Chinese porcelain in his *Novus Atlas Sinensis* (1655), and added:

> Yes, and that which seems even more wonderful is, that pieces, secured together with copper thread, keep the moisture and do not leak. Those who have any knowledge of the art of mending porcelain go all over China continually and use a very fine bone, generally called a drill, with which to make

very small holes. Its point is of diamond, like those with which to write on glass, or rather like those in use in Milan for boring rock-crystal.[11]

This early reference to the 'stitching' or riveting of broken china was quoted by Father Athanasius Kircher, another Jesuit missionary to China, in his *Verheerlykt China* (1667). Part of Kircher's book was translated in an appendix to John Ogilby's version of another Dutch book, Nieuhof's *An Embassy from the East India Company of the United Provinces to the ... Emperor of China* (1668). Mr Geoffrey Wills, who gives these references in an interesting article, commits himself to the rash observation: 'It would seem that there are no references to riveting having been done in England before Victorian times. ... The names of men who may have specialized in the work are unknown, and will probably never come to light.'[12] As we have seen, however, John Parry styled himself a riveter; and the fact that he does not feel it necessary to enlarge on this makes it likely that riveting was a well-known method of repairing broken wares. There also exists a Niderviller porcelain figure, modelled by Lemire *c.* 1765–70, of a china-mender carrying a pair of bellows, a basketful of broken china, and, in his hand, a barber's bowl clearly showing the rivets with which it has been mended.[13] The bowl in Plate 199 shows the unsightliness of this method. Iron was also used for replacing handles and spouts (Plate 200) and knops (Plate 199). Basketwork handles were also made. Wealthier owners of more valuable pieces sometimes had them repaired with silver, as with the banding and strapping of a Chinese-made punchbowl (Plate 197) in the Preston Hall Museum, Stockton-on-Tees. In this case, the bowl was made *c.* 1735, while the silver bears the Sheffield hall mark for 1843–4; but it must be remembered that some wares were originally sold mounted in silver, as Turner and Abbott's advertisements prove.

We can, then, make a clear social distinction between two kinds of repair: expensive reinforcement of valuable pieces which would be hard or impossible to replace; and cheap first-aid for ordinary wares to avoid the expense of buying replacements. Ris-Paquot, with a tantalizing absence of reference to original sources, describes how the growth in France of a repairing trade of the latter type caused friction with the Paris faienciers:

C'est vers le commencement du xviiie siècle que datent les premiers essais du raccommodage de la faïence. Paris fut la ville qui vit surgir ces premières expériences. Elles consistaient à tirer parti de la faïence cassée en rajustant ses fragments au moyen d'un simple fil d'archal. L'honneur de cette découverte revient de droit à un homme Delille, natif du petit village de Montjoye, en Normandie. Cette industrie naissante qui était appelée à venir en aide aux petites bourses en leur évitant une lourde dépense, ne tarda pas à prendre une grande extension qui s'accrut de plus en plus en raison même de la modicité de ses prix et de l'immense service qu'il rendit dans un grand nombre de cuisines et de petits ménages. Cette vogue ne fut pas longtemps à causer aux fabricants faïenciers un tort si considérable qu'elle les effraya des le début.[14]

Ris-Paquot adds that the manufacturers met in great numbers to discuss how to put an end to what they called 'une concurrence' (competition). They decided to initiate a law suit against the restorers. They did so, but lost, and the trade of faience restorer was decreed free to all. Here again we see the French desire to have things in black and white, and to bring about change by a dramatic showdown. In England, a characteristic compromise was reached, when china sellers advertised on their trade-cards that they were willing to undertake repairs,[15] thus doing themselves out of one kind of business to obtain another.

In the nineteenth century, the art of restoration kept pace with the growing interest in collecting. An *Essai sur l'Art de Restaurer les Faïences, Porcelaines, etc.* was published by P. Thiaucourt in 1865. In an introduction to this small book, the prolific Baron Davillier gave his usual jocose résumé of the situation:

Chacun aujourd'hui veut se *mettre en faïence*, comme on disait sous Louis XIV : ne soyons pas trop sévères contre ce que les profanes appellent la manie des *pots cassés*.

Ris-Paquot's *Manière de restaurer soi-même les faïences, porcelaines, etc.* appeared a few years later, teaching the amateur how to make a bow-drill (Plate 201) and to restore handles and other parts (Plates 202–3). Professionals, at the same time, had to become more expert, well versed in the characteristics of the antique wares they were asked to restore. H. van Koert (Plate 192) who had his restoring establishment at No. 167 Ebury Street not long after George Moore had his *Conversations* at No. 121, is dressed like a cabinet minister, with a high starched collar, while his two assistants look as if they have been reincarnated from the eighteenth century and the Renaissance respectively. Evidently the status of the restorer had improved as he had become more specialist.

It was no great step from restoring part of a figure or pot, to 'restoring', or resurrecting, the whole thing. Replicas, when marked with the maker's name, are 'reproductions'; when not so marked, they are 'forgeries' or 'fakes'. Like restorations, reproductions and fakes naturally became more common as the number of collectors grew. Lady Charlotte Schreiber's son, Montague Guest, wrote of his mother's collecting days as an arcadian time: 'Any person with a very small amount of knowledge could go round the old shops and pick up the untold treasures of to-day for the most trivial sums; there was an enormous supply, and very little demand, in consequence, the "fake" hardly existed.'[16] Guest would have needed to go no further than the Memoirs he was editing to learn what an industry faking porcelain had already become in his mother's lifetime:

May 17, 1877: Next we walked down to the station again, and proceeded to St Amand, in the neighbourhood of which are M. Bettignies Works. His family were the original proprietors of the Tournai in its palmy days, some century since. They have been at St Amand some 60 years. Pourbaix had given us a note to him, and after having walked up to his 'fabrique' in a pouring rain, he received us very politely, and showed us everything without reserve. First he took us to see his rooms full of finished pottery and porcelain; the latter consists of white pieces, 'pâte tendre' copied from the old Sèvres, which he told us was bought by dealers in Paris to be there painted (and marked with X) and duly sold as old. Some of the forms are very fine indeed, and most of them are exact copies of old Sèvres. Among them were a few figures and groups, and we were especially interested in spying out two hexagonal covers, which could only have been made for imitation of Worcester vases, and many oviform vases, etc., which are evidently made to imitate Worcester and Chelsea. All he could tell us was that they all went to Paris 'to be decorated and sold as old'.

Lady Charlotte was not an easy person to hoodwink, but even she fell victim to a forgery by Samson of Paris, the most notorious of all porcelain fakers:

February 14, 1878: We took the cover of one of our newly purchased vases to Samson's, who owned himself the maker of it. So those vases have proved themselves all wrong and cannot go into the collection. I fear we shall lose heavily on them, but they are so pretty that I regret them more for their beauty than for the money's worth. This has been rather a costly lesson.

The late Wallace Elliott wrote to Messrs Samson in 1937 or slightly before, asking for information on the history of the firm, the nature of its productions, and on its trade and factory marks. 'In doing this I used all the tact of which I am capable, and after a long interval and somewhat to my surprise I received a very courteous reply enclosing six foolscap

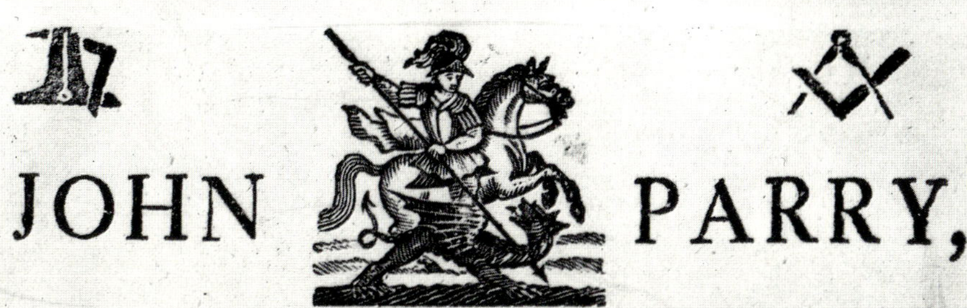

JOHN PARRY,

CHINA BURNER AND RIVETER,

No. 9, *Hatton Wall, Hatton Garden,*

Tea-pots handled and ſpouted, Glaſs Ornaments and Luſtres cleaned or repaired.

Pomatums ſold wholeſale and retail by the Maker.

N. B. Muſic provided for Town or Country on the ſhorteſt Notice by the above JOHN PARRY.

Improv'd by me the Eſculapian art,
Of healing fractures, curing ev'ry part;
Of your frail earthen veſſels; frail, tho' fair,
Your china with your perſons I compare;
And if requeſted, will, my art profound,
Employ to cure each fracture and each wound.
Bring then not, broken limbs and broken pates,
But broken diſhes, ſaucers, cups, and plates,
With all the miſchiefs which ſuch frames befall
I'll burn them well and ſurely cure them all.

1793

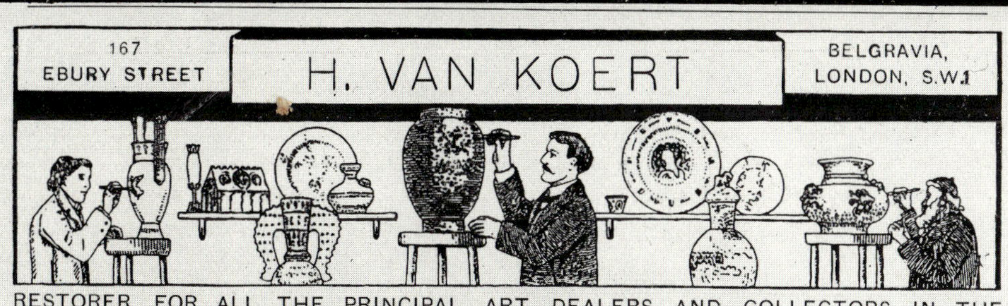

191 (top) Trade-card of John Parry, porcelain repairer, 1793. See p. 300.
192 Advertisement of H. van Koert, china restorer, from *The Connoisseur*, 1901. See p. 303.

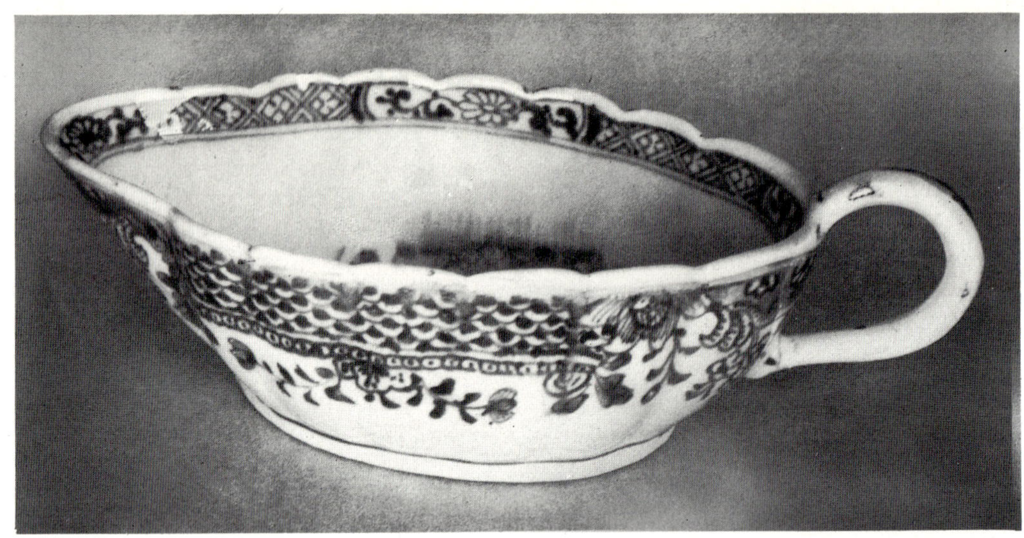

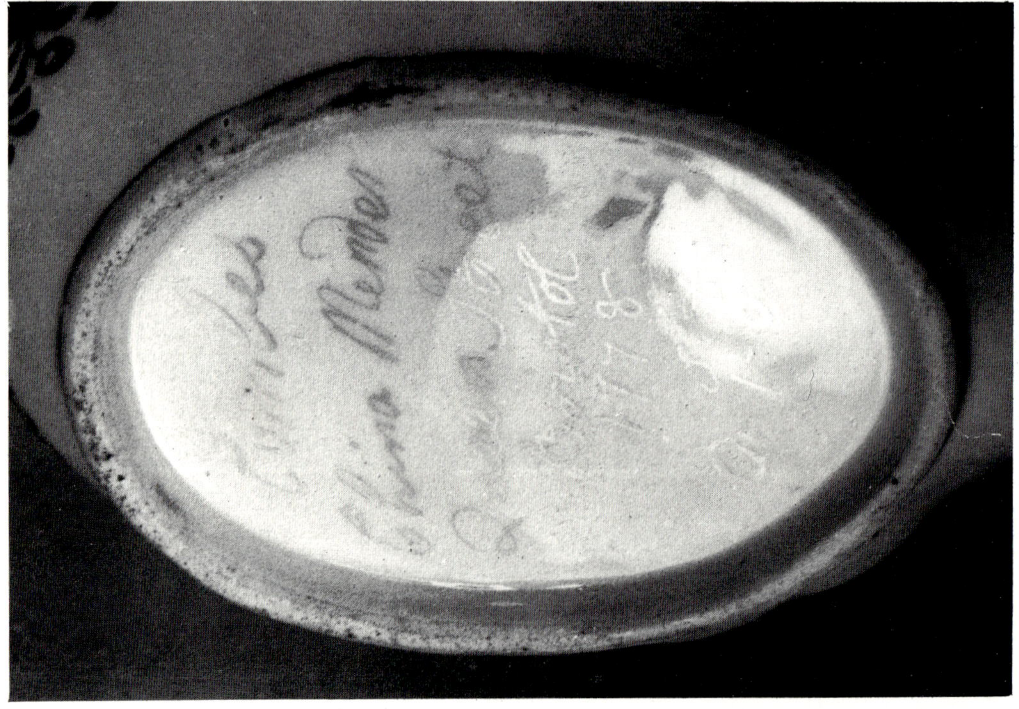

193 and 194 Chinese blue and white sauceboat, *c.* 1775, length $7\frac{3}{4}''$, base $4''/2\frac{3}{4}''$. It was repaired by Coombes of Bristol, and the inscription on the base reads, 'Coombes China Mender Queen Street Bristol 1778 1s.od.' See p. 301.

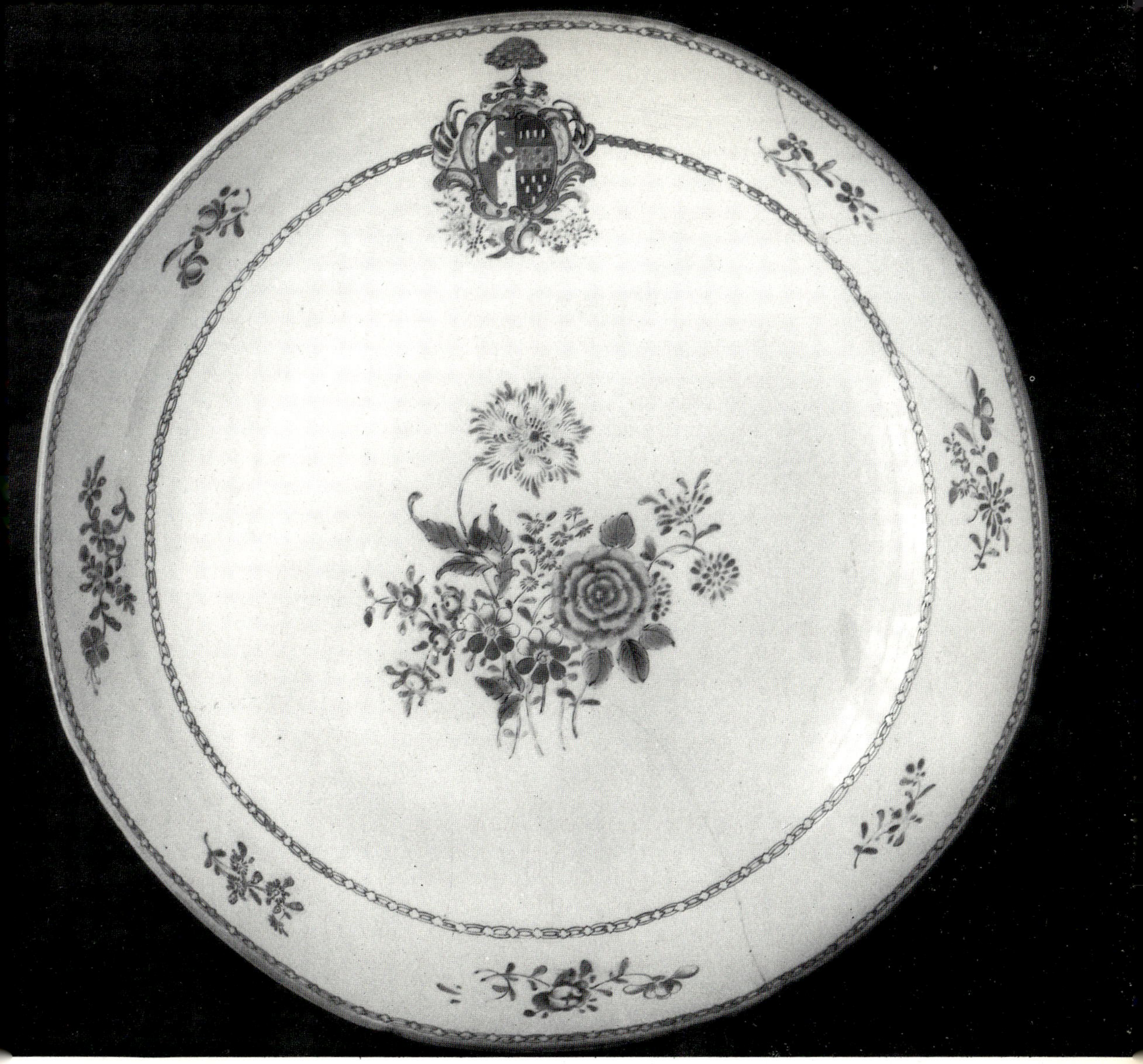

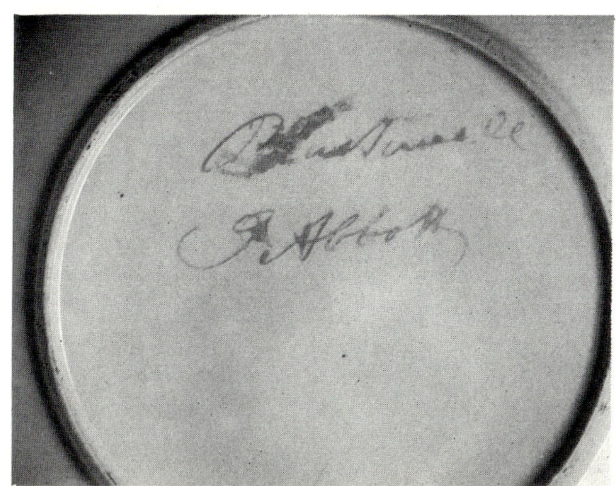

195 and 196 Chinese plate, *c.* 1760–70, diameter 9″, repaired in the eighteenth century by 'J. Abbott'. The dexter, or husband's coat on the shield, is that granted to John Hurst of Welbury, Hertfordshire, in 1715. The sinister, or wife's coat, is that of Lee of Shropshire. The crest is that used by the Hurst family of Horsham Park, Sussex.

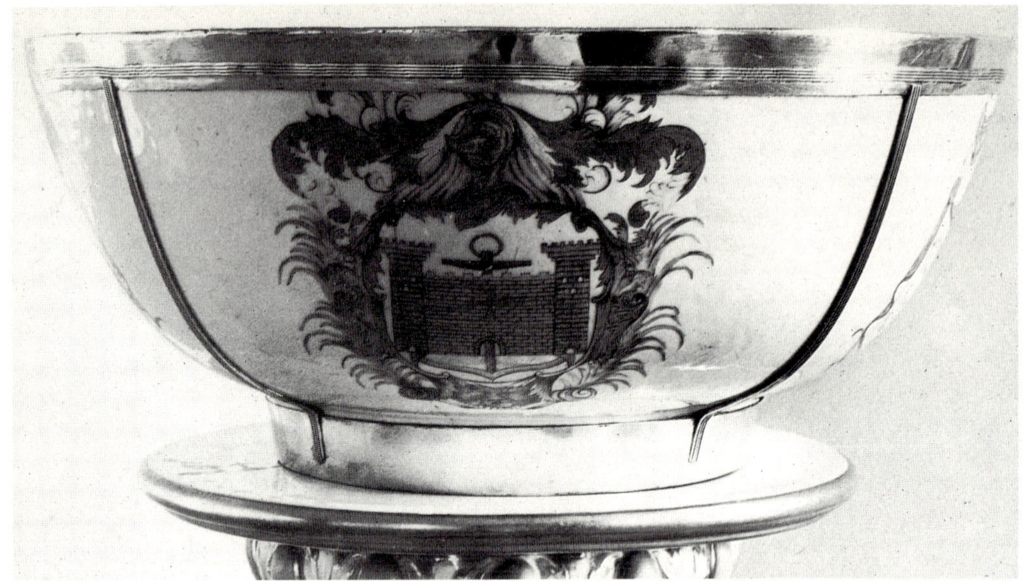

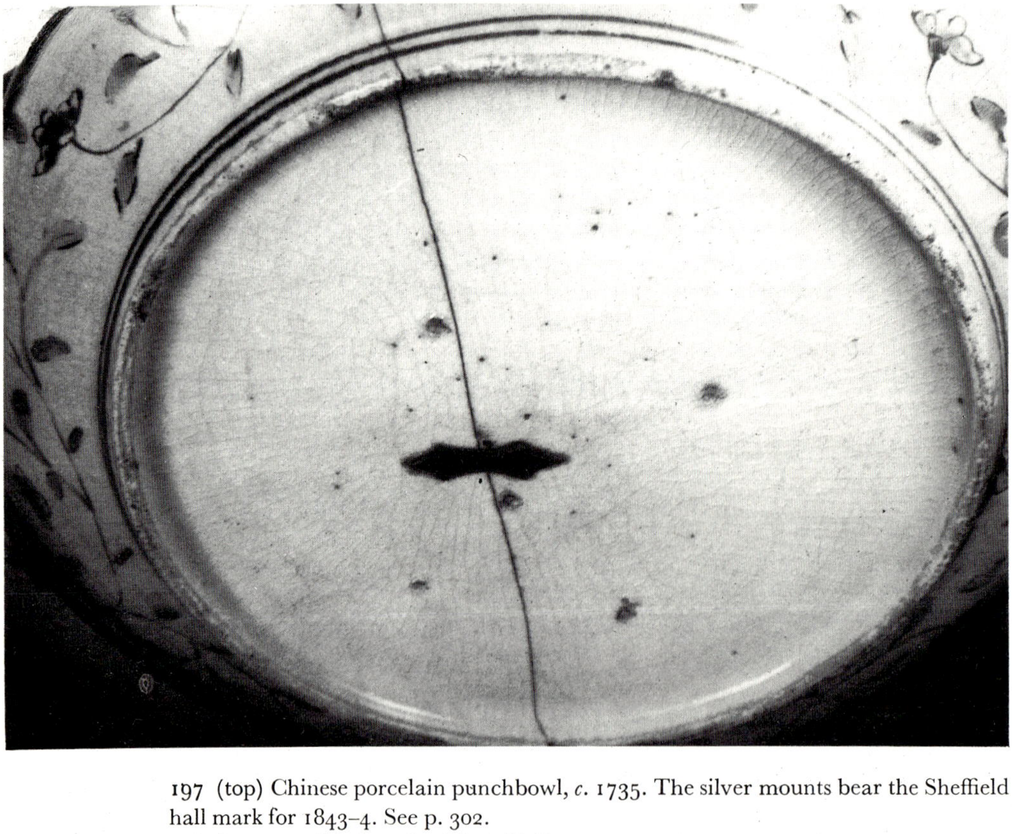

197 (top) Chinese porcelain punchbowl, *c.* 1735. The silver mounts bear the Sheffield hall mark for 1843–4. See p. 302.
198 Japanese dish, length of rivet $\frac{7}{8}''$. See p. 302.

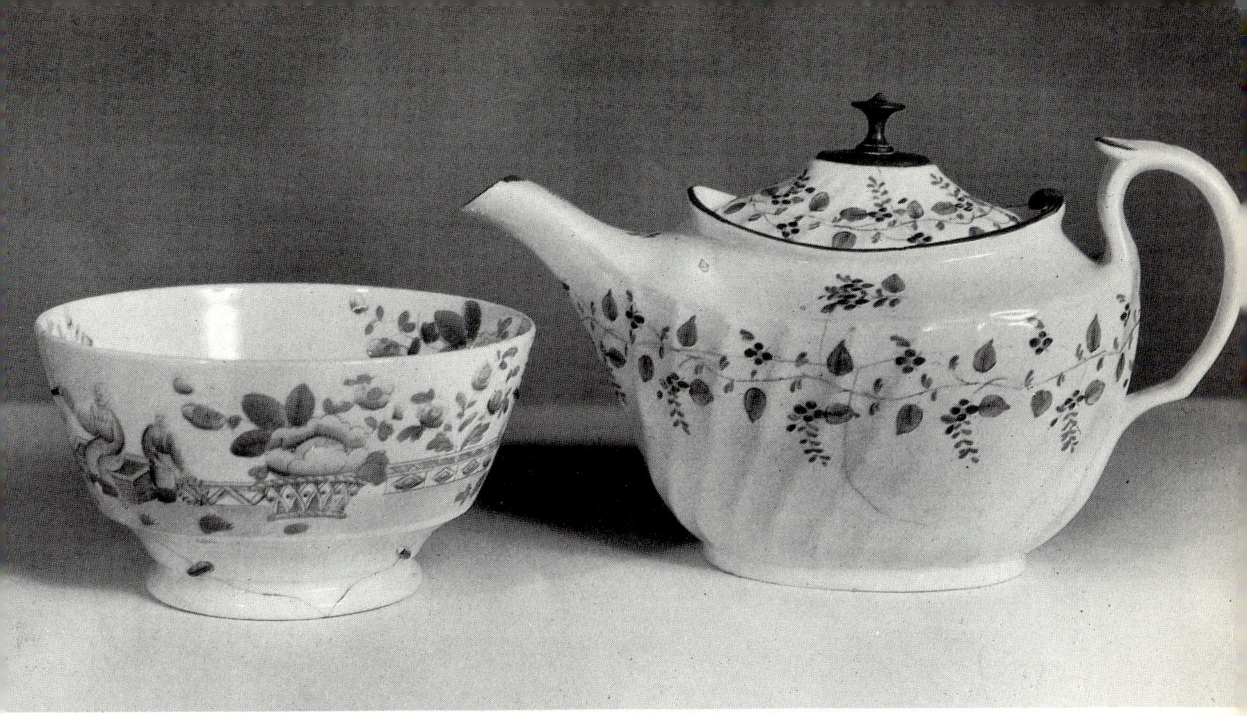

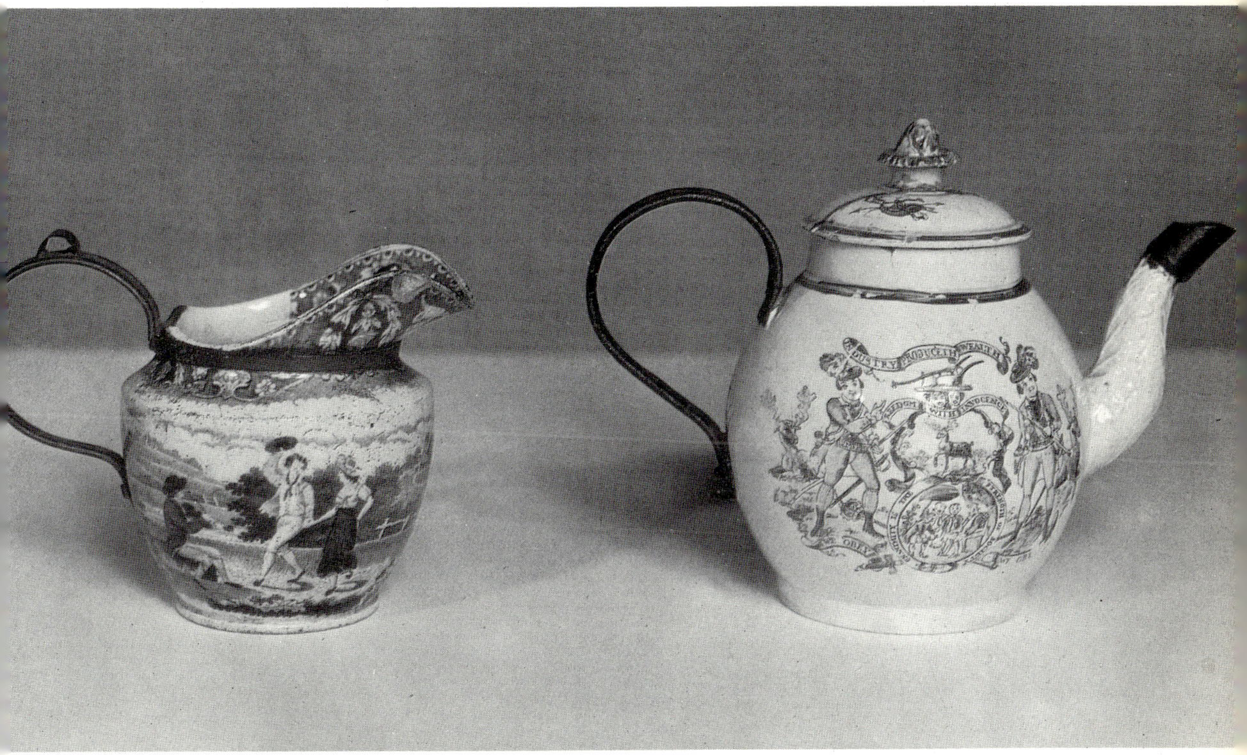

199 and 200 Metal repairs: (above) two nineteenth-century Staffordshire pieces, the *sucrier* mended with rivets, the teapot with a metal knop; (below) nineteenth-century Staffordshire creamer with metal handle, and eighteenth-century creamware teapot with metal handle and spout. See p. 302.

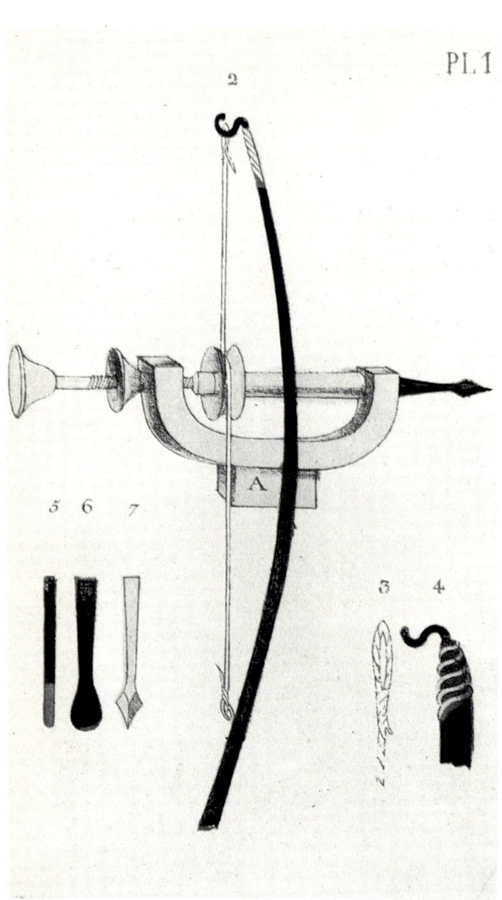

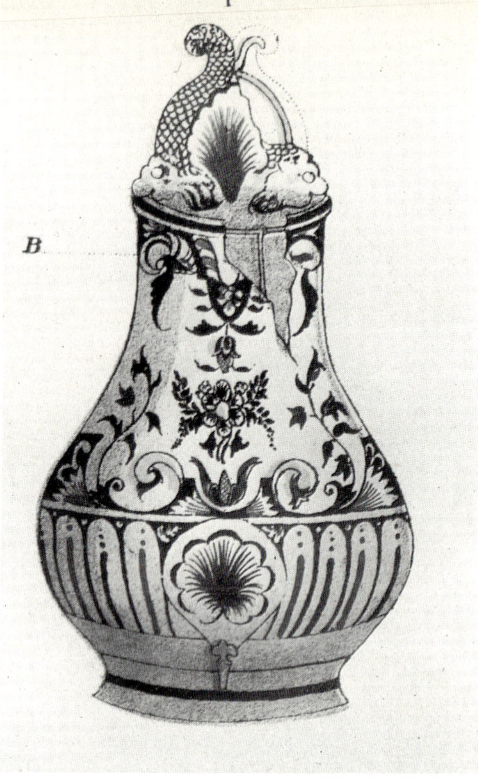

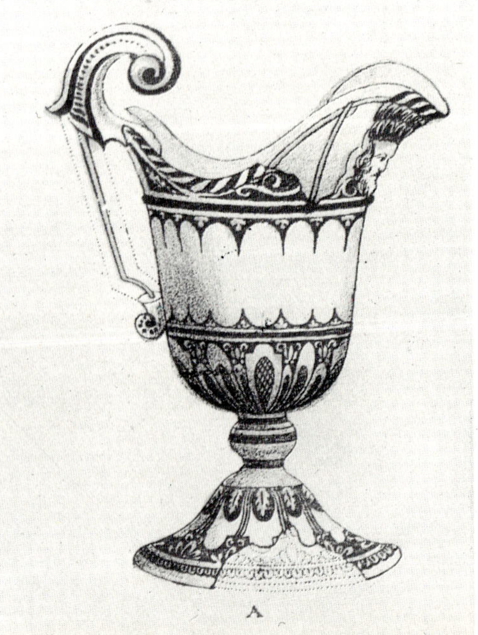

201–3 Do-it-yourself repairs: plates from Ris-Paquot's *Manière de restaurer soi-même les porcelaines, faïences, etc.* (1876): (above left) a bow-drill for drilling holes to take rivets; (above right) a Rouen *fontaine* and (right) a Rouen *casque*, both with repairs strengthened with copper wire. See p. 303.

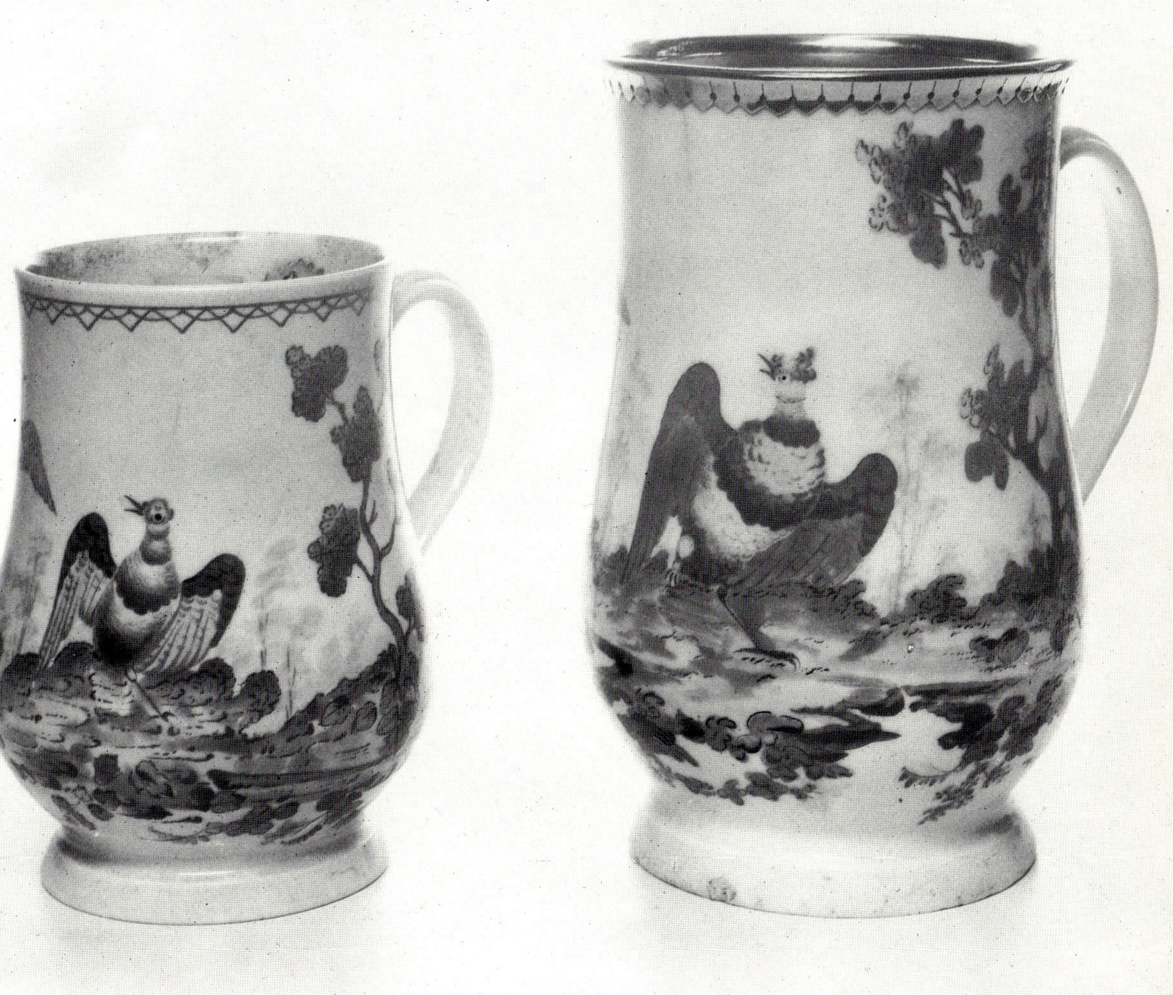

204 (left) A fake Plymouth mug by Samson of Paris, and (right) a genuine Plymouth example. See p. 313.

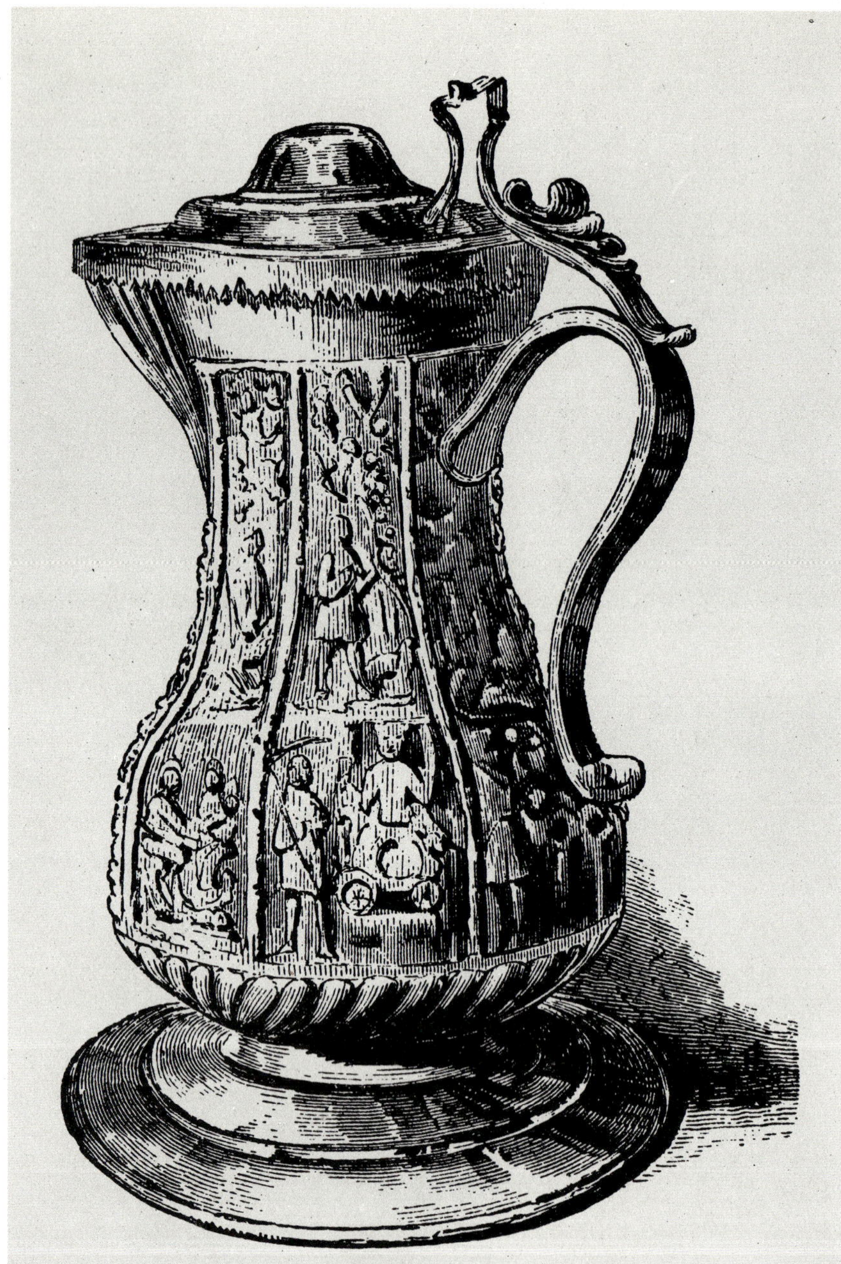

Fig. 115. "Shakspeare's Jug." (Mrs. Fletcher, Gloucester.)

205 An eighteenth-century Staffordshire jug which in the mid-nineteenth century was put on show as 'Shakespeare's Jug' and recorded as such by Marryat in the first edition of his *Pottery and Porcelain* (1857). The jug is now in the Rous Lench Collection. See pp. 316–17.

pages in which I was given all I asked for.' The House of Samson, he learnt, was founded in 1845 by Edmé Samson at No. 7, Rue Béranger. Edmé was only a decorator of china. It was his son Emile (1837–1913) who first began to reproduce early porcelains, earthenwares and enamels. Mr Elliott was given a romantic story of how the idea of manufacturing reproductions first came to Emile Samson. It may be true. Samson was gazing one day at some Limoges porcelain in the window of a shop in the Rue Paradis when he overheard a gentleman, speaking in a strong foreign accent, say to his companion: 'I have an incomplete service which was given by Catherine II to my parents, and I am looking for an artist capable of understanding its beauty, in order to complete it and to make me another one, of which I will make a present to the Czar.' Emile Samson then approached the stranger, 'who was none other than a Grand Duke of Russia', and offered his services. A specimen plate was executed, and 'His Highness was so charmed with the work that he gave him the commission and further entrusted him with big orders intended for the Russian Court, and he remained a faithful client right up to the outbreak of the Revolution'.[17] After Emile's death in 1913 his son Léon took over the factory and at his death in 1923 he was succeeded by his son. Samson's reproduced Chinese, Meissen, Sèvres and English porcelain, Strasbourg faience and European enamels. Whether, as Mr Elliott's informant claimed, these were always marked with a 'S', is questionable. Since Samson's reproductions are of hard paste, the copies of soft-paste factories such as Chelsea and Bow are easy to detect; those of hard-paste factories such as Plymouth and Bristol (Plate 204) are more dangerous.

Forgers so quickly altered their productions to satisfy the changing tastes of collectors, that fakes give a clear indication of what those tastes, at different periods, were. In his admirable book *Fakes: A Handbook for Collectors and Students* (1948), Dr Otto Kurz has shown how in the late eighteenth and early nineteenth centuries Greek vases were appreciated by collectors for their subject matter, not for the quality of the painting. (Though artists such as Flaxman and Carstens found in Greek pots an aid to the simplification and refinement of the linear style.[18]) Thus a geniune Greek amphora fraudulently painted with the happy reunion of Eros and Psyche found an admirer (it even got into the Vatican Collection) because it confirmed a literary theory then widely held. To the adherents of this theory Apuleius's fairy tale of Amor and Psyche was not a creation of the Hellenistic age but an old Indo-European myth. An early vase with this subject was therefore welcomed as proof that the story had already been current in Plato's time.[19] The occupational vice of the collector – wishful thinking – is the forger's chief ally.

The Sèvres fashion of the early nineteenth century was indulged by the Paris dealers Pères and Ireland, who had bought up a large number of the 'seconds' which had accumulated at the Sèvres factory during the eighteenth century and which were sold off by the new Director, Alexandre Brongniart, in auctions from 1804 onwards. These 'seconds' were in white. Pères and Ireland employed a decorator named Soiron, who had worked at Sèvres, to paint them in the early styles. In London, white Sèvres procured by Baldock of Bond Street was decorated by Richard Robins, formerly of Pinxton, and his partner, T. M. Randall. Randall sometimes painted on genuine Sèvres porcelain from which the decoration had been skinned with acid. Wares of this kind, according to Litchfield, were known in the trade as 'Quakers'[20] – an allusion to Randall's religion. But there was apparently no fraudulent intention. Chaffers quotes a dealer as saying in 1859, the year of Randall's death, 'The Old Quaker stands first, at the top of the tree, but he will not put the French mark on his ware or I could sell any quantity of it at the tip-top price old Sèvres sells for.'[21]

By the middle of the century, the maiolica craze was in full career. *The Morning Post* of 29 December 1857 describes the consternation caused in Florence by the publication of the second edition of Joseph Marryat's book, which exposed some of the fakes:

> The second edition of Mr Joseph Marryat's *History of Pottery and Porcelain* has fallen like a bomb among both the buyers and sellers of 'modern antiquities' in Florence. One great millionaire, as renowned for his collection of crockery as for his command of cash, has at once countermanded all orders for further purchases of majolica. Curiosity-dealers who a couple of months ago were asking 100 l for a cracked plate, are now willing to take a hundred pence. In so thoroughly exposing, in his classical work, the manufacture of spurious majolica long carried on here, Mr Marryat has performed a signal service to the admirers of fictile art.

Marryat suffered by his own exposé. After the Bernal sale prices had risen day by day. At Florence thirteen plates were sold for 39,000 francs. But after that, because of the public distrust of maiolica aroused by Marryat's book, values rapidly declined, and at the public sale of his collection in February 1867, two companion plates, which had fetched £40 and £50 respectively at the Bernal sale, were sold for £23 and £27. It was as though a prophet, after denouncing heathen idols, had been unable to win credence for his own god, on the grounds that all gods were now suspect.

A skilful forger of majolica was Torquato Castellani (b. 1846), whose grandfather, Fortunato Pio Castellani (1793–1865), had rediscovered the forgotten Etruscan technique of granulation, while his father, Alessandro, owned a famous collection of majolica auctioned in 1878. Some of Castellani's works show Quattrocento youths in profile, and Dr Kurz has pointed out that this exemplifies a characteristic turn in the collectors' taste. For the older generation the masterpieces of Italian ceramics were the rich mythological compositions of Urbino dishes, the so-called 'Raphael ware'. But this taste was succeeded by a vogue for portraits, reflected also in the collecting of Quattrocento paintings, where the demand for portraits caused so many imitations that 'genuine examples are now definitely in the minority'.[22] On a dish in the Musée Cluny at Paris the Uffizi portrait of Raphael appears in a slightly embellished version. Such copies of famous paintings are not found on genuine majolica. At the beginning of the twentieth century certain collectors turned their attention towards 'primitive' majolica – the Tuscan wares of the fourteenth and early fifteenth centuries. Like the collectors of Chinese porcelain who were turning from K'ang Hsi to Sung, they were learning, after a century of elaboration and excess, to appreciate simplicity. A large number of the Tuscan originals, however, were fragments brought to light by excavation, and the complete vessels had to be made to order – usually from book illustrations.

Joseph Marryat, who had brought fire and brimstone into the majolica forger's den, attacked the counterfeiters of Italian porcelain with a similar crusading zeal – but this time it was misdirected, and Marryat became responsible for a fallacy which still, despite elucidation by the late Arthur Lane,[23] bedevils the collecting of Italian porcelain. In the second edition of his book (1857), Marryat wrote:

> About ten years ago a dealer of Leghorn used to order once a year a set of embossed teacups resembling the Capo di Monte, which he procured from La Doccia at two dollars each, and, in the course of the bathing season, managed to dispose of as genuine for about twelve. Upon this discovery, the manufactory began to make this ware extensively upon its own account, and it became a most profitable trade, the Neapolitan factories having long ceased to manufacture any. From further inquiries we ascertain that this china has, since the last half of the last century, been occasionally made from the identical moulds of the Capo di Monte, which have been at La Doccia as far as the memory of the oldest sculptor, now 86, extends. No trace of them exists

in the records of the establishment, but it is supposed that the Senator Lorenzo Ginori, who had constant relations with Naples on account of his coral fisheries, must have procured them in one of his journeys to that place.

This fact would establish the identity of the Doccia with the Capo di Monte china, but it does not render it less a subject of regret that the Marquis should have given an opening for the fraud by not at first affixing to his pieces the mark of the Doccia manufactory.[24]

The speculations are reasonable; the exposition is sound; the facts are totally wrong.

By 'embossed' wares, Marryat meant those decorated in low relief with miniature mythological, religious and hunting subjects, but such wares were never made at Capodimonte. In the eighteenth century they were made, as documents discovered by Marchese Ginori-Lisci and Arthur Lane show, at Doccia. So in the nineteenth century Doccia was not forging Capodimonte; it was merely reproducing its old wares, apparently in some cases from the original moulds. But imitations of the pseudo-Capodimonte relief wares were made in Paris and Germany (by Ernst Bohne and Sons of Rudolstadt and others).

The catalogue of the British Museum Exhibition of Forgeries and Deceptive Copies held in 1961 quoted the remark of a well-known museum official, that 'every director has a bust of Flora[25] waiting for him at the end of the corridor'. Marryat had one waiting for him, in the shape of the celebrated 'Shakespeare Jug' (Plate 205). In the first edition of his book (1850), he illustrated this stoneware jug, and wrote of it:

Shakespeare's jug, which has been carefully preserved by the descendants of the immortal bard since the year 1616, is, perhaps, the most remarkable example of the Elizabethan Pottery now existing. The shape partakes very much of the form of the old German or Dutch ewer, without, however, the usual top or cover; the one now attached to the jug being a modern addition of silver, with a medallion bust of the poet in the centre, beautifully executed, and inscribed 'WM. SHAKESPEARE, AT THE AGE OF FORTY' ... as regards the degree of perfection which English Pottery had attained in the Elizabethan age, an inspection of this Jug will justify the presumption, that her court was not less tastefully provided in that respect than those of the Continent....[26]

The jug, said Marryat, had been exhibited in the west of England. In a long footnote, he quoted from a handbill printed by Mr Bennett of Tewkesbury, which included a farcical pedigree tracing the jug back to Shakespeare's sister Joan; it only stopped short of saying that this was the very pot which greasy Joan keeled. The handbill added that the jug had been 'long ago noticed and described by Sir Richard Phillips, in the *Monthly Magazine*, and in Mr Bennett's *Tewkesbury History and Register*.'[27]

Between the first edition of his book (1850) and the second edition (1857), Marryat was tactfully informed that moulds for similar jugs undoubtedly of eighteenth-century manufacture, from the collection of Enoch Wood, were to be seen in the Museum of Practical Geology. It is a tribute to Marryat's scholarship and open mind that 'Shakespeare's Jug' went into inverted commas in the second edition, and that the revised attribution was given. But, wormwood and gall, he had to record in the same edition that 'A fac-simile of Shakespeare's jug has been made by Kerr, Binns, and Co., of Worcester, copied with great accuracy from the original in the possession of Mrs Fletcher of Gloucester'.[28] (This fact was omitted from the third edition of 1868. Self-mortification can go too far.)

Marryat's howler teaches at least two lessons: never trust family tradition; and never trust a silver mount. In as little as half a century, family tradition can become grossly distorted, by accident and design. The silver mount is a particularly clever device of the forger. Would I waste a silver mount, he seems to ask, on a spurious object? In the National Maritime Museum, Greenwich, London, is a Turner jug with a silver mount claiming in Gothic characters that Nelson drank his grog out of it each night on *Victory*, and that he presented it to Hardy on his deathbed.

What redress had society against the forger? A curious incident is recorded by Lady Charlotte Schreiber, who was friendly with the respected Victorian dealer Mortlock and who sometimes acted as an agent for him on the Continent:

> December 2, 1879: A curious trial is coming on. A lady is trying to prevent Mortlock from copying some of the old shapes, saying it depreciates the value of some ancient specimens she possesses. We are doing all we can to find him other pieces of the same form and decoration to prove that hers are not at all unique. Indeed the pattern is a very well known one, but as it always will happen, we cannot lay our hands upon a specimen at this moment. I found a saucer of the same in the autumn, and now the search is for a cup. Ivor is also interesting himself in the question. We think it is most meritorious of Mortlock to produce these revivals of the ancient taste, which can only tend to the improvement of art, and we are constantly lending him examples for that purpose. They are far from being forgeries, as the name of the manufacturer is always added, besides which no connoisseur could ever mistake them for antiques.

Perhaps Lady Charlotte was successful in her search, as this case never seems to have reached the courts.

One which did, was the case of Dickins *v.* Ellis (1908). A well-known dealer had employed Ellis, a personable confidence-trickster, to foist on to the founder of Dickins and Jones large quantities of fake Meissen and Sèvres porcelain. The fraud was not discovered until the executors' sale. In the ensuing law-suit, Professor Brinckmann, Director of the Hamburg Museum, and Frederick Litchfield, the English authority, appeared for the plaintiff. As Litchfield recalled in *The Connoisseur* of 1917, they caused 'quite a sensation' by producing in court white groups in imitation of Meissen made at Potschapel in Saxony, where they could still be purchased cheaply.[29] Ellis had judgment given against him for £20,000. He was later indicted for fraud, but escaped on a technicality. The original instigator of the fraud escaped altogether.

If human justice failed, there was always divine retribution. For what else can we see in the fate of Ferruccio Mengaroni (1875–1925) who was killed when a huge head of Medusa, which he had made in della Robbia style, fell on him?[30]

14 Art Nouveau

Ten years ago, a social history of ceramics would not have contained a chapter on *art nouveau*. At that time the style, insofar as it was given any consideration by art historians, was viewed as a prolonged decadence, the *fin de siècle*, an unfortunate phase art went through before being rescued by Frank Lloyd Wright, Gropius and the cubists.[1] Since then there has been a formidable *art nouveau* revival, reflected in dress, poster design, the antiques market and the publication of books such as Robert Schmutzler's *Art Nouveau* (1964), Maurice Rheims's *L'Art 1900* and *L'Objet 1900*, and – less luxurious but more acute – Mario Amaya's *Art Nouveau* (1966). Today *art nouveau* is seen as the style which emancipated art from an anecdotal or narrative approach and finally from representation itself; the first style which set out consciously to react against precedent and trained the spectator to look for innovation; the style which rejected the bourgeois division between fine and applied arts; an abstract decorative movement which heralded Van der Rohe's Barcelona chair (1929) and Saarinen's Kennedy Airport (1961) – not to mention Frank Lloyd Wright, Gropius and the cubists.

The claims made for the influence of *art nouveau* may not be excessive; but they tend to distort our appreciation of the style itself as a phenomenon of its time. Since simplicity has been the rule from the 1930s onwards (the dominant modern shape is the rectangle of the skyscraper) modern critics emphasize the austere side of *art nouveau* – the 'soberness of purpose, if not of mood, of the pure Arts and Crafts exponents',[2] the cleanness of Ashbee's and Dresser's silver designs, of Mackmurdo's and Voysey's furniture and textiles. *Art nouveau* is thus thought significant because it established 'a whole new vocabulary of rectilinear functional form, which made possible the language of the Bauhaus and contemporary design.'[3] But while this simplicity may have been the best aspect of *art nouveau*, it was not the most typical; and it is the typical which a social historian must consider first, before discussing the sports. A tour of the stalls and shops which specialize in *art nouveau* today will scarcely reveal one Mackmurdo-style chair or Dresser toastrack to a thousand objects of tortured complexity and over-elaborate decoration.

At its mildest, *art nouveau* was a kind of drugged rococo.[4] While the rococo curvetted, span itself into arabesques and other vivacities, *art nouveau* languished in loops, tendrils and unctuous coils. If the shell, with its brittle, bony whorls, is the archetype of rococo, the 'shell-like ear', with its fleshed curlicues and pendulous lobe, may be taken as the microcosm of *art nouveau*. The Vincennes *vase à oreilles*[5] of the eighteenth century only timidly anticipates a motif made explicit by an Italian architect of 1900 when he took literally the saying that 'walls have ears' and designed an immense bronze ear as the doorbell of an *art nouveau* house in Milan.[6]

But the same style was capable of a more spirited decadence. From smoothing green hair, simpering and writhing in ecstasies of narcissism, it would suddenly be rearing from scimitar waves, bubbling, gurgling, undulating obscenely, hovering and swooping on bat pinions. The passive *art nouveau* oozed, distended, fell into sensuous swoons; the vicious *art nouveau* flung itself into wild tarantellas, dervished itself into 'the delirious trance of death'.

Two typical *art nouveau* vases are shown in Plate XIV. The bat on the larger work is a recurring motif. M. Rheims, who illustrates a gold goblet decorated with a spreadeagled bat,[7] writes: 'Ces animaux, chargés de bien de crimes, ont fait en tout temps l'objet de légendes et d'illustrations terrifiantes.'[8] But it was not until the nineteenth century[9] that stories of the vampire bats of the South American forests reached Europe, giving the little blind flying mouse a reputation for sinister perversity quite acceptable to the decadents: 'Holy Roman Vampire', suggested Wilde. (Perhaps it is no accident that a 'Batman' cult should have accompanied the *art nouveau* revival?) It is a pity that *Die Fledermaus* was written as a comic opera by the younger Strauss, and not as an epic by Wagner. If opera and oratorio are characteristic baroque music, and Mozart is a rococo genius, Wagner is surely the composer most representative of *art nouveau*. One can imagine a film of *art nouveau* shapes in violent movement set to the vertiginous orchestration of *Lohengrin* or *Tannhäuser*. At the Royal Lancastrian Pottery, Gordon Forsyth painted the Ride of the Valkyries in high *art nouveau* style on a

Art Nouveau

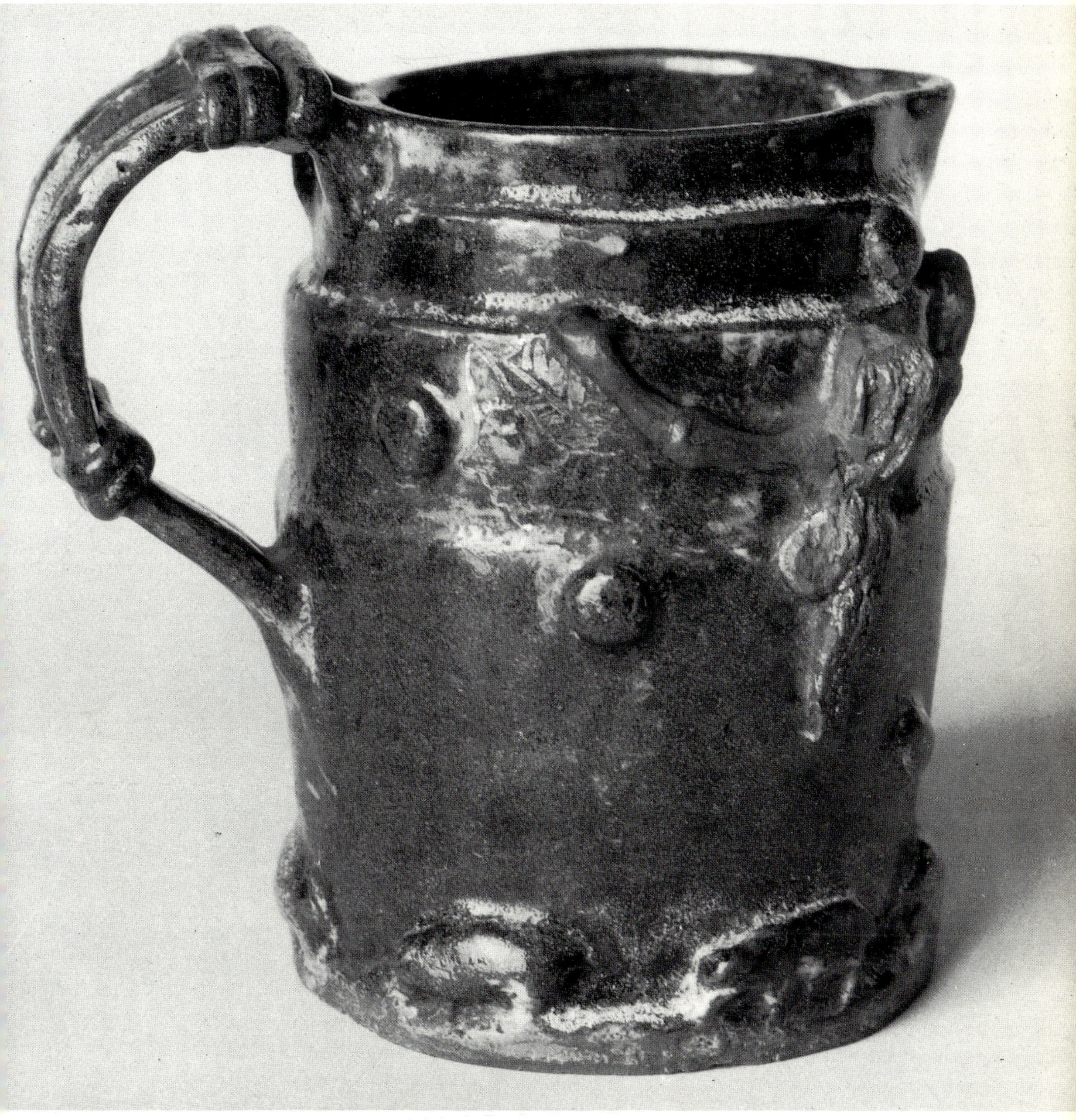

206 Pottery mug modelled by Gauguin. Fired by Chaplet about 1886–7. Height 6″. See p. 332.

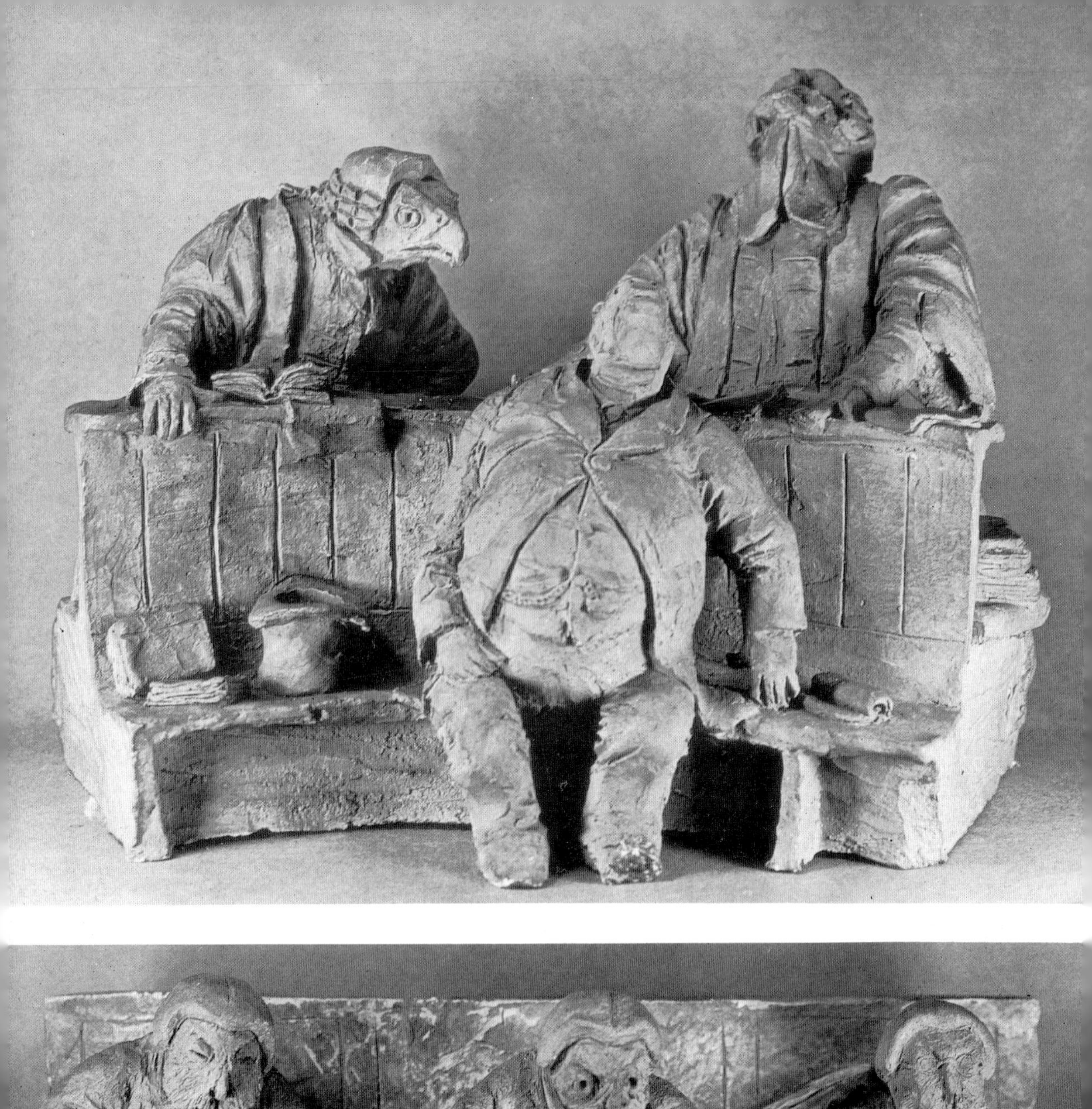

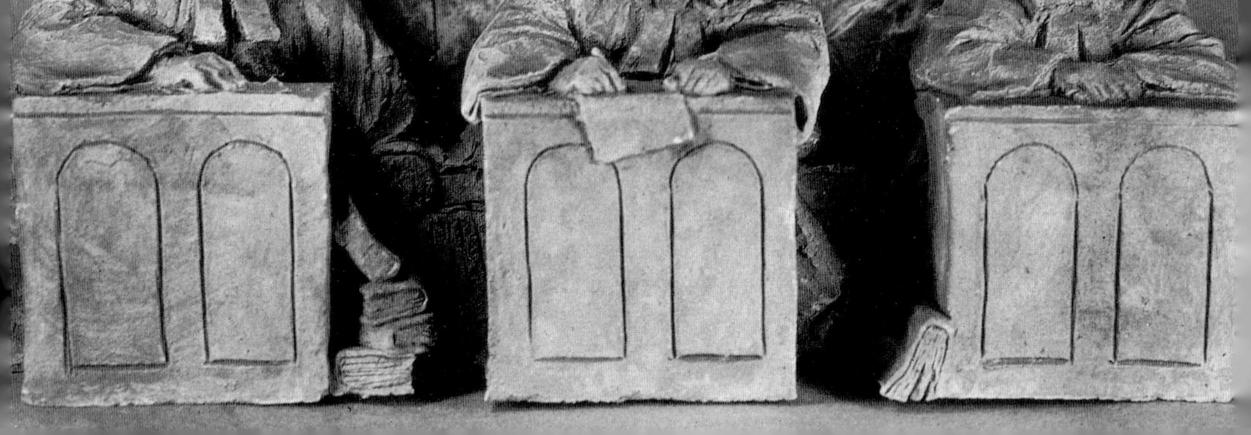

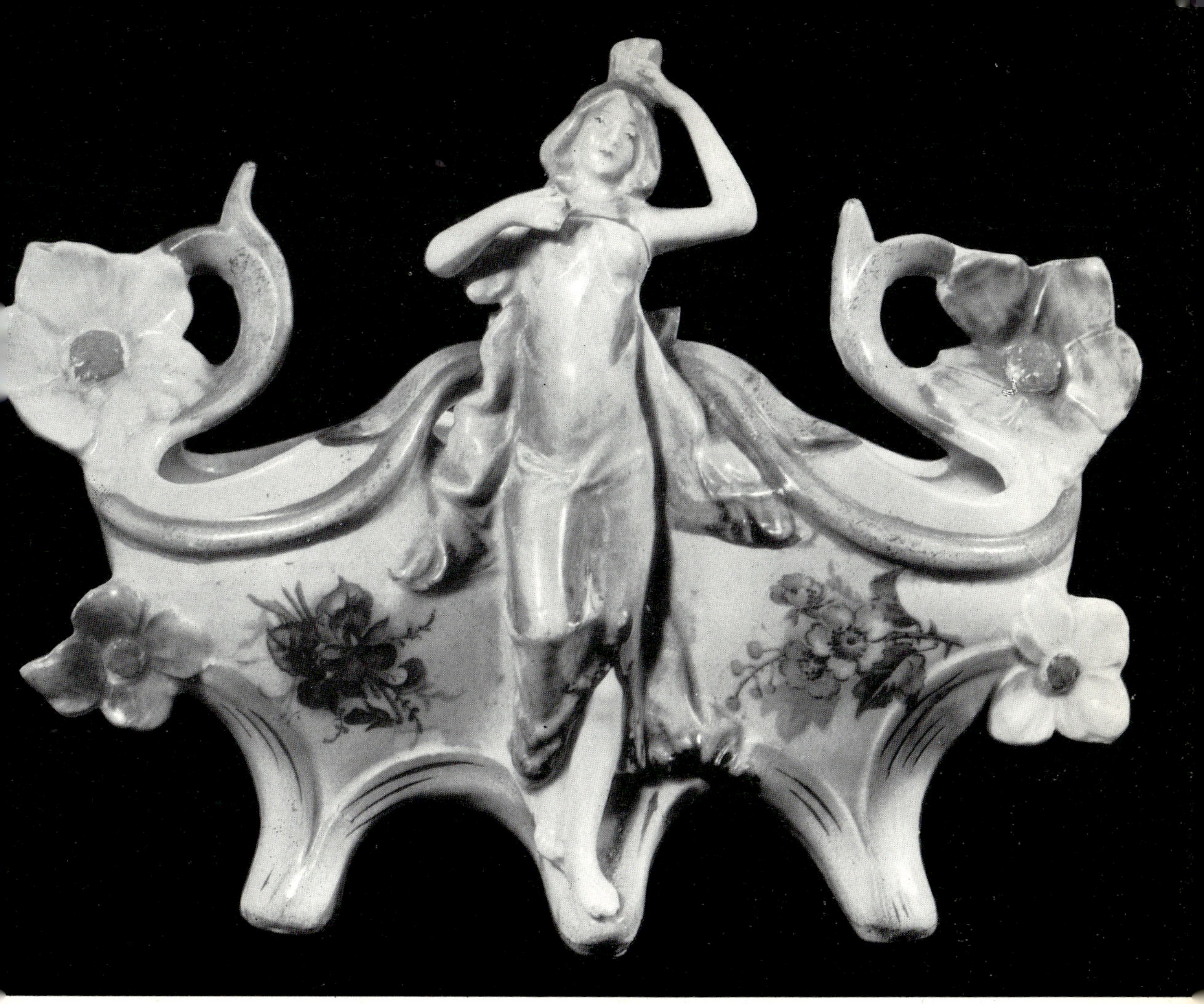

209 Vase, probably French, late nineteenth century. Length 9″, height 6¾″. See p. 329.
210 (right) Ironstone plate with design in Japanese style by Félix Bracquemond. Made by Barluet and Company at Montereau, late nineteenth century. Diameter 10¾″. See p. 332.

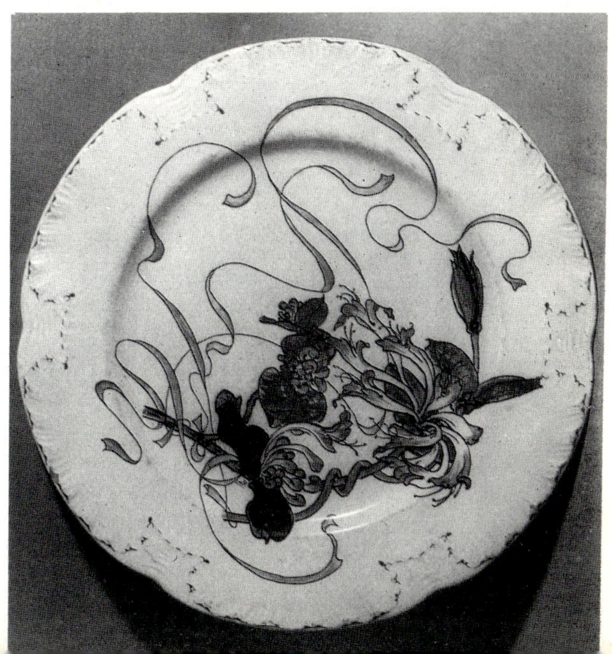

207 and 208 (opposite) Terracotta group of 'The Tichborne Trial', modelled by Randolph Caldecott. Height 8″. The three judges, Lord Chief Justice Cockburn, Justice Mellor and Justice Lush are shown as owls, the claimant is a turtle, and the counsel, Mr Hawkins and Dr Kenealy, are respectively a hawk and a cockerel. See p. 331.

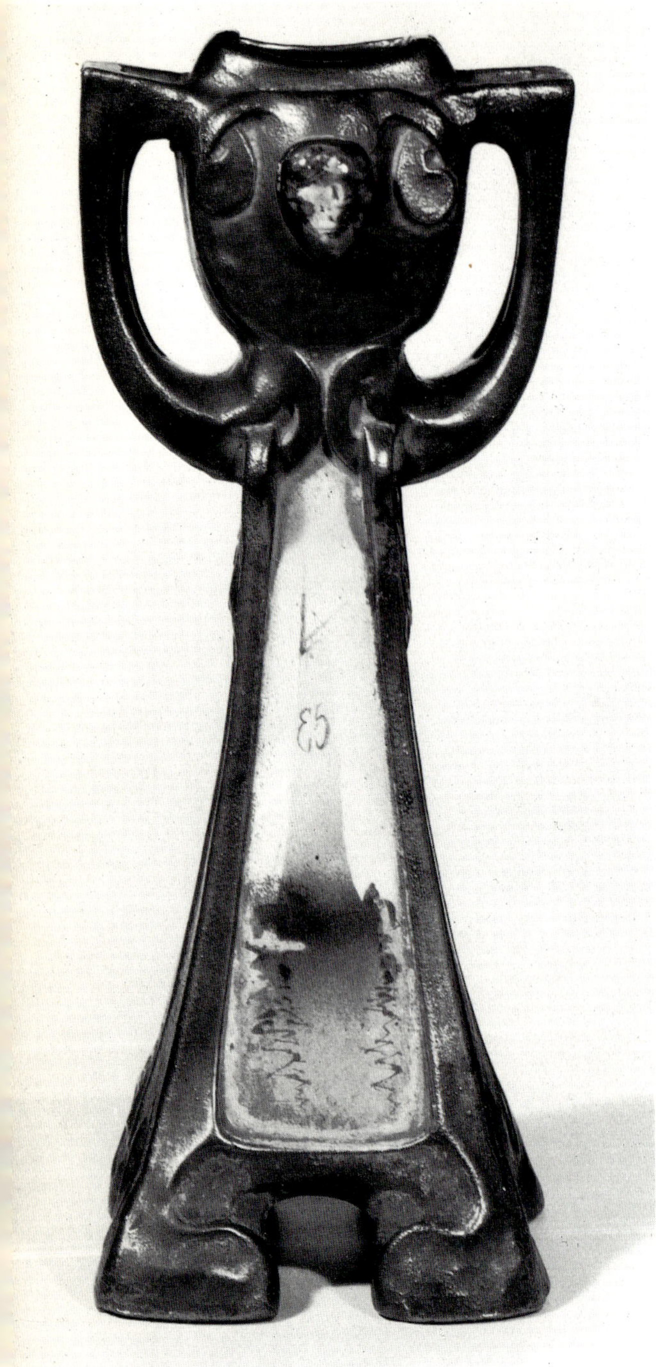

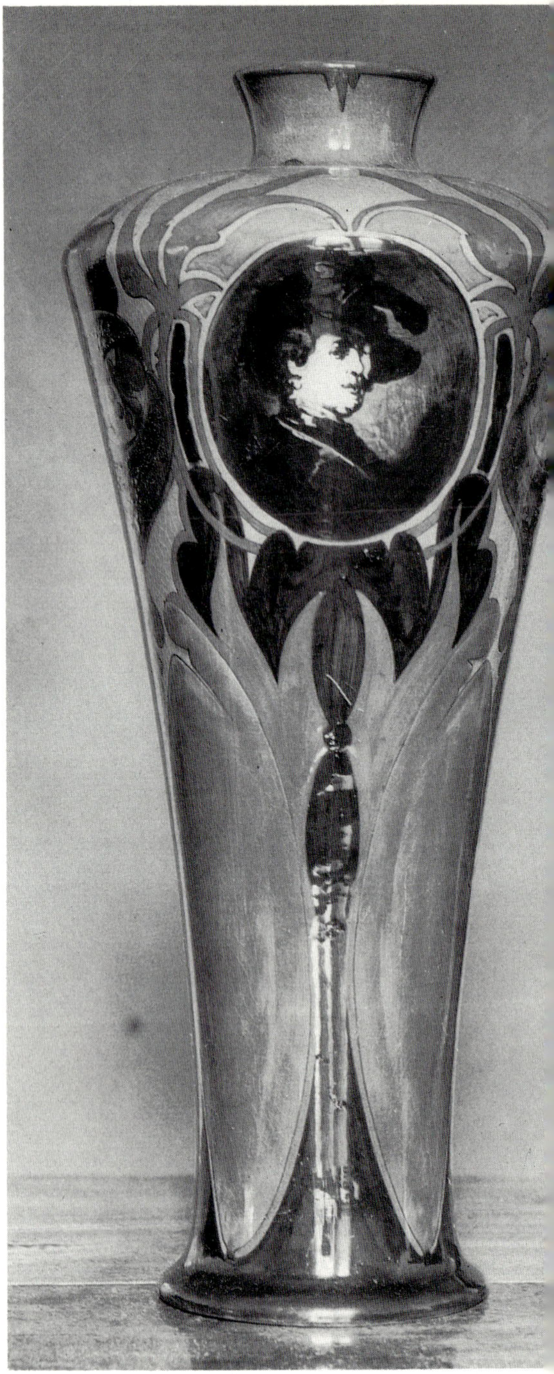

211 (left) Pottery vase made at the Bretby Art Pottery, late nineteenth century, and decorated, over the bronze glaze, with sailing scene in red and yellow enamels. Height 11″. See p. 329.

212 (right) Large vase in *art nouveau* style, showing the use of photographic techniques on ceramics. Height 14″. See p. 338.

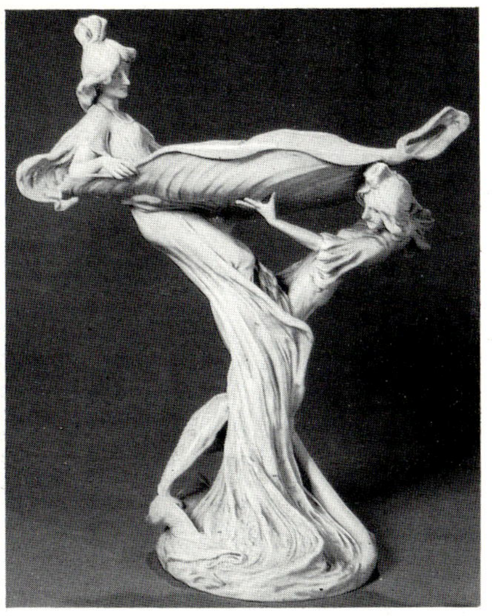

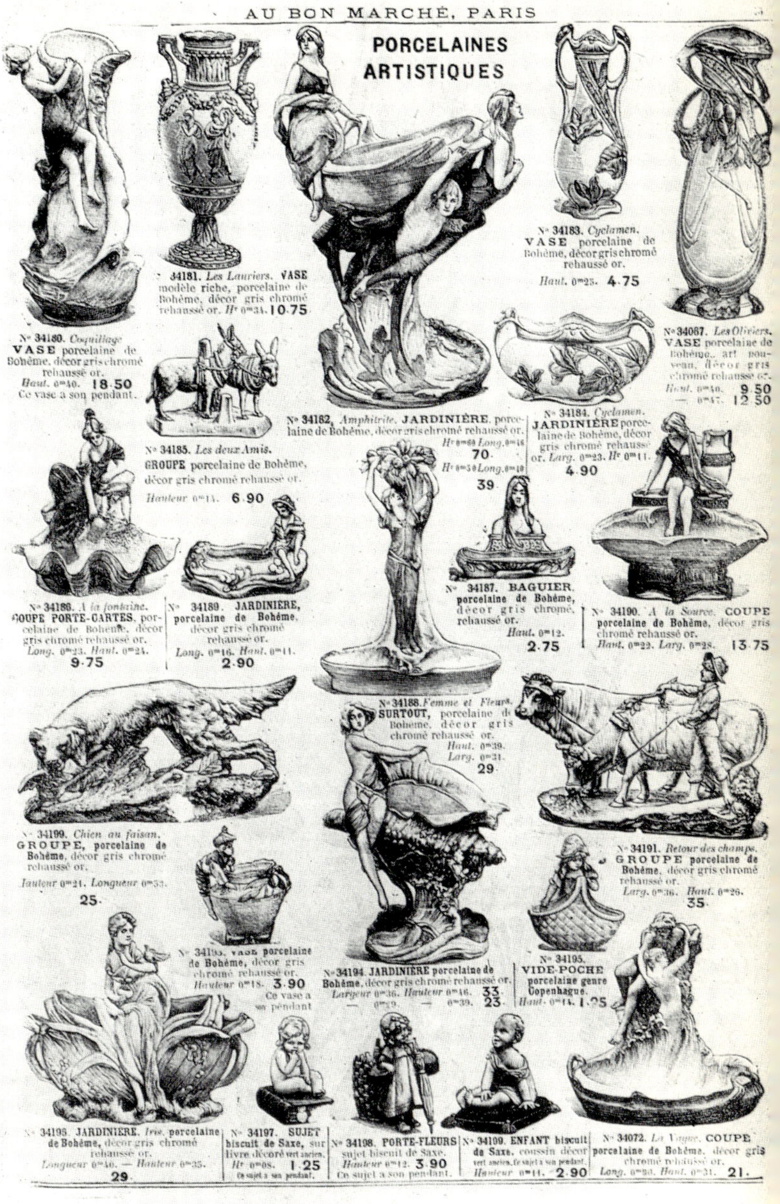

AU BON MARCHÉ, PARIS

PORCELAINES ARTISTIQUES

Nº 34180. *Coquillage.* **VASE** porcelaine de Bohême, décor gris chromé rehaussé or. *Haut.* 0m40. **18.50** Ce vase a son pendant.

Nº 34181. *Les Lauriers.* **VASE** modèle riche, porcelaine de Bohême, décor gris chromé rehaussé or. *Hr* 0m34. **10.75**

Nº 34182. *Amphitrite.* **JARDINIÈRE**, porcelaine de Bohême, décor gris chromé rehaussé or. *Hr* 0m60 *Long.* 0m46 **70.** *Hr* 0m50 *Long.* 0m40 **39.**

Nº 34183. *Cyclamen.* **VASE** porcelaine de Bohême, décor gris chromé rehaussé or. *Haut.* 0m25. **4.75**

Nº 34067. *Les Oliviers.* **VASE** porcelaine de Bohême, art nouveau, décor gris chromé rehaussé or. *Haut.* 0m40. **9.50** — 0m47. **12.50**

Nº 34184. *Cyclamen.* **JARDINIÈRE** porcelaine de Bohême, décor gris chromé rehaussé or. *Larg.* 0m23. *Hr* 0m11. **4.90**

Nº 34185. *Les deux Amis.* **GROUPE** porcelaine de Bohême, décor gris chromé rehaussé or. *Hauteur* 0m14. **6.90**

Nº 34186. *A la fontaine.* **COUPE PORTE-CARTES**, porcelaine de Bohême, décor gris chromé rehaussé or. *Long.* 0m23. *Haut.* 0m24. **9.75**

Nº 34189. **JARDINIÈRE**, porcelaine de Bohême, décor gris chromé rehaussé or. *Long.* 0m16. *Haut.* 0m11. **2.90**

Nº 34187. **BAGUIER**, porcelaine de Bohême, décor gris chromé, rehaussé or. *Haut.* 0m12. **2.75**

Nº 34190. *A la Source.* **COUPE** porcelaine de Bohême, décor gris chromé rehaussé or. *Haut.* 0m22. *Larg.* 0m28. **13.75**

Nº 34188. *Femme et Fleurs.* **SURTOUT**, porcelaine de Bohême, décor gris chromé rehaussé or. *Haut.* 0m39. *Larg.* 0m21. **29.**

Nº 34199. *Chien au faisan.* **GROUPE**, porcelaine de Bohême, décor gris chromé rehaussé or. *Hauteur* 0m21. *Longueur* 0m33. **25.**

Nº 34191. *Retour des champs.* **GROUPE** porcelaine de Bohême, décor gris chromé rehaussé or. *Larg.* 0m36. *Haut.* 0m26. **35.**

Nº 34193. **VASE** porcelaine de Bohême, décor gris chromé rehaussé or. *Hauteur* 0m18. **3.90** Ce vase a son pendant.

Nº 34194. **JARDINIÈRE** porcelaine de Bohême, décor gris chromé rehaussé or. *Largeur* 0m36. *Hauteur* 0m46. **33.** — 0m29. — 0m39. **23.**

Nº 34195. **VIDE-POCHE** porcelaine genre Copenhague. *Haut.* 0m14. **1.25**

Nº 34196. **JARDINIÈRE.** *Iris.* porcelaine de Bohême, décor gris chromé rehaussé or. *Longueur* 0m40. — *Hauteur* 0m35. **29.**

Nº 34197. **SUJET** biscuit de Saxe, sur livre décoré vert ancien. *Hr* 0m08. **1.25** Ce sujet a son pendant.

Nº 34198. **PORTE-FLEURS** sujet biscuit de Saxe. *Hauteur* 0m12. **3.90** Ce sujet a son pendant.

Nº 34199. **ENFANT** biscuit de Saxe, coussin décor vert ancien. Ce sujet a son pendant. *Hauteur* 0m11. **2.90**

Nº 34072. *La Vague.* **COUPE** porcelaine de Bohême, décor gris chromé rehaussé or. *Long.* 0m30. *Haut.* 0m31. **21.**

213 and 214 Page from the Christmas catalogue of Au Bon Marché, 1907, showing 'Porcelaine de Bohême': (left) a Royal Dux Bohemia vase, height 19″, of the kind illustrated in the catalogue.

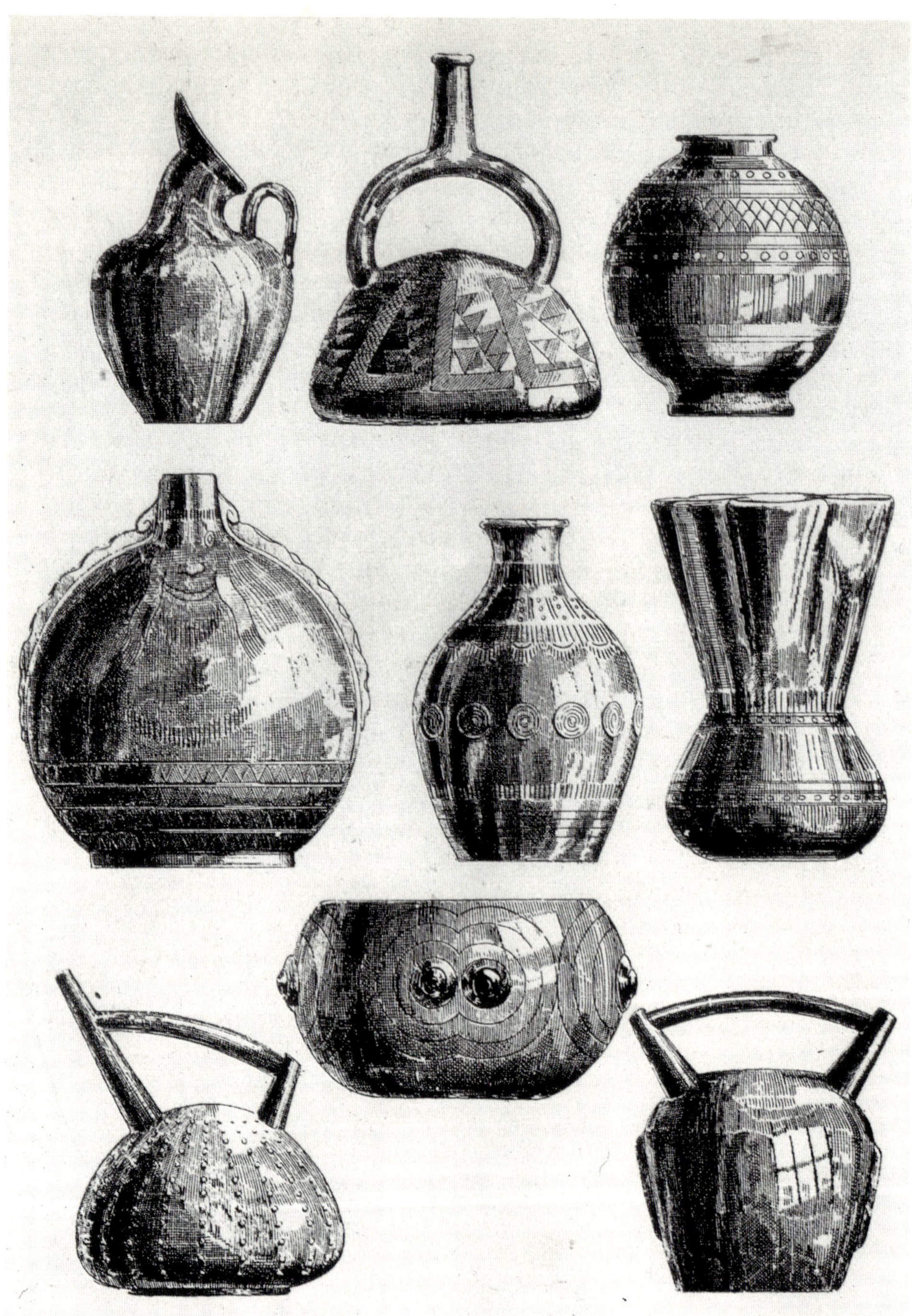

215 Dr Christopher Dresser's Linthorpe Art Pottery, in Peruvian Shapes. See p. 336.

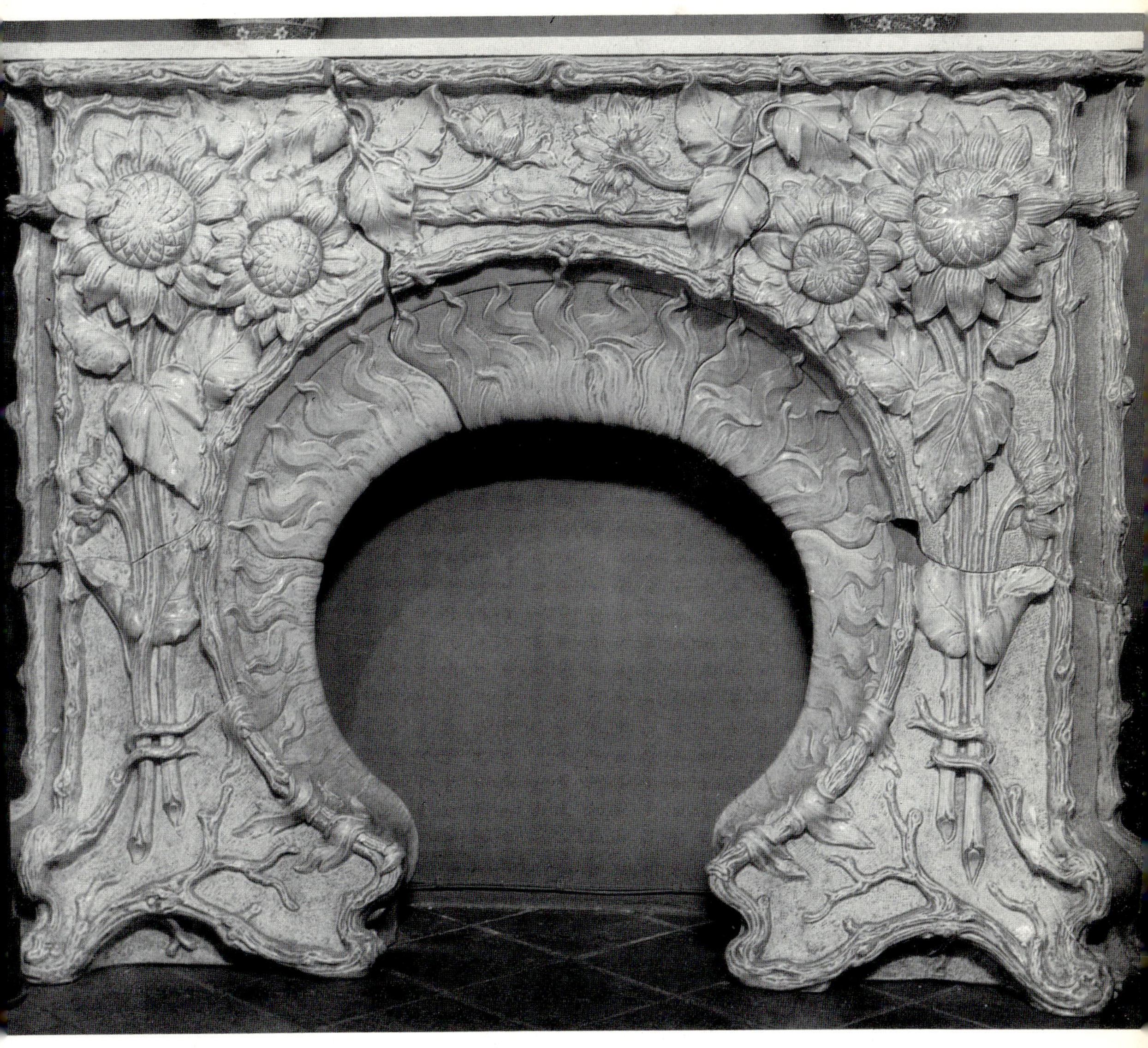

216 Chimneypiece decorated with sunflowers in relief, stoneware with ochre glaze, perhaps French, *c.* 1880–90.

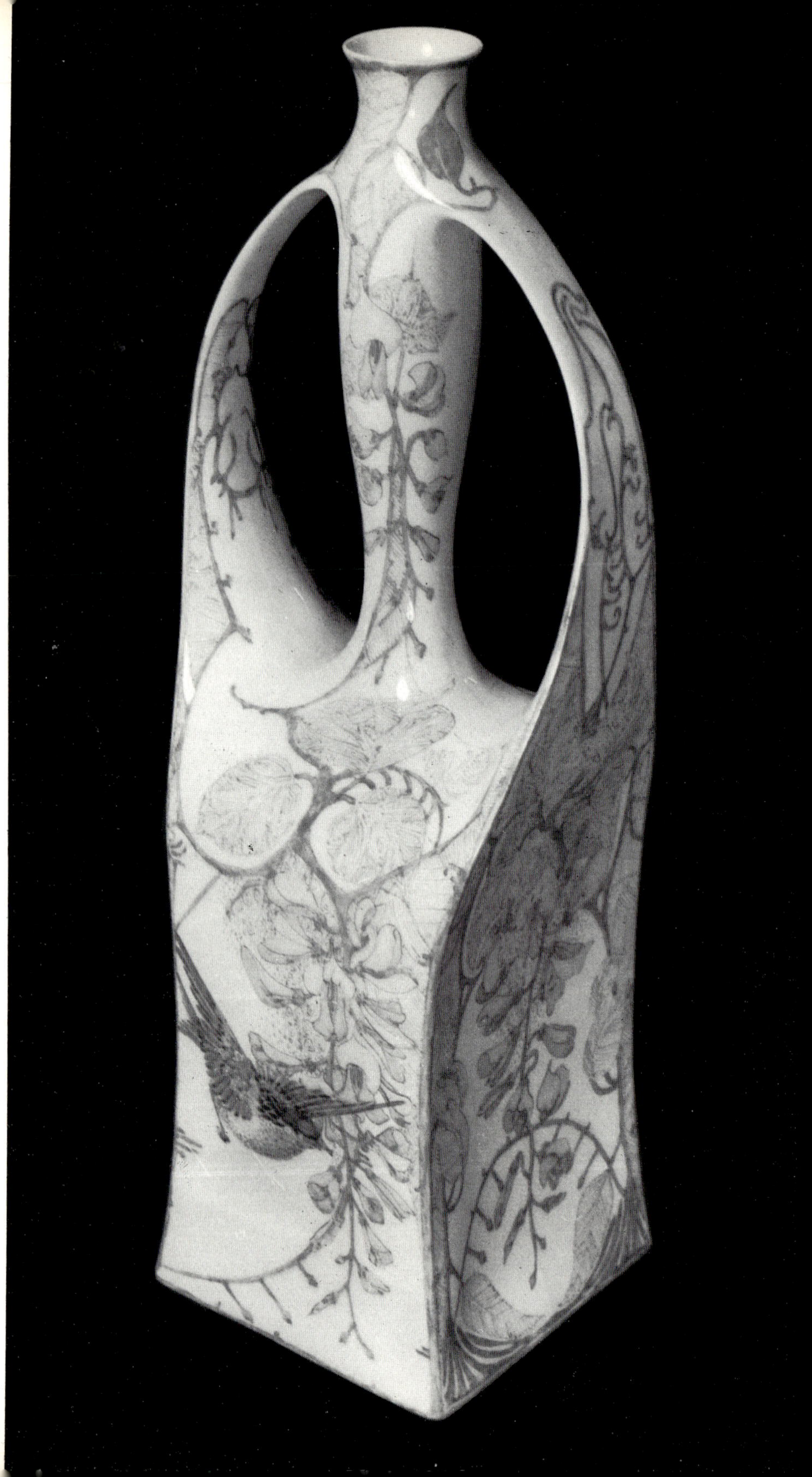

217 Rozenburg vase with decoration designed by Juriaan Kok. See p. 334.

vase now in the possession of Lord Dunsany. Recalling Hitler's admiration for Wagner's music, we may well consider it the aspect of *art nouveau* most prophetic of the thirties.

The other case in Plate XIV, with its quaint handles, actress's head and rising tide of aniline purple, gives little impression of that concern for unity and harmony which the champions of *art nouveau* claim for the style. One would scarcely suspect that Dr Christopher Dresser had ever exercised an influence over the Bretby works which produced the vase shown in Plate 211. We are back to the 'intricacy' that Hogarth prescribed for the rococo. Three more Hogarthian precepts, in favour of 'tender tints', 'serpentine lines' and 'disproportion', are flagrantly obeyed in the little boudoir vase of Plate 209. The central figure, in a pale lilac gown, is dwarfed by flowers which might have come from a paradise designed by Walt Disney.

At the same time, there was a movement towards simplicity, far from esoteric, and sometimes consciously democratic. Its leader was Henri Van de Velde (1863–1957), a Belgian designer much influenced by the ideas of William Morris. His influential *Formules* contained this indictment of a Meissen tureen:

> Voyez : Elle est un vaste dôme, dont tout le poids est supporté par des dauphins qui mettent en croix des queues éployées de feuilles de céleris. Sur le galbe du dôme s'ébattent des cygnes blancs, rangés en audacieuse posture, poitrines bombées et ailes au vent ; ils tendent tout l'effort de leurs longs cous vers des guirlandes de fleurs et de fruits mêlés de coquillages et de crustacés. Et, sur les côtés, deux sirènes retiennent ces guirlandes qu'elles pressent contre leur poitrine ! Celles-ci s'offriront ensuite aux mains des serveurs qui écraseront de leurs doigts ces chairs pâles et fragiles : car ces sirènes sont les anses de cette soupière dont le couvercle est une vraie apothéose : Amphitrite et l'Amour voyageant sur le dos d'un dauphin rouge et géant qui souffle par le nez deux jets d'une masse verte si épaisse qu'il ne peut y avoir de doute pour personne que cette soupière contient de la soupe aux choux ! Notre raison se révolte contre pareil mensonge, contre pareille folie.[10]

Van de Velde's own design for a teacup and saucer is plain and rhythmic. The curve of the handle is continued in the curve of the painted pattern.

Where did the new simplicity come from? Its pioneers were three children's book illustrators – Kate Greenaway, Walter Crane and Randolph Caldecott. One would as probably look for the dark origins of vorticism in the drawings of Beatrix Potter (in whose works, after all,

Mr Graham Greene has detected a period of deep psychological disturbance).[11] Huysmans mentions all three in his *L'Art Moderne*. In each case, significantly, he compares them with Japanese artists. Of Crane's *The Fairy Ship* he writes:

> C'est une petite merveille d'observation, un tour d'adresse de dessin, enlevant d'un coup de crayon les poses les plus effacées et les plus simples du corps, un tour d'adresse tel qu'il faut, pour en trouver un aussi expressif et aussi agile, recourir aux albums japonais d'Hokkei et d'Okou-Saï.[12]

He found Kate Greenaway's *Under the Window* (translated into French as *La Lanterne magique* and into German as *Am Fenster*) full of 'inchassables souvenirs des albums d'Okou-Saï'.[13]

> Puis quel art de la décoration dans cet album, quel art de la mise en page, quelle incessante variété dans les motifs d'ornement, empruntés aux fruits, aux fleurs ... quelle diversité dans la ligne du cadre qui change à chacune des feuilles du livre ! [14]

As for Caldecott's drawings, they 'semblent alors crayonnés par l'un des artistes de Yeddo'.[15]

All three were concerned with ceramic design. Kate Greenaway's prize-winning tile of 1864, which Dr Schmutzler regards as the shy début of *art nouveau*,[16] makes use of flats of colour enclosed by a strong outline of sinuous geometry – a form of design which probably owed more to Owen Jones's *Grammar of Ornament* than to the colour prints of Hokusai and Utamaro. Her influence was certainly stronger than might be expected from the trivial scope of her works. Lasenby Liberty, in the *British Warehouseman* interview already mentioned, said: 'I have never met her but I have always had the greatest admiration for Kate Greenaway's work. She was one of the earliest and most powerful popular educators in my colour theories, with her simple little outline drawings.'[17] So Miss Greenaway, whom Lady Dorothy Nevill used to invite to matinees 'to take her out of herself', became a European influence, one of the inspirers of *le Stile Liberty*. In England her designs were copied directly on Beardmore's Sunderland Art Ware.

Walter Crane drew designs for Pilkington's Royal Lancastrian Pottery, including one for a peacock plate.[18] Like the bat, the peacock, symbol of narcissism, is a recurring motif in *art nouveau* ceramics and in the style as a whole: Whistler's Peacock Room and Beardsley's *The Peacock Gown* are the most famous examples. E. Brain and Company, of the Foley China Works, Fenton, introduced a 'Peacock Pottery'. The brand mark is itself an imaginative *art nouveau* design; the feather-tips, usually an excuse for chromatic orgies, are simply indicated as white excavations.[19]

Randolph Caldecott modelled birds as part of the capitals of the pillars in Lord Leighton's Arab Hall,[20] for which De Morgan supplied tiles. But Caldecott's ceramics have not a trace of *art nouveau* feeling. His terracotta models, such as the group of the Tichborne trial (Plates 207–8) are grotesqueries in the manner of Tinworth. His use of anthropomorphic animals and birds shows the influence of the French sculptor Dalou, under whom he studied when Dalou was in England.[21]

But the influence of Caldecott's book illustrations on *art nouveau* was important. When he died, prematurely, in 1886, a fourteen-page obituary appeared in the *Gazette des Beaux Arts*. It described him as one of:

> ... les chefs de la jeune école anglaise qui promettaient de donner à l'art de leur pays une impulsion nouvelle et de l'empêcher, par le souffle de leur talent nourri aux sources vives de la nature, de se figer encore une fois dans les formules banales de la convention, ou de s'abandonner aux séductions subtiles et dangereuses de l'École pré-raphaëlite dans son évolution définitive.[22]

Beside the starchy composure of Kate Greenaway's drawings and the militant effeteness of Walter Crane's, Caldecott's designs seem to lack any quality of distinction. He seems a Bowdlerized Victorian Rowlandson. Yet the obituary singles out two qualities which at the time seemed not only distinctive, but revolutionary: rejection of convention, and recourse to nature, both now regarded as essential aspects of *art nouveau*. The same obituary reveals that:

> Victor Hugo s'intéressait beaucoup aux dessins de notre humoriste, surtout aux Picture Books: un ami intime de l'artiste, M. Armstrong, directeur du musée de Kensington, sérait arrangé pour envoyer régulièrement au grand poète, par l'entremise de M. Lockroy, les premiers exemplaires tirés de ces albums.[23]

From another source we learn that the greatest artist associated with *art nouveau* – Paul Gauguin, himself a potter – admired Caldecott's work. A. S. Hartrick, in his autobiography, *A Painter's Pilgrimage Through Fifty Years* (1938), records that:

> In art, Gauguin's greatest contempt was reserved for the schools and academic art generally. This, of course, is now all 'vieux jeu'. But I had one

conversation with him, illustrating this side of him in a very unexpected way. He had been making some drawings of geese which he showed me. He then produced one of Caldecott's coloured books, in which some geese were depicted in the artist's very characteristic way. These he praised, almost extravagantly as it seemed to me. 'That,' he said, 'was the true spirit of drawing.' [24]

But the strength of *art nouveau* did not come entirely from the books of babes and sucklings. Japanese art, in which Huysmans found parallels for all three artists, was the cardinal influence. Félix Bracquemond, as we have seen, was the first to appreciate Japanese prints, when in 1856 he bought a series of Hokusai *mangwa* from the dealer Delâtre. It is not surprising, therefore, to find a fairly direct derivation from Hokusai in Bracquemond's ceramics (Plate 210). Bracquemond was the artistic director of the *atelier* of Haviland at Auteuil. The potter Ernest Chaplet, who had become acquainted with him during the siege of Paris in 1871, entered Haviland's factory in 1875. They experimented together with the so-called 'barbotine', a technique invented by Théodore Deck which made it possible to give the faience a wider range of colours by replacing glazes with a white slip which could be coloured by any oxide. Bracquemond inspired Chaplet with his passion for Far Eastern art – ceramics as well as prints – and Chaplet made tall, simple vases decorated with glazes in the Japanese manner. It was Bracquemond, too, who introduced Gauguin to Chaplet. In the summer of 1886, after he had shown his work at the eighth and last Impressionist Exhibition, Gauguin wrote to his wife:

> M. Bracquemond le graveur m'a acheté avec enthousiasme un tableau 250 Frs et m'a mis en relations avec un céramiste qui compte faire des vases d'art. Enchanté de ma sculpture il m'a prié de lui faire à mon gré cet hiver des travaux qui vendus seraient *partagés de moitié*. [25]

Gauguin's first pieces – fifty-five in number – were fired in the winter of 1886–7. They were unsaleable, and even Bracquemond was not impressed. None of the pieces was thrown on a wheel, and Gauguin later explained that it was his aim 'donner à l'art de la céramique un élan nouveau par la création de nouvelles formes faites a la main'.[26] He wished 'remplacer le tourneur par des mains intelligentes qui puissent communiquer au vase la vie d'une figure'.[27] So with Gauguin's ceramics we again encounter the perennial conflict between potting and sculpture. It was because Chaplet was 'enchanté de ma sculpture' that he had thought Gauguin might make a ceramist. Gauguin wanted to use the clay for making anything but pots. He used it to create a relief surface for painting on; he stuck his vases with wholly unsuitable modelled motifs – a burnous-clad Algerian horseman after Delacroix, a ballerina after Degas; and he used it for sculpture pure and simple. In the *art nouveau* period, ceramics for the first time gain the ascendancy over sculpture. Instead of pottery imitating sculpture, as in the eighteenth century adaptations of Il Fiammingo, sculpture adopts the fluency of ceramics, whether in Dalou's monkeys or Rodin's burghers. Alternatively, sculptors adopt the ceramic medium. As with the rococo, pliable clay, so easily teased into fanciful or grotesque shapes, is a more suitable medium for *art nouveau* than marble. Jean Carriès (1856–94), who began as a sculptor, abandoned stone in favour of stoneware – 'ce mâle de la porcelaine, cette matière noble que nul ne peut dominer s'il n'est un maître ouvrier ... pâte divine, silice mystérieuse qui, sous l'habile pression des doigts prend des formes si diverses, si exquisement gracieuses, qui résiste aux températures énormes, qui s'assimile des émaux chargés de chaux et s'épanouit sous l'aspect enchanteur d'un fruit mûr ou d'un caillou précieux, modelé par la joie ou le besoin de l'homme'.[28] While Carriès modelled in the most masculine form of porcelain, A. Léonard, at Sèvres, used the most feminine, white bisque, for his four dancing figures. Another sculpturesque work is Capeque's 'Riddle of Life' (Plate XV), which shows the characteristic *art nouveau* preoccupation with the enigmatic and ambivalent, exhibited also in Franz Metzner's *Sphinx des Lebens*[29] and in Gauguin's *Oviri* figure, which he asked to be placed on his grave.[30]

Gauguin was the greatest artist who applied himself to ceramics in the *art nouveau* period, but he was not the greatest potter. Except where they become full sculpture, as in the superb 'Black Venus', his ceramic works are technically inept, full of whimsy and highly unfunctional. Only fragments of the greater Gauguin are embedded in these mock Toby jugs and puzzle-pots. Gauguin was an experimentalist, and not all experiments can be successful. But bad works sometimes demonstrate period style better than good ones. Like his Pont Aven paintings, Gauguin's pots show the influence of cloisonné enamels; the garish colours are imprisoned in cells. Japanese prints taught the same lesson, that which Kate Greenaway had learnt more demurely from the *Grammar of Ornament*. The strong contour became an evident characteristic of *art nouveau*.

Other French potters – Chaplet, Delaherche, Dammouse, Dalpeyrat,

Madame Moreau-Nélaton – made simple pots in Japanese style. The model was good, but the derivation was excessive. This suggestion was made in the Catalogue of the Exposition Universelle of 1878:

> Depuis la fin de XVIIe siècle, la céramique européenne est restée sous le joug asiatique. Notre époque aura vu le goût japonais se substituer tout à fait au goût chinois, et le persano-arabe occuper uniquement des fabriques entières.... En résumé, une céramique très brillante, très variée, mais surtout imitative, voilà la céramique française. Dans le détail des couvertes, nous sommes arrivés à n'avoir presque rien à envier a l'Asie. Mais comme décors, nous n'avons rien trouvé de français, d'européen, de décisif depuis le XVIIIe siècle.[31]

The artist potters showed the way. It was left to the factories to take it. The public was not purist. It did not demand to drink its tea from reproduction Japanese teabowls with richly slubbered glazes. It wanted ceramics which would be perfectly functional yet novel in form and decoration. As the 1878 catalogue said, 'La formule d'un décor européen correspondant à nos besoins, à nos habitudes, aux objets usuels de notre existence reste encore à découvrir'.[32] Two factories in particular showed how it could be achieved. The *Grossherzogliche Majolika-Manufaktur* at Karlsruhe, under its director Max Läuger, produced tall, slender vases boldly decorated with swaying trees and grasses. Tiles were the factory's mainstay; a fireplace design of skeletal trees in the snow[33] is typical. It might almost have been adapted from a Van Gogh painting. But perhaps the most successful of all *art nouveau* ceramics are the table wares (Plate 217) designed by J. Jurriaan Kok for the Rozenburg factory at the Hague. A paper-thin porcelain, pressed into shapes which still seem astonishingly modern despite the *art nouveau* bias of flame-like stopples and handles, was decorated with a flaring, manic line. Structural starkness was combined with a crazily erratic design of dragonfly antennae, crab claws, asters, starfish, snowflakes, tentacles, convolvuli, mazes of querulous or demented doodling. It was a compromise with none of the tame concessions of a compromise. The *mise en assiette* was brilliant; Jurriaan Kok's deployment of the blank space was as masterly as his draughtsmanship. And these were not the unique works of a dedicated studio potter. They were mass-produced table wares.

Throughout the period, eminent artists were turning to ceramic work. Among them were Paul Baudry, well-known for his allegorical paintings in the Opéra and Palais de Justice in Paris, and Paul Helleu, the portraitist and watercolourist. J. F. Willumsen, the sculptor, was inspired by Gauguin's work in his experiments with stoneware at the Bing and Groendahl Ceramics Works, Copenhagen. Jean Gauguin (Paul Gauguin's son) worked under him for a time. Ernst Barlach, a German sculptor turned potter, wrote a book, *Keramik, Stoff und Form* (1908), which influenced the development of ceramics in Germany. The Bohemian sculptor Václav Mařan became professor at the Ceramics School at Bechyně. The growth of such schools shows the increasing status of ceramics. At Teplice, also in Bohemia, there was a famous Ceramic Trade School which in 1898 came under the direction of Robert Stübchen-Kirchner, the painter and architect. In England, the Lambeth School of Art, under John Sparkes, was a nursery for Doulton's. Henri Van de Velde opened a seminar at Weimar in 1902, which later became a school of applied art. The Bauhaus was its direct descendant.

In Copenhagen, Thorvald Bindesbøll, son of Gottlieb Bindesbøll, the architect of the Thorvaldsens Museum, Copenhagen, made ceramics which anticipate modern design more, perhaps, than those of any other *art nouveau* potter. Hermann Kähler's lustre decoration at Nestved, Denmark, and the painting of Carl Mortensen and Gerhard Heilmann on Copenhagen porcelain, all belong to the more austere *art nouveau.* Copenhagen was the least reactionary of the great European factories. Its icy paste, so suitable for models of polar bears, penguins and seagulls, is still in use, and modern Copenhagen models are virtually indistinguishable from those illustrated in Borrmann's *Moderne Keramik* of 1902. Here, too, the Japanese influence was strong: Borrmann illustrates a 'Vase, Moven und Meereswelle, nach einem Motiv des Hokusai gemalt von Arnold Krog (1888)'.[34]

In England, J. C. Cazin, the French landscape painter, worked for Doulton in *sgraffito* techniques which influenced the Barlow sisters and the Martin brothers. At Paris, where he had studied painting under Lecoq-du-Boisbaudran, Rodin's teacher, he had been instructed in potting by Houry of Sèvres. He came to London at the time of the Franco-Prussian War, and set up an art school with his fellow student Legros.

For the historian of *art nouveau*, the collaboration of Dr Christopher Dresser with Henry Tooth at Linthorpe, Middlesbrough-on-Tees, and later at Bretby, Burton-on-Trent, is a fascinating example of theory in practice. Dresser did more than any other Englishman to make Japanese design popular in England, partly by his *Japan, Its Architecture, Art and Art Manufactures* (1882) and his other books on ornament, and partly by importing Japanese works of art for his firm, Dresser and Holme of Farringdon Road, London. The influence of Japanese art is especially apparent in his own silver designs.[35] But in designing ceramics he was more influenced by Peruvian and Mexican wares. Gauguin had fallen under the same influence, as his guardian Gustave Arosa had a collection of pre-Columbian pottery. Here again there is a prophetic suggestion of the 1930s, when Mexican art is a powerful influence on architecture, when men like D. H. Lawrence and Middleton Murry think of Central America as a suitable site for utopias, and Aldous Huxley achieves a more private but more immediate El Dorado with mescalin.

Apart from its importance in art history (which can be overestimated, since Dresser's designs, however well they illustrate his seminal theories, are often undeniably cranky) Linthorpe is socially interesting as the first example of a ceramics factory specifically founded to bring relief to an area hard-hit by industrial depression. In his *Nineteenth-Century English Ceramic Art* (1911), J. F. Blacker wrote:

> Dr Dresser – the well-known architect and ornamentist – when in Middlesbrough some time ago, was struck with the misery then prevailing in the district through the temporary slackness of the iron trade, and, upon seeing clay on the Linthorpe estate, suggested to Mr John Harrison, the owner of the ground, the starting of a Pottery, with the view of giving labour to idle hands, and of alleviating to some extent the misery which prevailed in the district. Mr Harrison at once consented to act on the suggestion, raised the necessary buildings, called to his aid a most efficient manager – Mr Henry Tooth, to whom I owe these notes – and surrounded himself with an excellent and skilled staff of potters; and he also arranged with Dr Dresser that he should become the permanent Art Director of the works.[36]

The foundation of Linthorpe (1880) has more in common with the lavish philanthropic gestures of the Baroness Burdett-Coutts and other Ladies Bountiful than with the socialism of Bernard Shaw or even William Morris. But Dresser was evidently a good radical all round. His radicalism extended to choice of clay. He despised the European factories for insisting on white china – 'they make the mistake,' he said, 'of confusing whiteness with cleanliness.' For his part, he was content to use the common brick-clay of Linthorpe, unadulterated. Possibly, too, this was the first time that Japanese wares, rather than the doctrines of William Morris, had influenced anyone in favour of a natural use of natural materials: Dresser had visited Japan in 1876.

He also insisted that pottery should be made with a view to its setting – the ordinary home:

> Makers of such English pottery as is intended for the decoration of our houses have hitherto erred, to a great extent, in the effort to obtain excellence by introducing too much detail and excessive finish into their works. It must ever be borne in mind that whatever is intended to play a part in the decoration of a room should be so bold in effect, or so 'broad' in treatment, that it can be seen together with the furniture, and other objects when the room is viewed as a whole.[37]

Ceramics, then, were to be more democratic, more adapted for common use. The old division between 'decorative' and 'useful' wares was becoming less distinct. In their self-conscious naked simplicity, Dresser's Linthorpe wares point towards the unashamed appearance of rectilinear form in ceramics in the 1930s. Dresser's aesthetic philosophy is behind the 1930s wares: however unsuitably ceramics might embody the flat-sided form, they must be made in that style to harmonize with the décor of the room. 1930s vases by Midwinter had exactly the shape of cinema wall sconces. Historical pastiche was replaced by a contemporary pastiche.

The breakdown of the old bourgeois distinction between the arts and the crafts, 'fine' and 'applied' art, became complete with the collaboration of André Matthey (1871–1921) with Pierre Bonnard, Maurice Denis, André Derain, Pierre Laprade, Maximilien Luce, Aristide Maillol, Odilon Redon, Georges Rouault, Paul Signac, Cornelius Van Dongen and Maurice Vlaminck. Matthey had begun as a stone mason. While serving as a soldier at Auxerre he came across a handbook on pottery, and decided to become a potter. When he left the army, he set up a kiln and experimented with stoneware, already made popular by Carriès. He exhibited for the first time at the *Salon des Indépendants* in 1901. Then he turned to faience, which offered more scope for painting. He exhibited a collection of ceramics, many decorated by his artist friends, at the *Salon d'Automne* in 1907. These works were signed by the artists and marked with the discreet monogram 'A.M.'. Later, Matthey found that he wanted to express his own ideas in ceramics, and began to work on his own again. (In 1909 he held a successful exhibition of his work at the *Musée Galliera*.) But the old snobbish barrier between the 'pure' artist and the potter was down for good. Picasso is only the best known of the twentieth-century artists who have made pottery a second canvas.

There was a new coalition of potters with architects and engineers. It was not only that tiles were being used more and more for both interior and exterior decoration. Two Parisian firms, Emile Muller and Alexandre Bigot, specialized in architectural ceramics. Muller made a huge frieze and pyramids for the entrance hall of the Palais des Beaux Arts; a statue of Narcissus for the garden of the Musée du Luxembourg; balusters for the first platform of the Eiffel Tower. A. Charpentier, who modelled the Narcissus, also made a small stoneware kiosk for the entrance to the Esplanade des Invalides at the 1900 Paris Exhibition. Charpentier's colossal relief, 'The Baker'[38], was made for the west façade of St Germain des Prés. Bigot's firm also made friezes and plaques for the 1900 Exhibition.[39] Max Läuger of Karlsruhe, himself an engineer and architect, was the most prolific of the interior designers.

Science was revolutionizing the arts as it had not done since the early years of the Industrial Revolution. Seurat and Monet experimented with the spectrum palette. The invention of photography – instantaneous Pre-Raphaelitism at the press of a button – had an effect on painting 'compared with which,' one art historian has claimed, 'the effects of the fall of Constantinople, the genius of Titian or the Council of Trent will appear negligible'.[40] Some artists, such as Ingres[41] and Frith, attempted to rival daguerreotype definition; others, such as Corot[42] and the Impressionists, learnt light effects from the muzzy backgrounds of photographs. Finally, 'artistic' photographers imitated Corot's paintings[43]: an example of 'full circle' analogous to that by which Chinese porcelain painters of the eighteenth century eventually began to imitate European decoration after a long period of European derivation from Chinese wares.[44]

Photography had a wholly unfortunate effect on ceramics. It led to the manufacture of what Mr Geoffrey Godden has christened 'photoceramics'.[45] Dr Helmut Gernsheim, in *The History of Photography* (1955), mentions that an unworked patent for firing photographs was taken out as early as 1849 in the names of Fox Talbot and Thomas Malone.[46] Mr Godden has some marked Minton plates bearing year cyphers of 1884, still with the original paper labels of the Ceramic, Stained Glass and Vitrified Photograph Company, of 19 Finsbury Circus, London, EC. The brown photographic image of a painting transferred to a Dutch vase (Plate 212) mars the unity of the design.

The scientific advances which had most effect on the art of ceramics were those in chemistry. 'I am more of a chemist than most potters,' boasted William De Morgan, 'and more of a potter than most chemists.' But the two studies had always been close. By a decision similar to that of John Philip Elers two centuries before, Alexandre Bigot left his post as *Professeur de Chimie et Physique à l'Ecole Alsacienne* to experiment with pottery, after seeing the Chinese and Japanese wares at the Paris Exhibition of 1889. William Burton of the Royal Lancastrian Pottery studied chemistry in Professor Thorpe's laboratory at the Royal School of Mines. (There he became a friend of H. G. Wells, who later described him as 'Old Burton, Ruskinised, biblical as became a man from John Bright's Manchester, and very eloquent and copious'. Both wore bright red ties and read papers to the Fabian Society.) In 1871 Dimitri Mendeléeff published his *Periodic Table of the Elements*. The elements were placed in the order of their atomic weights in horizontal octaves, the rows being placed under each other with the lightest elements in the top row and the heaviest at the bottom. They were thus grouped both horizontally and vertically. Abraham Lomax, who was an employee at the Royal Lancastrian Pottery (the factory for which Walter Crane designed) at the turn of the century, has shown what Mendeléeff's *Table* meant to the potter:

> I was intensely interested in this periodic table. It made a powerful impression on me. I revelled in Mendeléeff's *Principles of Chemistry* for it was a superb treatise on the subject. I read and studied it with avidity, and, in consequence, became steeped in knowledge of the similarity of elements in the vertical columns. The table was a fine tool for me and I made great use of it and was rewarded beyond my expectations. It led me to think that elements might be substituted for others; for instance, that strontia or baryta could replace lime.... Of course, I was well aware that no two elements are alike in all respects and therefore I should probably find some differences in the products of such substitutions. It was these differences that I sought to find, and the search for them led to great discoveries.[47]

By this method of substitution, new glazes were perfected, more iridescent, less subject to crazing, more glossy, more matt, or more opaque. Similar improvements were being made in the United States. At the Rookwood Pottery, where some fine *art nouveau* wares were made, the glittering crystalline 'Aventurine' glaze was invented in 1884.

The concentration on new glaze effects, on colour and iridescence, reinforced in ceramics the principle of abstraction which emerged from all the complexities of *art nouveau* as its most important legacy to the twentieth century. Gauguin was the first to use the word 'abstraction' in its modern sense, when he said of a self-portrait: 'Le dessin est tout à fait special (abstraction complète) ... Les yeux, la bouche, le nez sont comme des fleurs de *tapis persans*.'[48]

It is again Abraham Lomax of the Royal Lancastrian Pottery who gives us two revealing examples of the new abstraction in force in ceramics. On 14 August 1910 the whole of the British section of the Brussels Exhibition was destroyed by fire. Pilkington's lost several examples of Lancastrian ware. Mr Sheppard, the firm's London area manager, who was on holiday in Belgium, sent back newspapers containing photographs of the ruined buildings showing the bent and twisted steelwork:

> These provided a *motif* for Gordon Forsyth which he developed in the grand manner. He painted a large vase with leaping, surging, swirling tongues of lurid flame licking the distorted girders. It was an exceptionally fine piece of lustre ware, superb with the glow of fires and flames of gorgeous colour.[49]

The other passage also concerns Forsyth:

> As he was responsible for everything pertaining to the art side of the ware, he naturally searched for new clay-shapes. His procedure was to sit beside Radford (the thrower) whilst many small pieces were thrown. Radford called these pieces *twifflers* (trifles); Forsyth called them 'sketches in clay' and from them evoked new shapes.[50]

An almost exact parallel in painting is the *blottesque* method of Cozens, by which blots were thrown at random on to a sheet of paper and then formed into a coherent scene; but since in this case abstraction was the result, perhaps the most apt comparison is with Paul Klee's cheeky manifesto: 'I let a line go for a walk.' An art founded on the arbitrary would be the complete negation of historical precedent. Again we recall Hogarth's *The Analysis of Beauty* and the word with which he epitomized the rococo: 'wanton'.

Notes

I SOCIAL STATUS OF THE POTTER

1 This quotation is taken from an anonymous London translation of 1705 (British Museum 1475.a.69), pp. 29–30. Although there is an excellent translation by Professor Wilmer Wright (University of Chicago Press, 1940), I have preferred the 1705 version because it is so nearly contemporary with Ramazzini's work.
2 *Ibid*, pp. 32–3.
3 *Loc. cit.*
4 *Loc. cit.*
5 *Loc. cit.*
6 *Loc. cit.*
7 *Essai sur les Maladies des Artisans par Ramazzini. Traduit du Latin avec des Notes et des Additions par M. de Fourcroy*, 1834 edn, p. 36n.
8 C. Turner Thackrah, *The Effects of the Principal Arts, Trades and Professions ... on Health and Longevity*, 1831, p. 59.
9 J. T. Arlidge, *Hygiene, Diseases and Mortality of Occupations*, 1892, p. 312.
10 *Ibid.*, p. 310.
11 *Ibid.*, p. 313.
12 *Ibid.*, p. 317.
13 *Ibid.*, p. 318.
14 By W. B. Honey, *Transactions of the English Ceramic Circle*, No. 2, 1934, p. 8.
15 Simeon Shaw, *History of the Staffordshire Potteries*, 1829, p. 119.
16 Published in *Memoirs of George Elers, 1777–1842*, 1903, p. 278. Perhaps it is to the same picture that reference is made in the *Memoirs* of Richard Lovell Edgeworth, 1820, i, 78–9: 'Paul Elers Esq. [John Philip's son, and Edgeworth's father-in-law] was descended from a German family of some opulence. How or why the family of Elerses came into England I know not; but I know, that some of them were favourites of the Elector of Mentz, of whom they had several pictures; I remember one in particular, that had been dismantled of some diamonds, which, from their setting, were probably of great value.'
17 Published in *Memoirs of George Elers, 1777–1842*, 1903, p. 285.
18 Lady Holland, *A Memoir of the Rev. Sydney Smith*, 1855, ii, 202–3.
19 *Ibid.*, ii, 220.
20 James Boswell, *Life of Samuel Johnson*, 1824 edn, iii, 325.
21 Ramazzini, *op. cit.*, p. 32.

22 *Vide*, Flaubert, *Sentimental Education*, 1964 edn, p. 120:
'It may have been the thought of Madame Arnoux which made him stop outside a second-hand dealer's shop, at the sight of three china plates. They were decorated with yellow arabesques, with a metallic sheen, and they cost three hundred francs apiece. He had them put on one side.
' "If I were you," said Deslauriers, "I'd prefer to buy myself some silver plate." '

23 W. Cooke Taylor, 'Notes on the Application of the Arts of Design to Manufacturing Industry in France: Sèvres', *Art Union Monthly Journal*, vol. ix, 1847, p. 113.

24 From *The Escorial* (1860) by G. M. Hopkins. See *Poems of Gerard Manley Hopkins*, ed. W. H. Gardner, 1956 edn, p. 14.

25 See also Longfellow's poem *Keramos*, which contrasts Palissy's humble situation with his moral nobility. (*The Poetical Works of Longfellow*, 1916 edn, p. 725.)

26 Moncure Daniel Conway, *Travels in South Kensington*, 1882, p. 59.

27 Simeon Shaw, *History of the Staffordshire Potteries*, 1829, pp. 108–9.

28 *Ibid.*, pp. 128–9.

29 Conway, *op. cit.*, pp. 59–60.

30 Arthur Lane, *Italian Porcelain*, 1954, p. 45.

31 Simeon Shaw, *op. cit.*, p. 229.

32 Voltaire, *Letters Concerning the English Nation*, ed. Charles Whibley, 1926 edn, pp. 5–6.

33 John Houghton, FRS, *A Collection for Improvement of Husbandry and Trade*, No. 189, 13 March 1695–6, p. 1.

34 See B. Hillier, *The Turners of Lane End*, 1965, pp. 84–5.

35 Dr John Moore, *A Journal During a Residence in France*, 1794, i, 10.

36 See Siegfried Ducret, *German Porcelain and Faience*, 1962, pp. 17–18.

37 *Selected Letters of Josiah Wedgwood*, ed. Ann Finer and George Savage, 1965, pp. 75–6.

38 See *The Diary of Sylas Neville, 1767–1788*, ed. Basil Cozens-Hardy, 1950, p. 9:
'Mon. Jun. 1.1767. Went to James St, Golden Square to see some white Dresden china with hawks, herons etc. engraved by Baron Burt [*sic*: perhaps an editor's misreading] Canon of Hildersheim [*sic*], who is the only person that possesses the art.'

39 See C. A. A. Disbrowe, *Old Days in Diplomacy*, 1903, p. 179.

40 Dorothy Margaret Stuart, *The Daughters of George III*, 1939, pp. 37–8.

41 See *The Connoisseur*, November 1901, for an illustration of this service.

42 Quoted in *Selections from the Letters and Correspondence of Sir James Bland Burges, Bart.*, ed. James Hutton, 1885, p. 295.

43 Quoted *loc. cit.*

44 See Geoffrey Wills, 'Pots for Painting', *Proceedings of the Wedgwood Society*, No. 3, 1959, p. 152.

45 China-painting was also popular in America. See Katharine Morrison McClinton, 'American Hand-Painted China', *The Spinning Wheel*, April 1967, pp. 10–12.

46 On Stacy Marks, see B. Hillier, 'The St. John's Wood Clique', *Apollo*, June 1964, pp. 490–5.

47 William Owen, *Songs of Labour*, 1884. Quoted by his son, Harold Owen, opposite the title page of *The Staffordshire Potter*, 1901.

2 THE END OF THE BAROQUE

1 In 1644, while in Rome, John Evelyn wrote in his diary: 'Bernini ... gave a Publique Opera ... where in he painted the scenes, cut the Statues, invented the Engines, composed the Musique, writ the Comedy & built the Theater all himselfe.' (*The Diary of John Evelyn*, ed. E. S. de Beer, 1955, ii, 261.)

2 Rudolf Wittkower, *Art and Architecture in Italy, 1600–1750*, 1958, p. 178.

3 Mr John Mallet of the Victoria and Albert Museum has made a study of the Fiammingo variants and derivations, and I am very much indebted to him for information on this subject.
4 The *St. Andrew* is illustrated by Arthur Lane, *Italian Porcelain*, 1954, Plate 58.
5 A white Meissen example is illustrated by George Savage, *Porcelain Through the Ages*, 1961 edn, Plate 20a.
6 R. Nisbet Bain, 'Poland and the Saxon Kings', *Cambridge Modern History*, 1909 edn, p. 198.
7 *The Works of Sir Charles Hanbury Williams*, 1822, ii, 211–12.
8 Eberhard Hempel, *Baroque Art and Architecture in Central Europe*, 1965, p. 72.
9 Illustrated by Sponsel, *Der Zwinger*, 1924.
10 Hempel, *op. cit.*, p. 201.
11 Quoted by Klaus Lankheit, *Florentinische Barockplastik*, 1962, p. 136.
12 Illustrated by Arthur Lane, *Italian Porcelain*, 1954, Plate 56.
13 Three of the porcelain figures – Spring, Summer and Winter – are illustrated by Lankheit, *op. cit.*, Plates 167–9.
14 Quoted by W. B. Honey, *Dresden China*, 1934, p. 20.
15 Not Amsterdam, as given by Honey, *op. cit.*, p. 46.
16 See Peter Thornton, *Baroque and Rococo Silks*, 1965, p. 141n.
17 Eberhard Hempel, *op. cit.*, p. 193.
18 B.M.Add.MSS.34, 788, p. 51. (Transcript of Victoria and Albert Museum copy.)
19 See Harold Newman, 'Reveille for Veilleuses', *Apollo*, February and March 1955, pp. 35–9, and 71–5. Also his book *Veilleuses* (1967).
20 See Siegfried Ducret, 'Bourdalous', *Bulletin de la Société des Amis de la Céramique Suisse (Freunde der Schveizer Keramik)*, December, 1953, pp. 15–17.
21 See E. S. Auscher's chapter on 'L'Hygiène à la Cour du Grand Roi' in his *La Céramique au Château de Versailles sous Louis XIV*, 1903. I am also indebted to N. M. Penzer, 'The Silver Chamber Pot', Part ii, *The Antique Collector*, December 1958, pp. 228–9.
22 See Arthur Lane, *French Faience*, 1948, p. 19.
23 Quoted Eberhard Hempel, *op. cit.*, p. 10.
24 *Op. cit.*, p. 31.

3 PORCELAIN

1 John Goldsmith Phillips, *China Trade Porcelain*, 1956, Plates 37 and 38.
2 Michel Beurdeley, *Porcelain of the East India Companies*, 1962, Figs. 60 and 61, Plate XIV, Figs. 80 and 82.
3 Sir Algernon Tudor-Craig, *Armorial Porcelain of the Eighteenth Century*, 1925, discusses these services.
4 *Ibid.*, p. 17.
5 See Jean McClure Mudge, *Chinese Export Porcelain for the American Trade, 1735–1835*, 1962.
6 See Bredo Grandjean, *Dansk Ostindinsk Porcelaen Importen fra Kanton ca. 1700–1822*, 1965.
7 See J. A. Lloyd Hyde and others, *Chinese Porcelain for the European Market*, 1946.
8 A brief account of the raising of the ships and of their contents is given in *The Sunday Times* (London), 18 December 1966.
9 Michel Beurdeley, *op. cit.*, Plate XIX.
10 *Ibid.*, Fig. 70.
11 *Ibid.*, p. 119.
12 Cosmo Monkhouse, *Chinese Porcelain*, 1901, Fig. 47.
13 See 'Recollections of a Lecturer', *Apollo*, February 1942, p. 58.
14 Stendhal, *Le Rouge et Le Noir*, trans. Margaret R. B. Shaw, 1953, p. 376.
15 At p. 35.

Notes for pages 68–89

16 J. Ovington, MA, An *Essay upon the Nature & Qualities of Tea*, ed. Augustine Birrell, 1928, p. 2.

17 Duncan Forbes, *On the State of the Revenue of Scotland*, quoted in *The Culloden Papers*, ed. Duff, 1815, pp. 192–3. In *The Culloden Papers* this memorial is dated 'about 1742', but Mr George Menary points out (*The Life and Letters of Duncan Forbes of Culloden*, 1936, p. 143n.) that Tweedale's reply of 17 February 1743 proves that it was written on 1 January 1743.

18 Jonas Hanway, *Essay on Tea*, 1757, ii, 272.

19 *Op. cit.*, ii, 75.

20 Samuel Johnson, Review of Hanway's Journal and Essay on Tea, *Works of Samuel Johnson*, ed. Robert Lynam, 1825, v, 653.

21 Agnes Repplier, *To Think of Tea!*, 1933, p. 61.

22 John Galt, *Annals of the Parish*, Everyman edn, 1926, p. 11.

23 *A Frenchman in England, 1784. Being the Mélanges sur l'Angleterre of François de la Rochefoucauld.* Ed. from the MSS. by Jean Marchand, trans. S. C. Roberts, 1933, op. 23.

24 For tea importation figures, see Elizabeth Boody Schumpeter, *English Overseas Trade Statistics, 1697–1808*, 1960, pp. 52–5.

25 For information on tea taxes, I am indebted to Frank Tilley, *Teapots and Tea*, 1957, p. 79 *et seq.*

26 Gervas Huxley, *Tea in Porcelain.*

27 Duncan Campbell, *A Poem on Tea*, 1735, p. 17.

28 John, Lord Hervey, *Political Epistle to the Queen on her Commanding Lord Hervey to Write no More*, 1736. Quoted, John, Lord Hervey, *Memoirs of the Reign of George the Second*, 1884 edn, ii, 326.

29 *Reminiscences and Recollections of Captain Gronow*, 1892 edn, i, 284–5.

30 *The Diary of John Hervey, First Earl of Bristol*, 1894 edn, p. 136.

31 *Court and Private Life in the Time of Queen Charlotte; Mrs. Papendiek's Journals*, 1887, i, 181. Attention was first drawn to this reference by Geoffrey Wills, in *Apollo.*

32 Quoted by G. Schiedlausky, *Tee, Kaffee, Schokolade*, 1961, p. 19.

33 William Prescott, *The Conquest of Mexico*, quoted by Arthur Knapp, *The Cocoa and Chocolate Industry*, 1930, p. 16.

34 Quoted by Baron Davillier in his Preface to the 1870 edn of Pierre de Frasnay's poem *La Fayence*, pp. 8–9.

35 *Ibid.*, p. 10.

36 Edmond Barbier, *Chronique de la Régence et du Règne de Louis XV*, 1857 edn, vii, 200–1.

37 Tallement des Reaux, 'L'Archévèque de Reims', *Historiettes*, 1834 edn, ii, 198.

38 The affinities of early Chelsea porcelain with silver are discussed by Arthur Lane, *English Porcelain Figures of the Eighteenth Century*, 1961, pp. 57–9.

39 Nancy Mitford, *Voltaire in Love*, 1957, pp. 239–40. (An accurate paraphrase of Longchamp and Wagnière, *Mémoires sur Voltaire*, 1826, ii, 195–7.)

40 See M. Kayserling, *Moses Mendelssohn, Sein Leben und Seine Werke*, 1862, p. 268; A. H. Japp, *German Life and Literature*, 1880, p. 184; and A. H. Japp, *Industrial Curiosities*, 1880, p. 106.

41 See Sotheby's catalogue, 12 October 1965, Lot 91.

42 See Constance Hill, *Juniper Hall*, 1904.

43 Augustus Hare, *The Story of My Life*, 1896, ii, 58.

44 See B. Hillier, 'A Unique Copeland Chimneypiece', *The Connoisseur*, January 1966, p. 32.

4 THE ROCOCO

1 William Hogarth, *The Analysis of Beauty*, ed. Joseph Burke, 1955, p. 159.

2 H. Butterfield, *Napoleon*, 1939, p. 16.

3 Arno Schönberger and Halldor Soehner, *The Age of Rococo*, 1960, p. 8.

4 Voltaire, *Letters Concerning the English Nation*, ed. Charles Whibley, 1926, p. 98.
5 Quoted by Fiske Kimball, *The Creation of the Rococo*, 1943, p. 107.
6 M. E. J. Délécluze, *Louis David, Son Ecole et Son Temps*, 1855, p. 82n.
7 Kimball, *op. cit.*, p. 155.
8 The late W. B. Honey made a detailed study of the use of engravings by potters (*European Ceramic Art*, 1952, pp. 201–4), and I am much indebted to this work.
9 Schönberger and Soehner, *op. cit.*, p. 7.
10 In his introduction to Hogarth's *Analysis of Beauty*, 1955, p. xx.
11 *Op. cit.*, p. 36.
12 *Ibid.*, p. 42.
13 *Ibid.*, p. 59.
14 *Ibid.*, p. 132.
15 See John Mallet, 'Hogarth's Pug in Porcelain', *Victoria and Albert Museum Bulletin*, April 1967, vol. ii, No. 2, pp. 45–54.
16 W. B. Honey, *German Porcelain*, 1947, p. 9.
17 Hogarth, *op. cit.*, p. 62.
18 Quoted by R. Pfnor, *Receuil d'Estampes Relatives à l'ornementation des Appartements*, 1871, p. 67.
19 See Hellmuth Vriesen, 'Neue Theaterkupfer Aus Der Werkstatt von Martin Engelbrecht,' *Maske und Kothurn*, vi, 1960, pp. 276–9.
20 An essay in *The World* of 8 February 1753, first quoted in this connection by the late Mrs Arundell Esdaile, in *The Observer*, 22 June 1924.
21 *Loc. cit.*
22 James Woodforde, *The Diary of a Country Parson*, ed. John Beresford, 1931, p. 92. (4 September 1783.)
23 Quoted by George Savage, *Seventeenth and Eighteenth Century German Porcelain*, 1960, pp. 132–3.
24 *The Diary of John Evelyn*, ed. E. S. de Beer, 1959, p. 284. (25 March 1650.)
25 Quoted by Hugh Honour, *Chinoiserie*, 1961, p. 54.

5 FOLK POTTERY

1 At p. vi.
2 Walter Sickert, *A Free House*, ed. Osbert Sitwell, 1947, p. 48.
3 See Chapter 13, pp. 298–9.
4 Josef Vydra, *Painting on Folk Ceramics*, 1950, pp. 27–8.
5 André Malraux, *The Voices of Silence*, trans. Stuart Gilbert, 1954, p. 287.
6 Bernard Rackham and Herbert Read, *English Pottery*, 1924, p. 22.
7 *Ibid.*, p. 21.
8 Vydra, *op. cit.*, p. 24.
9 *Op. cit.*, pp. 26–8.
10 See Arthur Lane, *French Faience*, 1948, p. 35.
11 This kind of jar is also the subject of Pirandello's short story *La giara* ('The Jar'), first published in the *Corriere della sera* of 20 October 1909. See Luigi Pirandello, *Short Stories*, ed. Frederick May, 1965, pp. 80–91.
12 Vydra, *op. cit.*, p. 17.
13 William Shakespeare, *King Henry VI*, Part II, Act iv, scene ii.
14 Ralph Thoresby, *Diary*, ed. Joseph Hunter, 1830, ii, 168.
15 Illustrated by Reginald Haggar, *Staffordshire Chimney Ornaments*, 1955, Plate 14.
16 See *ibid.*, Colour Plate 5, and pp. 91, 92, 94, 112 and 126.
17 See B. Hillier, *Master Potters of the Industrial Revolution; The Turners of Lane End*, 1965, Plates 17a and 17b, and pp. 10, 14 and 18.

18 See *Good Words*, 1 March 1869.

19 Though it must be added that Gladstone exaggerated the significance of the 'Beer and Bible' alliance: see H. J. Hanham, *Elections and Party Management*, 1959, pp. 221–5.

20 See B. Hillier, 'Mrs Graham Greene's Collection of Dolls' Houses', *Apollo*, January 1963, p. 26.

21 T. E. Lawrence, *Seven Pillars of Wisdom*, 1964 edn, p. 447.

6 WEDGWOOD, NEO-CLASSICISM AND THE INDUSTRIAL REVOLUTION

1 Probably William Chatterton, described in Poll Books of 1754 and 1774 as a potter; he was apprenticed to Richard Frank on 14 November 1741. (W. J. Pountney, *Old Bristol Potteries*, 1920, p. 202.)

2 Quoted by E. H. W. Meyerstein, *A Life of Thomas Chatterton*, 1930, p. 23. Meyerstein plausibly suggests in a manuscript note in a British Museum copy of this book (Ref: 10858.f.28) that 'The child had probably seen the large engraving (W. H. Toms after James Starvart 1745) of the South Prospect of St. Mary Redcliff, where an angel with a trumpet in the [*word indecipherable*] points with a quill to the [*word indecipherable*] name on a scroll inscribed THIS/ /FABRICK/was/FOUNDED/BY/Simon/de Barton/1292.' Meyerstein further adds: 'This detail does not appear in Halfpenny's smaller version of the same, that which Chatterton is supposed to have seen. Simon de Barton is the hero of the Rowley poem called "The Tournament".'

Another possibility, however, is that Chatterton had seen the Worcester King of Prussia mug, actually dated 1757 – the year his own delft cup was painted – which bears a transfer print of Fame – an angel with two trumpets. (See Cyril Cook, *The Life and Work of Robert Hancock*, 1948, Item 56.)

3 See Thomas Bateman, *Antiquities of Lomberdale*, 1855, p. 297.

4 'A correspondent of Willis's Current Notes writes: "Howell, who wrote the introduction to the Life and Adventures of Alexander Selkirk, printed in Edinburgh in 1829, discovered Selkirk's grand-nephew in the person of John Selcrag, a teacher at Canon Mills, near Edinburgh. He was in possession of two relics which had formerly belonged to Selkirk – a walking-stick and his flip-can, which was of brown stoneware, holding a pint. It was inscribed:

> Alexander Selkirke, this is my one [own],
> When you take me on bord of ship,
> Pray fill me full with punch of flipp.
> Fulham.

This stone-ware jug was obtained from the Fulham Pottery about the middle of 1703, while waiting for the equipment and sailing of the Cinque Ports galley, to which he had been appointed sailing-master, and doubtless accompanied him on his voyage to Juan Fernandez, and was highly venerated in the family; it was kept locked up for fifty years by one of his nieces." ' (Annie Trumbull Slosson, *The China Hunters' Club*, 1878, p. 54.)

5 James Orton's Memoirs of the late Reverend Dr Philip Doddridge, prefacing *The Works of the Rev. P. Doddridge, D.D.*, 1802, i, p. 18.

6 *Intimate Society Letters of the Eighteenth Century*, ed. Duke of Argyll, 1910, i, 81.

7 Sheridan Le Fanu, *Uncle Silas*, 1904 edn, pp. 381–2.

8 Edward Gibbon, *Autobiography*, ed. Bernard Groom, 1930, p. 127.

9 Flaxman to Romney, 25 May 1788. (Quoted by W. G. Constable, *John Flaxman*, 1927 p. 32.)

10 Quoted *ibid.*, pp. 33–4.

11 Quoted by David Irwin, *English Neo-Classical Art*, 1966, p. 59.

12 Wedgwood to Bentley, 12 September 1776. (WMSS.E.18693–25.)

13 Wedgwood to Bentley, 19 June 1779. (WMSS.E.18898–26.)
14 See Alison Kelly, *Decorative Wedgwood*, 1965, Plates 44 and 45.
15 Gibbon to Sheffield, 12 September 1792. (*Letters of Edward Gibbon*, ed. J. E. Norton, 1956, iii, 271.)
16 See p. 78.
17 Wedgwood to Bentley, 2 August 1770. (WMSS.E.18314–25.)
18 Wedgwood to Bentley, 16 October 1778. (WMSS.E.18855–26.)
19 Quoted by D. Marshall, 'London and the Life of the Town', in *Johnson's England*, ed. A. S. Turbeville, 1933, i, 187.
20 Quoted by Alison Kelly, *op. cit.*, p. 90.
21 Wedgwood to Bentley, 1771. (Quoted by Alison Kelly, *op. cit.*, p. 58.)
22 Wedgwood to Bentley, 14 January 1775. (Quoted by W. G. Constable, *John Flaxman*, 1927, p. 8.)
23 This letter is reproduced, with the sketch, in the *Art Journal*, 1912, p. 83.
24 Most valuable work has recently been done on the Herculaneum factory by Mr Alan Smith of the Liverpool Museum, who has been very generous in giving me information incorporated in the passage which follows.
25 See B. Hillier, *Master Potters of the Industrial Revolution; The Turners of Lane End*, 1965, pp. 81–2, note 30.
26 See *loc. cit.*
27 For a 'Pergolesi suite' see Byron Webber, *James Orrock, R.I., Painter, Connoisseur, Collector*, 1903, ii, Plates facing pages 18 and 28.
28 Arthur Young, *Travels in France, etc.*, ed. Thomas Okey, 1934, p. 249.
29 Arthur Lane, *Italian Porcelain*, 1954, p. 62.
30 Walter Pater, 'Winckelmann', *The Renaissance*, ed. Sir Kenneth Clark, 1964, p. 193.
31 See W. B. Honey, *European Ceramic Art*, 1952, p. 417.
32 See Siegfried Ducret, *German Porcelain*, 1962, Plate 104.
33 On Rambouillet, see Johannes Langner, 'Architecture Pastorale sous Louis XVI', *Art de France*, 1963, 171–86.
34 On Raincy, see Jean Feray, 'A Wedgwood Dairy in a French Collection', *The Connoisseur*, August 1957, p. 21.
35 On the Brocklesby and Lady Spencer diaries, see Alison Kelly, *Decorative Wedgwood*, 1965, pp. 121, 122, 129 and Plates 58, 60 and 61.
36 Wedgwood to Bentley, 9 April 1773. (WMSS.E.18455–25.)
37 *Loc. cit.*
38 Quoted by Cyril Cook, *The Life and Work of Robert Hancock*, 1948, pp. 63–4. The mug to which Carlyle referred is now in the British Museum.

7 THE FRENCH REVOLUTION

1 An attempt at this subject has been made by H. T. Parker in his *The Cult of Antiquity and the French Revolutionaries* (1937). Mr Parker mentions two contemporary writers who acknowledged the classical influence, Regnaud de Saint-Angély and Volney. The Rev. John Chetwode Eustace comments unfavourably on it in his *Letter from Paris* (1814, p. 49). But the most brilliant discussion of the topic is by Karl Marx in *The Eighteenth Brumaire of Louis Bonaparte*, first published in 1852. It is also the subject of an essay by Harold Rosenberg, 'The Resurrected Romans', in *The Tradition of the New*, 1959, pp. 154–77.
2 See Thomas Hobbes, *Leviathan*, ed. Michael Oakeshott, 1957, pp. 140–41, and 214.
3 Act iii, scene i.
4 See H. Morse Stephens, *Orators of the French Revolution*, 1892, i, 413.
5 On the work of this terracotta sculptor, whose kiln may still be seen at the Château de Chaumont, see A. Villers, *Jean-Baptiste Nini; ses Terres Cuites* (1862).

6 E. Bersot, *Etudes sur le XVIIIe siècle*, 1855, p. 65. Champfleury confirms this story (*Faïences Patriotiques*, 1875 edn, p. 57); he had met 'un vieillard qui me disait la tenir du peintre à qui le vase avait été commandé. Il me citait même le nom de l'artiste.'

7 Arthur Young, *Travels in France, etc.*, ed. Thomas Okey, 1934 edn, p. 83.

8 Chavagnac and Grollier, *Histoire des Manufactures Françaises de Porcelaine*, 1906, p. 216.

9 *Ibid.*, p. 220.

10 See Verlet, 'Le Grand Service de Sèvres du Roi Louis XVI', *Faenza*, N 4–6, 1948, pp. 120–21. Also the *Catalogue of the Bearsted Collection; Porcelain; Upton House*, prepared by Mr John Mallet, who kindly drew my attention to this material.

11 Champfleury, *op. cit.*, p. 368.

12 *Ibid.*, p. vi.

13 'Plusieurs de nos artistes français, dans les peintures, les sculptures et les gravures nombreuses qui se sont faites depuis le commencement de la révolution, se sont servis de la forme du bonnet phrygien, pour décorer la tête de la figure même de la Liberté. Séduits par le galbe recherché de ce bonnet efféminé, que les monumens antiques nous ont conservé sur les têtes gracieuses des Paris et des Ganimède, ils n'ont pas réfléchi que rien n'est moins fait pour désigner la liberté que le bonnet phrygien; que c'est une coëffure d'Asie; que jamais la liberté n'habita ces contrées; que la partie asiatique de la Grèce même n'avoit pu conserver la sienne, et que les rois esclaves, exposés aux arcs-de-triomphe de Rome, sont coëffés d'un bonnet presque semblable.' (A. E. Gibelin, Peintre d'Histoire, *De l'Origine et la Forme du Bonnet de la Liberté*, L'an IV de la République, p. 24.)

14 Quoted Champfleury, *op. cit.*, p. 205.

15 For other ceramics commemorating Wilkes, see G. Wooliscroft Rhead, 'Wilkes and Liberty', *The Connoisseur*, No. 48, 1917, p. 149.

Incidentally, Wilkes, like Robespierre, did not believe in dressing or living like *sans-culottes*. He was a famous dandy. His taste in ceramics was not austere. On 29 May 1770, he wrote to his daughter, 'I wish you to inquire about China handles of St. Cloud porcelain for knives and forks, and the price. I would purchase three dozen of the large sort, both knives and forks, and two dozen for the desert, if they do not come too dear, and have them mounted in England.' (John Almon, *Correspondence and Life of John Wilkes*, 1805, iv, 34.) On 12 June 1770 he wrote to her again on the same subject, 'When I mentioned St. Cloud, it was by inadvertence; I meant Seve, to which place, as I remember, the manufacture of Vincennes is removed.' (*Ibid.*, iv, 49.) In his will, he left quantities of Wedgwood ware to his daughters (see *ibid.*, v, 91.)

16 Illustrated by Champfleury, *op. cit.*, Plate 12.

17 Edmund Burke, *Reflexions on the French Revolution*, 1929 edn, p. 7.

18 See Champfleury, *op. cit.*, p. 376.

19 *Loc. cit.*

20 See Arthur Young, *Travels in France, etc.*, ed. Constantia Maxwell, 1929, p. 324.

21 George Rudé, *The Crowd in the French Revolution*, 1959, p. 43.

22 'La Bastille et les Faienciers', *La Révolution Française*, 1881, i, 115–22.

23 Wedgwood to Darwin, July 1789. (*Correspondence of Josiah Wedgwood, 1781–94*, ed. Lady Farrer, 1906, p. 92.)

24 *Ibid.*, p. 96.

25 See B. Hillier, *Master Potters of the Industrial Revolution: The Turners of Lane End*, 1965, Chapter VII.

26 Geoffrey Wills, 'John Flight of Worcester', *The Connoisseur*, No. 119, 1947, p. 92.

27 An exception to English conservatism and anti-Revolution feeling was John Hurford Stone, who went to Paris in 1792, and was active in support of the Girondins. As a partner of Athenase Coquerel and of François-Antoine Legros d'Anisy, he was responsible for introducing transfer-printing in French ceramics, on the class of wares from various factories loosely known as 'Creil wares' because Creil was the first factory in the field. (See

Dictionary of National Biography, 'John Hurford Stone'; and Cynthia Postan, 'Political Exile and Ceramic Pioneer', *Antique Collector*, April 1960, pp. 68–73.)

28 Abbé Cochet, *Galerie Dieppoise*, 1862, p. 108.

29 Quoted Champfleury, *op. cit.*, p. 320.

30 See Serge Grandjean, 'Napoleonic Tables from Sèvres', *The Connoisseur*, No. 143, 1959, p. 151.

31 See Serge Grandjean, 'The Wellington-Napoleonic Relics', *The Connoisseur*, No. 143, 1959, pp. 223–30.

8 NORTH AMERICA

1 See Warren E. Cox, *The Book of Pottery and Porcelain*, 1945, ii, 979.

2 Discovered by Gilbert Cope of West Chester, Pa., and published by E. A. Barber, *The Pottery and Porcelain of the United States*, 1901 edn, p. 54.

3 Gabriel Thomas, *Historical Account ... of Pensilvania*, 1698, p. 29.

4 Arthur W. Clement, *Our Pioneer Potters*, 1947, pp. 2–3.

5 Llewellyn Jewitt, *The Ceramic Art of Great Britain*, 1878 edn, i, 134.

6 Dewilde seems to have remained in America after the Coxe pottery closed. The name of John Dewilde, 'Pot-maker', appears in a list of freemen of New York City under the date of 18 January 1697–8. The estate of John Dewilde of Doctors Creek, Monmouth County, New Jersey, was inventoried on 26 April 1704. (Clement, *op. cit.*, pp. 3, 4, 7 and 9.)

7 Discovered by John D. McCormick of Trenton, and published by E. A. Barber, *op. cit.*, p. 55.

8 Quoted by Harold Donaldson Eberlein and Roger Wearne Ramsdell, *The Practical Book of Chinaware*, 1948, p. 28.

9 Francis S. Drake, *Tea Leaves*, Boston, 1884. (No copy in British Museum.)

10 'In Camden, New Jersey, is still preserved the little Oriental china tea set, with decorations in underglaze blue and red, from which William Penn drank when he went to have tea with Friend Cooper; that fixes the date not later than 1701, when Penn went back to England, never to return to his "Holy Experiment".' (Eberlein and Ramsdell, *op. cit.*, p. 68. Three pieces from the tea-set are illustrated by them, at Plate 119b.)

11 See Esther Forbes, *Paul Revere and the World he Lived in*, 1942, pp. 380–2.

12 *Loc. cit.*

13 *Colonial Records of Georgia*, i, 427–8.

14 *Ibid.*, v, 139, 141.

15 *Ibid.*, v, 196.

16 *Ibid.*, xxii, Part 2, p. 291.

17 *Ibid.*, iv, Supp., p. 169.

18 *Ibid.*, iv, Supp., p. 205.

19 *Ibid.*, iv, Supp., p. 220.

20 *Ausfuehrliche Nachrichten von den Saltzburgischen Emigranten*, Halle, 1743, ix, 1148. Discovered by G. A. R. Goyle (Rudolph P. Hommel) who has written on Duché in *Chronicles of the Early American Industries*, vol. i, Nos. 9, 10 and 11, November 1934 to May 1935.

21 *Colonial Records of Georgia*, i, 428.

22 *Ibid.*, i, 427.

23 *Ibid.*, xxiv, 341.

24 The patent is quoted in full by Llewellyn Jewitt, *The Ceramic Art of Great Britain*, 1878 edn, i, 112.

25 P. J. B. Du Halde was a Jesuit missionary, whose *Description ... de l'empire de Chine*, published at Paris in 1735 and in English translation at London in 1738, contained a description of the composition and manufacture of Chinese porcelain.

26 Presumably the East India Company.

27 John Prideaux, *Relics of William Cookworthy*, 1853, p. 12.
28 *Diary of the First Earl of Egmont*, ii, 230, 15 November 1741.
29 Robert Dossie, *Handmaid to the Arts*, 1758, ii, 338.
30 Quoted Barber, *op. cit.*, p. 91.
31 *Loc. cit.*
32 Discovered by Charles Henry Hart of Philadelphia and published by E. A. Barber, *op. cit.*, pp. 91–2.
33 Quoted *ibid.*, p. 93.
34 Quoted by Arthur W. Clement, *op. cit.*, p. 61.
35 *Loc. cit.*
36 The petition is given in full by Barber, *op. cit.*, pp. 93–5.
37 Quoted by Clement, *op. cit.*, p. 61.
38 In their petition to the Pennsylvania Assembly, Bonnin and Morris said they had 'expended great Sums in bringing from London Workmen of acknowledged Abilities....' (Barber, *op. cit.*, p. 94.)
39 Against this, Josiah Wedgwood, in his *Address to the Workmen in the Pottery on the Subject of Entering into the Service of Foreign Manufacturers* (1783, p. 8), refers to eight Staffordshire workmen who went over to the Philadelphia factory.
40 I am indebted to Mr Hugh Tait who arranged for these pieces to be examined.
41 Quoted by Barber, *op. cit.*, pp. 99–100.
42 See Moon, *The Morris Family of Philadelphia.*
43 Quoted by E. A. Barber, *op. cit.*, p. 96.
44 *Loc. cit.*
45 Quoted by Arthur Clement, *op. cit.*, p. 62.
46 *Ibid.*, p. 64.
47 Quoted by William Flinn Rogers, 'Life in East Tennessee near End of Eighteenth Century', *Publications of the East Tennessee Historical Society*, 1929, i, 29.
48 *Records of the Moravians of North Carolina*, ed. Adelaide L. Fries (quoted by Carl Bridenbaugh, *The Colonial Craftsmen*, 1961, p. 28.)
49 *Loc. cit.*
50 Quoted by Eliza Meteyard, *Life of Josiah Wedgwood*, 1866, ii, 475.
51 Wedgwood to Thomas Bentley, 3 March 1778. (*Selected Letters of Josiah Wedgwood*, ed. Ann Finer and George Savage, 1965, p. 217.)
52 Presumably at Bonnin and Morris's Southwark factory.
53 In the *Boston Evening Post* of 15 May 1769, appeared an advertisement asking for samples of white clays and fine white sand, to be submitted for examination. On 16 October of the same year, the following advertisement appeared:

> 'Wanted immediately at the new Factory in New Boston, four Boys for Apprentices to learn the Art of making Tortoise shell, Cream and Green Colour Plates, Dishes, Coffee and Tea Pots, Cups and Saucers, and all other Articles in the Potter's Business, equal to any imported from England.' (Quoted by Eberlein and Ramsdell, *The Practical Book of Chinaware*, 1948, p. 294.)

54 Perhaps a reference to Duché's factory at Savannah, of which earthenware was the main product.
55 Possibly the factory set up by Bartlem, the Staffordshire potter, in 1766.
56 Lord Sheffield (J. B. Holroyd), *Observations on the Commerce of the American States*, 1784, p. 21.
57 Quoted by Eberlein and Ramsdell, *op. cit.*, pp. 73–4.
58 See William G. Keener, 'Ohio Potters and Potteries', *The Spinning Wheel*, July-August 1963, p. 47.
59 These included a pitcher modelled by Josiah Jones in 1861 to commemorate the shooting of Colonel E. E. Ellsworth at Alexandria, Va., during his attempt to tear down the Confederate flag from a building. This piece is illustrated by Barber, *op. cit.*, p. 452.

60 A full description of the service is given by Mrs Annie Trumbull Slosson, in *The China Hunters' Club* (1878) and by E. A. Barber, *op. cit.*, pp. 190–91.
61 George Ward Nichols, *Pottery: How it is made*, 1878, p. 87.
62 Quoted by Eberlein and Ramsdell, *op. cit.*, p. 34.
63 *Loc. cit.*
64 From a letter written by Cartlidge to Mr Geoffrey Godden, and quoted by that author in *Antique China and Glass under £5*, 1966, p. 70. The italics are mine.

9 MARKETING

1 See Maurice Keen, *The Outlaws of Medieval Legend*, 1961, pp. 18–19, 23–4, 56, 73, 116–18, 131, 146 and 216.
2 Dr Robert Plot, *Natural History of Staffordshire*, 1686, p. 124.
3 John Byng, *A Tour of the North*, 18 June 1792.
4 *The Life of Thomas Holcroft*, ed. Elbridge Colby, 1925, i, 29–30.
5 *Ibid.*, i, 33.
6 The belligerent potter-pedlar in the ballad of *Robin Hood and the Potter* refused to pay toll to the outlaw, and won his respect by beating him in a fight:

And ar Roben meyt get het agen,
Hes bokeler at hes feete,
The potter yn the neke hem toke,
To the gronde sone he yede.

That saw Roben hes men,
As thay stode ender a bow;
Let us helpe owr master, seyed Lyttel John,
Yonder potter els well hem sclo.

7 Noah Heath (born *c.* 1780) is the subject of an essay by Henry Wedgwood, *Romance of Staffordshire*, ii, 101.
8 Henry Wedgwood, *Romance of Staffordshire*, i, 64–5, This book is very rare. The British Museum has only odd volumes; so far as I know, Mr E. N. Stretton owns the only complete set of Henry Wedgwood's *Romance of Staffordshire* (three volumes) and his *Staffordshire: Up and Down the County* (three volumes).
9 Henry Wedgwood, *Romance of Staffordshire*, 1879, i, 56.
10 *Loc. cit.*
11 John Mottley, *Joe Miller's Jests*, 1739, ed. Robert Hutchinson, 1963, pp. 22–4.
12 Jonathan Swift, *Directions to Servants*, 1959 edn, pp. 56–7.
13 *The Lover*, 18 March 1714. (*Works of Joseph Addison*, ed. Richard Hurd, 1900, iv, 322–3.)
14 Quoted S. Rubinstein, *The Street-Trader's Lot*, 1947, p. 109.
15 Godard d'Ancour, *Thémidore*, 1760 edn, i, 9–10.
16 *Ibid.*, ii, 24.
17 Jacques Rochette de la Morlière, *Angola*, 1751 edn, p. 10.
18 Illustrated by Hugh Honour, *Chinoiserie*, 1961, Plate 34.
19 Longchamp and Wagnière, *Mémoires sur Voltaire*, 1826, ii, 177–80.
20 Philip Thicknesse, *Observations on the Customs and Manners of the French Nation*, 1766, p. 36.
21 Philip Thicknesse, *A Year's Journey Through France and Part of Spain*, 1777, ii, 167.
22 See Chapter 12, pp. 268–9.
23 Quoted by Paget Toynbee, *Strawberry Hill Accounts*, 1927, p. 52n.
24 Quoted *loc. cit.*
25 i.e., glost, or glazing kiln.
26 Wedgwood to Cox, 13 June 1768. (*Selected Letters of Josiah Wedgwood*, ed. Finer and Savage, 1965, p. 64.)
27 Illustrated by B. Hillier, *Master Potters of the Industrial Revolution: the Turners of Lane End*, 1965, Plate 25b.
28 Jane Austen, *Northanger Abbey*, 1955 edn, p. 144.
29 At pp. 8–9.

30 Robert Southey, *Letters from England*, ed. Jack Simmons, 1951, p. 191.
31 See A. T. Hazen and J. P. Kirby, *A Bibliography of the Strawberry Hill Press*, 1942, pp. 238–9.
32 William Andrews, *Curious Epitaphs*, 1899 edn, pp. 13–14.
33 On Luny, see *Transactions of the Devonshire Association*, xviii (1886) 442–9, and xix (1887) 107–90.
34 *La Foire de Beaucaire*, 1708, p. 10.
35 Arthur Young, *Travels in France*, ed. Constantia Maxwell, 1929, p. 102.
36 D. H. Lawrence, *Sons and Lovers*, 1933, p. 84.
37 George C. Williamson, *Murray Marks and his Friends*, 1919.
38 Illustrated *ibid.*, illustration facing p. 40.
39 Vol. ii, p. 195.

10 REVIVALS – GOTHIC AND OTHERWISE

1 Stephan Tschudi Madsen, *Sources of Art Nouveau*, 1956, p. 84.
2 The following is a list of the exhibitions from 1845 until the end of Victoria's reign:
1845–6 Manchester Exhibition of British Industrial Art.
1849 Birmingham Exhibition.
1851 Great Exhibition of the Works of Industry of All Nations, London.
1853 Dublin International Exhibition.
1855 Paris International Exhibition.
1862 London International Exhibition.
1865 Dublin International Exhibition.
1867 Paris Universal Exhibition.
1871, 1872, 1873, 1874 South Kensington International Exhibitions, London.
1873 Vienna Universal Exhibition.
1876 Philadelphia Centennial Exhibition.
1878 Paris Universal Exhibition.
1887 Manchester Royal Jubilee Exhibition.
1893 Chicago World's Columbian Exhibition.
1900 Paris Universal Exhibition.
1900 Vienna Secession Exhibition.
1901 Glasgow International Exhibition.
3 Geoffrey Godden, 'A unique pair of Exhibition vases', *The Connoisseur*, April 1963, p. 237.
4 Exactly the same idea is expressed in Wassily Kandinsky's *On the Spiritual in Art* (written in 1910, first published in 1912): 'Every cultural period creates art of its own, which can never be repeated again.... For example, it is impossible for us to relive or to feel the inner spirit of the ancient Greeks. The sculptor's attempts to employ Greek principles can only achieve a similarity in form, while the work itself remains for all time without a soul. Such imitation resembles the antics of apes. Externally, the animal's movements are almost like those of human beings. The monkey sits and holds a book an inch from its nose, turns the pages, makes thoughtful faces, but there is no sense or meaning in any of these actions.' (First English edn, 1946, p. 9.)
5 Owen Jones, *The Grammar of Ornament*, 1868, p. 1.
6 When the Oxford School of Modern History was established in 1862, J. R. Freeman suggested that it would be 'an easy school for rich men'. (R. W. Southern, *The Shape and Substance of Academic History*, 1961, p. 11.)
7 Quoted by Mario Amaya, *Art Nouveau*, 1966, p. 6.

8 Notably, the Church Building Society, founded in 1818, the Oxford Movement, started in 1833, the Cambridge Camden Society, active from 1840, and the Oxford Society for Promoting the Study of Gothic Architecture, of which Ruskin and the Archbishop of Canterbury were members.

9 Sir Kenneth Clark calls the Arts and Crafts Movement 'perhaps the most promising and most disappointing child of the Gothic Revival'. (*The Gothic Revival*, 1962 edn, p. 223n.) Dr Madsen writes that 'The Gothic Revival, as developed by Morris, is the forerunner and the actual basis of the Arts and Crafts Movement'. (*Sources of Art Nouveau*, 1956, p. 94). Morris had trained in the office of the Gothic Revivalist architect George Street.

10 On the subject of these chessmen, I am indebted to an excellent article by Norman Stretton, 'Some Notes on the Flaxman Chessmen', *Proceedings of the Wedgwood Society*, No. 1, 1956, pp. 31–3.

11 Later Sir Herbert Croft (1751–1816). See *Dictionary of National Biography*, Sir Herbert Croft. It is interesting to note that Croft contributed an article on chess to Richard Twiss's *Book on Chess* (1787–9); but the Wedgwood chessmen are not mentioned.

12 Almost certainly John Folgham, Case and Cabinet Maker, of 81 Fleet Street, who wrote on 'Wednesday 16th 1788' to Byerly, Wedgwood's nephew: 'J. Folgham presents Compliments to Mr. Byerley – & requests the favour he will exchange the two largest of these, for two exactly the same size as the small ones, – as they are too large for our Case; he also desires Mr. Byerley will let him have 4 Setts (or 6 if possible) of Chess Men by Friday next – if you have them – Our Man will bring them with him.' (Quoted by Norman Stretton, *op. cit.*, p. 33.)

13 Croft is chiefly remembered for the Life of Young which he contributed to Johnson's *Lives of the Poets*. Burke said of it: 'It is not a good imitation of Dr Johnson; it has all his pomp without his force; it has all the nodosities of the oak without its strength. ... It has all the contortions of the Sibyl without the inspiration.' (Quoted D.N.B.)

14 Quoted Norman Stretton, *op. cit.*, pp. 31–2.

15 *Op. cit.*, p. 32.

16 Quoted by Alison Kelly, *Decorative Wedgwood*, 1965, p. 116.

17 Quoted by Norman Stretton, *op. cit.*, p. 32.

18 *Loc. cit.*

19 *Loc. cit.*

20 W. G. Constable (*John Flaxman*. 1927, pp. 21n. and 22n.) points out that Mr J. D. Holmes, who had made a special study of the Flaxman chessmen, had discovered at University College, London, a study of a horse and rider which evidently served as a basis for the design of the knight. He had also shown that a figure of a bishop in Wells Cathedral was the model for Flaxman's chessman bishop.

21 William Hone, *Year Book*, 1838, p. 562. The illustrations of Flaxman chessmen are at pp. 559, 560, 591, 592, 593 and 594.

22 For the information on Wallace Martin which follows, I am much indebted to Charles R. Beard, *A Catalogue of the Collection of Martinware formed by Mr Frederick Nettlefold*, 1936.

23 'For the execution of the decorative sculpture, Mr. Thomas (acting of course under the direction of Sir Charles Barry) was alone responsible, and probably at the time no one was better qualified to undertake it.' (Charles L. Eastlake, *The Gothic Revival*, 1872, p. 185n.)

24 Charles Beard, *op. cit.*, p. 4.

25 See Sir Kenneth Clark, *The Gothic Revival*, 1962 edn, pp. 206–7.

26 *Strand Magazine*, October 1891.

27 See the author's article on Tinworth, *The Times*, 25 April 1964.

28 Charles Beard, *op. cit.*, p. 30.

29 See Chapter 4, p. 102.

30 Gleeson White, 'The Rococo, and After', *The Quarto*, 1896, pp. 14–15.

31 *Ibid.*, pp. 15–16.
32 Eberhard Hempel, *Baroque Art and Architecture in Central Europe*, 1965, p. 20. He adds: 'No matter how hard we may try to be fair to this nineteenth-century revival, there is little chance that it will ever again be appreciated – the note of insincerity is too obvious.'
33 Walter Pater, *The Renaissance*, 1964 edn, ed. Sir Kenneth Clark, p. 78.
34 *Loc. cit.*
35 See the author's article on Bingham, *The Times*, 16 November 1963.
36 Quoted by Hugh Wakefield, *Victorian Pottery*, 1962, p. 84.
37 See Norman Stretton, *op. cit.*, p. 33.
38 Charles Beard, *op. cit.*, p. 25.
39 *Op. cit.*, p. 30.
40 *Loc. cit.*
41 Wakefield, *op. cit.*, Plate 70.
42 Abraham Lomax, *The Royal Lancastrian Pottery, 1900–1938*, 1957, p. 42.

11 ARTIST POTTERS IN ENGLAND

1 James McNeill Whistler, *Mr. Whistler's Ten O'Clock*, 1888, p. 15.
2 Quoted by William Gaunt, *The Pre-Raphaelite Tragedy*, 1942.
3 and 4 These dots are George Moore's, and do not represent omissions from the original text.
5 George Moore, *Confessions of a Young Man* (1886), 1939 edn, p. 104.
6 Oscar Wilde, 'The Critic as Artist', *Essays by Oscar Wilde*, ed. Hesketh Pearson 1950, pp. 108–10.
7 'No artist expects grace from the vulgar mind, or style from the suburban intellect.' 'In England, the arts that have escaped best are the arts in which the public takes no interest.' (Oscar Wilde, 'The Soul of Man under Socialism', *ibid.*, pp. 252 and 248.)
8 William Morris, *Art and the Beauty of the Earth*, a lecture delivered at Burslem Town Hall on 13 October 1881, 1898 edn, p. 12.
9 A. M. W. Stirling, *William de Morgan and His Wife*, 1922. All other unascribed quotations in this chapter relating to De Morgan are from the same source.
10 Reginald Blunt, *The Wonderful Village*, 1918, p. 174.
11 It was built on orchard land in 1878–81 for 'artistic people of moderate income' at the instigation of Mr Jonathan Carr, from designs by Norman Shaw and others. A contemporary account is given in an essay, 'Bedford Park', by Moncure Daniel Conway, published in the same volume as his *Travels in South Kensington.* (1882).
12 'Narcissus' by John Betjeman, *London Magazine*, October 1965.
13 Blunt, *op. cit.*, p. 180.
14 Halsey Ricardo also carried out some ambitious architectural designs with Wedgwood plaques, at Buckminster Park, Leicestershire. (See Alison Kelly, *Decorative Wedgwood*, 1965, pp. 131–2 and Plates 72 and 73.) Ricardo used 'multicolour tiles' (perhaps by De Morgan?) in his interior decoration of Lytton Strachey's home at Lancaster Gate. (See Michael Holroyd, *Lytton Strachey*, 1967, i, 28.)
15 Holbrook Jackson, 'Martinware', *T.P.'s Magazine*, November 1910.
16 *Ibid.*
17 See *The Times*, 16 November 1963.
18 The first Josiah Wedgwood had forbidden this practice. In 1777, referring to busts of Shakespeare and Garrick, he had written to his partner Bentley: 'You will see by looking under the shoulder of each that these heads are modeled [*sic*] by *Wm Hackwood*, but I shall prevent his exposing himself again now I have found it out. I am not certain that he will not be offended if he is refus'd the liberty of putting his name to the models which he

makes quite new, & I shall be glad to have your opinion upon the subject. Mine is against any name being put upon our articles besides W & B, & if you concur with me I will manage the matter with him as well as I can.' (*Letters of Josiah Wedgwood, 1772–1780*, ed. Lady Farrer 1903, ii, 287–8.)

As late as 1889, in Henry Arthur Jones's play *The Middleman* (a huge box-office success), the following conversation takes place between customer, proprietor and workman at a pottery:

LADY UMFRAVILLE: Ah, Mr. Blenkarn! That lovely dinner service Mr. Chandler gave us was your workmanship, wasn't it? (CYRUS *assents.*) I'm glad you put your own mark on it!

JOSEPH CHANDLER (*shows annoyance*): Ah-ra-Blenkarn – ah-ra I think that's rather an absurd practice of yours, putting your own private mark on your best pieces. It's not necessary – not necessary – I wouldn't do it again if I were you!

CYRUS BLENKARN: Very well, sir. (*His face falls; he shows intense disappointment.*)

(Henry Arthur Jones, *The Middleman*, 1907 edn, p. 27.)

19 William Morris, *Art and the Beauty of the Earth*, a lecture delivered at Burslem Town Hall on 13 October 1881, 1898 edn, p. 22.

20 *Loc. cit.*

21 See Roy Andrew Miller, *Japanese Ceramics*, 1960, pp. 17–18.

12 COLLECTORS

1 Lord Macaulay, *History of England*, 1855 edn, iii, 56.

2 See Arthur Lane, 'Queen Mary's porcelain collection at Hampton Court', *Transactions of the Oriental Ceramic Society*, vol. 25, 1949–50, pp. 21–31.

3 In the Wardrobe accounts of Madame Ann von Goltstein, Privy Purse to Queen Mary, the following entry occurs: 'I do hereby certify that there is due to Adrianus Koex of Delft for Dutch china of English money 122 l. 14s. 9d.' (British Museum, Add. MSS. No. 5751.)

4 E. F. Gersaint, *Catalogue Raisonné des Differens Effets Curieux et Rares Contenus dans le Cabinet de feu M. le Chevalier DE LA ROQUE* (1745).

5 *Poetical Works of Robert Browning*, 1951 edn, ii, 566.

6 Petite Edition of the *Works of La Fontaine*, 1744, letter 24, ii, 157.

7 Dr Martin Lister, *A Journey to Paris in the Year 1698*, 1699, p. 35.

8 1878 edn, by Edouard Fournier, p. 227.

9 *Ibid.*, p. 216.

10 See *Le Cabinet du Duc d'Aumont et les Amateurs de son Temps*, ed. Baron Davillier, 1870, pp. i–xii.

11 *The Spectator*, 18 March 1714.

12 It is interesting to find Horace Walpole writing to Sir Horace Mann on 29 November 1781: 'It there any china left in the Great Duke [of Tuscany]'s collection, made by Duke Francis the First himself? Perhaps it was lately sold with what was called the refuse of the wardrobe, whence I hear some charming things were purchased.'

13 Robinson first made this point in the *Catalogue* of the Soulages collection (December 1856), p. 1.

14 From Swift's *Journal to Stella:*

15 September 1710: 'I am resolved to bring over a great deal of china. I loved it mightily today.'

6 October 1710: 'Sir Andrew Fountaine came this morning, and caught me writing in bed. I went into the city with him; and we dined at the Chop-house with Will Pate, the learned woollen-draper: then we sauntered at China-shops and booksellers. . . .'

26 October 1710: 'What do I know whether china be dear or no? I once took a fancy for resolving to grow mad for it, but now it is off; I suppose I told you in some former letter.'

15 Horace Walpole to the Countess of Upper Ossory, 20 June 1781.

16 This picture was drawn to my attention by John Cornforth, 'Drayton House, Northamptonshire', iv, *Country Life*, 3 June 1965, p. 1346.

17 Quoted *loc. cit.*

18 Quoted *op. cit.*, p. 1348.

19 When, in 1764, Conway was dismissed from the command of his regiment and from his post as Groom of the Bedchamber, a pamphleteer named William Guthrie justified the dismissal in his *Address on the late Dismission of a General Officer*. Walpole rushed to Conway's defence in a *Counter-Address*. Guthrie was not slow to detect the fire behind the smoke, and in his *Reply to the Counter-Address* sneered that 'The passionate fondness with which the *personal* qualities of the officer in question are continually dwelt on, would almost tempt me to imagine, that this arrow came forth from a female quiver. ... I will not follow the Author of the Counter-Address through that detail of personality, pleasing as the theme may be to him, into which his zealous affection for the gentleman in question has betrayed him. One of the beaux esprits of the present times, has christened this regard, calling it, with a feigned concern, "an unsuccessful passion, during the course of twenty years".'

20 'Horry is gone a progress into Northamptonshire to Lady Betty Germaine's. Is it not surprising how he moves from old Suffolk on the Thames to another old goody on the Tyne; and does not see the ridicule which he would so strongly paint in any other character?' George Williams to George Selwyn, 18 July 1763 – Jesse, *George Selwyn and his Contemporaries*, i, 252.)

21 'I almost think there is no wisdom comparable to that of exchanging what is called the realities of life for dreams. Old castles, old histories, and the babble of old people, make one live back into centuries, that cannot disappoint one.' (Walpole to Montagu, 5 January 1766.)

22 R. W. Ketton-Cremer, *Horace Walpole*, 1964 edn, p. 36.

23 *Ibid.*, p. 112.

24 A word coined by Swinburne from Walt Whitman's equivocal series of poems, *Calamus*. A pun on 'catamite' was presumably intended. (See Geoffrey Faber, *Jowett*, 1957, p. 370.)

25 Mr Ketton-Cremer writes: 'It is difficult to explain why, apart from its obvious dramatic qualities, this repulsive story should have held so much interest for Walpole'. (p. 251.) If this seems unduly innocent, Fanny Burney (who borrowed the Queen's copy) went to the opposite extreme: 'I felt a sort of indignant aversion rise fast and warm in my mind, against the author of a story so horrible: all the entertainment and pleasure I had received from Mr Walpole seemed extinguished by this lecture, which almost made me regard him as the patron of the vices he had been pleased to record'. (*The Diary and Letters of Madame d'Arblay, edited by her Niece*, 1842, iii, 234–6.)

26 Robert Southey, *Letters from England*, ed. Jack Simmons, 1951, p. 116.

27 Mark Twain, *A Tramp Abroad*, 1880, pp. 179–80.

28 In his will (Somerset House, signed 12 March 1757, proved 27 July 1757) Byng left to his nephew, John Byng, the third son of his brother Robert Byng, among other things 'the three cases of white china handled knives and forks and the spoons belonging thereto and all my china in my house in Berkeley Square'. To Augustus John Hervey he left 'my French clock ornamented with Dresden flowers'.

29 Walpole to Mann, 3 March 1757; (quoted Ketton-Cremer, *op. cit.*, p. 203.)

30 Lord Macaulay, 'Horace Walpole', *Critical and Historical Essays*, ed. F. C. Montague, 1903, i, 544–5.

31 I am indebted to Mr Paul Grinke for drawing my attention to this reference.

32 Walpole to George Montagu, 30 May 1751. (*Horace Walpole's Correspondence*, ed. W. S. Lewis, 1941, ix, 114.)

33 *Catalogue raisonné d'une Collection considerable de diverses Curiosités en tous Genres, contenues dans les Cabinets de feu Monsieur BONNIER DE LA MOSSON, Bailly & Capitaine des Chauffes de la Varenne des Thuilleries & ancien Colonel du Régiment Dauphin* (1744).

34 'Sir Joseph Banks possessed a fine collection of Oriental porcelain. It went by bequest to Sir E. Knatchbull, and was removed to Mersham Hatch, near Ashford, the ancient mansion of the family.' (Joseph Marryat, *A History of Pottery and Porcelain*, 1868 edn, p. 304.)

35 See Soame Jenyns, *Japanese Porcelain*, 1965, pp. 7, 56 and 228, and Plates 8a and 8b.

36 Richard Bateman's collection was sold by Christie's in May 1774. An incomplete catalogue is in the British Museum.

37 Audrey Harrison, only daughter of Edward Harrison of Balls, Hertfordshire; she was wife to Charles, third Viscount Townshend, and mother of George, first Marquis of Townshend, and of the celebrated Charles Townshend.

38 *The Works of Sir Charles Hanbury Williams*, 1822, i, (73–78).

39 W. F. Mavor, *New Description of Blenheim*, 1806 edn, pp. 55–6.

40 Cyrus Redding, *Memoirs of William Beckford*, 1859, ii, 301.

41 *Dictionary of National Biography*, William Beckford.

42 Joseph Marryat, *A History of Pottery and Porcelain*, 1868 edn, p. 306.

43 'Mr Griffiths I need not mention, you know he hath one of the warmest places in my heart.' (Wedgwood to Bentley, 16 February 1765. Quoted by W. Carew Hazlitt in his Introduction, p. xi, to Wainewright's *Essays*, 1880 edn.)

44 Oscar Wilde, 'Pen, Pencil and Poison', *Essays*, ed. Hesketh Pearson, 1950, p. 90.

45 Jesse, *Beau Brummell*, 1927, i, 276.

46 *Ibid.*, i, 277.

47 *Ibid.*

48 *Reminiscences of Captain Gronow*, 1892 edn, i, 284–6.

49 T. H. S. Escott, *Society in the Country House*, 1907, p. 424.

50 Sir Guy Laking, *The Sèvres Porcelain of Buckingham Palace and Windsor Castle*, 1907, p. xii.

51 See Hugh Tait, 'Sèvres Porcelain in the Collection of the Earl of Harewood', *Apollo*, June 1964, January 1965, June 1966.

52 B. Hillier, 'The Dolly Monologues', *Cornhill Magazine*, Spring 1967.

53 Ralph Nevill, *Life and Letters of Lady Dorothy Nevill*, 1919, p. 190.

54 *Ibid.*, p. 188.

55 See *Punch*, LXXIX, p. 194. (30 October 1880.)

56 Roger Lancelyn Green, *Andrew Lang*, 1962 edn, p. 62.

57 Henry Treffry Dunn, *Recollection of Dante Gabriel Rossetti and his Circle*, 1904, pp. 49–50.

58 *Transactions of the English Ceramic Circle*, vol. iv, part 4, p. 21.

59 Quoted by Marcel Valotaire, *La Céramique française Moderne*, 1930, pp. 9–10.

60 Quoted George Somes Layard, *The Life and Letters of Charles Samuel Keene*, 1892, pp. 228–9.

61 Lionel Tollemache, *Talks with Mr Gladstone*, 1898, p. 29.

62 *Ibid*, pp. 29–30.

63 Sir Arthur Conan Doyle, 'The Illustrious Client', *The Complete Sherlock Holmes Short Stories*, 1928, p. 1100.

64 See George D. Painter, *Marcel Proust*, 1966 edn, i, 211. Montesquiou was not even at the charity bazaar, but that did not prevent his enemy Jean Lorrain from describing the famous cane as 'that battle axe for live ladies and tongs for removal of the corpses of dead ones, henceforth so dismally celebrated in the annals of masculine elegance'.

65 Quoted by Alison Adburgham, *A Punch History of Manners and Modes 1841–1940*, 1961, p. 115.

66 Vincent O'Sullivan's *A Book of Bargains* had appeared in 1896, with a frontispiece by Beardsley, but the bargains were of the pact-with-the-Devil type.

13 REPAIRS, REPRODUCTIONS AND FAKES

1 Godard d'Ancour, *Thémidore*, 1760 edn, i, 26–7.
2 For example, it is prescribed for Molière's *Malade Imaginaire* by his physicians.
3 W. J. Pountney, *Old Bristol Potteries*, 1920, p. 116.
4 See Hugh Owen, *Two Centuries of Ceramic Art in Bristol*, 1873, p. 239.
5 See H. Boswell Lancaster, 'China to Mend', *Apollo*, vol. xlv, 1947, pp. 107–8.
6 I am indebted for information on repairers to Geoffrey Wills, 'Old and New Ways of Mending China', *Country Life*, 4 December 1958, p. 1328; and Mr Wills has kindly lent me relevant illustrations for this book.
7 Robert Dossie, *Handmaid to the Arts*, 1758, ii, 28.
8 *Loc. cit.*
9 Quoted by Geoffrey Wills, *op. cit.*, p. 1331.
10 *Loc. cit.*
11 *Ibid.*, p. 1327.
12 *Loc. cit.*
13 Illustrated by C. Michael Newman, 'The Beginnings of Hard-Paste Porcelain in France', *Antique Collector*, June 1961, p. 116, Fig. 5.
14 O. E. Ris-Paquot, *Manière de restaurer soi-même les Faiences, Porcelaines, etc.*, 1876 edn, p. 17.
15 See Aubrey Toppin, 'The China Trade and Some London Chinamen', *Transactions of the English Ceramic Circle*, No. 3, 1935, Plate xxiii.
16 *Lady Charlotte Schreiber's Journals*, ed. Montague Guest, 1911, i, xxvii–xxviii.
17 See Wallace Elliott, 'Reproductions and Fakes in English Eighteenth-Century Ceramics', *Transactions of the English Ceramic Circle*, No. 7, Vol. 2, 1939.
18 See R. Rosenblum in *Art Bulletin*, December 1957, p. 279.
19 Dr Otto Kurz, *Fakes: A Handbook for Collectors and Students*, 1948, p. 228.
20 William Chaffers, *Marks and Monograms*, 1874 edn, p. 747n.
21 *Loc. cit.*
22 Kurz, *op. cit.*, p. 249.
23 See Arthur Lane, *Italian Porcelain*, 1954, pp. 39–40.
24 At p. 332.
25 A bust attributed to Leonardo which became the subject of a sensational controversy when it was bought, in 1909, for the Kaiser Friedrich Museum in Berlin by Murray Marks's friend, Wilhelm Bode. It was later claimed that the bust was in fact the work of Richard Cockle Lucas, whose son, Albert Durer Lucas, said he had helped his father to make it in 1846.
26 At p. 57.
27 At p. 58.
28 Marryat, 1857 edn, p. 147.
29 Frederick Litchfield, 'Imitations of Dresden', *The Connoisseur*, No. 49, 1917, p. 213.
30 G. Ballardini, *Maestro Ferruccio Mengaroni, Maiolicaro di Pesaro,* (*Collana di Studi d'Arte Ceramica*, v, 1929, p. 11.)

14 ART NOUVEAU

1 Honourable exceptions are: Fritz Schmalenbach, *Jugendstil*, 1935; Nikolaus Pevsner, *Pioneers of the Modern Movement*, 1936; H. F. Lenning, *The Art Nouveau*, 1951; Thomas Howarth, *Charles Rennie Mackintosh and the Modern Movement*, 1952; and T. S. Madsen, *The Sources of Art Nouveau*, 1956.
2 Mario Amaya, *Art Nouveau*, 1966, p. 42.
3 *Ibid.*, p. 156.

4 Mario Amaya makes the interesting point that the two styles lasted about the same length of time. (*Ibid.*, p. 14.)

5 See W. B. Honey, *French Porcelain*, 1950, p. 16. T. H. White, in an excellent chapter on 'Ears' in *The Age of Scandal* (1966 edn, pp. 212–18) suggests that an erotic interest attached to the ears in the eighteenth century because these organs were associated with punishment: the cutting off of ears in the pillory. And he points out that the War of Jenkins's Ear (1739) is the only war on record which has taken its name from a part of the human body.

6 Maurice Rheims, *L'Art 1900*, 1965, p. 109. When Gauguin, the leading symbolist in art, made the 1889 self-portrait in stoneware, he modelled himself without ears. Mrs Merete Bodelsen suggests that this symbolized Gauguin's renunciation of the outward world. She adds: 'That Gauguin a few months after Van Gogh's act of self-mutilation introduced a reference to the latter into his self-portrait shows that he connected this act in his mind with the symbolist theory his portrait was meant to express, viz. that the artist should shut himself out from the world of the senses. Whether Van Gogh really – perhaps in a panic that Gauguin might desert him – performed his act of symbolic castration as a crazy reaction to his friend's artistic creed, must remain a matter for conjecture.' (Merete Bodelsen, *Gauguin's Ceramics*, 1964, p. 216, n. 61.)

7 Maurice Rheims, *L'Objet 1900*, 1964, Plate 41.

8 *Ibid.*, p. 79.

9 Douglas Hill and Pat Williams, *The Supernatural*, 1965, pp. 288–9.

10 Henri Van de Velde, *Les Formules de la Beauté*, 1923 edn, p. 11.

11 'The creation of Mr. Puddle-Duck marked the beginning of a new period. At some time between 1907 and 1909 Miss Potter must have passed through an emotional ordeal which changed the character of her genius.' (Graham Greene, 'Beatrix Potter', *The Lost Childhood*, 1962 edn, p. 125.)

12 J. K. Huysmans, *L'Art Moderne, Oeuvres Complètes*, ed. Lucien Descares, VI, p. 219.

13 *Ibid.*, p. 222.

14 *Ibid.*, p. 223.

15 *Ibid.*, p. 231.

16 Robert Schmutzler, *Art Nouveau*, 1964, p. 98.

17 *British Warehouseman*, February 1895, p. 23.

18 See Mario Amaya, *op. cit.*, p. 42.

19 See J. F. Blacker, *Nineteenth-Century English Ceramic Art*, 1911, p. 511.

20 Henry Blackburn, *Randolph Caldecott: A Personal Memoir of his Early Art Career*, 1886, p. 196.

21 *Ibid.*, p. 111.

22 *Gazette des Beaux Arts*, April 1886, p. 327.

23 *Ibid.*, p. 338.

24 At p. 33.

25 Quoted Merete Bodelsen, *Gauguin's Ceramics*, 1964, p. 11.

26 Quoted *ibid.*, p. 18.

27 *Loc. cit.*

28 Quoted by Marcel Valotaire, *La Céramique Moderne*, 1930, p. 21.

29 Illustrated by H. Borrmann, *Moderne Keramik*, 1902, Plate 97.

30 Mrs Bodelsen has more to say on Gauguin's taste for the ambivalent: 'The Oviri figure is known both from paintings, drawings and woodcuts. A drawing in the Louvre, which appears in a copy of "Le Sourire", written in Gauguin's own hand, bears the following cryptic text: "Et le monstre, étreignant sa créature, féconde de sa sémence des flancs généreux pour engendrer Séraphitus Séraphita." Gauguin here apparently refers to Balzac's Swedenborgian novel "Seraphita", thus suggesting with this figure of woman and animal the theme of the "androgyne", which we found him mention already in his

letter to Madeleine in 1888. The preoccupation of the symbolists with the hermaphrodite is exemplified by Sar Peladan, who in 1888 founded the Ordre Kabbalistique de la Rose-Croix. His book "Curieuse" has much in common with Balzac's Séraphitus-Séraphita and he later on devoted a whole volume to the subject with his "l'Androgyne". Here then Gauguin touches on an ideology that has its roots in contemporary literary symbolism and occultism. That, however, the attraction of *l'androgyne* was not merely a literary attitude, but something that came to colour his whole conception of primitive life, appears from the passage in "Noa Noa" where he suddenly sees the young Tahitian who walks in front of him in the ravine as a hermaphrodite (cf. his earliest MS. of Noa Noa "... son souple corps d'animal avait des gracieuses formes, il marchait devant moi sans sexe." and the comments he makes in a note: "le côté androgyne de sauvage – le peu de différence de sexe chez les animaux.").'

(Merete Bodelsen, *Gauguin's Ceramics*, 1964, p. 149.)

31 Quoted, Marcel Valotaire, *La Céramique Moderne*, 1930, p. 13.

32 *Loc. cit.*

33 See H. Borrmann, *Moderne Keramik*, 1902, Plate 60.

34 *Ibid.*, p. 84.

35 See Nikolaus Pevsner, 'Minor Masters of the XIXth Century. IX. Christopher Dresser, Industrial Designer', *Architectural Review*, 1937, p. 183; and Shirley Bury, 'The Silver Designs of Dr. Christopher Dresser', *Apollo*, December 1962, p. 766.

36 At p. 406.

37 Quoted by J. F. Blacker, *Nineteenth-Century Ceramic Art*, 1911, p. 410.

38 Illustrated by H. Borrmann, *op. cit.*, Plate 27.

39 *Ibid.*, Plate 28.

40 Robin Ironside, 'Painting', in *The New Outline of Modern Knowledge*, ed. Alan Pryce-Jones (1956), p. 279.

41 'If we compare Ingres' *Odalisque* which was painted in 1814 with *La Source* which was painted in 1856, we feel that the differences cannot wholly be explained by the reflection that Ingres was thirty-four when he painted the first picture and was suffering a little from senile concupiscence when he painted the second. ... Ingres, there is no doubt, was much influenced technically by daguerrotypes in later years. ...' (R. H. Wilenski, *The Modern Movement in Art*, 1927, pp. 95–6.)

42 *Ibid.*, p. 97ff.

43 *Ibid.*, p. 98n.

44 See Chapter 3, p. 67.

45 Geoffrey Godden, *Antique China and Glass under £5*, 1966, p. 78.

46 At p. 279.

47 Abraham Lomax, *Royal Lancastrian Pottery, 1900–1938*, pp. 137–8.

48 Quoted Merete Bodelsen, *Gauguin's Ceramics*, 1964, p. 186.

49 Lomax, *op. cit.*, p. 46.

50 *Ibid.*, p. 111.

Select Bibliography

Alison Adburgham, *A Punch History of Manners and Modes, 1841–1940*, London, 1961.

Mario Amaya, *Art Nouveau*, London, 1966.

Godard d'Ancour, *Thémidore*, The Hague, 1760 edn.

William Andrews, *Curious Epitaphs*, London, 1899 edn.

Duke of Argyll, *Intimate Society Letters of the Eighteenth Century*, London, 1910.

J. T. Arlidge, *Hygiene, Diseases and Mortality of Occupations*, London, 1892.

E. S. Auscher, *La Céramique au Château de Versailles sous Louis XIV*, Paris, 1903.

Ausfuerliche Nachrichten con den Saltzburgischen Emigranten, Halle, 1743.

Jane Austen, *Northanger Abbey*, London, 1955 edn.

G. Ballardini, *Maestro Ferruccio Mengaroni, Maiolicaro di Pesaro*, 1929.

E. A. Barber, *The Pottery and Porcelain of the United States*, New York, 1901 edn.

Edmond Barbier, *Chronique de la Régence et du Règne de Louis XV*, Paris, 1857 edn.

Thomas Bateman, *Antiquities of Lomberdale*, Bakewell, 1855.

Charles R. Beard, *A Catalogue of the Collection of Martinware formed by Mr Frederick Nettlefold*, London, 1936.

La Foire de Beaucaire, Amsterdam, 1708.

E. Bersot, *Etudes sur le xviiie siècle*, Paris, 1855.

Michel Beurdeley, *Porcelain of the East India Companies*, London, 1962 edn.

Henry Blackburn, *Randolph Caldecott: A Personal Memoir of his Early Art Career*, London, 1886.

J. F. Blacker, *Nineteenth Century Ceramic Art*, London, 1911.

Reginald Blunt, *The Wonderful Village*, London, 1918.

Merete Bodelsen, *Gauguin's Ceramics*, New York, 1964.

H. Borrmann, *Moderne Keramik*, Berlin, 1902.

James Boswell, *Life of Samuel Johnson*, London, 1824 edn.

Carl Bridenbaugh, *The Colonial Craftsmen*, Chicago and London, 1961.

Sir James Bland Burges, *Selections from the Letters and Correspondence*, ed. James Hutton, London, 1885.

Edmund Burke, *Reflexions on the Revolution in France*, London, 1929 edn.
Herbert Butterfield, *Napoleon*, London, 1939.
John Byng, *The Torrington Diaries*, ed. C. Bruyn Andrews, London, 1934–8.

Cambridge Modern History.
Duncan Campbell, *A Poem on Tea*, London, 1735.
W. Chaffers, *Marks and Monograms*, 15th edn., vol. ii revised by G. Godden, London, 1965.
Champfleury (i.e. Jules Husson), *Histoire des Faïences Patriotiques sous la Révolution*, Paris, 1867.
R. J. Charleston (ed.), *English Porcelain, 1745–1850*, London, 1965.
Chavagnac and Grollier, *Histoire des Manufactures Françaises de Porcelaine*, Paris, 1906.
Sir K. Clark, *The Gothic Revival*, London, 1962 edn.
Arthur W. Clement, *Our Pioneer Potters*, New York, 1947.
Abbé Cochet, *Galérie Dieppoise*, Paris, 1862.
W. G. Constable, *John Flaxman*, London, 1927.
Moncure Daniel Conway, *Travels in South Kensington*, London, 1882.
Cyril Cook, *Life and Work of Robert Hancock*, London, 1948.
Warren E. Cox, *The Book of Pottery and Porcelain*, New York, 1945.

M. E. J. Delécluze, *Louis David, Son Ecole et Son Temps*, Paris, 1855.
C. A. A. Disbrowe, *Old Days in Diplomacy*, London, 1903.
Philip Doddridge, *Works*, ed. James Orton, London, 1802.
Robert Dossie, *Handmaid to the Arts*, London, 1758.
Francis S. Drake, *Tea Leaves*, Boston, 1884.
Siegried Ducret, *German Porcelain and Faience*, London, 1962 edn.
Henry Treffry Dunn, *Recollections of Dante Gabriel Rossetti and his Circle*, London, 1904.

Charles Eastlake, *The Gothic Revival*, London.
H. D. Eberlein and R. W. Ramsdell, *The Practical Book of Chinaware*, Philadelphia and New York, 1948.
Earl of Egmont, *Diary*, ed. R. A. Roberts, London, 1920–3.
George Elers, *Memoirs, 1777–1842*, ed. Lord Monson and Granville Leveson-Gower, London, 1903.
T. H. S. Escott, *Society in the Country House*, London, 1907.
John Evelyn, *Diary*, ed. E. S. de Beer, Oxford, 1955.

Sheridan Le Fanu, *Uncle Silas*, London, 1904 edn.
Flaubert, *Sentimental Education*, London, 1964 edn.
Esther Forbes, *Paul Revere and the World he Lived in*, Boston, 1942.

John Galt, *Annals of the Parish*, London, 1926 edn.

William Gaunt, *The Aesthetic Adventure*, London, 1945.
—, *The Pre-Raphaelite Tragedy*, London, 1942.
Edward Gibbon, *Autobiography*, ed. Bernard Groom, Oxford, 1930.
—, *Letters*, ed. J. E. Norton, London, 1956.
A. E. Gibelin, *De l'Origine et la Forme du Bonnet de la Liberté*, Paris,.
Geoffrey Godden, *Antique China and Glass under £5*, London, 1966.
—, *Encyclopaedia of British Pottery and Porcelain Marks*, London, 1964.
—, *Illustrated Encyclopaedia of British Pottery and Porcelain*, London, 1966.
—, *Victorian Porcelain*, London, 1961.
Bredo Grandjean, *Dansk Ostindinsk Porcelaen Importen fra Kanton ca. 1700–1822*, Copenhagen, 1965.
Roger Lancelyn Green, *Andrew Lang*, London, 1962.
Captain Gronow, *Reminiscences*, London, 1892 edn.

Reginald Haggar, *Concise Encylopaedia of Continental Pottery and Porcelain*, London, 1960.
—, *Staffordshire Chimney Ornaments*, London, 1955.
H. J. Hanham, *Elections and Party Management*, London, 1959.
Jonas Hanway, *Essay on Tea*, London, 1757.
Augustus Hare, *The Story of My Life*, London, 1896 edn.
A. T. Hazen and J. P. Kirby, *A Bibliography of the Strawberry Hill Press*, Yale, 1942.
Eberhard Hempel, *Baroque Art and Architecture in Central Europe*, London, 1965.
John, Lord Hervey, *Memoirs of the Reign of George the Second*, London, 1884 edn.
Constance Hill, *Juniper Hall*, London, 1904.
Bevis Hillier, *Master Potters of the Industrial Revolution: the Turners of Lane End*, London, 1965.
Thomas Hobbes, *Leviathan*, ed. Michael Oakeshott, Oxford, 1957.
William Hogarth, *The Analysis of Beauty*, ed. Joseph Burke, London, 1955.
Thomas Holcroft, *Life*, ed. Elbridge Colby, London, 1925.
Lady Holland, *A Memoir of the Rev. Sidney Smith*, London, 1855.
W. B. Honey, *Dresden China*, London, 1934.
—, *European Ceramic Art*, London, 1951.
—, *French Porcelain*, London, 1950.
—, *German Porcelain*, London, 1947.
Hugh Honour, *Chinoiserie*, London, 1961.
John Houghton, F.R.S., *A Collection for Improvement of Husbandry and Trade*, No. 189, London, 1695–6.
J. K. Huysmans, *Oeuvres Complètes*, ed. Lucien Descares, Paris.
J. A. Lloyd Hyde and others, *Chinese Porcelain for the European Market*, 1946.

David Irwin, *English Neo-Classical Art*, London, 1966.

A. H. Japp, *German Life and Literature*, London, 1878.
—, *Industrial Curiosities*, London, 1880.
Soame Jenyns, *Japanese Porcelain*, London, 1965.
Heneage Jesse, *Beau Brummell*, London, 1927 edn.
Llewellyn Jewitt, *The Ceramic Art of Great Britain*, London, 1878 edn.
Samuel Johnson, *Works*, ed. Robert Lynam, London, 1825.
Owen Jones, *The Grammar of Ornament*, London, 1868.

M. Kayserling, *Moses Mendelssohn, Sein Leben und Seine Werke*, 1862.
Maurice Keen, *The Outlaws of Medieval Legend*, London, 1961.
Alison Kelly, *Decorative Wedgwood*, London, 1965.
R. W. Ketton-Cremer, *Horace Walpole*, London, 1964 edn.
Fiske Kimball, *The Creation of the Rococo*, New York, 1943.
Arthur Knapp, *The Cocoa and Chocolate Industry*, London, 1930.
Otto Kurz, *Fakes: A Handbook for Collectors and Students*, London, 1948.

Sir Guy Laking, *The Sèvres Porcelain of Buckingham Palace and Windsor Castle*, London, 1907.
Arthur Lane, *English Porcelain Figures of the Eighteenth Century*, London, 1961.
—, *French Faience*, London, 1948.
—, *Italian Porcelain*, London, 1954.
Klaus Lankheit, *Florentinische Barockplastik*, Munich, 1962.
D. H. Lawrence, *Sons and Lovers*, London, 1933 edn.
T. E. Lawrence, *Seven Pillars of Wisdom*, London, 1964 edn.
George S. Layard, *Life and Letters of Charles Keene*, London, 1892.
Dr Martin Lister, *A Journey to Paris in the Year 1698*, London, 1699.
Abraham Lomax, *The Royal Lancastrian Pottery, 1900–38*, London, 1957.
Longchamp and Wagnière, *Mémoires sur Voltaire*, Paris, 1826.

Stephen Tschudi Madsen, *Art Nouveau*, London, 1967.
—, *Sources of Art Nouveau*, London, 1956.
André Malraux, *The Voices of Silence*, trans. Stuart Gilbert, London, 1954.
Wolf Mankowitz and Reginald Haggar, *Concise Encyclopaedia of English Pottery and Porcelain*, London, 1957.
Joseph Marryat, *A History of Pottery and Porcelain*, London, 1857 and 1868 edns.
Karl Marx, *The Eighteenth Brumaire of Louis Bonaparte*, trans. Eden and Cedar Paul, London, 1926.
George Menary, *Life and Letters of Duncan Forbes of Culloden*, London, 1936.
E. H. W. Meyerstein, *A Life of Thomas Chatterton*, London, 1930.
Roy Andrew Miller, *Japanese Ceramics*, Tokyo, 1960.
Nancy Mitford, *Voltaire in Love*, London, 1957 edn.
Cosmo Monkhouse, *Chinese Porcelain*, London, 1901.
George Moore, *Confessions of a Young Man*, London, 1939 edn.
Dr John Moore, *A Journal during a Residence in France*, London, 1794.

Jacques Rochette de la Morlière, *Angola*, Paris, 1751 edn.
William Morris, *Art and the Beauty of the Earth*, London, 1898.
John Mottley, *Joe Miller's Jests*, ed. Robert Hutchinson, London, 1963.
Jean McClure Mudge, *Chinese Export Porcelain for the American Trade, 1735–1835*, New York, 1962.

Ralph Nevill, *Life and Letters of Lady Dorothy Nevill*, London, 1919.
Sylas Neville, *Diary, 1767–88*, ed. Basil Cozens-Hardy, London, 1950.
Harold Newman, *Veilleuses*, London, 1967.
George Ward Nichols, *Pottery: How it is Made*, New York, 1878.

J. Ovington, *An Essay upon the Nature and Qualities of Tea*, ed. Augustine Birrell, London, 1928 edn.
Harold Owen, *The Staffordshire Potter*, London, 1901.
Hugh Owen, *Two Centuries of Ceramic Art in Bristol*, London, 1873.

George D. Painter, *Marcel Proust*, London, 1966 edn.
Mrs Papendiek, *Journals*, London, 1887.
H. T. Parker, *The Cult of Antiquity and the French Revolutionaries*, New York, 1937.
Walter Pater, *The Renaissance*, ed. Sir Kenneth Clark, London, 1964 edn.
R. Pfnor, *Receuil d'Estampes Relatives a l'ornementation des Appartements*, Paris, 1871.
John Goldsmith Phillips, *China Trade Porcelain*, Cambridge, Massachussets, 1956.
Luigi Pirandello, *Short Stories*, ed. Frederick May, London, 1965.
Dr Robert Plot, *Natural History of Staffordshire*, Oxford, 1686.
W. J. Poutney, *Old Bristol Potteries*, Bristol, 1920.
William Prescott, *The Conquest of Mexico*, London, 1843.
John Prideaux, *Relics of William Cookworthy*, London, 1853.

Bernard Rackham and Herbert Read, *English Pottery*, London, 1924.
Bernadino Ramazzini, *De Morbis Artificum*, Padua, 1700.
Tallement de Réaux, *Historiettes*, Paris, 1934 edn.
Cyrus Redding, *Memoirs of William Beckford*, London, 1859.
Agnes Repplier, *To Think of Tea!*, London, 1933.
Maurice Rheims, *L'Art 1900*, Paris, 1965.
—, *L'Objet 1900*, Paris, 1964.
O. E. Ris-Paquot, *Manière de Restaurer Soi-Même les Faïences, Porcelaines, etc.*, Paris, 1876 edn.
François de la Rochefoucauld, *A Frenchman in England, 1784*, ed. Jean Marchand, London, 1933.
Harold Rosenberg, *The Tradition of the New*, New York, 1959.
George Rudé, *The Crowd in the French Revolution*, London, 1959.

Select Bibliography

George Savage, *Eighteenth-century English Porcelain*, London, 1952.
—, *Eighteenth-century German Porcelain*, London, 1958.
—, *Porcelain through the Ages*, London, 1961.
—, *Seventeenth and eighteenth century French Porcelain*, London, 1960.
G. Schiedlausky, *Tee, Kaffee, Schokolade*, Nuremberg, 1961.
Robert Schmutzler, *Art Nouveau*, London, 1964 edn.
Arno Schönberger and Halldor Soehner, *The Age of Rococo*, London, 1960 edn.
Lady C. Schreiber, *Journals*, ed. Montague Guest, London, 1911.
Elizabeth Boody Schumpeter, *English Overseas Trade Statistics, 1697–1808*, Oxford, 1960.
Simeon Shaw, *History of the Staffordshire Potteries*, Stoke-on-Trent, 1829.
Lord Sheffield (J. B. Holroyd), *Observations on the Commerce of the American States*, London, 1784.
Walter Sickert, *A Free House*, ed. Osbert Sitwell, London, 1947.
Annie Trumbull Slosson, *The China Hunters' Club*, Boston, 1878.
Robert Southey, *Letters from England*, ed. Jack Simmons, Oxford, 1951.
Sponsel, Der Zwinger, *Dresden*, 1924.
Stendhal, *Le Rouge et Le Noir*, trans. Margaret R. B. Shaw, London, 1953.
H. Morse Stephens, *Orators of the French Revolution*, London, 1892 edn.
A. M. W. Stirling, *William De Morgan and his Wife*, London, 1922.
Dorothy Margaret Stuart, *The Daughters of George III*, London, 1939.
Jonathan Swift, *Journal to Stella*, Oxford, 1948 edn.

C. Turner Thackrah, *The Effects of the Principal Arts, Trades and Professions ... on Health and Longevity*, Leeds, 1831.
Philip Thicknesse, *A Year's Journey through France and Part of Spain*, London, 1777.
Gabriel Thomas, *Description of Philadelphia*, London, 1697.
Ralph Thoresby, *Diary*, ed. Joseph Hunter, London, 1830.
Peter Thornton, *Baroque and Rococo Silks*, London, 1965.
Frank Tilley, *Teapots and Tea*, London, 1957.
Lionel Tollemache, *Talks with Mr Gladstone*, London, 1898.
Donald Towner, *English Cream-coloured Earthenware*, London, 1957.
—, *The Leeds Pottery*, London, 1963.
Paget Toynbee, *Strawberry Hill Accounts*, London, 1927.
Sir Algernon Tudor-Craig, *Armorial Porcelain of the Eighteenth Century*, London, 1965.
A. S. Turbeville (ed.), *Johnson's England*, London, 1933.
Mark Twain, *A Tramp Abroad*, London, 1880 edn.

Marcel Valotaire, *La Céramique française moderne*, Paris, 1930.
Henri van de Velde, *Les Formules de la Beauté*, Paris, 1923 edn.
A. Villers, *Jean-Baptiste Nini: Ses Terres Cuites*, Paris, 1862.

Voltaire, *Letters Concerning the English Nation*, ed. Charles Whibley, London, 1926 edn.
Josef Vydra, *Painting on Folk Ceramics*, London, 1950.

Hugh Wakefield, *Victorian Pottery*, London, 1962.
Horace Walpole, *Letters*, ed. W. Lewis, New York and London, 1926 onwards.
Dr Bernard Watney, *English Blue and White Porcelain*, London, 1963.
—, *Longton Hall Porcelain*, London, 1957.
Byron Webber, *James Orrock, R.I., Painter, Connoisseur, Collector*, London, 1903.
Henry Wedgwood, *Romance of Staffordshire*, Stoke-on-Trent, 1879.
—, *Staffordshire, Up and Down the County*, Stoke-on-Trent, 1879.
Josiah Wedgwood, *Address to the Workmen in the Pottery on the Subject of Entering into the Service of Foreign Manufacturers*, Newcastle, Staffordshire, 1783.
—, *Correspondence*, ed. Lady Farrer, London, 1906.
—, *Selected Letters*, ed. Ann Finer and George Savage, London, 1965.
James McNeill Whistler, *Mr Whistler's 'Ten O'Clock'*, London, 1888.
Oscar Wilde, *Essays*, ed. Hesketh Pearson, London, 1950.
R. H. Wilenski, *The Modern Movement in Art*, London, 1927.
John Wilkes, *Correspondence and Life*, ed. John Almon, London, 1805.
Sir Charles Hanbury Williams, *Works*, London, 1822.
George C. Williamson, *Murray Marks and his Friends*, London, 1919.
Rudolf Wittkower, *Art and Architecture in Italy, 1600–1750*, London, 1958 edn.
James Woodforde, *The Diary of a Country Parson*, ed. John Beresford, Oxford, 1931.

Arthur Young, *Travels in France, etc.*, ed. Constantia Maxwell, London, 1929; also Thomas Okey edn., London, 1934.

Newspapers and periodicals consulted:
Antique Collector
Antiques
Apollo
Architectural Review
Art de France
Art Journal
British Warehouseman
Bulletin de la Société des Amis de la Céramique Suisse
Chronicles of Early American Industries
Colonial Records of Georgia
Connoisseur
Cornhill Magazine
Faenza
Gazette des Beaux Arts

Good Words
London Magazine
Maske und Kothurn
Proceedings of the Wedgwood Society
Publications of the East Tennessee Historical Society
Punch
The Quarto
La Revolution Française
The Spectator
The Spinning Wheel
Strand Magazine
Sunday Times
The Times
Times Literary Supplement
T.P.'s Magazine
Transactions of the Devonshire Association
Transactions of the English Ceramic Circle
Transactions of the Oriental Ceramic Society
Victoria and Albert Museum Bulletin
The World

Index

Index

Index

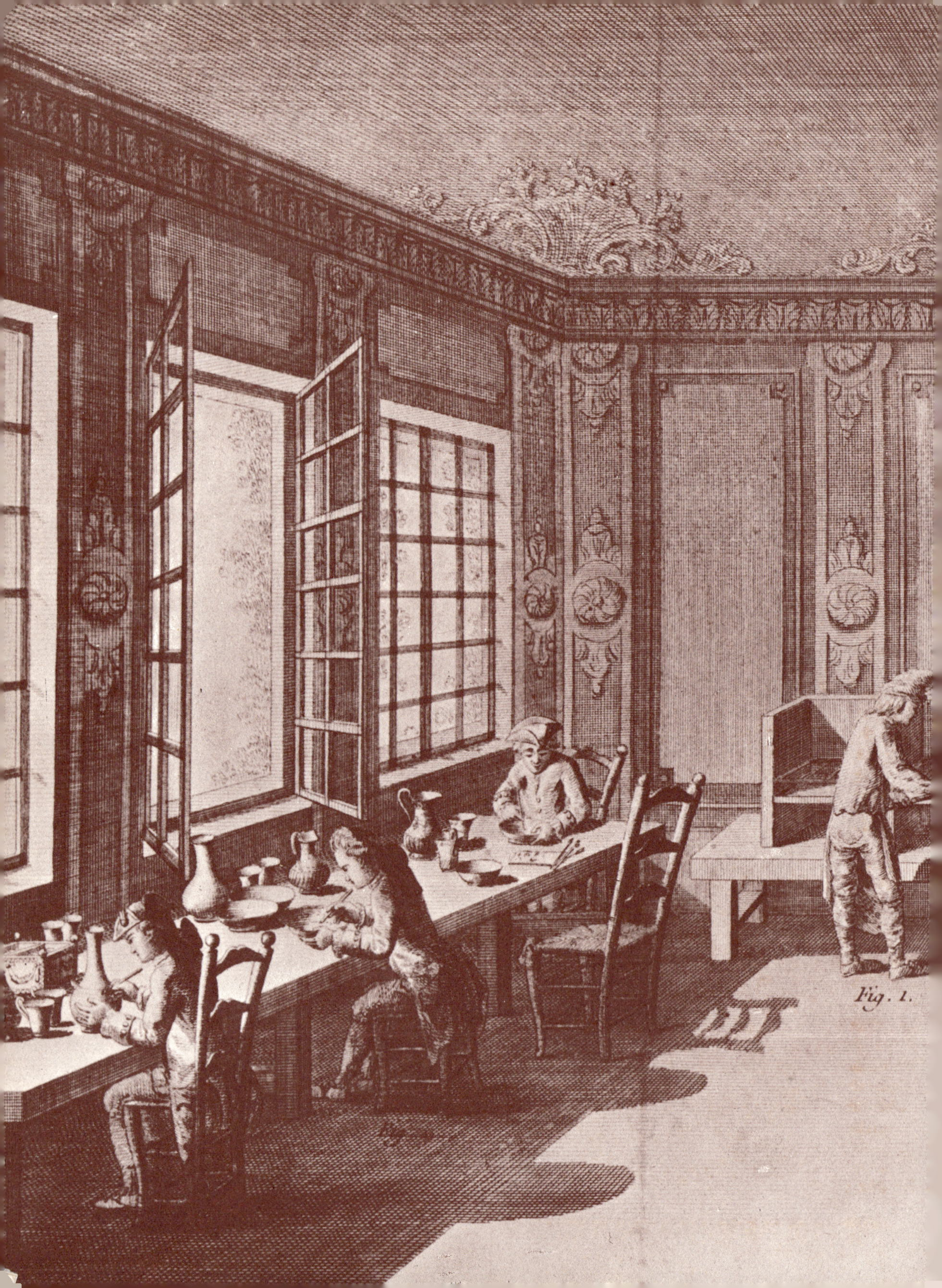
Fig. 1.